Industrial conflict

Industrial conflict

A comparative legal survey

EDITORS
Benjamin Aaron and K. W. Wedderburn

AUTHORS
Benjamin Aaron
Xavier Blanc-Jouvan
Gino Giugni
Thilo Ramm
Folke Schmidt
K. W. Wedderburn

Crane, Russak & Company, Inc.
New York

First published 1972

ISBN 0–8448–0156–9

L/C Number 72–94300

Published in the United States of America by
Crane, Russak & Company, Inc.
52 Vanderbilt Ave.
New York, N.Y. 10017

Printed in Great Britain

Contents

Chapter 2 Methods of industrial action: courts, administrative agencies, and legislatures

by Benjamin Aaron, *Director of the Institute of Industrial Relations and Professor of Law, University of California, Los Angeles, U.S.A.*

Chapter 3   The peace obligation

by Gino Giugni, *Director of Advanced School for Labour Law and Professor of Labour Law, University of Bari, Italy*

Chapter 4   The effect of industrial action on the status of the individual employee

by Xavier Blanc-Jouvan, *Professor of Law, University of Paris I, France*

Chapter 5   The legality of industrial actions and methods of settlement procedure

by Thilo Ramm, *Professor of Labour Law and Civil Law, University of Giessen, Federal Republic of Germany*

Chapter 6   Industrial action, the State and the public interest

by K. W. Wedderburn, *Cassel Professor of Commercial Law, University of London, at the London School of Economics, England*

Editorial preface

The authors of the present volume joined together in 1966 to collaborate on research in the field of comparative labour law and industrial relations. Two preceding volumes, *Employment Grievances and Disputes Procedures in Britain*, by K. W. Wedderburn and P. L. Davies, and *Labor Courts and Grievance Settlement in Western Europe*, edited by Benjamin Aaron, were published by the University of California Press in 1969 and 1971, respectively.

The present volume is a more truly 'comparative' work than either of its predecessors, which consisted, essentially, of national reports on labour dispute settlement procedures. The subject of industrial conflict has been divided into six major topics, each of which is dealt with in a separate chapter covering the pertinent law and practice in the six countries included in the survey: Britain, France, West Germany, Italy, Sweden and the United States. Each author is responsible for his own chapter; but in the preparatory work each of us drew upon the knowledge and criticisms of our colleagues to a very great extent, so that the book may in general be regarded as the product of the group as a whole. The authors have, in this attempt at a piece of comparative research, endeavoured to show how similar kinds of employer–employee and employer–trade union relationships in the six countries have been influenced by different historical and cultural factors, leading to the development of a rich variety of governmental and private mechanisms by which these relationships are regulated. Our joint studies were completed in October 1971, and, with the exception of a few footnotes, the text represents the result of our work at that date.

The study was made possible by a grant from the Ford Foundation; the authors gratefully acknowledge this assistance. We also express our thanks for the substantial help supplied in the final stages of our work by the staff of the Institute of Industrial Relations, University of California, Los Angeles.

B.A.
K.W.W.

List of abbreviations

ACLI	Associazione Cristiana Lavoratori Italiani (Italian Christian Association of Workers)
AD	Arbetsdomstolens Domar (Swedish Labour Court Reports)
AFL	American Federation of Labor (U.S.A.)
AUEW	Amalgamated Union of Engineering Workers (Britain)
BAG	Bundesarbeitsgericht (Federal Labour Court) *and* Entscheidungen des Bundesarbeitsgerichts (decisions of the Federal Labour Court)
BDA	Bundesvereinigung der Deutschen Arbeitgeberverbände (German Confederation of Employers' Associations)
BGB	Bürgerliches Gesetzbuch (German Law Code)
B Verf GE	Bundesverfassungsgericht (Federal Constitutional Court) *and* Entscheidungen des Bundesverfassungsgerichts (decisions of the Federal Constitutional Court)
CBI	Confederation of British Industry
CFDT	Confédération Francaise Démocratique du Travail (French Democratic Confederation of Workers)
CFTC	Confédération Francaise des Travailleurs Chrétiens (French Confederation of Christian Trade Unions)
CGT	Confédération General du Travail (French General Confederation of Labour)
CGIL	Confederazione Generale Italiana del Lavoro (Italian General Confederation of Labour)
CIO	Congress of Industrial Organisations (U.S.A.)
CISL	Confederazione Italiana dei Sindacati dei Lavoratori (Italian Trade Unionists Confederation)
CUB	Comitate Unitari di Base (Italian Shop-floor Committees)
D	Dalloz (France)

DAG	Deutsche Angestelltengewerkschaft (German White-Collar Workers' Union)
DATA	Draughtsmen and Allied Technicians Association (Britain)
DB	Der Betrieb (journal)
DGB	Deutscher Gewerkschaftsbund (German Federation of Trade Unions)
ENI	National Institute for Hydrocarbon Industry (Italy)
FIOM	Federazione Operaie Impiegati Metallurgici (Engineering Workers' Federation: affiliated to CGIL)
FMCS	Federal Mediation and Conciliation Service (U.S.A.)
FO	Force-Ouvrière (Workers' Confederation; France)
Gesamtmetall	Gesamtverband der metallindustriellen Arbeitsgeberverbände (Confederation of German Engineering Employers' Associations)
IRI	Industrial Recovery Institute (Italy)
ILO	International Labour Organisation
JCP	Juris-Classeur Périodique
JCP ed. CI	Juris-Classeur Périodique, édition Commerce et Industrie
LMRA	Labor Management Relations (Taft-Hartley) Act (U.S.A.)
LMRDA	Labor Management Reporting and Disclosure (Landrum-Griffin) Act (U.S.A.)
LO	Landsorganisationen i Sverige (Swedish Confederation of Trade Unions)
NIRA	National Industrial Recovery Act (U.S.A.)
NIRC	National Industrial Relations Court (Britain)
NJA	Nytt juridiskt arkiv. (Swedish Supreme Court Reports)
NLGA	Norris-La Guardia Act (U.S.A.)
NLRA	National Labor Relations (Wagner) Act (U.S.A.)
NLRB	National Labor Relations Board (U.S.A.)
NUGMW	National Union of General and Municipal Workers (Britain)
RdA	Recht der Arbeit (German Labour Law Review)
RGL	Revista Giuridica del Lavoro (Italian Labour Law Review)
RGSt	Entscheidungen des Reichsgerichts in Strafsachen (decisions of the Supreme Court in penal cases)

RGZ	Entscheidungen des Reichsgerichts in Zivilsachen (decisions of the Supreme Court in civil cases)
SACO	Sveriges Akademikers Centralorganisation (Swedish Confederation of Professional Associations)
SAF	Svenska Arbetsgivareföreningen (Swedish Employers' Confederation)
SOC	Social Chamber of Court of Cassation (France)
SR	Statstjänstemännens Riksförbund (National Swedish Federation of Government Officers)
TCO	Tjänstemännens Centralorganisation (Swedish Central Association of Salaried Employees)
TGWU	Transport and General Workers' Union (Britain)
TUC	Trades Union Congress (Britain)
UIL	Unione Italiana del Lavoro (Italian Workers Union)
UIMM	Union des Industries Métallurgiques et Minières (Engineering and Mining Industries Association)

I

Industrial action:
the role of trade unions and
employers' associations
by Folke Schmidt

Introduction

This first section in our study of six countries, namely Great Britain, the Federal Republic of Germany, France, Italy, Sweden and the United States, is intended to serve two purposes. First, it will give the reader an introduction to the other sections by presenting basic data on trade unions and employers' associations. Secondly, it will aim at analysing certain questions such as the strength of the trade unions, their aims and strategies, their control over strikes, and the relationship between the organizations and their members and the relationship between the two sides, the unions and the employers.

Each country has a character of its own, and the problems are interwoven with one another in a complicated national fabric. The author has chosen to give a country-by-country presentation. There is a closer relationship between some of the countries than between others and for this reason Great Britain and the United States, Sweden and West Germany, France and Italy might be looked upon as three different families, and these family relationships have decided the order in which the countries appear in the chapter. Within each of the six-country presentations the material is, when possible, organized in the same sequence. At the end there follows a section containing some conclusions.

Britain

THE FIGHT AGAINST RESTRICTIONS ON UNION ACTIVITIES

There are specific reasons why the situation in Britain should be presented before that in the other five countries. For our study the indisputable claim of seniority is of minor significance. The long history of the British trade unions has, however, one characteristic feature, namely the constant struggle against interference with union activities. Until the commencement of the

Industrial Relations Act 1971, this struggle was successful in so far as the unions had themselves immunity from tort liability and their officials and members were protected within the framework of the famous golden formula of the Conspiracy and Protection of Property Act, 1875, and the Trade Disputes Acts of 1906 and 1965: 'an act done . . . in contemplation or furtherance of a trade dispute'.

The Trade Union Act of 1871 had the same protective goals as the Trade Disputes Acts. Trade unions were not criminal, nor were they unlawful for civil purposes. Further, it was laid down that 'any agreement made between one trade union and another' was not enforceable (sec. 4(4)). The view of the trade union world and of most managers was that collective agreements were not legal contracts and that no legal action could therefore be brought if a union failed to observe agreed procedures. This appeared to be so, quite apart from the 1871 Act, for the reason that the parties never intended to make them binding. As Wedderburn concludes, very few collective agreements were enforceable as legal contracts.[1]

As we shall find from our study of the situation in Sweden and West Germany, the structure and the strategy of the unions are influenced by the policy of organized employers. Thus the Swedish Employers' Confederation has forced upon the Swedish unions a centralization which might not have been altogether in the interest of the unions. In Britain, as we shall see later on, employers' associations are weak and are more concerned with the day-to-day work than with long-range planning. The British unions have enjoyed freedom to shape their own policy and they remain organizations under popular control, very little influenced by pressure from the side of the employers.

The Industrial Relations Act 1971, an enactment more ambitious than any other piece of legislation in the six countries covered by the present study, sets out to change this state of affairs. The status of trade unions and employers' associations is redefined. A distinction is drawn between registered and unregistered organizations: the former are to be subject to strict rules with regard to membership and funds, the latter will remain in their present legal twilight. But after the repeal of the Trade Disputes Acts of 1906 and 1965 and of the Trade Union Act of 1871, the unregistered union will, before the newly established Industrial Court, be deprived of some of its protection.

Registration is voluntary. As an incentive to register, the union is offered a number of advantages. Among these are the following: the availability of the agency shop agreement, whereby the union will have the opportunity of collecting appropriate contributions from non-members, too (secs. 11–16); the possibility of being recognized as the sole agent of a bargaining unit (secs. 44–50); certain limits on awards of compensation made by the new Industrial Court against a union (sec. 117); protection from certain unfair industrial practices (esp. secs. 96, 97(3)); and immunity of its officials in case of proceedings with respect to actions taken by the official within the scope of his

1. K. W. Wedderburn, *The Worker and the Law*, 2nd ed., Penguin Books, 1971, pp. 171–80; *Ford Motor Company* v. *A.E.U.* [1969] 2 Q.B. 303.

authority (sec. 101(4)). Further, the right to organize as substantiated in a protection against dismissals because of union activities is conferred on members of registered unions only. Moreover, only registered unions will continue to enjoy the extensive tax exemptions given to union income applied in payment of provident benefits.

Another change concerns the collective agreement. Every collective agreement made in writing after the commencement of the new Act is presumed to be intended by the parties to be a legally enforceable contract unless it contains a clause which provides to the contrary, i.e. excludes legal effect. What the practical effect of this rule will be remains to be seen. The majority of the trade unions have requested (September 1971) that their collective agreements shall contain an exclusion clause and so far they have encountered little resistance from the side of the employers.

CRAFT, INDUSTRIAL AND GENERAL UNIONS. UNION MEMBERSHIP

The craft union,[2] which has its roots deep in history, is intended exclusively for skilled workers, and often unskilled and semi-skilled workers at the same workplace are organized in other unions, as is still the case in the shipbuilding and building industries. The existence of craft unions partly sets the pattern for the multi-unionism which constitutes one of the characteristic features of the British labour market and the existence of which explains some of the unrest caused by strikes in different sectors of an industry or a plant. However, there is an increasing tendency for craft unions to develop larger units, e.g. through the amalgamation of several trades or the enrolment of workers with lower grades of skill. The total membership of craft unions is declining.

There is in Britain no industrial union in the German sense which claims to organize all workers within an industry, including even the salaried employees. The nearest approach is the National Union of Mineworkers, which represents all colliery manual workers, including craftsmen. It enjoys sole recognition by the National Coal Board in respect of the majority of weekly-paid industrial grades (in the main foremen and supervisors) and is also recognized jointly with the Clerical and Administrative Workers' Union and the National Association of Clerical and Supervisory Staff as representing substantial numbers of clerical workers in the industry.[3] It is interesting to note that the formation of an industrial union was related to the nationalization of the coal mines by the Coal Industry Nationalisation Act 1946. Since nationalization the union has, through a series of demarcation agreements, amalgamations and arrangements for dual membership, succeeded in eliminating a large number of other unions claiming representation at colliery level. There are a few other industrial unions, such as the National Union of Tailors and Garment Workers and the National Union of Boot and Shoe Operators.

The classification into craft unions and industrial unions applies only to a

2. See, on what follows, H. A. Clegg, *The System of Industrial Relations in Great Britain*, Oxford, 1970, pp. 40 ff.
3. See Ministry of Labour, *Industrial Relations Handbook*, London, 1961, p. 68.

minority of the total union membership. The three largest unions are in fact general unions: the Transport and General Workers' Union (TGWU) (1,638,000 members in 1971), the Amalgamated Union of Engineering Workers (AUEW) (1,400,000 by 1971), and the National Union of General and Municipal Workers (NUGMW) (853,000). These unions concentrate on certain sectors, the first, for instance, being mainly concerned with road transport and work in the docks, and the last with manual work in municipal employment. But according to Clegg, the three general unions referred to are represented in almost every industrial sector in the Standard Classification.

An increasing role is being played by the unions of white-collar workers, among them the Association of Scientific, Technical and Managerial Staffs (membership 200,000). Furthermore, the existence of a very large number of localized unions should be mentioned.

The Donovan Report[4] summarized the situation at the end of 1966 as follows. There were 574 trade unions, with a total membership of 10,111,000. Unions varied in size from unions with a few hundred members to the TGWU and the AUEW, each with a membership exceeding one million. One half of all trade unionists were in the nine largest unions and four-fifths were in the 38 largest unions.

In 1971 there were a little more than 500 unions; 142 of them were affiliated to a central organization, the Trades Union Congress (TUC), and these unions had a total membership of over 10 million employees. The TUC has a broader membership than its Swedish counterpart, the LO. The TUC, unlike the LO, comprises unions of white-collar workers as well as blue-collar workers.

The figure of about 10 million unionists in 1966 should be compared with the figures for the total work force that year, viz. 14 million manual workers and 9 million white-collar workers.

A striking illustration of the multiplicity of unions in Britain is given in a Government social survey of 1968.[5] An inquiry was made among a sample of shop stewards in six major trade unions.[6] The shop stewards[7] were asked how many unions besides their own had manual workers in their workplace.[8] Their answers are found in Table 1 on p. 6.

It is the aim of the 1971 Industrial Relations Act to reduce multi-unionism by various devices. A registered union may apply to the Industrial Court when the employer is unwilling to enter into an agency shop agreement (sec. 11(2)). Upon the request of the Court the Commission on Industrial Relations, a newly established statutory body, has to take a ballot of the workers

4. *Royal Commission on Trade Unions and Employers' Associations 1965–1968.* Chairman: The Rt. Hon. Lord Donovan, HMSO, 1968, para. 28.
5. Governmental Social Survey, *Workplace Industrial Relations*, 1968.
6. The Transport and General Workers' Union, the Amalgamated Engineering Union, the National Union of General and Municipal Workers, the Electrical Trades Union, the National Union of Railwaymen, and the Amalgamated Union of Building Trade Workers.
7. Except those in the National Union of Railwaymen.
8. Governmental Social Survey, op. cit., p. 18.

Table 1 *Number of unions with manual-worker members*

	%
None other than own	17
1 other	21
2 others	18
3 ,,	16
4 ,,	11
5 ,,	8
6 ,,	3
7 or more others	5
Don't know	1
Total	100

falling within the range specified in the application or a larger unit determined by the Commission. If in the ballot a qualified majority of the workers vote in favour of an agency shop, a duty is imposed upon the employer to enter into an agency shop agreement. A similar procedure applies when a trade union applies for recognition as sole bargaining agent. In some situations, however, these procedures may have the opposite effect of increasing competition between unions if several unions compete for such a status. The statute pays no regard to the voluntary methods developed by the TUC for settling inter-union disputes over membership under the Bridlington Agreement of 1939 and the amendments to the TUC rules of 1969.[9]

THE STRUCTURE OF BRITISH UNIONS, WITH PARTICULAR REFERENCE TO THE ROLE OF SHOP STEWARDS

The organizational structure shows a marked similarity in all unions.[10] All have a conference which meets annually or, more rarely, biennially or even triannually. In most cases the conference is elected directly by the members, though some unions have a system of indirect election by divisional committees. Every union has an executive responsible to the conference. All unions have a general secretary, normally elected by the members, though in some cases he is appointed by the executive. The other full-time officers are generally appointed by the executive.

The union has local branches. In general, the branch is based on the members' places of residence, and not on their places of work. The members are convened to meet at regular intervals. However, attendance is low, and the branches have lost some of their earlier significance. In part this can be explained by the fact that many activities have become centralized.

Of critical importance are the shop stewards, who are lay representatives

9. See, on these agreements, Wedderburn, op. cit., pp. 467, 475.
10. On what follows see in particular Clegg, op. cit., and J. Hughes, *Trade Union Structure and Government*, Royal Commission Research Papers 5, 1967.

operating at the place of work. Normally the shop stewards are elected by the members of the union in the shop by a 'show of hands'. Regular re-election appears to be the general practice.[11] Union rule books and formal procedure agreements are not accurate guides to the role played by shop stewards as workplace representatives. Many important aspects of their job are not regulated by rule, and many stewards enjoy *de facto* privileges in the workplace that are not embodied in procedure agreements. From the union point of view the shop steward has the function of collecting contributions together with that of recruiting new members.[12] In relation to management the steward is a spokesman for the workers in negotiating over rates of pay, fringe benefits and conditions of work generally, and taking up grievances and complaints with the foremen; he represents individual workers who have been disciplined by the management, and supplies information about the works' rules and management concern over breaches. W. E. J. McCarthy[13] states in his Research Paper for the Royal Commission that shop stewards often back their demands with various types of collective sanctions, of which the 'unconstitutional strike' is only the most immediate and apparent. The steward cannot be considered a representative of the union and be compared to a union officer. Rather it would seem that the shop steward has a dual role. Perhaps he is primarily the representative of a local informal work group, but also accredited by his national union.

PATTERNS OF COLLECTIVE BARGAINING

The modern union has two basic functions, that of collective bargaining and that of strike leadership. Ordinarily these functions are closely integrated with each other. The right to strike is an essential element in a system of collective bargaining aiming at voluntary settlements. According to the philosophy of liberal economists the balance of economic warfare depends upon the power of the union. The threat to strike is the most persuasive argument for a fair settlement.

In Britain collective bargaining is a well-established institution. Although there are plant agreements, in many sectors the industry-wide national agreement dominates the scene. In the collective agreement are laid down the length of the normal working week, the regulations for overtime, the ordinary pay for workers of different grades, and other substantive conditions of work.

The Royal Commission under the chairmanship of Lord Donovan, which had to consider the role of trade unions and employers' associations in promoting the interests of their members and in accelerating the social and economic advance of the nation, was particularly concerned about the fact

11. W. E. J. McCarthy, *The Role of Shop Stewards in British Industrial Relations*, Royal Commission Research Papers 1, 1966, para. 66.
12. See, on these matters, McCarthy, op. cit.; W. E. J. McCarthy and S. R. Parker, *Shop Stewards and Workshop Relations*, Royal Commission Research Papers 10, 1968, and Commission on Industrial Relations Report No. 17, *Facilities afforded to shop stewards*, 1971, Cmnd. 4668, secs. 46–85.
13. op. cit., para. 2 E.

that there are two partly autonomous systems, one formal and one informal.[14] The formal system is centred upon the industry-wide collective agreement. The informal system is created by the actual behaviour of trade unions and employers' associations, managers, shop stewards and workers.

The observation with regard to the existence of two industrial-relations systems is probably of universal validity. What worried the Royal Commission was the great gap between these systems. The industry-wide collective agreement does not give more than a minimum level. The earnings of the worker are to a large extent dependent upon additions in the form of piecework rates and other incentive earnings. There is a continuous workplace bargaining which is largely autonomous in relation to the bargaining related to the industry-wide collective agreement. In his evidence to the Commission, Allan Flanders[15] describes the workplace bargaining as 'fragmented' because it is conducted in such a way that different groups in the works get different concessions at different times.

THE STRIKE RECORD, WITH PARTICULAR REFERENCE TO UNOFFICIAL STRIKES

The number of disputes over industry-wide issues which lead to industrial action was until recently fairly small. The overwhelming majority of all strikes arise from workshop and factory disputes.

The relation between official and unofficial strikes has a bearing upon this state of affairs. If a strike has its cause in a dispute over an industry-wide issue, it is ordinarily an official strike, while the greater part of strikes on workplace issues are unofficial. Statistical figures are presented by Benjamin Aaron in Chapter 2. There it will be found that unofficial strikes have been about six times as numerous as official strikes. Generally unofficial strikes are shorter than official ones and the total number of working days lost is not more than twice as great. The incidence of unofficial strikes is higher than statistics suggest. Many relatively small strikes are never reported. In addition, there are other forms of workshop pressure: working to rule, go-slows, and so on.

SYMPATHETIC ACTIONS

According to Marxist socialism all the workers constitute a separate class involved in a permanent state of social warfare against capitalism. The strike therefore has a justification not only as an element of a bargaining procedure aiming at voluntary settlements but as an attack against the employer as an enemy of the working class. Even among non-Marxist labour leaders there is a feeling that workers can never be detached lookers-on but have a duty to support any of their fellow workers who are engaged in industrial action.

British labour has been less influenced by Socialism than have the labour movements of Sweden, Germany and France. Possibly this is one of the

14. See the Donovan Report, paras. 46 ff.
15. Donovan Report, para. 67.

reasons why actions in solidarity between workers in different industries have been comparatively rare. It is difficult to give a clear picture, since no figures are given either in the Report or in the Research Papers of the Royal Commission. Most likely the figures are low, since it seems to be a part of British philosophy to solve industrial conflicts one by one as they occur. However, it should be recalled that the General Strike of 1926, which brought out nearly two million workers, was a sympathetic action called by the T U C in support of the coal miners in their struggle against wage reductions.

THE RELATIONSHIP OF THE UNIONS TO THE LABOUR PARTY

The links between the trade union movement and the British Labour Party are numerous and well-established. Indeed, the Labour Representation Committee of 1900, which was the precursor of the Labour Party, was set up by a conference of trade unions and socialist bodies. The trade union movement of today sponsors M.P.s and provides substantial financial support to the Party. In applying their funds for political purposes the unions are subject to special regulations set out in the Trade Union Act, 1913. The resolution for the furtherance of such objects has to be approved by a ballot of the members. A member has the right to contract out of contributing to the political fund; the contracted-out member may not be victimized, and contribution to the fund must not be made a condition for admission to the union.[16] The law with regard to political funds stays as it was with the commencement of the Industrial Relations Act, 1971.

UNION RULES WITH REGARD TO STRIKE INITIATION AND STRIKE SETTLEMENT. STRIKE BENEFITS

Some short comments will here be made on union rules for the procedure of strike initiation and strike settlement and for distribution of strike benefits, as well as on the enforcement of a strike through the disciplining of strike-breakers.

Once again, in Britain there is no general procedure to be found in all union rule books for the initiation or settlement of disputes. Several unions, in fact, if their rule books are to be believed, have no procedure laid down for these matters.

In 1970 the T U C conducted a survey of union rule books on the provisions made for strike initiation and settlement. In all, 115 rule books were examined, representing a total membership of 8,483,062. A considerable number of books, representing, in particular, unions of non-manual workers, had no rules relating to procedure in these matters. Thirty rule books provided for a strike ballot, though some only in situations where a national strike of the union was envisaged. In five cases the executive council had discretionary power to order a ballot. Only two unions, with a membership of 388,601 to-

16. Trade Union Act, 1913, secs. 3(1), 4(1). See, too, Royal Commission, *Written Evidence of the Chief Registrar of Friendly Societies*, paras. 28 and 29.

gether, provided for a ballot to end a strike; one further union (membership 62,000) had discretion to order a ballot in that situation.[17]

It is usual for British unions to provide strike benefits. However, these, though greater than unemployment benefits, constitute only a small drain on the union funds compared with provident benefits. According to the 1968 Report of the Registrar of Friendly Societies, covering a total membership of 8,529,000, the expenditure on benefits was as follows:

	£
Provident benefits (this includes benefit for sickness, accident, death, superannuation, etc.)	10,454,000
Unemployment benefits	478,000
Dispute benefits	1,162,000

Union contributions in Britain are generally low. The annual average contribution in 1969 was £4 8s. 7d. (£4·43) per member, which represents a sum of somewhat less than 10p (2 shillings) a week. The normal Transport and General Workers' Union rate is 12½p (2s. 6d.) a week. Even in unions of professional, higher paid workers, the rate is low. In the Association of Scientific, Technical, and Managerial Staffs the rate is 12½p a week, and in the National Union of Teachers it is £5·25 (5 guineas) a year (=fractionally over 10p a week).

Often British unions do not have very substantial means available to meet the needs arising in case of a strike. Some notes on the postal strike of 1971, which lasted from 19 January to 8 March, will illustrate the problems encountered when a union has to rely upon help from other sources. The postal strike involved about 170,000 workers, and about 7 million working days were lost. The union had only £300,000 in its strike fund and this money was spent on advertisements in the national press in support of the strike. The union was able to raise £210,000 in gifts from other unions and £356,000 in loans. Over £10,000 was collected from the public.[18] From these funds the union paid 'hardship benefits', mostly to single persons who had no other source of income. Strikers with dependants actually had to live on what was paid to their families in supplementary social benefits.

DISCIPLINARY MEASURES AGAINST STRIKE-BREAKERS

Where a union has called a strike in an industry, in a plant or a department, all workers employed by the employer involved in the dispute are expected to join. A person who stays at work or does the work of a striker is regarded as a 'scab', little better than a deserter from an army.

In addition to social ostracism the union can take disciplinary measures against the strike-breaking member, since his conduct can be treated as an infringement of the rules. There may be a specific rule detailing strike-break-

17. cf. Wedderburn, op. cit., p. 228.
18. The TUC was involved only to the extent of giving advice and moral support to the union.

ing as an offence, or it may be what is known as a 'blanket' offence, that is to say, 'conduct detrimental to the interests of the union', or words to that effect. Rule 22(I) of the Amalgamated Engineering Union is a particularly comprehensive example of the latter:

> any member who, in the opinion of his branch or the Executive Council, shall have injured or attempted to injure the union, or worked or acted contrary to the interests of the union or its members, or attempted to break up or dissolve the union . . . or otherwise brought the union into discredit . . . may be expelled or otherwise dealt with by the Executive Council.

A TUC survey of the disciplinary rules of 118 of the 150 affiliated unions, with a total membership of 8,404,910, found that only three unions (with 12,000 members) had no powers to take disciplinary action. Six of the remainder had no power of expulsion. All the remaining 109 unions had a 'blanket' provision.[19]

Union officials have pleaded that the relations between the union and its members should be considered a sphere protected against actions in court. In applying the law before the 1971 Act, the courts disregarded this objection and took jurisdiction over actions by members for wrongful expulsions.[20] The rule book was considered a legally binding contract between the member and the union.[21] Certain judges have recently regarded the rule book as more than a contract when asserting judicial control.[22]

The judicial tendency is paralleled by the Industrial Relations Act, 1971, which imposes new controls on the rules and practices of all unions, registered and unregistered. In the Act disciplinary actions against union members are dealt with exhaustively. The member must be given a reasonable time to prepare his defence, and he must be afforded a full and fair hearing. The union is not allowed to take against a member disciplinary action which the court in its discretion declares to be unfair, and in particular no action may be taken in a number of cases, among them a member's refusal to take part in a political strike or a strike which would constitute an unfair industrial practice (sec. 65(7)). For practical purposes, after the commencement of the Act the expulsion of a strike-breaker will be justified only where the strike was authorized by the union, and the expulsion was held fair by the court.

The principles of conduct embodied in the Act also regulate the right to gain membership. Any person who applies for membership and belongs to the profession or category which the union is intended to represent may not be excluded from membership by way of any arbitrary or unreasonable discrimination (sec. 65(2)). Thus the union rule book is construed as a contract which confers rights upon third parties.

19. TUC Report, 1969, para. 36, p. 142.
20. See Wedderburn, op. cit., pp. 230 ff.
21. *Lee* v. *Showmen's Guild of Great Britain* [1952] 2 Q.B. 329.
22. *Edwards* v. *S.O.G.A.T.* [1970] 3 W.L.R. 713.

ADDITIONAL COMMENTS ON UNOFFICIAL STRIKES, INCLUDING
THE ROLE OF SHOP STEWARDS

The 'unofficial' strike calls for some additional comments. This is the British
term for what the Americans call the 'wildcat' strike. The word 'unofficial'
here has exactly the meaning normally connoted by the term, being applied
to a strike which has not been recognized by the union as a union action. Thus,
by definition any strike ordered by a union's official organ is excluded. But the
fact that a strike is initiated by a group of workers in a plant does not mean
that the strike cannot become official through subsequent recognition by the
union. Such recognition may follow when the strike has come to an end, with
the effect that the strikers will then be entitled to strike benefits. The dividing
line is not always quite clear. Indeed, there are cases when the union has not
declared the strike 'official' but is negotiating with the employer for its
members and paying 'hardship' benefits.[23]

The ordinary unofficial strike concerns a dispute at the plant level for a
group of workers. The character of the unofficial strike is analysed by W. E. J.
McCarthy in his Research Paper concerning the role of shop stewards.[24] He
points out that unofficial strikes vary in character. Sometimes the strike is
used as an act of demonstration. It indicates to management that something
ought to be done, and done quickly, to try to satisfy a particular group. For
this purpose the strike does not need to last more than a few hours, and the
usual procedure is to return to work as soon as some assurance has been given
that a particular problem will receive immediate attention. McCarthy raises
the question whether the unofficial strike may be considered a 'spontaneous'
action and finds that this is certainly not true as a general statement. Some of
the strikes covered by his study, like other sanctions which were employed –
such as overtime restrictions or 'go-slows' – were not purely spontaneous
demonstrations. One such was a strike in the confectionery industry over
piece rates, where it was consciously decided to impose pressure at a time of
maximum seasonal demand. Other strikes have occurred in the docks, where
the urgency of certain cargoes increased the effectiveness of strike action at
particular periods. The investigators had come across strikes that were
strategic in the sense that they represented a deliberate show of force. In
other words, quite apart from the merits of the grievance involved, or even the
need to use strike action in order to put the necessary pressure on management, it was felt by stewards and their members that there was a need to prove
to management that effective strike action was possible in respect of a particular group.

McCarthy emphasizes that the role of the shop steward in this context is
difficult to define. 'First, while it was true that shop stewards acted often as a
restraining influence it was not clear that they generally did so. In fact they
played every possible role: from the steward, in local government, who decided, on his own initiative, that there must be an immediate demonstration

23. See, for example, the T U C Report 1970, para. 72, p. 176.
24. op. cit., paras. 41 ff.

against a management decision, and very decidedly led his members out, to the steward, in confectionery, who pleaded with his members not to strike, and persuaded them to return to work before he had even seen management.'

EMPLOYERS' ASSOCIATIONS

Before presenting the role of British employers' associations it should be mentioned that the ordinary national collective agreement, like the ordinary plant agreement, is valid indefinitely. Unlike American, Swedish and German employers, British employers have been more interested in the bringing about of an effective procedure for the settlement of disputes as they occur than in agreements that wages and conditions of work are definitely settled for a specific period of time, still less they have made it a condition *sine qua non* that a peace obligation should be incumbent upon the parties.

In the pamphlet *Fair Deal at Work*, in which one finds the Conservative Party's recipe for industrial prosperity in Britain, there are some critical comments on employers' associations. It is asserted that hitherto their policies have been largely defensive.[25] By making the collective agreement a legally enforceable contract the party, on achieving power, has, it is claimed, endeavoured to create a new situation. The Industrial Relations Act does not touch upon the question whether the collective agreement shall be valid indefinitely or for a definite period of time; in *Fair Deal at Work* the American collective agreement is mentioned as an illustration of a more efficient arrangement.[26]

The majority of British employers are members of employers' associations, although a number of firms – big ones as well as small – prefer to remain outside. Some of the employers' organizations combine the functions of an employers' association with that of a trade association, and some of them operate solely as employers' associations. The most important ones, such as the Engineering Employers' Federation and the Federation of Building Trade Employers, are nation-wide. The Confederation of British Industry (CBI) is a top organization with a membership of 108 organizations. Individual companies, too, are admitted to membership.

Incidentally, in the Industrial Relations Act employers' associations are placed on a par with unions. A distinction is drawn between registered and unregistered associations. With regard to right to membership the association is submitted to rules similar to those applicable to unions.

The national employers' association concerned has the responsibility for the collective bargaining. The CBI does not intervene in the conduct by employers' associations or individual companies of their own affairs. Nor does it maintain a fund to indemnify employers against loss due to industrial disputes.[27] Compared with the Svenska Arbetsgivareföreningen (the Swedish

25. *Fair Deal at Work*, Conservative Party, 1968, p. 58.
26. op. cit., p. 28.
27. Royal Commission, para. 748.

Employers' Confederation) or even with its German and French counterparts, the CBI has very little authority over its members.

The Royal Commission conducted two studies, one of which concerned a selected number of employers' associations, while the other was a survey of opinions among officials of such associations.[28] Together, these studies give a good picture of British employers' policies.

Both studies revealed that only very few employers' associations seek to determine more than a part of their members' total wage bill. One association, the National Federated Electrical Association, constituted an exception. It aimed at the prevention of local additions and a member was not allowed to remain in the Association if he wished to implement a different policy in his firm. All the other associations allowed for local bargaining by shop stewards, even if this resulted in wide disparities between earning levels among members.[29]

It is the aim of the associations to prevent the occurrence of strikes and other industrial actions involving refusal to work according to the employers' wishes. The ordinary approach in case of a strike was to contact the local trade union official with a view to seeking his cooperation in getting the men to return to work before recommencement of negotiations on the dispute, supplemented in some cases by similar action at national level. The general attitude was that negotiations should not continue 'under duress' while the men remained on strike. However, this did not prevent informal contact with the trade union to 'clarify the issues', and possibly to indicate the lines on which a settlement might be obtained. The author of the Research Paper does not state whether this applies to unofficial strikes only, but that qualification seems to follow from the context.

In addition to assistance in negotiations, some associations, as the Engineering Employers' Federation and the National Federated Electrical Association, operate indemnity funds. Payments may be claimed under certain conditions when production is interrupted by a strike. The present author has no information as to the virtual importance of such insurance against strikes except for a statement in the Research Paper that 'they do not compensate the member for loss of profits or loss of orders, which may be the most serious effects'.[30]

There is very little information in the Research Papers of the Royal Commission on the use of lockout or threat of lockout as countermeasures to strikes. If there is a local strike involving a department of a plant or a group of workers, the usual practice is to keep the remaining part at work so long as layoffs are not necessitated because of lack of raw material or power. Ordinarily the employer does not lockout other workers for the purpose of bringing pressure upon those involved in a strike.

It is not the part of the policy of employers' associations to resort to lockouts in disputes over national agreements. The only national lockout for nearly

28. V. G. Munns and W. E. J. McCarthy, *Employers' Associations*, Royal Commission Research Papers 7, 1967.
29. Research Papers 7, paras. 26–8.
30. ibid., para. 215.

half a century occurred in 1967. The Shipbuilding Employers' Federation reacted to an official strike of members of the Draughtsman and Allied Technicians Association (DATA) at one shipyard in N.E. England by 'suspending without pay' (as they put it) all 1,800 members of DATA employed in member firms. The lockout, which the union regarded as in breach of procedure, lasted about ten weeks and was finally settled by making an increased offer to the original strikers, not to be paid till a later date. The lockout could hardly be described as a success for the employers, who were initially determined that they should not be 'picked off' company by company by the union.[31]

To conclude, the policy of British management differs from that which later will be seen to be followed by Swedish or German management. British employers' associations are still satisfied with the function of the expert adviser in collective bargaining and negotiations over grievances.

AUTHOR'S COMMENTS

Trade unions and employers' associations are opposed powers. The workers organize in order to achieve strength in bargaining for improvements of the conditions of work; once they have organized the single employer may find himself too weak to resist pressure and he therefore prefers to join with other employers. Again, the fact that employers organize on an industry-wide basis may affect the structure of the trade union movement. A feedback of this kind is a characteristic feature of the Swedish labour market, where the overwhelming majority of all manual workers are organized in industrial unions.

As already mentioned, the formation of the Union of Mineworkers came soon after the nationalization of the coal mines, which implied that the control of the coal-mining industry, earlier split on a number of private firms, was vested in one body, the National Coal Board. The present author is not prepared to answer the question whether the amalgamation on the side of the workers was an effect of the merger on the side of the employers, nor whether a slight decrease in the number of stoppages of work by miners can be explained by the contraction in mining employment.[32] Except for this example, very little backfeeding has been found during our study of the British scene. British employers' associations are weak, and compared with Sweden and Germany the trade unions have been allowed to shape their policies without being under heavy pressure from organized employers.

There is another feature closely related to weakness in management which is even more important from the point of view of our subject, namely the existence at the shop level of a strong semi-independent organization under the leadership of the shop stewards. The workers refuse to submit to control

31. DATA was in 1971 involved in a lockout of its members by Rolls Royce, over a local claim by Coventry employees. Once again the dispute ended with an increased offer to the original disputants.
32. According to H. A. Turner, the contraction in mining employment does not provide a sufficient explanation. See Turner, *Is Britain Really Strike-prone?*, Cambridge U.P., 1969, p. 25.

from their own union as well as from management. Some unions, such as the TGWU, have tried to meet the situation by closer collaboration between officials and shop stewards and by regular references for discussion with the members during negotiations. It remains to be seen whether the Industrial Relations Act will, as predicted in *Fair Deal at Work*,[33] make industry's task easier through its approach of legal regulation by 'strengthening the hands of employers, trade unions and individuals who resist irresponsible, subversive or unconstitutional action'.

The United States of America

CONGRESSIONAL POLICIES ON LABOUR RELATIONS

The history of American trade unionism basically resembles that of British unionism. The Common Law prohibition against restraints of trade was reinforced by a federal enactment, the Sherman Antitrust Act of 1890. In the Danbury Hatters' case of 1908,[34] the Supreme Court found that the Sherman Act was applicable to organized labour. The leaders of trade unions were constantly subjected to civil actions in court, and, as stated by Charles O. Gregory,[35] during the latter part of the nineteenth century the American courts developed a control upon unionism that was far more effective than any criminal-law device – the labour injunction.

As in Britain, the American unions had to persuade the legislature to curtail the power of the courts. The first piece of legislation, the Clayton Act, was passed in 1914. It was at that time hailed by Samuel Gompers, the president of the American Federation of Labor (AFL),[36] as labour's Magna Carta. However, it proved to be ineffective. The excessive use of injunctions was done away with by the Norris–La Guardia Act, 1932. The net effect of this Act, again according to Gregory,[37] 'was to establish the coercive techniques of labour unions on a par with those of business associations at common law'.

In the United States the legislature has played an active role which had no counterpart in Britain until the introduction in December 1970 of the Industrial Relations Bill. From detached neutrality Congress shifted to a pro-labour attitude. This swing was foreshadowed by the Railway Labor Act of 1926. The right to organize was laid down in sec. 7 of the National Industrial Recovery Act, 1933. It is true that this Act was invalidated as unconstitutional by the Supreme Court in 1935.[38] However, this did not change the policy of Congress on this point. Indeed, the right to organize was given teeth by the National Labor Relations (Wagner) Act (NLRA) which was passed only a

33. op. cit., p. 29.
34. *Loewe* v. *Lawlor*, 208 US 274 (1908).
35. Charles O. Gregory, *Labor and the Law*, Norton (2nd rev. ed. with 1961 supplement), 1961, p. 15.
36. ibid., p. 159.
37. ibid., p. 191.
38. *Schechter Poultry Corp.* v. *United States*, 295 US 495 (1935).

few months after the decision of the Supreme Court. In sec. 1 of this Act it was declared to be the policy of the United States to eliminate the causes of certain obstructions by 'encouraging the practice and procedure of collective bargaining and by protecting the exercise by workers of full freedom of association, self-organization, and designation of representatives of their own choosing, for the purpose of negotiating the terms and conditions of their employment or other mutual aid or protection'.

The present law, the Labor-Management Relations (Taft-Hartley) Act (LMRA) 1947, has basically the same aims. The Taft-Hartley Act, however, takes the view that industrial strife is due not only to the activities of some employers but also to certain practices by the labour unions. For this reason the definition of unfair labour practices in sec. 8 comprises both employer and union activities. Further, in sec. 7, which deals with the right to self-organization, it is provided that individual employees have the right not only to engage in concerted activities but also to refuse to do so. Mistrust of unions is the background of another piece of legislation, the Labor-Management Reporting and Disclosure (Landrum-Griffin) Act (LMRDA) 1959. Its basic aim as expressed in sec. 2(c) is *inter alia* 'to eliminate or prevent improper practices on the part of labor organizations, employers, labor relations consultants, and their officers and representatives which distort and defeat the policies of the Labor-Management Relations Act'.

WHY DID NOT AMERICAN TRADE UNIONISM DEVELOP INTO A POPULAR MOVEMENT?

There was a time – the early Roosevelt era – when students of social history might have expected the union movement to win over the whole of the American labour force. In 1933, after a period of recession in the 1920s, the membership of American trade unions was less than 3 million. During the second part of the 1930s and the first part of the 1940s there occurred an increase in total membership to about 13 million. To some extent this remarkable development was due to the growth of the established unions within the American Federation of Labor. More significant, however, was the creation of new unions and their penetration into new industrial areas. As stated by Millis and Montgomery,[39] the appearance of new unions in previously unorganized or almost unorganized industries and trades was significant as a manifestation of the spread of organization-mindedness among the American workers. In the mass-production industries, such as iron and steel, motor-car production, electrical and radio manufacturing and aluminium production, hundreds of thousands of workers were drawn into strong industrial unions. The majority of these were affiliated to the Congress of Industrial Organizations (CIO), created in 1936.

However, in the middle of the 1950s the peak was reached and, although in

39. Harry A. Millis and Royal E. Montgomery, *Organized Labor*, 1945, p. 198.

1968 the total figure was higher than before or about 19 million, this figure represented a lower percentage of the total labour force than in the middle 1950s. Thus the percentage of union members among those employed in non-agricultural enterprises was 34 per cent in 1955 and 28 per cent in 1968.

In their recent study *Labor and the American Community*, Bok and Dunlop[40] raise the question why American unionism, unlike the union movement of Western Europe, did not develop into a popular movement. According to these scholars, in Europe labour movements arose against the backdrop of a feudal tradition that denied workers access to economic opportunity or political power. The sense of working-class solidarity, of separateness from the rest of the community, had not the same fertile ground in a society like that of America, which stressed the ideas of classlessness and of individual initiative, a society in which the workers enjoyed the right of suffrage and the opportunity for a free public education.[41] The present author submits that other factors, too, have been relevant, such as the scarcity of manpower and the ample opportunity of employment for skilled workers, and the permanent existence of a minority of black people and poor immigrants to whom no attention has been paid, at least until recently.

THE AMERICAN TRADE UNION

In the United States there are a considerable number of craft unions, many of them with a long history, and a limited number of industrial unions, such as the Auto Workers' Union, the Mine Workers' Union and the Steel Workers' Union. Further, there is one big union, the Teamsters' Union, which might be classified as a general union. It has a core of truck drivers but organizes workers within warehouses and other affiliated industries.

The concentration on certain sectors such as transportation, communications and public utilities, or construction and certain manufacturing industries like the automobile industry, the electrical industry, the steel industry, and its almost total insignificance within other sectors, such as trade and agriculture, are characteristic features of American labour unionism. Where union membership exists, it often tends to be 100 per cent. As will be explained in detail in the next paragraph, the American local union represents all employees within the appropriate bargaining unit, and some sort of union security clause prescribing that union membership shall be compulsory or that union dues shall be deducted from the wages of all employees is a regular part of the collective agreement.

It should be mentioned that the figures of membership given above are figures measured by payment of dues. The statistics of union membership

40. Derek C. Bok and John T. Dunlop, *Labor and the American Community*, 1970, p. 48 and p. 388. For a comparison of American and European trade unionism, see the study by Everett M. Kassalow, *Trade Unions and Industrial Relations: An International Comparison*, New York, 1969, pp. 5 ff.
41. Bok develops the same ideas in his paper, 'Reflections on the distinctive character of American Labor laws', 84 *Harvard Law Review*, p. 1400 (1971).

therefore include a considerable number of individuals who actually have not joined a union, and have not voted for the union in an election organized by the National Labor Relations Board.

The structure of the American trade union is very much the same as that of the British: a national union – often called international because of membership in Canada – with branches, called locals. The majority of the national unions are affiliated to a head organization, the AFL-CIO – a merger of two earlier federations, the AFL and the CIO. As in Britain, the federation has mainly policy-making functions and has very little to do with the actual bargaining. The relation between the national union and its locals is different from that in Britain. Most of the collective agreements are plant agreements entered into by locals, and therefore the power naturally gravitates to the local. As stated in the section dealing with Britain, there exists in that country a dual system, a formal one embodied in the collective agreement and an informal one constituting a sort of 'cease fire' arrangement at the plant level. The American labour market does not suffer from such dualism; the local with its elected officers controls the bargaining, and the American shop steward has a subordinate position compared with his British colleague. The American union where it exists is a strong organization. The average number of full-time officials may be used as an index. There is about one official to every 300 members, a ratio which is not reached by any Swedish union and should be contrasted with the British ratio, 1:3,000.[42]

It is very difficult to generalize about the self-conceived role played by the American union official. Nevertheless one might distinguish two major types. The first is the leader who regards himself as a super business agent whose principal job is to maximize the economic benefits accruing to his members; most of the presidents of unions affiliated to the old AFL were of this type. The other is a leader who sees himself as representing a wider constituency than the members of his own union and is interested not only in their welfare but also in the general improvement of social conditions in the community as a whole. The late Walter Reuther, president of the United Auto Workers, was the foremost example of this latter type.

When emphasis is on the role of the union with regard to strikes, the business–agent philosophy holds undisputed sway. There is not a single union in the United States which has made it part of its constitution to change basically the present economic and social system of the country. Political strikes as a means of protesting against the government are virtually unknown.

THE BARGAINING UNIT

The system of bargaining is backed up by the legislators. According to the Taft-Hartley Act, 1947, the employer has a duty to bargain collectively with

42. See the Donovan Report, para. 701. Bok and Dunlop, op. cit., p. 54 footnote, refer to a figure that the ratio of officers in Britain should be 1:2,000. This figure however, is not correct.

the representative of the employees, and a union which has the support of the majority in the appropriate unit is the exclusive representative of all employees, members as well as non-members (sec. 9(a)). In the absence of an agreement between the parties, a special authority, the National Labor Relations Board, may be called upon to determine 'the unit appropriate for the purpose of collective bargaining' and to direct a secret ballot in order to find out whether the union commands, as claimed, the support of the majority. As already indicated, the union, once voted in, frequently secures its position by some union security clause in the collective agreement, but there are many agreements without any form of security provisions.

With regard to the question what constitutes a unit for the purpose of collective bargaining,[43] the Board considers it a primary concern to group together only employees who have a substantial mutual interest in wages, hours and other conditions of employment. Guidelines are laid down in the Taft-Hartley Act. The unit should be 'the employer unit, craft unit, plant unit, or subdivision thereof' (sec. 9(b)). Regard must be paid to the position of the employees in the social hierarchy. Thus a unit may not include both professional and non-professional employees unless the majority of the professional employees vote for inclusion in such a unit. Skilled workers, too, are in certain cases protected against being included in a larger unit. According to the Board's construction of the Act, an 'employer unit' may include a multi-employer bargaining unit. Unlike the other bargaining units, the multi-employer unit is consensual. In the opinion of the Board it must be made manifest that all employers who are members of the group intend to be bound in future collective bargaining. The consent of the union is also required.

THE AMERICAN COLLECTIVE AGREEMENT

The insistence of the union upon a detailed control of management is a typical feature of the American collective agreement. Thus a seniority clause or some other job-security clause is a part of almost every collective agreement. The student of the American scene raises the question to what extent this should be credited to the Taft-Hartley Act. Have unions been favoured by the fact that certain matters are subjects of compulsory bargaining ? Generally speaking, the words of the statute in sec. 8(d)(1), that the bargaining shall concern 'wages, hours, and other terms or conditions or employment' are given a rather broad interpretation.

The ordinary American collective agreement is an agreement for a specified period of time with a 'no-strike clause', and the agreement is a contract binding at law. However, disputes arising under the contract are not, as in Sweden and Germany, ordinarily adjudicated by the courts. An arbitration clause is a regular part of the agreement. In *Steelworkers* v. *Warrior Gulf & Navigation Co.*, (1960) 363 US 574, the US Supreme Court emphasized

43. See Bok and Dunlop, op. cit., pp. 95 ff., and the article 'The Board and Section 9(c)(5): Multilocation and Singlelocation Bargaining Units in the Insurance and Retail Industries', 79 *Harvard Law Review*, February 1966, pp. 811 ff.

that the hostility demonstrated by courts toward arbitration of commercial agreements has no place in labour-management relations. A collective agreement is an effort to create a system of industrial self-government, and the arbitration machinery lies at the very heart of that system. A court will therefore order a party to submit a dispute to arbitration, and it is exclusively for the arbitrator to decide the merits of the dispute. The actual effect of the American arbitration system is to move the final stage of the grievance procedure to the plant. As mentioned earlier, the union is the exclusive representative of all the employees before the arbitrator.

MISTRUST OF UNION LEADERSHIP

The author has emphasized the strength of American unions, where they exist. There are many cases, however, where a union has been voted in with a narrow margin and a large minority remains outside it. Under these circumstances it might not seem paradoxical to suggest that mistrust of union leadership is another feature characteristic of the United States. There is a strong belief in democratic procedures which give the members power to protect themselves against irresponsible leaders. This is shown not only in rules that the officers shall regularly come up for reelection, but also in the collective bargaining procedure. Ordinarily the negotiators of a bargain conclude a tentative agreement, and the contract is not made final until ratified by the principals. A majority decision is the ordinary procedure. On this point, too, Congress has expressed its view. In the Taft-Hartley Act, sec. 203(c), the federal mediator is instructed to seek to induce the parties to solve the dispute by means not involving resort to strike or lockout, including submission to the employees of the employer's last offer for approval or rejection in a secret ballot. It should be added, however, that the method of submitting a last offer is confined almost exclusively to 'emergency disputes', where it is a required part of a special procedure (sec. 209). In the ordinary non-emergency dispute the mediator rarely suggests a vote on the last offer, since it has been learnt by experience that the result is often a rejection by a large majority.

STRIKE BENEFIT PROGRAMMES. DISCIPLINARY MEASURES
AGAINST STRIKE-BREAKERS

If a strike occurs the union is expected to support its members. A survey of strike benefit programmes among 113 national and international unions published in 1968 by the National Industrial Conference Board,[44] shows a varied picture. The majority, 70 unions, with a total membership of 11·6 million, have formal, centrally-based strike benefit programmes, and six others reported informal strike-assistance procedures. The 37 remaining unions surveyed indicated that they had no strike benefit programmes at the national or international level. The amount of benefit and the waiting period

44. National Industrial Conference Board (Miscel. Public.), *Union Initiation Fees, Dues and Per Capita Tax; National Union Strike Benefits,* 1968, pp. 29 ff.

differ from programme to programme; in some cases the members are entitled to benefits as a matter of right, in other cases the payment depends upon need. It should be noted that the duty to perform picketing is often a requirement for the receiving of strike benefits.

Having in mind the fact that the American union is the exclusive representative of all employees and that ordinarily even non-members pay dues to the union, one might have expected that strike benefits would be extended to non-members as well. However, this is not always the case. When 46 national and international unions were asked whether strike benefits were given to non-members, 23 said that non-members could, under certain circumstances, receive benefits. An equal number made no such provision.

In the present study it is not possible to probe more deeply into this subject. Compared with Sweden, the American strike benefit programmes with some exceptions cannot be considered highly developed. On the other hand, the existence of large national funds is not so important in a country where the emphasis is on local bargaining and therefore only a part of the members of a union can be expected to be on strike at the same time. Further, under those circumstances, members on strike will often find outside work.

During the strike no one is allowed to cross the picket line. Naturally, continuance at work is regarded as constituting treason to the union. Under the Taft-Hartley Act, the union is entitled to prescribe its own rules with respect to retention of membership (sec. 8(b)(1)(A)). A person who considers himself unjustly expelled from a union may file a charge of unfair labour practice against the union with the National Labor Relations Board. However, the Board has been reluctant to take up these cases and has done so quite recently only on a highly selective basis. The member may, if he so prefers, sue in court for damages, but in this case the court will normally require that the plaintiff shall have exhausted all his internal remedies.

Expulsion from a union because of violation of the union rules regarding participation in a strike will not entitle the union to require the employer to dismiss his employee. It will not help the union that the employer has signed a union shop agreement. In the Taft-Hartley Act (sec. 8(a)(3)(ii)(B)) it is laid down that the employer is not allowed to discriminate against an employee for non-membership, if membership was terminated for reasons other than failure to pay a reasonable initiation fee or reasonable dues. From the union's point of view, therefore, it is sometimes more profitable to fine the member than to expel him.[45, 46]

COALITION COLLECTIVE BARGAINING

The agreement covering a plant unit entered into with the union local is the usual type of agreement. However, bargaining by larger units is far from

45. The leading case on this question is *NLRB* v. *Allis-Chalmers Mfg. Co.*, 388 US 175 (1967).
46. The union's power to expel a member as a disciplinary measure and the prerequisites for the levying of union fines are extensively discussed by William B. Gould in 'Some limitations upon union discipline under the National Labor Relations Act: The radiations of *Allis-Chalmers*', *Duke Law Journal*, 1970, pp. 1067 ff.

unusual. In the first place, it should be noted that a collective agreement for all employees of a company or for all manual workers may often involve a high level of centralization. Thus, contracts with giants like the Ford Motor Company and the United States Steel Corporation comprise a great number of plants at different places and have an actual coverage larger than that of many industry-wide agreements. Secondly, there is coalition bargaining going on within a considerable number of industries, such as railroads, coal, glass, pottery, stovemaking and wallpaper. Thirdly, there are multi-employer dealings on a regional basis in several industries, varying from hosiery and textile-dyeing to shipbuilding. Sometimes there is to be found at the local level a multi-employer association which consists of groups covering different industries in a given locality. The most famous example is the San Francisco group. The employers have instituted master agreements establishing uniform conditions. Almost 75 per cent of the employees who are covered by collective agreements in San Francisco work under the terms of various master agreements negotiated by their unions with a number of different employer associations.

There are no recent figures as to the number of workers covered by agreements negotiated between trade unions and formal or informal employer groups. In 1947 the number of workers under all types of union agreements was 15 million; 4·5 million or about 33 per cent of them were subject to multi-employer agreements.[47] The present situation is not radically different.

Unlike the earlier experience in Sweden, multi-employer bargaining has been considered to favour the interests of the unions in particular. The A F L - C I O has established an Industrial Union Department which is trying to persuade affiliated unions to join in coordinated bargaining. Particularly they have aimed at centralized bargaining with companies having a great number of widely-spread factories. An example is provided by the bargaining in 1965– 66 over a contract with General Electric, where a coalition committee was formed embracing eight international unions. In other cases the employers found it in their interest to stick to coordinated bargaining. Thus the members of the San Francisco group have instituted their master agreement in order to prevent the union from obtaining concessions from various enterprises above the established level.

RETALIATION BY EMPLOYERS

Generally, the strike is as wide as the bargaining union. If the union should choose to call out only members in key positions, the employer can be expected to answer with a lockout of all employees who are union members. A national or international union may try to apply what is called wage-leader bargaining or 'whipsawing'. The union selects an employer whom the union thinks vulnerable and at the same time prosperous enough to pay, and strikes

47. U. S. Department of Labor, Bureau of Labor Statistics, *Collective Bargaining with Associations and Groups of Employers*, Bulletin No. 897 (1947).

against him if he is not willing to yield. When an agreement is reached, other firms are expected to follow the lead. Within some industries it is an accepted pattern that small firms follow the agreements of the giants. Thus, for many years, in the steel industry the contract of the United States Steel Corporation has served as a wage leader.

The employer may retaliate against the whipsawing union, particularly when the company owns a number of plants, by simply moving production from one plant to another. Another approach is to refuse to bargain over 'national' demands or, when demands are presented during plant bargaining, to try to embarrass the spokesmen of the union by treating them as 'strangers'. The possible use of actions for injunctions based on the claim that the company is guilty of unfair labour practice complicates the picture. The ultimate weapon of the company is, of course, to keep offers short and in the event of a strike to pay the costs of a prolonged shut-down.[48]

In a study aiming at comparisons it should be stated that sympathetic strikes and sympathetic lockouts are rare. As mentioned before, American union leaders are not swayed by the spirit of solidarity between all members of the working class which is such an essential part of European unionism and which in exceptional circumstances has been held to justify resort to a general strike. In the United States, a fairly frequent type of sympathetic action is a refusal to cross a picket line at the premises of another employer. It should be added that the sympathetic strike or a sympathetic lockout may constitute a breach of contract as a violation of the no-strike (no-lockout) clause of the collective agreement.

EMPLOYERS' MUTUAL AID PROGRAMMES

As already indicated, membership of a national or international union means that the individual is part of a mutual aid arrangement. Generally there are local and national strike funds available. If only part of the union's membership is on strike or subject to lockout, which is the normal situation in the United States, the members on strike can expect that the other members will contribute if local and national funds are insufficient to meet the needs.

Does membership of an employers' association give the member firm the corresponding advantage of mutual aid in case of a labour dispute? Some British associations operate indemnity funds. As we shall see in the two following sections of this chapter, in Sweden and Germany the compensation against losses because of labour conflicts is a central function of an employers' association. In the United States, employers' associations, with some exceptions, do not engage in such activities. The railroad carriers and the airline carriers have entered into mutual aid pacts. Both these groups of employers are covered by the Railway Labor Act, a counterpart to the Taft-Hartley Act, but proceeding from the assumption that labour disputes in transpor-

48. The strategies on both sides are described by George H. Hildebrand, 'Cloudy future for coalition bargaining', *Harvard Business Review*, November–December 1968, pp. 114 ff.

tation industry always constitute a national emergency. This explains some circumscribing conditions in the mutual aid pacts, which will be mentioned later on. Under the railroad agreement, each member contributes to an insurance fund. When a member is hit, he is paid compensation sufficient to cover his fixed costs and his daily expenses. In the airlines agreement, it is laid down that if a member is struck, the other members shall turn over any extra revenues resulting from carrying his traffic, after a deduction for increased costs.[49]

The validity of employers' mutual aid programmes can be disputed from a number of points of departure, some of them peculiar to the two programmes just mentioned, some of them pertinent to all employers' mutual aid programmes. The unions have claimed that the agreements violated the employer's duty under sec. 2 of the Railway Labor Act – a duty 'to exert every reasonable effort to make and maintain agreements concerning rates of pay, rules, and working conditions, and to settle all disputes, . . . in order to avoid any interruption to commerce or to the operation of any carrier growing out of any dispute between the carrier and the employees thereof'. Further, the unions have argued that, because of statutory provisions, the pacts required approval of the Interstate Commerce Commission or of the Civil Aeronautics Board, respectively. An objection of more general application is the following one. The aid programme may cause an interruption of commerce constituting a violation of the provisions of the Sherman Antitrust Act. So far, when tested by courts all these arguments have been rejected. However, it should be noted that neither of the two aid programmes can be invoked by a member merely because he has been struck. Rather, each sets up conditions to the right of subsidy. Thus, under the railroad agreement, the right arises when a strike (*a*) is contrary to the provisions of the Railway Labor Act, (*b*) is to enforce demands contrary to the recommendations of an Emergency Board convened pursuant to the Railway Labor Act, or (*c*) is in resistance to the application of recommendations of the Emergency Board.

AMERICAN STRIKE RECORD – AUTHOR'S COMMENTS

It is well known that the United States has a higher figure for working days lost because of labour disputes than have many other countries, Britain included. For various reasons one might have expected another state of affairs. In the United States union membership is not very high compared with Britain, Sweden or Germany; in 1966 it represented only 28 per cent of all those employed in non-agricultural enterprises. On the other hand, unofficial strikes do not occur as often as in Britain.[50]

The explanation of the high number of days lost in ordinary lawful strikes

49. For a more detailed discussion of the operation of both the airlines and the railroad plan, see Comment, 38 *New York University Law Review*, 1963, pp. 126 ff.
50. Bok and Dunlop state that strikes that shut-down operations during the term of a collective-bargaining agreement, including wildcat stoppages, have largely yielded in private industry to the discipline of the grievance procedure and arbitration over the interpretation and application of the agreement. See Bok and Dunlop, op. cit., p. 252.

must be looked for elsewhere than in union membership. Here the author makes reservations before proceeding further on this subject: the forming of an opinion ought properly to be based on a deeper insight into American society than he can claim to possess. Even then, the distinguishing of major factors in a complicated pattern of social interrelations must often be a kind of guesswork.

With these reservations in mind one may recall what has been said above about the reasons why the American unions did not develop into a popular movement, as did the unions in Western Europe. The prototype of the American trade union is the union of skilled workers, constituting socially a middle-class element.

When explaining the strife in the labour market another factor mentioned by Bok and Dunlop should be particularly emphasized, namely the widespread opposition to the unions manifested by employers. Its importance can be seen from the ease with which unions can usually organize blue-collar workers once management has been persuaded to remain neutral.[51] It is against this background one should assess the validity of the common statement that unions have come to stay. In America management does not, as in Sweden, look upon the union as a stabilizing factor which he is happy to negotiate with. The American employer bargains with the union because he is forced to do so.

From this it is natural to pass on to another observation made by Bok and Dunlop[52] concerning serious interruptions arising from attempts to change the structure of bargaining and in particular the unions' attempts to extend the system of coalition bargaining. They present a long list of disputes which in the last years have attracted much public attention. The most glaring example is the strike in the copper industry in 1967–68, which lasted eight months. The four major companies resisted to the union's claim of company-wide collective joint bargaining. Their strategy of exhausting the resources of the union proved successful.

This leads to the comment that a further development of bargaining, industrywise or companywise, for larger units than at present may eliminate a number of causes of disputes and focus attention on wages and additional benefits. In certain contexts it is easier to come to an agreement on what an industry can pay than on what an employer, who has been selected as wage leader, should pay.

Other factors explaining the unrest are at work in situations, too, where the bargaining follows the established pattern. The wisdom of a system of ratification – incidentally such a system has recently been introduced in Italy – may be doubted. It implies that each settlement has to be sold ('marketed') twice, first to the representatives and then to the members.

One should keep in mind that the members will seldom take a settlement against the advice of their leaders. Rejections are numerous, particularly so

51. Bok and Dunlop, op. cit., pp. 49 f., and Bok in 84 *Harvard Law Review*, 1971, p. 1413.
52. ibid., pp. 256 ff. See also, Hildebrand, op. cit., pp. 120 ff.

when the union representation was not unanimous in its acceptance, and one cannot exclude the possibility than an employer who is faced by the risk that the union members will reject his offer will withhold something which he might otherwise have given, and that the union leaders will be less willing than otherwise to take responsibility.[53] It should be noted that in Sweden the national board of the union always has the constitutional power to sign an agreement without previous submission to the members, and that in Germany a qualified majority is a condition for the continuance of a strike.

Another relevant feature of American labour relations is the unwillingness of the employer to close down his plant in case of a strike. Not infrequently, the American employers try to keep production going with the help of un-organized workers. In the historical part of this section the author mentioned that Congress shifted from detached neutrality to a pro-labour attitude with the introduction of the Industrial Recovery Act, 1933, and that the approach of the Taft-Hartley Act was basically the same. However, this Act is Janus-faced. Its policy is to protect not only the right of the individual to organize but also his 'right to refrain from' union activities. As a part of this policy a union member who stays at work is – as mentioned before – protected against dismissal even if he has been expelled by the union as a 'strike-breaker'. This last comment does not add much that is new to what has already been said. In most countries the loss of working days due to industrial disputes is to a large extent a consequence of a dual distrust; a distrust on the part of employers towards unions, and a distrust by union members of union leadership.

Sweden

THE CONDITIONS UNDER WHICH TRADE UNIONISM BEGAN

It is easier to describe the role of the unions in Sweden than that of unions in the United States. This is so not only because the present author is now on his home ground and because Sweden with its 8 million inhabitants obviously cannot offer such a wide spectrum as can a country of 200 million people. The chief reason is rather that the existence in Sweden of certain well-established patterns is due to a long evolutionary process which has not been disrupted by wars, revolutions or serious economic crises. Sweden's record of industrial peace, so often noted by foreign observers, is to be explained as a product of history and not by reference to certain qualities of the Swedish people.

In Sweden the conditions under which trade unionism began were more favourable than in most other countries. Swedish trade union leaders were not called upon to defend themselves in court to the same extent as they had to do in Britain and in the United States. The common law of Sweden is alien both to the idea that combined action as restraint of trade constitutes a

53. See William E. Simkin, 'Refusals to ratify contracts', *Industrial and Labor Relations Review*, July 1968, pp. 518 ff., p. 535 in particular.

tort – the lawfulness of an act is judged by itself even if the defendant was taking part in a concerted action – and to the idea that interference by a third party in a contractual relationship is a wrong – thus, as a matter of principle, no sanction can be applied against a trade union leader who has induced a worker to commit a breach of his employment contract. For many years there was felt to be a need for statutory restrictions on the use of industrial actions, but from the point of view of those in power the results were very meagre owing to dissension as to what methods should be applied.

Further, both politically and economically, Swedish employers have never played a role comparable to that of American businessmen. In the Swedish Parliament the farmers, the small entrepreneurs, and the royal officials played the leading parts until 1932. In that year the Social Democratic Party came into power, where, save for one short interval in the summer of 1936, it has stayed ever since – albeit sometimes with a narrow majority margin and sometimes in coalition with other parties. Actually there were not so many big enterprises in Sweden, and in time some of the most important ones, such as the principal railways, the liquor and tobacco monopolies and many of the power plants, came to be State-owned.[54]

The Swedish union movement for industrial workers acquired its present shape, with national unions affiliated to a confederation, Landsorganisationen i Sverige (LO; Swedish Confederation of Trade Unions), at the end of the nineteenth century. The LO was constituted in 1898.

Swedish employers as a defence measure joined together in 'strike insurance societies'. The Svenska Arbetsgivareföreningen (SAF; Swedish Employers' Confederation) was founded in 1902.

THE SWEDISH TRADE-UNION MOVEMENT AS A POPULAR MOVEMENT

It is not easy to give a complete explanation why the Swedish trade unions, and those of manual workers particularly, present such a uniform picture. Great importance must be attached to the early socialist propaganda according to which all workers constitute a social class oppressed by the capitalists. The conditions of individuals could be improved by pressing the employers as an opposite party to yield to the demands of the union and ensuring that achievement of these ends should not be hampered by competition between individual workers. The close relationship with the Social Democratic Party is another characteristic feature. Indeed, at the constituent assembly of the LO in 1898, it was laid down that every union associated with the LO should join the Social Democratic Party within a period of three years. It is true that this decision was never enforced. Soon, collective membership with the Party was secured by other means. In 1900 the LO decided that it should encourage local branches of national unions to join the local labour commune and in that way achieve membership of the Social Democratic Party. The local labour

54. cf. Theodore J. Schneyer, 'Administrative responsibility in Swedish public enterprise. The problem of complex goals', 14 *Scandinavian Studies in Law*, 1970, pp. 169 ff.

communes still form the backbone of the Party. Since 1908, however, the individual trade union member has been entitled to contract out of collective membership.

The L O, whose membership consists almost exclusively of manual workers, had in 1970 1·7 million members. This means that in practically all industries more than 90 per cent of the workers belong to an L O union.

A distinctive feature of the Swedish labour market is the line of demarcation between manual workers, on the one hand, and white-collar workers and public officials, on the other. The unions of white-collar workers began to gain ground in the 1930s.[55] The organizational pattern is less uniform than that of the manual workers. Within private industry two unions dominate the picture: the Union of Clerical and Technical Employees in Industry with 193,000 members and the Union of Supervisors with a membership of 64,000. Within the public sector the employees are divided between a number of unions. Manual workers and officials in the lower grades are organized in two unions, the Swedish State Employees' Union and the Swedish Municipal Workers' Union, both affiliated to the L O. State officials and municipal officials in the middle grades constitute two powerful blocs loosely united with the salaried employees and the supervisors in a confederation called Tjänstemännens Centralorganisation (T C O; Swedish Central Organization of Salaried Employees). There is another federation of State employees, Statstjänstemännens Riksförbund (S R; National Swedish Central Organization of Salaried Employees), consisting mainly of officers in the armed forces and high-ranking employees of the State railways and the postal service. In addition there is a confederation of qualified professional people, Sveriges Akademikers Centralorganisation (S A C O; Swedish Confederation of Professional Associations) with a membership of, 104,000, representing such groups as lawyers, social scientists, social workers, civil engineers, medical doctors, high-school teachers, and university professors and lecturers. The T C O unions are, like the S R and S A C O, politically neutral.

Among white-collar workers and public officials the proportion of union membership is not so high as it is among manual workers, possibly 70 per cent compared with 95 per cent. According to statistics relating to 1970, the total membership of Swedish unions is about 2·4 million out of a work force of about 3·6 million, representing a ratio of 69 per cent. None of the other five countries covered by our study comes close to that figure.

PATTERNS OF COLLECTIVE BARGAINING

Ordinarily the Swedish collective agreement governs the relations between the parties for a definite period of time, e.g. for one, two, or three years. According to the Collective Agreements Act of 1928, sec. 4, a peace obligation

55. For white-collar unionism in Sweden, see Nilstein, 'White-Collar Trade Unions' in *Contemporary Developments in Industrialized Societies*, Sturmthal (ed.), Chicago, 1967, pp. 261 ff.

is incumbent upon the parties and their members. For practical purposes the Act implies – the details will be dealt with in a later chapter[56] – that resort to economic action during the period of validity of the agreement is not allowed except in the case of sympathetic actions. The idea that peace shall prevail for the period agreed upon was accepted by the parties even before the introduction of the Act of 1928.

Constitutionally, the power of collective bargaining lies in the hands of the national union, and the national agreement for an industry is the prototype of the Swedish collective agreement. One would therefore expect some open conflicts when new national agreements are negotiated. However, where private industry is concerned – the unrest in the public sector will be discussed later on – one has to go back to the year 1953 in order to find an open conflict of that kind. The Food Workers' Union gave notice of a strike at the slaughterhouses from 7 April 1953. The SAF answered with a lockout by their member firms of all workers coming under the jurisdiction of the Food Workers' Union. The conflict lasted for five weeks. In 1955 there arose a similar situation in another industry. The Pulp and Paper Workers' Union with some 40,000 members gave notice of a strike. Again the SAF hit back, but this time on a much larger scale. Notice was given of a general lockout covering about 500,000 workers. Under these threats peaceful agreements were reached simultaneously for a number of industries. According to the yearly report of the SAF the employers had, by threatening a lockout, succeeded in causing the unions to scale down their demands considerably.

From 1956 there have been continuous central negotiations for all workers in private industry. The negotiations have resulted in joint recommendations from the LO and the SAF to affiliated organizations on both sides to make national agreements within a framework laid down in the recommendations. Generally the periods have covered one or two years, but the agreements of 1966 and of 1971 were both for a three-year period. The SAF and the LO have come to agreement without resort to economic action, and with two exceptions, the above-mentioned agreements of 1966 and of 1971, even without threat of resort to such action.

In the spring of 1971 the situation was more tense than on earlier occasions. Negotiations for a new central agreement between the LO and the SAF had been pending since the late autumn of 1970 and the collective agreements had expired around the turn of the year. The National Collective Bargaining Office, which represented the State in negotiations with the unions of State employees, had launched a policy of favouring the lowest-paid groups in order to diminish the gap between the earnings of those at the top and those at the bottom. The LO unions, who had been frustrated in earlier attempts to establish equalization, wanted a coordination between the public and the private sectors. They therefore refused to present definitive wage claims until a settlement for the public sector was within reach. SACO and the SR – the unions of qualified people and of certain other categories of officials – had

56. See Chapter 3.

called strikes, the Office had hit back with lockouts covering, among other groups, university and high-school teachers, two categories with a large SACO membership. The strikes came to have serious effects on the whole community – a strike among railway employees had brought to a stop all passenger traffic and most heavy goods traffic as well. In this situation the Government, as will be described in Chapter 6, introduced a Bill which was passed by Parliament on 11 March and came into force the following day. The Government was granted power to renew certain collective agreements for a period of six weeks. SACO and SR were forced back to work.

Several committees of mediators were in action. The mediators for the State sector presented a final proposal on 13 May. Now the LO was prepared to disclose its wage claims. During the night of 3–4 June the mediators for the private sector declared that they were unable to reconcile the conflicting views. Immediately the LO took action and on 4 June it recommended its members to ban all overtime work. Contrary to its earlier policy in similar situations, the SAF decided not to escalate. The LO proceeded on its way and recommended affiliated unions to give notice of strikes at a selected number of firms covering about 10 per cent of the membership in private employment. Again the SAF preferred to abstain from countermeasures. On 16 June the SAF declared its intention to compensate those of its members who would suffer from the strikes. Eventually, on 22 June a settlement was reached in accordance with the recommendations of the mediators.

Certainly this agreement of 1971 between the SAF and the LO was a compromise. Compared with the contemporary settlements for the State and the municipal sectors it was a victory for the employers, who at least in part were able to reject the claim for total coordination. For those who intend to resort to economic action, the end of June is a bad period in an affluent society like Sweden. Around 1 July most of industry shuts down for a period of four weeks in order to allow for the statutory period of vacation. Thus the SAF could take the position that they would wait and see. The LO people would have placed themselves in a rather awkward position if the strikes had come into effect at a time when they would hurt those members of the general public who were on vacation more than they would organized employers.

As already indicated, within the public sector the situation has been more troublesome. Under two Acts of 1965, the State Officials Act and the Municipal Officials Act, which came into force on 1 January 1966, the earlier system of unilateral regulation of conditions of employment was replaced by a system admitting collective bargaining and resort to industrial action in disputes over salaries and other matters of remuneration. The State, through its agent the National Collective Bargaining Office, has applied methods similar to those of the SAF. When in autumn of 1966 SACO, the Swedish Confederation of Professional Associations, called a strike at some university departments and some high schools, the Office imposed a lockout on all SACO teachers. The lockouts of early 1971 have been mentioned before. The unrest within the public sector has been due to two main reasons, one being the claim of small groups, like marine pilots and locomotive engineers, to have negotiating rights of their own, and the other the unwillingness of officials in the higher grades to yield to the salary-equalization policy of the National Collective Bargaining Office.

PROCEDURE FOR STRIKE INITIATION AND RATIFICATION OF SETTLEMENTS

The constitutions of the unions affiliated to the LO are in most cases framed in accordance with a model constitution and all contain essentially the same elements. Thus the goal of the Swedish Metal Workers' Union is to organize all workers over 15 years of age employed in the metallurgical industry in a common organization embracing the whole country in order to promote by all available means the organizational, economic and social interests of the members.

There are strict provisions concerning a procedure for decisions with regard to recourse to industrial action. A strike can be initiated by a branch or by some other local unit. If more than two-thirds of those concerned have voted for a stoppage of work, the matter must be submitted to the board of the national union, which decides whether and when action shall be taken. The board is entitled to take the initiative on its own without putting the issue to a vote.

Ordinarily there are also provisions with regard to the acceptance of a new agreement. Until 1969 the constitution of the Metal Workers' Union prescribed that each new agreement should be ratified in a secret ballot unless it had been entered into before the expiration of an earlier agreement. The practical effect of this clause was not what one might have expected. The national board found the procedure of ratification inconvenient and arranged that the old agreement should continue to apply pending negotiations. Under the new constitution of 1969, a decision as to whether the new agreement should be put to a vote or not falls within the discretion of the board of the union.

There is no provision to the effect that the continuance of a strike presupposes the existence of a qualified majority. The vote on ratification is consultative. In the early days of trade unionism this was not always the case. In the light of earlier experiences of prolonged and costly conflicts, the constitution of the LO was amended in 1941. It was made a condition for membership of the LO that the constitution of the affiliated union should give the board the power to take the ultimate decision in matters concerning notice of termination of collective agreements, or acceptance or rejection of proposals to such agreements, and of resorting to industrial action.

THE ROLE OF THE LO WITH REGARD TO STRIKE INITIATION

With regard to strikes and other offensive actions the LO plays an important role, although the constitutional power to take the ultimate decision lies in the hands of the national union. Because of its membership of the LO the national union has certain obligations incumbent upon it. It is not entitled to order a strike involving more than 3 per cent of its membership without the prior consent of the Secretariat, i.e. the governing body of the L O. Even a strike of smaller proportions than this requires the consent of the Secretariat, if the strike is expected to cause a lockout of more than 3 per cent of the membership or of members of other affiliated unions. That this was a disputed point will be seen from the following extract from the L O constitution. In order to protect the national union against unwanted intervention it is laid down that the L O may not refuse permission unless 'the strike is expected to cause considerable disadvantages for other affiliated unions or for the trade union movement as a whole, or is considered to be an action against the interests of the nation'.

STRIKE BENEFIT PROGRAMMES

The union has a duty to support members engaged in strike or exposed to lockout. The L O will grant financial aid to affiliated unions involved in open conflicts, provided that the strike was duly authorized. The main financial burden falls on the national union, and the L O does not enter until the strike has lasted for some time. Thus a member of the Metal Workers' Union is entitled to benefits from his union from the seventh day after his entry into the conflict. According to the constitution of the L O, its aid programme comes into effect from the third week.

Union membership dues in Sweden are generally considerable, on average 400–500 kronor a year, and the Swedish unions aim to build up substantial strike funds.

The following figures from the L O Annual Report 1953 on the dispute in which the Food Workers' Union was involved will give some idea how the system operates. The stoppage of work lasted five weeks and involved members employed by firms affiliated to the S A F. Benefits were paid for 547,000 days to a total amount of 4·96 million kronor.

The main sources were as follows:

	Skr. mill.
Union Fund	2·96
Levy from members not involved in the strike	0·92
L O	0·67
Levy from members of the Nordic Food Workers' Union	0·33
Contributions from other unions	0·05

DISCIPLINARY MEASURES AGAINST STRIKE-BREAKERS

Swedish unions are well disciplined and able to bring strong social pressure upon unorganized workers. Therefore, within the L O sector one can expect

100 per cent participation in every strike which is officially authorized. Since a serious incident in 1931, when military forces were used to protect strike-breakers, the Swedish employers have actually adopted a policy of closing down the plant when a strike occurs.

The situation within the public sector is more complicated. In the conflicts with the SACO groups in 1966 and 1971, the National Collective Bargaining Office locked out only those who were SACO members, requiring unorganized employees within the units concerned to remain in work. SACO, in its strike declaration of 1971, declared that non-union members were welcome to join; they were even offered strike benefits.

Among manual workers it is the general opinion that a person who has acted as a strike-breaker has violated the fundamental duty of solidarity incumbent upon every member of the working class. In earlier days it often happened that a strike-breaker was followed from one workshop to another and harassed by fellow workers until the blacklisting was forgotten or formally withdrawn after the strike-breaker had made a public apology at a meeting of the union. In the Basic Agreement between the SAF and the LO of 1938, which has been adopted as a collective agreement within most parts of private industry, there are provisions which limit the use of direct action. In this document it is stated that after a labour dispute has been settled no action of retaliation should be resorted to against anyone because of his relationship to the dispute. Today one seldom hears about blacklisting of strike-breakers. Most likely they seldom occur.

Like the British courts, the Swedish courts have exercised jurisdiction over actions by members for wrongful expulsions on the assumption that the individual member has, by his application for admission, submitted himself to the terms of an agreement embodied in the constitution of the union. It is generally acknowledged that strike-breaking constitutes a serious wrong and that exclusion may follow as a disciplinary action.

Swedish courts have proceeded further than the English courts did before the coming into force of the Industrial Relations Act 1971. Without any statutory support the courts have taken jurisdiction over claims by outsiders to gain membership. The case 1948 NJA 513 concerned an action laid by a Norwegian bricklayer who had been refused admission to the Bricklayers' Union. According to the grounds for the decision of the Supreme Court, the character and scope of the operation of the union had resulted in a situation where workers in the masonry trade were essentially dependent upon membership of the union for obtaining employment and consequently for securing a livelihood. In consideration of this fact and in accordance with the principle, laid down in the constitution, that the union was to be an open organization, the local branch of the Bricklayers' Union could not reject applications for membership without valid reasons.[57] There is no reported case concerning the question whether a strike-breaker may bring an action for readmission. Most

57 See Folke Schmidt, *The Law of Labour Relations in Sweden*, Harvard U.P., 1962, pp. 81 ff.

likely, the court would sustain his action, basing its decision on the above-mentioned philosophy, expressed in the Basic Agreement, that after the settlement of a labour dispute retaliation should not be resorted to against anyone because of his relationship to the dispute.

THE WILDCAT STRIKE

Every year a number of wildcat strikes occur in Sweden. The ordinary wildcat strike is of short duration, lasting only a few hours or one or two days. The workers revolt against a supervisor or a time-study man or to express their dissatisfaction with an offer of a new piece rate. Until very recently the number of days lost was not very great and from an overall view was almost insignificant. In the last two or three years, however, the situation has changed. Since the autumn of 1969 there have been a number of incidents. Local groups of workers have gone on strike for long periods with the aim – not always clearly articulated – of improving the conditions of the national collective agreement.

The most remarkable incident was the strike, lasting from the middle of December 1969 to early in February 1970, by 5,000 miners at the State-owned iron-ore mines in the north of Sweden. The boards of the branches concerned were for all practical purposes brushed aside by a strike committee, which held regular meetings and put various proposals to the vote. Following the pattern laid down by the SAF that in case of unlawful strikes negotiations must not take place under duress, the management explained that they did not intend to bargain before the men returned to work. However, in the end the management yielded and entered into informal talks with a committee composed of 21 representatives of the strikers and six representatives of the local branches concerned. Even the LO gave the strikers quasi-official recognition. During the last phase the deputy president of the LO, Mr Kurt Nordgren, acted as adviser to the delegation.

EMPLOYERS' ASSOCIATIONS

The SAF, the Swedish Employers' Confederation, is a tightly knit organization. It is composed of a number of sectoral associations. Each firm, however, has a double affiliation. It is at the same time a member of such an association and a part-owner of the Confederation. The power of policy-making is vested in the Board of the SAF and its General Council.

A firm or a sectoral association wishing to enter into a collective agreement with a trade union is obliged to submit the draft agreement to the Board of the SAF for its approval. The SAF has the power to exercise a strict control of economic actions undertaken by its affiliates. A sectoral association or a firm may not order a lockout without the consent of the Board or the General Council. After a decision of the General Council, the SAF has the right to call a lockout involving even an association which has not given its consent.

During a strike or a lockout at a member firm no employer may directly or indirectly offer work or any other support to workers involved in the strike or the lockout.

Analogously to a trade union, the SAF has the power to discipline, by imposing expulsion, a member disobeying a lockout order. Damages may also be claimed from the violator.

Each firm affiliated to the SAF pays an annual due. Out of the surplus of the paid-in dues there has been built up a compensation fund, which at the end of 1968 had assets of about 500 million kronor. In addition each member has to sign a guarantee bond. The aggregate liability sums of the bonds constitute a fund which can be used as additional security for the payment of compensation to firms involved in labour disputes. In the constitution it is laid down that in case of stoppage of work an affiliated firm is entitled to compensation for each working day to an amount related to the wage sum. At present it corresponds to an average of 5 kronor a day per worker, a sum which is far from sufficient to cover the actual loss. However, the Board is allowed to give additional compensation, and in order to stop the flood of wildcat strikes the SAF on 23 January 1970 issued a declaration that member firms hit by labour disputes would be fully compensated for all losses, including loss of profit.

West Germany

THE POINT OF DEPARTURE

On the downfall of the Third Reich in 1945, Germany had to start from scratch. The line of demarcation between the American, British and French forces and the Soviet occupying forces soon split the realm into two countries. The cities had been largely destroyed by the bomb attacks and whatever still remained in the factories was dismantled and moved to other countries. The administration was run by the occupying powers. Certainly, those who were building the new West Germany acted under strong pressure from these powers, and from the USA and Britain in particular. However, there was no uncritical acceptance of American or British institutions. Rather, the builders of the new society looked to the Weimar Republic of 1919–33 for their model. They asked why it was that a basically democratic system like that of the Weimar Republic had been unable to withstand the Nazis. The inheritance from the Nazi period, 1933–45, was to be renounced, and there were to be created democratic institutions that would be strong enough to resist attacks from the extreme left as well as from the extreme right.

The student of West German labour relations will find hardly anything borrowed from American or British counterparts. If any similarity exists at all between Germany and any of the other five countries here studied, it is with Sweden. One can point to the fact that for centuries there has been a lively cultural exchange between Germany and Sweden, and that until 1933 Swedish trade-union leaders and Swedish employers had close personal contacts with their German colleagues, not to mention the ties between Social Democratic politicians of both countries.

LABOUR AND MANAGEMENT ORGANIZE AND JOIN IN NATIONAL CONFEDERATIONS

In the beginning the trade-union people were in a more favourable position than the employers. In West Germany they were made welcome to organize the workers in the shops, whereas in the first few years the employers, because of the denazification programme, were not allowed to engage in organizational activities.

The Deutsche Gewerkschaftsbund, (DGB; The German Federation of Trade Unions) was created in 1949 and Die Bundesvereinigung der Deutschen Arbeitgeberverbände (BDA; The German Confederation of Employers' Associations) was established in 1950. A characteristic feature of these two organizations is their effort to settle their mutual disputes peacefully by themselves through negotiations conducted with the advice of conciliators. This policy was laid down in a document signed at Hattenheim on 12 January 1950, the so-called Hattenheimer Agreement.[58] The confederations made an urgent joint request to their affiliated organizations to create machinery for joint conciliation. They subscribed to the policy of self-government by the 'Sozialpartner' and pointed out that State interference for regulation of wages and conditions of employment was inconsistent with this policy. The Hattenheimer principles were restated during the conversations at Limburg in 1951 and were replaced by the Margarethenhof Agreement of 1954. The newly established Federal Government followed the advice of the *Sozialpartner* and adopted a policy of non-interference. The Chancellor of the Bund stated in a declaration of 29 October 1953, that the Government intended to act in the full assurance that 'the Sozialpartner would be able to reconcile their interest in trustful cooperation without disruptions of the economy and disturbance of the community caused by serious labour conflicts'.[59]

THE 'EINHEITSGEWERKSCHAFT' AND THE DGB

The occupation powers had a vested interest in the coming into being of free trade unions, since such unions were considered to be a basic element of a democratic society. For natural reasons, however, the Powers were against strong centralized unions because of a possible misuse of power, and they preferred local unions. The German union leaders for their part wanted to build up larger units as quickly as possible. The new leaders were of opinion that the splits in the union movement had been one of the reasons why the Nazis came to power. The unions of the new Federal Republic were to be

58. The signatories to this declaration were the DGB and die Vereinigung der Arbeitgeberverbände. Die Vereinigung der Arbeitgevbererbände adopted its present name, Die Bundesvereinigung der Deutschen Arbeitgeverberbände, BDA, at an assembly in November 1950. See Gerhard Erdmann, *Die Deutschen Arbeitgeberverbände*, 1966, p. 231.
59. Quoted from *Jahresbericht der Bundesvereinigung der Deutschen Arbeitgeberverbände 1. Dezember 1952–30. November 1953*, p. 11.

based on the principles of all-embracing scope and of neutrality as to political ideology. The new leaders were successful, at least in part.

The unions affiliated to the DGB dominate, with a total membership at the end of 1969 of 6·7 million. However, there are several independent unions. A rather weak Christian federation exists with a membership of around 200,000. More important, the Deutsche Beamtenbund (the German Federation of Officials), with a membership of 730,000 and goals less militant than the DGB unions, forms a unit on its own. Further, there exist a number of organizations of white-collar workers. The Deutsche Angestelltengewerkschaft (DAG; Union of German Salaried Employees) embracing some 600,000 members is the most important one.

The DGB is a confederation of a number of industrial unions, such as IG Metall (Metal Workers), IG Bau, Steine, Erden (Building and Construction Industries) and IG Bergbau (Mine Workers). There are federal unions, too, for employees in commerce, banking and insurance, and for employees in teaching and scientific occupations. There is one general union, namely the Gewerkschaft Öffentliche Dienste, Transport und Verkehr; it comes second in membership among the DGB unions and embraces employees in federal, state and municipal service, as well as employees in land and maritime transport.

The DGB union is an *Einheitsgewerkschaft*, i.e. a unified union. Compared with the unions of the Weimar Republic the *Einheitsgewerkschaft* represents an innovation in the following respects:

(*a*) many of the earlier unions were unions representing a trade,
(*b*) in the Weimar period there were separate unions for manual workers, clerical workers, and public officials, and
(*c*) the earlier unions were split along political lines into socialist, Christian, and liberal unions.

In 1955 the total number of union members represented 33 per cent of all employees. As in the United States, union membership is unevenly distributed. The Mine Workers' Union (IG Bergbau und Energie), with a membership of 80 per cent, has a higher proportion than any of the other unions. The Metal Workers' Union (IG Metall) has 46 per cent, whereas the union of workers in the building and construction industries (IG Bau, Steine, Erden) covers no more than about 18 per cent of all employees. In Germany, too, the total membership rate has declined somewhat, from about 33 per cent in 1955 to about 30 per cent in 1970.

With regard to the distribution of power the structure in Germany corresponds to that obtaining in Britain. The DGB has, like the TUC, mainly policy-making functions. Affiliated unions pay a quarterly contribution of 0.15 DM per member to a federal *Solidaritätsfonds*. In the event of wage movements of general importance financial aid can be paid to the conflict-stricken union. Contributions may come from other unions, too. However, this is regarded as an exceptional step. Each national union operates independently. Upon inquiry, IG Metall informed the present author that so far it has never supported other unions financially.

It should be mentioned that the DGB constituent assembly of 1949 adopted a code of conduct in labour disputes[60] which deals in detail with the initiation and the continuation of strikes. According to the constitution of the DGB this code is binding on all affiliated unions.

Membership of a German DGB union can be compared to membership of a Swedish LO union. In both countries the unions claim to represent the workers as a social class with interests opposed to those of capitalism. It is hard to say why membership should be so much lower in Germany than in Sweden. It cannot be explained, as in the United States, by the unwillingness among employers to recognize the unions. The typical German collective agreement is a regional agreement. Even the Building and Construction Workers' Union, which represents about 18 per cent of all employees, is signatory to a number of regional collective agreements. It is a common saying among Swedish trade union people that the German inertia may be related to the fact that the works committee (*Betriebsrat*) of a plant is very influential and that therefore the individual employees are more concerned with their representation on the works committee than with their representation on the board of the local union. However, this cannot explain the dilemma of the German union leaders. Through an historical accident[61] the workers within the coal and steel industries were granted greater powers of codetermination than were the workers in other industries, and as we have seen before the unions which organize these industries – the Mine Workers' Union and the Metal Workers' Union – have membership rates above the average.

THE POLICY OF THE GERMAN TRADE UNION MOVEMENT

The Declaration of Principles adopted at the constituent assembly of the DGB at Munich in 1949, states that the trade union movement shall aim at a radical change of society. Workers who are trade union members should, it states, have codetermination not only in social matters but also in management. Basic industries, such as mining, steel, the large chemical concerns, the supply of energy, should be made public property. In the following years there has been a debate in progress between the traditionalists represented by the leaders of the metal workers and the chemical workers, on the one hand, and the reformers represented by the Building Workers' Union, on the other hand. The former group has advocated that the principles laid down at the Munich conference should still apply, the latter has expressed the opinion that the trade union movement should face the fact that it is actually operating within a capitalist society. As expressed by one of its leaders, Georg Leber, at a union congress in 1963, the union is acting as a *Sozialpartner* and as such it is an *Ordnungsfaktor*, i.e. the union is assigned supervising functions. The oppo-

60. *Richtlinien des Deutschen Gewerkschaftsbundes zur Führung von Arbeitskämpfen, beschlossen vom Gründungskongress des Deutschen Gewerkschaftsbundes,* Munich, October 1949.
61. The 'Ruhrgebiet' belonged to the British zone and its administration was more pro-labour than was the administration of the American zone.

sed characteristics of the traditionals, who are militant, and the reformers, who believe in the idea of 'Sozialpartner'-ship, are to be traced back to the earlier split between socialist and Christian trade unions. The new programme adopted at Düsseldorf in 1963 is an attempt to arrive at a compromise between these views.[62]

Doubt has been expressed whether a union like the Building Workers' Union, with a membership rate in 1961 of about 18 per cent, is capable of serving as an effective party to the bargaining.[63]

IG METALL AS SIGNATORY TO COLLECTIVE AGREEMENTS

In the absence of studies on the German trade union movement in general, its aims and its place in the community, the author will concentrate his presentation upon one important section of the German labour market, namely the metallurgical industry.[64] It follows from what has been said before that it will be a picture of a union governed by traditionalists.

As has been indicated earlier, bargaining in West Germany is generally conducted at a regional level. Often the *Land* or a similar geographical unit, constitutes the region. Thus Nordrhein-Westfalen, Bayern, Hessen and Schleswig-Holstein are bargaining regions. There are separate sets of agreements for white-collar workers and for blue-collar workers. The agreements for blue-collar workers of Nordrhein-Westfalen give an idea of the pattern applied. In the *Manteltarifvertrag* (the basic collective agreement) norms are laid down concerning hours of work, additional pay for overtime, the period of vacation, etc., and in the *Lohnrahmenabkommen* (agreement on job classification and piece work) rules are embodied concerning the classification of work and the amount of work expected in cases of piece-rate payment, etc., and in the *Lohnabkommen* (agreement on rates of pay) the hourly wage rates and the piece-rate guides are given.[65]

The three agreements have different periods of duration, the *Manteltarifvertrag* lasting for three years, the *Lohnrahmenabkommen* for two years, and the *Lohnabkommen* for one year.

The Essen, Hagen, Cologne and Münster section of IG Metall is a signatory to all three agreements. There are two signatory associations of employers to the *Manteltarifvertrag*, namely the Metal Trades Employers' Association of Nordrhein-Westfalen and the Iron and Steel Trades Employers' Association

62. See Hans Limmer, *Die deutsche Gewerkschaftsbewegung*, Munich 1966, pp. 84 ff., p. 86, pp. 115 f. and p. 132 in particular.
63. ibid., pp. 133 f.
64. The author has been in correspondence with the IG Metall, the DGB, the Gesamtverband der metallindustriellen Arbeitgeberverbände (the Confederation of Employers' Associations in the Metallurgical Industry) and the BDA, and has studied their annual reports and several pieces of source material with which he has been generously provided by these organizations.
65. For a description of the German collective agreements, see G. Giugni, *L'évolution des negotiations collectives dans les industries du charbon et de l'acier dans les Pays membres de la CECA (1959–1963)*, Luxemburg, 1968.

of the Bund. The Metal Trades Employers' Association of Nordrhein-Westfalen is the signatory to the *Lohnrahmenabkommen* and the *Lohnabkommen*.

RULES REGARDING INITIATION AND CONTINUATION OF STRIKES

In the constitution of I G Metall there are embodied rules with regard to the initiation and the continuation of strikes which correspond to the requirements of the DGB code of 1949 mentioned above in the section dealing with Einheitsgewerkschaft and DGB (see p. 38). A stoppage of work requires a decision of the national board. A proposal for a strike may not be adopted unless in a secret ballot 75 per cent of the members concerned have cast their votes in favour of the proposal. Even the continuation of a strike requires a 75 per cent majority.

In the Strike Directives of I G Metall the procedure is laid down in detail. The regional board concerned may request permission from the national board to arrange a strike ballot (*Urabstimmung*) subject to the following preconditions:

1. That negotiations have broken down.
2. That the collective agreement has come to an end.
3. That the peace obligation has ceased to exist.[66]

When the votes have been counted, the national board decides whether and when a strike shall take place. In the event of a strike all members are ordered to report daily at the local headquarters. The local branch decides whether unorganized workers shall be allowed to join as new members. The branch is recommended not to accept new applicants. Pickets are posted at the entrances of all plants which are affected. The pickets have to peacefully advise those prepared to work not to enter the employer's premises. Workers who for specific reasons are not covered by the strike are to be given special passes.

The strike-benefit programme is well established and the funds of I G Metall are considerable. According to the constitution the striker is entitled to benefits related to the income upon which his dues were computed. The payment of union contributions for a period of three months is a condition of the right to strike benefits. The amount of the benefit is related to the number of months for which contributions have been paid. A worker who has paid more than 36 monthly contributions is entitled to the maximum. The strike benefits are substantial. Thus a member with a gross monthly income of DM 1,000 receives – provided he has made more than 36 contributions – DM 156 a week as long as the strike lasts. Those who have families to support receive additional benefits.

66. The preconditions mentioned must be read against the background of a judgment of the Federal Labour Court of 31 October 1958 (*Entscheidungen des Bundesarbeitsgerichts*, vol. 6, pp. 321 ff.). Before the peace obligation had ceased to apply, the Schleswig-Holstein region of I G Metall had proposed a 'Urabstimmung' and the national board had granted its consent. These decisions, which were made public, were considered to constitute breaches of the peace obligation. An objection that they were exclusively internal matters was rejected. The judgment of the Federal Labour Court has been heavily criticized by the unions.

From the report for the years 1954/55[67] the author has selected two cases in order to demonstrate how the system of 'Urabstimmung' works. The Württemberg-Baden section gave notice of termination. The agreement expired on 31 May 1954. On 5 June the conciliation board met. An offer of the employers was submitted to the members concerned and was rejected by 83 per cent. In this situation the Prime Minister of Württemberg-Baden interfered and called the parties to a meeting. The employers raised their earlier offer, and in a second ballot the new offer was accepted by 57·4 per cent of the votes against 42·6 per cent. With this the dispute, in which about 130,000 workers had been engaged, was settled.

The same year there arose in Bavaria a dispute covering 212,000 employees. The I G Metall section for Bavaria had given notice of termination. The employers refused to make any offers and even refused to come to a meeting to which the parties were called by the Bavarian Minister of Labour. On 29 and 30 July a ballot took place. Of 137,000 members 111,000, or 90 per cent, voted for a strike, and the strike came into effect a few days later. The employers now made considerable concessions. On 26 and 27 August representatives of the parties under the chairmanship of the Minister made a proposal for the settlement of the strike. The proposal was submitted to a vote. The report of I G Metall states: 'At the fixed date the workers cast their votes and, in spite of a four weeks' strike, 52·8 per cent of those on strike were in favour of a continuation. However, the constitutional condition (75 per cent) was not met and the strike was called off.'

German trade unions take the same view as trade unions of other countries. A member who has acted as a strike-breaker may be excluded on the ground that he has committed a breach of his duties as a member.

As in other countries, the German courts take jurisdiction over actions by members for wrongful expulsions.[68]

THE WILDCAT STRIKE

The low membership rates do not seem to hamper the German unions in their control of members, and the wildcat strike is not regarded as a serious prob-

---

67. *Geschäftsbericht 1954/55 des Vorstandes der Industriegewerkschaft Metall für die Bundesrepublik Deutschland*, pp. 83 ff.
68. The court will always try whether the procedural rules for expulsion laid down in the union constitution were properly applied. The courts are also competent to invalidate a decision on the ground of substantial unfairness. Some decisions of the *Reichsgericht*, the Supreme Court of the Weimar Republic, are still considered leading cases. Thus, Thilo Ramm quotes a decision of 1933 (*Entscheidungen des Reichsgerichts in Zivilsachen*, vol. 140, p. 24. See Thilo Ramm, *Einführung in das Privatrecht*, vol. 3, 1970, p. 857); the case concerned the expulsion of a doctor from a medical association. According to the *Reichsgericht* the courts were competent to intervene if the association was influential and the member was caused harm with regard to important social relations ('in wichtigen Lebensbeziehungen'), provided there had been gross unfairness or a serious misuse of power. Nipperdey summarizes the present situation as follows. The court tries whether the expulsion from a trade union is a justified sanction considering the circumstances of the case (H. C. Nipperdey, *Lehrbuch des Arbeitsrechts*, second part, vol. 1, 1967, p. 187).

lem. The author has no information as to the frequency of what in Sweden is considered the typical wildcat strike, a flaring up of workers who revolt against a foreman, poor piece rates or an unjust dismissal. If the number of such incidents is proportionately smaller than in Sweden, this may be explained by reference to the role of the German works councils, the quality of the methods of settling grievances at the plant level, and legal sanctions to which the strikers might be exposed.

On one point there is a clear parallel to Sweden, namely the *Lohnexplosion* (the wage explosion) in the latter part of 1969.[69] Early in August 1969, I G Metall and the Confederation of Metal Trades Employers' Associations entered into new collective agreements. As from 1 September wages were increased by 8 per cent. In some other industries, too, wage increases of 8 per cent were granted. The movement for a revision of all collective agreements irrespective of their expiry dates started with a wildcat strike over a local issue at a steel factory and spread to the whole iron and steel industry. Soon coal and power plants were also involved. More than 150,000 employees were on strike. The employers yielded and the workers were paid even for days lost. The concessions were made against the protest of the BDA, which claimed that even an unexpected boom could not as a matter of principle justify renegotiations of a collective agreement before the date of expiry. However, it was admitted that agreements entered into during the recession of 1968 were in need of revision. The author of the BDA report concluded that the wildcat strikes had come as unexpectedly to the trade unions as to the employers.

EMPLOYERS' ASSOCIATIONS

German employers' associations have a very complicated organizational structure, at least within the metallurgical industry. The individual firm is a member of a regional association. All the regional associations of a *Land* or a similar geographical unit constitute a federation. Thus, the Verband metallindustrieller Arbeitgeberverbände Nordrhein-Westfalen is a federation of regional employers' associations within Nordrhein-Westfalen. The *Land* federations of the metallurgical industry are affiliated to the Gesamtverband der Metallindustriellen Arbeitgeberverbände (Gesamtmetall; the Confederation of Metal Trades Employers' Associations). The federal top organization, the BDA, has both employers' associations and federations as members.

Like the DGB, its counterpart within the union movement, the BDA has policy-making functions. In its constitution it is expressly provided that the independence of its members in the field of collective bargaining must not be restricted by the BDA or its organs. Gesamtmetall, too, has principally policy-making functions. On matters concerning social benefits it has, however, the wider power of taking care of the interests of employers in the metal trades. The principal collective bargaining is done by the regional associations.

---

69. The following is based upon the *Jahresbericht der Bundesvereinigung der Deutschen Arbeitgeberverbände 1. Dezember 1968–30. November 1969*, pp. 64 ff., and Dieter Schneider and others, *Zur Theorie und Praxis des Streiks*, 1971, pp. 316 ff.

However, the BDA and Gesamtmetall are engaged in coordinating activities which make them power centres of great importance.

According to the BDA report for the period December 1952–November 1953 the policy of self-government by the 'Sozialpartner' should be based on mutual respect. 'A state of balance of the two forces must exist; if it does not, the weaker party will be the victim of the stronger and partnership will be replaced by its mortal enemy, the claim of power.'[70] The establishment of strong industrial unions, like I G Metall, was felt as a threat and for the purpose of bringing about the proper state of equilibrium the regional associations of employers were recommended to constitute 'Gefahrengemeinschaften' (risk communities).

The idea of risk communities was pushed forward the next year under the impetus of a declaration by one of the leaders of I G Metall in connection with a strike in the Bavarian region. The German trade union movement would, it was held, achieve its aims more effectively by industrial actions or threat of such actions than by peaceful cooperation. In a memorandum of November 1954, the members of the BDA were recommended to establish strike protection funds at the bargaining units and supplementary risk communities of the industries concerned.[71] An additional step was taken by the BDA in 1954 with the institution of a permanent coordination committee.

The memorandum of November 1954 was replaced in June 1961 by a 'Memorandum on Solidarity between Employers'. Guidelines for the desired cooperation have been laid down in the *Instrumentarium* of 12 October 1965.

According to the memorandum of 1961, a membership firm has to pay regard to the interests of a stricken firm. An employer is not allowed to engage strikers, to entice a customer to leave a stricken membership firm, or to transfer his own orders to other firms. Employers' mutual aid programmes operate at three levels:

1. The regional association establishes a strike protection fund, and each membership firm is required to contribute.
2. The 'Gefahrengemeinschaft' will operate at the national level and take care of the interests of the industry concerned.
3. The *Schutzgemeinschaft* (protection community) is a fund common to several industries based upon contributions from the *Gefahrengemeinschaften*.

Because of the wildcat strikes in 1969 the BDA has issued a document on 'The Solidarity of Members in the event of Wildcat Strikes' of 5 August 1970. The members are encouraged to enter into additional arrangements for mutual aid. The principles of conduct laid down in the 1961 memorandum are restated. The 1970 document, however, does not deal with defensive measures exclusively. It calls attention to the fact that the cause of a wildcat strike is often to be found in a local issue. A wage dispute may have its cause less in a

70. *Jahresbericht der Bundesvereinigung der Deutschen Arbeitgeberverbände 1. Dezember 1952–30. November 1953*, p. 11.
71. *Jahresbericht der Bundesvereinigung der Deutschen Arbeitgeberverbände 1. Dezember 1953–31. Dezember 1954*, pp. 23 f.

feeling that payment is too low than in a conviction that it is unjust. The employer should do his best to eliminate unjustifiable differences with regard to performance ratings.

As in Sweden, organized employers regard the lockout as a measure for bringing about equilibrium ('Kampfparität') and employers may have recourse to sympathetic lockouts as well. However, the use of sympathetic lockouts is carefully circumscribed by constitutional provisions. Assume that after a breakdown of the bargaining over a regional agreement the Federation of the Metal Industry of Nordrhein-Westfalen were to regard a lockout of all the workers within the industry as a suitable countermeasure. The decision of the federation would have to be carried by a majority of four-fifths of the regional associations. The individual firms will still not be bound to take action. A decision of the regional association is required. There are no sanctions attached to the obligation to follow the instructions of the regional association.

STRATEGIES

In order to give an idea of the strategies of the two 'Sozialpartner' in the metal trades, I G Metall and Gesamtmetall with its affiliated associations, the author will present the steps on each side which preceded the new agreements in the years 1962 and 1963. At the end of 1961, I G Metall gave notice of termination of the agreements on paid holidays for all regions and of the agreements on wages for the regions of Bavaria, Württemberg-Baden and Berlin. Gesamtmetall interpreted these steps as attempts at national bargaining over wages and upon its instructions notice was given in respect of those regional wage agreements to which I G Metall had not given notice. *Urabstimmung* took place within two regions. The employers escalated the conflict by giving notice of a lockout covering two other regions. Upon the initiative of the Prime Minister of Baden-Württemberg, Dr Kiesinger, negotiations took place. Later agreements were reached for two regions, Nordwürttemberg-Nordbaden and Südwürttemberg-Hohenzollern. These agreements served as models for the bargaining over the remaining agreements.

In 1963 the matter came to open conflicts. I G Metall was the initiator of strikes at a number of important factories in the regions Nordwürttemberg-Nordbaden and Südwürttemberg-Hohenzollern. The employers retaliated with lockouts which came into effect in the region Nordwürttemberg-Nordbaden on 1 May and in Südwürttemberg-Hohenzollern on 4 May. The workers of the region Nordrhein-Westfalen had an *Urabstimmung* and voted in favour of a strike. In this situation the Minister of Economics of the German Federal Republic, Professor Erhard, intervened, and under his chairmanship the parties came to an agreement on 7 May.[72]

The board of I G Metall comments in its report on the 1963 conflict as follows. For the first time since 1928 the employers had resorted to lockouts as a reply to a number of strikes of limited character. The attempts at inter-

72. The report of these incidents is based upon the *Jahresbericht der Bundesvereinigung der Deutschen Arbeitgeberverbände*, 1961/62 and 1962/63.

vention did not, as earlier, stop at the level of the government of the *Land* concerned. The Chancellor of the Federal Republic and the Federal Minister of Economics had considered the conflict as a matter of concern to them. Now the members of the union had learned that the strike and the lockout were powers of unequal weight. 'By treating socially unequal measures as equal in character, equality before the law has not been created, rather it has been destroyed. The position of the weaker party has been worsened instead of being improved.'[73]

COMMENTS

Of the six countries which are the objects of our study, West Germany has the lowest rate for working days lost in industrial disputes; the German figure – 32 days per 1,000 employees – is even lower than the Swedish one, 40.

There are many reasons to point to. One possible explanation is the lack of activity of those unions which have low membership rates. A union like I G Bau, Steine und Erden (Building and Construction Industries), with a rate of about 18 per cent, might find it necessary to refrain from industrial actions and to confine itself to the more modest role of an *Ordnungsfaktor* (peace officer).

The student of the reports of the board of I G Metall will find that a union governed by traditionalists is more aggressive and that strikes are not infrequent. However, whether the strike covers a number of selected plants or a region, ordinarily it does not last very long. The parties are generally able to compromise and come to an agreement, often along the lines of suggestions made by the Prime Minister or the Minister of Labour of the *Land* in which the dispute is located. Compared with the United States the student notes the absence of any prolonged strike undertaken because the union is fighting for its existence.

With regard to the role of the union – the subject of the present chapter – the following points in particular may be noted. The German union, as an *Einheitsgewerkschaft*, represents all employees of an industry. There are no craft unions which, like the British unions, claim that certain sectors belong to their members exclusively. Further, the rules of initiation and continuation of strikes are very strict, possibly even stricter than the corresponding Swedish rules. As a matter of principle a majority of 75 per cent must support the strike at any stage. The ultimate power to call the strike lies with the national board and is not a matter for the regional board representing the bargaining unit concerned.

The German employers are organized on a regional basis. There are, however, permanent organs for cooperation between the regions. Thus Gesamtmetall is, in spite of its limited constitutional powers, a coordinating factor comparable to I G Metall on the union side. The German Confederation of

73. *Geschäftsbericht 1962, 1963 und 1964 des Vorstandes der Industriegewerkschaft Metall für die Bundesrepublik Deutschland,* sec. 4.

Employers' Associations, the federal BDA, is a much more active organization than is the corresponding union federation, the DGB.

It is the credo of the BDA that an equilibrium should be created by coordinated actions and by the establishing of strike indemnity funds. The present author is not competent to judge whether such an equilibrium actually exists. He is, however, inclined to believe that the employers have slowly turned the scales in their favour.

Another reason for the German appeasement should also be mentioned. Students of the German situation have often emphasized the role played by the works councils. The day-to-day settlements are often reached after deliberations with the works council, which in many factories, although legally independent, functions as a branch of the national union concerned.

France

THE STRIKE AS DISAPPROVAL OF AUTHORITY

The situation in France differs from that of the four countries dealt with earlier. In the United States, in Sweden and in West Germany, the strike is ordinarily a means which the union may use in order to bring pressure on the other party at the bargaining table. The same applies to Britain, at any rate as far as official strikes are concerned. In all these countries the strike is a recognized part of an established system of self-government practised by the parties of the labour market. In France, on the other hand, the strike has been regarded as an action by individual employees joined by other employees. Sometimes it is initiated by a union, but just as often it is spontaneous in its initial stages and later on is made a matter of concern to one or more unions. It has been looked upon as a revolt by the individuals against the power of the employer, which they feel to be too onerous.

It is true that in the last few years there seems to have been a change. More often than before, strikes are called by the unions and they have become an established part of the strategies and tactics of collective bargaining. In French law certain legal effects are attached to the recognition of a union by the authorities at the national level or the company level as belonging to the category of 'les plus représentatives' (those who are truly representative). A piece of legislation of 1963 is indicative of the tendency to assign important functions to the unions. According to the Act of 31 July 1963, concerning certain modalities in cases of strikes within the public services, notice of a strike has to be given five working days in advance. The notice must emanate from a union which at the national level belongs to the category of 'les plus représentatives' of the workers concerned. Thus the representative unions are the only ones that have the right to call a strike. However, the statements of the sociologist Jean-Daniel Reynaud in his study of the trade unions in France of 1966[74] still apply:

74. Jean-Daniel Reynaud, *Les Syndicats en France*, 1966, p. 141.

Each strike is a demonstration of strength and an open disapproval of authority; it has for the strikers – if not a revolutionary flavour, at all events the character of a liberation from the yoke. Violent or orderly, bitter or good-humoured, spontaneous or planned, the French strike is never the disciplined action of a troop which takes the steps designed by its leaders, each striker having the labour code in his hand, the economic data in his head, and the contract of employment in his pocket. The strike is the materialization of agitation and the concordance of different displeasures. The strong force that will be displayed is never easy to appraise.

To the French people there is nothing paradoxical in the fact that the strike as a challenge to the established society is a fundamental right as laid down in the Preamble of the Constitution of 27 October 1946, and confirmed by the Constitution of 1958.

There are two events in the history of the French labour movement that are of paramount importance, namely the incidents of 1936 and of 1968. On both occasions, under the pressure of factory occupations, big employers had to yield. Thus as an effect of the 1936 revolts the collective agreement in its present shape was recognized, and legislation was passed to give workers two weeks' paid holiday and a 40 hour week.

In 1936 labour enjoyed governmental support. The 'Front Populaire' – a coalition of communists, socialists and radicals – was in power. In 1968 labour was in opposition to the Gaullist government. As we all know, the whole of France was paralysed by strikes from the middle of May until early in July. In the metallurgical industry alone, where the strike lasted from 13 May to 2 July, it covered about 2·1 million employees. At an early stage a meeting was held in the presence of the Prime Minister, and in the Protocol of Grenelle certain concessions were made.[75] One of the many achievements, besides considerable wage increases, was the recognition of the right of the trade union to establish a branch in each plant and to appoint representatives, principles which were embodied in the Act of 27 December 1968, regarding the implementation of union rights in the plants.[76]

THE PLURALISM OF FRENCH TRADE UNIONISM

Pluralism is a characteristic feature of the labour movement in France. French pluralism should not be confused with British multi-unionism. It reflects the fact that French labour leaders have not been able to establish the industrial 'Einheitsgewerkschaft' of the German type. There are several confederations claiming to represent the same constituencies. The following are the most important:

75. The Protocol of Grenelle (le Procès-Verbal de Grenelle) was never signed by any of the parties who took part in the conference. It was made public in the morning of Monday, 27 May, by the Prime Minister M. Pompidou, as a 'projet de protocole d'accord'. See *Le bilan social de l'année 1968. Revue pratique de droit social*, Paris, 1969, p. 41.
76. Loi no. 68–1179 du 27 décembre 1968 relative à l'exercice du droit syndical dans les entreprises.

1. Confédération Générale du Travail (CGT;
2. CGT – Force-Ouvrière (FO;
3. Confédération Française Démocratique du Travail (C.F.D.T.;

The CGT has the largest membership. Although politically independent, it is dominated by a Communist minority. In its policy the CGT is influenced to a greater degree than the other two confederations by the revolutionary tradition of the French trade union movement, according to which the strike is a preparation for the revolt, as in the formula of Griffuelhes, an old CGT leader: 'Strikes are necessary gymnastics in the same way as army manoeuvres are the gymnastics of war.'[77] As a matter of principle the CGT still refuses to take any responsibility for the capitalist society.[78]

The CGT-Force-Ouvrière was formed by a minority which broke away from the CGT in 1947. Like the CGT, it is politically independent, although definitely anti-Communist. The Force-Ouvrière is more willing to take part in a constructive dialogue with management than is the CGT.

The CFDT, which comes second in membership, is also politically independent. It has its origin in a Christian trade union movement. It is in many respects as radical and militant as the CGT, which it temporarily joins in industrial actions.

It is difficult to give figures regarding the degree of unionization. A reasonable estimate would be 25 per cent of the total work force.[79] But figures concerning the membership of French unions are meaningless in the absence of regular payment of dues. However, it is possible to get an idea of the influence of one union compared with others from figures relating to the elections of employee representatives in the plant ('délégués du personnel' and members of the 'comité d'entreprise'), since all employees take part in these elections and in the first ballot a candidate must be supported by a union belonging, at the company level, to the category of 'les plus représentatives'.

PATTERNS OF COLLECTIVE BARGAINING

The French collective agreement is governed by detailed statutory regulations. But in contrast to the situation obtaining in the United States, Sweden and Germany, a peace obligation is ordinarily not embodied in the agreement. According to art. 5 of the Act of 1950 on collective agreements and on procedures governing collective labour disputes, the parties are required immediately to submit their disputes to conciliation by a committee of conciliators. It is true that conciliation is made compulsory, but this does not imply that industrial action has to be postponed. Nor are there any statutory provisions to the effect that notice shall be given beforehand, with the exception of a piece of legislation mentioned before. According to the Act of 31 July 1963, regarding certain modalities of strikes involving public services, the union is required to give five full days' notice.

77. The quotation is taken from J.-D. Reynaud, op. cit., p. 62.
78. cf. François Sellier and André Tiano, *Économie du travail*, 1962, p. 356.
79. Hélène Sinay, *La grève* (*Traité de droit du travail*, vol. 6), 1966, p. 48.

A no-strike clause in a collective agreement for a year or any substantial period would be considered invalid as constituting an infringement upon the fundamental right to strike.[80] However, a clause providing that action should be postponed for a while would most likely be considered legally binding. However, French unions, and the CGT in particular, are critical of such commitments. The CGT has refused to sign the so-called 'contrats de progrès' offered by the Government in 1969 and 1970 for nationalized industries; this was the case, for example, with the agreement for the Electricity, one of the largest enterprises of France, in which was embodied a clause stating that the union must give three-months' notice before resorting to a strike on matters covered by the agreement. And in the interests of the right to strike, the CGT in its Programme of December 1969 calls for the repeal of the Act of 1963 regarding certain modalities of strikes involving public services.

THE CGT AND THE CFDT – TWO CONFEDERATIONS OF UNIONS

The CGT and the CFDT are composed of a number of federations. Generally a federation represents the workers of an industry, but the organizational principles vary and in some cases it represents a craft. In the federation are grouped a number of unions established at regional or local levels. The union, or *syndicat*, constitutes the basic element. The union as a regional or local organization may have branches at the plants. In the Act regarding the implementation of union rights in the plants there are provisions laying down that the enterprise shall afford certain facilities to the branch.

Decentralization is the acknowledged principle. The regional branch enjoys a considerable degree of independence, even on matters like the initiation of strikes. The confederation has mainly coordinating functions.

French confederations and national unions have very small financial resources. The contributions are low compared with the dues payable to an American or Swedish trade union – the CGT recommends a due of one hour's pay per month – and they are not paid regularly. The individual feels free to leave his union at will, and membership fluctuates from time to time. According to Reynaud, the French unions are, together with the Italian unions, the poorest in Europe.[81]

THE STRIKE AND ITS TERMINATION

There are no statutory provisions with regard to the procedure of the initiation, the administration, or the bringing to an end of a strike. And there is very little on these matters in union constitutions or rule books. The confederation, the national union or the regional branch may initiate a strike.

The union may organize a secret ballot. This is not, as in Germany, exclusively a matter of concern to the members but is a referendum. The fact that the union leaders will have an opportunity of presenting the issue to a larger

80. Sinay, op cit., pp. 211 ff.
81. J.-D. Reynaud, op. cit., p. 124.

audience than their own membership is, from the union's point of view, one of the advantages of the system, since the success will depend upon whether non-members are willing to join in. It is not certain that the union will follow the advice of the referendum. Sellier and Tiano[82] mention that nine referenda were organized at the Renault plants in the years 1947–55. Of these, two were against the proposition, seven in favour of it. In the two cases where the majority had voted against, the workers went on strike despite this decision; and in three of the cases where the vote was favourable, no strike followed.

Often strikes are spontaneous. Indeed, the two successful general strikes of 1936 and 1968 were both, in their initial stages, spontaneous actions. It should be mentioned that the general strike of 1946, called by the CGT, was a failure, partly because of a split which led to the withdrawal of the reformist minority and the creation of the CGT-Force-Ouvrière.

Certainly, sometimes unions take action against those who organize strikes which have not been properly sanctioned. But more often the union officers listen and try to find out whether individual strike actions will arouse a favourable response. In that case the union may in great haste declare the strike a matter of concern to it. The action will be endorsed by at least one of the three main confederations, possibly by all of them. The following incident from the strike period of 1968 illustrates the position of French unions leaders. M. George Séguy, Secretary-General of the CGT, went to the Renault factories at Boulogne-Billancourt in order to announce as a victory the concessions made in the Protocol of Grenelle, but was to his surprise met with a chilly reception. He recovered himself quickly and acted as if he too, were against a return to work.

During a strike an *ad hoc* strike committee may be appointed. If the strike is endorsed by several confederations, an inter-union committee will be constituted. However, a large proportion of all strikes are actions of short duration, one or two days, and in such a case one can hardly expect there to be any formal election of a strike committee or appointment of an inter-union committee.

Often a strike is joined only by a part of the work force. Sometimes the union cannot expect more than 30 per cent participation. Certainly, a participation of 100 per cent is rare. There are many circumstances that may influence the situation, among others whether the strike will be endorsed by all the confederations concerned. In a great number of cases the action is sanctioned only by some unions – generally the more aggressive ones, such as the CGT and the CFDT – while other unions urge their supporters to remain at work.

The union leaders do not always have the power to bring the strike to an end after a settlement. The settlement of the 1936 strikes by the Matignon agreement of 7 June was a success in this respect. In the agreement, which was signed in the presence of the Prime Minister by representatives of the Confederation of French Employers and of the CGT, was embodied a request by the representatives of the workers that the strikers should take decisions to

82. Sellier and Tiano, op. cit., p. 464.

return to work. The appeal of the famous labour leader Maurice Thorez – 'il faut savoir terminer une grève' – was followed within 48 hours. The failure, on the other hand, of M. Séguy in 1968 has been mentioned before.

There is nothing peculiar in the fact that French unions are reluctant to sign even favourable agreements. J.-D. Reynaud comments sarcastically:

> When a strike has to be called or a protest is to be manifested, there is a race among the union leaders to gain the initiative for their own union and to be able to present themselves as representing the union which has extracted the benefit of the movement. When, on the other hand, it comes to signing a document accepting a compromise which will not satisfy all demands, there is instead a competition to be the last one. The first signatory is responsible for the concessions. The others may accuse him of breaking the unity of the workers, though later they may themselves sign because of constraint or pressure.[83]

Incidentally, the French legal system favours such an approach. When one union has signed an agreement it becomes binding upon all employers covered by the agreement and must be applied to all employees (Code du travail, book 1, article 31 e).

The ordinary French union has no funds from which strike benefits can be paid. The contributions of the members are spent on salaries to a few full-time officers and on the union press. Thus the strikers are dependent upon their own means and upon what they are able to collect from sympathizing groups of workers or from the public. In order to win the fight the leaders therefore have to ask other workers and the public for financial support. There are exceptions, however. Some unions, CFDT unions in particular, have built up strike funds which have given the national unions greater power than before to control local strike actions.[84]

In the case of a prolonged strike the workers will naturally run into debt. The Protocol of Grenelle was remarkable from the point of view that it dealt with compensation for days lost, too. It was provided that days lost because of stoppage of work should be made up for later on. Fifty per cent was to be paid in advance. In the settlements on return to work advances were actually granted which later on were only in part recovered. In *Le bilan social de l'année 1968*, a collection of documents published by the CGT, the commentator declares that the actual payment for days lost was one of the great achievements of the workers.[85]

DISCIPLINING STRIKE-BREAKERS

Like trade unions of other countries, the French trade union may expel members who have acted as strike-breakers. It is not disputed that the local civil court (*tribunal de grande instance*) has jurisdiction over a suit by the member

83. J.-D. Reynaud, op. cit., p. 169.
84. See Reynaud, op cit., pp. 126 f.
85. *Le bilan social de l'année 1968. Revue pratique de droit social*, Paris, 1969, p. 185.

against the union for wrongful expulsion. It is a settled opinion that the court is entitled to check that procedural rules have been strictly applied and that facts have been proven when contested. Whether the courts have the power to try whether the facts constitute a substantive ground for expulsion is a more complicated matter.[86] The answer to this question is not very important, however, in a system like that obtaining in France, with a number of competing unions. The strike-breakers are generally members of another union or have no union affiliation.

EMPLOYERS' ASSOCIATIONS

In contrast to the organizations of labour, where the power lies in the regional or the local unit, French employers' associations are principally national sectoral associations.[87] The Union des Industries Métallurgiques et Minières (UIMM), representing the metallurgical and mining industries, is by far the most important one. Dealing with labour relations is only one of a number of activities performed by the UIMM and its affiliated associations. In France collective bargaining is focused at the regional level, but the UIMM provides its members with qualified experts and documentation in a way which permits effective coordination.

The Central Federation of French Management (Conseil National du Patronat Français) exerts certain activities, too. Thus there exist a number of multi-industrial agreements of which those concerning pensions and additional unemployment benefits are particularly important.

However, in case of a strike the French employer does not get any financial support from other employers. No strike indemnity funds have been established, nor are the organizations active in raising contributions for firms hit by strikes.

THE LOCKOUT AS A DEFENSIVE WEAPON

In France, unlike Sweden and West Germany, the lockout is not a recognized means of industrial action. This does not mean that lockouts do not occur. In the 1950s and 1960s employers sometimes reacted against new forms of strikes, such as *la grève tournante* (the tactic of short strikes which are repeated again and again), by locking out their employees. Only rarely has the lockout been used for offensive purposes.

The legality of the lockout has been much debated. Some legal writers have claimed that the German principle of *Kampfparität* should apply. Other writers, among them Paul Durand in his *Traité de droit du travail*,[88] have held that this is a false analogy. The strike is a counterweight designed for persons who as employees are placed in a state of dependence. Its purpose is to establish an

---

86. See J. M. Verdier, *Syndicats* (*Traité de droit du travail*, vol. 5), 1966, pp. 266 ff.
87. See, on what follows, Reynaud, op. cit., pp. 38 ff.
88. op. cit., vol. 3, 1956, p. 898. cf. Hélène Sinay, op. cit., pp. 333 ff.

equilibrium between two social parties of unequal economic power. The lock-out would create a dominance of the employer.

Further, the freedom to strike is a fundamental right confirmed by the Constitution. There is no law on the statute book upon which to base a claim of recognition for the lockout. In these circumstances the lockout should be analysed in the light of the contractual relationships concerned. This individualistic approach is natural in a country with a large number of competing unions, where even the strike is basically considered as a set of individual acts. According to the French law of employment contracts the employer has a duty to provide the employee with work. Indisputedly the lockout, as a unilateral act, constitutes a breach of this duty. As a matter of principle the employee is entitled to damages as compensation for his loss of earnings.

The courts have rejected the idea of the lockout as a sort of employer's strike and have applied the individual approach. In a number of decisions the Cour de Cassation (the French Supreme Court) has laid down the doctrine that in case of a lockout the employer is in fault against each individual who has suffered loss and that consequently he must pay wages for days lost.[89] Action for reversal is rejected when the employer is able to prove that his failure to supply work was due to *force majeure*, e.g. in cases where a strike in one department has caused work in another department to be discontinued owing to lack of material. In some other situations, too, the employer has been held to have a proper excuse, as in cases where work has not been started up again immediately after a strike because of a need for reorganization. With regard to the question whether the employer may retaliate against a strike which is illegal because of its character (i.e. a political strike) or because of the means applied (*la grève tournante*), the law is not settled.

A COMPARISON BETWEEN FRENCH AND BRITISH TRADE UNIONS

Even more than in Britain the typical strike in France is of the short 'flaring up' kind. In connection with this one should stress the strength of the trade union movement in Britain at the shop level, and in France at the local or the regional level. If one compares the relations between the national union and those at the shop level, one observes the difference that in France the national union never contests the authority of those at the shop level. The French confederation or national union has its happiest moments when it is leading a strike supported not only by its own members but also by non-union workers as well as members of other unions.

There is another, and possibly even more important, difference between France and Britain with regard to the shop level namely the absence in France of permanent bargaining. This observation should be related to a statement made at the beginning of this section (p. 47) that in France the strike is not part of an established system of self-government. However, regard must be paid to the evolution since the events of 1968. Permanent bargaining (*con-*

89. See Sinay, op. cit., pp. 348 ff., and G. H. Camerlynck and Gérard Lyon-Caen, *Précis de droit du travail*, 1970, pp. 548 f.

certation permanente) was one of the solutions then offered by President de Gaulle.

Verdier in his study *Syndicats* (1966) comments on the two main streams, the revolutionary and the reformist, which coexist in the French trade union movement. According to Verdier,[90] the reformers tend to dominate. The communist CGT of today is more cooperative than was the non-Marxist CGT of 1914. In her study *La grève* (1966) Hélène Sinay[91] emphasizes the fact that strikes nowadays seldom take place without union orchestration.

J.-D. Reynaud[92] notes the same trend but is less optimistic than Verdier. He characterizes the situation within the plant as a permanent guerilla war between labour and management. The decisions concerning day-to-day problems are made by management over the heads of those concerned. Unsettled matters are stacked up until the last straw breaks the camel's back, and one day the workers are on strike again.

The studies of Verdier and of Reynaud were published in 1966. Considering the events in the spring of 1968, Reynaud's sceptical approach was well-founded. What happened that year – the recognition of the right of the trade union to appoint representatives in each plant – and what has happened since may have improved the climate and made possible a constructive dialogue between management and labour. On this the present author is not qualified to express an opinion.

Italy

INTRODUCTORY REMARKS

Following the French pattern, the Italian Constitution of 1948, in its Art. 40, establishes a right to strike which must be exercised within the limits of the laws that are to regulate it. These laws, however, have not yet been enacted. A distinction is drawn between the legitimate and the illegitimate strike. In a number of decisions the courts have attempted to define the limits of the legitimate strike. The practice, however, is not consistent.

In 1970 a statute on the rights of the workers was enacted for the purpose of protecting the freedom and the dignity of the workers at the workplace, the right to organize, and the right to engage in trade union activities. The statute contains rules concerning workers who have taken part in a strike. They are intended to improve the protection of the legitimate strike but do not contribute to the laying down of a demarcation line. It is still the task of the courts to determine whether a strike is legitimate or not. Some legal writers, indeed, claim that all peaceful industrial activities are legitimate.

The 1970 statute has had a tremendous impact as regards the protection of

90. Verdier, op. cit., pp. 40 f. cf. pp. 29 ff.
91. Hélène Sinay, op. cit., p. 44.
92. J.-D. Reynaud, op. cit., pp. 217 f.

the right to strike. Its Art. 28 grants the lower courts, which are single-judge courts, the power to issue injunctions against actions of the employer aiming at restrictions of trade union freedom and of the right to strike. In the period May 1970–May 1971 more than 100 injunction orders were issued, revealing a more liberal approach to the right to strike among the members of the bench than had been shown in earlier decisions of the higher courts. Thus in cases where an employer has countered a *grève tournante* with a lockout, many lower courts have ordered the employer to cease and desist from his action.

As in France, the strike may be characterized as an action by an individual employee joined by other employees. This is also the view of Italian legal writers and of the courts, or at least the great majority of these. It should be noted, however, that under the new law an action for injunction has to be brought into the court by a union. But this does not change the basic principle that the right to strike is an individual right, even though the strike itself is a collective action.

THE UNION AND THE STRIKE

In Italy the unions have been more dominant than in France. Until 1968 the great majority of the strikes were union actions. In the rare cases of wildcat strikes or other spontaneous actions, it is usual for all the unions to come forward without delay to endorse the strike. It should be mentioned that since the beginning of the 1960s the rivalry among the unions, previously considerable, has decreased.

In 1968, under the influence of the French events in May and the students' riots in France, Germany, Italy and other countries, there occurred a wave of spontaneous industrial actions directed against big industry.[93] At the workplaces new forms of organizations emerged, such as the Comitati Unitari di Base (CUB). In the beginning the Comitati and similar organizations challenged the leadership of the unions. But gradually the unions gained control. When, in the 'hot autumn' of 1969, the bargaining over the most important national agreements – such as those of the metallurgical industry, the chemical industry, housebuilding and road construction – took place, the unions were back in the saddle and were able to obtain considerable concessions. In various ways the union leaders demonstrated their strength and control over the masses, and the many small leftist fractions were isolated. The point to be made is that the unions regained leadership after a process of reorganization and of reconsideration of strike tactics.

First, there was a spreading of the practice of general meetings in the factory open to all workers. At these meetings the union men had to face their constituents. They were forced to represent all the workers irrespective of union affiliation. In the metallurgical industry, for example, the discussions over the claims which had to be presented during the negotiations over the new agree-

93. See Gino Giugni, 'L'automne chaud syndical', *Sociologie du travail*, 1971, pp. 159 ff.

ment took place in crowded assemblies, where union leaders offered the workers different choices on basic issues like equalization.

An additional feature was the establishment of the office of shop steward, especially in the bigger factories. Spontaneously the workers of a department, an assembly line or some other subdivision of a plant appointed a representative. This movement took different shapes, elections on a union ticket, or on a white ticket, etc. The newly-elected stewards cooperated with union representatives, and according to the present trend they jointly constitute a factory council recognized by the national metal workers' unions as their local representation. The same pattern has spread to other industries.

A new procedure of strike decision-making emerged during the coming into being of the agreement for the metallurgical industry. The strike was called by a joint meeting of the three national unions, but its implementation was left to the factory representatives and the meetings of the workers. There were a few national strikes and a number of *grèves tournantes*. Where the latter were concerned, the workers decided the distribution of idle hours between different departments and periods.

ITALIAN TRADE UNIONS—SPLITS AND MERGERS

As in France, there are several trade union confederations. The most important of these is the General Confederation of Labour (CGIL); it is made up of Communists and Socialists, the Communists being in the majority and representing, according to a rough estimate, about 75 per cent. Second in order of importance is the Confederation of Workers' Unions (CISL), made up of Catholics and a minority of Socialists, and third comes the Italian Workers' Union (UIL) – a federation which more or less corresponds to the French CGT-Force-Ouvrière. This classification of political kinship is, however, rather superficial. Thus, the National Metal Workers of the CISL can hardly be defined as a Catholic union. Several of their leaders, former Christian Democrats, have moved to the left – some of them to the extreme left. As an indication of the swing among Catholic workers it should be mentioned that the ACLI (Associazione Cristiana Lavoratori Italiana), a non-union association, earlier one of the most powerful supporters of the Christian Democratic Party among workers, has adopted a new approach favouring the idea of Socialism. Recently the Pope stated that the ACLI should not be considered a Catholic organization.

In the Italian union blue-collar and white-collar workers meet. It is hard to give precise figures for membership, but it may be estimated that the CGIL has 3·5 million members, the CISL 2·3 million, and the UIL rather less than 1 million; this means that about one-third of the work force are union members. Membership declined in the period 1953–58, but since then, and particularly in the years 1969–70, it has increased considerably. When one speaks of Communist domination within the CGIL one should keep in mind the fact that the confederation refuses to follow instructions from abroad and that both the confederation and the Italian Communist Party condemned the Soviet invasion of Czechoslovakia in 1968. The CGIL, jointly with the two other confederations, has adopted the rule of *incompatibilità*, which means that a union official is not allowed to hold certain political positions; he may not, for example, be a member of Parliament or sit on the executive board of a political party. At present the extension of this principle to lower political positions is under debate.

In 1944, after the liberation from the Fascist regime, a unitarian confederation was established by the *patto di Roma*, signed by representatives of Communist, Socialist, and Christian Democratic labour leaders. In 1948–50, there occurred a series of splits which brought about the formation of the CGIL, the CISL and the UIL. In the 1950s, the rivalry between them was strong. The Italian employers applied policies of discrimination against the Communist-dominated CGIL or against trade unionism in general, policies which were supported by the US agencies in Europe.

In the second half of the 1960s, the idea of a merger of the three confederations gained ground. Many meetings took place at the top and these resulted in a formal non-rivalry agreement. In 1968 and 1969, years of unrest in the labour market, a unitarian front was established, emanating from the ground level; it was supported in particular by the younger generation, which had not experienced the years of the cold war. This trend towards unification was visible in the metallurgical industry. At the frequent general meetings of workers in the bigger factories a unified front of the three national unions, the CGIL, the CISL and the UIL, emerged. For several years past, the strikes in the metal industry have been called by the three federations jointly. Incidentally, similar practices apply to most other industries. In the years 1969 and 1970 the executive boards of the three confederations, the CGIL, the CISL and the UIL, jointly called several general strikes on political issues. In 1966 discussions started on the question whether a merger was possible. Gradually, unity became an accepted slogan. Some common services, such as research, have been established. The unions of some industries have jointly undertaken to publish periodicals, and the joint publication of a monthly review by the three confederations has been decided upon. The process of integration slowed down in the summer of 1971. On the other hand, the three national unions within the metallurgical industry decided to merge before the end of 1972; but this merger was replaced by a federation of the three confederations.

PATTERNS OF COLLECTIVE BARGAINING

The Italian collective agreement is not governed by statutory regulations. The Act of 1970 tries to remove obstacles to union activities in the workplace but does not enter into the domain of collective bargaining. In legal writing and court practice the collective agreement is recognized as a civil-law contract binding both upon the parties to the agreement and their members. Thus, Italian law applies the same combined theory of the collective agreement as Sweden.

The Italian national agreement is for a specific period of time, ordinarily two or three years. Up to 1970 the system of collective agreements constituted a hierarchy. At the top were the interprofessional agreements covering a field like industry or commerce; these were especially important in the years after the war. They still exist but their impact has decreased. At the second level, which is the paramount one, were the national industry-wide agreements, among them the agreement of the metallurgical industry covering 1·3 million workers, and playing the role of leader; and at the third and lowest were shop agreements for specific subjects designated for company bargaining by the national agreement. This system of bargaining at three levels, which is called the 'contrattazione articolata', came into being, together with a no-strike clause, in 1962 during the negotiations over a new national agreement for the metallurgical industry. In the 'hot autumn' of 1969 the system of articulated bargaining disintegrated, but as yet it is not clear by what system it will be replaced. In 1969 the employers in the metallurgical industry urged a redefinition of the subjects of local bargaining. They were willing to extend the scope of such bargaining, but only within frames laid down in a national agreement. The unions, for their part, claimed freedom of negotiation at the shop level without restrictions as to choice of issues, even with possible overlappings between the two levels. This issue has remained unsettled, and what happens today is that unions bargain over and call strikes at the shop level in disputes not only over matters not dealt with by the national agreement (no one could question their right to do so) but also over matters settled in the national agreement. Employers allege that this is a violation of existing agreements, the unions deny it. Actually, negotiations do go on and bargains are made. In 1968, company agreements entered into were 3,900, covering 1·6 million workers; 3,400 agreements were made in 1969, workers covered being 1·3 million; and in 1970 the number of workers covered was 1·6 million by 4,300 agreements being made, most of them touching upon matters beyond the limits prescribed in articulated bargaining. The actual number of workers covered by company agreements at any time is higher than the figures given since several agreements remain in force for more than one year.

Furthermore, the emergence of a body of shop stewards has created a new level of informal bargaining at the very bottom. In conclusion, it may be stated that bargaining goes on permanently and not only, as before, in the period after the expiration of a collective agreement. As in England, there is a trend towards supplementing union bargaining with informal bargaining at the shop level.[94]

THE ITALIAN UNION: FINANCES, POSITION IN THE PLANT

As has been shown above, the Italian union movement has passed from a stage of centralization and of splits between competing confederations to a stage of decentralization and unification. One of the reasons for centralization was that

94. cf. François Sellier, 'Les transformations de la négociation collective et de l'organisation syndicale en Italie', *Sociologie du travail*, 1971, pp. 141 ff.

in 1944 the union movement, as in Germany a year later, had to be rebuilt from above. In Italy, this process was often initiated by the political parties, which supplied the unions with money and leadership. Later a new generation of union leaders, recruited within the unions and often trained at union schools, took over.

The Italian unions are not wealthy. The contributions of the members are estimated to vary from 0·5 to 1 per cent of the wages. By means of collective agreements, however, the system of check-off has been introduced, securing new resources for the union. It is possible that Reynaud's opinion that the Italian unions, together with the French unions, are the poorest ones in Europe is no longer valid. As yet the number of full-time union officials is not high.

It should be mentioned that, in the Act of 1970 and in a number of recent agreements for various industries or company agreements, provisions are laid down that a certain number of paid hours shall be assigned to the shop representatives of the union for the performance of their duties. The Fiat factories with their 180,000 employees provide an example. In the agreement a total of 1 million paid hours are assigned to the union representatives. According to the Act of 1970 even time spent at meetings held during working hours has to be paid by the employer up to a limit of ten hours annually per worker.

STRIKE PROCEDURES

In its Art. 51, the constitution of the CGIL, drafted before the split of 1945, imposed upon the affiliated unions the duty of negotiating a dispute before calling a strike and laid down that the strike must be approved by a majority of union members. According to Art. 52, strikes in public utilities were permitted only in exceptional circumstances and they required the authorization of the national union concerned. These articles, which now are practically forgotten, bore the hall-mark of the Catholic wing of trade unionism. It is strange to find that the constitutions of the two confederations which emerged out of the split, the CISL and the UIL, contain more sober rules. It should be mentioned that the constitutions of most affiliated national unions generally follow the pattern of the confederation.

The executive committee of the union calls the strike. As mentioned before, the three confederations nowadays often cooperate, decisions to call a strike being taken at joint meetings of the executive committees of the three confederations or of representatives of the three unions concerned. It has also been indicated earlier that the unions apply a strategy of calling all workers of an industry on strike for a limited number of days, e.g. three or four working days; the union takes the decision upon a *grève tournante*, leaving it to the plant representatives or/and to the meeting of the workers to fix the time for and the distribution of the hours on strike. It should be added that, with the system of fractional bargaining, strikes over local disputes are frequent. In most cases such strikes are sanctioned by the union, more or less willingly.

When a settlement was reached, up to the events of 1968–69, it was ordinarily signed at the negotiation table by the representatives of the unions joined by a selected number of members. Nowadays, ratification of the settlement is almost invariably required. In the case of a national agreement general meetings at the workplaces take place, and at these the draft agreement is put to the vote. The system is not favoured by the employers, who are afraid of rejections necessitating a second round of negotiations. However, by signing the settlement the union leaders have informally committed themselves to work for ratification, which almost invariably takes place. There are no procedural rules with regard to the meetings of workers. The decision is carried by a simple majority.

As in France, there are no funds from which strike benefits can be paid, although some unions had such funds before the Fascist regime destroyed the freedom of the unions. There are many reasons why the Italian unions have not followed the German pattern. Among these are the unwillingness of the members to pay contributions, the fear of the Communist Party that rich trade unions may develop into independent power centres, the generally held idea that a rich union will be slow in taking offensive action, and the feeling that the individual member ought to make a sacrifice. In these circumstances the strategy of short strikes and *grèves tournantes* is easy to explain.

THE ADMINISTRATION OF A STRIKE

In the event of a strike all workers, members as well as non-members, are expected to join in. Picket lines are organized and transgressors may be exposed to violence. Employers not infrequently try to challenge the union and to continue operations, although the hiring of replacements does not occur. However, participation is rarely total, and among white-collar workers there are many who are more inclined to stay at work. During the strikes of the 'hot autumn' of 1969, however, participation was high, even among white-collar workers.

The strike-breaker is generally a non-union member, and expulsion would not be the appropriate sanction. Instead, all kinds of ostracism are practised.

A SUMMARY

The foregoing sections may be summarized as follows. Earlier the unions were looked upon as associations of individual members, and the doctrine regarding the effect of the collective agreement was based upon the idea of the privity of contract. There was, however, a dualism embodied in the union movement. The unions were expected to represent a larger group, the CGIL unions the working class, and the CISL, among its first generations of leaders, the category concerned, e.g. the workers of an industry. In the last few years the Italian unions have been involved in a process of transition. The union is developing into a popular movement representing all workers employed in the plant and in the industry.

EMPLOYERS' ASSOCIATIONS

In Italy there are separate confederations of employers representing industry, commerce and agriculture, respectively. The name of the confederation of industrial enterprises is Confindustria. In addition there is an association of banks and there are a few other associations, some of them with overlapping jurisdictions. At the provincial level the industrial employers are organized in an association common to all enterprises in the province. The provincial associations are affiliated to Confindustria. Moreover, there are several national sectoral associations affiliated to Confindustria. However, the associations of the metallurgical industry are not engaged in labour relations. For negotiation purposes an *ad hoc* committee is appointed composed of representatives of the enterprises which are members of the provincial associations concerned.

Special mention should be made of the fact that the great majority of the bigger companies in various industries are State-owned. They are controlled by central State agencies to which the shares are assigned. The most important of these agencies are the IRI (Industrial Recovery Institute) and the ENI (National Institute for Hydrocarbons). The IRI controls companies within steel, mechanical engineering and public utilities, such as navigation, highways, the telephone service, radio and television; the ENI is concerned with hydrocarbons, oil, the chemical industry, textiles, and mechanical engineering units. The IRI has established an employers' association, Intersind, which is also open to other State-owned companies; the ENI has an employers' association of its own. In the 1960s the role of these associations and of Intersind in particular became preeminent. In 1962 they started negotiating separate collective agreements. Usually their bargaining took place ahead of that of private industry, and often the Intersind agreement for the metallurgical industry has set a pattern for the corresponding agreement of private industry.

In the 1950s Confindustria was a very powerful organization, both politically and economically. It was the only bargaining agent of affiliated enterprises. The creation of Intersind, with the enlargement of State participation, deprived Confindustria of its monopoly. When, with the introduction of the system of articulation, bargaining at the shop level came into existence, Confindustria tried to retain its power by prescribing that shop agreements should be negotiated by its provincial branches. Today the representatives of the enterprise actually make the final decision regarding the settlement, and this decision is endorsed by the provincial association of Confindustria.

Intersind has to face similar problems of authority in local bargaining. Since all the members have the same owner, the State, a consistent policy is easier to apply.

There are no funds to indemnify employers against loss due to industrial disputes.

Resort to countermeasures against strikes and other industrial actions is legally restricted. According to a decision of the Constitutional Court (1960 no. 29), a lockout would not fall under criminal sanction, yet the lockout was considered illegal and a breach of the individual contract of employment. The lockout constituted a *mora creditoris*, i.e. the creditor's refusal to cooperate in order to make performance possible. With the introduction of the Act on the rights of the workers of 1970, a lockout might be subject to an injunction, and criminal sanctions are applied in case of non-compliance. The employers claim the right to shut down the plant as a countermeasure to unlawful actions such as the *grèves tournantes* (considered illegal by the Corte di Cassazione), sabotage, violence, or factory occupation. As in France, the shutting down of a plant may be held justified because of the illegality of the acts of the workers or because these acts have caused impossibility of performance.

Conclusions

In a comparative study of unions it is natural to look first at their membership rates. As we have stated, great differences exist in this respect. In Sweden almost every employee is assumed to belong to a union; among blue-collar workers in industry the actual figure is as high as 95 per cent, and of the total work force union members represent about 70 per cent. Britain comes next with a membership rate of about 40 per cent. The figure for Germany is around 30 per cent and that for the United States is a little below that figure. It would be meaningless to give corresponding figures for France and Italy, since in these countries union membership has a different meaning from what it has, for example, in the United States. Union membership of a French or an Italian union is more like membership of a party organization. A union with a small number of members which embarks on industrial action may have the support of a strong majority.

Undoubtedly the Swedish unions are strong both economically and politically. In any attempt to measure the importance of the role played by the unions of the six countries, possibly Britain should be placed next. The whole industrial life of Britain is based upon the philosophy that management and labour are parties to a continuous bargaining process and that the parties are able themselves to settle all disputes as they arise without any external help. The main weakness in the British system is, as indicated in the Donovan Report, its duality, the existence side by side of a formal system and an informal one. The formal system is administered by the unions and focused upon the industry-wide collective agreement. The control of the union is insufficient when it comes to the informal bargaining at the shop level. Power centres around the shop steward, the representative of the group, who, although accredited by the union, often acts on his own initiative.

There are some similarities between the German and the American big industrial union, such as their coverage of both blue-collar and white-collar employees and their lack of political affiliation. But the differences are perhaps more important. In saying this I am not thinking exclusively of the concentration on centralized bargaining in Germany and on company bargaining in the United States. The figure of 30 per cent membership in Germany means something different from the corresponding American figure. In Germany trade unionism is spread all over the field while in the United States it is concentrated in certain areas. Thus the German unions of the building industry, which represent only about 18 per cent of the workers of the industry, are parties to collective agreements. Nothing similar exists in the United States. The explanation is probably that trade unionism has come to be socially accepted in Germany – the trade union is useful even in the opinion of the employer as an *Ordnungsfaktor*, i.e. as a supervisor of the collective agreement. An American employer would not assign such a function to the union unless he took it for certain that the union represented the majority of the employees.

As already indicated, France and Italy represent another kind of unionism. The unions are avant-gardist; their leaders are first and foremost political leaders and not business agents bargaining for day-to-day improvements, although the trend in both countries is towards integration in the established society. However, it would be altogether wrong to believe that the low membership rates, the poverty and the splits along political lines mean that French or Italian unions are weaker than American trade unions. Indeed there is reason to believe that on some occasions these peculiarities are assets rather than drawbacks. In a critical situation unions of different confederations may join, establish a unified front, and expose a revolutionary force to which there is no counterpart in the history of American trade unionism since the second world war. The incidents in France in the spring of 1968 constituted a revolution brought about by the peaceful means of a general strike. The incidents in Italy in the autumn of 1969 had a less revolutionary trend and more the character of an economic industrial action. They demonstrated, however, the capacity of leadership of minority unions.

Incidentally, what makes the Swedish L O, with its membership of blue-collar workers, stronger than almost any other confederation of unions is the combination of a high membership rate, substantial financial resources, and *de facto* political affiliation with the party which is in power.

A union's strategies and tactics depend not only upon its own resources but also upon the policies of the employers. If a line has to be drawn between countries where employers' policies have influenced the unions and those where this has not been the case it will pass between Sweden and Germany, on the one hand, and the remaining four countries, on the other. A union movement which meets a unified front of employers and is invited to bargain on an industry-wide basis will find that power has to be given to the national board of an industrial union. It is not unlikely that the leaders on both sides will, in the process of bargaining, develop a feeling of having a common interest at stake, namely an interest in making settlements without interference from the State. They may, as unions and employers in Sweden and Germany have done, subscribe to a policy of self-government of labour relations by the *Sozialpartner*.

In this context attention should be called to the role played by the sympathetic lockout in Sweden and in West Germany. Any student of the social history of Sweden will know that after the general strike in 1909 the union movement would have been wiped out had not Swedish managers found it in their interest to continue in their recognition of the unions as guarantors of industrial peace. The sympathetic lockout which forms the backbone of the Swedish Employers' Confederation is a powerful weapon comparable to the nuclear bomb. The present author fully subscribes to the statement of the French scholar Durand that the analogy between the strike and the lockout is a false one. The lockout is far more powerful than the strike. The recent policy of the Swedish Government to resort to lockouts against the unions of officials in professional grades has placed these unions in a very critical position with a substantial decline in membership as a prospective effect.

This leads to a comment on American labour relations. The difficulties of American unionism in gaining ground in new fields may be ascribed to special circumstances, in particular: (i) its lack of devotion to a political programme – political affiliation need not necessarily mean Socialism, the French Christian unions provide evidence of an alternative; and (ii) the resistance to and mistrust of unions among American employers. Bok and Dunlop[95] emphasize the latter point when they mention how easily unions can organize blue-collar workers once management has been persuaded to remain neutral.

My presentation of the situation of each of the six countries has focused upon the question how the unions and employers' associations regard the use of strikes and other industrial actions. Strikes occur in all countries; in some they are frequent, in others less so. The lockout plays a role particularly in countries with strong centralized employers' associations as in Sweden; in other countries, e.g. France and Italy, lockouts are subject to legal restrictions.

It would have been interesting to seek a correlation in the six countries between union membership, union structure and union financial resources, on the one hand, and the number of days lost because of industrial disputes, on the other. Such correlations, however, are very difficult to discover. The existence of strong unions within certain sectors of American industry may explain why some strikes are so costly. They are of such a kind that only a strong union can afford them. On the other hand, as will be demonstrated by statistical data in Chapter 2, the number of days lost in industrial disputes is low in Sweden and in Germany. Indisputably, Swedish and German unions are equal in strength to American unions. Furthermore, France and Italy, countries in which the unions are split into a number of competing confederations whose membership generally speaking is low and whose financial resources, at any rate in the case of France, are almost non-existent, have a greater proportion of days lost in industrial disputes than have Sweden and Germany. One would be inclined to offer an explanation opposite to the one presented with regard to the American scene. French and Italian unions call strikes because they are poor.

Two general observations should be made, however. In Britain there is a close relationship between the structure of the trade union and the occurrence of 'wildcat' strikes. The union is weak at the shop level. Bargaining is continuously going on between management and the shop steward as spokesman

95. Bok and Dunlop, op. cit.

of the workers. The shop steward often backs up his demands with various types of strikes of which – as stated by McCarthy in his research paper for the Royal Commission – the 'unconstitutional' strike is only the most immediate and apparent.

There is a fundamental difference between the bargaining systems of countries like the United States, Sweden and Germany, where the unions have accepted the idea of a collective agreement for a specific period of time with a no-strike clause or a peace obligation implicitly embodied in the agreement, and those of countries like Britain, France and Italy. In the three first-mentioned countries conflicts tend to occur in periods when a collective agreement has expired and the parties have not as yet negotiated a new contract. During the period when a contract exists the disputes tend either to be postponed or to be solved peacefully as in the United States by recourse to arbitration or as in Sweden and Germany by resort to court action. Possibly the difference between the two groups of countries is due not so much to differences in the legal systems as to differences in the approach of their trade unions. The French Communist-dominated CGT refused to sign the so-called *contrats de progrès* offered by the Government for a certain nationalized industry, the Electricity, on the ground that in the agreement there was embodied a provision that the union must give three months' notice before resorting to strike on matters covered by the agreement. The British trade unions, which are supposed to be more peaceful than French and Italian unions, are at present taking the same view in the face of the new Industrial Relations Act. The majority of them have demanded that their collective agreements shall contain an exclusion clause. Thus they insist upon contracting out from the peace obligation – one of the big innovations of the Act – even from the peace obligation for a limited period which otherwise might have followed from a duty prescribed in the procedure to negotiate an issue before resorting to action.

Industrial actions can be used for different purposes. It is everywhere recognized that the individual employee is the weaker party in the employment relationship. In order to exert economic power he needs to be backed up by other employees. Many people seem to assume that the two sides are countervailing powers and that the scales are equally balanced when on one side there is a coalition of the workers in the shop and on the other side is the employer. It has been held that this balance of power will cease to exist when local unions join together in national unions and national unions form federations. In order to create a new state of equilibrium the employers will have to join together on their side; this is the philosophy upon which Swedish and German employers base their associations. The author is not willing to subscribe to any doctrine of equilibrium, *Kampfparität*, since ordinarily one side of the scales will have more weight in it than the other and which side this is will depend upon the circumstances. Indisputably, however, a fundamental purpose of industrial action is to back up demands with economic pressure.

Not all strikes can be explained as having the primary purpose of demonstrating economic strength or rather as showing a capacity to cause harm to the other party. Several other categories of strikes can be distinguished.

Sometimes strikes are acts of protest. A strike may be a spontaneous reaction against conditions that the workers find intolerable. It may be addressed not only to the employer but also to the public, it may, as in the case of a political strike, be directed to the Government of the country or of another country. While actions to bring pressure upon the other party to the bargaining occur everywhere, the strike as a manifestation of a protest is more typical of some countries than of others. In the United States, in Britain, in Sweden and in the German Federal Republic there are relatively few strikes of this kind. In France and Italy they dominate the picture. As we have seen, the French sociologist Jean-Daniel Reynaud has stated that 'each strike is a demonstration of strength and an open disapproval of authority; it has for the strikers – if not a revolutionary flavour, at all events the character of a liberation from the yoke'.

A third type of strike consists of strikes for recognition. The United States might be called the homeland of this kind of strike. In that country, strikes for recognition often occur, despite legislation (which is being enforced by a special board) aimed at securing recognition by managements and imposing on managements a duty to bargain. Immobility is a characteristic feature of all established systems. An example is provided by the great number of serious interruptions which have been caused by attempts to change the structure of bargaining and in particular the attempts of unions to introduce coalition bargaining in new fields.

Sweden, too, has – albeit to a smaller extent – suffered for the same reason. Many of the strikes of unions within the public sector have been called in order to gain recognition as a party to a collective agreement.

The fourth and last category of industrial actions consists of actions which aim at coordination. A union which has entered into agreement with one firm wants to make this agreement a wage leader. Other employers are told that they must pay the same wages, otherwise the union will call a strike. Certainly strikes of this kind are frequent in most countries. However, it is not the strike but the lockout which is of particular interest in this context.

From its initiation in 1902 the policy of the SAF, the Swedish Employers' Confederation, has aimed at protecting their members against what managements in general consider excessive wage claims. According to the constitution of the SAF a member firm is not entitled to enter into a collective agreement without the consent of the SAF. When a national union has brought pressure for higher wages by calling strikes in a selected number of firms, the SAF has hit back by imposing lockouts on members of the union who are employed at other member firms. It is possible that the whole system of centralized bargaining would never have been established had not Swedish employers consistently pressed upon the LO unions their demand for coordination. The lockouts within the public sector early in 1971 had the same aim of coordination. They intended to force upon SACO and SR, two federations of professional workers, the policy of equalization. The employees in the lower grades were offered proportionately higher wage increases than those in the higher grades for the purpose of diminishing the gap between them.

German employers subscribe to the idea of coordination, too, although as yet the sympathetic lockout has not had the same practical application in Germany as in Sweden.

2

Methods of Industrial Action: Courts, Administrative Agencies, and Legislatures
by Benjamin Aaron

Introduction

As the title of this volume implies, we are concerned with the various manifestations in the specific countries included in this comparative survey of interruptions in the normal relations between employers, employees, and unions, as well as with the extent to which Governments seek to regulate the forms of industrial action resorted to under such circumstances.

The varieties of industrial action treated in this study have been shaped and influenced by many factors in addition to constitutional provisions, legislation, and court decisions; their ultimate origins are part of 'the seamless web of history,' and their present manifestations are understandable only as parts of the entire political, economic, and social framework within each country. The picture we present must necessarily be drawn in broad strokes; readers wishing more detailed information about laws and practices in the individual countries covered by this survey are referred to more specialized studies.

The patterns of development of the forms of industrial action in the six countries are an interesting mixture of similarity and diversity. The basic forms – the strike and the lockout – are to be found in each country, but the laws regulating their use are anything but uniform. The same may be said of the numerous other forms of industrial action, most of which may be characterized generally as variations of these two main themes. More detailed analyses of selected aspects of these phenomena are presented in the subsequent chapters of this volume.

Patterns of industrial conflict[1]

Any research on this subject must take into account the study by Arthur M. Ross and Paul T. Hartman. They accumulated roughly comparable strike data

1. In discussing the *incidence* of industrial disputes resulting in work stoppages, no distinction is made between strikes and lockouts. Most countries do not differentiate between the two forms of industrial action in reporting their statistics. See International Labor Office (I L O), *Yearbook of Labor Statistics* (1958), p. 693.

for fifteen countries, including the six covered by the present survey; grouped all but three of the countries (none of which is involved in this study) into four main 'patterns'; and formulated some tentative explanations of why a particular country fell within a designated pattern. Although their monograph included no data for any year after 1956, it still provides an interesting, though controversial, analytical tool for the purposes of our study.

In constructing their statistical comparison, Ross and Hartman did not use the three annual measures universally employed: the number of strikes, which they termed 'not particularly informative in itself';[2] the number of workers involved, which tells whether strikes are large or small; and the number of man-days of idleness within establishments directly involved, which indicates whether the strikes are short or long. Instead, they used these data and others to construct six more sophisticated standards of measurement. The first, intensity of union organization, shows union membership as a percentage of non-agricultural employment. The authors thought this standard significant because in periods of both rapid organization and loss of membership strikes tend to increase, whereas, when union membership has become stabilized, strike activity generally declines.

The second standard, membership involvement ratio, represents the sum of all workers involved in all strikes during one year, divided by the average number of union members during that year. This was deemed by the authors to be one of the most revealing measures of industrial conflict because it shows the frequency with which union members are called out on strike, whether for many small stoppages or for a fewer number of larger ones.

Employee involvement ratio, the third standard, represents the ratio between the number of workers involved in strikes and the number of non-agricultural employees. The authors noted that in using this standard some account had to be taken of two facts not reflected in the data: first, that strikes by agricultural workers sometimes occur; second, that some workers may strike more than once in any given year.

The fourth standard, duration of strikes, was constructed by dividing the number of workers involved into the number of working days lost in a particular year, thus yielding the statistic of the amount of time lost per striker. Of this standard the authors remarked: 'the duration of strikes is one of the most significant measures of industrial conflict from a behavioristic as well as an economic standpoint. Certainly the diversity in the meaning of the strike from one country to another, or from one period of time to another, shows up most dramatically in variations of length.'[3]

The fifth standard, membership loss ratio, or the ratio between the number of union members (in hundreds) and the number of working days lost, shows

A. M. Ross and P. T. Hartman point out that 'there are two parties to every dispute, in equal disagreement with each other. . . . Therefore the strike is really a bilateral suspension of work, although it is generally described as a unilateral act. . . . [W]e are using the term *strike* to designate all work stoppages, including lockouts initiated by employers.' *Changing Patterns of Industrial Conflict*, Wiley, 1960, p. 3.
2. op. cit., p. 10.
3. op. cit., p. 24.

the average loss of time as a result of strikes per hundred union members. The sixth standard, employee loss ratio, shows the average lost time from strikes per 100 non-agricultural wage and salary earners. These two standards give a rough indication of the economic impact of strikes.

On the basis of data organized in accordance with the foregoing standards of measurement, Ross and Hartman posited their four principal 'patterns':

(*a*) North Europe – First Variant;
(*b*) North Europe – Second Variant;
(*c*) Mediterranean–Asian;
(*d*) North American.

In addition, there is also a category for 'Special Cases and Mixed Situations.' They described the characteristics of North Europe – First Variant, which they found applicable to Germany and Britain (as well as to Denmark and the Netherlands), in part as follows:[4]

> This pattern . . . is characterized by a nominal propensity to strike [defined as a membership involvement ratio averaging less than three percent annually subsequent to 1947] and a low or moderate duration of strikes ['low' being defined as less than five days; 'moderate,' as an average duration of more than seven but less than ten days]. These countries have mature labor movements with firm and stable relationships. . . . Leadership conflicts are subdued; there is one dominant federation. . . . The Communist faction has been notably weak. . . .
>
> By virtue of industry-wide negotiations and the influence of central federations, collective bargaining functions have become highly centralized [in varying degrees]. . . . There are strong labor or social democratic parties, which have organized or at least participated in the government except in postwar Germany.
>
> There is a fair amount of public enterprise in the United Kingdom, but not a great deal in [Germany]. . . . Neither is there much reliance on the State for defining important conditions of employment. On the other hand, [Britain and Germany] . . . have had active programs of intervention in bargaining disputes. Compulsory arbitration was practiced in the United Kingdom until 1951, and the machinery was retained on a voluntary basis in a number of key industries. . . . The [collective bargaining agreement] 'extension' system is also used in Germany.

The authors placed Sweden (and Norway) in the North Europe – Second Variant. The distinguishing characteristic of this pattern is very infrequent but long stoppages, 'long' being defined as an average duration in excess of 14 days. In most other respects, the authors found close similarity between the first and second variants, the only significant difference being that in the latter the Government generally maintains 'a hands-off policy in labor-management controversies'.[5] Ross and Hartman conceded that this disparity was hardly

4. op. cit., pp. 73–4.
5. op. cit., p. 74.

sufficient to explain sizeable differences in the average duration of strikes between the two patterns, and suggested that variations in 'industry mix' and other causes might have affected the results.

The Mediterranean–Asian pattern included France and Italy (as well as Japan and India). The characteristics of this pattern were described by the authors in part as follows:[6]

Participation in strikes is very great [averaging from 22 to 62 per cent of union membership each year, 1947–56]. Labor movements entered the phase of mass organization, or reorganized from scratch, subsequent to World War II. Union membership does not involve an important personal or financial commitment and has often been an ephemeral phenomenon. Rival unionism and internal leadership conflicts have been endemic; there has been a powerful Communist faction . . . which has made chronic use of the massive demonstration stoppage as an agitational tool.

Labor-management relations . . . are weak and unstable. The unions have not really been accepted by employers and are not in a position to negotiate on an equal basis. Although the forms of multi-employer bargaining are used . . . the subject matter of bargaining is rather insubstantial. The significant conditions of work, for the most part, are either set by government or remain within the employer's control. The unions are normally too poor to undertake long strikes.

. . . [T]hese countries have two or more left-wing parties affiliated with different branches of the labor movement. They are bitterly divided. . . . As a consequence, conservative governments have . . . [remained in power]. No single labor party has come sufficiently close to political power that a strike policy of its affiliated unions has been affected. . . .

There is a surprising amount of public enterprise in France [and] Italy. . . . [U]nionism is so weak in the industrial sphere that unrest is focused on the political process. Thus labor protest is frequently directed against the government, a further reason for the popularity of brief demonstration strikes.

The North American pattern is represented by the United States (and Canada). They noted that the labor movement in the United States, insofar as large-scale organization is concerned, is younger than those in North Europe and older than those in the Mediterranean–Asian group. The propensity to strike was rated as moderately high (15·4 per cent of union membership), and intensity of organization as becoming more stable since the 1940s. According to the authors, the status of union leadership in the United States at the outset of the 1960s was in transition: Communist influence had ceased to be a significant factor; the American Federation of Labor (AFL) and the Congress of Industrial Organizations (CIO) had reunited; political rivalry within the unions had diminished. Another apparently irreversible development was the

6. op. cit., pp. 75–7.

acceptance and incorporation of unions into the industrial system. Collective bargaining was typically decentralized and most agreements were negotiated for single-employer units. Important conditions of employment were determined largely by private agreement rather than by government; no labor party had emerged; the central orientation of the labor movement was industrial rather than political; and the United States maintained a *laissez-faire* policy toward most types of industrial disputes. All of these factors helped to explain the relative frequency and long duration of strikes.

The foregoing patterns described by Ross and Hartman, with a few exceptions, were consistent with the history of industrial relations in the six representative countries as of the time the authors' study was written. All have been altered in some respects, and some quite substantially, by subsequent developments.

The validity of the Ross–Hartman strike data, which provided the basis for the classification of each country into its particular pattern, is not easily demonstrated – a fact which the authors candidly admitted. The complexities and shortcomings of international strike statistics for comparative purposes are well known. For example, the International Labor Organizations (ILO) strike statistics include only the total number of industrial disputes which resulted in a stoppage of work, and the number of working days involved and working days lost. Disputes 'of small importance' and 'political strikes' are frequently not included. In some cases the data do not cover workers 'indirectly affected'; in no case, apparently, do they cover workers in *other establishments* indirectly affected, as, for example, when auto workers are idled because of a steel strike. Various methods are used to calculate the number of working days lost, and these data, as well as the statistics of workers involved, 'are often approximations only'.[7]

Of even greater significance are the differences between countries in the minimum size of the stoppage reported. The United States, for example, excludes disputes involving fewer than six workers or lasting less than a full day or workshift. Britain, on the other hand, does not count disputes involving fewer than ten workers or lasting less than one day, unless they result in a loss of more than 100 working days. Germany excludes disputes lasting less than one day, regardless of the number of workers involved, unless a loss of more than 100 working days results. So far as it appears from the ILO data, France, Italy, and Sweden report all strikes, regardless of their purposes, duration, number of workers involved, or working days lost. Apart from these differences, it must be assumed that within each country some fairly large stoppages may occasionally go unreported, while a number of incidents that would ordinarily not be considered as strikes nevertheless find their way into the statistics.[8] In respect of political strikes, too, there is a problem, because the

7. ILO, op. cit., p. 693.
8. For a discussion of the relative value of international strike statistics for comparative purposes, as well as for differing interpretations of those statistics, compare H. A. Turner, *Is Britain Really Strike Prone?*, Cambridge U.P., 1969, pp. 16–20, with W. E. J. McCarthy, 'The Nature of Britain's Strike Problem' (1970), p. 8, *British Journal of Industrial Relations*, 224, 226–30.

determination whether a strike is 'political' or 'economic' is necessarily an arbitrary one that is likely to be applied inconsistently as between countries and even within a single country.

Despite these obvious limitations, Ross and Hartman[9] concluded that the international statistics were usable, for the following reasons:

> When all is said, the dissimilarities in methods and definitions are not very great. Furthermore, the conclusions reached in this study do not require a high degree of precision in the basic data. The recorded differences in experience among the several groups of countries are so great as to outweigh the relatively minor discrepancies and ambiguities in the statistics.

The Royal (Donovan) Commission on Trade Unions and Employers' Associations also made use of the ILO strike statistics and similarly noted the limitations of the data previously mentioned. The Commission concluded, however, that the ILO figures 'give a broadly accurate picture'.[10]

Unfortunately, it has not proved feasible to bring all of the six Ross–Hartman comparative measurements up to date. This is so because the statistics of union membership which they used were, by the authors' own admission, imprecise and unreliable. They noted such deficiencies as 'inflated membership claims on the part of some unions, incomplete coverage of labor organizations in the reports of some Governments, gaps in certain time series, and inconsistent definitions of union membership'.[11] Accordingly, the only three of their computations that have been brought up to date are those concerning the duration of strikes, the employee involvement ratio, and the employee loss ratio. Table 1 indicates, for each of the six countries, the average days lost per striker for the years, 1957–68. The data are presented in 6- and 12-year averages. Column 4 gives the Ross–Hartman corresponding data for the years, 1948–56.

Table 1

	1957–62 (days) (1)	1963–68 (days) (2)	1957–68 (days) (3)	1948–56 (days) (4)
Britain	3·4	2·9	3·2	4·3
France	1·3	1·3	1·3	2·9
Germany*	6·4	3·9	4·9	9·9
Italy	4·6	3·5	3·9	2·7
Sweden	14·7	12·1	12·6	22·6
United States	17·5	15·4	16·3	14·6

* Figures after 1960 include West Berlin.
Sources: Ross and Hartman, Table 4, p. 27; US Bureau of Labor Statistics, *Labor Developments Abroad*, February, 1970, pp. 19–22.

9. op. cit., pp. 184–5.
10. *Report of Royal Commission on Trade Unions and Employers' Associations, 1965–1968*, Chairman, Rt. Hon. Lord Donovan, HMSO, 1968 Comnd. 3623, para. 364.
11. op. cit., p. 187.

If one compares the figures in the first three columns of table 1 with the 1948–56 averages in column 4, it will be seen that the trends described by Ross and Hartman, to be discussed in greater detail below, continued without significant change during the period 1957–68.

Table 2 indicates, for each of the six countries, the employee involvement ratio, that is, the number of workers involved in industrial disputes as a percentage of non-agricultural employment, for the years, 1957–68. The data are presented in 6- and 12-year averages. Column 4 gives the Ross–Hartman corresponding data for the years 1948–56.

Table 2

	1957–62 (1)	1963–68 (2)	1957–68 (3)	1948–56 (4)
Britain	6·5	4·2	5·3	2·7
France	13·9	15·7	14·9	26·4
Germany	0·3	0·5	0·4	1·0
Italy	20·9	28·1	24·7	28·0
Sweden	*	0·2	0·1	0·4
United States	2·9	3·1	3·0	5·1

* Less than one-tenth of 1 per cent.
Sources: Ross and Hartman, Table 3, p. 23; US Bureau of Labor Statistics, *Labor Developments Abroad*, February, 1970, pp. 19–22.

Table 3 indicates, for each of the six countries, the employee loss ratio, that is, the working days lost per hundred non-agricultural wage and salary earners, for the years 1957–68. The data are presented in 6- and 12-year averages. Column 4 gives the Ross–Hartman corresponding data for the years, 1948–56.

Tables 2 and 3 show, with minor exceptions, a continuation of the trends revealed by the Ross–Hartman data. They noted that the proportion of wage and salary earners going on strike had fallen since the prewar period in a number of countries, including Britain, Germany, Sweden, and the United States. In each case the trend was explained by a declining *membership* involvement rate, by which they meant that recourse by union members to strikes was declining. The authors characterized the ratio between the number of strikers

Table 3

	1957–62 (1)	1963–68 (2)	1957–68 (3)	1948–56 (4)
Britain	22·3	12·7	17·3	10·6
France	17·7	20·3	19·0	68·2
Germany	2·5	1·9	2·1	5·9
Italy	93·4	98·6	96·0	44·5
Sweden	0·8	2·2	1·5	8·1
United States	51·5	47·6	49·5	75·0

Sources: Ross and Hartman, Table 6, p. 32; US Bureau of Labor Statistics, *Labor Developments Abroad*, February, 1970, pp. 19–22.

and the number of union members in Germany and Sweden as 'nominal', that is, averaging less than 3 per cent annually since 1947. In other words, the authors concluded that in these countries recourse to strikes had been largely eliminated. The membership involvement ratios in France and Italy, on the other hand, were characterized as 'high', that is, averaging from 22 to 62 per cent annually since 1947. For the same period, average annual membership involvement ratios in Britain and the United States were characterized as 'moderate' – 5·9 per cent for Britain, and 15·4 per cent for the United States. Because the duration of stoppages in Britain had been so brief, however, the authors felt 'justified in saying that the strikes have been largely eliminated in that country';[12] and because the ratio in the United States had dropped from 26 per cent in 1945–47 to about 10 per cent in 1954, they felt it could no longer be said that American unionists have an unusually high propensity to strike.

Although, for reasons previously given, we have no membership involvement figures for the period after 1956, the Swedish *employee* involvement rate continued to decline through 1968. Ross and Hartman found, on the other hand, that the degree of participation had risen greatly in several countries, including France, and attributed this to more intensive organization of workers, as well as a greater propensity to strike. But this trend was more than offset by large membership losses suffered by unions in France, and in Italy as well; hence, employee involvement ratios had declined sharply in both countries. Table 2 shows that the decline levelled off in the 12-year period since 1956.

In respect of employee loss ratios, Ross and Hartman noted that in the period 1948–56, the relative loss in the majority of countries had been running below the 1927–47 period, despite the higher rate of union membership. In the more recent of the two periods, only the United States had two days' idleness annually per union member; at the other extreme, Britain, Germany, and Sweden averaged less than one-quarter day per member. Table 3 shows that this trend has not been reversed in any of the six countries. More importantly, the authors observed:[13]

> In not a single country has the average been as high as one day per wage and salary earner per year, and in the majority it has been less than half a day. We cannot think of any other major source of loss – including unemployment, industrial accidents, and the common cold – having a smaller relative effect. It is not the economic effect of strikes in general, however, but the political effects of particular strikes and groups of strikes that have been most significant.

The truth of that statement is demonstrated most dramatically, perhaps, in Sweden during the years 1970–71. Even with the unusual rise in strike activity in that country, the number, duration, and economic impact of strikes have not been nearly so significant as the challenge presented by a few key

12. op. cit., p. 19.
13. op. cit., p. 29.

strikes to the existing collective bargaining system and to the Government itself.

The Donovan Commission, as previously noted, made certain international comparisons of strike statistics for the years 1964–66, inclusive, derived from ILO data. Table 4 presents the comparative average annual figures collected by the Commission for the six countries for stoppages due to industrial disputes in mining, manufacturing, construction, and transport. Column 4 represents data for the years 1963–67, as compiled by the British Government and included in its White Paper, published in 1969.[14]

Table 4

	No. of stoppages per 100,000 employees (1)	Average no. of persons involved per stoppage (2)	Average duration of each stoppage in working days (3)	No. of working days lost per 1,000 employees (4)
Britain	16·8	340	3·4	184
France	21·8	1,090	0·8	347
Germany	N.A.	N.A.	3·6	34*
Italy	32·9	720	5·3	1,045
Sweden	0·5†	570†	15·4†	26†
United States	13·2‡	470‡	14·2‡	934‡

N.A. Figures not available.
* Average for 1963-66 only. Figures for 1967 not available.
† All industries.
‡ Including electricity, gas, water, sanitary services.
Derived from Donovan Commission Report, p. 95; British White Paper, Appendix 2, p. 38.

Of the six countries, Britain and the United States have the most difficult strike records to interpret, in part because of their definitions of strike (or lockout) for reporting purposes. The British picture is further complicated by the relatively large number of 'unofficial' strikes. The Donovan Commission defined an 'official' strike as 'one which has been sanctioned or ratified by the union or unions whose members are on strike, all others being unofficial'. It went on to point out that 'unofficial' strikes 'are also in practice usually . . . unconstitutional' in the sense that they take place in disregard of an existing agreement laying down a procedure for the attempted settlement of a dispute before strike action is taken'.[15] On the basis of data supplied by the Ministry of Labour, the Commission reported that for the years, 1964–66, 'the overwhelming majority of stoppages – some 98 per cent – are due to unofficial strikes. Over these three years each unofficial strike involved on average about 300 workers and lasted a little over 2½ days. By contrast each official strike involved on average approximately 1,370 workers, lasted nearly three times as long, and caused the loss of over twelve times as many working days.'[16] The

14. *In Place of Strife: A Policy for Industrial Relations* (1969), Comnd. 3888.
15. op. cit., para. 367.
16. op. cit., para. 368.

Commission also reported that whereas official strikes had not shown any consistent tendency to increase in the years, 1960–66, 'unofficial strikes have shown a strong general upward trend in numbers in recent years'.[17]

This is not the proper place to debate the uses and abuses of the unofficial strike in Britain, or the relative seriousness of its impact on the British economy. Developments during the years since 1956, however, do cast serious doubt on the validity of the following conclusions reached by Ross and Hartman:[18]

> . . . British labor has largely abandoned the strike as a tactical instrument in pressing its purposes. The age and stability of unions, the sophistication of employers, the improvement of bargaining machinery, the activities of government, the political aims of the labor movement and the success of the Labour Party are all involved. The 'unofficial strike' – a protest directed against union leadership rather than employers – is the safety valve of the system. . . .

At the very least, one is entitled to conclude from evidence now available that British labor has resorted increasingly to the 'unofficial' strike as 'a tactical instrument in pressing its purposes'; that there is more appearance than substance in the 'sophistication' of British employers; that the bargaining machinery – at least the 'formal' kind – has not noticeably improved; and that the 'unofficial' strike is by no means directed exclusively, or perhaps even primarily, against the union leadership. If these conclusions are substantially correct, then Britain probably does not fit the Ross–Hartman North Europe – First Variant pattern, but should be included with Australia, Finland, and South Africa in the category reserved for Special Cases and Mixed Situations.

So far as the United States is concerned, although in terms of annual number of strikes and number of working days lost it leads all other countries, the number of man-days idle as a percentage of estimated working time is small. For 1946, the greatest strike year since the end of the Second World War, that figure was 1·04 per cent; for the years, 1957–70, the average figure was 0·16 per cent. Those figures help to explain the judgment of Ross and Hartman that employers and union officials were 'almost unanimous in opposing stronger forms of intervention in peacetime,' and that the 'informed public' appeared generally to 'countenance a considerable volume of strike activity as an incidental cost of a free-enterprise system.'[19]

Recent events, however, may force a modification of that judgment. In 1970 strike idleness amounted to 0·34 per cent of working time – the highest rate since 1959. In 1971 strikes or threatened strikes in the public sector, in transportation, especially railroads, and in the maritime (including longshoring), copper, telephone, and steel industries, among others, have given rise to a considerable public outcry and demands for strike curbs of various sorts. The

17. op. cit., para. 370.
18. op. cit., pp. 89–90.
19. op. cit., p. 169.

Government presently has before Congress a Bill to avoid or suppress strikes in the railroad, airline, trucking, and maritime industries. As inflation and unemployment continue to mount in the United States, so does the popular tendency to blame these phenomena on the system of collective bargaining and the various forms of industrial action. It is conceivable that Congress may eventually conclude that the present system costs more than it is worth.

The case of Sweden is somewhat different because of the unusual degree of employer–union conflict in the two years, 1970 and 1971. According to information from the National Mediation Office and the *Svenska Arbetsgivareföreningen* (SAF; Swedish Employers' Confederation), in 1970 there were 216 wildcat strikes with 157,000 man-days lost, all in private or State-owned industry.[20] Of all these days lost about 100,000 were attributed to a two-month strike of the workers in the State-owned mines in the north. They were essentially unauthorized strikes. The strikes were mainly for higher pay and directed against the centralized system of bargaining.

The stoppage of work in 1971 was of a somewhat different character. The unions of State officials in professional grades protested against the Government policy of equalizing by diminishing the gap between State employees in the higher and in the lower brackets. More detailed information concerning industrial conflict in the public sector is given in Chapter 6.

The years since 1956 have brought great changes in strike patterns in France and Italy, and many of the 'characteristics' of the Mediterranean–Asian pattern noted by Ross and Hartman no longer apply, if, indeed, they ever did. To begin with, it seems to have been a mistake to link France and Italy with Japan and India; the labor movements and collective bargaining systems in the latter two countries are sufficiently different to have dictated against such a grouping. Second, it would be quite wrong, at least today, to say that the subject matter of collective bargaining in France and Italy is 'rather insubstantial', that most unions in those countries are 'not in a position to negotiate [with employers] on an equal basis', or that they are 'so weak in the industrial sphere that unrest is focused on the political process', which the authors apparently and rather surprisingly consider to be completely distinct from industrial action.

Third, in respect of strike action in France and Italy, it is no longer true that strikes are merely 'demonstrations' for political purposes. As will be discussed in greater detail later in this chapter, in Italy the short, repetitive stoppage is now a calculated display of union bargaining power; in France, where union control of strikes is minimal, the workers themselves have resorted to brief, sporadic strikes to secure collective bargaining demands as well as for political purposes. One must conclude, therefore, that the Mediterranean–Asian pattern posited by Ross and Hartman is no longer a valid or useful description for our purposes.

20. cf. B. C. Roberts. 'Social Cost of Bargaining: A European Perspective' (1971), *Monthly Labor Review*, 56, 57: 'During 1970 there were some 160 illegal strikes in Sweden, mostly for higher pay and directed against the centralized system of bargaining.'

The principal conclusion reached by Ross and Hartman was that the strike (and lockout), as an instrument of industrial action, has been 'withering away'. They found that in almost all of the 15 countries studied by them, membership involvement has been declining since 1900, and the duration of strikes has been greatly curtailed in every nation which has kept records of strike activity going back that far. The exceptions were the countries in the Mediterranean–Asian group, including France and Italy, 'where the brief and massive work stoppage is used as a protest demonstration'.[21] They assigned three primary reasons why the strike 'has been going out of style':[22]

> First, employers have developed more sophisticated policies and more effective organizations. Second, the state has become more prominent as an employer of labor, economic planner, provider of benefits, and supervisor of industrial relations. Third, in many countries (although not in the United States) the labor movement has been forsaking the use of the strike in favor of broad political endeavors.

A critique of this analysis and of the assumptions upon which it is based will be reserved for the concluding portion of this chapter.

Methods of industrial action by employees and unions

This section is primarily descriptive; it is designed to acquaint the reader with the variety of forms of industrial action resorted to by unions and their federations, and by individual employees. It excludes, for the most part, references to public officials and employees, so-called 'political' strikes (including the general strike), industrial action tending to create an 'emergency', and governmental sanctions applicable to illegal conduct. Each of these subjects is discussed in detail in later chapters of this volume.

FORMS OF EMPLOYEE RESISTANCE

All 'job action' by employees does not take the usual form of strike, picket line, or boycott; nor does it necessarily involve union activity. 'Working to rule' is a form of passive resistance to, or aggression against, authority, occasionally resorted to by both organized and unorganized workers. It is particularly effective in jobs governed by rules, normally honored in the breach, relating to inspection, observance of safety precautions, and making out reports.

Another universal form of passive job action is consciously retarding the pace of work. This technique is known by a variety of names, such as 'go slow', 'ca canny', 'soldiering', or 'working without enthusiasm'. Thorstein Veblen

21. op. cit., p. 39.
22. op. cit., p. 42.

applied to this and similar forms of behavior the terms, sabotage[23] – which he defined as 'the conscientious withdrawal of efficiency', and which he found to be a common practice among all classes of society.

This technique, also, is not restricted to union members, as S. B. Mathewson's classic study of American practices demonstrated conclusively 40 years ago.[24] William E. Leiserson went further and suggested that non-unionists tended to restrict production more than unionists:[25]

> Trade-union restriction is ordinarily enforced by agreements with employers which usually come to public notice. In fear of the condemnation of public opinion, responsible leaders of labor organizations use their influence to reduce the restrictive practices of their members. Non-union workers have no such restraining influence, except as the management is on the watch; but this is offset by an amazing amount of encouragement of restriction by the workers' immediate foremen and supervisors.

Studies in the United States reveal that widespread and effective use is made of plant-wide slowdowns when grievances on manning and work standards are under discussion.[26] In Britain McCarthy's research paper on shop stewards for the Donovan Commission reported that plant-wide restrictions on output as a deliberate bargaining tactic were relatively rare, but that 'spasmodic "go slows" and restrictions occurring ... among relatively small groups' were common. Moreover, he reported difficulty in distinguishing, sometimes, 'between the planned control of output by a work-group, for the purpose of stabilizing earnings, or qualifying for overtime, and the deliberate use of output restrictions as a bargaining weapon.'[27]

Individual employees engaging in slowdowns are normally subject to disciplinary action by their employer. If the slowdown is by concerted action, it is usually equated with a strike and treated in the same manner. French law, as we shall see, accords the broadest protection of the right to strike, but slowdowns are forbidden. According to André Brun,[28]

> [s]uch strikes have always been disapproved by the *Cour de cassation*, which considers that it amounts to disloyalty to go through the motions of performing one's contract whilst actually holding back one's efforts. It is thus a partial failure to carry out the obligations of the contract of employment.

23. The origin of the word is commonly traced to the act of a French workman in throwing his wooden shoe (*sabot*) into the machinery and stalling it in an effort to induce the employer to grant certain demands. 'Sabotage', in *Encyclopaedia of the Social Sciences*, 1934, Vol. XIII, p. 495. *See also* T. Veblen. 'On Sabotage', *The Engineers and the Price System*, New York, 1921, p. 1.
24. S. B. Mathewson. *Restriction of Output Among Organized Workers*, New York, 1931.
25. W. E. Leiserson. 'The Economics of Restriction of Output,' in Mathewson, op. cit., pp. 160, 163.
26. See S. L. Slichter, J. J. Healy, and E. R. Livernash. *The Impact of Collective Bargaining on Management*, The Brookings Institution, 1960, p. 670.
27. W. E. J. McCarthy. *The Role of Shop Stewards in British Industrial Relations*, HMSO, 1966, p. 20.
28. 'The Law of Strikes and Lock-outs in France', in O. Kahn-Freund (ed.), *Labour Relations and the Law*, London, 1965, p. 193.

In Italy, the practice of working to rule is observed mainly in public employment. In this case a defense of its legality would hardly be tenable.[29] From 1948 until the early 1950s, 'non-cooperation' became an official form of industrial action, but was rejected not only by employers, but also by the minority unions. It consisted primarily of refusals to perform any duties not strictly related to a worker's job, to make minor repairs of machines, and working to rule. In practice, however, non-cooperation frequently tended to become a slowdown, which was regarded as illegal by the courts. Consequently, the practice disappeared around 1953.[30] At present, there is a frequent resort to slowdowns or to the practice of omitting one essential operation. Workers on piecework sometimes engage in a *piecework strike*, which consists of producing an amount necessary to earn base pay but not enough to earn any incentive pay. Decisions in respect of the legality of such piecework strikes are not reported; however, they probably uphold their legality.

STRIKES IN GENERAL

In modern times the strike has, in most countries, become associated almost exclusively with some form of union activity. In essence, it is a temporary concerted cessation of work, in which regard it is to be distinguished from a voluntary and unilateral termination of employment by employees acting independently. Strikers act in concert, with the intent to return to the jobs which they have temporarily ceased to perform; the purpose of the typical strike is to force some concession from the employer in respect of union recognition, wages, hours of work, or some other term or condition of employment.

In most countries the 'right' (or liberty) to strike, subject to varying degrees of limitation, is guaranteed by constitution, statute, administrative decree, or judicial decisions. In the United States, for example, the National Labor Relations (Wagner) Act (NLRA), which does not apply to Federal Government, state, county, or municipal workers, expressly guarantees and protects the right to strike, subject to procedural limitations; state and other Federal laws and judicial decisions grant similar rights to employees in the private sector not covered by that statute. On the other hand, the United States Supreme Court has held that the Constitution does not confer the absolute right to strike.

As in the other five countries included in our survey, the law in the United States distinguishes also between permissible and prohibited strike objectives and strike tactics. Most of this law is spelled out in Federal statutes, but states still have the authority to exercise their police powers to prevent, for example, breaches of the peace.

In France, the right to strike is guaranteed by the Constitution of 1958; strikes do not constitute a breach of individual contracts of employment, nor can they be made the basis for disciplinary dismissals. So basic is the right to

29. G. Giugni. *Diritto sindacale*, Bari, 1969, p. 214.
30. See L. Mengoni in *Grève et Lock-out*, Luxembourg, 1961, p. 270.

strike that it can be exercised with impunity in the face of procedural requirements, such as compulsory conciliation, designed to forestall its use. On the
other hand, French case law declares some strikes unlawful because of the
means employed or the objective sought, and penalties are prescribed under
the criminal law for the commission of such unlawful acts.

France is the conspicuous exception to the generalization that in modern
times strikes have become associated almost exclusively with some form of
union activity. Neither French practice nor French law conforms to that statement. Strikes are frequently initiated and administered by unorganized workers or by a minority within one of several unions representing workers in the
struck enterprise. The laws recognize no necessary link between strikers and
unions; therefore, procedural requirements, such as strike votes, are not prescribed, and legal sanctions against either individual strikers or the unions to
which they belong are barred by the constitutional guarantee of the absolute
right to strike.

The status of the strike in Italy is no less unique than it is in France. Article
40 of the Constitution of 1948 guarantees the right to strike, but only within
the ambit of contemplated future legislation to regulate its exercises. Such
legislation, however, has never been passed; so the task of defining, in legal
terms, what is meant by 'the right to strike' has been assumed by the courts.
The question whether Art. 40 is self-implementing or requires legislation to
make it fully effective has been resolved in favor of the former interpretation;
courts have defined the nature of the constitutional right to strike on numerous
occasions since 1951. In general, the right is defined as the power, collectively
and by agreement, to abstain from work in order to further economic interests.
The Italian courts have also created distinctions between legitimate and illegitimate strike objectives and strike tactics. Earlier decisions held that an
'economic interest' had to be concerned with a matter subject to a collective
bargaining agreement with an employer. A decision by the Constitutional
Court in 1962, however, extended the definition to cover socio-economic
interests, that is, interests which lie beyond the gates of the factory.[31] Economic strikes by Government employees that do not affect 'functions or services
essential to social life' are considered to be protected by Art. 40. This question
is discussed in greater detail in Chapter 6. The area of strikes goes even beyond
this field to embrace self-employed independent contractors, professional
workers such as doctors and attorneys, salesmen, and sharecroppers. As to
these persons, the law is completely unclear. A majority of legal commentators,
however, are inclined to restrictive reading of Art. 40 in this respect.[32]

In Germany the status of the strike also has its peculiar features, although
there are some similarities with the situations in both France and Italy. Unfortunately, because the constitutional provisions relating to the subject are
ambiguous, the decisions of the courts are divided, and the discussion of labor

31. Corte Costituzionale, 1962, No. 123.
32. L. Mengoni. *Grève et Lock-out*, p. 264; G. Pera, 'Lo Sciopero e la Serrata' in
Nuovo trattato di diritto del lavoro, L. Riva Sanseverino and G. Mazzoni, Vol. 1,
Padova, 1971, p. 565. *Contra*: G. Branca in *Rivista di diritto civile*, 1968, I, p. 151.

law is still dominated by conceptual legal thinking, which is far from unanimous, it is difficult to generalize about the status of the strike in that country. The Federal Constitution of 1949 (known as the 'Basic Law') provides in Art. 9:[33]

1. All Germans have the right to form associations and societies.
2. Associations, the objects or activities of which conflict with the criminal laws or which are directed against the constitutional order or the concept of international understanding, are prohibited.
3. The right to form associations to safeguard and improve working and economic conditions is guaranteed to everyone and to all trades and professions. Agreements which restrict or seek to hinder this right are null and void; measures directed to this end are illegal.

According to Ramm, what the Basic Law guarantees 'is not a right [to strike], but only a freedom to strike and to lock out. This freedom is only one aspect of the general freedom to act, *i.e.*, to do what is not forbidden,[34] and this is a freedom enjoyed by individuals and groups and therefore by labor organizations.'[35] The courts, however, have asserted the right to restrict this freedom. The most important limitation imposed is that a strike is illegal unless supported by a trade union. In the case of a legal strike, the individual striker, as in France, is held not to have breached his contract of employment simply because he failed to give the requisite contractual notice to his employer. The German Federal Labor Court (*Bundesarbeitsgericht*) has held that a strike does not terminate, but merely suspends, the strikers' contracts of employment. Employers may not dismiss individual strikers, but they are allowed to resort to a lockout, which can result in either the suspension or collective dismissal of the employees. Moreover, a 1960 decision of the Federal Labor Court permitted the employers to 'split' the lockout into a number of 'successive, partial lockouts with notice,'[36] thus, in effect, permitting individual dismissals. On the other hand, the employer cannot claim damages against strikers for failure of the latter to give notice of their suspension of services. This point is discussed at greater length in Chapter 5.

From a purely legal point of view, the problems concerning strikes and strikers in Sweden are similar to those of the other European countries. During the latter part of the nineteenth century, there was a transition from the formal contract of employment, regulated by the Statute of Laborers, to the so-called 'free' contract, which dispensed with the prior formalities and provided, typically, for an indefinite rather than a fixed period of employment. In

33. German Information Center, *The Basic Law of the Federal Republic of Germany*, New York, 1962. The accuracy of the translation of para. 3 is disputed by Ramm for reasons discussed by Wedderburn in Chapter 6.
34. Article 2(1) of the Basic Law provides: 'Everyone has the right to the free development of his personality insofar as he does not violate the rights of others or offend against the constitutional order or the moral code.'
35. 'The Restriction of the Freedom to Strike in the Federal Republic of Germany', in *Labour Relations and the Law*, O. Kahn-Freund (ed.), London, 1965, p. 203.
36. Ramm, op. cit., p. 205.

the absence of legislation, questions arose as to what law should govern these free contracts.

Since the early years of the present century, collective bargaining has been the established pattern in Sweden. Unlike the situation in the United States, the institution was firmly established prior to the enactment of legislation. Even before the adoption of the Collective Agreements Act of 1928, the collective bargaining parties had implicitly acknowledged that each has the right to resort to industrial action in order to obtain an acceptable agreement, but that both have the obligation to refrain from such action to alter an existing agreement during its normal term. As discussed in greater detail in Chapter 4, Sweden was the first country to take the view that strikes do not breach the employment relationship, but only suspend it. Employment agreements regularly require that employees must give a minimum period of notice before leaving their jobs. For blue-collar workers this period was one week until 1964, when it was extended to two weeks. The question whether blue-collar workers can strike without notice has been much disputed since the early part of the century. In respect of white-collar workers, the Labor Court held in the *Bank Clerks* case[37] that the collective bargaining parties had intended to make industrial action lawful regardless of the notice requirement. The Mediation Act of 1920 was amended in 1935, and as a substitute for regular notice it required that the party intending to strike (or lock out) must give the opposite party and the mediator of the district a minimum notice of seven days. Although this procedural rule is generally observed,[38] a violation does not constitute a breach of the collective bargaining agreement, nor does it affect the validity of the offensive action under the Collective Agreements Act. Thus, the strikers are considered to retain their status as employees of the struck employer. In this respect the Swedish law differs sharply from the American; workers in the United States who strike in violation of the notice requirements of the Labor Management Relations (Taft-Hartley) Act (LMRA) lose their status as employees and their right to reinstatement at the termination of the strike.

The right to strike, in Britain, has never been granted explicitly by law; instead, a series of statutes enacted in the last 100 years have relieved strikers from the sanctions which would otherwise attach to their actions under the Criminal and Civil Law. The Industrial Relations Act 1971, which embodies some substantive and procedural provisions similar to those in the American NLRA and LMRA, does not have any exact counterpart to sec. 7 of the NLRA. Section 167(1) of the Industrial Relations Act defines 'strike' as

37. AD 1948: 47.
38. Chapter II, Art. 8 of the Basic Agreement of 1938, as amended, provides in part:
   Strikes, lockouts, boycotts, or any other similar forms of direct action – even if otherwise permissible under Swedish law or under any collective bargaining contract – must not be resorted to because of any given dispute: . . . .
   (3) unless, following due negotiations, a written notice of the action contemplated has been served on the opposite trade federation not later than three months from the day when the negotiations . . . shall be deemed as having been finished. . . . Quoted in Schmidt, *The Law of Labor Relations in Sweden*, Harvard U.P., 1962, p. 270.

a concerted stoppage of work by a group of workers, in contemplation or furtherance of an industrial dispute, whether they are parties to the dispute or not, whether (in the case of all or any of those workers) the stoppage is or is not in breach of their terms and conditions of employment, and whether it is carried out during, or on the termination of, their employment.

Section 5(1) gives every worker 'the right to be a member of such [registered] trade union he may choose', or to refuse to be a member of either a registered or unregistered union[39]; but it says nothing about the right to engage in concerted activities with other workers for their mutual aid or protection. Nor does the Act contain an affirmative guarantee of the right to strike, which must be inferred from the provisions defining certain kinds of action as unfair industrial practices.

In most occupations[40] the law grants to every employee, acting individually or in combination with others, the right to cease work upon the giving to his employer of the required notice under the contract of employment. Upon the expiration of the notice, he may lawfully stop working.

As in the other European countries, the legal relation between collective industrial action and the individual employee in Britain is conceived in terms of the individual contract of employment. In the case of a strike, the legal question is whether the worker has terminated his contract or has broken it. Because a worker must ordinarily give due notice in order to terminate his contract lawfully, the determination whether a strike is to be considered 'lawful' or 'unlawful' will depend upon the giving of the correct period of notice by the individual workers or their bargaining representative. Accordingly, the consequence of a legal termination of an individual contract of employment, at least until recently, has been the outright termination of the contract, rather than its suspension, as is the case in France, Italy, Germany, and Sweden. In strict legal theory, therefore, if the worker subsequently returns to work, he does so as a new employee, without any of the benefits he has accumulated in the course of his prior period of employment.

On the other hand, if insufficient notice has been given, or if a strike has been called without any notice, the employees are regarded as having breached their individual contracts, and the employer is entitled to terminate them forthwith. If he elects to do so, the consequences to the employees are the same as if they had lawfully terminated their employment contracts. Alternatively, the employer may elect to sue the striking employees for damages for breach of contract.

As is so often the case in Britain, however, actual practice does not conform to legal theory; it is, in fact, exceptional for an employer to exercise his legal rights even in the case of an 'unlawful' strike. Similarly, when striking employees have lawfully terminated their employment contracts by giving adequate notice, it is the accepted practice for all parties to treat pensions, senior-

39. The vital significance of the new system of registration under the 1971 Act is explained in Chapter 1.
40. Strikes by certain categories of employees treated differently under the 1971 Act are discussed in Chapter 6.

ity, and other accumulated rights as though continuity of employment had never been broken. Thus, in Britain as well as in the other countries included in this survey, it is clearly understood by all parties that strikers do not intend to sever their relationship with the employer.

The decision in *Rookes* v. *Barnard* ushered in a new trend in legal theory. In that case the plaintiff alleged intimidation by illegal means, which meant that he had to prove that the threatened strike would itself have been unlawful. Inasmuch as inadequate strike notice had been given, the question to be considered related to the legal effect of the threat to breach the contracts of employment. In the Court of Appeal, Lord Justice Donovan expressed the view that 'no-one seems yet to have thought that a strike itself in breach of contract is unlawful, and at this time of day I do not think it is'.[41] The House of Lords thought otherwise, however, and held the threatened strike to be a form of unlawful intimidation.

In *Stratford & Son, Ltd.* v. *Lindley*, involving what had theretofore been regarded as a 'lawful' strike, Lord Denning, M.R., held that 'a "strike notice" is nothing more nor less than a notice that men will not come to work. In short, that they will break their contracts. . . .'[42] The effect of this decision was to abolish the previous distinction between 'lawful' and 'unlawful' strikes based on the giving of adequate notice. However, three years later, in *Morgan* v. *Fry*, Lord Denning drew back somewhat from his previous position, and concluded that a strike notice does not terminate a contract of employment, but merely suspends it. 'In practice this would mean', the Donovan Report observes, 'creating a new right of unilateral suspension, since either side to the contract of employment could exercise the right without the consent of the other, the employee by striking, the employer by locking out.'[43]

Although there are a number of theoretical and practical objections to such an approach, which would require a fundamental change in the present law of contract,[44] the new Industrial Relations Act takes a long step in that direction. Section 147 reads in part:

> (1) Due notice given by or on behalf of an employee of his intention to take part in a strike shall not, unless it otherwise expressly provides, be construed –
>
> (*a*) as a notice to terminate his contract of employment, or
> (*b*) as a repudiation of that contract. . . .
>
> (5) In this section 'due notice', in relation to an employee, means notice of a duration not less than that which (whether by virtue of any enactment or otherwise) he would be required to give to terminate his contract of employment.

41. [1963] 1 Q.B. 623, 683.
42. [1965] A.C. 269, 285.
43. op. cit., para. 942.
44. See, e.g., K. W. Wedderburn, *The Worker and the Law*, Penguin Books, 1971, pp. 109–11, 193–6, and the Donovan Report, para. 943. See also the discussion in Chapters 3 and 4.

Section 147(2) provides that the action of an employee in taking part in a strike, after due notice of his intention to strike has been given, '. . . shall not be regarded as a breach of his contract of employment . . .' in any action in contract or tort, or for breach of contract involving injury to persons or property; nor shall it be regarded as the unfair industrial practice of knowingly inducing or threatening to induce another person to break a contract under the very important sec. 96(1). Nevertheless, sec. 147(4) states that

> nothing in subsection (2) of this section shall be taken to exclude or restrict any right which an employer would have apart from that subsection to dismiss (with or without notice) an employee who takes part in a strike.

And sec. 147(3) declares:

> Subsection (2) of this section shall not apply to any action by an employee which is contrary to a term of his contract of employment (including any term implied or incorporated in that contract by reference to a collective agreement) excluding or restricting his right to take part in a strike.

Wedderburn emphasizes that, at Common Law, although an employer was no longer free to terminate strikers' contracts for fundamental breach, there had been no alteration in the Common Law position that even a strike which did not terminate the contract of employment constitutes some kind of breach of contract. Moreover, the strike is still considered an 'unlawful means', upon which liability for the torts of conspiracy and intimidation may be predicated in the High Court. But in that jurisdiction protection is given in industrial disputes against tort liability in sec. 132(3) of the 1971 Act. The National Industrial Relations Court (NIRC) does not, of course, apply the law of tort, but rather, the new law of unfair industrial practices.

SPECIALIZED FORMS OF STRIKES

The strike is a flexible instrument, capable of assuming a number of different guises and adaptable to a number of different objectives. Some types are, of course, more common than others. For example, the *sympathetic strike* is known in all six countries covered by this survey. A sympathetic strike is a concerted work stoppage by employees of one employer to express solidarity with striking employees of another employer, and to exert indirect pressure on the other employer. In the United States, sympathetic strikes are relatively uncommon because of the prevalence of no-strike clauses in collective bargaining agreements and the legislative prohibition against 'hot cargo' clauses in such agreements. An example of a lawful sympathetic strike would be one by a group of unorganized workers in support of a strike by the organized employees of the same employer caused by that employer's unfair labor practice.

In Britain the broad definition of 'trade dispute' in the 1906 Act clearly makes sympathetic strikes lawful, subject, of course, to the limitations on all strike activity discussed above. As stated by Citrine:[45]

> ... where there is a trade dispute between an employer and his own workmen, the fact that other workmen, who have no quarrel with their own employers and no direct quarrel with any other employer, join in the dispute in sympathy, does not alter its character, and they, too, will be entitled to the protection of the Act.

But forms of sympathetic action which interfered with commercial contracts were actionable as torts, receiving no protection from the old Acts. Furthermore, liability would arise if the acts done were held to further some predominant object other than a trade dispute, even though done in the course of that dispute: for example, acts done to punish a third-party employer who had intervened.[46] Even after 1971, the old law of tort would apply to such a case because the acts would not be done in furtherance or contemplation of an 'industrial dispute'.

The Industrial Relations Act 1971 introduces three major 'unfair industrial practices'. Section 97 makes unlawful the organizing, financing, or threat to call any strike (whether notice is given or not), any 'irregular industrial action' defined in sec. 33(4) (below, p. 92), or any lockout, which has as its principal purpose the assistance of another person whose acts constitute an unfair industrial practice under the Act. Thus, if a strike were unlawful for any of the manifold reasons which could make it an unfair practice, a secondary boycott in its support would itself become unlawful. An exception to this rule is made for the registered union if its conduct consists in supporting action that is unlawful by reason only of infringement of sec. 96 (the unfair industrial practice of inducing breach of a contract), a provision inserted in order to enable such a union to turn 'unofficial' strikes by its members into 'official' strikes without risk of liability under sec. 97. Secondly, sec. 96 makes unlawful inducing breach of contract, except for the registered trade union.

Thirdly, sec. 98 makes it an unfair industrial practice to take or threaten to take action by way of a strike, irregular industrial action, or lockout with the principal intention of frustrating performance of a commercial contract with an 'extraneous party'. In the British situation this liability will be of particular importance in the case of sympathetic or 'solidarity' action. Section 98(2) provides that a person shall be regarded as 'extraneous' if he is not a party to the dispute and if 'he has not, in contemplation or furtherance of that dispute, taken any action in material support of a party to it'. Otherwise, the definition of 'extraneous party' in sec. 98(3) is wide; it includes, for example, even an 'associated employer,' defined in sec. 167(8) as one who has direct or indirect control of the business of the primary employer, or who is, together with the primary employer, directly or indirectly controlled by a third person. No special protection is given to registered unions under sec. 98, which is

45. N. A. Citrine, *Trade Union Law*, Stevens, 1960 edn., p. 506.
46. Wedderburn, op. cit., pp. 334, 357.

aimed at limiting sympathetic ('secondary') boycotts and strikes. This means that there is no protection of the common British phenomenon of one section of a large union (e.g., drivers employed by a supplier) refusing to do work that would assist an employer in a dispute with another section of the same union or another union. Thus, sec. 98 of the Act takes the place of, and even slightly extends, the old tort liability of interfering with commercial contracts.

In Sweden the SAF early took the view that sympathetic lockouts should be used as the means of defense against strikes directed against individual members. The claim that resort to sympathetic action should be permitted even during a period in which a collective agreement was in force was reluctantly accepted by the *Landorganisasjonen i Sverige* (LO; Swedish Confederation of Trade Unions, as a justification for sympathetic strikes, and for the general strike as the ultimate remedy. When the Minister of Social Welfare introduced the Bill on Collective Agreements in 1928, he noted that both the collective bargaining parties agreed on the permissibility of sympathetic lockouts or sympathetic strikes. Accordingly, such actions were made unlawful only when a party took action in order to assist others in cases in which those others were themselves forbidden to take offensive action. Thus, a sympathetic strike to assist strikers involved in a lawful dispute remained lawful. Indeed, resort to sympathetic action on both sides may be looked upon as the 'backbone' of a highly centralized system of bargaining.

Similarly, although the procedure in Chapter II of the Basic Agreement of 1938 between the SAF and the LO contains detailed rules on the peace obligation, it does not apply to the taking of 'sympathetic actions'. Conversely, the national agreement for agriculture provides, by implication, that sympathetic strikes are prohibited for the duration of the agreement.

It may be inferred from the present legal status of strikes in general in Germany that sympathetic strikes are probably illegal. By definition, such a strike involves a dispute that cannot be terminated by a collective bargaining agreement between the sympathetic strikers and *their* employer. Also, given the prevailing attitude of the labor courts toward strikes, it seems more than likely that the *ultima ratio* theory would be invoked to declare sympathetic strikes 'socially inadequate.'[47]

Sympathetic strikes are relatively infrequent in France, except during periods, such as 1936 and 1968, when strike waves engulfed the entire nation. When sympathetic strikes do occur, however, they present no special legal problem. As in Sweden, the only test is whether the original strike is lawful or unlawful; its legal status will govern that of the sympathetic strike.

The status of sympathetic strikes in Italy is not entirely clear. It was previously assumed that, in order to be a lawful 'economic' strike, the stoppage must aim at achieving something which is in the power of the strikers' own employer to grant. Also, it was argued that Arts. 503 to 505 of the Penal Code, which declare illegal and punishable political and sympathetic strikes and

47. This subject is discussed in further detail in Chapters 5 and 6.

lockouts, are still in force. In 1962, these articles were the subject of a decision by the Constitutional Court, which sustained their constitutionality. The Court held, however, that Art. 505 is not applicable to sympathetic strikes when the interests of the sympathetic strikers and those whom they support are so interdependent that both groups will suffer unless they are permitted to act in concert.

A much debated question is whether, in certain situations, the interests of the sympathetic strikers and those whom they support are really interdependent. The Corte di Cassazione (Court of Cassation) has held that when different productive units have a common financial ownership, strikers in one productive unit may lawfully strike in sympathy with those in the other.[48] On the other hand, mere membership by the sympathetic strikers in the same confederation to which the primary strikers belong has been held not to be a sufficient interdependent interest to justify a sympathetic strike.[49] In the opinion of some scholars, however, the workers' judgment must determine the question whether interests are so interdependent as to justify a sympathetic strike.

SPORADIC STRIKES

The *sporadic strike* also takes a variety of forms and is known by a number of terms, such as 'hit-and-run' strike, 'switch-strike,' 'rolling' or 'rotating' strike (*grève tournante*), *débrayages* (repetitive work stoppages), and the like. The purpose underlying all forms is to disrupt production or service either without actually leaving the work place or by leaving it only briefly. In the United States such activities are not protected by law, and the principal legal question they present is whether the action constitutes an unfair labor practice under the NLRA. If it does, the dispute falls within the exclusive jurisdiction of the National Labor Relations Board (NLRB) or, if the matter is referred to arbitration, within the concurrent jurisdiction of the Board and the arbitrator. If the action does not constitute an unfair labor practice, any legal challenge to the employer's retaliatory measures is a matter either for arbitration or for the courts.

In Britain this type of industrial action would now appear to fall within the definition in sec. 33(4) of the Industrial Relations Act 1971 of 'irregular industrial action short of a strike'; that is,

> ... any concerted course of conduct (other than a strike) which, in contemplation or furtherance of an industrial dispute, –
> (a) is carried on by a group of workers with the intention of preventing, reducing or otherwise interfering with the production of goods or the provision of services, and
> (b) in the case of some or all of them, is carried on in breach of their contracts of employment or (where they are not employees) in breach of their terms and conditions of service.

48. Corte di Cassazione, 1963, No. 2036.
49. Corte di Cassazione, 1963, No. 2283.

In certain circumstances, both irregular industrial actions and strikes are regarded as unfair industrial practices. For example, such action by a union (as well as a lockout by an employer) designed to influence the regular procedures governing the establishment of an agency shop is declared in sec. 16 to be an unfair industrial practice. The same is true in respect of pressures on an employer to infringe on rights of workers (sec. 33), and of pressures by employers or unions to frustrate procedures governing questions of recognition of sole bargaining agent and of collective bargaining (secs. 54–5). It should be borne in mind that, insofar as strikes are concerned, the giving of notice or the existence of a negotiated procedure or of a no-strike duty are immaterial; all strikes for the forbidden purposes are unfair industrial practices.

Complaint of an unfair industrial practice may be filed under sec. 101(1) of the 1971 Act with the newly created National Industrial Relations Court by 'any person' against whom the practice was directed. If the NIRC finds that the grounds of the complaint are 'well-founded' and that relief would be 'just and equitable' (section 101[2]), it may grant relief in the form of a declaratory judgment of the rights of the disputants, an award of compensation, or a 'cease-and-desist' order against the respondent (sec. 101[3]). Section 101(4) provides that in any proceedings on a complaint against an official of a trade union or an employers' association in respect of action taken by him in his official capacity, if it is shown that he did in fact act within the scope of his authority, he shall be subject neither to an order to pay damages nor to an order to cease and desist. This immunity does not extend, of course, to the trade union or the employers' association on whose behalf he acted.

The kinds of sporadic strikes referred to above commonly occur in Sweden between the lapse of an old collective bargaining agreement and the execution of a new one. Folke Schmidt also refers to a form of 'secret' strike, known as 'desertion of the workshop', in which the workers, by prior arrangement, give notice and leave, one by one. This conduct is illegal if there is a collective agreement in force.

For the reasons previously given, sporadic strikes are probably illegal in Germany and are, in any case, uncommon. In France, *débrayages* and *grèves tournantes* (those affecting, one after another, various units of industry, e.g., a particular bus service or assembly line; or the various employees within a particular firm, e.g., welders, fitters, and electricians, in turn) are very important. They are designed to force management to make concessions while, at the same time, reducing the workers' loss of earnings to a minimum. All forms of these strikes are lawful, unless they seriously disorganize production or service. The question whether such strikes so seriously disrupt the enterprise as to become abusive is left to the courts to decide. The courts thus have great power, but in most cases they tend to be lenient toward the workers.

In Italy there has been increasing resort to *scioperi articolati*. The legality of these short 'rotating' or 'rolling' strikes is much debated. Employers retaliate by imposing discipline on those engaged in this form of stoppage. Following the imposition of such measures, however, or the refusal to pay wages to workers forced by the strike of others to be idle, or a lockout, many unions have filed claims under Art. 28 of the new Workers' Statute of 1970. Article 28 of this Statute provides that if an employer takes actions 'intended to prevent or restrict the exercise of trade union freedom and activities as well as the right to strike,' he may, at the instance of the local or national unions involved, and after a hearing, be ordered by the local judge (*pretore*) 'to cease and desist from the illegitimate actions and to eliminate their effects'. The judgment of the *pretore* may be appealed within 15 days to a court of first instance (*tribunale*), which renders 'an immediately enforceable decision'. It is a crime for an employer to refuse to comply with the decision of either the *pretore* or the *tribunale*. Decisions of the *pretori* have tended to recognize the illegality of such measures, but have often been based on such issues of fact as whether there was work available.[50]

Those decisions of the *pretori* do not repudiate, even in respect of *sciopero articolato*, some basic principles laid down by the Corte Costituzionale,[51] according to which it is up to the strikers to avoid material damage, dangers to safety, and deprivation of essential goods to the community protected by the constitution itself, as a consequence of the strike.

But the majority of the *pretori* did not follow the established doctrine of the Court of Cassation which had given rise to a harsh debate among legal commentators.[52] This doctrine was that of 'equality of damages'; that is to say, that a strike is lawful insofar as the non-performance of work is balanced by the non-payment of wages. When consequences go further (for example, disorganization of production, bottlenecks in production, impossibility of resuming work immediately after the cessation of the strike, and physical damage to equipment) the strike is considered illegal. This doctrine has led to a condemnation of the *sciopero articolato*, and now to a conflict between the lower and higher courts.

A form of secret or disguised strike, sometimes practiced by employees who are prohibited by law from taking such industrial action, is known in the United States as the '*sick-out*'. As the name implies, the employees, by prior and concerted agreement, fail to report for work and notify their employer that they are too ill to work. This tactic is particularly effective for short periods, owing to the difficulty of proving that an employee was not in fact sick.

A less drastic form of industrial action, fairly common in the United States, Britain, and Italy, is the *concerted refusal to work overtime*. This is obviously legal unless the duty to work overtime is provided for in the applicable collective

---

50. With some limitations. In one case it was held that the strikers had a duty to inform the employer about the program of the *sciopero articolato*. On the other hand, the employer has a duty to reduce damages to the extent possible. See F. de Ambri Corridoni, F. Fabbri, G. Veneto, 'Rassegna critica delle decisioni concernenti la legge', 20/5/1970. n. 300, in RGL, 1970, II, p. 834.
51. Corte Costituzionale, 1962, No. 124.
52. The leading case is Corte de Cassazione, 3 March 1967, No. 512. Among legal writers, see G. Pera, 'Lo Sciopero e la serrata', in *Nuovo trattato de diritto del lavoro*, pp. 617 ff., and the sharp criticism of Ghera, 'Considerazioni sulla giurisprudenza in tema di sciopero', in ISLE *Indagine sul sindacato*, pp. 388 ff., in which he asserts the possibility of resorting in some cases to liability for tort.

agreement or individual contract of employment. In Italy, the refusal to work overtime is considered by the Supreme Court to be as unlawful as the *sciopero articolato*. In fact, it often results in a *sciopero articolato*.

SIT-DOWN STRIKES

Although it remains today little more than a symbol of the world-wide labor unrest in the 1930s, the *sit-down strike* once represented one of the most effective forms of industrial action ever devised. Bernstein[53] gives the following description of this phenomenon, which achieved its apotheosis in the automobile industry in the United States.

> The workers took physical possession of the plant and its machines, ceased productive labor themselves, and prevented others from engaging in such labor. Since in the classic form the basic issue was recognition, the workers sat down until the employer agreed to deal with their union. There were variations for lesser matters. The 'quickie', a sit-down that lasted only a few minutes or an hour or two, was usually a protest against the speed of the assembly line. The 'skippy', which bordered on sabotage, was a refusal to assemble every sixth fender or to tighten every fifth bolt.
>
> From labor's point of view, the sit-down was marvellously effective. It brought production to an immediate and total halt. . . . But unlike the conventional walkout, it allowed the employer no choice over whether he would operate or shut down, and thereby it automatically eliminated the scab [strikebreaker, blackleg]. Picketing, with its accompanying legal complications, became unnecessary. . . . In a large, integrated manufacturing operation, such as auto production, a relatively small group of disciplined unionists could cripple an entire system by seizing a strategic plant.

In 1937 – the highwater mark of the sit-down strike in the United States – there were 477 such strikes, in which almost 400,000 workers participated. In 1939, however, when the sit-down wave had ebbed, the Supreme Court ruled that this form of industrial action was illegal. The Court said in part:[54]

> The seizure and holding of the buildings was itself a wrong apart from any acts of sabotage. But in its legal aspect the ousting of the owner from lawful possession is not essentially different from an assault upon the officers of an employing company, or the seizure and conversion of its goods, or the despoiling of its property or other unlawful acts in order to force compliance with demands.

In France, the sit-down strike (*grève d'occupation* or *grève sur le tas*) enjoyed a similar vogue. In 1954 Lorwin recalled the 1936 sit-downs as 'the greatest and easiest triumph of labor memories', representing 'working class unity as well as working class power.'[55] The 'first fine careless rapture' of the 1930s, however, could not be recaptured in the postwar period.

53. I. Bernstein, *Turbulent Years*, Houghton-Miflin, 1970, p. 499.
54. *NLRB* v. *Fansteel Metallurgical Corp.*, 306 US 240, 253 (1939).
55. Val R. Lorwin, *The French Labor Movement*, Harvard U.P., 1954, pp. 236–7.

In dealing with sit-down strikes the French courts have concentrated their attention on the attitude of the individual worker, rather than on the legality of the strike itself. This is natural, because in French law the only sanctions available apply to individuals rather than to unions. A kind of modified sit-down strike occurs frequently, taking the form of strike meetings held on company time and property. Whereas such tactics would be regarded with the utmost seriousness in the United States, they are not uncommon in France, largely because most strikes are only partial strikes. Thus, typically, some workers continue to perform their assigned tasks while others in the same enterprise are on strike. So long as the strikers do not interfere with others' freedom to work, their activities will be regarded as lawful. Recently, in a few isolated cases, however, strikers not only occupied the employer's premises while refusing to work, but also imprisoned some management representatives in their own offices in an effort to force them to make concessions. These tactics are clearly unlawful, and are denounced not only by the courts, but by the unions as well. Yet, somewhat paradoxically the unions vigorously oppose any sanctions against workers guilty of such tactics and, while refusing to condone them, may oppose any attempted discipline of the workers who have engaged in such conduct by the employer.

In Britain the sit-down strike was less common because it was so obviously illegal. Under Common Law it would constitute not only a probable breach of contract but also an undeniable tort (trespass), which was not protected by the 1906 Act even in trade disputes. According to Citrine,[56]

> if employees 'down tools' in breach of contract, their implied authority to remain on the employer's premises is automatically brought to an end, and it is their duty to leave the premises as soon as is reasonably possible. If they [do not] . . . they are liable for trespass, and the fact that they have remained in order to persuade others to cease work will not excuse them, but, on the contrary, may aggravate the tort.

Sit-downs are illegal in Italy under both Civil and Criminal Law. In Civil Law, the remedy is a possessory action, which may be enforced by the police. The preconditions for such actions, however, are rather intricate; indeed, they were developed centuries ago for quite different purposes and cannot be easily accommodated to industrial action. In the Criminal Code there is a specific provision (Art. 508) against occupation of land and factories. This provision is Facist in origin and the courts have almost always avoided invoking it. They have preferred, rather, to base their decisions on 'violation of the domicile', 'trespass to land or building', or 'use of violence in disturbing the peaceful possession of land'. Generally speaking, Italian courts are unwilling to apply criminal statutes to this type of action, especially when it is taken to resist mass layoffs. Public opinion in such cases is overwhelmingly with the workers. One lower court went so far as to lay down the new doctrine that

56. op. cit., p. 458.

occupation is legal when it is pursued to achieve basic rights guaranteed by the Constitution.[57]

Neither in Sweden nor in Germany has there been any resort to sit-down strikes.

ECONOMIC AND 'UNFAIR LABOR PRACTICE' STRIKES

In the United States a sharp legal distinction is made between *economic strikes* and *'unfair labor practice' strikes*. The former are over the terms and conditions of new agreements ('interests'); the latter are in response to conduct by the employer which the law denominates an unfair labor practice. Despite the confusing terminology, an 'unfair labor practice' strike is not itself an unfair labor practice; it is, rather, a lawful strike caused by the unlawful conduct of the employer. The legal consequences stemming from this distinction are considerable. Economic strikers, although retaining their status as employees, may be permanently replaced during the strike. Their right to reinstatement when the strike is over (in the absence of any intervening unfair labor practice by the employer) is dependent upon their unconditional offer to return to work and the existence of an available vacancy. If no present openings exist, they are entitled only to preferential consideration (as against applicants who were not previously employed by the employer) for future vacancies. Unfair labor practice strikers, on the other hand, are completely protected against replacement. At the conclusion of the strike, they are entitled to reinstatement, normally with back pay for the time lost, even if the employer must discharge replacements hired during the strike in order to make room for them.

It should be borne in mind, however, that the commission of an unfair labor practice by either an employer or a union is not the equivalent of a breach of the collective agreement. (Individual contracts of employment, except in a few specialized categories of managerial employees, do not exist in the United States in any practical sense. Except as specified by collective agreements or regulated by statutes prescribing minimum terms and conditions, the circumstances of employment are determined exclusively by the employer. In case of any alleged violation of terms, the employee's right to relief is predicated either on the collective agreement or on the statute, not on an individual contract of employment.) For example, an employer's breach of the collective agreement that does not involve interference, restraint, coercion, or discrimination relating to union activity is not an unfair labor practice and will not be cognizable by the NLRB. The employee or his union will typically handle such a question in the grievance and arbitration procedure prescribed by the collective agreement. If such a procedure is not provided for, an action may be filed in court.

The new British Industrial Relations Act 1971 apparently makes no distinction between breaches of collective agreements and unfair industrial

57. Pretore, Rome, 16 March 1970.

practices. Section 36 states that it shall be an unfair industrial practice for any party to a collective agreement

(*a*) where the agreement is a legally enforceable contract, to break the agreement, or

(*b*) where part (but not the whole) of the agreement is a legally enforceable contract, to break that part of the agreement.

The whole question is, of course, new in Britain, where collective agreements were not previously enforceable by law, but only by industrial action. Section 34 of the new Act now provides, however, that every collective agreement executed in writing after the effective date of the Act which

does not contain a provision which (however expressed) states that the agreement or part of it is intended not to be legally enforceable, shall be conclusively presumed to be intended by the parties to it to be a legally enforceable contract.

In none of the other four countries in our survey does the law recognize a separate category of illegal conduct known as an 'unfair labor (or industrial) practice'.

WILDCAT STRIKES

Another form of strike common to all countries in this survey is the *wildcat* strike, which, in its simplest terms, is one not authorized, called, or ratified by a union. In the United States such strikes occur every year, but in terms of numbers and economic impact they are not of great significance. The chief targets of wildcat strikes are either the employer, for some action he has taken or refused to take, or the parent union, against which the strikers are rebelling. Often, however, a wildcat strike will signify the rejection by the strikers of the terms of a new collective agreement entered into by the employer and the parent union. Less frequently, unorganized workers will engage in a spontaneous strike against an employer over some grievance. In all cases, unless the employer has committed an unfair labor practice, the strikers will be subject to discipline by the employer, up to and including discharge. If a collective agreement with a no-strike clause is in effect, and if the union does not disavow the strike and order the strikers to return to work, it may be liable in damages to the employer.

In Britain, as has already been noted, the overwhelming number of strikes are 'unofficial' or 'unconstitutional', and may therefore be classified as wildcat strikes. We have previously expressed some serious doubt that these strikes are primarily acts of rebellion against union leadership, as asserted by Ross and Hartman. Indeed, the unofficial strike seems to have been incorporated into that second, 'informal' system of industrial relations referred to by the Donovan Commission, and to be directed as much or more toward employers at the plant level than toward union leadership at the national or regional level. At this stage one can only speculate as to the effect, if any, that the 1971 Act will have on this peculiarly British phenomenon.

In Sweden, wildcat strikes are illegal, and the question most commonly considered by the Labor Court is whether and to what extent labor unions or their officers are liable for damages resulting from such strikes. In general, it may be said that Swedish law requires unions and their officers to take positive steps to repudiate and to halt these illegal stoppages. Failure to do so will ordinarily result in liability. The individual strikers themselves are, of course, subject to discipline and, under sec. 8 of the Collective Agreements Act, may be ordered to pay damages not exceeding 200 kronor.

In Germany, wildcat strikes are, *ipso facto*, illegal because only a union can call a legal strike.

The very concept of the wildcat strike is unknown in French law because there is no essential link between any strike and a union and, as we have seen, most strikes are not initially called by unions and are frequently engaged in by nominally unorganized workers. This is not to say that what are known as wildcat strikes in other countries do not occur in France; they occur quite frequently, but are usually called by a different name, such as 'surprise strikes' or 'lightning strikes'.

In Italy, we are told by Giugni, the prevailing opinion is that 'to be lawful, a strike does not have to be called by a union'.[58] In a decision to that effect the Court of Cassation also held that the calling of a lawful strike does not have to be preceded by an attempt at conciliation. (A similar rule obtains in France.) Notice is not required except, as the Constitutional Court has indicated, when advance warning is necessary to prevent damage to equipment or threats to personal safety.[59]

JURISDICTIONAL STRIKES

The *jurisdictional* or *demarcation* strike is associated primarily with the United States and Britain, especially the former. The principle of jurisdiction lies at the very foundation of trade union structure in the United States and constitutes one of its most important distinguishing features from a comparative point of view.

Jurisdiction is considered by American unions to be a property right; the union charter defining jurisdiction serves as a kind of title to ownership. John T. Dunlop[60] has pointed out that the concept of jurisdiction as property was emphasized by a provision of the A F L constitution referring to encroachment on a union's jurisdiction as a trespass.

The implications of this view of jurisdiction are profound. If a union claims a property right in certain types of work, it conceives of this right as being paramount over not only the claims of a rival union, but also the wishes of the men actually performing the work.

58. 'The Right to Strike and Lock-out Under Italian Law', *Labour Relations and the Law* (ed. Kahn-Freund), p. 214.
59. Corte Costituzionale, 1962, No. 24; see also G. Giugni, *Diritto Sindacale,* op. cit., p. 206, and Ghera, *Considerazioni sulla giurisprudenza,* op. cit.
60. 'Jurisdictional Disputes', *Proceedings of New York University Second Annual Conference on Labor,* 477, 482 (1949).

Strikes arising out of disputes between rival unions in the United States over the *representation* of workers have declined sharply since enactment of the NLRA procedures for peacefully determining questions of representation by secret ballot elections. The merger of the AFL and the CIO and the observance by most of its affiliates of 'no-raiding' pacts have also contributed to this trend. The classic jurisdictional dispute in the United States, however, is not over which union represents the workers, but over which of two or more unions of organized workers is entitled to perform the work. This kind of work-assignment dispute is the product of both the extensive degree of craft union organization in the United States and the declining number of jobs resulting from technological advances and new forms of economic and industrial organization. Thus, jurisdictional strikes have erupted most frequently in the building and construction, printing, railroad, and entertainment industries.

American unions have never defended jurisdictional strikes with any real fervor, and have tried to avert them by establishing conciliation and arbitration procedures among themselves and with employers. The NLRA also declares strikes to compel an employer to assign work to one group of employees rather than to another an unfair labor practice, unless the work in question is covered by the Board's certification of the striking union as the exclusive representative of the employees involved. If an employer files an unfair labor practice charge against a union based on an alleged illegal jurisdictional strike, the statute declares that the Board 'is empowered and directed to hear and determine the dispute,' unless within ten days after notice that the charge has been filed, the parties present satisfactory evidence to the Board that the dispute has been resolved.

Despite its purported application of a number of different criteria, the NLRB almost invariably awards the work to the union representing the employees who were originally assigned the work by the employer. In relative terms, the number of such cases is not great. For the fiscal year 1969, the NLRB took formal action in only 86 instances.

The situation in Britain is rather different than in the United States. As reported by Wedderburn, '[t]he old type of "demarcation" dispute about "who-does-what" [so important in the United States] is declining. It is not multi-unionism which is the worse problem. It is conflict and competition *between* overlapping unions.'[61] Thus, it is the interunion competition for members and for recognition that has caused the difficulty in Britain, whereas these types of problems have been pretty well regulated in the United States by procedures administered by the NLRB.

Recognizing the seriousness of these controversies, the Trades Union Congress (TUC), under the so-called 'Bridlington Agreement' of 1939, regulates the relations of overlapping unions and, through its Disputes Committee, decides between two affiliated unions in disputes about who should organize a group of workers. In 1956 only four cases were heard, whereas 66 cases were

61. op. cit., p. 466 (italics in original).

decided in the period 1966–69. In 1969 the TUC adopted a new rule that all official stoppages resulting from interunion disputes must be reported to the TUC General Council; no union may initiate such a strike until the Council has investigated the dispute and, if need be, referred it to the Disputes Committee. If an interunion dispute leads to an unofficial strike, the unions concerned must take 'immediate and energetic steps' to obtain a resumption of work.[62] Sanctions against offenders are in the nature of 'moral suasion', similar to those traditionally invoked by the AFL–CIO in like cases.

The Donovan Commission reported that of the 2,196 unofficial strikes that took place in Britain during the period, 1964–66, some 57 stoppages, or 2·6 per cent, grew out of demarcation disputes. A majority of the Commission were of the opinion that demarcation disputes 'are not nearly as costly in terms of working days lost as they used to be'.[63] This observation was in partial response to a recommendation of a three-man minority on the Commission that demarcation disputes between trade unions in which the employer is neutral should be excluded from the definition of 'trade dispute' in the 1906 Act, which included 'any dispute between employers and workmen, or between workmen and workmen, which is connected with the employment or non-employment, or the terms of employment, or with the conditions of labour, of any person.' In rejecting this proposal, the majority declared 'that it would be difficult to distinguish and define a demarcation dispute in which an employer was completely neutral and that as productivity bargaining spreads employers are likely to become more involved in defining the duties of particular workers'.[64]

The 1971 Act may possibly ameliorate interunion disputes over membership and recognition. Sections 44–50 establish procedures for application for and designation as 'sole bargaining agent'.[65] This appears to be an adaptation of the procedure for determining the 'exclusive bargaining representative' in the United States, although there are important differences between the two.

The 1971 Act does not define 'trade dispute'; however, it introduces a new term, 'industrial dispute,' which replaces the definition of 'trade dispute' in the 1906 Act, now repealed. 'Industrial dispute' is defined in part as

> a dispute between one or more employers or organizations of employers and one or more workers or organizations or workers, where the dispute relates wholly or mainly to . . .
> (c) allocation of work as between workers or groups of workers. . . .

The phrase, 'or between workmen and workmen', is omitted from the definition of 'industrial dispute' in the 1971 Act. It remains to be seen whether

62. Wedderburn, op. cit., pp. 474–5.
63. Donovan Report, para. 820.
64. ibid.
65. But cf. 'Bridlington Principles and the TUC Disputes Procedure', in *General Council's Report 1971* (103rd Annual Trades Union Congress, 6–10 September, Blackpool), paras. 87–110, discussing possible impacts of the 1971 Act.

the British courts will use this change of language as the basis for finding that a demarcation dispute is not an 'industrial dispute' under the new law.

In Sweden, the Congress of the L O has adopted certain principles for the guidance of affiliated unions in demarcation disputes. The L O constitution provides that a dispute between affiliated unions must be submitted to the Secretariat for trial and decision. The decision of the Secretariat is binding upon the parties.

Jurisdictional disputes within other fields are generally settled peacefully between the parties. The white-collar workers unions have entered into several agreements on demarcation issues between themselves. On some occasions, the agreement provides for double membership. For example, under the agreement in 1968 between the Union of Clerical and Technical Workers in Industry and the Journalists' Union the former union is responsible for the building up of a strike fund and for the unemployment insurance fund, and it therefore receives for this purpose one-third of the contribution of the members. The remaining two-thirds is split equally between the two unions.

BOYCOTTS

A boycott is 'a concerted effort to withdraw and to induce others to withdraw from economic or social relations with offending groups or individuals.'[66] Stated in another way, it is 'a combination formed for the purpose of restricting the markets of an individual or group of individuals.'[67] Although widely used for many centuries in one form or another, it is today associated primarily with industrial action by unions. (When used by employers, the boycott is commonly referred to as a *blacklist*.) In the United States the boycott, which has been an important union weapon since the days of the Knights of Labor, has been accorded a wide variety of treatment by legislatures and the courts. At Common Law, state and Federal courts applied the terms 'primary' and 'secondary' to boycotts. These two adjectives did not really describe the nature of the boycott, but were merely shorthand terms for legal conclusions: 'primary' boycotts were lawful, 'secondary' boycotts were not. Generally, 'primary' boycotts were directed solely against the employer with whom the union had its dispute, whereas 'secondary' boycotts were directed at one or more employers other than the one with whom the union had its dispute, in an effort to compel the others to put economic pressure on the 'primary' employer to come to terms with the union. The chief objection to the word 'secondary' was and is that it lumps indiscriminately into one category both employers who are truly 'strangers' to the dispute, or wholly neutral, and those who have a community of interest with the struck employer and who may, in fact, be his 'allies'.

Federal legislation restricting the use of the boycott made its appearance with the L M R A amendments to the N L R A in 1947. The statute did not define 'secondary boycott'; instead, it prohibited specific activities and ob-

66. 'Boycott', in *Encyclopaedia of the Social Sciences*, 1934, Vol. II, p. 662.
67. L. Wolman, *The Boycott in American Trade Unions*, Baltimore, 1916, p. 12.

jectives. The Congressional purpose, however, was clear: to prevent a union engaged in a 'primary' strike against employer A from putting pressure on him by inducing the employees of employer B to stop work with the object of compelling B to cease doing business with A. But as worded, the statutory provisions did not wholly effectuate its purpose. Consequently, the Act was again amended by the Labor-Management Reporting and Disclosure (Landrum-Griffin) Act in 1959 (LMRDA). Unions are now forbidden by sec. 8(*b*)(4)(i) of the amended NLRA

> to induce or encourage any individual employed by any person engaged in commerce or in an industry affecting commerce to engage in a strike or a refusal in the course of his employment to use, manufacture, process, transport, or otherwise handle or work on any goods, articles, materials, or commodities or to perform any services ... where ... an object thereof is
>
> (B) forcing or requiring any person to cease using, selling, handling, transporting, or otherwise dealing in the products of any other producer, processor, or manufacturer, or to cease doing business with any other person. ..

Violation of this provision is, of course, an unfair labor practice, subject to a cease-and-desist order by the NLRB. Beyond that, however, the LMRA provides, in sec. 303(b), that any person injured in his business or property by reason of an unlawful boycott may sue for damages. Whether a union has in fact engaged in an unlawful boycott is frequently a close question; hence, it is possible that the same situation may be judged differently by the NLRB in an unfair labor practice proceeding and by a court in an action for damages.

It is somewhat ironic that farm workers, who, for the most part, are not 'employees' covered by the NLRA and have been deprived of its guarantees of the right to organize and to bargain collectively, have recently profited by their freedom to engage in boycotts, which are illegal if conducted by employees covered by the Act. A long and bitter dispute between the Farm Workers Union and California grape growers was recently won by the union, largely as a result of the efficacy of its efforts to persuade both distributors and consumers not to handle or eat 'non-union' grapes.

Britain has no legislation outlawing boycotts as such. In recent years, however, conduct that would be called a 'secondary' boycott in the United States has been declared unlawful by the British courts on several different grounds: that no trade dispute existed; that the conduct constituted a 'direct' inducement to breach a contract to the detriment of a third party; or that the conduct constituted an 'indirect' inducement by 'illegal means', namely, the breach of individual contracts of employment outside the context of a labor dispute.

In 1970 the High Court went so far as to grant a *mandatory* injunction on an *ex parte* application by an employer (i.e., without the union being heard); but this form of remedy for interference with commercial contracts was held by the Court of Appeal to be too extreme.[68] The Industrial Relations Act 1971

---

68. See *Boston Deep Sea Fisheries Ltd.* v. *TGWU*, 1970 (the 'Hull Trawlers' case), described in Wedderburn, op cit., pp. 381–5.

provides protection in the High Court for the tortious liabilities of conspiracy to injure, inducement to break any contract, or threats to break a contract, always providing that no extraneous illegal means are used and that the defendant has acted in furtherance of an industrial dispute (sec. 132).

After 1971, liabilities for 'unfair industrial practices' before the N I R C will take the place of the old tort liabilities. That court, however, is not allowed to make interim orders *ex parte*; the defendant must be given an opportunity to put his case, as provided in Schedule 3, para. 22(3) of the Act of 1971. As we have already seen secs. 96, 97, and 98 can all affect the legality of a boycott by introducing liability, respectively, for inducing breach of contract, for assisting anyone committing an unfair practice, and for preventing performance of commercial contracts with extraneous parties. Whereas the registered union is protected against liability in sec. 96 and partially protected under sec. 97 (see p. 90), it receives no exemption from liability under sec. 98. Furthermore, where under this last section industrial action becomes unlawful by reason of prevention of performance of contracts between the employer and an extraneous party, *both* the primary employer *and* the extraneous third party can, under sec. 105(5), sue the union or other defendants before the N I R C claiming an order or an award of compensation or both. The practical effect of these sections of the new Act will no doubt depend on the use that is made of them. It may be noted, however, that although employers may well refrain from hasty litigation which could inhibit settlements of disputes with the unions organizing their employees, extraneous third parties may feel no similar constraint about bringing actions under sec. 98, inasmuch as their main interest will be to recover compensation for the loss suffered in industrial disputes to which they were not in law a party.

The boycott is frequently used in Sweden, although in a somewhat more limited fashion than in the United States. Chapter IV, Art. 1, of the Basic Agreement specifically recognizes '*direct action* [including strikes and boycotts] *against a neutral third party* ("secondary action")', which it defines as 'an action which, in the case of a dispute, may be directed against anyone who is not a party to the dispute, for the purpose of bringing pressure to bear on one party for the benefit of the other party.'[69] Article 8 provides that direct action may not, with certain exceptions, be directed against a neutral third party in disputes over the negotiation of new collective bargaining agreements, over the negotiation or application of individual employment contracts, 'in competitive disputes regarding the possibility of employment', or for the purpose of inducing a party 'to join or to prevent him from leaving a trade organization'.[70]

There are two exceptions to this provision. Article 9 specifies that it shall apply only to third parties who remain neutral, and spells out with great particularity who shall be considered 'non-neutral'. Article 10 provides that, notwithstanding the prohibition in Art. 8 against direct action against a neutral third party in a dispute over the negotiation of a new agreement, such action

69. Quoted in Schmidt, op. cit., p. 274 (italics in original).
70. Quoted in Schmidt, op. cit., p. 275.

(limited to strikes, lockouts, 'blockades', and boycotts) may be resorted to solely for the purpose of assisting either party to the dispute by extending its original scope (sympathetic strike or boycott).

Finally, the Basic Agreement also provides, in Art. 7, that in cases in which direct action against another party is prohibited by other provisions in the Agreement, by other collective contracts, or by law, such action may not be directed against a neutral third party.

According to Folke Schmidt, the chief purpose of a union boycott in Sweden is to deprive the employer of necessary manpower. Therefore, it is a common practice to impose a boycott at the same time that a strike is called; all workers are asked not to accept employment with the employer against whom the action is directed. If any workers refuse to go out on strike or accept employment as strike-breakers during the strike, the boycott is extended to them also, and union members will not work with them. This form of blacklist used to be widely publicized, and continued even after the dispute was over and until the offending workers apologized at a union meeting. Today, however, the blacklist ends when the dispute ends; Chapter IV, Art. 4 of the Basic Agreement provides:[71]

> After a labour dispute has been settled, direct action for purposes of re-taliation must not be resorted to, either against anyone who has been a party to the dispute or against anyone else because of his relationship to the dispute.

Boycotts of goods have 'practically disappeared' in Germany, we are told by Ramm. 'One reason is that the boycott of goods is impossible if the enterprise concerned does not produce an end product. The blacklisting of employers makes no sense if there is no "reserve army of workless persons" anxious to occupy the jobs deserted by the men on strike and if the specialization of labour has reached a point at which it prevents the hiring of alternative labour.'[72] Doubtless, the low level of strike activity, generally, as well as the practice of extension of major collective bargaining agreements throughout the industry by ministerial decree, also help to explain the low incidence of boycotts.

Boycotts are not widely resorted to in France, either. In most instances, what is involved is a form of individual blacklisting. Prior to 1884, blacklisting was a criminal offense; now it is so regarded only when it constitutes 'an act of intimidation calculated to fetter the exercise of a person's freedom to work.'[73] Under a law of 1956 blacklisting is immune from civil liability only in two cases:[74]

> 1. As a punishment of a union member. In such a case blacklisting is simply a disciplinary measure against a member who has disobeyed union

71. Quoted in Schmidt, op. cit., p. 274.
72. 'The Restriction of the Freedom to Strike in the Federal Republic of Germany', in *Labour Relations and the Law*, Kahn-Freund (ed.), p. 201.
73. Brun, op. cit., p. 99.
74. ibid.

instructions, but these instructions must be properly based on considerations arising out of employment.

2. As a protection of its members' material or non-material interests against third parties. It may thus be used against an employer who is not observing the terms of a collective agreement.

This law merely confirms the previous case law founded on the theory of abuse of the right not to hire or the right to dismiss.

Blacklisting is forbidden, however, for the purpose either of preventing the hiring of a nonmember or procuring his dismissal. This is because French law strictly protects every employee's right to join or not to join a union. Thus, resort to the blacklist is infrequent, because it so often conflicts with the right to organize or the freedom to work. Also, blacklisting for purely political reasons is illegal.

The boycott is not used in Italy. A 1969 decision of the Constitutional Court held that the crime of boycott still exists, unless the boycott is limited to mere propaganda; and even then if the propaganda is disseminated by unions and political parties, it may be unlawful.[75] This decision might now be considered to be in conflict with Art. 1 of the Workers' Statute, previously cited, which guarantees, among other things, the right of workers freely to express their thoughts at the places where they work.

HOT CARGO

Another form of boycott practiced in the United States, Britain, and Sweden is an embargo on 'hot', 'blacked' or 'infected' goods, that is, those produced or handled by an employer whom the union has declared to be 'unfair'. In the United States so-called 'hot cargo' agreements, permitting workers to engage in this form of 'secondary' boycott, have been declared illegal and unenforceable; moreover, it is an unfair labor practice on the part of both employers and unions who enter into such agreements. *A fortiori*, it is an unfair labor practice for a union to put economic pressure on an employer to compel him to enter into an illegal 'hot cargo' agreement.

The law, however, recognizes some exceptions. The statutory prohibition is against agreements to cease dealing in the products of 'any other employer' or with 'any other person'. The refusal by employees to handle 'struck work' (lateral boycott) is not unlawful, because an employer who agrees to finish such work automatically becomes an ally of the struck employer. It cannot be said, therefore, that pressure has been put on 'any other employer'. Also, if two or more companies are closely integrated in respect of ownership and control, they are generally regarded as one 'person' so far as the 'hot cargo' prohibition is concerned.

The statute also specifically exempts collective bargaining agreements in the construction industry relating to 'the contracting or subcontracting of work to be done at the site of the construction, alteration, painting, or repair of a

75. Corte Costituzionale, 17 April 1969, no. 84.

building, structure, or other work.' Thus, construction workers may lawfully refuse to work with non-union employees of a subcontractor at the job site or to handle any materials worked on by them. There has been considerable litigation involving the legality under the 'hot cargo' prohibition of 'work preservation' clauses, that is, those providing that no member of a contracting union will be obliged to handle prefabricated building materials on construction sites. The United States' Supreme Court has ruled that if the boycotted work has been traditionally performed at the job site, the work preservation clause is not an illegal boycott.

A second exemption applies to subcontracting in the garment industry, in which much of the manufacturing is done by jobber-contractors. Given the highly competitive condition of the industry, contractors tend to seek advantages by forcing down wages and undermining working conditions; the garment unions have been compelled, therefore, to make the jobbers responsible for policing the collective bargaining agreements, and the law permits them to do so.

In Britain, the refusal of workers to handle 'blacked' goods is traditional. At this stage in the development of the law, it is difficult to determine the legality of such action. It depends upon whether the workers taking such action are themselves parties to a trade dispute; whether their pressure on their employer or fellow workers constitutes a knowing 'inducement' to breach supply or employment contracts, and if so, whether the inducement is 'direct' or 'indirect'. One question of particular interest involves the inducement of breaches of contract not yet made. The law before 1971 is discussed by Wedderburn:[76]

> In *Thomson* v. *Deakin* . . . Lord Justice Jenkins had stressed that general statements such as 'X is black' were not inducements to unlawful action. And all the books had said that liability could not arise where no contract existed between the parties. To this the . . . case of [*Torquay Hotel Co. Ltd.* v. *Cousins*] adds a critical qualification when the employer is seeking an injunction and alleges that the union officials have shown an intention to procure breach of contracts *if* he makes any. Apparently, in such a case it will count against the union officials that they do not add, when announcing 'X is black', some phrase to say: 'But if you have or make commercial contracts with X we will not make you break them'. This change is crucial, for it would allow injunctions to remove the power behind 'blacking' altogether.

Sec. 96 of the 1971 Act may create constant risk of illegality to unregistered unions.

In Sweden, a 'common case is the refusal to handle so-called infected goods, that is to say, goods originating from or intended for another business in which a strike or lockout is going on'.[77] This refusal is typically accompanied by an

76. op. cit., pp. 375–6 (italics in original).

appeal to workers engaged in transporting, loading, and unloading to refuse to handle the 'infected goods.' The rules and practices governing such action are the same as for boycotts generally, as previously described.

PICKETING AND HANDBILLING

In none of the six countries in this survey has picketing been so widely and extensively resorted to by unions or been so prolific of litigation as in the United States. The picket line is a ubiquitous and familiar feature of the American scene. It is an almost invariable concomitant of the strike, largely because of the efforts by so many struck employers to continue operations during the strike. Even in the highly organized industries such as automobiles, steel, and rubber, in which no attempt is made to operate during a strike, token picket lines are maintained.

Another kind of picket line is frequently set up for *organizational* purposes. The picketing union may or may not represent a majority of employees in the picketed establishment, and a question sometimes arises whether the union is trying to compel the employer to recognize it as the bargaining representative, even though the employees do not want to be represented by that union, or whether the picketing is to compel the unwilling employees to join the union. In either of these two cases the union's conduct would constitute an unfair labor practice.

Still another kind of picketing is ostensibly for the *protection of labor standards*. In this case the union's picket signs will usually advise the public that the wages, hours, or conditions of work at the picketed establishment are substandard. Here again, a question may arise whether the true purpose of the picketing is to obtain recognition and bargaining representation rights for a group of workers whom the union does not actually represent. If that proves to be the case, the union's conduct constitutes an unfair labor practice.

Early decisions held, in effect, that peaceful picketing was a contradiction in terms (one federal court declared it to be no more possible than 'chaste vulgarity, or peaceful mobbing, or lawful lynching'[78]), and that all picketing was illegal. Judicial attitudes toward picketing began to change in the 1930s, however, and by 1940 the Supreme Court's opinion in *Thornhill* v. *Alabama* discussed peaceful picketing as a form of freedom of speech protected by the First and Fourteenth Amendments of the Constitution. In 1941 the Court went still further, proclaiming that the public policy of a state prohibiting peaceful picketing by non-employees of the picketed establishment was a 'ban of free communication ... inconsistent with the guarantee of freedom of speech'.[79]

By 1950, however, the pendulum had swung back considerably. In two cases decided in that year the Supreme Court declared that 'while picketing has an

77. Schmidt, op. cit., pp. 162–3.
78. *Atchison, T. and S. F. Ry* v. *Gee*, 139 Fed. 582, 584 (C.C.S.D. Iowa 1905).
79. *AFL* v. *Swing*, 312 US 321, 325 (1941).

ingredient of communication it cannot dogmatically be equated with freedom of speech'[80]; that 'picketing is more than speech and establishes a *locus in quo* that has far more potential for inducing action or non-action than the message the pickets convey'[81]; and that states may ban peaceful picketing for an unlawful objective, so long as the balance struck between the conflicting interests involved is not 'so inconsistent with the rooted traditions of a free people that it must be found an unconstitutional choice'.[82]

The manner of picketing has always been subject to local regulation. *Mass picketing*, which is patently designed to prevent ingress or egress from the picketed establishment rather than simply to publicize a labor dispute, is an unfair labor practice (restraint or coercion) under the NLRA, and is usually a misdemeanor under local ordinances against breach of the peace. Although both the NLRB and the courts have come increasingly to recognize that the conduct and language of the picket line should not be judged by the standards of the drawing room, the repeated use of obscene or threatening epithets, the following of strike-breakers to their homes, or similar acts are held to be illegal. Striking employees engaged in picket line violence or other illegal conduct may be dismissed by the employer for cause.

Generally, the number of pickets allowed at each entrance of the picketed establishment is limited, and usually the pickets are required to keep moving. Typically, the pickets carry signs, announcing that a dispute is in progress, although signs stuck in the snow or placed on the back of parked automobiles have been held sufficient evidence of picketing even though no pickets were physically present. It is only rarely possible to learn from the signs what the dispute is about. Frequently, the pickets pass out leaflets to passers-by, giving their side of the dispute. This process is known as *handbilling* and is given broader latitude than picketing.

Congress included in the LMRA amendments to the NLRA, in 1947, specific limitations on peaceful picketing. These were expanded, in 1959, by the LMRDA amendments to the NLRA. As it now stands, the statutory law regulating peaceful picketing is a labyrinth of principal and dependent clauses, modified by a bewildering number of provisos, that has challenged the comprehension of even the most astute specialists in the field. The following summary of the proscribed objectives of peaceful picketing must be understood, therefore, to be a simplified explication of the gross anatomy of the statute, rather than a dissection of its infinitely complex substructures.

It is an unfair labor practice to picket for any of the following purposes:

1. to compel any employer or self-employed person to join any labor or employer organization or to enter into any 'hot cargo' agreement;

2. to compel any person to cease dealing in any way with the products of any *other* business, or to cease doing business with any *other* person, or compelling any *other* employer to recognize or bargain with a particular union as the repre-

80. *International Bhd. of Teamsters* v. *Hanke*, 339 US 470, 474 (1950).
81. *Building Service Employees Int'l Union* v. *Gazzam*, 339 US 532, 537 (1950).
82. *International Bhd. of Teamsters* v. *Hanke*, 339 US 470, 474 (1950).

sentative of his employees unless that union has been duly certified as the representative of those employees by the NLRB (these prohibitions are not applicable to 'primary' picketing);

3. to compel any employer to recognize or bargain with a particular union as the representative of his employees if another union has been so certified;

4. to compel any employer to assign particular work to employees in a particular union or in a particular trade, craft, or class, rather than to employees in another union or in another trade, craft, or class, unless the employer is failing to comply with an order or certification of the NLRB assigning such work to the picketing union. (This provision relates to 'jurisdictional' or 'demarcation' disputes.)

All of the preceding four paragraphs, however, are subject to the proviso that the prohibition does not apply to 'publicity, other than picketing, for the purpose of truthfully advising the public, including consumers and members of labor organizations', that the products involved are produced by an employer with whom the union has a 'primary' dispute and are distributed by another employer. However, such publicity, too, is forbidden, if it has 'an' effect, even if only incidental, of inducing 'any individual employed by any person other than the primary employer in the course of his employment to refuse to pick up, deliver or transport any goods, or not to perform any services, at the establishment of the employer . . . [engaged in distributing the products involved].'

Complicated though the foregoing proviso is, it was complicated still further by a 1964 decision of the United States Supreme Court, holding that a union may *picket* a distributor to persuade consumers approaching the store not to purchase a product produced by an employer with whom the union has a dispute. This form of picketing is known as *product picketing*. The Court chose to ignore the plain meaning of the statutory phrase, 'publicity, other than picketing', offering the factually inaccurate explanation:

> When consumer picketing is employed only to persuade customers not to buy the struck product, the Union's appeal is closely confined to the primary dispute. The site of the appeal is expanded to include the premises of the secondary employer, but if the appeal succeeds, the secondary employer's purchases from the struck firms are decreased only because the public has diminished its purchases of the struck product. On the other hand, when consumer picketing is employed to persuade customers not to trade at all with the secondary employer, the latter stops buying the struck product, not because of a falling demand, but in response to pressures designed to inflict injury on his business generally. In such case, the Union does more than merely follow the struck product; it creates a separate dispute with a secondary employer.[83]

83. *NLRB* v. *Fruit and Vegetable Packers and Warehousemen*, Local 760, 377 US 58, 72 (1964).

The statutory regulation of organizational picketing is also quite complex. Simply stated, it prohibits picketing or threats to picket any employer, for the purpose of compelling him to recognize or bargain with a union as the representative of his employees, unless the union has already been certified by the NLRB as such representative, in any of the following instances:

1. the employer has lawfully recognized (the employer may voluntarily 'recognize' a union representing a majority of his employees, but only the NLRB can 'certify' that a union represents a majority of employees in an 'appropriate bargaining unit') another union and a question of representation may not appropriately be raised at that time;

2. a valid NLRB election has been held within the preceding 12-month period; or

3. the union has pickcted without filing a petition with the NLRB (which could then peaceably resolve the representation issue in accordance with statutory procedures) within a reasonable period, not to exceed 30 days.

In the case of 3, above, the initiative rests with the employer; the NLRB will do nothing unless and until the employer files an unfair labor practice charge against the picketing union. At this point, the picketing must stop (if the union does not stop, the NLRB must seek an injunction against it), and the NLRB will then direct an election to determine the wishes of the employees of the picketed establishment. As usual, however, there is a proviso to the statutory provision just summarized, to the effect that it does not prohibit 'any picketing or other publicity for the purpose of truthfully advising the public (including consumers) that an employer does not employ members of, or has a contract with a labor organization'. But that proviso is subject to still another, which prohibits the otherwise permissible picketing if it has 'an effect' of inducing 'any individual employed by any other person in the course of his employment, not to pick up, deliver or transport any goods or not to perform any services'.

The hostility of Common Law judges and early legislation in Britain even to peaceful picketing is well-known. The modern law on the subject began with the Trade Disputes Act of 1906. Section 2 of that statute provides:

> It shall be lawful for one or more persons, acting on their own behalf or on behalf of a trade union or of an individual employer or firm in contemplation or furtherance of a trade dispute, to attend at or near a house or plant . . . merely for the purpose of peacefully obtaining or communicating information, or of peacefully persuading any person to work or abstain from working.

The usual forms of nonpeaceful picketing – mass picketing, physical molestation, threats of violence, and the like – are not protected by the statute, but are now civil offenses only. Some forms of peaceful picketing, however, may

still constitute the Common-Law tort of nuisance, even if carried out in furtherance of a trade dispute. In the 1966 case of *Tynan* v. *Bolmer*, the defendant led 40 pickets in a continuous circle around a factory. Incoming trucks
were stopped and presumably asked not to make deliveries, but no serious
obstruction of anyone was proved. Nevertheless, the Recorder found as a fact
that the object of the pickets was to 'seal off the highway', and the High Court
subsequently found that such a purpose was unlawful and a nuisance. Section
2 of the Trade Disputes Act 1906, which, with only minor amendment, is incorporated in sec. 134 of the Industrial Relations Act 1971 which makes it
lawful 'for one or more persons . . . in contemplation or furtherance of an
industrial dispute, [to] attend at or near a house or place where a person
works or carries on business . . . only for the purpose of peacefully obtaining
information from him or communicating information to him, or peacefully
persuading any person to work or abstain from working.' In the *Tynan* case,
however, the High Court raised as the first question whether the conduct of
the pickets would have been legal at Common Law. It concluded that at
Common Law the conduct would have been a nuisance and unlawful, and
that therefore sec. 2 of the 1906 Act did not apply. A confused observer from
another country can only inquire exactly what kind of conduct sec. 2 was
designed to protect; but if he is an American, he will at once recall how the
United States Supreme Court similarly construed and applied sec. 20 of the
Clayton Act of 1914 so as to deprive it of any real significance.

It remains to be seen what practical effect the *Tynan* decision will have. According to Wedderburn,[84] however, 'in practice workmen do picket in rather
more effective fashion than the *Tynan* decision allows and sensible experienced police officers often take no action so long as there is no violence or
other serious obstruction in fact.'

Picketing does not appear to be as widespread a custom in Sweden as it is
in the United States and Britain. Folke Schmidt[85] mentions that in connection
with boycotting non-union enterprises, 'the trade union may post pickets in
front of a restaurant [for example] in order to distribute messages to the effect
that the restaurant staff are unorganized and consequently are enemies of the
trade-union movement'.

Neither the Swedish Collective Agreements Act nor the Basic Agreement
contains any provisions directed at picketing as such. Picketing is not practiced
in Sweden because it is unnecessary; in the case of a strike or lockout employers do not attempt to continue operations.

Picketing in France has the same legal status as sit-down strikes. Theoretically, the emphasis is on the individual picket's intent; practically, it is on his
conduct. French law makes it a crime to interfere with the exercise of any
person's freedom to work; yet the right to strike is given broad protection. The
offense consists in exerting unlawful pressure on nonstrikers. In fact, only
when violence, duress, threats, or fraudulent conduct are involved is there a
violation of the Criminal Code. In determining whether picketing is criminal,

84. op. cit., p. 326. Since 1971 picketing a residence is not allowed.
85. op. cit., p. 165.

the courts distinguish between peaceful (*défensif*) picketing and offensive (*aggressif*) picketing. An example of this rather unsatisfactory distinction is given by Brun:[86]

> If the pickets at the gates remain passive they do not commit the crime of interfering with freedom to work. But if, on the other hand, they are threatening in their demeanour, if they cause non-strikers to fear that they will come to some harm, the strike pickets commit the offence laid down in the [Criminal] Code.

In Italy picketing is lawful, provided it is peaceful, that is, limited simply to propaganda. Non-peaceful picketing is a criminal offense. Mere passive resistance, however, such as forming a 'human wall', has been held not to be criminal. Inasmuch as the formation of a 'human wall' is plainly designed to prevent persons from entering an establishment, as well as to propagandize a dispute, the decisions are explainable only on the ground that Italian judges do not like to apply criminal sanctions to this type of activity.[87] No cases have yet arisen involving the physical prevention of goods from being taken from a plant, either by a *sciopero articulato* or by peaceful obstruction short of a strike at the last stage of the production process.

In Germany, picketing was suppressed from at least 1869 until 1918, when the Reich Trade Order was abolished. Today, peaceful picketing, according to Ramm, should be protected by the principle of free speech, and in the case of a union strike, by the right to organize guaranteed by the Basic Law. The German courts, however, have construed rather broadly the employer's right to a free and secure access to his premises. As in the United States, questions whether unlawful provocations, insults, or threats of force have been committed are largely determined by the judiciary.[88]

Methods of industrial action by employers and employers' associations

We have already seen that employers, either singly or through their associations, often take industrial action against unions or against their unorganized employees, either as a reaction against offensive measures taken against themselves or as offensive measures of their own. The principal tactics discussed in this chapter are employer espionage; blacklisting, intimidation, and coercion of employees; interference with union organization efforts; interference with or domination of unions; lockouts, and various forms of legal actions, the most common of which are the filing of unfair labor practice charges with an administrative agency or complaints with a labor court or regular court, and suits for injunctions, damages, or both. Disciplinary action (including dismissal) is treated in Chapter 4. Initiation of legal actions and criminal charges against employees or unions is discussed in Chapter 5.

86. op. cit., p. 196.
87. Pret. Pinerolo, 31 May 1966.
88. The subject is also discussed in Chapter 5.

EMPLOYER ESPIONAGE; BLACKLISTING, INTIMIDATION, AND
COERCION OF EMPLOYEES.

Hostile actions by employers against employees in order to punish them for
engaging in union activities, or to prevent them from doing so, date back to the
earliest beginnings of unionism in each of the six countries covered by this
study. The laws in all six countries now protect workers against most of these
aggressive actions; but although the more flagrant resort to such tactics is
seldom found any more, isolated instances still occur.

In the United States all these forms of hostile actions, and numerous variations of them, were commonly practiced by large numbers of employers until
1937, when the original National Labor Relations (Wagner) Act was declared
constitutional by the Supreme Court. That Act makes all these tactics unfair
labor practices. The usual remedies include an NLRB order to 'cease and
desist' from resorting to such tactics and to post notices to that effect throughout the establishment. Employees who have been discharged or who have been
denied employment because of their lawful union activities are entitled to
reinstatement or to be employed at the first available opportunity, as the case
may be, with back pay.

In Britain union retaliation against hostile acts by employers against employees has historically taken the form of self-help, rather than resort to the
courts. Now, for the first time, the Industrial Relations Act 1971 sets forth
rights of workers, defines certain unfair industrial practices, and establishes a
tribunal (NIRC) to hear and adjudicate complaints arising under the statute.
Section 5(2) (Rights of Workers) makes it an unfair industrial practice for an
employer, or for any person acting on behalf of an employer:

(*a*) to prevent or deter a worker from exercising . . . [the rights 'to be a
member of such [registered] trade union as he may choose' and take
part in its activities and, subject to the requirements of (approved post-
entry closed shop or agency-shop) agreements, to be a member of no
(registered or unregistered) union or to refuse to be a member of any
particular union], or

(*b*) to dismiss, penalize or otherwise discriminate against a worker by reason of his exercising any such right, or

(*c*) [subject to the requirements of union security agreements] . . . to refuse to engage a worker . . . [because of his membership or nonmember-
ship in any trade union or in a particular trade union].

Section 33(3) makes it an unfair industrial practice for any person, including any trade union or trade union official, among other things to call or
threaten to call a strike or any irregular industrial action if the principal purpose of such action is knowingly to induce an employer to take any action
which would be an unfair industrial practice under sec. 5(2).

In Sweden, the right of association is protected by the Act of 1936, as amended. Section 3 provides in part:[89]

89. Act Respecting the Right of Association and the Right of Collective Bargaining,
dated 11 September 1936, as amended by Acts of 17 May 1940 and 27 April 1945,
ILO authorized translation, ILO Legislative Series 1936 (Sweden 8), 1940 (Sweden
3), with amendments incorporated, quoted in Schmidt, op. cit., pp. 251, 252.

The right of association shall be deemed to be infringed if measures are taken either by employers or by employees to constrain any employee or employer . . . to refrain from becoming a member of or to resign from an association, to refrain from exercising his rights as a member of an association, or to refrain from working for an association or for the formation of an association. . . . The right of association shall be deemed to be infringed even if the measures in question have been taken under a clause of a collective contract or any other contract.

Violators of this right, which presumably would include any employer engaging in the hostile actions presently under discussion, are liable for damages.

Article 9 of the Basic Law of the German Federal Republic, previously quoted (p. 85), declares that measures directed to the restriction or hindrance in the exercise of the universal right 'to form associations to safeguard and improve working and economic conditions' are illegal. This would seem to cover all of the hostile actions by employers presently under discussion.

In France, as we have seen, both the freedom to organize and the freedom to work are given broad protection. A Law of 27 April 1956, modifying sec. 1a, book 3, of the Labor Code provides:

It is forbidden for any employer to take into consideration the membership in a union or the exercise of a union activity, to make any decision concerning the hiring, organization and distribution of work, training, promotion, remuneration, and the granting of social advantages, discipline and dismissal. . . .

The employer or his representatives shall not use any form of pressure in favor of or against any union.

Any measure taken by the employer contrary to the previous paragraphs shall be regarded as abusive and give rise to damages.

These provisions are not waivable [*d'ordre public*].

The Italian Workers' Statute of 1971 provides a number of specific protections to workers against hostile actions by employers. Article 1 (Freedom of Opinion) provides in part: 'Workers, without distinction as to political, union, or religious opinions, shall have the right to freely express their thoughts at the places where they work. . . .' Article 2 (Security Guards) provides in part: 'The employer is forbidden to assign . . . guards . . . to the surveillance of work activities, and the guards may not enter the premises where such activities are performed, during the performance of work, other than in exceptional cases of specific and justified needs pertaining to [the protection of company property].' Article 3 requires that the 'names and specific duties of personnel assigned to the surveillance of work activities shall be communicated to the workers concerned'. Article 4 (Audio-Visual Installations) declares that the 'use of audio-visual installations and other equipment for controlling the activity of workers from a distance is forbidden'. It also provides that installations and equipment of control 'considered necessary in the interests of organization and production purposes, or in connection with work safety, but which may also be used to control the workers' activities, may be installed only upon prior agreement with trade union plant representations [*sic*] or, in their absence, with the Plant Internal Committee'. If no agreement can be reached, the matter may be referred by the employer to the Labor Inspectorate for determination, subject to appeal by the employer or by either the union representatives or the Plant Internal Committee. Article 8 forbids employers, 'for recruitment purposes as well as during the employment relation, to carry out enquiries, also through third parties, concerning the political, religious or union opinions of the worker. . . .'

The detailed manner in which these protections are set forth suggests that hostile actions by employers designed to discourage union activity continue to be a problem in Italy.

INTERFERENCE WITH UNION ORGANIZATION EFFORTS

In none of the six countries covered by our survey does this form of interference constitute a problem even remotely approximating the magnitude of that in the United States. Among the reasons for this are the traditional hostility of American employers to union organization; the difficulty unions have always had in organizing the unorganized; and the tremendous importance of successful organization and certification of the union by the NLRB to the future conduct of the enterprise.

The choice of a bargaining representative (which then becomes the exclusive representative of all employees in the appropriate bargaining unit, whether or not they are members of the union so selected) is normally accomplished by a secret-ballot election conducted by the NLRB. The election may involve one or more unions, but employees are always given the option to vote for no union. In the period preceding the election, the unions involved and, usually, the employer propagandize the employees in a variety of ways (including direct solicitation; distribution of literature to individual employees at or near their place of work, or at their homes; telephone calls; meetings; and advertisements in the news media) in an effort to influence their votes. The extent of leeway permitted employers under these circumstances has remained a matter of intense controversy since the NLRA was enacted in 1935, and has resulted in a veritable flood of Board and court decisions, many by the Supreme Court. The subject is far too complex to be dealt with comprehensively in this chapter; we can do no more than outline its scope.

Prior to the LMRA amendments in 1947 the NLRB tended to restrict employers to absolute neutrality in the election process. In this it was supported in principle by the Supreme Court. Congress became disturbed, however, over the conflict between this policy and the employer's constitutional right of free speech; accordingly, it added the following amendment to the NLRA in 1947:

> The expressing of any views, argument, or opinion, or the dissemination thereof, whether in written, printed, graphic, or visual form, shall not constitute or be evidence of an unfair labor practice . . . if such expression contains no threat of reprisal or force or promise of benefit.

In construing and applying that language the Board has successfully established the rule that some employer (and union) expressions, although not constituting an unfair labor practice, are sufficient to justify the invalidation of the election on the ground that they have materially affected the ability of the employees to exercise a free choice. The Board has so far been unsuccessful, however, in distinguishing in any satisfactory way between threats and 'statements of legal position' or 'predictions' of the consequences of a favorable vote for the union, or between coercive anti-union propaganda and permissible adverse comments about union policies or personnel. Similarly, the Board has had difficulty in establishing a credible rationale for decisions that unlawful interference with the election process may result from the granting of wage or fringe benefits 'with no strings attached', even though it has been supported in this regard by the Supreme Court.

A major controversy has surrounded the practice of many employers to give privileged, anti-union speeches to 'captive' audiences of employees on company time and property immediately prior to an election.

The present rule adopted by the NLRB permits employers to make such speeches, and does not require them to offer unions equal time; but neither employers nor union may make such speeches within a 24-hour period immediately prior to the election; and if such a speech is made, the election will be held invalid. The Board bases this policy on the questionable judgment that such speeches 'have an unwholesome and unsettling effect and tend to interfere with that sober and thoughtful choice which a free election is designed to reflect.'[90]

In order to offset the advantage to the employer presumably resulting from his opportunity to address captive audiences of his employees prior to the 24-hour period, the Board requires every employer, within seven days from the date of the Board's order directing that an election be held, to furnish the union or unions involved with a list of the names and addresses of all employees qualified to vote in the election. The unions thus have an opportunity to communicate with the employees away from the plant. In addition, employees (as distinguished from union organizers who are not employees) have the right in most cases to solicit employees and distribute literature in the plant, or directly outside the plant on company property, but not on company time.

Flagrant abuses by the employer of any of the aforementioned rights not only constitute an unfair labor practice, but are increasingly being made the basis by the Board for orders directing the employer to recognize and bargain with a union, even when the union has lost the representation election.

INTERFERENCE WITH OR DOMINATION OF UNIONS

This practice by employers is also associated chiefly with the United States, although instances can doubtless be found in France and Italy. Article 17 of

90. Peerless Plywood Co., 107 NLRB 427, 429 (1953).

the Italian Workers' Statute specifically forbids employers and employers' associations 'to establish or support, by financial means or otherwise, labour unions'. Interference includes illegal assistance and preferential treatment. Domination implies that the labor organization is the mere creature of the employer, incapable of independent action to protect or preserve the rights of its members.

In the United States, both forms of activity are employer unfair labor practices, subject to cease-and-desist orders by the NLRB. In the increasingly rare cases of domination, the dominated union may be ordered disestablished by the Board. Prior to enactment of the NLRA, American management resorted widely to the establishment of 'company unions' or 'employee representation plans' in an effort to forestall genuine collective bargaining. This practice has virtually disappeared in the last 20 years. The same is true, although to a lesser extent, of employer efforts to interfere with the employees' free choice of bargaining representatives, either by helping one of two or more rival unions or by rendering illegal financial or other assistance to the certified bargaining agent. In the former situation the employer who strays too far beyond the bounds of neutrality may be held to have committed an unfair labor practice, or may cause a representation election to be set aside. An employer who renders illegal financial assistance to a union is guilty of a misdemeanor punishable by fine and imprisonment.

LOCKOUTS

Of the various forms of industrial actions by employers and employers' associations, the lockout is the most universal. It is or has been used with varying degrees of frequency in all six countries. Although an effort has been made in some of the countries to distinguish between 'offensive' and 'defensive' lockouts, these characterizations are generally more confusing than helpful. Whatever the ostensible reason for the lockout, its basic purpose is to place the employer or employers' association in a more advantageous position *vis-à-vis* the employees, union, or labor federation involved in the dispute.

It is somewhat ironic that in the United States, where employer resistance to unionism has been so persistently vigorous and successful, the lockout is used even less frequently than, for example, in Sweden. Indeed, since the enactment of the NLRA, the lockout has been viewed with great suspicion by both the NLRB and the courts, and its legality under modern legislation has been established comparatively recently. The reason probably is that in earlier times the lockout was a particularly brutal weapon, designed not so much to bring about a satisfactory settlement of a dispute from the employer's point of view as to crush incipient unionization or a strike by getting rid, once and for all, of all 'troublemakers'. Chronic unemployment being a characteristic of the American economy, employers never had to worry about securing replacements for the men they dismissed. Lockouts also worked great hardship on the workers' families, many of whom, in the early days, lived in company-owned houses, from which they were summarily evicted when the lockout was declared. Consequently, until relatively recently in the United States, the lockout carried an aura of disrepute that has only gradually been dissipated. Today, the lockout is considered a perfectly respectable form of industrial action, but one that may be used only in carefully defined situations.

There are several versions of the lockout, as used in the United States. One type is the offensive bargaining lockout, which was long considered an unfair labor practice under the NLRA. More recently, however, the Supreme Court has held that an employer's lockout during a labor dispute, in support of his bargaining position, is not *per se* illegal; the test of legality is the motive of the employer. If undertaken for legitimate business purposes and with no intent to destroy the union, this type of lockout is held not to interfere with the right to strike and not hostile to collective bargaining.

Another type of lockout is one to prevent economic loss because of a strike. The employer's right to prevent such loss may be balanced against the employees' right to strike; and in the case of predictable unusual economic hardship the employer may shut down his plant to avert that result.

The third variation of a lockout is the defensive attempt to maintain the integrity of multi-employer bargaining units, which usually are combinations of small employers, in the face of an attack by a large and powerful union. A frequent union tactic in such cases is the 'whipsaw' strike (i.e., a strike against one member of the unit at a time). As a counter to the union's actions, the employers give advance notice that a strike against one will be treated as a strike against all, and that if one member of the multi-employer unit is struck, all the others will immediately lock out their employees. Under these circumstances, such a lockout has been held to be legal. Also, absent any evidence of an unlawful motive, the hiring of temporary replacements during a defensive lockout by nonstruck employers is not an unfair labor practice.

In some instances an employer may respond to a strike by moving the plant or simply going out of business. It is not an unfair labor practice for an employer to close his entire business, even if he does so because of hostility to unionism. But closing *part* of a business will be held to be an unfair labor practice if the purpose is to discourage unionism in any of the employer's remaining plants and if the employer may reasonably have foreseen that effect. Similarly, when an employer moves his plant in response to union economic pressure (a phenomenon known as a 'runaway shop'), the move will ordinarily be presumed to be prompted by anti-union animus, and therefore an unfair labor practice, unless the employer can produce convincing evidence of an overriding business necessity.

Most employers faced by a strike, however, do not retaliate by locking out their employees, or moving their plants, or going out of business; in the great majority of cases they either voluntarily cease or reduce operations until the strike has been settled or try to maintain operations during the strike. In the latter case employers sometimes offer special inducements to keep non-strikers on the job, to persuade strikers to return to work, and to recruit replacements for strikers. The legality of such inducements depends upon the employer's motive, an issue commonly litigated before the NLRB and reviewed by the courts. In some instances, however, the employer's action is said to carry its own *indicia* of illegal intent; that is, the normal and foreseeable consequence of his inducement is held to be a derogation of this employees' right to strike, guaranteed by the NLRA. If the inducement offered by the employer is only arguably illegal, he must still offer affirmative proof of a good-faith motive; and if he fails to do so, the NLRB may find his conduct to be an unfair labor practice without affirmatively proving a bad-faith motive.

In Britain, the test of the legality of lockouts has been whether they effected a breach of contracts of employment. The 1971 Act undertakes to spell out the circumstances under which a dismissal by way of a lockout is permitted. Section 167(1) defines 'lockout' as

> action which, in contemplation or furtherance of an industrial dispute, is taken by one or more employers, whether parties to the dispute or not, and which consists of the exclusion of workers from one or more factories, offices or other places of employment or of the suspension of work in one or more such places or of the collective, simultaneous or otherwise connected termination or suspension of employment of a group of workers.

Section 25(1) provides that the dismissal of one or more employees at the beginning or during the course of lockout '. . . shall not be regarded as unfair if the employee is offered re-engagement as from the date of resumption of work'.

Section 25(3) defines an 'offer of re-engagement' to an employee as '. . . an offer (made either by the original employer or a successor of that employer or by an associated employer) to re-engage that employee, either in the position which he held immediately before the effective date of termination or in a different position which would be reasonably suitable to him.'

Section 26(2) provides that if the principal reason for dismissing an employee is that on the date of dismissal he was taking part in a strike or other industrial action, the dismissal shall not be considered unfair unless one or more of the employees of the same (original) employer, who also participated in the same industrial action, were not dismissed for that reason, or if they were dismissed for that reason, were offered re-engagement at the termination of the industrial action, whereas the claimant was not. The dismissal will also be considered unfair if the principal reason for which the claimant was dismissed was that he exercised, or indicated his intention to exercise, any of the rights (previously mentioned) conferred upon him by sec. 5(1) of the Act.

In Section 24(6) the standard by which the dismissal shall be judged to have been fair or unfair, 'having regard to the reason shown by the employer,' is declared to be '. . . . whether in the circumstances he acted reasonably or unreasonably in treating it as a sufficient reason for dismissing the employee; and that question shall be determined in accordance with equity and the substantial merits of the case.'

The lockout is relatively uncommon in Sweden, although its use is prohibited only in aid of others who may not themselves commit offensive actions. The rules laid down in the Collective Agreements Act and in the Basic Agreement take into consideration the possibility of a sympathetic lockout. Swedish employers do not find it necessary to resort to lockouts very frequently, however, because of the powerful *in terrorem* effect of their possible use. According to the constitution of the SAF, no lockout may be imposed by a branch association or individual firm affiliated with the SAF without the prior consent of the Federation's Board or General Council. Once a lockout (or strike) is in effect, however, no employer is allowed, directly or indirectly, to offer work or any other support to any union or its members involved in the dispute.

Reference has previously been made, in the discussion of strikes, to the preferential judicial treatment accorded lockouts in Germany, in comparison with strikes. The subject is discussed further in Chapter 5.

Employers may also lawfully engage in a sympathetic lockout in support of other employers in the same region. Unions do not have a corresponding freedom to call sympathetic strikes, not only because, as previously noted, unofficial stoppages are prohibited, but also because strikes are commonly organized on a regional basis anyway.

The status of the lockout in France is completely different from that in the United States, Britain, Sweden, or Germany. In France, the lockout is not considered the legal counterpart of the strike; it is, in fact, illegal except as an extreme measure in exceptional circumstances. The Court of Cassation has held a lockout to be lawful in the case of *force majeure*, such as a strike that causes the entire plant to shut down, or in the case of a refusal by the workers to perform the duties covered by their contracts of employment in a conscientious manner, as when they engage in slowdowns or *débrayages*.

Thus both 'offensive' and sympathy lockouts are illegal in France; an employer guilty of such conduct must reimburse his workers for the time they have lost. Blanc-Jouvan has commented that the law and practice in respect of lockouts demonstrates, among other things, the essential looseness of employer organization in France and the lack of centralized authority. The lockout, when resorted to, represents the decision of the individual employer; typically, he neither asks for nor receives advance approval or even advice from his association, and he neither expects nor receives any support from his fellow-employers once the lockout has begun.

The law of lockout in Italy is very similar to the law of France. Article 502 of the Penal Code treated both the strike and the lockout, for economic reasons, as crimes. The position of the lockout remained uncertain until a 1960 decision by the Constitutional Court declared Art. 502 unconstitutional. In respect of the lockout, this conclusion was inferred from Art. 39 of the Constitution, freedom of organization, on the ground that this freedom implies the freedom (but not the right) of industrial action as well. The Court, although holding that the law making the strike a crime was incompatible with Art. 40 of the Constitution, stopped short of ruling that a right of lockout existed. The present situation is stated by Giugni:[91]

The lockout is considered as an act the legal characteristics of which are to

91. 'The Right to Strike and Lock-Out Under Italian Law', *Labour Relations and the Law* (ed. Kahn-Freund), pp. 217–18.

be derived from an application of the general principles of law. Generally speaking, it constitutes a failure on the part of the employer to perform his contract, more precisely perhaps it is a *mora accipiendi* on his part. One can therefore say that a lockout is in a position analogous to that of an unlawful strike, without however being a criminal offence: it is an exercise of a freedom, but not an exercise of a subjective right.

A 1967 decision of the Constitutional Court, however, held that a lockout in protest against the Government, unrelated to labor relations, is still a crime under Art. 505 of the Penal Code. A defensive lockout in the face of an unlawful strike has often been regarded as legal.[92] The present trend of the courts seems to be in the direction of upholding the legitimacy of lockouts compelled by necessity.[93] In this respect, however, it is really not a lockout, but, rather, the inability to continue the operation. We may say, therefore, that in Italy the lockout, as such, is becoming irrelevant in legal terms.

Conclusion

One of the commonest failings of even the most careful writers in the comparative field is to succumb to the temptation to make facile assertions or broad generalizations about countries other than their own. Scholars of comparative labor law and industrial relations are no exception. The dangers of reliance on dubious analogies, as well as the insidious influence of unconscious cultural bias, are illustrated in the following statement by Ross and Hartman:[94]

> Likewise there are evident national differences in the ability to develop viable compromises. Compromise is the essence of collective bargaining ... in the ... sense that the bargaining system itself represents a settlement of the basic power issues between Labor and Capital. It is a well-established fact that collective bargaining does not thrive on a diet of principles. In fact, one of the great virtues of collective bargaining is that it permits the formulation of limited issues which are amenable to resolution and blurs over large differences of principle which can never really be settled. ... [W]e may confidently state that the willingness to 'muddle through' is unevenly distributed over the globe. For example, the graceful retreat of the English from India and Burma may be contrasted with the debacles suffered by the French in Indochina and Algeria.

Collective bargaining does indeed involve compromise, a fact repeatedly stressed by many observers; but the Swedish experience suggests that a collective bargaining system can 'thrive on a diet of principles', provided that the

92. App. Milano, 20 November 1964; Corte di Cassazione, 2 December 1964.
93. See courts' decisions quoted in F. de Ambri Corridoni, F. Fabbri, G. Veneto, *Rassegna critica*, op. cit. By necessity is not meant 'impossibility' in the naturalistic sense, as in the Roman law tradition. But on the other hand, 'necessity' does not mean a higher economic cost. See Pera in *L'esercizio del diritto di sciopero*, Milano, 1968, with a good list of cases.
94. op. cit., p. 174.

diet is supplemented with adequate portions of common sense and mutual forebearance.

The reference to 'muddling through' is essentially meaningless. If the expression is equated with compromise, then all six countries have demonstrated the ability to 'muddle through'; for in each there is some form of collective bargaining system that is functioning. To be sure, collective bargaining in France is not the same as it is in Britain, but if one is to judge the new British Industrial Relations Act by the reaction of trade union leaders, it is an even greater debacle for British unionism than the loss of Burma and India was for the Empire. The United States is another case in point. Experience under the emergency disputes procedures of the Railway Labor and Taft-Hartley Acts is a classic example of 'muddling through' and demonstrates a flexibility and pragmatism that a man from Mars would think impossible of a country that persists in prolonging its participation in a foreign conflict which has brought about the greatest military and political debacle in its entire history.

Of considerably more importance than their misuse of analogy, however, is the authors' questionable conclusion that strikes and lockouts, as instruments of industrial action, are 'withering away'. Aided by more than a decade of hindsight, we can see that their judgment appears to have been wrong, and it may be useful to examine some of the assumptions that led them into error.

One assumption was that the growth in the number of white-collar and professional employees in the labor force and in labor unions has contributed to the decline in the propensity to strike. Ross and Hartman[95] took for granted 'that these groups, as well as female workers, are disinclined to strike. . . . Where the white-collar workers make up a large proportion of union membership, either the strike weapon is seldom used or else stoppages are typically brief.' As we know, however, strikes among white-collar and professional workers are on the increase, especially in the United States, in which they were a negligible factor a decade ago. Nevertheless, the overall strike pattern in the United States has not changed, thus belying the significance which the authors attributed to the fact that white-collar unionism is much less important in Finland, Canada, and the United States, the only countries in which, according to their study, strikes are relatively frequent and also relatively long.

One is forced to conclude that the propensity to strike is a fluctuating phenomenon for which we do not have any really reliable explanation. The hypothesis that it goes down as the level of white-collar and professional unionism goes up will not hold water, and the same may be said for the idea that the propensity is in inverse proportion to the level of affluence within a given country. The most one can say is that the propensity to strike seems to be linked in some way with political, economic, and social unrest, which may be the result of a wide variety of causes.

Another assumption was that a revolutionary change in employer policies has contributed to the decline of the strike. But the evidence hardly supports

95. op. cit., p. 45.

the claim that employers in the 'older industrialized countries' have generally accommodated themselves to unionism and collective bargaining, or that unions are now 'accepted as a permanent, and perhaps even a welcome, part of the enterprise'.[96] In varying numbers and degrees, employers in all six countries in our study are resigned to the necessity of dealing with unions; it is doubtful, however, that unions are 'welcomed' by a majority of employers in any of the countries.

The theory advanced by Ross and Hartman that unions in Europe and the United States were tending increasingly to abstain from strike action of their own volition was a logical deduction from data then available. Because strikes are expensive to unions and their members, causing forfeiture of all cash income for the period of the stoppage, they argued 'that unions would endeavor to develop better methods, particularly as real incomes rise'.[97] Moreover, a 1948 study of strike statistics for Britain, France, Germany, Sweden, and the United States,[98] seemed to show that the 'outcome of work stoppages generally has not been favorable to unions',[99] and that long strikes, in particular, have at all times been less successful than short strikes. Furthermore, major strike waves in the United States, Britain, France, Italy, and Sweden during this century have all resulted in substantial setbacks for unionism. It was therefore not unreasonable to assume that this experience would bring about a change in union ideology; and from there it was an easy transition to the declaration that modern unions, except for those under Communist leaderships, have sharply limited the use of the strike, and have sought, instead, to achieve broad economic and social changes through political action.

But here again we have confirmation of Holmes' aphorism that a page of history is worth a volume of logic.[100] In the case of France and Italy, where loss of cash income during a strike is indeed a serious problem for workers, the response has not been to abandon the use of the strike weapon. On the contrary, unions and workers have resorted increasingly to short strikes. These strikes may no longer be viewed solely as spontaneous 'demonstrations'; in Italy, for example, they are increasingly being used as calculated displays of bargaining power. Moreover, strange as it may seem to an American observer, striking workers in both France and Italy almost always demand payment for the time on strike as a condition of settlement, and frequently obtain at least partial reimbursement.

As for political action, we have previously noted that in Britain the political activity of unions has been largely for the purpose of counteracting the effects of hostile legislation and court decisions. This still appears to be true, and it would be quite wrong to assume that British trade unionists, any more than unionists in the other European countries, have chosen political action as an

96. Ross and Hartman, op. cit., p. 47.
97. op. cit., p. 55.
98. K. Forchheimer, 'Some International Aspects of the Strike Movement: The Results of Labour Disputes'. *Bulletin of the Oxford University Institute of Statistics*, Vol. 10 (Sept. 1948), p. 295.
99. ibid., p. 55.
100. *N.Y. Trust Co.* v. *Eisner*, 256 US 345, 349 (1921).

alternative to strikes and related activities. It would be more accurate to say that both political and industrial action are used, frequently in a coordinated way, to gain particular objectives.

Even the common assumption about the use of industrial action in the United States needs substantial revision in the light of developments in the last decade, and more particularly in the last few years. Although American unions still have greater economic power than political power, the role of the AFL-CIO and its affiliates in national politics is becoming increasingly more important. At the same time, the position of a number of large American firms in respect of the world market has substantially deteriorated, productivity in the United States has declined, and in 1971 the American balance-of-payments deficit was the greatest in its modern history. In that year the Government instituted more rigid wage and price controls than any attempted since 1951–52. Public tolerance of strikes in strategic industries has become increasingly strained, and the possibility of further legislative curbs on industrial action cannot be completely discounted. It may well turn out, therefore, that unions in the United States will increase their political activities and resort less frequently to industrial action, at least in the short run. On the other hand, if Government policies are regarded as oppressive and unfair, there is at least the possibility that American unions will resort, for the first time, to a series of essentially political strikes by way of protest.

We noted earlier that Ross and Hartman cited the larger role now played by the State in national collective bargaining systems as an important factor contributing to the decline of the strike. Their thesis was that as *laissez-faire* policies have 'gone out of fashion' and governments have assumed a 'more influential role in the economy', the strike has been pushed into a 'less prominent position'; that although strikes against public enterprises are not unknown, 'brief demonstration strikes are more common than real contests of economic strength, and political solutions are even more likely'; that '[w]here the state plays an active role in economic planning, it has a strong motive to ensure that its plans are not frustrated'; and that '[t]hrough protective legislation and social security programs, the state disposes of issues that might otherwise be the focus of labor-management conflict'.[101]

The foregoing observations were evidently made with Sweden, Britain, and the United States primarily in mind. The authors did not foresee the extensive resort to strikes by Government employees in those three countries in the past two years, discussed in Chapter 6. Similarly, they failed to account for the possibility, which has since become a reality, that the continuing search by most industrialized countries for some sort of workable incomes policy would result in confrontations between Governments and organized labor and heightened strike activity, even in a country such as Sweden, in which unions have a strong bond with the dominant political party. Moreover, the authors' thesis is, as we have seen, completely wrong in respect of France, where union efforts to secure major changes in wages, hours, and working conditions

101. op. cit., pp. 50–1.

through collective bargaining have tended to center on Government enterprises, which are the pattern-setters for private industry. Also, the authors seem to have placed too much confidence on the efficacy of Government dispute-settlement programs in reducing the volume of strike activity. In this regard, their assertion that in the United States the Railway Labor Act 'for the most part . . . has been successful in preventing major strikes' was a most unfortunate example, as events in recent years have illustrated so dramatically. Similarly, Britain's Government machinery for settling disputes has not proved notably successful, and even Sweden had its problems in 1970–71.

Finally, one must question the assumption that the power of the State to affect the workers' economic welfare is so pervasive that union efforts to do so through collective bargaining and industrial action have become less important. If this were true, one would have expected the efforts to curb inflation by the Governments of Sweden, Britain, and the United States, among others, to have been more successful than they presently are. Collective bargaining continues to exercise profound, and to some extent uncontrollable, influences on productivity and the phenomenon of 'wage drift'.

The foregoing discussion indicates the risks involved in making any kind of generalization in the field of comparative labor law and industrial relations. Nevertheless, the evidence derived from the experience in each of the six countries included in this study supports at least one general observation: strikes, lockouts, and related forms of industrial action, far from 'withering away', have undergone changes in each country to insure their survival and continued use, despite the revolutionary or evolutionary changes in the industrial relations systems in those countries. It is more likely than not that they will continue to do so.

3

The peace obligation
by Gino Giugni

The sources and general features of the peace obligation

The present chapter is devoted to the limitations on the right to strike which are set by the parties themselves through collective agreements.[1] The most important of these limitations is the peace obligation which may also assume other designations, such as 'no-strike' clause (USA), 'truce' clause (France, Italy). In any case, it consists of an undertaking by a trade union and/or the workers not to take industrial action during the life of an agreement or during the course of a procedure. Theoretically, a peace obligation could be laid down in a specific agreement without any connection with the determination of wages, hours, or of other work conditions or of procedures for the settlement of disputes.

However, the latter case is not realistic, although its formulation will be of some help when we face the problem of the legitimacy of the peace obligation in so far as it implies a waiver of the right to strike – a much debated issue especially in Italy and France where the right to strike is recognized by the Constitution. Limitations on industrial action by way of autonomy may consist not only of the above-described 'no-strike' obligation, but also of limitations placed upon the methods or procedures of taking industrial action.

Although limitations of this kind are always brought about through industrial autonomy, the source which gives them a legal effect may also be a statute or principle of law, no matter what the intention of the parties was. Thus, where it is assumed, as we shall see later on, that every collective contract implies a peace obligation, the source of the latter may be found in the legal fiction of the implied terms (or invisible clauses[2]) of the agreement or in the general legal principle *pacta sunt servanda*. In this case, the peace obligation exists because it is imposed by law, but a contract is always necessary. We

1. Another important source of self-imposed limitations may be internal union rules. They do not fall under the scope of the present chapter, although mention should be made of the issue as to whether they give rise to *a right* of the counterpart to their observance.
2. A. Suviranta, 'Invisible clauses in collective agreements', in Vol. 9, *Scandinavian Studies in Law*, Stockholm, 1965, p. 177 ff. The author classifies the following kinds of 'invisible clauses': (p. 184) (*a*) rules of law; (*b*) implied terms, deriving from the construction of the inexpress intention of the parties, and including *naturalia negotii*; (*c*) clauses and implied terms of employment contracts, whose generality might 'perhaps sometimes have the specific effect of collective agreement clauses'.

may easily construe the situation as a natural effect, determined by law, of an agreement between the parties.

Even more important, is the case which occurs when the law expressly attaches the peace obligation to collective agreements. We should mention the Swedish Act on collective agreements of 22 June 1928, sec. 4; the British Industrial Relations Act 1971, sec. 36, relating to legally enforceable contracts; the American Labor Management Relations Act (LMRA), sec. 8(d); and finally Art. 31(9) of the first book of the French Labour Code.

The case which seems unique is the one provided for by sec. 37 of the British Act of 1971. This section regards areas of industrial relations not covered by suitable procedure agreements, or covered by agreements which are unsuitable for the purpose of settling disputes or grievances 'promptly and fairly'. It must also be proved that there are grounds for believing that the maintenance of orderly industrial relations is seriously impeded so that there have been substantial losses of working time (sec. 37(5)). This case is put on the same ground (sec. 37, 1(*b*)) with the one of recourse to industrial action contrary to the terms or intentions of an agreement – but this appears indeed as a very different hypothesis.

The Industrial Court, after a rather intriguing procedure (sec. 41 (2)), may issue an order imposing a compulsory procedure on the parties which will have the effect of a legally enforceable contract, '. . . as if a contract consisting of those provisions *had* been made between those parties.'* These provisions, which are by their nature legally binding, would probably include an obligation not to take industrial action. This is an unusual combination of the contractual and the statutory sources of the peace obligation. In fact, the Industrial Court is granted the power to create a procedural machinery, probably including a peace obligation, which the parties have to operate as though it had been agreed by them.

To summarize what we have said so far, we should point out that the ban on strikes or limitations on the way in which strikes are conducted may arise from collective agreements or from union rules. In the case of collective agreements such limitations originate

(*a*) from statutory provision;
(*b*) or, by implication, from principles of law, such as *pacta sunt servanda*;
(*c*) from explicit clauses of the agreement.

We have now to draw a distinction as to whether such limitations arise from substantive agreements (the ones dealing with wages and working conditions) or from procedural agreements, or, of course, from agreements which combine substantive and procedural rules.

Such a distinction may assume a remarkable importance, when, as we shall see, the peace obligation is treated as a *quid pro quo* – perhaps the consideration of the contract or, at Civil Law, its *causa*.[3] In these cases, the finding of the

* Author's italics.
3. For a clear distinction of the two concepts (consideration and cause), among the large bibliography, it suffices to refer to: *Le droit français*, R. David (ed.), II, Paris, 1960, p. 159–60.

obligations undertaken on the employers' side in return for the peace obligation may have relevant consequences as regards the assessment of liability for
violations.

Finally, a basic distinction must be recalled, namely the one between relative and absolute peace obligation. This distinction, originated in Germany,[4]
has a wide application. The 'relative' obligation covers only the matters settled
in an agreement, whereas the 'absolute' one has a wider scope, which may
resort to a prohibition of all industrial actions during an agreement. The
'absolute' or enlarged (*erweiterte*) obligation occurs more often in procedural
agreements, or is attached to procedure clauses of them. We shall see, however,
that in these cases it may not be proper to speak of a true 'absolute' peace
obligation (p. 170).

An enquiry into the legal framework and industrial practice of the six
countries would reveal profound differences between them. The reasons for
such differences may be found in the following aspects:

1. The general legal set-up of each country

The first difference is due, of course, to the demarcation line between Common
Law and Civil Law. Many pronounced differences also occur within these
general categories, while similarities are probably more frequent than in other
branches of law. This may be due to a uniformity impact of industrialism,[5]
but the main reason is probably the young age of labour law, and especially of
the law of collective labour relations. By approximation, we may allocate Italy
and France on one side, Germany and Sweden on another, and the US and
UK (after the new Act) on another. We shall also briefly take into consideration the situation of the UK before the 1971 Act was passed, when the position
of that country was almost unique and not comparable to any other.

2. The systems of industrial relations

It is only possible to quote a few significant examples. Countries like the
United States, with a prevailing system of company agreements, do not have
the problem of a connection between various levels of negotiation, whereas in
France and Italy the issue arises as to whether a peace obligation negotiated
in a national agreement is binding for a supplementary company agreement or
shop agreement. A similar problem can arise in Britain in respect of plant
bargaining.

Another point may be made as concerns the duration of agreements. Where
they have an expiry date the peace obligation may have a very different
meaning to the situation when an agreement can be terminated at any time.
The structure itself of the collective contract may bring about significant di-

---

4. See, among the early legal writers, H. Sinzheimer, *Der korporative Arbeitsnormen-
vertrag*, II, Leipzig, 1908, p. 197 ff.
5. This, in general terms, is the thesis of the well-known *Industrialism and the Industrial Man* by C. Kerr, J. T. Dunlop, F. Harbison, C. Myers, New York, 1964.

versities. When a contract is in the form of a 'code' for the industry or company – that is to say, it is presumed that it will cover the whole area of employment relations (e.g., Sweden, under the debated theory of implied management rights, see p. 136) – the nature of the peace obligation may differ widely from a situation where there is no single contract, but successive agreements on different matters.

3. Ideological or political factors

These may influence the consensus of trade unions *vis-à-vis* the idea itself of a truce in industrial warfare. Revolutionary unionism may just reject this idea, whereas a cooperative labour movement may focus on it as a bulwark of collective bargaining itself. On the other hand, a pragmatic but very militant labour movement may reject the peace obligation, not for reasons of principle, but just in order to avoid legal liabilities.

Features of contractual limitations: countries at Civil Law

Taking into account the shaping force of the factors set out above, we can now try to analyse, country by country, their frequency and the typical characteristics of limitation on the right to strike. For purposes of presentation, we shall classify the countries into two groups: Civil Law and Common Law. These two classifications will be considered in this and the following section. The reader, however, will become aware, confirming a previously made statement, of the fact that the demarcation line of these two groups is less meaningful as regards the institutions of collective bargaining and industrial action as it is with regard to remedies and sanctions.

GERMANY

The practice of including a 'no-strike' clause in the *Tarifverträge* (collective agreements) was not unknown from the very beginning of collective bargaining practice in Germany. But more than the bargaining practice, the legal theory was influential, especially with Professor Hugo Sinzheimer,[6] in the first decade of the century, when it came to construe the collective agreement as an exchange for better conditions of work with a peace obligation. Therefore, the peace obligation entered into the *causa* of the contract – a traditional Civil Law concept, much debated in itself, which we assume here as the essential terms of a contract (e.g., among the contracts of exchange: a thing *v.* a price: contract of sale; work *v.* wages: contract of employment; better work conditions *v.* peace obligation: collective contract).

Given that, and rejecting the theory of agency laid down at an earlier date by Lotmar[7] which was not embraced by the courts, the legal commentators came to the conclusion that the collective agreement was binding only at the

6. op. cit.
7. See P. Lotmar, 'Die Tarifverträge zwischen Arbeitgebern und Arbeitnehmern', in *Archiv für soziale Gesetzgebung und Statistik*, Berlin, 1900.

collective level (employer or employers' association, and trade unions). The practical result was that the peace obligation was the only part of the agreement endowed with actual legal efficacity. On the other side, the *Durchführungspflicht* (duty to perform) engaged the employers' associations to perform their specific duties and the *Einwirkungspflicht* engaged them to induce compliance from their members. But the practical significance of all this was very poor, since no action could be taken by the unions or by the employee against the non-compliant employer, while violations of the 'duty to perform' by the employers' associations were of minor importance.

The ordinance of the revolutionary Government on collective agreements enacted in 1918, and never repealed until the Nazi regime, accepted the suggestions of the legal commentators and gave the agreement a direct effect on the contracts of employment. The theory of agency was rejected,[8] but the normative effect of the collective agreement was reached through statutory provision which granted the collective contract the power to replace all less favourable conditions set down in individual contracts of employment.

The 1949 Act on collective agreements, which was slightly amended in 1969, followed the same pattern. It is remarkable to say that neither Acts codified the peace obligation – the 1918 Act was enacted during the revolution[9] and aimed only at strengthening the binding force of agreements on the side of employers; the 1949 Act was built on the same pattern, and in this the unions opposed the express inclusion of the peace obligation.

As a matter of fact, substantive agreements never express a 'no-strike' clause, but, on the firm foundation of the traditional doctrine, this is assumed as a natural effect of the agreement, or, better, as a necessary element of it.[10] On this ground, legal writers deem also the peace obligation to be unwaivable and it is stated similarly in sec. 4 of the Swedish Act on collective agreements; the prevailing opinion is that the scope of the peace obligation can be enlarged, not restricted.

The peace obligation assumed as implied in all agreements is *relative* to the matters settled in the agreement itself. The issue as to what should be meant by 'settled matters', a very debated one also in other countries, was raised among legal writers,[11] but no recent cases are recorded on this subject.[12] There

8. This repulsion to the doctrine of agency still prevails. Recent efforts were made to resume it with regard to the binding effect of the collective contract *upon the employees*. See T. Ramm, *Die Parteien des Tarifvertrags*, Stuttgart, 1961, p. 70 ff.

9. For a comparative explanation of the political background of Swedish and German Acts on collective agreements see F. Schmidt, 'Ein Vergleich zwischen der deutschen und der schwedischen Gesetzgebung über Kollektiv verträge, in *Festschrift für H. C. Nipperdey*, II, München u. Berlin, 1965, p. 609 ff.

10. Only one dissenting opinion is recorded, and it is the one by R. Strasser, *Die Rechtsgrundlage der tariflichen Friedenspflicht*, in RdA, 1965, p. 401 ff. This author assumes that the existence of the peace obligation depends upon the intention of the parties, which may be implied as well. With regard to the other countries such a construction will appear as the most common.

11. For example, a very extensive notion of 'settled matters' was proposed by E. Gift, *Probleme der Friedenspflicht*, DB, 1959, p. 651 ff.; *contra* A. Hueck–H. C. Nipperdey, *Lehrbuch des Arbeitsrechts*, II, Berlin und Frankfurt, p. 317.

12. See Hueck–Nipperdey, op. cit., p. 317.

is consensus, however, on the point that the peace obligation ought not to be interpreted extensively. Silence of the agreement on a subject matter does not mean, under given factual circumstances, that there was an intention to consider the matter itself as settled. Another point is that the peace obligation would cover all matters connected (*im Zusammenhang*) with a main one.[13] The peace obligation, finally, does not apply to sympathetic strikes, the legality of which will depend on different grounds.

The so-called *absolute* clauses, covering all industrial action during the life of an agreement regardless of the matter, can be found actually only in procedural agreements which provide for conciliatory steps in case of negotiations of a new agreement or its completion. Such clauses always expressly set out a prohibition of all industrial actions (*Kampfmassnahmen*) until the procedure has been fully exhausted. An agreement of this kind, with a scope extended to the whole industrial sector, was signed, for example, in 1954 in Margaretenhof in the common intent to pursue 'social peace'.

It is important to bear in mind from now on that the well-known decision of the Federal Labour Tribunal on the Schleswig-Holstein case of 1958 (discussed later, see p. 153) stated that a prohibition of industrial action (*Kampfmassnahmen*), no matter if absolute or relative, would involve also strike balloting. This was held to be a breach of the peace obligation, in so far as it was sufficient to break the state of peace at the work place. One may wonder whether, under this assumption, all preparatory acts like meetings, propaganda, etc., instrumental to the calling of a strike, would not fall into the domain of the 'no-strike' pledge.

There is no doubt that the peace obligation in Germany would not allow renegotiation with resort to industrial action at different levels, like a shop agreement supplementary to a regional one.[14] The works' councils, on their side – as stated in para. 59 of the 1952 Works' Constitution – are not entitled to negotiate on matters usually settled by collective contracts in the proper sense, and therefore could not resort to industrial action. Finally, a strike supporting a grievance against an employer is deemed to be unlawful (under the doctrine of social adequacy (*Soziale Adäquanz*)[15]) in so far as other remedies are available, namely the resort to Labour Courts.

The almost general consensus about the peace obligation as an essential part of the collective contract and the extensive interpretation laid down by courts reflects a tendency towards a very prudential use of the strike weapon. The sociological concept of the strike as an *ultima ratio* clearly seems to be the underlying motivation of court decisions, legal writers and even trade unions' practices and internal rules. Such internal rules, which may be very restrictive in public utilities and for those who the Swedish Act of 1928 defines as 'protective workers', far from having a sheer internal relevance might

13. See for a critical appraisal, T. Ramm, *Kampfmassnahmen und Friedenspflicht im deutschen Recht*, Stuttgart, 1962.
14. See Chapter 5, p. 267. On the pattern of collective bargaining in Germany see Chapter 1, p. 40.
15. See also p. 163, and more extensively Chapter 5, p. 268. On the notion of *Soziale Adäquanz* (social adequacy) see Hueck–Nipperdey, op. cit., p. 1000.

even, through the doctrine of social adequacy, lay the foundation for a liability in tort towards the employer.

SWEDEN

The early collective agreements in Sweden, as in the other countries, consisted mostly of summary price lists and provisions on hours of work. The enlargement in scope, both in terms of including other working conditions and in terms of including a peace obligation, procedures for negotiation, etc. originated mainly from the employers.[16] This development in Sweden took place as early as the first decade of this century, and the collective agreement, in spite of the lack of specific legislation and its uncertain nature at Civil Law, was recognized by the Supreme Court in 1915 as binding at law, and implying an obligation to refrain from work stoppages during the life of the agreement.[17]

In this specific case, however, the action was dismissed because the strike in question was a sympathetic action, namely the taking part in a general strike of 1909. The Supreme Court considered sympathetic action to be outside the scope of the limitations on industrial action contained in the collective contract.

It was in 1928 that collective agreements were covered by a special statute. The two Acts on collective agreements and on the Labour Court, both of that year, aroused strong opposition among the labour movement, but actually they should have worked satisfactorily during the following years as the Confederation of Trade Unions ended up by supporting the Acts. But the general climate was also changing, and in 1938 relations between the two parties had become so constructive as to allow the stipulation of the Basic Agreement, still the main foundation of labour relations in Sweden.

The Labour Court sits in Stockholm and its task is that of examining and settling questions relating to collective agreements.[18] As far as we are concerned, it is sufficient to say that this Labour Court has jurisdiction over disputes concerning (Art. 11):

1. The validity, contents or interpretation of a collective agreement;

OMISSIS

3. The consequences of an action which is deemed to be contrary to the collective agreement or the aforesaid Act

Article 4 of the Act on collective agreements of 22 June 1928 contains an exhaustive definition of a peace obligation which is worth quoting here.

Employers or employees who are bound by a collective agreement may not, during the period of validity of the agreement, take part in a stoppage of

---

16. See F. Schmidt, *The Law of Labor Relations in Sweden*, Harvard U. P., 1962, p. 28.
17. Decision 1915, NJA, 233.
18. See F. Schmidt, in *Labor Courts and Grievance Settlement in Western Europe*, B. Aaron (ed.), Berkeley – Los Angeles, 1971, p. 198.

work (lockout or strike), blockade, boycott, or other offensive action of a similar nature:

1. on account of a dispute respecting the validity, existence or current interpretation of the agreement, or on account of a dispute as to whether a particular action constitutes an infringement of the agreement or the provisions of this Act;
2. in order to bring about an alteration in the agreement;
3. in order to enforce a provision which is to come into operation on the expiration of the agreement; or
4. in order to assist others in cases in which those others may not themselves commit offensive actions;

OMISSIS

The provisions of this section shall apply even to agreements which contain clauses contrary thereto. If a collective agreement contains provisions imposing obligations which are more far-reaching, these shall apply.[19]

In the case of Sweden we may find confirmation of the fact that statutory peace obligations have always been the product of action taken by conservative rather than by pro-labour political groupings. As already mentioned, the 1918 statute passed in Germany did not contain any such provision, in spite of the well-entrenched doctrine of peace as an essential element of the collective agreement. This was probably due to the fact that the order was passed during the revolution, while the statute of 1949 partially repeated the same structure, and, in any case, the legislation met with union opposition to an open recognition of the peace obligation. In the United States sec. 301 of the LMRA (Taft-Hartley Act) was introduced in 1947. The case in Britain, 1971, needs no comment.

The correct interpretation of the above-mentioned Article 4 should throw light on some important features of this statutory rule. First, according to subsec. (1) industrial actions over conflicts of rights are not admitted in so far as a peaceful procedure is provided for through the Labour Court. It is not easy to define a dispute over rights, and the Swedish lawyers are well aware of this. Thus, it is admitted that a strike against an employer who is not complying with an obligation is not a dispute over rights or a conflict of rights, unless the employer objects to his obligation with legal counter-arguments. This would be what, in Italian collective bargaining practice, is often called a dispute over application as distinct from a dispute over interpretation.[20] Needless to say, such a distinction is extremely narrow, and often not practicable at all.

Furthermore, a dispute over rights may even arise if an employer objects to the expiration of a contract that could end in the prorogation of the peace obligation, even though the court may finally reject the employer's argument.[21]

19. The English version of the excerpts from the two Acts mentioned in the text is quoted from F. Schmidt, *The Law of Labor Relations in Sweden*, p. 243 ff.
20. See also the same distinction in the USA, as drawn in *Local 174, Teamsters v. Lucas Flour Co.*, 369 US 95 (1962), referred to in Chapters 5 and 6.
21. See F. Schmidt, *The Law of Labor Relations in Sweden*, p. 182.

To summarize, if we take the distinction, basic to Swedish law, between conflicts of rights and conflicts of interests, we see that Art. 4 very clearly forbids industrial action both in the former and the latter, in as much as conflicts of interest would produce an alteration to the agreement. Subsections 2 and 3 of the article mentioned are apparently inferred from the general principle *pacta sunt servanda*. 'Alteration', however, does not mean addition, and therefore the statutory peace obligation in Swedish law should be regarded as relative to the contents of the agreement. Besides, subsec. 4 follows the principle laid down by the 1915 case (p. 134), holding that sympathetic action can be treated as a breach of contract only when action is taken in order to support a party in breach.

Granted that the statutory peace obligation is relative only to settled matters, it is the definition of the contents of the collective agreement itself and therefore of what has to be meant by settled matters which has appeared to be a difficult issue, and one on which the Labour Court has had to take many decisions.

We may mention the case AD 1947:51[22] when the court rejected a claim against a union for taking action to determine a wage tariff for a locality not provided for by the collective agreement. Even more interesting is the case of a boycott against an employer (AD 1933:159) in order to force him to reinstate dismissed workers. The Swedish Labour Court reasoned in the following way: according to general rules of private law in the employment relationship, it is ordinarily embodied that an employer is entitled to certain prerogatives, among these the right to dismiss a worker upon notice without giving any reason for his dismissal. These prerogatives become implied in the collective agreement. An offensive action by a union because of the dismissal of some workers during the period of validity of a collective agreement thus constitutes an infringement upon the manager's prerogatives embodied in the contract and implies therefore a breach of the peace obligation.

This solution given by the Labour Court has not gone without criticism.[23] It closely resembles, in its practical effects, the view of some American scholars, according to which management prerogatives are residual to the matters laid down in the collective contract and lay out the scope of bargaining during the life of the agreement.[24] What follows is that the acceptance of the above-mentioned doctrine of the Swedish Labour Court would change the peace obligation into an absolute one, at least for matters internal to the company or companies involved. This may happen to be the inevitable conclusion of a doctrine based on the recognition of invisible clauses in collective agreements.[25]

This conclusion is strictly connected, however, to the one concerning what exactly is meant by 'questions settled in a collective agreement'. The issue, as

22. See F. Schmidt. op. cit., p. 184.
23. ibid., p. 185.
24. See also, p. 146. A flexible interpretation of this principle is invoked by P. Prasow and E. Peters, *Arbitration and Collective Bargaining*, McGraw–Hill, New York, 1970, p. 32–3, under the authority of the leading scholar H. Shulman.
25. See A. Suviranta, op. cit., mainly, p. 211 ff.

we shall see, is common to other countries as well, but we find it dealt with extensively by Scandinavian scholars. In fact, during negotiations, claims may be advanced which are later discarded in order to reach a final settlement. Dropping a claim does not necessarily mean leaving it unsettled, but it may have the very different meaning of postponing it until the next negotiations. Professor Suviranta[26] is prepared to support the 'commonly accepted proposition that the legal peace obligation is but relative', and would draw a distinction between

(i) collective agreements aimed at a complete regulation of the employment relationship covered by them (the agreements the author has defined as a 'Professional Code', known particularly in France, Italy and USA[27] and
(ii) the agreements which do not have this aim.

An agreement of the first kind would not leave 'unsettled questions' and, as the author admits, at least in this case, the peace obligation would become absolute. We may object that no agreement usually defines itself as 'a complete regulation', thus one should anyway resort to an extensive and hard enquiry into the intention of the parties.

Section 4 of the Collective Agreements Act clearly states that the peace obligation is to be read into each collective agreement and contrary clauses are void. This peace obligation is considered as a minimum since the parties can impose obligations which are more far-reaching. This happens not infrequently in Sweden. First of all, we should mention procedural agreements, the best example of which is the Basic Agreement negotiated by the two confederations in 1938, which is still the basis of industrial relations in Sweden. Article 8 of this Agreement provides for prohibition of any direct action when the appropriate procedure laid down in the agreement has not been followed, and before each party has fulfilled his duty to negotiate as ruled by this agreement. According to Art. 14 of the Labour Courts Act, a suit should not be brought before the Labour Court before negotiations have taken place.

Besides this agreement, which is very important for its general coverage, we have contractual peace obligations provided for in branch agreements, as in the seamen's ship officers' and ship engineers' agreements and in the national agreement for agricultural workers. The meaning of such clauses is mainly to enact an absolute peace, including sympathetic actions.[28] Furthermore, at the end of 1965, before the commencement of the State Officials Act which legalized strikes in the public sector, an agreement was entered into between the national bargaining office representing the State and the confederations of State employees. In this Basic Agreement the procedure was laid down for exemptions in case industrial action would threaten essential public interest. The protection of essential needs for the community is provided for also by

26. op. cit. On the issue of the meaning of the 'settled questions', see also F. Schmidt in *Labor Courts and Grievance Settlement in Western Europe*, p. 211.
27. G. Giugni, *L'evolution des négociations collectives dans les industries du charbon et de l'acier dans les Pays membres de la CECA*, Luxembourg, 1968 (ron.) p. 37.
28. See F. Schmidt, *The Law of Labor Relations in Sweden*, p. 200.

Art. 9 of the Basic Agreement of 1938, which draws a definition of 'protective workers',[29] namely of the workers whose operations are required to continue also during a strike. This portion of the agreement is often implemented by local agreements.

FRANCE

France is one of the two countries, which fall under the scope of our study, where the right to strike is constitutionally recognized. This will open the question as to whether a peace obligation is conceivable in so far as it implies a temporary waiver of the right to strike. Although this is a widely accepted conviction (p. 151), clauses of peace or clauses regarding the procedure of strikes are far from being unknown, and above all, the wording of Art. 31(q) of the first book of the Labour Code lays down the basis for the construction of a relative peace obligation implicit in all collective contracts. This statutory provision spells out that 'parties to the collective agreement (*convention collective*) are bound to do nothing which could prevent its loyal performance'. We must remember that this term applies to a specific type of contract with national or regional scope, but the above-mentioned rule may also refer to all kinds of collective agreements (e.g., to company agreements).

This obligation lies in fact under many restrictions concerning, on the one hand, its scope, and on the other hand, its effectiveness. First of all, there is no doubt that it is relative in nature, and, according to legal commentators,[30] it allows that:

(a) a strike supporting a claim for more favourable conditions than those fixed in the *convention collective* would be lawful because the *convention collective* is only concerned with minimal conditions; even a strike for an increase of actual wages would be admitted since actual wages in France are very often much higher than contractual wages. The Court of Cassation, however, rejected the application of this principle to a case concerning claims for increases of actual wages. We should remember that the same attitude was taken by the German Federal Court (p. 133).

(b) A strike against a violation of the agreement would be lawful.

(c) A strike in support of a conflict of interpretation would likewise be lawful, with the only exception of bad faith – namely a conscious claim for a change under the guise of a conflict of interpretation.

This cautious, if not restrictive interpretation of Art. 31(q) is undoubtedly due to the preoccupation with preserving the constitutional right to strike. But it is also easy to discover the influence from an ideological background characterized by the lack of consensus over the ideal of social peace and by the ad-

29. See F. Schmidt, op. cit., Appendix, p. 202 for the text.
30. See H. Sinay, 'Le droit de grève', in *Traité de droit du Travail*. G. H. Camerlynck (ed.), V I, Paris, 1966, p. 216; M. Despax, 'Conventions collectives', ibid., V I I, Paris, 1966, p. 272 ff.

herence of the labour movement to the idea of a class struggle. Moreover, we must remember the deep-rooted tradition of syndicalism in France. The ideological background is completely different from the Swedish or German one, countries whose legal institutions are aimed, with a majority consensus among the labour force, at preserving social peace. It is also far removed from the American idea of collective bargaining for industrial peace. We shall find, however, it has many features in common with Italy.

From the point of view of effectiveness, Art. 31(q) only binds the trade unions. A wildcat strike would never be a violation of this Article. Furthermore, the parties are not obliged to adhere to active behaviour, but only to abstain from certain kinds of action. The union, namely, is not bound to take action in order to prevent or to stop a strike, but only not to support a strike. In industrial relations practice this means that the union can surreptitiously promote a strike, or intervene opportunely in support of a settlement, in return for substantial concessions, taking advantage of the wildcat strike. In other words, the wording of Art. 31(q) allows for many loopholes.

In collective agreements, 'no-strike' clauses and clauses aimed at ruling the conduct of a strike are very rare at the national level, but more frequent at the enterprise or shop level (*accords d'entreprise* or *d'établissement*). A factual enquiry shows that the practice of these clauses is relatively recent. On the other hand, one must bear in mind that collective bargaining developed very slowly in France and it has acquired a very important role virtually only since the 1950s and especially in the second half of that decade, and after.[31]

A straight 'no-strike' clause is, however, very infrequent. We should mention the agreement at the Peugeot Company in the early 1960s which banned strikes and lockouts for the whole duration of the agreement if they were called for a reason outside the scope of the enterprise or outside the economic (*professionels*) interests of the employees, but it allowed participation in short national strikes due to economic reasons. Furthermore, in the case of conflicts inside the enterprise, industrial action could be taken only after a special procedure of conciliation had been followed. Such an agreement is rather peculiar because the underlying intention is to isolate the personnel from the employees of other companies or industries, whereas it does not, in the last resort, ban strikes over questions arising inside the enterprise. To a certain extent it is therefore just the opposite of a common 'relative' 'no-strike' obligation, whereas the prohibition of strikes not concerning the economic interests of the employees of the company looks like a piece of an 'absolute' 'no-strike' clause. It is apparent that these classifications, worked out by German legal writers, although very useful for descriptive purposes, are not always workable in reality.

Other clauses lay down a 'no-strike' obligation of a procedural nature. In the Company Messier agreement of 1964, which was followed by many other agreements in important companies, a very broad clause prohibited the resort to strike until all possibilities for a settlement deriving from law, agreements,

31. G. Giugni, op. cit., p. 24.

etc., had been exhausted. The French Confederation of Christian Trade Unions (Confédération Française des Travailleurs Chrétiens (CFTC) – now entitled Confédération Française refused to sign the 'Accord Messier' because of such unusual limitations on the right to strike. Such a limitation is quite rightly considered a severe one, and of doubtful legality, because the exhaustion of all possible channels of conciliation could take a long time and would virtually curb the right to strike.[32] On the other hand, such a limitation is a *quid pro quo* for remarkable concessions in terms of the recognition and protection of union shop stewards, and the facilities for their activities.

The typical 'no-strike' clause banning strikes over questions settled in the agreement, seems in fact to be very rare, partly because it would look like a repetition of Art. 31(q), and partly because the unions are usually hostile towards such a clause. In the 'agreements of progress' (a formula which circulated in France at approximately the same time as the idea of 'productivity agreements' gained popularity in Great Britain) with the Electricité de France, a procedural 'no-strike' clause of a relative kind was signed at the end of 1969. It provided for a period of three months' notice, during which negotiations had to take place. The General Confederation of Labour (CGT) refused to endorse such an attack on the right to strike and a referendum among the employees later justified this militant position.

On the contrary the ground has been more fertile for clauses concerning the way in which strikes should be conducted. Even national collective contracts (*conventions collectives*) contain rules concerning a delay that must elapse before a strike is implemented. The delay is 5–10 days in general and is sometimes connected with the exhaustion of a contractual procedure. In this case the peace obligation becomes a procedural one. At the company level similar procedural rules are often found, with, additionally, a few clauses concerning other aspects of the implementation of strikes. The above-mentioned Messier agreement provided for a referendum, if it was requested by 50 per cent of the shop stewards.

In food companies, notice is not infrequent in order to avoid the destruction of perishable goods. The maintenance of crews in order to avoid the destruction of perishable materials is also provided for. Finally, there are also agreements which limit the use of the right to strike to economic aims, or ban slowdowns (*grève perlée*), which the courts for their part have deemed unlawful.

However, the frequency of company agreements containing rules concerning the right to strike should not be taken as indicating a trend. In fact, company agreements themselves are still rare, and in those that exist most do not contain any clause regarding industrial action. It could be said, however, that limitations to the right to strike were a return to the recognition of company bargaining, at a time when the position of the unions in general was still weak. It will not be difficult to draw a parallel here with the vicissitudes in Italy.

32. See H. Sinay, op. cit., p. 207.

ITALY

In spite of the political tradition of Italian unionism, we find that the 'no-strike' clause was not unknown even from the beginning. In the celebrated agreement of 1906 between the metallurgical union (FIOM) and the Italia Company in Turin (one of the earlier automobile companies, later absorbed into Fiat)[33] we can read a clear-cut 'no-strike' undertaking with the acceptance of liability by the union and even a cash deposit in the bank in order to cover this liability. This was the *quid pro quo* for significant concessions like recognition of the shop stewards and the union shop. It is remarkable that the agreement stated that the participation in general strikes should not be considered as a breach of the obligation. This agreement gave rise to a great deal of debate both within the labour movement and in the business world. The left wing of the labour movement accused the signatory union of pursuing a policy of peace and cooperation with capitalists. But even in the business *milieu* the company itself found strong opposition because it had accepted the principle of company agreement without the intermediary of an employers' association, and it had recognized the union at the company level. This new policy of management met with support from the progressive liberals, but it proved to be too far in advance of the stage of maturity reached by the employers' class as a whole. The strength of opposition resulted in the agreement being terminated only one year after it had been brought into force.

Apart from this case which gave rise to such heated debate, we find scattered examples of 'no-strike' clauses in minor shop agreements. During the corporate State, 1926–44, strikes and lockouts were outlawed and furthermore, the 1926 statute made the unions responsible for non-compliance with the provisions of agreements, but it must be remembered, at any rate, that strike action was prosecuted as a crime in itself.

The restoration of trade-union freedom in 1944 brought with it the growth of national agreements which initially covered the whole area of industry (commerce, agriculture, etc.). In 1946 we find the provision for a wage truce[34] which was actually motivated by the engagement of all political groupings, including the Communist Party, in a policy of industrial recovery. After this instance the peace obligation disappears, to be resurrected only in 1960. It is worth mentioning, however, that the existence of a peace obligation was argued by the Supreme Court[35] from an agreement of 1950 – replaced in 1965 with amendments, but now overcome by subsequent statutes – which provided for arbitration on individual dismissals[36] and it stated in its foreword '. . . the

33. P. Spriano, *Socialismo e classe operaia a Torino dal 1892 al 1913*, Torino, 1958, p. 175 ff.
34. Concordato interconfederale del 27. 10. 1946 per la disciplina del trattamento economico dei lavoratori dell'industria.
35. Corte di Cassazione, 29 aprile 1959, n. 1285. A mention of procedural clauses is made by G. Ghezzi, in *L'esercizio del diritto di sciopero*; edited by the Istituto di Diritto del Lavoro dell'Università di Firenze, Milano, 1968, p. 73.
36. See G. Giugni, in *Labor Courts and Grievance Settlement in Western Europe*, p. 318.

common purpose of the parties to prevent the unrest stemming from such events which frequently lead to open conflict.'

Furthermore, we can mention here practices of exemption of protective workers from the strike, especially known in steel and later (1966), and consolidated into national and company agreements,[37] and of the rules laid down by railwaymen unions. Finally, we add another rule which broke down at the end of the 1960s. It was the unusual one of 'non-negotiation during a strike' – a practice which we find, however, in Sweden,[38] only with regard to wildcat strikes – which also became 'non-mediation during a strike' in the Government's attempts at conciliation.

At the beginning of the 1960s, starting with a few company or shop agreements which began to flourish at that time, explicit 'no-strike' clauses were resumed, and the very important milestone of the national agreement for the metal-mechanical industry of 1962/3[39] contained a clause which was repeated by almost all successive national agreements. It was more or less in terms of a reciprocal engagement by the employers to respect and obtain compliance with the terms of the agreement, and for the unions not to take action that would change or supplement what had been agreed in the national and supplementary company agreements which were recognized at this time. The employers' obligations were of the *Durchführung* and *Einwirkung* type, undertakings to perform and to obtain performance from the engaged employers. The union obligation was really a relative 'no-strike' or peace obligation. This clause aroused a debate which we shall come to later. Suffice it to say here that its motivation was a *quid pro quo* for recognition of shop bargaining. When, at the end of the decade, no agreement was reached as to the scope of shop bargaining in the hard-fought conflict over the new contracts for the metal-mechanical industry, the peace obligation itself broke down.

As to the nature of a relative peace obligation, the wording of the clause usually left no doubt,[40] even though, since the Italian collective contracts touch upon a wide variety of matters and belong to the type of the 'professional code' (p. 137), the general impression was that an 'unsettled question' would have been a rare bird.[41] Also this assumption was to be challenged by the events following 1968.

Mention should also be made to the procedural clauses included in collec-

---

37. See G. Giugni, *L'evolution des négotiations collectives*, idem., p. 165 ff. In the Cogne steel company an agreement of 1960 provided that production should not have been suspended in short strikes at the blast furnaces, but that the company should pay a sum to a fund for social welfare as a compensation for the profit realized out of the partial implementation of the strike.

38. See Chapter 1, p. 35.

39. 1962: State-owned companies; 1963: private companies. See G. Giugni, 'Recent Trends in Collective Bargaining in Italy' (1971), Vol. 104, in *International Labour Review*, 1971.

40. See G. Giugni, *L'evoluzione della contrattazione collettiva nelle industrie siderurgica e mineraria (1953–1963)*, Milano, p. 78.

41. See G. Giugni, in *La categoria e la contrattazione collettiva*; edited by the Istituto di Diritto del Lavoro dell'Università di Firenze, Milano, 1964, p. 342.

tive contracts,[42] the most important of which were once again in the metal-mechanical workers' agreements of 1966, where it is stated that if a collective dispute arises during the life of the contract, negotiations should take place at the local level, and in the event of failure, 15 days must elapse before strike action can be taken.[43] Of course, such a procedure would apply to disputes not covered by the general 'no-strike' clause: for example, disputes over matters to be negotiated at the shop level and disputes over the interpretation or application of the collective agreement. As a matter of fact, this clause was not very clear and the construction given to it for the purpose of this presentation is already in itself a rationalization of its wording. It was introduced in 1966 and only two years later met with the strong revival of labour struggles, as a result of which it has never really operated in practice.

The present situation is open to many constructions and is in fact typical of a transitional period, where established rules of behaviour in bargaining have been broken and not yet replaced by new rules.

The static conception of law held by most jurists engenders in them a sense of uneasiness which often leads to over-simplification of problems, such as the jurists who, having assumed the non-existence of a peace obligation, come to challenge even the existence of a collective contract, as binding at law.[44]

The whole issue is not so simple, and must be considered by pointing out at least two sub-problems. Taking a national agreement with a fixed term – like the agreements in metal-mechanical industry – we must ask first whether or not resort to industrial action before the expiration date of the agreement would be lawful. Then we have the issue, which is the real one, of the possibility of reserving for industrial action at other levels, mainly at the shop level – either for new matters or for improvement of conditions laid down in the national contract.

As for the first issue which is the most intriguing, but the less realistic, we should take the reference to the principle that *pacta sunt servanda* as an approximate and erroneous over-simplification, because there is no statutory provision, as in France, nor is there a legal construction like the one circulating among German legal scholars by which one should read the peace obligation as an invisible clause into the agreement. Furthermore, it would be contradictory, if the problem was merely one of discovering the intention of the parties, to take this obligation as an unexpressed intention, when the unions, during the latest negotiations, flatly rejected any such obligation. During the pilot negotiations for the metal-mechanical industry in 1969[45] the whole problem of relations between levels of negotiation was left aside; but

42. Often procedures provide for examination by a joint committee. See Annex 3 to nation-wide collective agreement 1.12.1969 for chemical industry.
43. See Art. 16 common part, of the nation-wide collective agreement 15.11.1966 for State-owned metal-mechanical industry.
44. See G. Ghezzi, *Osservazioni sul metodo dell'interpretazione giuridica nel diritto sindicale*, in Rivista Trimestrale di Diritto e Procedura Civile, 1970, p. 409 ff.; U. Romagnoli, 'Il contratto collettivo difficile', in *Politica del Diritto*, 1971, p. 71 ff.
45. The settlement for State-owned companies preceded the settlement for private companies by two weeks. Differences are slight.

we have also seen that the peace obligation had come to life eight years before as a return of the recognition of shop bargaining. It therefore seems realistic to admit that no peace obligation is placed on the trade unions, but the collective agreement still remains a legally enforceable contract in so far as it engages the employers to abide by its terms until the expiration date. This would not be contradictory to any principle at law because contracts as a source of obligation for only one of the parties are far from being unknown – the large majority of French collective agreements are undoubtedly one-sided – and also for the different reason that if a *quid pro quo* is to be found, it may be, as it was written right after the conclusion of the agreement,[46] not the peace for the future, but the cessation of the state of strike at present.

Another construction is possible, as well. There is a striking difference in the way in which negotiations were conducted and the way in which the agreements were later written. Negotiations arrived at a three-year agreement on specific points, and if we enquire into the intention of the parties, it would not be difficult to state that there was no intention, on the part of the unions, of considering that those matters of the expired agreement which were not changed should fall under the three-year term. In fact, these negotiations were more similar to the patterns of bargaining in countries where it is a succession of partial agreements, than to the traditional idea of a 'professional code' for industry to be re-enacted at each term of expiration, of course with amendments. From this point of view, we might conclude that the 1969 agreements were also binding for the unions for the term, but only for the matters which were specifically agreed upon. In fact, so far no attempt was made to renegotiate at the national level before expiration any part of the 1969 settlement. We are not required anyhow to take a position here among the mentioned possible constructions.

At the shop level, however, recent experience shows a growth of agreements containing:

(*a*) clauses which are improvements on the corresponding ones in the national agreement
(*b*) clauses touching on new matters – i.e. issues outside the 1969 agreements which have remained unchanged (like the working environment, job classifications, incentive payments, etc.).

The legitimacy of the former claims can be inferred, as in France (p. 138), from the principle of more favourable treatment, though many agree with plausible arguments that such a principle would legalize better conditions, but not the resort to industrial action in order to get them during the life of an agreement, both at the national and company level. As far as the latter are concerned, the legitimacy of such action could be inferred either by the bold denial of any peace obligation in the recent agreements, or by the opinion that the peace obligation was anyhow restricted to matters actually settled in the last round of national bargaining.

46. See G. Giugni, 'L'autunno caldo sindacale' in *Il Mulino*, 1970, p. 24 ff., now reprinted in *Sociologie du travail*, 1971, p. 71 ff.

Features of contractual limitations: countries at Common Law

UNITED STATES OF AMERICA

In the United States we find the peace obligation, commonly called the 'no-strike' obligation, both in the LMRA, applicable to enterprises operating in inter-state commerce, and in contractual practice, where it began to appear above all since the Second World War, when arbitration, under the influence of the War Labor Board, started to spread quickly. The 'no-strike' clause became common, however, only after the enactment of sec. 301 of the LMRA, in 1947, providing for liability of unions in case of breach of contract.

In the antecedent period, in case of violation of a 'no-strike' clause, the liability of the unions depended largely upon their legal status, which was not uniform. Lacking a 'no-strike' clause, only a minority opinion deemed the contract itself to imply a peace obligation.

A statutory regulation is explicitly inferred from the duty to bargain, which, according to the NLRA, sec. 8(d) 'shall also mean that no party to such contract shall terminate or modify such contract, unless the party desiring such termination or modification. . . .' Sec. 8(d) goes on to state terms and procedures for termination by stating particularly that no resort to strike or lock-out should be allowed for a period of 60 days after written notice of termination or modification is given, or until the expiry date of the contract, whichever occurs later. As a sanction it is provided that the employee who engages in a strike within this period shall lose his status as an employee for the purposes of the Act, what may bring about a termination of the relation of employment.[47] This is the statutory setup which is concerned only with the event of a strike aimed at termination or modification of an existing collective contract. It is evident that we are dealing here with a relative peace obligation which, as we have already seen in the case of Sweden, is enforced by an explicit statutory provision.

A more extensive obligation may arise from a collective contract dealing with striking over grievances or even over unfair labour practices on the part of the employer. The latter is deemed to be legal in relation to the statutory peace obligation contained in sec. 8(d).[48] Strikes over grievances should on the other hand be considered legal if not prevented by a 'no-strike' pledge. We shall discuss later on the connection between the 'no-strike' clauses and the contractual grievance procedures.

Whether a collective agreement includes a 'no-strike' clause or not, and if it does, whether the clause is relatively broad or narrow depends largely on the economic strength of the collective bargaining parties. If the union is very strong and the employer is very weak, the collective agreement may contain no peace obligation, which means that the union will be free to strike over grievances during the life of the agreement – but not over modifications of the agreement – sec. 8(d). On the other hand, if the employer is very strong and the union very weak, the collective agreement may contain a very broad 'no-

47. See Chapter 4, p. 212.
48. *Mastro Plastics Corp.* v. *NLRB*, 350 US 270, (1956).

strike' clause (sometimes referred to as a 'wall-to-wall' clause). In such extreme cases, as we have seen, even a strike against an unfair labour practice by the employer could resort to being illegal. Such clauses would meet the qualification of absolute peace obligations, not even necessarily connected (a rare case indeed) with procedural provisions. There are instead a few instances of a 'no-strike' clause which, since it was not connected with arbitration, is lifted after compliance with a specific procedure. Finally, there are very few cases, and these are usually found in the public utilities, where binding arbitration is provided even in the final stage of the process of making an agreement, with an agreed ban on strikes or lockouts. This case implies a waiver of the right to strike which would be inconceivable in most of the other countries under consideration.

A very serious problem arises, as in other countries, concerning the matters covered by a 'no-strike' obligation. The doctrine of the reserved prerogatives of management[49] will propose that all that has not been settled remains in the management's prerogatives, and cannot be negotiated until the expiration of the agreement. Here we come very close to the similar theory of the embodied prerogatives, with which we became acquainted in the section on Sweden (p. 136). Both doctrines undertake to construe the 'no-strike' obligation as an absolute one. A recurrent issue for the USA is, for instance, the one concerning the power of management of contracting-out jobs, if it is not expressly limited by the collective agreement.

The opposite opinion will deem that matters unsettled in the agreement may be negotiated during the life of it. This is the policy of the NLRB.[50] If a question is open to negotiation, and assuming that the other party has a duty to bargain, it follows that it is up to the union to take action. The construction of the intention of the parties by the NLRB has been very cautious, requiring a 'clear and unmistakable' language in order to express the intention to waive the right to negotiate over specific matters.[51] The use of recurrent expressions like 'all management rights not given up in the contract are expressly reserved to it' may not be sufficient.[52]

Even the 'zipper clause', as is called the statement that a contract represents the complete expression of the agreements of the parties, was held to not imply a clear and unmistakable waiver.[53] In the Jacobs Mfg. Co. case it was held that sec. 8(d) does not relieve an employer of the duty to bargain 'as to subjects which are neither discussed nor embodied in any of the terms and conditions of the contract'.[54]

---

49. An accurate analysis of the different points of view appears in C. J. Morris (ed.), *The Developing Labor Law*, Washington, BNA, 1971 p. 477 ff.; J. T. McKelvey (ed.), *Management Rights and the Arbitration Process*, Washington, BNA, 1956. See also p. 136, n. 24.
50. C. J. Morris (ed.), *The Developing Labor Law*, p. 478, n. 23. Such policy was endorsed by the Supreme Court in *NLRB* v. *C & C Plywood Corp.*, 385 US 421 (1967), cited by Morris, ibid., p. 479, n. 245.
51. Cases quoted ibid., p. 333, n. 403.
52. *Proctor Mfg. Co.*, 131 NLRB 1166 (1961).
53. *New York Mirror*, 151 NLRB 834 (1965).
54. *NLRB* v. *Jacobs Mfg. Co.*, 196 F. 2d 680 (2d Cir. 1952).

There is a clear-cut tendency, therefore, to construe the 'no-strike' obligation as a relative one, and to interpret the intention of the parties with restrictive criteria. Starting from the assumption that a union has a right to bargain, even though upon mandatory subjects broadly defined by sec. 8(d) of the NLRA, any restriction is construed as a waiver, and, as such, evaluated with extreme carefulness.

The finding out of what is meant by 'unsettled matters' open to negotiation gives interesting guidelines also for comparative purposes. Thus, it was held that where a subject has been discussed but is not covered by the subsequent agreement, negotiation would be prevented only if the union 'consciously yielded' its position.[55] Mere silence or inaction is not 'conscious exploration'[56] unless the employer gave a full explanation for rejection, and the silence might have meant conscious acquiescence.[57] A demand withdrawal without 'full discussion' would not imply a settlement.[58]

Connection with arbitration procedures raises a number of similar issues. The 'no-strike' clause, which extends to all forms of industrial action – not only the refusal to work – has usually been construed as a *quid pro quo* for the arbitration clause. In several important agreements, e.g. in the automobile industry, some matters are not submitted to arbitration and the union therefore retains the right to strike over these issues. Here we face a clear-cut relative peace obligation. However, where a grievance procedure culminating in arbitration exists, a quasi-absolute peace obligation, with the only exceptions pointed out further on, seems to be presumed unless otherwise stated by the parties concerned.

The theory of the connection between the 'no-strike' clause and the arbitration clause – in Civil Law terms we could speak of *causa* of the contract – has gone so far that the 'no-strike' clause has been inferred by the courts even if it is not written into an agreement, which, however, provides for arbitration. The leading case was *Local 174, Teamsters* v. *Lucas Flour Company*,[59] where a statement of policy was made according to which 'the contrary view would be completely at odds with the basic policy of national labour legislation to promote the arbitration process as a substitute for economic warfare'.

We have the reverse situation when a 'no-strike' clause is provided for, but specific issues are expressly excluded from arbitration procedure. But if an exclusion is not expressed, or if the wording is obscure, preference must be given to the extensive coverage of arbitration,[60] because arbitration, unlike commercial disputes, is a substitute not of the judicial process but of industrial warfare. This point of view is in fact rather questionable because, before the

---

55. *New York Mirror, supra*, note 7.
56. Various cases quoted by Morris, op. cit., p. 335, note 417.
57. *Speidel Corp.*, 120 NLRB 733 (1968).
58. *Beacon Journal Publishing Co.*, 164 NLRB 734 (1967).
59. 369 US 95 (1962). The 'no-strike' obligation was, however, attached to a clause regarding arbitration of differences of interpretation. The court extended the scope of the obligation.
60. *United Steelworkers* v. *Warrior & Gulf Navigation Co.*, 363 US 574 (1960).

Lincoln Mills case,[61] it was recognized that judicial adjudication on merits, although not frequent, could replace arbitration if this had not taken place.

Finally, the Supreme Court[62] held that a standard 'no-strike' clause would be construed to apply only to the 'economic relationship' between the parties, and that a 'compelling expression' of a broader intent was needed before a waiver of the right to strike over an unfair labour practice could be inferred. It does not seem that the same conclusions could be reached for a sympathetic strike, which is 'unprotected' by law, or for other industrial actions outside the 'economic relationship' between the parties. This same conclusion could have been reached in the UK before the 1971 Act, on the grounds of statutory reference to 'industrial dispute' or 'trade dispute'.

What seems remarkable, and will be mentioned again later, is this link between the procedural part of the agreement and the 'no-strike' clause, which will similarly appear in some way in the case of Great Britain, while a comparison can also be made with the bargaining practice in Italy, where the peace obligation was tied within a more comprehensive collective contract to the clauses which recognized the right to bargain collectively at the shop level. All these constructions may be compared in their turn with the German traditional one, according to which the peace obligation is the return for the whole collective agreement as such.

As to the way of carrying out a strike, it is rarely a matter for contractual obligations. Protective work may be maintained as a current practice, but in a restricted way. During a steel strike, for instance, blast furnaces, unlike those in other countries, cease to operate.

GREAT BRITAIN

In the UK the 'no-strike' or peace obligation clause in collective agreements is often present, most usually in the form of a procedure which should be exhausted before industrial action is taken. Such procedure clauses can be found both in industry-wide and in company agreements. It was such a clause, for instance, which gave rise to the famous Ford case.[63] The court concluded with the reaffirmation of the principle that collective agreements were not binding by law, and therefore no breach of agreement could be legally enforceable against the union which had called for a strike.

In order for the parties to be bound by the peace obligation – here we mean 'bound' either by honour or by law – it has to be written into the agreement. These clauses generally refer to matters settled in the agreement (relative peace obligation) but there can also be a general prohibition on all industrial action for the duration of the agreement, particularly in company contracts. The peace obligation in procedural clauses or in procedural agreements may

61. *Textile Workers* v. *Lincoln Mills*, 353 US 448 (1957).
62. *Mastro Plastics Corp.* v. *NLRB*, 350 US 270 (1956).
63. *Ford Motor Co. Ltd* v. *Amalgamated Union of Engineering and Foundry Workers and the Transport and General Workers Union* (1969) 1 WLR 339. See an extensive appraisal of the case in K. W. Wedderburn, *The Worker and the Law*, Penguin Books, 1971, p. 172 ff.

consist of an agreement to follow a procedure for 'all questions arising between the parties', and not to resort to industrial action during such procedure. We can therefore speak of a peace obligation with its scope restricted to the duration of the procedure, similar to some German instances referred to previously.

In recent times, and before the enactment of the Industrial Relations Act 1971, the tendency has been towards an expansion of these clauses. This tendency ran parallel to a slight increase in the number of agreements with a fixed term. This slight increase of 'no-strike' clauses also corresponds to the Government's suggestions, and to the attempt made, for instance, by 'productivity agreements' to contain social unrest and to increase efficiency. On the other hand, since the collective agreement was not normally enforceable at the collective level, by signing such clauses the unions did not assume any liability, and as we shall see, even if legal liability existed, it was limited by the immunity granted in the past.

The entire picture may change with the new Act. This Act was aimed principally at enforcing sanctions against breaches of the Act itself, and in particular against breaches of the peace obligation. The first step was therefore to declare the agreement binding at law. The solution reached seems like an attempt to compromise with a deep-rooted tradition to the contrary. According to sec. 34(1) a written agreement '. . . shall be conclusively presumed to be intended by the parties to it to be a legally enforceable contract' unless it states that it, or part of it, is intended not to be legally enforceable. This statement, which would exclude legal enforceability, must also be included in written decisions taken by voluntary joint negotiating bodies if they are not to be subject to a similar presumption (sec. 35).

Assuming that the agreement is binding at law[64] sec. 36 declares a breach of the agreement to be an unfair industrial practice, the consequences of which will be considered later on.

The obligation placed upon the union is not only not to act in breach of the agreement, but also to take all such steps as are reasonably practicable for the purposes of preventing its officials from taking any action contrary to this undertaking, of preventing its members from taking any such action, and finally of ensuring that such action, once taken, is not continued. This obligation is far-reaching and it appears broader in scope than the corresponding peace obligations of other countries in so far as in the wording of sec. 36(2)(b) and (c), it places the union under an obligation to ensure that its members carry out their duties regularly and comes near to a guarantee obligation. Much will depend, of course, on the interpretation of the concept of 'reasonably practicable steps'. It should be pointed out that sec. 36(2)(a) forbids '. . . any

64. At present many agreements (approximately 100) now being made provide for an exclusion clause. Furthermore the Annual TU Congress 1971 gave mandatory instructions for inclusion of this clause. Typical exclusion clauses are: 'this agreement does not in any way constitute a legally enforceable agreement between the parties' or 'this agreement is binding in honour but is not intended to constitute a legally enforceable agreement between them', etc.

action contrary to an undertaking given by that party and contained in the collective agreement . . .'. The wording of the Act, here, is not completely clear, since it can be stated that the 'undertaking . . . contained in the collective agreement' should be just an express peace obligation. If this interpretation is correct, we should still return to the principle that a peace obligation under the old law and under the new Act must always be expressly spelt out.

Under the new Act, it seems likely that a sympathetic or political strike in breach of a 'no-strike' clause would also be an unfair labour practice because no reference is made in sec. 36 to 'industrial dispute'. Under the old law such a reference might have had relevant consequences.

But the Industrial Relations Act is more far-reaching. In the above-mentioned secs. 37–41, the Industrial Court is empowered to give an order which will be read into the collective agreement, as if it had been agreed upon by the parties, and the object of which would be a procedure for the settlement of disputes. In so far as it is common practice that the duration of a procedure would imply the suspension of industrial action, one could argue that the final result of the imposed procedure would be a peace obligation imposed by authority. But still one may wonder if it should be expressed or not. This peace obligation could cover all matters settled in substantive agreements and also, depending on the policies of the public bodies concerned, 'all other matters'. This might bring about an absolute peace obligation imposed by authority. It is not the task of this essay to give a full account of the intriguing procedure. Suffice it to say that the Industrial Court, once addressed by one of the parties to the agreement or by the Secretary of State, after a summary examination of the case to ascertain the existence of the required *prima facie* reasonable grounds, namely of the *fumus boni juris*, must refer it to the Industrial Relations Commission, which will lay down the appropriate proposals and lead sessions with the parties in order to work out a legally enforceable agreement concerning the procedural machinery. Once this has been done, the Commission will report to the Industrial Court, which will issue a binding order if it deems it necessary. Sanctions will be considered subsequently.

Considering that collective bargaining has traditionally prevailed at the national level, the problem of new claims on the shop floor may arise, but it does not appear that this would bring with it the dramatic consequences which have been typical in Italy. It is generally assumed that on questions not covered by the agreement, bargaining and strikes may occur. This is also the case when a clause of the agreement is questioned, namely where a conflict of interpretation arises. We should remember that the distinction between the conflicts of interest and conflicts of right is not usually recognized in British practice.[65]

As regards the way in which a strike is conducted, it appears to be a matter of industrial practice rather than of collective bargaining. The practice of

65. See K. W. Wedderburn, 'Conflicts of "Rights" and Conflicts of "Interests" in Labor Disputes', in *Dispute Settlement Procedures in Five Western European Countries* (B. Aaron ed.), Los Angeles, 1969, p. 65 ff.

maintaining protective workers in order to avoid damage or danger to safety is observed, but it is possible that during a severe conflict the union may threaten to stop this practice.

The legitimacy of the peace obligation

The issue of the legality of the 'no-strike' obligation would arise when the right to strike was recognized by legal provision which could not be waived by the parties. As a matter of fact, the issue was raised only in France and in Italy, where the right to strike is recognized by the Constitution. However, provided that in the other countries a right to strike is recognized either directly or indirectly by the statutory law, the same issue might have been raised there. If it was not, that may be due to the fact that the right to strike was recognized (as in Sweden) by the same source that gave full recognition to the peace obligation, or that it was construed (as in Germany) leaving untouched the current principle of the peace obligation as a necessary element of the agreement.[66] When such a strict legal analysis fails to give the reason for the recognition of the full legitimacy of the peace obligation, the fact that such an issue was never raised is an evidence, at least, of a 'political' consensus, which deprives the legal argument of any actual value.[67] By rejecting any abstract approach to the problem, we shall therefore deal only with the case of France and of Italy.

The solution given by the French courts was rather empirical, having mainly to deal with clauses placing limitations on the procedure, or connecting the exercise of the right to strike to conciliatory steps. The Cour de Cassation,[68] constantly followed by subsequent decisions, ruled that such limitations could be admitted in so far as they were precisely defined, with specific attention to the cooling-off period imposed on the parties and to the duration implied in a duty to abstain from action during conciliatory steps. If such periods exceeded a reasonable duration, the clause would not be legitimate. In other words, conventional limitations are upheld provided that they do not result in a waiver of the right to strike and/or that they do not make its exercise too difficult.[69] We do not know about decisions concerning a true 'no-strike'

66. We assume that the main feature of the right to strike is the immunity from the consequences deriving from the abstention from work, namely from the non compliance with the obligation to work. Such a doctrine was clearly stated by the distinguished Italian scholar Piero Calamandrei (*Significato costituzionale del diritto di sciopero*, in R G L 1952, I, p. 243 ss.). The immunity produces the suspension of the obligation itself, which is recognized, as an effect of the strike, in all countries under survey, with the exception of the UK, overcome, although in not clear and unquestionable terms, by the Act of 1971. See Chapter 4, pp. 144, 201.

67. This may be the case of the USA, where the right to strike may be easily inferred from the NLRA, and mainly from secs. 7, 8(a), and 13, although the existence of a constitutional protection was rejected in *United Federation of Postal Clerks* v. *Blount*, 325 F. Supp. 879 (DDC), *aff'd per curiam*, 92 Sup. Ct. 80 (1971). See Gregory, *Labor and the Law*, New York, Norton, 1961, p. 511.

68. Six decisions of 5 May 1960, in *Juris-Classeur Périodique*, 1960, II, 11692.

69. See H. Sinay, 'Le droits de grève', op. cit., p. 211 ff. In the same sense, M. Despax, 'Convention Collectives', in *Traité de droit du Travail* (G. H. Camerlynck ed.), VII, Paris, 1966, p. 270 ff.; *Contra* P. Durand, *Traité de Droit du Travail*, III, Paris, 1956, p. 597.

clause, but we should remember that it could be conceived as an extension of Art. 31(q) of the Labour Code, and it might fall under the previously mentioned principle of reasonableness applied to contractual limitations. Of course, one could also question the constitutionality of Art. 31(q) in so far as an implied waiver to the right to strike can be construed from an obligation to loyal performance. This issue does not, however, seem to have been raised.

The legality problem of the peace obligation aroused bitter debate in Italy, but did not give rise to a corresponding number of court decisions. The explanation is easy. Disputes in court are so long-lasting[70] that parties generally come to an agreement before a decision is taken. The lower courts came to conflicting opinions, which, however, should also be related to differences in the factual situation and in the wording of agreements. In 1959 the Corte di Cassazione[71] read an implied peace obligation in the above-mentioned agreement for dismissals in industry (p. 141). But the issue of constitutionality had not been raised by the defendants. A very recent decision[72] took the stand that 'no-strike' clauses were legitimate.

The debate, which continues among legal writers, may be summarized as follows:

1. A peace obligation is a waiver of the right to strike which in itself is not waiverable. Therefore it is void.[73]
2. A strike is not an end in itself but merely the instrument which can be negotiated for a return. At any rate, the 'no-strike' clause must be express. In as far as it means a limitation of a constitutional right it cannot be construed as an implied term of the agreement.[74]
3. The 'no-strike' obligation belongs only to the obligatory part of the collective agreement and is therefore only binding for the trade union.[75] According to now prevailing opinion, the union does not have the right to strike, which remains freely available to the individual workers. Therefore the union does not in fact negotiate the right to strike, but its capacity to call a strike – a step which is not necessary to carry on a strike. The individual on a wildcat strike would not violate the collective agreement, and he would only respond to his union if he is a union member.
4. A variation on the second and third points would be that the peace obligation is a *quid pro quo* for some specific concessions and that it is concerned only with these concessions. On the other hand, the intention of the parties

70. See G. Giugni, in *Labor Courts and Grievance Settlement in Western Europe*, p. 271.
71. Corte di Cassazione, 29 aprile 1959, n. 1025.
72. Corte di Cassazione, 10 febbraio 1971, n. 357. We should remember that such a question cannot be brought before the constitutional court because the latter only has jurisdiction on statutory law and not on contracts. Only the ordinary courts can void a clause of a contract.
73. U. Natoli, *La c.d. Friedenspflicht nel diritto italiano del lavoro*, in R G L, 1961, I, p. 319 ff.
74. G. Ghezzi, *La responsabilità contrattuale delle associazioni sindacali*, Milano, 1962, p. 180.
75. G. Ghezzi, *Autonomia collettiva, diritto di sciopero e clausole di tregua (variazioni critiche e metodologiche)* in Rivista Trimestrale di Diritto e Procedura Civile, 1967, p. 152 ff.

and the wording itself of most 'no-strike' clauses points out a commitment limited only to the unions.[76]

This doctrine may be the more realistic because, as we have already mentioned, the peace obligation was conceived as a return for recognition of shop bargaining, and it fell down only when no agreement could be reached on a new bargaining system in 1969.

It would finally be even more realistic to take the peace obligation as a moral obligation, binding by honour. In fact, its violation was very frequent, but resort to legal action was very rare. There is a trend of thought in Italian labour law which argues that some trade union activities, including some clauses in agreements, are not necessarily to be considered as binding at law, or at least, that they may have a two-fold nature, in which the practice of resorting to remedies internal to the industrial relations system prevails over the practice of resorting to the courts.[77] In order to set aside the binding nature at law of a 'no-strike' obligation, it would, however, be necessary for a declaration of intent to be made by the parties. Alternatively, a behaviour of the parties, even after the stipulation (Art. 1362 of the Civil Code) implying clearly and unmistakably the same intent, could lead to the same conclusion.

The contents of the peace obligation and the subjects bound by it

There is no doubt that in all the countries we have taken into consideration, when, as is usual, the peace obligation is binding at law, it provides an undertaking between the contracting trade union or unions and the employers' association or the individual employer if he is the other contracting party. The trade union, however, is liable for its own behaviour, namely for infringements committed by its officials while acting on its behalf. Even though it is theoretically conceivable, there is never any guarantee concerning the behaviour of the workers themselves, for example, in the case of a wildcat strike. However, the duties imposed on the union by the agreement may vary in scope. We have already seen that in France the union is only bound by a negative obligation to do nothing which might hamper the loyal performance of the agreement. A wildcat strike would not place it under any obligation to take up a position against the strike: it would merely have to abstain from supporting it.

The point of view held by the German courts seems more extensive. In the famous Schleswig-Holstein case,[78] it was held that even preparatory acts like a referendum were a breach of contract. There is no doubt that a positive undertaking would be required to halt stoppages called in breach of contract. The union should, for instance, disown the strike, or take disciplinary action against its members who have taken part in it. A similar duty is clearly stated in the Swedish Act on Collective Agreements of 1928, Art. 4, sec. 2, which asserts

76. G. Giugni, *Diritto sindacale*, Bari, 1969, p. 108 ff.
77. G. Giugni, *Introduzione allo studio della autonomia collettiva*, Milano, 1960, p. 93 ff.
78. Decision of the BAG, 31.10.1958 in AZR (632/57).

that 'an association which is itself bound by collective agreement should be bound to endeavour to prevent its members from committing unlawful, offensive actions, or, if such actions have already been committed, to endeavour to cause such members to cease committing such actions'. Such an obligation should not be construed as a liability for the result (namely, the cessation of the illegal stoppage), but as a duty on the part of the union to do everything that can be reasonably expected of it to achieve such a result.

Although Italian legal doctrine did not pay much attention to this problem, we can take this as the most plausible solution applicable in this country as well, since most peace clauses state a duty to comply with the agreement and to get members to comply with it.

In the United States more emphasis is perhaps placed on the positive duty of the union to order strikers back to work and to take disciplinary measures against those who do not comply. In the United Kingdom, as we have seen, under the Industrial Relations Act, sec. 36(2), the union is under a duty '. . . to take all such steps as are reasonably practicable for the purposes' of preventing anyone, purporting to act for the union or any member, from taking any action contrary to an undertaking in the agreement and of securing that the action is not continued. This provision, although not very clear, is undoubtedly broad in its scope, but does not mean a guarantee of performance from the workers. We should add that sec. 96, while stating that inducement or threat to break a contract would be an unfair industrial practice, describes such a behaviour (among other items) as 'calling, organizing, procuring or financing a strike'.

In conclusion, we may say that on this point comparison shows a rather uniform legal setup, with France in the most cautious position as regards the nature of the precise duties implied in the statutory peace obligation.

If the peace obligation were taken as binding only for the contracting party, it could not have an effect on the contract of employment. This doctrine has been predominant in Germany, where, as we have seen (see above, p. 132) the peace obligation was construed from the very beginning as a return for the obligation to comply and to get member employers to comply. It should be noted, however, that this doctrine was integrated with the doctrine of the third beneficiary. In the case of the peace obligation, the third beneficiary would be the employer who then had the right to exact compliance from the contracting union. For this reason, the employer was in a position to sue the union, but still not able to take any action against employees because the 'no-strike' clause would be detrimental to them, and their willingness to accept it would have to be expressed. The gap was in fact filled by the Labour Courts, by stating, through the doctrine of Social Adequacy, that individual workers were liable in tort. The employer, however, would not be bound to comply with the benefits *vis-à-vis* the individual employees. Such a paradox was challenged by Professor Ramm[79] who proposed to apply the agency doctrine to the employers' association.

79. T. Ramm, *Die Parteien des Tarifvertrags,* p. 84 ff.

The situation is quite different in Sweden, where a combined theory is laid down by law (Statute of 1928, Art. 2) meaning that the collective agreement is also binding both for collective parties and for members of employers' associations, and trade unions.

Thus the individual union member is bound himself by the peace obligation. According to Professor Schmidt[80] this rule was consciously aimed at by the legislature, wishing to favour the unions through binding their members to the obligations undertaken by the unions themselves.

The theory of agency, which makes the collective agreement binding for individual employers and employees, has practically always been followed in Italy, but since the 1960s the legal doctrine has resumed the old distinction, received by Germany as far back as the 1900s, between the obligatory and the normative part of the agreement.[81] If this distinction is taken rigidly, the peace obligation would remain outside the scope of the contract of employment.[82] There is a large amount of uncertainty on this point. In fact, such a distinction should not prevent specific clauses of the obligatory part of the agreement from having an ambivalent effect, as we have seen in Swedish legislation. It is interesting to note that the few court decisions on this subject matter are all on disputes between the employer and an individual worker. Actions for damages against unions were often brought, but always withdrawn.

In fact, in our specific case the adherence to this rigid division of the collective contract draws a fair amount of support from a consideration of the intention of the parties. This seems to have been in the sense of imposing an obligation only on the unions in return for certain benefits such as the recognition of shop bargaining, which can only have an indirect impact on the contract of employment.

Furthermore, the wording of the agreement is usually in the sense of an obligation imposed upon the collective parties.[83] The Corte di Cassazione[84] recently upheld the legitimacy of a 'no-strike' clause and its binding effect upon the individual workers, although, in the specific case, the wording of the agreement was probably far from being aimed at such an effect.

80. F. Schmidt, *The Law of Labor Relations in Sweden*, p. 112.
81. See O. Kahn Freund, Introduction to *Labour Relations and the Law*, London, 1965, p. 1 ff.
82. This is the main argument of Ghezzi, *Autonomia collettiva*, idem., p. 152 ff. It is worth mentioning that the Constitutional Court always applied this distinction when it had to decide over questions arising from the 1959 Act on minimum labour standards. The Act gave all existing collective agreements a general binding effect, as they were law, but the Constitutional Court restricted this effect to the 'normative' part. Considering the 'no-strike' clause, in fact its extention to associations not parties to the collective agreement and to their members would have been unquestionably unconstitutional. Such a question did not, however, come before the Court. See G. Giugni, in *Labor Courts and Grievance Settlement in Western Europe*, p. 303.
83. Thus in the case of the metal-mechanical industry, which was the most important.
84. Decision of 1971, mentioned above, p. 152, n. 72. On the case, where the existence itself of a peace obligation was doubtful, see the discussion in *L'esercizio del diritto di sciopero*, idem., p. 47 ff. The text of the alleged 'no-strike' clause was the following: 'The stipulating agents of the workers (the unions) acknowledge that with the present agreement claims advanced by employees . . . are fully satisfied.' The agreement covered the Pirelli Company.

In spite of the constitutional recognition of the right to strike, French law does not exclude the liability of the individual employees. Even though the theory of agency seems to be on its way out, and seems to have been abandoned in favour of the normative theory, the 'no-strike' clause is recognized (unlike the situation in Germany) as having a binding normative effect. However, the courts (p. 151, n. 68), strictly follow the civil rule of liability for fault made on the distinction between strikers who are conscious of committing a breach of contract and mere participants, to whom malice of aforethought could not be imputed.

The case of the United Kingdom seems to be rather different. Before the 1971 Act, given that suspension doctrine had been rejected,[85] and given that the union is commonly agreed not to bargain as the agent of its members,[86] the breach of a 'no-strike' clause would have had the same effect. It should be pointed out that it was recognized during the *Rookes* v. *Barnard* case that the employer, in order not to lose his labour force, usually did not terminate employment contracts, as he has the power to do. In other words, it was up to the employer to draw consequences from the breach of contract *vis-à-vis* his employees. On the other hand, such a situation may be assumed as typical for all countries, mainly when their economies operate at full employment.

At any rate, the matter of whether or not a 'no-strike' clause may be binding as an implied term or even as an expressly incorporated term of the contract of employment depends also on the wording of the clause. The example quoted by Professor Wedderburn[87] of the clause which came from the famous *Rookes* v. *Barnard* case contained the following wording: 'The employers and the employees undertake that no lockout or strike shall take place.' A clause with different words might be less appropriate for incorporation into an individual employment contract. The issue of whether incorporation into the contract of employment takes place or not, although it may have been of no importance as regards the consequences to the individual strikers, since the *Rookes* v. *Barnard* case had become much more important. On that occasion a *threat* to induce workers to breach the contract of employment was deemed actionable in tort, in spite of the immunity granted by the 1906 Act for *inducement* to some person to break a contract of employment. As is well known, after the final decision of the case, an Act was passed in 1965 which removed any liability in disputes based on an alleged threat to breach a contract of employment.

Under the 1971 Act, if due notice is given – and this is the notice laid down in case of termination of employment – strike action will not be construed as a breach or a termination of the contract although protection against dismissal is rather restricted (sec. 26(2)). Section 147 appears, anyhow, to partially embrace the doctrine of suspension.[88]

Now, the issue of the incorporation of the 'no-strike' clause really becomes

85. See K. W. Wedderburn, *The Worker and the Law*, p. 109.
86. See ibid., p. 185.
87. See ibid., p. 195.
88. See Chapter 4, p. 201.

a basic one in so far as a strike does no longer break the contract of employment, but this may be an independent effect stemming from the incorporation of the 'no-strike' pledge into the contract of employment. According to sec. 20(2)(*b*) and (*c*) the employer is required to communicate in writing (see Contracts of Employment Act 1963) details of the procedure for redressing any grievance.[89] The written communication would provide strong evidence that, if a peace obligation is part of a procedure agreement, it is incorporated with the latter into the contract of employment.

Section 147(3) is very clear as to the consequences of a violation of a peace obligation. It states that what we have just identified as an acceptance of the doctrine of suspension would not apply if the action undertaken by the employee were '. . . contrary to a term of his contract of employment (including any term implied or incorporated in that contract by reference to a collective agreement) excluding or restricting his right to take part in a strike.' Moreover, if *inducement* to break the contract of employment came from a non-registered organization or from any other person, it will be an unfair industrial practice (sec. 96).

It appears, however, that the impact of the 'no-strike' pledge on the individual contract of employment could still be avoided, either by wording the peace obligation in such a way that it would not be construed as placing any obligation on individual workers or by stating in the individual contracts of employment that it is not binding. Inclusion of the procedural agreement through the written statement of the terms of employment could not, however, be avoided (sec. 20(2)(*b*) and (*c*)), nor could the resort to use of the procedure as laid down in sec. 37 and following sections. The above could, as we have seen, result in a peace obligation being written into the collective agreement, but even in this case it would not be certain that the peace obligation was binding for the union and/or the employees; this would depend once more on the wording of the clause concerned. The Act seems to have bypassed all uncertainties as to whether procedural rules might be incorporated into an individual contract, a question which arose mainly in relation to the Terms and Conditions of Employment Act of 1959.[90] In the British Law, the distinction between obligatory and normative parts of collective contracts may be useful for the purpose of classification, but not at all for the purpose of legal construction.

As we have seen, in the United States, sec. 8(d) of the NLRA prohibited industrial action in support of proposals to terminate or modify a collective agreement before its expiration. In addition, the great majority of agreements contain a 'no-strike' obligation which is almost invariably related to an arbitration procedure. The liability of the unions is clearly stated in sec. 301, which was introduced in 1947. It states that any labour organization which represents employees in an industry affecting interstate commerce may sue,

89. We shall remember that, according to the Contract of Employment Act 1963, an employer is required to give to his employees a written statement containing particulars of their terms of employment. The 1971 Act requires this statement to regard also the procedures for grievances.
90. See K. W. Wedderburn, *The Worker and the Law*, pp. 196–203.

or may be sued as an entity and on behalf of the employees for violation of collective contracts. It adds that any money judgment against the labour organization is enforceable only against the organization as an entity. This being the case, there seems to be little doubt that a breach of contract or a breach of the 'no-strike' obligation brings about consequences on the labour unions themselves, both in the specific case under sec. 8(d) (which can also be prosecuted as an unfair labour practice) and in the other cases as well.

The various remedies will be pointed out further on. We have to mention here, nevertheless, that under sec. 8(d) it is stated that an individual employee who takes part in a strike within the period of 60 days after notice of termination or modification shall lose his status as an employee. This is specified with reference to the sections of the Act which are aimed at protecting him from unfair labour practices, at preserving his right to vote during the strike, and at giving him the right to be reinstated after the strike is over, unless the job has been permanently refilled (see p. 145).

There was considerable debate during the 1930s as to the nature of the collective contract and its effects on the employment relation, and as a result of the lack of any specific legal regulation, doctrines which were well known in Europe at the time, such as the doctrine of agency or of the third beneficiary, were tested in the United States.[91] This debate seems to have vanished over the years as a result of the establishment of the consolidated opinion that the union is acting in bargaining as principal, not as agent,[92] and that the collective agreement has a normative force.

Furthermore, the rapid spread of arbitration procedures over grievances has practically deprived the debate as to the nature of the collective contract at Common Law of any meaning, since, in practical terms, a separate jurisdiction was set up, and the big issue which came before ordinary courts concerned the legal effect of arbitration clauses or awards and not one of the substantive rules of the agreements. Therefore, the issue of whether or not an employer could take action against his individual employees over the violation of a 'no-strike' clause has been diverted mainly to industrial jurisprudence.

There seems to be no doubt that strikes in violation of a statutory or of a contractual 'no-strike' undertaking would be an 'unprotected' activity under secs. 7 and 8(a) of the NLRA. The employer could react against the employee by discharging him, or by taking disciplinary action. Arbitration awards show a clear-cut orientation in this sense.[93] As for damages, courts are oriented to assume that sec. 301, which provides for action against unions, is also an exclusive remedy.[94] It is worth mentioning, furthermore, that an arbitration agreement might be broad enough to permit the umpire himself the assessment of damages.

---

91. See A. Lenhoff, 'The Present Status of Collective Contracts in the American Legal System', 39 *Michigan Law Review* 1109 (1941).
92. The leading US case in this sense is *J. I. Case Co.* v. *NLRB*, 321 US 332 (1944).
93. W. Gould, 'The Status of Unauthorized and "Wildcat" Strikes Under the National Labor Relations Act', 52 *Cornell Law Quarterly* 672, 702 (1967).
94. See *Local 174, Teamsters* v. *Lucas Flour Co.*, 369 US 95 (1962).

Legal remedies

In dealing with legal remedies for the violation of a 'no-strike' agreement, or, more generally, of self-imposed rules aimed at limiting the resort to strike, or at laying down rules for its exercise, we shall start with the Civil Law countries, including among them, at least in this respect, Sweden.

Speaking of the Civil Law countries we shall first consider those which have based their doctrine exclusively on contractual liability. The most accurate analysis of the consequences of violation of a contractual liability has perhaps been given by the Italian legal writers, in spite of the very poor number of decisions on the matter. Unions, although not incorporated, may be held responsible, together with their own assets, in a several obligation with their agents (Art. 37, Italian Civil Code). Action can be initiated by the employers' association, or by the individual employer as a member of the association, according to the principles of agency. An action from the former would be really unthinkable since an employers' association as such does not suffer any economic loss from a breach of contract of this sort. It might, however, if the violation is of major importance (Art. 1453 Civil Code), demand the termination of the agreement. Such a remedy might have been frequently resorted to when strikes at the shop level tended to assume a generalized character. But the remedy as such – and thus it will appear in the other countries as well – would usually boomerang, bringing about an even greater generalization of the struggle. Action on the part of the employer against the union for damages was thought to lead to poor results because of the low assets of the Italian unions. As a matter of fact, within a few years such assets have improved, because of the adoption of check-off devices. But if we take the doctrine which links the peace obligation to specific obligations binding the associations or the employers *vis-à-vis* the union itself, other remedies can be thought of, in terms of a partial lifting of obligations on the side of the employers; such would be a refusal to the full course of supplementary negotiations in multi-level agreements, or, as has actually been threatened on various occasions in the past, a suspension of the check-off service.

As far as the individual employee is concerned, he cannot be held responsible for a breach of the collective agreement, but rather for a breach of the incorporated terms in his own contract of employment, provided that the incorporation of the 'no-strike' pledge took place, which we deem hardly tenable. In this case, anyhow, action for damages would be possible, but since the essence of the right to strike is to give immunity from non-performance of work if the worker was held to have temporarily forfeited his right to strike, responsibility for non-compliance would be resumed. Absence from work, if it is considerable, can be disciplined or provide grounds for dismissal.[95]

We must remember, however, that collective agreements are binding only

95. *Law*, 15 July 1966, n. 604, makes a distinction between 'considerable non-compliance' as grounds for dismissal with notice, and the traditional concept of a 'just cause', more or less corresponding with the 'faute lourde' of the French law which provides grounds for dismissal without notice.

for members of both organizations. In fact, they are always applied to all workers depending on an employer bound by the agreement. Many doubts may arise as regards the 'no-strike' clause. If the 'outsider' worker benefits from the agreement, it might appear as an effect of the third beneficiary principle. This would not affect the peace obligation because of its detrimental character. But it is also argued that acceptance of benefits, even though not express, would imply acceptance and incorporation into his contract of employment of all the clauses of the collective agreement. In the latter case, the individual worker might be held responsible.

However, as we have already noticed (see p. 155) the liability of the individual worker is itself hotly debated and hardly tenable in spite of the contrary opinion of the only decision of the highest court.

French law moves on similar ground even though the implications drawn by authors and courts may be slightly different. There is no doubt that the union would be liable both to the employers' association and the individual employer,[96] but an action, apart from the small amount of union assets, also meets with a practical difficulty from the rule which partially prevents such assets from being distrained.[97] Specific performance, in a way not dissimilar to an injunction, would be admissible, but the sanction of *astreinte* (a judicial penalty) is usually deprived of practical effect.[98] Furthermore, suspension or termination of the undertakings of the other parties may be thought of, provided that, like in Italian law, the violation is remarkable enough.

As for the individual employee, his liability seems to be unquestioned as regards express 'no-strike' clauses. On the contrary, the obligation under Art. 31(q) of the Labour Code only concerns unions. The statute on collective agreements of 1950 gave official recognition to the doctrine of suspension which had been worked out long before then, by stating that 'a strike does not terminate a contract of employment except in the case of malice or serious misconduct (*faute lourde*)' (Art. 4). A strike in violation of contractual limitations would fall under the domain of this exception, and, furthermore, it would allow the employer to bring an action for damages. But what exactly is *faute lourde*? As we saw before, it would be based upon a subjective state of consciousness of the illegality of the action. Moreover, recent decisions, even though they do not concern our specific problem, have admitted that in the instance of an unlawful, but short, strike, *faute lourde* is not necessarily implied. If a serious breach is out of the question, however, disciplinary action can be taken, according to court decisions.[99] This opinion is criticized by Professor Sinay[100] on the grounds that the above mentioned Art. 4 only considers the *faute lourde*, which causes a disconnection of the contract, or, better still, as Professor Durand argued, it lays grounds for a dismissal for just cause.

96. See p. 151, n. 68.
97. Despax, *Conventions Collectives*, op. cit., p. 275. Code du Travail, III livre, Art. 13. Assets which cannot be distrained are estates, furnitures, libraries.
98. ibid., p. 82.
99. See Chapter 4, p. 218.
100. H. Sinay, 'Le droit de grève', op. cit., p. 303.

The reported opinion seems scarcely tenable because the *faute lourde*, under Art. 4, is related to the continuation of the employment relation. This does not mean that the employee who participates in illegal strikes of short duration, provided employment continues, cannot be submitted to minor disciplinary sanctions. It may be that the construction of Italian legal commentators (see p. 151) of the right to strike as an immunity from liability for non-compliance succeeds better in pointing out the consequences of an unlawful action not covered by the right to strike.[101]

In Sweden the liability may rest both with the association and the employees, the employee's liability being limited to 200 Crowns. This limit, which goes as far back as 1928, is equivalent to approximately two days' pay and it is therefore considered to be rather too low nowadays. However, when drafting the 1928 Act, the legislator realized that economic damages could either be too high for a trade union or for a worker, or, on the other hand, too low to give satisfaction to the wronged party and effectively penalize the guilty one.

For this reason it was established that the amount of damages could be reduced according to the circumstances, including the degree of culpability. In certain cases this could even extend to complete exemption from damages. But, if mitigation is something which also occurs in other countries, the provision for payment of damages 'other than those of a purely financial nature' is unique to Sweden. These are called general damages by the Labour Court, and in practice they are assessed according to the guilt of the party concerned[102] or – mainly in cases of violation of rules concerning wages, hours of work and working conditions – according to the interest of preventing the employer from continuation. General damages appear therefore more as a repressive sanction than as compensation for damages. General damages can, of course, also be granted to employers' associations. This is a very important point since, as we have seen, in the case of the violation of a peace obligation, in other countries, liability to the employers' associations was always a purely theoretical one, for they suffered no material damages.

It should also be remembered that the liability of a trade union may concur with the liability of the individual employees. In this case, if a strike was initiated by the workers and subsequently endorsed by the union, damages could be apportioned among the parties. It is a policy of the Labour Court not to assess damages against employees when an infringement is initiated by the union and the employees had acted on union orders. In case of a wildcat strike the union may be condemned for damages if it has not taken sufficient action.

There are other sanctions against unlawful actions which come under the power of the Labour Court. First, there is an injunction for the specific per-

101. Professor Sinay's (*Grève et lockout*, p. 306 ff.) assumption that non-performance of an obligation cannot be the grounds for a termination of the employment contract during a strike, because in such a case the contract is under suspension, is quite correct. But the basic issue still regards whether suspension is effective in case of an unlawful strike. On this point the opinion of this author seems rather ambiguous.
102. See F. Schmidt, *The Law of Labour Relations in Sweden*, p. 215 ff. to which we refer also for a broader description of the role of the Labour Court.

formance of an action, or for refraining from performing an action. In case of a wildcat strike, for example, a union official may be ordered to call strikers back to work. Infringement of an order of this kind brings about a penalty under general principles of Swedish law. This strongly resembles the penalty for contempt of court of the Common Law countries. The penalty imposed by the Labour Court cannot, however, consist of imprisonment, nor can the fine be converted into imprisonment. Rather frequently the Labour Court does not lay down any sanction, but in the case of non-compliance, the injured party may file subsequently a request to penalize the tortfeasor. According to a recent decision,[103] assessment of a fine cannot be attached to an order by the court that the individual worker shall return to work.

Another sanction, which in practice may be very effective, is a declaratory judgment; in many cases it would be impossible to distinguish between an injunction without an assessment of penalty and a declaratory judgment. Ultimately, we should also remember that the Collective Agreements Act, Art. 7, gives a specific application of the principle that an obligation need not be fulfilled if the other party has not fulfilled its own obligation. The Labour Court may either terminate an agreement or release the injured parties from their obligations, provided they are in some way connected with the obligation which has been violated. However, such a remedy is rarely resorted to, because the injured party can be damaged by the termination or suspension of the obligations of the other party. Assuming that the desire to take action against an employer is based on an alleged violation of his undertakings, under Art. 7 the union would in this case be released from its peace obligation, and it would regain complete freedom to take industrial action.

In conclusion we should mention that in terms of sanction against violations of collective agreements, Swedish law seems to have realized better than the others the specific nature of collective contractual relations, and at the same time it has succeeded in maintaining a favourable attitude to the weaker party. By and large in the other countries either traditional civil rules have to be enforced which do not fit into collective labour relations, or specific sanctions are enforced which show a tendency to favour the employer, or appear deceptively neutral, but nevertheless have the effect of strengthening the position of the stronger party.

The legal construction of the collective agreement in Germany, which has already been described, results in the liability for the peace obligation being limited to the union. Action may be taken also against the union by an individual employer according to the third beneficiary doctrine. In fact very few actions have been brought against unions. The most important was the one relating to the strike balloting called in the metal industry in Schleswig-Holstein in 1956. This case gave rise to much debate. In 1958 the Federal Labour Court judged the employer to be in the right,[104] but a claim was filed by the union with the Federal Constitutional Court. However, before a de-

103. AD 1970 no. 9.
104. See p. 153, n. 78.

cision was taken on the claim, a settlement was reached, and the long-lasting controversy was ended.

The resort to the doctrine of torts, with the application of paragraph 826 of the Civil Code (BGB), largely made by court law, is typical and unique of German law.[105] By implementing tort actions, an employer was enabled to take action against individual employees as well. The foundation of this doctrine is the *Soziale adäquanz* theory which we have already mentioned, but on our issue the courts did not hold a uniform position, and so far we have three cases on the one side and three cases on the other. When an action based upon *Soziale adäquanz* doctrine was brought, it was on the basis that a peace obligation, although it cannot be considered a breach of contract, as the employee is not a party to the collective agreement, is, however, a violation of a constitutional right of enterprise, derived from Arts. 2 and 12 of the Basic Law (*Grundgesetz*), which guarantees the right of enterprise.[106] Apparently German courts were willing to fill in the gap left by the construction of the collective agreement, with its rigid separation between the obligatory and normative sections.

Furthermore it may have seemed consistent with the general application of the theory of *Soziale adäquanz* as a limitation on the right to strike, to make use of it in the case of breach of agreement, especially since actions against unions had proved a somewhat ineffective remedy. Even the use of injunction[107] against infringements of the peace obligation does not seem unusual to German lawyers, although no case is recorded.

The prevailing opinion in Germany is that the existence of legal procedures would not remove the 'no-strike' obligation from the union, even in the event of non-compliance on the side of the employer or employers' association. It is only among lawyers that the doctrine of *Kollektives Zurückbehaltungsrecht* – collective withdrawal – was worked out[108] in order to show that this kind of stoppage was not a strike, but rather a refusal to perform on the grounds that the other party was not itself performing. Termination of the collective agreement because of non-compliance of one of the parties would also be possible, according to general principles, which we find applied, although in different ways, in all of the countries under survey. We should remember, however, that 'parties' to a peace obligation are in Germany only the collective ones. Therefore, a single employer could not resort to this remedy, and only a violation concerning the generality of workers covered by the agreement could allow the employers to take action, through their association, for termination of the agreement.

In the United Kingdom the problem of legal remedies is rather complex. The liability of the trade unions was excluded by the old law both as a con-

---

105. See Chapter 5, p. 268.
106. See Chapter 5, p. 267 ff. The author warns that such arguments may just be found as *obiter dicta* in a few decisions of the Federal Labour Court. The reported opinion is taken for granted by Hueck–Nipperdey, op. cit., p. 995, who mentions a rich bibliography.
107. Chapter 5, p. 315.
108. Chapter 5, p. 295.

tractual liability (sec. 4(4)) of the 1871 Act, provided that the parties to the agreement were 'trade unions', that is to say labour unions and in some cases, employers' associations,[109] and as a tortious liability (1906, sec. 4). The liability of individuals – like union officials – however, remained, although they received a certain protection for actions committed in furtherance of labour disputes.

The Industrial Relations Act openly states that, if the parties have not stated their intention for the contract not to be legally enforceable (see p. 149), a breach of a collective agreement would be an unfair industrial practice.[110] We should remember that the parties are obliged to 'take all such steps as are reasonably practicable' in order to prevent members and others from taking such action (sec. 36(1) and (2)). Section 96 goes further, and profiting from the experience of the case law of the 1960s it defines that 'any person, in contemplation or furtherance of an industrial dispute, who knowingly *induces* or *threatens* to induce another person to break a contract to which that other person is a party',* is committing an unfair industrial practice. However, immunity is given to registered trade unions or employers' associations, their officials and other agents. We should add that by 'contract' this section does not mean a collective agreement, but means any other contract, including a contract of employment. The latter, however, may incorporate clauses from a collective agreement, perhaps including a 'no-strike' clause – or a procedural clause. Liability for torts in the High Court (sec. 132) for inducement and threats of a breach of contract in contemplation or furtherance of an industrial dispute is still excluded. So it is in industrial disputes for '. . . interference with the trade, business or employment of another person, or with the right of another person to dispose of his capital or his labour as he wills.' Such a tortious liability may exist only in the case of inducement to break a peace obligation for some purpose other than industrial disputes.

It should be added that the old immunity under the 1906 Act for trade unions is not provided for under sec. 36 even for registered trade unions. Thus a breach of the agreement – unlike inducement to break a contract of employment – would make the union fully liable. It would have been strange if immunity were provided for, as the Act is aimed chiefly at imposing a legal responsibility for breach of agreements.

The Act also provides two other remedies. The first (sec. 41) is that the Industrial Court may impose a peace obligation where procedural agreements are non-existent or defective. This has already been analysed (see p. 150) as legal source for the peace obligation. Secondly, when a complaint of an alleged violation is submitted to the Industrial Court, it may grant the following remedies (sec. 101):

(*a*) a declaratory order;

* Author's italics.
109. See K. W. Wedderburn, *The Worker and the Law*, p. 179.
110. A breach is, however, subject only to a declaratory order if it is of an agreement made between a union and employers' association before the repeal of the 1871 Trade Union Act (sec. 105(6)).

(b) an award of compensation – but the compensation awarded against a registered trade union is limited to an amount related to its membership, which ranges between £5,000 to £100,000 (sec. 117(2)).

No limit is provided for in respect of unregistered organizations. It is also worth remembering that even the maximum limits apply only to each separate complaint, while one action may include many complaints of unfair industrial practices;

(c) an order to refrain from continuing to take action, namely an injunction.

We now come to the liability of individuals. Under the old law which held that a strike brought about a breach of the contract of employment, participation in a strike in violation of a 'no-strike' obligation could, besides causing loss of work, bring about an action for damages. The courts in fact limited damages[111] to the amount corresponding not with the loss of production, but with the production of the individual worker involved, or with the cost of his replacement. The Industrial Relations Act, sec. 147, seems to embrace the theory of suspension,[112] at least on the condition that due notice must be given by the worker or on his behalf, due notice being read as the notice required for termination of employment, and provided, of course, that no binding 'no-strike' obligation is broken. Liability for tort, as pointed out by the much debated courts' policies during the 1960s, would, on the contrary, have much larger scope, covering all the damages suffered by the other party, but the Industrial Relations Act, as we have just seen, has considerably restricted the scope of this liability. As regards the right of the injured party to refuse performance of its obligation, this is a remedy never resorted to by an employer, because it would merely succeed in enlarging the scope of the conflict.

On the contrary, the effectiveness of a lifting of the 'no-strike' obligation might become very relevant if the claim for the *status quo* clause, recently put forward by the unions, would be accepted. Under such a clause, management would have to consult with the union before making any change in working conditions. If the employer does not honour such obligation the union would be released from the peace obligation under ordinary principles of the law of contracts.

It is interesting to note that the frequent violation of the peace obligation in Italy and its present rejection are based on the assumption of continually changing conditions of work on the initiative of the employer, so that, according to the argument of the unions, any peace obligation would operate under the assumption of the *status quo*. Such as assumption, which renders the peace obligation almost useless, goes far beyond the present claim of British labour. On the contrary, the German doctrine of 'collective withdrawal' (p. 163) although rooted in similar principles, has narrower scope, in so far as it would only regard violations on the side of the employer, not changes in work conditions which fall under the managerial prerogatives.

The recent legislation in the United Kingdom, as is well-known, was at

111. See *NCB* v. *Galley* (1958) 1 W L R 16.
112. See Chapter 4, p. 201.

least partially inspired by the American LMRA. Thus, the idea itself of unfair industrial practices strongly corresponds with the well-experienced notion
of unfair labour practices in the United States. Unlike Great Britain, however, American statutory law is much more restrictive. In the case foreseen
by sec. 8(d) of the NLRA, the employer is relieved of any liability relating to
his duty to bargain and the union may be prosecuted for unfair labour
practice. If an employee loses his status during a labour dispute, he will have to
bear the consequences mentioned above, practically a termination of the employment relation (see p. 158).

This is not, however, the main feature of the American law. A strike against
a statutory (sec. 8(d)(4)) or a contractual 'no-strike' obligation, would expose
the union to liability for breach of contract (sec. 301), and the employer would
be able to sue the union for damages. The union must take responsibility for
the acts of its agents, but an order to pay damages is only enforceable against
the organization as an entity and against its assets. Jurisdiction rests with the
ordinary courts.

The most important issue is again, however, the one of resort to injunction.[113] In the case of a strike in violation of a peace obligation, such a
remedy, the effect of which goes far beyond that of an award of damages,
should not be used according to the specific prohibition provided for in sec. 4
of the Norris-La Guardia Act 1932. Given that a strike is illegal when it
breaks a 'no-strike' pledge, we have also seen that a general 'no-strike' clause,
or at least an extension of it, can be inferred by the mere existence of an arbitration procedure.[114]

The limitation on industrial action is therefore considerably extended and,
provided that the agreement has an arbitration clause, as is generally the case,
any strike for 'economic reasons' might fall under the policies of the court, as
laid down in the Lincoln Mills case,[115] to enjoin the union to arbitrate the
dispute.

But all this does not yet mean that a strike is enjoinable in itself. Even
though the Norris-La Guardia Act banned the use of injunctions by Federal
courts, the state courts used to grant injunctions under the above-mentioned
circumstances, bringing about an unbalanced distribution of power between
the state and Federal jurisdictions. The situation became even more intriguing since the unions, according to the American rules of procedure,
were able to remove cases to the Federal Court. The most recent decision of
the US Supreme Court[116] was reached by a divided vote and it reversed an
earlier decision which had endorsed the doctrine that an injunction could not
be issued in the case of a breach of a 'no-strike' clause in order to terminate a
stoppage.[117]

The Boys Market decision made the point 'that the unavailability of equitable relief in the arbitration context present, a serious impediment to the

113. See the extensive treatment of this sanction in Chapter 5, p. 315.
114. See *Local 174, Teamsters* v. *Lucas Flour Co.*, 369 US 95 (1962).
115. *Textile Workers* v. *Lincoln Mills*, 353 US 448 (1957).
116. See *Boys Market Inc.* v. *Retail Clerks, Local 770*, 398 US 235 (1970).
117. See *Sinclair Refining Co.* v. *Atkinson*, 370 US 195 (1962).

congressional policy favouring the voluntary establishment for the mechanism for the peaceful resolution of labor disputes'.

Consistent with this statement of policy, the decision made a strike in breach of the peace obligation enjoinable. Violation of an injunction would be punishable by contempt of court which may even lead to imprisonment. In fact, the courts show a marked preference for fines, as imprisonment tends to make martyrs of the union officials and also to embitter the dispute.

A dispute over the right of the union to strike may also be decided by declaratory judgment, a kind of judgment which is provided for by a statute (Federal Declaratory Judgment Act).

As regards the individual employees, as we have seen (p. 158) the power of the employer to take disciplinary action or to discharge them seems to be unquestionable. Discharge will be frequent even in the case of a short strike, because the ground of it is the participation to the strike in itself, not, as e.g., it is for Italy, the absence from work no longer covered by the immunity deriving from the legitimate exercise of the right to strike.

Finally, the effect of a peace obligation can be suspended by the illegal behaviour of the other party. In the United States, a strike against an employer's unfair labour practice was not deemed to be illegal by the leading decision in Mastro Plastics.[118] There are, however, contracts which expressly provide for 'no-strike' pledges to be lifted in the case of violation on the other side, especially in the case of non-compliance with the grievance procedure.[119]

Conclusions

The issue of the peace obligation, or, more generally, of the contractual limitations on industrial action, but primarily on the right to strike, cannot be singled out of the general context of industrial relations in which it appears. That is to say, the peace obligation is first of all a political problem, and thus may affect either the attitude of the State or of the two parties at the bargaining process, or of all of them.

Such a peace obligation – or 'no-strike' agreement – in fact, would always require the existence of an agreement between the parties. But its source may be the common intention of the parties, either express or implied, or may be a public policy, laid down by statute or by judge-made law. This happens when the peace obligation has a mandatory effect in any collective agreement, no matter what the intention of the parties will be, or even when their intention is to the contrary.

Such a compulsory peace duty exists in almost all of the countries under consideration, although with very diversified features. Italy, almost, is the only exception, although France runs very near to it. The 1928 Act on collective agreements in Sweden; sec. 8(d) of the NLRA in the USA; Art.

118. See *Mastro Plastics Corp.* v. *NLRB*, 350 US 270 (1956).
119. See some examples in C. W. Summers and H. H. Wellington, *Labor Law*, Foundation Press, New York, 1968.

31(q) of the 1950 Act on collective agreements in France; an old-established legal construction of the collective contract in Germany: all of these are sources of the peace obligation which stand above the intention of the parties, and sometimes may run against it. In Sweden and in the USA, the statutory peace obligation is unwaivable, as a principle of public policy, and the same rule applies in Germany, under judge-made law. In the United Kingdom the 1971 Act does not flatly provide for a compulsory peace obligation, but the Industrial Court is empowered, after an intricate procedure, to write it into the agreements.

Experience shows that this principle of public policy was almost always laid down with restrictive purposes towards industrial action, and, generally, against a strong opposition by labour unions. The only exception might seem to be Germany, where the doctrine of the peace obligation as a necessary element of the collective agreement was worked out amongst legal commentators, who were mainly socialist. But it is worth mentioning that the unions opposed the insertion of this principle into the statutes on collective bargaining, perhaps in order to keep the door open to possible changes either in legal thinking or in industrial practice. The provision of the French Labour Code, finally, is so limited in scope and in its actual possibilities of implementation, that it has appeared almost irrelevant for the labour unions and did not arouse strong opposition.

The peace obligation may thus be a result of action taken by the Government which is hostile to labour. It is a limitation upon industrial action, similar to other limitations. However, such a limitation may come to be either accepted or tolerated by the unions, in so far as they come to share with the Government an ideal of 'social peace'. Sweden and Germany seem to be the best example. For Sweden one must not overlook the fact that the 1928 Act included the lockout within the scope of the peace obligation, and that lockout in that country is still a weapon of some importance in the conduct of industrial relations.

This attitude by unions may also be due to the fact that 'no-strike' obligations are often, in many countries, voluntarily entered into. In the USA, for example, the 'no-strike' pledge has gone far beyond the scope of sec. 8(d), which regards only action to modify or terminate an agreement, and tends to cover the whole area of grievances. In the UK, clauses of this kind have been rather frequent, although they were not binding at law but, with a few exceptions, only by honour. They have been frequent mostly in procedural agreements. In Italy in the 1960s the 'truce clause' flourished, without any pressure by the Government.

The underlying political motivation may be different: when connected to a procedural clause the temporary suspension of industrial action is an expression of confidence in negotiation and in reciprocal goodwill. This is the case of the UK. In other countries, the peace obligation may be conceived merely as a return for some concession, and its binding force as a contract derives from its function as a *quid pro quo*. Such has been the grievance arbitration process in the USA, the recognition of collective bargaining and union representation at the shop level in Italy during the 1960s. The *quid pro quo* function is a very important basis for the construction of the intention of the parties, but additionally it has a special meaning in terms of countervailing bargaining powers. In so far as a 'no-strike' obligation is not mandatory, a union can use it as a price for concessions. This means that when such an obligation becomes mandatory, the unions come to lose some of their bargaining power. It would not be contradictory for them, therefore, to fight against a statutory peace obligation, and, in the meantime, to make use of the latter at a return to the bargaining table.

But the attitude of trade unions may happen to be openly hostile to the idea itself of a temporary waiver of the right to strike. This attitude prevails among French unions, and, after the big strikes of 1969, which have deeply changed the system of industrial relations in Italy (provided that a 'system' still exists), it has become a widespread policy of the unions in Italy, so that the peace obligation tends to disappear from collective agreements. Such an opposition has a strong ideological background: a 'no-strike' clause appears to be a surrender towards the class enemy. But there is also an unexpressed reason for this attitude, namely the inability of the unions to get their members and, moreover, the workers who are not members, to comply with the undertaking of making no resort to industrial action. It has already been remarked how in France and in Italy it is the individual worker, not the union, who owns the right to strike. Furthermore, the right to strike in these countries is expressly protected by the Constitution, so that even a temporary waiver, even if offered in return for consistent advantages, according to some legal opinions, might be unlawful, for constitutional rights are unwaivable.

These different attitudes, which underlie a different value system, may even appear from the semantics. The expression 'peace' obligation comes from Germany, and it bears some flavour of an idea of cooperation between labour and capital, at least in the effort to minimize the industrial conflict. The strike as *ultima ratio* has become in that country an entrenched principle both for courts and for the majority of unions. Instead, the mere reference to a 'no-strike' pledge shows a realistic and empirical approach to the issue. The use of the term 'truce clause', rather common in Italy and in France, is consistent with the tenets of the class struggle where you may have truce or armistice, but never *peace*. And, as a matter of fact, since the 'peace' is temporary, the use of the word itself is rather misleading in all cases.

The 'peace' obligation can therefore be based upon a legal effect of the collective agreement, or find its proper source in the intention of the parties. There is a widespread opinion, however, that any agreement should take along with it a waiver of industrial action. This opinion is based upon the assumption, as old as the law is, that *pacta sunt servanda* (agreements have to be complied with). This is a rough oversimplification and generalization. What has to be found out in any specific case is what kind of an agreement has to be complied with. And, if in Germany legal thinkers connect the peace obligation to the concession offered by the other party as a return or a *quid pro quo*, this is not exactly what French or Italian legal commentators have assumed, at least in majority. A collective contract may be a one-sided contract, with obligations only from the employers' side – or, if we want to find out what is the return or the *quid pro quo*, we may assume that a contract is entered into in order to bring to an end a conflict, but not in order to get a guarantee that other conflicts will not occur until the expiration. This is probably the best interpretation of the intention of the parties in the settlement of the conflicts of 1969 in Italy, when the 'no-strike' clause was practically abandoned.

The coverage of the 'no-strike' obligation is not uniform, and to a remarkable extent, diversities depend upon socio-political factors.

A basic classification, worked out in Germany, and largely adopted in the other countries, is the one based upon the distinction between relative and absolute peace obligation. The relative obligation covers only the matters settled in an agreement, the absolute one is aimed at banning all forms of industrial self-help for the duration of an agreement. Comparison shows that almost invariably the peace obligation, when provided for by a substantive agreement, will cover only the matters settled by it. An absolute peace obligation, in the sense of a temporary ban of all industrial actions, is usually found in procedural agreements. This is classified as an absolute peace obligation, since it covers any possible action, without a reference to settled or unsettled questions. But, at this point, it is suggested that the classification itself is misleading, in so far as procedural agreements, or procedural provisions with an attached 'no-strike' clause, are concerned. They are indeed a *tertium genus*, which aligns itself beside the relative and the absolute peace obligations. The procedural peace obligation does not ban industrial action, rather it provides for previous steps to be undertaken, before industrial action is resorted to. We have to emphasize the importance of such clauses: they are most frequent in the UK, they are widely spread in Germany, and not unknown either in Italy or in France.

The relative peace obligation, however, is the most frequent one, and, of course, the one which raises most issues. The majority of them regard what has to be meant by 'settled' questions, covered by the peace obligation. We can first mention the matters which are usually not covered by this obligation. They are usually matters which are external to the agreement itself. I mention the strikes against employers' unfair labour practices, deemed legal by the US Supreme Court (unless expressly waived by the agreement itself) which, with the American legal jargon, are identified as 'non economic' disputes. From this assumption in many countries it is inferred that sympathetic or even political strikes are no breach to a 'no-strike' pledge. We find, here and there, unusual exceptions in some company agreements in France, where the strike due to 'external' motivations is banned, while the one affecting labour-management relations in the particular company is subjected only to procedural requirements – although the legality of such agreements is undoubtedly questionable.

The relative peace obligation is by and large related to (*a*) modification or termination before the date of expiration of the agreement and (*b*) grievances concerning the application of the agreement itself. As far as modifications are concerned, the big issue is, of course, the one of finding out which are the settled matters, modification or termination of which is forbidden. The issue has been faced mostly by the N L R B in the U S A and in the Swedish Labour Court. In the U S A the prevailing policy of the Board is towards a very cautious and therefore restrictive interpretation of the intention of the parties. A settled matter is the one expressly provided for in the agreement, or that one which has been fully discussed by the parties and has been unmistakably waived by the claimant. Dropping a claim does not necessarily imply a waiver to it. This restrictive interpretation coexists with the opposite extensive policy of the US Supreme Court as regards the coverage of a 'no-strike pledge' connected to an arbitration provision. If this is not a contradiction, it may be conceived as a consistent policy aimed at restricting limitations upon industrial autonomy, unless they are framed within autonomous machineries, as the arbitration process.

In countries where multilevel bargaining exists (e.g. industry- and company-wide) the issue arises as to whether a settled question at the higher level may be negotiated, with possible resort to industrial action at the lower level. In so far as industry-wide agreements lay down minimal standards, one could argue for the legality of an action aimed at improvements at company or shop level. This view, however, was rejected by French courts, and would also have been hardly tenable in Italy during the 1960s, when company bargaining provided for only a few specific matters. A very brief mention should be made of a problem which has recently been raised by the British trade unions, and which is one of the factors underlying the agony of the peace obligation in Italy. This is the problem of the maintenance of self-imposed restrictions *vis-à-vis* substantial changes in industrial organization on the side of management. The *status quo* clause claimed by British unions or the *rebus sic stantibus* implied clause, invoked by the Italian unions in the past years as reasons for alleged violations of the truce, are a further challenge to management prerogatives. This is a well-known issue in the U S A, widely debated, and, of course, far from being solved.

As regards strikes over grievances, the peace obligation is usually connected with a procedure of previous negotiation, which may or may not end with arbitration. In the latter case the resort to action is thoroughly banned, unless specific exception is made by the parties; otherwise, the prohibition is just a temporary one. In countries where the distinction between disputes over interests and disputes over rights is well entrenched – and this is not the case in Great Britain, for example – a 'no-strike' pledge covering grievances over rights may be useless, in so far as resort to industrial action on such matters is *per se* forbidden. This is the case in Germany, where such strikes would fall under the *Soziale Adäquänz* doctrine. Nor is it the case either in Italy or France, where at least the prevailing opinion would uphold the legitimacy of such strikes, providing no contrary obligation was undertaken by the parties. In fact, 'no-strike' clauses related to grievance procedures are not infrequent, mostly so in Italy.

The peace obligation regards, from a broad point of view, all means of industrial action or of self-help. It may have a bilateral character, when it regards employers as well as unions or employees. However, a waiver to lock-out by the employers, probably with the only exception of Sweden, is practically meaningless, either because the lockout is *per se* unlawful (as in Italy), or because it is used only as a defensive weapon, and, as such, in most cases does not fall under the scope of the peace obligation: this may be the case in Germany. But, if we focus our attention on the strike and on the 'no-strike' pledge, we still have to tackle debatable issues, the most important of which is whether by strike we mean just the stoppage of work or the preparatory and instrumental actions as well, like the strike ballot or the workers' meeting or propaganda finally or picketing itself. The long-debated case of the strike ballot in mechanical plants of Schleswig-Holstein is a good example. The Federal Labour Court deemed that a strike ballot held before the expiration of an agreement is a breach of peace in itself. Under sec. 96 of the British Act of 1971 we find inducement to breach contracts of employment, and in other sections 'calling, organizing, procuring or financing a strike' which may be of significance. We may also reverse the terms of the issue, and wonder whether by right to strike we mean, according to the traditional view, just the right to refrain from work or also the right to use all means (legal, of course) necessary in order to organize and keep the stoppage going as well. On the other hand, a contractual limitation upon the right to strike is not necessarily a waiver of it, but may be restricted to the timing of it (notice; cooling-off periods: we find significant examples in France) or to the way of carrying it on. As regards the latter point, Sweden, with the Basic Agreement of 1938, and to a lesser extent Italy, with the agreements for the steel industry, have shown a specific interest in the matter of protective work, namely, the operations the interruption of which may bring about danger to safety or damage to equipment. The scope of contractual limitations therefore may be more restricted, and, in the meantime, wider than the one of the typical peace or 'no-strike' obligation.

We come now to the problem of the subjects which may incur liability in case of breach. There is no exception to the binding effect of a 'no-strike' obligation upon the union as party to the agreement. The obligation may be binding in honour when the agreement is not enforceable at law. This was the case, exceptional indeed, of the UK before the 1971 Act, and quite likely it will be also after the commencement of it. We find instead a variation in the degree of liability, as to what is required by the union in order to preserve peace. Variations run along a rather restricted range: from a mere duty to abstain from supporting the strike (French Labour Code) up to a duty to take all reasonable steps in order to prevent infringements (British 1971 Act). An obligation of guaranteeing behaviour of members is very nearly reached – but not quite. In any case, that would probably be an unbearable burden for the unions.

Apart from the almost unquestioned liability of the union, a liability of individual workers is recognized as well in most cases, and it may appear very important in case of wildcat strikes. A current construction of the collective agreement as a double-faced agreement, with one part (the obligatory) binding the collective parties, the other (the normative) the individual employers and employees, would seem to give a clear-cut answer: the peace obligation is included within the obligatory part, therefore it has no binding effect upon the individual workers. But this theoretical and syllogistic construction does not stand in the face of reality. In Germany, where this sharp distinction was worked out and is still assumed as a basic construction of the collective agreement, judge-made law reimposed the individual liability by resorting to the principles of torts. In Sweden, under the combination of the two parts of the agreement, the individual is responsible for his participation in the breach of peace. In the USA the industrial jurisprudence of arbitrators has recognized the right of the employer to discipline or to discharge the worker. In the UK the 'no-strike' clause may be construed as embodied into the contract of employment, and become binding at law for the individual worker, even though the collective agreement as such is only binding by honour. The 1971 Act seems to provide for the embodiment into contracts of employment of procedural agreements, which are the main source for 'no-strike' undertakings. French Courts have been cautious, but still uphold the liability of individuals if evidence of fault is given. Finally, in Italy, the question has been widely debated, and resort has been made also to the doctrine of separation between the two parties of the collective agreement. However, the most reasonable solution seems the one which releases the individual worker on the ground of analysis of the intention of the parties – the peace obligation of the 1960s, as we recalled, was agreed upon as a return for recognition of unions, not of individuals' rights. When statutes do not provide for such, attention must be paid to the intention of the parties. No solution may be inferred by an abstract construction of the 'concept' of collective contract and of its elements – a way of reasoning which is a product of the conceptualistic approach to law, still prevalent in some European countries.

In terms of legal remedies, ordinary civil law actions result in being rather ineffective. Actions for damages against unions everywhere raises sharp issues as regards the amount to be refunded, while, in the meantime, they often engender a feeling of victimization on the side of labour. Non-fulfilment or termination of the agreement may even be detrimental to the damaged party, because quite probably the conflict would become enlarged in its scope (all matters would become open to dispute) or in its area (the involvement of workers and/or unions who did not commit any infringement).

Disciplinary sanctions against individual workers usually appear more effective when and where they may be resorted to. The liability of the individual worker for violation of the peace obligation in some of the countries under survey is questionable in itself. When it is not, it is based either upon statutory provisions (Sweden) or on legal constructions (Germany) – but may as well depend on the will of the parties (UK or Italy), which has to be ascertained in each case. Furthermore, when the right to strike is deemed to be an unwaivable right of the individual, his liability cannot come into question. The foundation may be either a direct liability for violation of the collective agreement, as it is conceived in the USA, or of the contract of employment which has embodied the peace obligation (UK). Besides, such a liability may be founded upon non-compliance with the obligation to perform the work, once the immunity granted by the right to strike is lifted in the specific case. It should be remembered that Italy is the country where the doctrine of the right to strike as an immunity was better developed.

By far more effective remedies are actions for specific performance and the one for 'general damages', the latter known only by the Swedish law. Action for specific performance is provided for by the well-known remedy of the injunction. Its effectiveness is unquestionable, but its use in industrial disputes assumes the preeminence of the right to continue running the enterprise over the right to personal freedom. Therefore, when provided for, it is usually against trade unions, whereas individual workers who have infringed the peace obligation most times are covered by immunity (Germany, USA). General, non-material, damages are actually more a non-criminal penalty than a compensation for damages, and they are assessed by judges with large discretionary powers. This sanction is undoubtedly effective, and sticks to the nature of things, since it is aimed more at preventing or discontinuing an illegitimate conflict than at punishing it. Of course, it grants the judiciary a large regulatory power over the course of industrial relations, while, in spite of its non-criminal nature, it may engender victimization, and cause reactions far different from the expected restoration of 'peace'. In general terms, we may therefore remark that in its practical implementation, in some of the countries under survey the peace obligation, even though enforceable at law, operated more as a 'political' obligation between the parties, based upon their reciprocal good will. Resort to legal action, when undertaken, usually causes a more rigid attitude of the parties and possibly a delay in the settlement of the conflict.

The question to what extent the peace obligation has been able to shape a method of industrial relations is difficult to answer. The question itself refers back to the statements we made at the beginning: namely that the peace obligation, in spite of its ambitious denomination, is not an objective in itself but rather an instrument for the implementation of policies, of the State and of the bargaining parties, which may be remarkably different in relation to sociopolitical or cultural variables.

4

The effect of industrial action
on the status of
the individual employee
by Xavier Blanc-Jouvan

Introduction

The problem of the effect of industrial action on the status of the individual employee is in most countries a very significant one. On the practical level, it is an important source of litigation. On the theoretical level, it brings into play two essential preoccupations of labour law: to regulate industrial action in a satisfactory, well-balanced way, taking into account all opposing interests and to give to the employee a protected status, notably to guarantee to him, if not a real 'ownership' of his job, at least the minimum of security of tenure in employment that today constitutes a fundamental requirement of social policy.

There are two main reasons why industrial action must necessarily affect the individual status of the employee.

The first is that all forms of industrial action involving a stoppage of work – whether it is at the initiative of the employees (strike) or of the employer (lockout) – impair by themselves the normal execution of the contract of employment. Lawful or not, such a situation, as long as it lasts, cannot remain without consequences on the status of the employees – and, it must be said, not only of the employees who were directly engaged in the action (employees on strike or employees locked out), but of all the employees of the enterprise, even those who did not take part in the action, because they may have been impeded in the accomplishment of their work and they may have had to suffer indirectly from the action.

The second reason why industrial action normally produces an effect on the individual relation of employment is limited to the employees directly engaged in the action, but it is no less important. It is founded on the idea that such an action necessarily creates within the enterprise a state of tension, which may finally affect in a definitive way the status of the employee. This is true for strike and for lockout as well. In both cases, of course, the contract may be terminated by the employee – but it is more frequent that it be terminated by the employer, either as a reaction (in fact as a sanction) against the strike, or as a consequence of the lockout.

Yet there are still some differences, in that respect, between the various countries, according to whether their system of labour relations has a predominantly collective or individual structure. There are some countries in which the situation of employers and employees depends more on the respective force of the organizations to which they belong than on the individual contract by which they are bound. It is, then, at the collective level that all relations take place: both parties resort to collective weapons, and the law provides some collective sanctions, such as injunctions or damages, in case of unlawful action; therefore the problem of individual measures is not the most acute one. This is notably the case in countries like the US or Sweden. But there are other countries in which, on the contrary, labour relations are still predominantly located on the individual level and in which the contract of employment is still the main foundation of labour relations. Where this is so, it is by acting on the status of the individual worker that the employer normally tries to impose his will during the course of or at the end of the conflict – and it is therefore this status which must be the object of special consideration by law. There is no doubt that in France or in Italy, for example, the individual measures (such as the dismissal of an employee) are the only ones that are really effective in case of industrial action: it is consequently of primary importance that they be strictly regulated by statutes or by court decisions. It must be noted that in these countries the problem of the effect of industrial action on the individual contract of employment is one of the most important in the field, one of those which raises the most considerable amount of litigation; and in particular it is essentially in connection with this problem that the French and Italian courts have been led to establish a distinction between lawful and unlawful activities.

It so appears that the problem is more or less critical according to the countries considered. It must be added that it has also been more or less critical according to the epochs.

This is due to the fact that, in the beginning, in all countries, strikes and lockouts were forbidden and regarded as criminal offences. The penal sanctions which could then be pronounced against those who were engaged in such types of industrial action constituted such an effective deterrent that they usually made it unnecessary or inappropriate (according to the case) for the parties to resort to any sort of measure affecting the status of the employee: and the problem of the effect of industrial action on the contract of employment did not arise very often. When it arose, anyway, it was easily solved on the basis that the employee on strike could be immediately dismissed while the employer could not invoke the lockout to get rid of his employees nor to escape the normal obligations resulting from this contract (notably the obligation to pay the wages). Such a situation practically lasted during the major part of the nineteenth century. But it began to change when statutes were enacted in order to protect industrial action and decided that strikes and lockouts could no longer (except under special circumstances) be regarded as criminal activities. This happened in 1864 in France, in 1869 in Germany, in 1889 in Italy. It was at that time that it started to be important for the employers to react against the strikes by resorting to civil sanctions, such as the dismissal of the striking employees. And as the lockout ceased to be regarded as a crime, it started to be used more frequently and it inevitably involved consequences on the status of the employees. The problem of the validity of such measures – i.e., the problem of the effect of industrial action on the individual contract of employment – then arose in more acute terms than before. And it is still in these terms that it arises today.

This does not mean, however, that the solution of this problem has remained the same since the end of the last century. On the contrary, it has undergone an important evolution, which can be easily explained by the changes which have occurred in the structure of labour relations. It is important to note that this evolution has been practically the same everywhere – although it may have been quicker or slower in certain countries because of the legal tradition or of any other circumstances. At least the point of departure and the point of arrival are very largely similar. This is why it can be fairly said that the law of industrial action has gone through two important stages.

In the first stage, the law guaranteed only the freedom to resort to industrial action. This meant that strikes and lockouts were protected against the State; they could no longer give rise to criminal prosecutions; they could be ranked among civil liberties, although they were not protected against the other party to the individual relation of employment. There was no law limiting their use, but no law either limiting the resort to civil sanctions against them. This last point was particularly important. Neither the employee nor the employer could invoke any special privilege; they all remained subject to the ordinary rules of the civil law or common law of contracts. The employees on strike could be dismissed by the employer, and the employer, in case of a lockout, could be ordered to pay the normal wages to his personnel as though there had been no interruption in the work. There is no need to emphasize that such sanctions were commonly used and they constituted a very efficient weapon. The situation was undoubtedly justified at a strictly juridical level, by application of the classical principles of the law of contracts, especially to the extent that industrial action was analysed in individualistic terms: the participation in a strike or the lockout of an employee certainly was to be regarded as a breach of the individual contract of employment, giving rise to civil sanctions. But this solution also led, in practice, to very unfortunate consequences. The freedom to resort to industrial action was considerably impaired by the threat of sanctions taken by the other party, and the freedom to strike, notably, was of little interest for the individual worker who could fear to have his contract terminated and to lose his job.

All these reasons explain that the system has become more and more anachronistic and that, in a second stage of the evolution, it has been largely abandoned. This can be explained, not only by practical reasons (the necessity to assure the employee involved in labour dispute better protection against anti-union activities and, notably, a greater security of employment), but also by theoretical considerations on the true nature of industrial action. Even in the systems in which a strong emphasis is put on the employer-employee relationship, it has become progressively more obvious that such an action cannot be regarded only from the point of view of each individual engaged in it: it must rather be viewed as an action of a specific type, which has a predominantly collective character. Its effect on the contract of employment cannot therefore be defined according to the traditional scheme taken from the law of contracts; it must be determined by new, particular standards. In practically all countries, the freedom to engage in some types of industrial action has become a right. This right can be officially and expressly recognized by the Constitution itself, or it can be, more modestly, implied by the terms of some recently enacted statutes – sometimes even merely affirmed by the courts. But in any case, the idea has triumphed that it is a right, which means that it is protected not only against the State, but also against the other party to the employment relationship, in the sense that it cannot give rise on his part to any sort of civil sanction.

It would be, however, excessive to say that the previous system is no longer applied today. The 'right' granted by law is not – and cannot be – absolute and the protection against civil sanctions does not – and cannot – extend to all concerted activities. There are some of these activities which remain subject to the ordinary law of contracts. This is even the basis for a distinction between lawful and unlawful actions, a distinction that is quite different in each of the countries covered by this study. Naturally, this is extremely important as to the effect of the action on the status of the individual employee.

It so appears that this status is far from being as simple as it might seem at first sight. We must examine the situation, first, from the point of view of the maintenance of the employment relationship throughout the strike or the lockout, and, second, from the point of view of the consequences attached to this relationship: in fact, the rights and duties of each of the parties.

There is no doubt that such a study cannot be limited to legislation or court decisions – that is, to the law in the strict sense of the word. It is essential to see how this law is actually applied. Experience shows that there is sometimes, in that respect, a gap between theory and practice. It happens quite often, for example, that the employer does not make use of the power that is given to him by law to dismiss the workers engaged in a certain action; or that a collective agreement passed at the end of the conflict provides for the renunciation of each party to take any sanction against the other; or that the employer finally agrees to pay certain wages that he is not normally supposed to pay. Social pressure is more important in this field than legal theory, and none of the parties can ignore the ratio of forces nor the special requirements of labour relations before making a decision. This explains why the actual differences between the various solutions are often less important in practice than they could be if the law were to be strictly applied.

The effect of industrial action on the maintenance of the employment relationship

This aspect of the status of the individual employee is the most important, being the one that controls all the others. The problem is to know whether the employee remains an employee during the time the action takes place, and after it has ended. The solution may naturally be different according to the type of action considered and, in particular, it may be different for the strike and for the lockout. These activities are not really symmetrical, since the employer and the employee are not in a similar position in the labour market, and therefore they are not necessarily subject to symmetrical rules. On the contrary, the necessity of assuring to the worker a certain security of employment often leads in both cases to different solutions.

THE EFFECT OF THE STRIKE

The problem of the effect of the strike on the individual contract of employment can be set out in very simple terms. On one side, it is obvious that the strike constitutes a non-performance of the contract and it is normal that it produces consequences detrimental to the employee. But, on the other side, it is an activity that deserves protection – especially if the law purports to give to the worker a maximum of job security. One can easily understand why the solution of this problem is so complex.

Several systems are indeed conceivable. It is necessary to describe them briefly before examining to what extent they have been, or still are, in force in the various countries with regard to the different possible types of strikes.

Description of the various possible systems

The main opposition exists between the systems based on the idea of a termination of the individual contracts as a consequence of the strike and those based on the idea of a mere suspension.

(*a*) The termination of the contract is naturally the most rigorous solution for the employee because it deprives him of his job. But this termination itself can be legally justified on two different grounds, which involve different consequences. It may first be argued that the termination is due to the employee's initiative. Either the law requires that this employee give an explicit notice of termination before going on strike, in order to make this strike lawful, or it considers that the mere fact of going on strike, even without notice, implies a termination of the contract. In both cases, however, the result is the same: it is the employee who expresses his refusal of the present conditions of work and brings to an end his employment relationship with the intention of obtaining new conditions. The employer is only the victim of the strike, he can only accept as a fact the termination of the contract decided by the employee. Of course, at the end of the strike, he may rehire the workers who are willing to return to work; but this is merely an option for him, it is by no means an obligation: and if he takes this option, the reengagement will be made on the basis of a new contract of employment.

Such a termination of the contract on the part of the employee may certainly be unlawful (in which case the employee can be ordered to pay damages to the employer) – but it is normally lawful, especially in the case of a contract for an indefinite period, since it is admitted, as a matter of principle, that each party to such contract is entitled to terminate it by a unilateral decision at any moment. The only requirement may then be, for the party who terminates, to observe the period of notice prescribed for in statutory law, in the collective agreement or in the individual contract of employment, unless he is allowed, in the alternative, to pay to the other party a special compensation for summary termination.

This requirement is indeed already severe for the strikers: the previous notice may reduce the efficiency of the strike and the special compensation to be paid in replacement for this notice may constitute a heavy burden on the employees. Also, it is a great inconvenience for these employees to lose their right to certain payments (such as severance pay, for example) to which they would normally have been entitled if the contract had been terminated by the employer. Above all, the system may be criticized for two reasons: from a theoretical point of view, it is certainly contrary to the true intention of the workers. Nobody really believes that the employees who go on strike really want to terminate their contract; in fact, they precisely want to continue this contract since they want to obtain better conditions of employment. The system also appears unsatisfactory in practice, because it leads to an automatic termination of all the contracts and this is very prejudicial to the employees. Of course, the employer will eventually rehire most of these employees at the end of the action: but it will then be necessary to enter into a new contract and the employees will be deprived of all the advantages attached to their previous contract, particularly in the field of seniority.

Another possibility is to claim that the strike is only a just cause for the termination of the contract by the employer. As a concerted refusal to work, it is certain that the strike constitutes, on the part of the employee, a breach of contract. It is sometimes said that this breach automatically and by itself produces, as a consequence, termination of the contract, unless the employer expressly decides to continue the contract (with the possibility to pronounce lesser disciplinary sanctions): but such a solution is difficult to admit in any legal system, except in the case where it is expressly provided by statute.[1] More commonly, it is said that the breach of contract entitles the employer to dismiss the employee (and also to obtain damages if he has suffered economic loss). It is, then, the employer who takes the initiative of the termination. But this termination is in fact a sanction: not only is it lawful, but it is also justified by the non-performance of his obligation by the other party. Therefore the employer is excused from giving previous notice to the strikers or paying a special compensation for summary dismissal; similarly he is excused from paying any other of these compensations that are normally due to the employees when they lose their jobs (e.g. severance pay). Ordinary rules of contractual liability are here applicable against the workers who committed the breach. Such rules are only set aside when the strike itself has been called in

1. There are, however, some court decisions in France which have referred to this analysis in case of a *faute lourde* committed by the employee: cf. p. 217 *infra*.

response to a breach committed by the employer: for in this case, the stoppage of work can be regarded as a mere application of the *exceptio non adimpleti contractus* and it does not justify any sanction on the part of the employer.

Such an analysis, of course, makes possible a distinction between two categories of workers. The employer may choose as he pleases those that he wants to dismiss. For them the contract is definitely terminated and, if they are eventually rehired, it will be necessary to enter into a new contract. But for all the other employees who are not expressly dismissed (whether or not they are victims of other disciplinary sanctions), the contract continues; the employee keeps all the advantages attached to it (seniority) and, at the end of the strike, when he returns to work, he will not have to enter into a new contract.

This analysis, according to which the strike is a breach of contract, however, presents the great defect that it does not fit very well with the existence and the official recognition of a right to strike. Both propositions really seem contradictory. To the extent that the law expressly gives to the workers the right to exercise a pressure on their employer by ceasing work, in order to compensate for the unavoidable inequality that exists between both parties to the employment relationship, it appears difficult to admit that each worker is exposed to a sanction for his participation in the strike: there is a risk that the right to strike may become, in this case, completely meaningless and be reduced to nothing.

From a theoretical point of view, the contradiction can only be solved by the idea that the power given to the employer to discipline the strikers and the right given to the employees to call a strike are not situated at the same level. When the courts decide that the strikers can be dismissed by the employer, they consider the strike as an individual phenomenon, and look at its consequences on the individual relation of employment. On the contrary, when the legislature gives to the workers the right to strike, it regards it as a collective right.

More generally, we may say that all these doctrines leading to the conclusion that the strike involves termination of the contract (whether it be on the employee's or employer's initiative) seem perfectly justified as long as the strike is considered from an individualistic point of view. They are quite consistent with the classical conceptions of the civil law or common law of contracts. But they do not fit with the more modern analysis that tends to see the strike as a collective action of an original type – the analysis indeed which is implied by the laws recognizing the right to strike.

This theoretical objection to the traditional doctrine of termination of the contract as a consequence of the strike can be reinforced by obvious practical objections. It is clear that the termination of the contract, by one way or another, is very harmful for the strikers. One can wonder what interest the employees may have to organize a strike in order to improve their conditions of employment if they are threatened with the loss of this employment, and maybe the payment of damages to the employer.

Of course, such an inconvenience is somewhat reduced when the contract is not automatically terminated and the strike is only regarded as a breach that permits the employer to dismiss the worker. First, it is certain that the employer does not always use in practice the possibility he has to pronounce the dismissal and to sue for damages; he often prefers to ignore the breach and to continue with the existing contract. Of course, the mere fact that he can use this possiblity already places the worker at his complete discretion, and even if he does not dismiss or sue all the strikers, nor even a great number, but only some of them, he can do it in a discriminatory manner: he can make a distinction between the leaders of the strike and the mere participants: and this can be for him the pretext of anti-union activities. However, it is true that most workers will not in fact have to suffer from their participation in the strike. Secondly, the practice has developed for the employer and the strikers to include in the agreement entered into before the return to work a clause providing that no sanction will be taken against the strikers: and such clauses may be interpreted very broadly by the judges. It even happens that the courts construe the attitude of the employer during the strike in such a way that this employer is regarded as having implicitly renounced taking any sort of sanction against the strikers. The non-termination of the contract of employment then appears as being in conformity with the common will of the parties; in fact, it depends more on the ratio of their respective forces than on strictly legal considerations.

It should be added that some other ways can be found by the courts in order to avoid the termination of the contract as a consequence of the strike. For example, it is possible to give a large extension to the category of strikes that are regarded as responses to a breach committed by the employer and that are therefore justified. In other cases, it may be said that the strike was not voluntarily made by the employees and that it was imposed on them by a sort of *vis major* (picketing, impossibility of access to the plant, absence of means of transportation, threats of violence, etc.). Finally, it is possible to construe very narrowly the legal concept of strike and to exclude from this concept a certain number of activities that however constitute a cessation of work (short stoppages of work, cessation of work authorized by usages, etc.). But all these are only palliatives, which are not always available; they concern only a minority of strikes and therefore they cannot be regarded as really satisfactory.

(*b*) This is why another theory is often presented, that is based on the idea that the contract of employment is not terminated as a consequence of the strike. Of course, the execution of the contract is altered, since the work is not performed and, consequently, the wages cannot be paid; but the contractual relationship is not broken, it continues and still produces some effects during the strike. Furthermore, after the strike is over, the contract resumes its normal course, and all the advantages previously attached to it are retained by both parties. It is often said that the contract is suspended during the strike, and this theory is usually referred to as the theory of the suspension of the individual contract of employment (although the term is not always used). There is no doubt that it is more favourable to the employee than the theory of the termination of the contract, because it permits him to preserve his job.

Serious efforts are sometimes made to found this solution on the ordinary law of contracts and on an individual analysis of the strike. It is claimed that the strikers have no intention to terminate their contract, but only to improve its terms, so that it would be contrary to their will to break the employment relationship. But this analysis is not entirely convincing in view of the fact that no party to a contract is authorized to modify unilaterally the terms of this contract. The rule also applies to employees. If an employee wants to obtain better conditions of employment, he must first denounce the existing contract before trying to conclude a new one. The strike that is organized in support of a request for a modification of the present contract must normally be construed as a termination of this contract.[2]

In fact, it is certain that on the level of the individual employment relationship, the strongest arguments are in favour of the termination of the contract. It is only on the level of collective relations that the theory of the suspension of the contract may find a solid foundation. This is a new manifestation of the original character of labour law as compared with civil or common law. The basic idea is that the strike must be regarded as a collective phenomenon – the action of a group rather than of an individual; therefore it can only be subject to specific rules and not to rules provided for the individual employer-employee relationship. To the extent that a right to strike is officially granted by law, this right must normally be protected against the employer: this means that its exercise cannot produce as a consequence the loss of his job by the employee. Of course, this may be contrary to the ordinary law of contracts: but it is admitted that the collective right to strike given to the employees must prevail over the individual right to the execution of the contract given to the employer. The result is clear: as soon as the strike is regarded as lawful on the collective level, it can no longer be treated as a breach of contract and give rise to civil sanctions on the level of the individual relation of employment. The strike may be a non-performance of the contract, but it is not a breach of contract, because it is the exercise of a collective right. This right is an element of the legal status of the employee, to which all individual employment contracts implicitly refer. This is why it becomes impossible to claim that the contract has been broken because the right has been exercised.

Whatever is the theoretical justification for this doctrine of suspension of the contract, it is necessary to know exactly what consequences it involves from the point of view of the maintenance of the employment relationship. There can be no doubt, that in case of suspension the contract is not automatically terminated as a consequence of the strike and that it cannot be terminated by the employer as a civil or disciplinary sanction (that is, without previous notice). It is certain that if the employer dismisses the employee for the only reason that he participated in a strike, he commits an unfair or abu-

---

2. There are, of course, some strikes which do not tend to a modification of the terms of the employment contracts (political strikes, sympathetic strikes, etc.). In this case, it can really be argued that the strikers do not intend to terminate their contract. But it would be paradoxical indeed to secure a better protection for the strikers who deserve it the least, since they do not fight for economic reasons.

sive dismissal and he may be ordered to reinstate him or to pay him damages. But it remains a problem to know whether the employer still has the possibility to dismiss the employee on strike, after giving whatever previous notice is usually required, or to refuse to reinstate him, in spite of the fact that his contract is only suspended. There is, in that respect, a great variety of solutions. Between the systems admitting that the employer is still allowed to terminate the contract of the strikers – not as a sanction, but in application of the rule that any party to an employment contract which is not for a fixed term may, at any time and without any specific reason, terminate this contract – and those admitting that the employer cannot, under any pretext, dismiss the employees on strike, many intermediate positions can be found: it may be provided, for example, that the employer can only terminate the contract for economic reasons or in order to hire replacements. This shows that the protection granted to the strikers may be more or less complete. It is important to take into account, into that respect, the differences existing from one country to another – and also, in some cases, from one type of strike to another.

Termination or suspension of the contract of employment: these are the two main possibilities, and each one allows for important nuances in its application. It is now necessary to examine with more detail to what extent – and on what basis – each of these theories is now accepted in the various countries covered by this study. In that respect, it is essential to make a distinction between the different types of strikes, because the solution is not necessarily the same for the so-called 'lawful' and 'unlawful' strikes.

Broadly speaking, it can be said that all of the six countries which are here under consideration today accept the system of the suspension of the contract of employment as a consequence of the strike. But the reasons on which the system is based explain the limits brought to its application: the suspension is only accepted in case of a lawful strike, and it is therefore necessary to draw a borderline between those strikes and the unlawful strikes for which a system of termination of the contract is still applicable. In other terms, the suspension is only a principle, which suffers a good number of exceptions. Our purpose is to study the principle and to see what are its exact consequences from the point of view of the possibility of dismissal, before examining the limitations which are brought to its application in case of unlawful activities.

The principle of the suspension in case of a lawful strike

The principle of the suspension in case of a lawful strike is today accepted in most countries; at least it is accepted in the six countries covered by this study. In all of these countries, indeed, the evolution has been practically the same: it has gone from a system of termination of the contract (when the general feeling was hostile towards the strike and the classical conceptions of the law of contracts were predominant) to a system of suspension (now that the main preoccupation is to give to the employees a certain security of employment and that the 'right to strike' is officially recognized). But the evolution between these two extremes has been more or less rapid and it has followed different paths, because of the differences existing in the legal traditions and in the social backgrounds.

Sweden was probably the first country where the principle of suspension was accepted. Of course, the question of the effect of the strike on the individual contract of employment is a very old one. It began to arise as soon as the workers started to organize and engage in industrial action – that is, after the definitive abolition of the old regulation system by the Royal Ordinance of 18 June 1864 on the extension of freedom of trade. No doubt, strikers were then looked at with great mistrust. But the real problem was to know whether the resort to strike was consistent with the duties incumbent upon the employees under the employment contract. This problem became particularly acute during the later part of the nineteenth century, when the formal contract, strictly regulated by law, was gradually replaced by a 'free' contract of employment, which was not governed by any statutory provision. It was then necessary to determine which rule should apply – and notably whether the gaps in legislation should be filled with the help of analogies taken from the ordinary law of contracts.

The answer came rather early as to the particular point of the effect of the strike on the maintenance of the employment relationship. This is due to the fact that, for a very long time, the employers have implicitly acknowledged the right of the workers to resort to industrial action, with the exception of a pledge to refrain from action in order to bring about an alteration of the collective agreement. This approach to strike naturally implied that the strike did not disrupt the employment relationship. Its effect could only be suspensive, and that solution is still maintained today. Neither does the strike have the meaning of an automatic termination of the contract, nor does it constitute a breach that gives to the employer a ground to terminate it without notice. In the absence of legislation, the case law is now very clear on this point, and many decisions of the Labour Court expressly adopt the view that the strikers are still to be considered as being employed by their employer.[3] The only difficulty consists in determining the strikes to which this principle applies, and it is a difficulty to which we shall have to return.

Conversely, in the *United States*, it is the legislator that has had to intervene in order to impose the same solution. The system previously admitted was, of course, very prejudicial to the employees. Even after the courts had ceased to punish the strikers by criminal sanctions, they had continued to decide that these strikers could be subject to civil sanctions and that they could be discharged by their employer. This was, indeed, in conformity with the principle that each party to the employment relationship was allowed to terminate the contract at any time and without any condition of a previous notice: there was therefore no protection against the dismissal, in the case of a strike as in any other case, and the employer had a complete discretion in that respect.

The change came with the new legislation enacted at the beginning of the Roosevelt era and notably with the National Labor Relations (Wagner) Act

3. Cases cited in F. Schmidt, *The Law of Labor Relations in Sweden*, Harvard U.P., 1962 p. 203.

(NLRA) of 1935 – which is still in force today as part of the Labor-Management Relations (Taft-Hartley) Act (LMRA) of 1947, itself amended by the Labor-Management Reporting and Disclosure Act (LMRDA) of 1959. This Act is intended to protect the employees and to make effective their 'right . . . to engage in . . . concerted activities', as put by sec. 7 – more precisely their right to strike as reaffirmed by sec. 13. It therefore lays down some rules concerning the effect of the strike on the employment relationship. But it is to be noted that the problem is not dealt with in terms of contract, as in most other countries: the law of contract has indeed appeared insufficient and inadequate in this field, and it is true that the concept of an individual contract of employment has very little meaning in American labour law; this is why the Act does not refer to a real 'suspension' of the contract. The problem of the effect of the strike is treated, rather, in new and specific terms, more appropriate to labour relations, but it is clear that the result is about the same. The situation, in fact, can be summarized in two propositions.

The first one is that the workers who go on strike do not automatically put an end to their employment relationship: in fact, they do not lose their employee status. This results from sec. 2(3) of the NLRA, providing that 'the term "employee" shall include . . . any individual whose work has ceased as a consequence of, or in connection with, any current labor dispute'. Now the term 'labor dispute' is broadly defined in sec. 2(9) of the Act. It includes 'any controversy concerning terms, tenure or conditions of employment, or concerning the association or representation of persons in negotiating, fixing, maintaining, changing or seeking to arrange terms or conditions of employment, regardless of whether the disputants stand in the proximate relation of employer and employee.' This naturally includes all types of strikes. It so appears that the employee on strike remains an employee and preserves all rights to which employees are normally entitled.

But it is not enough to admit that the striker does not automatically lose his status; it is also important to determine whether he may be lawfully discharged by his employer. This involves the second proposition, according to which the employer is not entitled to dismiss an employee simply because of his participation in a lawful strike. The lawful strike is said to be 'protected' by the NLRA. If the strikers are regarded as exercising a right that is given to them by law, they cannot be punished by the loss of their employment. This implies several consequences. One is that if an individual contract of employment stated that participation in any strike would be a ground for discharge, this contract would certainly be void as against public policy; but it must be noted, in fact, that such contracts are extremely rare in practice, if indeed they exist at all. Another consequence is that if an employer actually discharges a worker for engaging in a lawful strike, he commits an unfair labour practice. The reason for this is that such a discharge results in discouraging union activity; it appears as an act of anti-union discrimination and falls under the provision of sec. 8(a)(3) of the NLRA, according to which 'it shall be an unfair labor practice for an employer . . . by discrimination in regard to hire or tenure of employment or any term or condition of employment to encourage or discourage membership in any labor organization.' As a consequence, it is admitted that the discharged worker is not deprived of his employee status: for the same sec. 2(3) of the NLRA, to which we have already referred, provides that 'the term "employee" shall include . . . any individual whose work has ceased . . . because of any unfair labor practice.' The employee therefore preserves all his rights as an employee; when the strike is over, he is entitled to reinstatement (provided, of course, he has made an unconditional offer to return to work)[4] and he can obtain, if necessary, an order of reinstatement by the National Labor Relations Board (NLRB); the employment relationship will then resume its normal course and it will be regarded as having never been broken. In fact, the impossibility – or at least the inefficiency – of the discharge as a consequence of the strike is all the more remarkable because, in normal situations, a discharge can always be effected by the employer and the legislation does not provide the employee with any protection against it.

It must be added, of course, that not only may an employer not discharge workers engaged in a lawful strike, but he may not impose any other sanctions that would have the effect of punishing them for participating in an activity protected by the NLRA. To do so would be to discourage union membership, in violation of sec. 8(a)(3) of the Act, and would therefore amount to an unfair labour practice on the part of the employer.

As can be seen, the situation in the United States corresponds exactly to that which is usually covered by the concept of suspension. Although the word is not used because it belongs to the terminology of contract, the reality seems to be the same. It is because the law is very clear and precise on this point that the problem of the effect of the strike on the individual employment relationship cannot be regarded as critical in the US, in spite of its practical importance and the considerable amount of litigation to which it gives rise.

The situation is also very clear in the three Western European countries – France, Italy and Germany – where the theory of suspension is adopted in express terms. The evolution, however, is more recent; it dates from the years after the Second World War and it has been to a large extent the consequence of the official recognition of the right to strike.

The movement started in *France*. Until then, however, it was admitted in French law that the strike resulted in the termination of the contracts of employment. Although the statutory law was silent on this point, the courts were unanimous in adopting this position. They did so, of course, before 1864, when the strike was expressly forbidden and regarded by Art. 414–16 of the Penal Code as a criminal offence, but they did not change their attitude after these articles had been abolished by the law of 29 May 1864 and the freedom to strike had been consequently recognized.

There has been, during all this period, some hesitation between the two possible explanations of this termination of the contract. The official doctrine was that the contract was terminated at the initiative of the employee, because this employee, when deciding to go on strike, automatically brought to an end

4. Provided also he has not been permanently replaced and he has not been discharged for cause: cf. pp. 208 and 211 *infra*.

his employment relationship. In spite of the fact that Art. 1780 of the Civil Code gave to the employee as well as to the employer the right to terminate his contract (when it was not for a fixed term) at any time by a unilateral decision, this termination by way of a strike was even sometimes regarded as unlawful (it surely was so before 1864, when the strike was a criminal offence; the question became doubtful afterwards) and, consequently, the employee on strike could be ordered to pay damages to the employer. Moreover, when the usages and later the statutory law and the collective agreements started to require that the party taking the initiative of the termination give previous notice or, failing that, pay a special compensation for summary termination of the contract, it was decided that the employee on strike did not escape this obligation. Anyway, the main point was that all the strikers were automatically deprived of their jobs. At the end of the strike, they could apply for rehiring, but the employer was under no obligation to accept them; and if he did so, he had to enter into a new contract with them.

This solution was strongly criticized because it was too severe for the employees. This is why a number of court decisions referred to another analysis, according to which the strike constituted a breach of contract, that made it possible for the employer to terminate the contracts in a lawful way, without running the risk of being sued in damages for abuse of the right to terminate the contract unilaterally and without even having to comply with the obligation to give previous notice (or to pay special compensation for summary dismissal). In other words, the strike only gave to the employer a ground for lawful and immediate dismissal. This solution progressively became the most frequently used. It was naturally more favourable to the employee, to the extent that this employee was not regarded as having taken the initiative of the termination: therefore he could not be sued in payment of a compensation for summary termination, and he could only be sued for damages if he had caused a special prejudice to the employer. Still more important, the employer could make a choice between the employees: he could retain some of them while discharging the others. For the workers who preserved their status as employees, the idea was that their contract was not terminated, but only suspended during the strike, so that it could resume its normal course after the strike had ceased, with all advantages attached thereto.

The courts even favoured this tendency to admit that the contract was merely suspended, not terminated. They often inferred from particular circumstances, and notably from the employer's attitude during or after the strike, that he preferred to ignore the breach and renounced his right to terminate the contracts of the strikers. They also used other palliatives in order to avoid the termination of the contract (notably by interpreting rather narrowly the concept of strike). Whereas, in practice, it is true that most strikers were not actually dismissed and that the suits in damages were extremely rare, the mere fact that they were possible and that the employer had a complete discretion in the use of such weapons was already very dangerous for the employees.

This is why even this solution was more and more criticized. The first reaction came from the legal writers. As soon as collective agreements started to develop, that is, after 1936, the labour unions also tried to impose some clauses departing from the system of termination of the contracts. It became more and more frequent, at the end of the strikes, to conclude agreements providing, explicitly or implicitly, that no sanctions would be taken against the employees who had participated in the strike. It is even fair to say that such clauses, when they existed, were usually construed very broadly by the courts. But this was, however, insufficent as a remedy: and the need was felt for a completely new solution.

This solution did not come from the ordinary courts, which remained, under the control of the Court of Cassation, adamant in their position; it came from the Superior Court of Arbitration, which was especially established in 1938 in order to settle definitely the collective labour disputes. In a famous case decided on 19 May 1939,[5] the Court laid down the principle that 'in the absence of any explicit or implicit intention on the part of the employees to give up their jobs, the strike should not in itself produce as a consequence the termination of the individual contracts of employment . . .'. The result was that the contracts could only be regarded as suspended. The court reaffirmed this position on several other occasions, only reserving the possibility of a different solution in case of an unlawful strike. The Court clearly placed the problem of the effect of the strike, not on the level of the individual labour relations and the law of contracts, but on the level of the collective labour relations and the disciplinary power of the employer.

This new development, however, was interrupted because of the war and the Superior Court of Arbitration ceased to function on 1 September 1939, before having had time to convince the ordinary courts. After the war came the official recognition of the right to strike. This right was even mentioned in the preamble of the Constitution of 1946 – preamble that is still in force today, since the present Constitution of 4 October 1958 expressly refers to it. Although nothing was said on the particular problem of the effect of the strike on the individual contract of employment, this affirmation of a right to strike – that was described as a 'fundamental right', one of those which are 'particularly necessary in our times' – appeared as the manifestation of a new psychological attitude towards the strike; it strengthened the old myth of the strike which had already played such an important role in the development of the French labour movement; and it made it more and more difficult to admit that the strike, being the normal exercise of a constitutional right (at least when it is lawful, which is the principle), could still constitute a breach of contract, giving rise to sanctions against the employee. The courts drew the normal inferences from this, and they openly resorted to the theory of suspension. The Court of Cassation itself rallied to this theory in a series of cases laid down in 1951,[6] expressly basing its decisions on the new constitutional provisions. It notably provided that 'the solemn affirmation by the Constitution of the right to strike, which has become a means to defend economic interests (*intérêts*

5. *Droit Social,* 1939, p. 199; *Gazette du Palais,* 1939, I, 903.
6. Soc. 1 June 1951, *Droit Social,* 1951, p. 530, 1st case; Soc. 18 June 1951, *Droit Social,* 1951, p. 532, 6th case; Crim. 28 June 1951, *Droit Social,* 1951, p. 542.

professionnels), cannot logically agree with the termination of the employment contract that would result from the exercise of this right'.

The facts on which these cases were based had taken place before 1950 – that is, before the enactment of the new statute which has set aside all hesitations and definitely solved the problem. It is actually sec. 4 of the important law of 11 February 1950, that expressly states that 'the strike does not break the contract of employment, except in case of serious misconduct (*faute lourde*) on the part of the employee'. Here again, the statute does not expressly use the word 'suspension': however, it is exactly the concept of suspension that is behind the legal formula. The Court of Cassation has affirmed in a case decided on 25 April 1952, that this sec. 4 was merely an official interpretation of the constitutional provision recognizing the right to strike. In fact, the principle of the suspension in case of a lawful strike is no longer disputed today. And the consequences of this principle are very clear: the employment relationship remains in existence, so that the contract can resume its normal course at the end of the strike. All advantages acquired by the employee before the strike are maintained after the strike, notably the seniority rights. The employer cannot terminate the contract on the basis only of the strike. He cannot even ask the courts to decide this termination (*résolution judiciaire*, as provided by Art. 1184 of the Civil Code for all sorts of contracts): for such a *résolution* is only possible at the request of one party when the other party has committed a breach of contract – and the strike in itself cannot be regarded as a breach. If the employer nevertheless dismisses the worker, he can be charged with 'abusive' termination of the contract. The only – but serious – shortcoming of the system lies in the absence of an effective remedy in such a case: French law does not admit the possibility of imposing the reinstatement on the employer and all the dismissed employee can finally obtain is damages (*indemnité de rupture abusive*) – which is quite unsatisfactory.

The evolution of the law has not been very different in *Italy*, and it has gone through the same steps. During most of the nineteenth century, the strike was also regarded as a criminal offence and the prohibition lasted even longer than in France (except in Tuscany, where it was lifted in 1853). After the promulgation of the Code of 1889, however, only the acts of violence were punished by penal sanctions. The strike was protected against the State and it was possible to speak of a freedom to strike. But the strike was not protected against the employer and, in the employer-employee relationship, the ordinary law of contracts remained applicable. The strike was only considered from an individualistic point of view and it was regarded as a breach of contract, except in the cases where it was imposed by a *vis major* (*force majeure*) or justified by a previous breach committed by the employer (in which situation it seemed possible to make application of the *exceptio non adimpleti contractus*).[7] The

7. It must be noted that the labour courts tried to favor the employees by resorting very often to this *exceptio non adimpleti contractus*. They considered that the *exceptio* could apply, not only when the strike was really a response to a breach committed by the employer, but also when it had been provoked by the resistance of the employer to fair revendications presented by the employees. But this was, in any way, insufficient as a palliative.

consequence admitted by the predominant case law – notably that of the Superior Courts and of the Court of Cassation of Rome – was that the contract could be terminated by the employer at his discretion and without notice, if, at least, the employee himself had not expressly manifested his intention to terminate it and given previous notice in that sense.[8] This consequence was so rigorous that, as early as the beginning of this century, the majority of the labour courts (*probiviri*) started to criticize the theory of termination and to support the theory of suspension, on the basis that the strike was to be viewed as a collective phenomenon rather than in the light of the ordinary law of contracts. They naturally exercised a strong influence,[9] but they could not finally overcome the resistance of the ordinary courts and of the Court of Cassation of Rome.

During the period of 1926–44, there was a return to the prohibition of the strike under penal sanctions (Law of 3 April 1925, Penal Code of 1930, Art. 502 *et seq.*). After the Second World War, this legislation seems to have been implicitly repealed by a decree-law of 23 November 1944, abolishing the corporative regime – and anyway a new stage in the development of the law of strike was inaugurated by the constitution of 27 December 1947, which officially recognized in its Art. 40 the right to strike in terms similar to those used by the French Constitution of 1946 ('The right to strike may be exercised within the ambit defined by statutory law'). As no statute was further enacted, it has been exclusively up to the courts to deduce the consequences of this broad affirmation – and there has been, of course, some uncertainty in the matter. It has even been claimed sometimes that Art. 40 of the Constitution was only programmatic and without immediate effect, but this argument was soon rejected: and since 1951, Art. 40 has been treated as a self-executing provision, embodying a legal principle and authorizing the free exercise of the right to strike. Later, many decisions have defined with more precision the extent of this right. As to the particular problem of the effect of the strike on the individual contracts of employment, the courts have constantly held that employees who go on strike in order to promote their collective interests do not commit a breach of contract: they enjoy, in fact, a sort of immunity which protects them from any measure of retaliation on the part of the employer. The result is that the strike (at least when it is lawful) does not produce the termination of the contract, but only its suspension – that is, the temporary paralysis of its execution. Therefore, the only problem is today to determine the exact limits of this lawful character of the strike: it is only on this point that some hesitations are still taking place. It so appears that the situation in Italy is probably the closest in that respect to the situation in France.

The principle of the suspension is also admitted today in *Germany*, but on rather different grounds. German law has also gone through the three main

8. Some decisions even admitted that, in case of a strike by the majority of the employees of an enterprise, all contracts of employment were terminated, even those of the workers who had not participated in the strike. Cf. Court of Cassation of Rome, 27 Dic. 1909, *Foro Italiano*, 1910, vol. I, col. 350 (cf. *infra*, footnote 76).
9. cf. E. Redenti, *Massimario della giurisprudenza dei probiviri*, Roma, 1906, p. 114–15.

stages that we have already described. Strikes, like other coalitions, were first regarded as criminal offences by the various German states. On 21 June 1869, the Trade Code (*Gewerbeordnung*) abolished this legislation and gave to all workers (except rural and domestic servants)[10] the freedom to form coalitions, including the freedom to associate and the freedom to strike (Art. 152). But this freedom was to be exercised within the framework of the ordinary law of contracts. And the courts decided that, according to this law, it was necessary for the employee to give notice of termination of the contract. If no notice was given (which was the most frequent situation, since the greatest number of strikes occurred spontaneously), the strike was regarded as a 'persistent refusal to work', which entitled the employer to dismiss the striker immediately, without notice.[11] In the first case, the contract was automatically terminated by the employee himself, while, in the second, there was only a possibility that it be terminated by the employer: but in any case, the striker was under a threat to lose his job whereas he had gone on strike precisely in order to improve the conditions of his employment. Furthermore, the employer had the possibility to counter-attack by way of a lockout, which was lawful, on the condition that it be preceded by a notice, and which also produced as a consequence the termination of the contracts of all the employees concerned: and such lockouts became rather frequent after 1890.

This system was all the more severe for the workers as it was accompanied by all sorts of discriminatory practices, such as blacklists, intended to discourage the workers from joining the trade-unions. The result was that requests started to be made for a change in the legislation, and notably for the recognition of a real right to strike that would be protected not only against the State (so that no penal sanctions would be available), but also against the employer (so that the strikers would not be subject to civil sanctions such as the dismissal without notice).

The change was particularly expected after the end of the First World War; and it is true that a few days after the outbreak of the Revolution of 15 November 1918, the employers' associations recognized unions as representatives of the workers and pronounced in favour of an unrestricted freedom of coalition. However, the Weimar Constitution of the Reich (11 August 1919) limited itself to affirming the 'freedom of combination (*Vereinigungsfreiheit*) for maintaining and promoting labour and economic conditions'; and it clearly results from the legislative history that 'combination' did not include strike. The freedom of combination was from now on construed as being protected against all measures by the employer (dismissal because of union membership was declared null and void by Art. 159 WCR) and it then became possible to speak of a 'right to organize'. But there was no change as to the strike. The ordinary

10. Until 1919 these workers remained under special servant codes legislated by the states.
11. In practice, until 1914, the notice usually required was so short (usually some hours, at most one day) that it made little difference for the workers to be dismissed after notice or immediately.

law of contracts remained applicable: a notice of termination was still required before the employee could legally join a strike, and sanctions such as dismissal were still available against those who went on strike without notice. In practice, this solution appeared very rigorous, in spite of the fact that the labour unions were often strong enough to impose, at the end of the strike, an agreement providing that all employees would be reinstated without suffering any sanction as a consequence of the strike.[12] It was supported by the largest sector of legal opinion, but it did not prevent this period from being characterized by a large number of labour conflicts, with strikes and lockouts.

The problem disappeared in 1933, with the establishment of the new regime: the strike then became in all cases unlawful. After the Second World War, some attempts were made in order to promote a certain number of reforms which had not been passed during the Weimar Republic, and notably the affirmation of a right to form coalitions that would include at the same time the right to organize and the right to strike. Several state Constitutions did expressly recognize this right to strike – although they usually restricted it to the strikes called by the unions[13] and often provided for the possibility of some limitations imposed by statute. Such a recognition clearly implied that the strikers should be protected against measures taken by the employers – i.e. against dismissals without notice for breach of contract. This interpretation, however, was denied by some authors such as Nikisch and Nipperdey,[14] who declared that the right to strike was nothing more than the freedom to strike and that, therefore, it did not protect the employee against a possible discharge. The legal opinion actually has always been divided on this point, and still today the matter remains doubtful.

But the most important problem is to know what is the Federal law in this field. As a matter of fact, the Bonn Basic Law of 23 May 1949 only contains an Art. 9, sec. 3, that recognizes the right to organize in nearly the same terms as Art. 159 WCR. It guarantees 'the freedom of combination for maintaining and promoting labour and economic conditions'. It had been planned to introduce in this same Art. 9, a sec. 4 that would have expressly recognized the right to strike in case of a union strike, but this project was finally given up because of the inability of the political parties to reach an agreement on the precise extent of such a right and the limitations that should be brought to it. Instead of adopting a broad formula, leaving the door open to further statutory enactments, as was the case in France or in Italy, the constituents preferred to leave out this sec. 4. It has been claimed sometimes that, in spite of the explicit intention of its authors as manifested in the legislative history, sec. 3 suffices in itself to imply the recognition of the right to strike (as well as the right to lockout), on the basis that such a right is included in the right to organize

12. Such clauses are called reinstatement clauses (*Wiedereinstellungsklausel*) or no-sanction clauses.
13. There was only one exception to this rule: the Constitution of Berlin admitted the right to strike without any limitation.
14. These two authors expressed this idea in two opinions, delivered in 1951 and 1953 respectively for the Federal Union of the German Employers' Association.

(conceived broadly as the right to form coalitions) and that, anyway, it is necessary for the regulation of collective agreements. But the Federal Constitutional Court has not yet had the opportunity to discuss this point. In fact, in the absence of express constitutional provision and of any other sort of legislation, the problem of the effect of the strike or the individual contracts of employment has mainly been left to the judges – and notably those of the Federal Labor Court.

Until 1955 this problem did not receive any clear-cut solution. The two opposite attitudes were expressed by two propositions: contractual obligation takes precedence over union obligation (*Vertragspflicht geht vor Verbandspflicht*) or conversely. But a very important decision was finally laid down on 28 January 1955 by the Big Senate of the Federal Labor Court, which definitively settled the matter. This was a case where the workers had gone on strike for a lawful purpose (in order to support a demand for better conditions of work) and under the sponsorship of their union, but without having given notice of termination of their contract within the prescribed time. The judges were, of course, in an interesting but delicate situation. They could have said that there was a gap in the Bonn Basic Law, so that they would have had to apply the constitutional provisions of the various states: but they definitely wanted to avoid this result. They could also have said that the 'social state' clause of the Bonn Basic Law protected at least the right to engage in a strike sponsored by the union (because the unions really exercise a 'social function'): but this also was contrary to one of the fundamental tendencies of the 'theoreticians' of labour law in Germany. In fact, the judges preferred to demonstrate that they were not bound by the text of the Constitution and that they had the power to create law if necessary. They knew the result that they wanted to reach – in fact, the abandonment of the theory of the termination of the contracts of employment and the adoption of the theory of suspension, at least in the case of a union strike. As they could not justify this result by a strictly legal reasoning founded on a particular statute or on the ordinary law of contracts, they expressly referred to a sociological analysis, based on the 'true nature of the strike'. They started with the idea that this strike – more precisely the union strike – is an original phenomenon, which is quite specific to labour relations and which cannot be analysed in classical terms; it is a collective action in which all individual actions of the participants are merged. Therefore, it is absurd to say that the strikers must give notice of termination of their contracts, and it is impossible to allege that, by exercising a freedom that is guaranteed to them by law, they commit a breach of contract that entitles the employer to dismiss them. Consequently there is no other alternative than to affirm that such a strike has merely a suspensive effect.

This recourse to a sociological analysis has naturally been criticized, not only because it led the Federal Labor Court to create new law (although, in fact, it can be claimed that the Court only granted to the unions a right that had already been given to them by some state Constitutions, but had been withheld so far by the lawyers), but also because it led to important restrictions both in the cases where this suspensive effect is admitted (it only applies to

union strikes when they are 'socially adequate') and in the consequences resulting from it (it does not deprive the employer of the right to decide a lockout in response): we shall come back to these two points later. It so appears
that the present system admitted in Germany is a sort of compromise: no
doubt, the principle is that of the suspension of the contract, but this principle
is limited in its application. The question is definitively solved in case law,
although, in the absence of legislation, there is a strong opposition on the part
of the legal commentators – an opposition that is particularly important in a
country where academic writers are very influential and where judge-made
law needs their approval in order to be regarded as customary law.

If the evolution has now come to an end in all of the five countries that we
have so far examined, it is still on the way in the sixth one: *Britain* – in spite of
the fact that the recent Industrial Relations Act contains important provisions
on this matter.

Although the freedom to strike is no longer disputed today, the problem of the
effect of the strike on the status of the employee is still conceived in the United
Kingdom in individualistic terms – and until recently, it remained almost exclusively subject to the ordinary law of contracts. In fact, in a strike situation,
there were two possibilities: (*a*) either the individual worker had himself
terminated his contract, or (*b*) he had acted in breach of it. In both cases the
result was the same for him: he was exposed to the loss of his employment.

The first possibility was that the striker himself terminated his contract.
Normally, when the contract is for an indefinite period (which is the most
frequent situation), each party can bring it to an end at any time, even without
any special ground, only by giving notice to terminate it. The length of such a
notice may be expressly set out in the written particulars of the contract; if
none is expressly agreed, it is that implied by the custom in the trade and, if
there is no custom, it is the period regarded as reasonable for ending the particular job; but, in any case, it cannot be less than a minimum provided by
statute. Under sec. 1(2) of the Contracts of Employment Act 1963, as amended
by sec. 19 of the Industrial Relations Act 1971, the minimum notice which
must be given by the employee is one week after 13 weeks of continuous employment. Such a rule naturally applies to the employee who goes on strike.
This employee must normally give notice to terminate his contract. If he does
so (either personally or through his representative, that is, the union), the
strike is regarded as lawful. In this case, there is no breach of contract, of
course; on the contrary, the contract has been fulfilled according to its terms.
But naturally, the notice produces its normal effects: the employment relationship is ended at the commencement of the strike, and continuity of employment is consequently broken. The employee loses all rights acquired under
his contract. If he is re-engaged by the employer at the end of the strike, he
will have to enter into a new contract and to acquire new rights. But the employer is by no means obliged to re-engage him: when the strike has ended, he
can actually pick and choose as he pleases among those who offer themselves
for reemployment.

The second possibility is that the employee does not fulfil his obligation to give notice to terminate the contract, either because he has only given inadequate notice (a notice which is not of the required length), or because he has not given any notice at all. Under these circumstances, of course, the situation is different. The strike is regarded as unlawful and the individual worker is said to be in breach of his contract of employment.

This breach is a fundamental breach, that gives to the employer an option. He may choose to regard the breach as a repudiation of the contract and to treat himself as no longer bound by this contract. In other words, he may terminate the contract of the striker. This termination is naturally justified by the breach already committed. That means that the employer is not subject in this case to the requirement of a previous notice: he can discharge the employee forthwith, without any delay. The strike, in fact, then constitutes a ground for summary dismissal. And this termination of the contract by the employer produces all the effects of a normal termination: it breaks the continuity of employment and it deprives the employee of all rights previously acquired; it also deprives him of his entitlement to redundancy payment. At the same time, of course, the employee can be sued by the employer for damages.

However, the employer may also choose, if he prefers, to waive the breach and to insist upon performance of the contract. To the extent that he does not obtain this performance, all he can do is to sue the worker on strike for damages for breach of contract,[15] thus ensuring that the contract is not terminated, the employment relationship is not broken.

Naturally, the employer is not obliged to take the same stand towards all strikers. He may freely choose among them those he wants to dismiss and those he wants to retain. He has a complete discretion in that respect.

Such was the legal theory until the Industrial Relations Act was promulgated. This theory seemed so severe for the individual employees that it could not be strictly followed in practice. It was very rare, in fact, that the employer actually exercised his rights, whether the strike was regarded as lawful or not. Where the strikers had terminated their contracts by giving adequate notice (which was, after all, rather exceptional), it was usual that they resumed normally their work after the strike had ended and that both parties acted in regard to pensions, seniority, etc., as though continuity of employment had never been broken by the strike. This was, in fact, in conformity with the true intention of all the persons concerned: for it is clear that strikers do not intend to sever their relationship with the employer, and the employer does not want either to regard this relationship as ended (in spite of all the statements that he can make during the strike and which are just a tactic of bargaining). Similarly, where the strike was unlawful, the employers usually did not take advantage of the possibility that was given to them either to terminate the con-

---

15. On the measure of damages in such a case, see *Ebb Vale Steel, Iron & Coal Co.* v. *Tew* [1935] 1 L.J.N. C.C.A.; *N.C.B.* v. *Galley* [1958] 1 W.L.R. 16; discussed in Grunfeld, *Modern Trade Union Law*, Stevens, 1966, pp. 325–9. It must be noted that such damages are usually very small: cf. K. W. Wedderburn, *The Worker and the Law*, 2nd ed., Penguin Books, 1971, pp. 115–16.

tract or to sue the employee for damages: for this would have impaired all chances of a peaceful settlement.

It is precisely this divergence between the reality and the legal theory that has caused some rethinking of the latter in the recent years. Doubts have been expressed about the validity of the strict legal analysis admitted so far and notably about its correspondence with the will of the parties. The problem especially arose in the case where the employee only gave strike notice – that is, a notice of withdrawal of labour, but not really a notice to terminate the contract. This situation was, in fact, the most frequent: and it was then neces-sary to construe this notice and to determine its effects with regard to the individual contract of employment. In strict legal terms, this notice was only a notice of intended breach: but it appeared difficult to admit that it should lead to the termination of the contract, because such a consequence clearly conflicted with the expectations and normal practice of both sides of industry. As put in the Donovan Report,[16] the employees in this case

> are not . . . really intending to repudiate the contract altogether – they simply want it modified. Nor does the employer in such a case regard the cessation of work as a repudiation of the contract, entitling him to rescind it. He really wants the contract to continue and he hopes to be able to come to terms over the modification which his employees are seeking. Only if this hope is finally dashed will questions of repudiation and consequent re-scission arise.

The first cases that were brought to the attention of the courts in that res-pect concerned unlawful strikes, that is, strikes where the employees had not given a notice of proper length. This was notably the case in *Rookes* v. *Barnard*. In the Court of Appeal,[17] Lord Justice Donovan strongly challenged the idea that a strike itself in breach of contract is necessarily unlawful. And in the House of Lords,[18] although the decision of the Court of Appeal was reversed, Lord Devlin picked up the same theme, affirming:

> It is not disputed that the notice constituted a threat of breach of contract by the members of [the union] . . . As Donovan, L.J., said in the Court of Appeal, the object of the notice was not to terminate the contract either before or after the expiry of seven days. The object was to break the con-tract . . . keeping the contract alive for as long as the employers would tol-erate the breach without exercising their right of rescission.

The matter was then pursued into the realm of what was hitherto thought 'lawful' strikes by Lord Denning, M.R., in *Stratford & Son Ltd.* v. *Lindley*,[19] where he said:

16. *Royal Commission on Trade Unions and Employers Associations 1965–1968*, HMSO, 1968, para. 939.
17. [1963] 1 Q.B. 623. For a full account of the case, see Wedderburn, op. cit., pp. 361 et seq.
18. [1964] A.C. 1129.
19. [1965] A.C. 269.

A week's strike notice is not be be construed as if it were a week's notice on behalf of the men to terminate their employment: for that is the last thing any of the men would desire. They do not wish to lose their pension rights and so forth by giving up their jobs. The 'strike notice' is nothing more nor less than a notice that the men will not come to work. In short, that they will break their contracts.

The irresistible conclusion of this new effort of legal reasoning to approximate to industrial practice was that all strikes, regardless of the question of notice, were to be considered 'unlawful' because they were in breach of the individual contracts of employment. It may be, of course, that this was more favourable to the employees, since the breach does not necessarily lead to a termination of the contract: it can be waived by the employer – in fact, it is normally waived and continuity of employment is not broken. But it could be objected that this analysis did not make any distinction between those who strike without notice and those who do give notice; and a certain feeling existed that where notices of proper length are given, such strikes should be accorded special status so as to distinguish them in law from 'lightning' strikes, which are, of course, nearly always unconstitutional and unofficial. In 1968, at any rate, Lord Denning specifically indicated that he had gone too far in *Stratford* v. *Lindley*. In *Morgan* v. *Fry*,[20] where proper notice had been given, he took a different and new position:

> Each side is . . . content to accept a 'strike notice' of proper length as lawful. It is an implication read into the contract by the modern law as to trade disputes. If a strike takes place, the contract of employment is not terminated. It is suspended during the strike and revives again when the strike is over.

This proposition that contracts of employment should not be terminated, but only suspended in all cases where strike notice of a sufficient length had been given was an innovation. But it has not been generally accepted and it has not become clear law. After all, Lord Denning was the only one of the three judges in *Morgan* v. *Fry* to present it.[21] Later, of course, it gained some support and a proposal was made in favour of its recognition in a statute. But this proposal was strongly criticized – notably by the Donovan Report, which openly pronounced against it, both for practical and theoretical reasons.[22]

From a practical point of view, it has been claimed that the adoption of this concept of suspension would give rise to considerable difficulties that are not resolved by *Morgan* v. *Fry*. Notably, it would be important to determine:. .

(*a*) to what strikes (and to what other types of industrial action) it applies
(*b*) whether the employer would still be allowed to dismiss instantly an em-

20. [1968] 3 All E.R. 452.
21. It is interesting to compare the opinion expressed by Lord Denning with the view of the two other judges in this case. Each one analysed the notice in his own way. Lord Justice Russel treated it as a notice of impending breach. Lord Justice Davies suggested that it was a termination of the existing contract and an offer to continue on new terms. See Wedderburn, op. cit., pp. 110–11, for a detailed consideration of the case.
22. op. cit., para. 943 et seq.

ployee for grave misconduct during the course of the strike and, if so, what kinds of act would constitute a 'grave misconduct'

(c) whether 'contracting out' of the system would be permissible, e.g. in collective agreements or in individual contracts of employment

(d) whether strikers would be free to take up other employment while their contract is suspended

(e) if all efforts to end the strike fail, upon what event would the suspension of the contract cease and be replaced by termination.

The Donovan Report even says that this list of practical difficulties that would derive from the adoption of the system of suspension is not exhaustive.

Still more important, however, in the Donovan Report's view, are the theoretical objections that may be opposed to this system of suspension. The idea is that there is no reason to create a right of unilateral suspension that the employee could exercise by striking without the consent of his employer: for any suspension of the contract must normally be by the mutual consent of both parties. The Donovan Report even rejects the argument that this concept of suspension really reflects the true intention of the parties – and it bases its argument on the fact that there are only two possible situations.

The first one is that in which the employee goes on strike in breach of his contract. As it is admitted in common law that none of the parties is entitled to break the contract unilaterally, it is normal that this breach produces consequences and that it gives to the employer the power to terminate the contract. Of course, it may very well be that this result is not exactly the one that had been wanted by the employee. But this is true in many other cases of breaches of contract – and even in contracts other than contracts of employment: the party who is responsible for the breach of contract does not want to end this contract – but, in fact, he acts in such a way that it gives to the other party the possibility to decide whether the contract will be terminated or not. There is no reason here which calls for a different solution.[23]

The second situation is that in which the employee gives notice to terminate the contract in accordance with the terms of this contract. Here again, it may very well be that both parties hope that the employment relationship will soon be resumed and not ruptured for good. Nevertheless, it can be reasonably said that, in such a case, the employee does wish to put an end to the existing contract as it is, even though he remains ready to conclude a new one on more favourable terms. And the employer has no choice but to accept the situation that the old contract is at an end, whatever his desire to retain his employee's services. All he can do to retain these services is to enter into another contract on new terms. This is why the Donovan Report[24] concludes: 'There seems to

23. This, of course, is true in Britain because there is no statute which expressly recognizes the right to strike in general terms. If such a statute existed, the problem would be raised in different terms and it might be necessary to adopt the theory of suspension. In countries such as France and Italy, for example, this adoption came just after the constitutional recognition of the right to strike.

24. op. cit., para. 948. The Report also uses an argument deduced from sec. 4 and 5 of the Conspiracy and Protection of Property Act 1875: cf. para. 949, op. cit.

us to be no need and no justification for ignoring the plain language of the notice to terminate the contract given by the employee' – more precisely for interpreting this notice as merely a notice of the intention to break the contract, as Lord Denning had proposed.

As to the case where the notice given by the employee is not quite clear, because it is only a notice of the intention to strike, the Donovan Report rejects the view (suggested by some commentators) that it should necessarily be construed as a notice of intended breach of contract. It says that, if this notice is not less in length than the notice required for termination of the contract and in the absence of any contrary intention clearly expressed, it ought to be treated as a notice of termination and produce the same effects.[25]

All these objections still stand today and they explain that the concept of suspension has not yet been able to triumph in the UK. However, the strong pressure that has been exercised in its favour explains the introduction in the new Industrial Relations Act of a section 147 which is fundamental in this matter. It may be said that this section goes a long way toward enacting the 'suspension' view – although the word 'suspension' is not used and the consequences are not exactly the same. Actually, this sec. 147 was only a minor provision in the initial Bill: but its importance has progressively grown in the course of the legislative procedure; and it is in its definitive form that it is closest to the theory of suspension (even though it does not go as far as the supporters of this theory would have desired).

It results from the new law that today there are no longer two, but three possibilites open to the strikers.

If the strikers still decide to give notice to terminate their contract, this notice will naturally produce its normal effects and the contracts will be terminated. This situation is indeed exceptional, but it may happen: some unions actually insist on giving such notices, even today.[26]

If the strikers do not give any notice at all or if they only give a notice which is not of the required length, the old situation also still prevails: the strike is regarded as a breach of contract and it produces all the consequences normally attached to this breach. It entitles the employer to dismiss – a dismissal which may not even be regarded as an unfair dismissal in the sense of sec. 22 and sec. 24 of the Industrial Relations Act.

But sec. 147 relates to a third situation which is the most important since it is the only one that does not lead to the termination of the contract. It is the situation where the strikers give a notice which is neither in its terms nor in its intent a notice to terminate the contract: it is only a notice of the intention to take part in a strike. If such a notice is given either by the employee himself or, on his behalf, by his representative (i.e. by the union) and if it is of a duration not less that than which (whether by virtue of any enactment or otherwise)

25. It has even been suggested to enact this in a law. But the Donovan Report raises the problem of the practicability of such an enactment.
26. Such a notice of termination may even be required by law. This is notably the case for seamen, to whom the Merchant Shipping Act, 1970, gives a statutory right to strike that they may exercise by giving 48 hours' notice, after mooring, to terminate their contracts.

this employee would be required to give to terminate his contract of employ-ment,[27] sec. 147(1) of the 1971 Act states that 'unless it otherwise expressly provides . . .', it shall be construed neither as a notice to terminate the contract nor as a repudiation of that contract.

This clause is extremely important: it makes clear that the employee who has given due notice of his intention to go on strike cannot be regarded as having himself terminated his contract. In its original version, however, the Industrial Relations Bill did not alter the common law position that the strike, if it does not produce termination of the contracts of employment, is still an action constituting some kind of breach of contract. It therefore did not remove the strict right of the employer to sue strikers in damages for breach of contract, nor eradicate the view that a strike was 'unlawful means' for the purpose of the torts of conspiracy and intimidation. But the final ver-sion of the Bill went further and provided in sec. 147(2) that, as a matter of principle, the action of an employee in taking part in a strike after due notice of his intention to do so shall not be regarded as a breach of his contract of em-ployment for the purposes of any proceedings in contract brought against him, nor any proceedings in tort, criminal proceedings based on sec. 5 of the Con-spiracy and Protection of Property Act, 1875,[28] or proceedings for unfair in-dustrial practice based on sec. 96 of the 1971 Act.

There is only one clear exception to this principle and it is provided by sec. 147(3). According to it, it remains possible to regard as a breach of contract '. . . any action by an employee which is contrary to a term of his contract of employment (including any term implied or incorporated in that contract by reference to a collective agreement) excluding or restricting his right to take part in a strike.' This is important, because a 'no-strike' clause is often con-tained in a procedure agreement and may be incorporated in the individual contracts of employment. In this case, participation in a strike will constitute a breach of contract, even though due notice has been given.[29]

Even outside of this case, it appears that the striker does not enjoy a com-plete protection – this is what makes the main difference with the true concept of suspension – for the law does not deprive the employer of his right to dis-miss the employee on strike. Section 147(4) expressly states that 'nothing in subsection (2) . . . shall be taken to exclude or restrict any right which an employer would have apart from that subsection to dismiss (with or without notice) an employee who takes part in a strike'. No doubt, the same Industrial Relations Act establishes, in its sec. 22(1), the right of the employee not to be

27. It results from this that the notice can be of different length for the various cate-gories of employees working in a same enterprise: professional employees, white-collar workers, manual workers, etc. This may give rise to difficulties if the notice is given on behalf of the employees by the union. Several notices must then be given at different times or, if only one notice is given, it must be of the greater length.
28. This text makes it a crime to break one's contract of employment wilfully and maliciously if there is reasonable cause to believe that the action will endanger life, cause serious bodily injury or cause the damage or destruction of valuable property.
29. It must also be noted that the protection granted by sec. 147 to the strike (as de-fined by sec. 167(1) of the Act) does not extend to 'irregular industrial action short of a strike' (as defined by sec. 33(4)).

unfairly dismissed, and it regards dismissal as an unfair industrial practice. But sec. 26 provides that dismissal of an employee for taking part in a strike (even if due notice has been given) shall not be regarded as unfair, except in very restricted circumstances – namely if it is shown that one or more employees who also took part in that action were not dismissed for that reason or, after having been dismissed, were offered re-engagement on the termination of the strike and that the reason (or at least the principal reason) for which the claimant was selected for dismissal or not offered re-engagement was his having exercised, or indicated his intention to exercise, any of the rights conferred on him by sec. 5(1) of the Act, that is,

(a) the right to be a member of such trade-union as he may choose;

(b) the right to be a member of no trade-union or other organisation of workers;

(c) the right to refuse to be a member of any particular trade-union or other organization of workers;

(d) the right to take part in the activities of a trade-union, or to hold office in this trade-union, etc.[30]

This provision under sec. 26 is very important indeed. It gives to the employer a large power to dismiss the workers engaged in a strike (even in a lawful strike), as long as he does not act in a discriminatory manner and with an anti-union purpose. This power is all the more dangerous because even the rules on the burden of proof are favourable to the employer. Of course, it is provided by sec. 24(1) that this employer must first give the reasons for the dismissal and establish that they are sufficient; but, in fact, it is very easy for him to find apparently legitimate grounds, such as a misconduct or a reduction in the labour force. In this case, it is up to the employee to prove that the dismissal is actually discriminatory according to sec. 26(2) and (3). The result is that all strikers are exposed to retaliatory measures on the part of the employer; and this is particularly true for union leaders, union representatives, shop stewards, etc., since none of them enjoys a special protection as is the case in other countries – France, for example. Of course, they always have the possibility to prove that they have been unfairly dismissed and that the termination of the contract by the employer constitutes an unfair labour practice, but this evidence may be difficult to bring.[31]

30. It clearly results from sec. 26 that the same rules here provided in case of a strike also apply in case of any 'irregular industrial action short of a strike'.

31. Section 106 of the Industrial Relations Act expressly provides that unfair dismissal is to be dealt with by complaint to an industrial tribunal. If the complaint is established, the tribunal may make, if it thinks it practicable to do so, a recommendation of reinstatement (subsec. (4)). If it does not do so, or the recommendation is not complied with, it shall make an award of compensation (subsec. (5)). By sec. 116(1), this compensation is to be such as the tribunal considers 'just and equitable' in all the circumstances, having regard in particular to any expenses reasonably incurred by the complainant in consequence of the act complained of and to the loss of any benefit which he might reasonably be expected to have had but for the act. Subsection (3) provides that the tribunal is empowered to reduce the compensation if it finds that the complainant has contributed to his own loss. If a recommendation of reinstatement has not been complied with because the complainant has unreasonably refused an offer on the terms of the recommendation, then his compensation will be reduced; otherwise, if

It is even possible to go further and say: not only the dismissal based on the participation of an employee in a strike is perfectly lawful, but it need not even be preceded by a notice on the part of the employer. This seems to result from sec. 147(4), which states that the employee may be dismissed 'with or without notice'. In spite of the appearances, it is not contrary to the principle laid down in sec. 147(2)(a), since this provision relates only to proceedings in contract brought *against* the employee: it may therefore be admitted that in all other respects the strike, even though due notice has been given, remains a breach of contract – which means that it can justify the immediate termination of the contract by the employer; it constitutes in itself a ground for dismissal without delay. At least this is the solution which seems to derive from the text of sec. 147; it will only be certain after it has been affirmed by the courts. At this point, it will be very clear that the system adopted by the Industrial Relations Act is quite distinct from the ordinary system of suspension of the individual contracts of employment: it is far indeed from giving a similar protection to the strikers.

In fact, this analysis of sec. 147 of the Act has already forced us to touch upon another subject, one on which we have to concentrate now.

The right to dismiss or refuse reinstatement in case of suspension

If we now suppose that the principle is that of the suspension, it remains important to determine what is exactly the situation of the employee with regard to dismissal or refusal of reinstatement (both problems are practically similar).[32] Of course, the fact that the employment contract is only suspended during the strike means, first, that it is not automatically terminated by the employee who ceases to work and, second, that it does not constitute in itself a ground for termination by the employer – that is a ground for dismissal. But the question remains to know whether, during the time the contract is suspended, the employer is authorized to resort to other grounds – notably economic or disciplinary grounds – to get rid of his employee or, at the end of the period of suspension, to refuse to reinstate him (with or without usual requirements such as previous notice, severance pay, redundancy payments, etc.) or whether there is an absolute prohibition to take any action against the strikers. In the first case, of course, the employee is only partially protected against the employer; in the second case, the guarantees he enjoys are much more complete and effective. The solution of this problem is very important in order to evaluate the real bearing of the principle of the suspension of the contracts of employment as a consequence of the strike.

---

the non-compliance is because of the employer's refusal, the compensation will be increased (subsec. (4)). Section 118 places a top limit on compensation of the amount equal to 104 weeks' pay for the complainant or £4,160, whichever is the less. It must be noted that this basis of compensation, though limited, is wider than that of common law damages: cf. *supra*, footnote 15.

32. There is no need to say that, during the time the contract is suspended, the employee himself is entitled to terminate it, on condition only that he observes the required period of notice. In fact, the normal rules of termination apply in such a case.

In that respect too, we find many differences according to the countries concerned, and there seems to be a slow gradation between them according to the effectiveness of the protection they grant to the strikers.

We shall not come back to the case of *Britain* – although it is in this country that the protection appears (at least in law if not in fact) the most insufficient. We already know, indeed, that the employer has a very large power to dismiss his employees on the mere basis of their participation in a strike, without even having to set forth economic or disciplinary motives. But this is precisely why the British system cannot be characterized as a true system of suspension of the employment contracts. It is only in the countries which openly admit the principle of suspension that we can verify the exact consequences of this principle as to the right of the employer to dismiss the striker or to refuse his reinstatement.

All these countries indeed decide that the strike does not constitute in itself a ground for dismissal – but that the dismissal remains possible for other reasons. The only differences existing between them relate to the sorts of reasons that may be invoked and, still more, to the party on which lies the burden of the proof.

It is in *Sweden* that the employer seems to have, in that respect, the largest power. All the regulation is based on the idea that, as a matter of principle, each party can terminate the contract of employment, even during the strike, the only condition being to give the required previous notice. Just like the employee who finds a new profitable job is entitled to give notice of termination during the strike, the employer can give notice of dismissal to his employees. There is, however, a limit to this right to dismiss: it cannot be used for the purpose of bringing pressure upon the other party to yield in the dispute. It is certain, for example, that the employer is not allowed to give notice to all the strikers or to the strike leaders as a method of retaliation, for this would clearly be an infringement of the right to organize (which right is not distinct, in Sweden, from the right to strike and is protected by law: sec. 3 of the Act concerning the right to organize and the right of collective bargaining, 1936). Although it is sometimes argued that the principle *inter arma silent leges* should apply in this case and that the employer should be permitted to use notices of termination as a means of economic action, the Labour Court has definitely taken the other view. But it remains true that it is not up to the employer to motivate his decision of dismissal by giving economic reasons – for example, the fact that a reorganization of his firm has reduced his need for manpower; it is only if an action is brought before the Labour Court that this employer will have to justify himself and to prove that he has an objective reason other than the strike or the union activity of the striker to dismiss him.

The same rules also apply when, at the end of the strike, the employer refuses to take the striker back to work and to replace him in his former position. Such a refusal is equivalent to a dismissal; it is valid under the same conditions. It must be noted, however, that, in fact, the matter is most often settled by a reinstatement clause which is a part of the new agreement. This clause may prescribe, for example: 'All workers for whom work can be provided are re-instated with priority. Workers who want to be reinstated shall report to the employer before a certain date.' Such a clause does put aside the ordinary rules of giving notice of termination. A worker who does not report ceases to be employed. The same is the case with workers who have reported their willingness to return, but for whom the employer is not able to provide work.

In most other countries, the principle is that the employer can dismiss the worker or refuse his reinstatement only if he has a ground for such a measure and if he can bring evidence of it. Even then, however, we find several nuances.

In *Germany*, the problem has not been extensively discussed and it does not seem to have ever been brought before the courts. There is no special rule, indeed, which applies in this case and it is necessary to refer to the ordinary law of dismissal as resulting from the 1952 law on Protection against Dismissal (*Kündigungsschutzgesetz*). The employer may always terminate the contract of employment by giving due notice, under the condition to indicate the ground on which he bases his decision, so that the court can verify whether this ground is valid or not and, consequently, whether the dismissal is justified or not. This regulation applies in case of strike. It can be said therefore that the striker does not enjoy a complete protection since he can be dismissed and lose his job; but the employer is far from having a complete discretion in that respect. In practice, the dismissal or the refusal of reinstatement will be regarded as valid only if it is founded on an economic necessity (surplus of personnel because of rationalization of the enterprise or hiring of permanent replacements) or on a misconduct on the part of the employee. It must be added that, in fact, the most important limitation brought to the protection granted to the employees on strike derives in German law from the possibility of a defensive lockout, which involves termination of the contracts of employment, not at the individual, but at the collective level. This is an effective way of retaliation, one to which we shall have to come back later.

In *Italy* and in *France*, the employees on strike seem to be still better protected against the dismissal or the refusal of reinstatement. The principle is that the employer is deprived of his right to terminate the contracts of the strikers, unless he proves very particular circumstances.

The solution was certain in *Italy* even before 1966, when the law granted to the employer the right to terminate *ad nutum* the contract of employment, by application of Art. 2118 of the Civil Code: it was then admitted that this right was suspended during the strike, because it was incompatible with the official recognition of the right to strike by Art. 40 of the Constitution. The situation is even clearer today, since the law of 14 July 1966 has abolished the right to terminate the contract *ad nutum*. It is now provided that the dismissal must be based either on a just cause (dismissal without notice) or, at least, on a justified motive (dismissal with notice), the burden of proof lying on the employer. If the employer does not comply with such a requirement, the dismissal is deprived of all effects and it can give rise, not only to damages, but also to reinstatement (Art. 18, Workers Statute, 1970). If the reason for dismissal is strike or other trade union action, the remedy of injunction is available (Art.

(28, ibid.). It therefore appears that dismissal of a striker or refusal of his reinstatement can be valid only if the employer brings evidence of a just cause or of a justified motive independent from the strike itself (for example, a grave misconduct on the part of the employee, such as a violation of the duty not to reveal industrial secrets).

In *France* the same result is reached through the theory of the abuse of the right to terminate the contract. We already know that, in normal circumstances, Art. 1780 of the Civil Code gives to the employers the right to terminate at any time the contracts of his employees, under the condition to give previous notice and, as the case may be, to pay the special compensation required by law (*indemnité de licenciement*). But it is clear that this right is not absolute and that the employer can make abuse of it: he is then liable for 'abusive dismissal' and he can be sued in damages by the dismissed worker. Normally, however, it is up to this worker to prove the existence of such an abuse – and this can be a difficult task for him. But the situation is different in case of a strike. It is admitted – as a consequence of sec. 4 of the law of 11 February 1950, which states that 'the strike does not break the contract of employment, except in case of *faute lourde* on the part of the employee' – that the right to terminate *ad nutum* the contract of employment is suspended during the strike. The courts therefore consider that, if the employer dismisses a worker during the strike or refuses to reinstate him, the abusive character of this measure can be presumed. This is a rigorous application of the theory of the abuse of rights. In case of a dispute before the court, it will then be up to the employer to prove either that the dismissal is justified by a *faute lourde* committed by the employee (this is a different problem, to which we shall come back later) or that it is justified by another reason quite independent from the strike (an economic reason or a misconduct that is not in relation with the strike). Many court decisions have made application of this principle, and they have also ruled that the employer is not entitled to refuse the reinstatement of the strikers on the basis that some replacements have been hired during the strike in order to maintain operations. Such replacements can only be hired on a temporary, not on a definitive basis. At the end of the strike, if it is not possible to give a job to all those who apply for it, preference must be given to the strikers. The refusal to reinstate a striker under the pretext that he has been replaced is normally regarded as *abusive* (although there are some contrary decisions of inferior courts on this particular point). It so appears that the protection granted to the employee on strike is rather complete in this system – at least theoretically.

We must consider separately the situation in the *United States,* because the problem here is raised in different terms – not in terms of possibility of dismissal, but in terms of bars to the reinstatement of the worker on strike. It is admitted, according to the NLRA, that the employee has normally a right to reinstatement at the end of the strike, at least in the case of a lawful strike. This right is something important (all the more because it can be readily enforced and it is not limited to the payment of damages, as in most countries) and rather exceptional in a country where the employment relationship can normally be brought to an end at any time, even without previous notice. It is intended to guarantee the free exercise of the right to strike and to protect the striker against retaliation by the employer. However, it appears that this right to reinstatement is not always absolute. Its exact extent depends on the type of strike – and here we find an important distinction between two types of lawful strikes.

If the strike has been caused or prolonged, in whole or in part, by an unfair labour practice on the part of the employer, it is normally called an unfair labour practice strike. An example would be a strike in response to an employer refusing to bargain in good faith, as required by the NLRA. It is clear that unfair labour practice strikers hold the highest status in respect to the rights retained. They have an absolute right to reinstatement if the strike was lawful in all other respects (i.e., if it was for a lawful purpose and lawfully conducted). The employer is required to take them back on their unconditional application for reinstatement. The fact that the workers, during the strike, have obtained employment in an equivalent job elsewhere does not constitute a bar to their reinstatement if they apply for it. And the right to reinstatement exists even if the jobs have been filled during the strike by replacements: the workers, in this case, can force the employer to fire the replacements. This is extremely important: it means that the unfair labour practice strikers can be temporarily replaced during the strike, but not definitively.

Some difficulties can arise, of course, at the end of the strike, if there are not enough jobs to give to all the strikers. This may be due, for example, to a bona fide reduction in operations. In this case, the reinstatement is not compulsory. But the employer is under the obligation to place the workers that he cannot reinstate on a preferential hiring list. Anyway, it is up to the employer to prove this impossibility of reinstatement, and the NLRB is rather severe on this point.

The other lawful strikes, which are not unfair labour practice strikes, are called economic strikes. They are those which have as their purpose the satisfaction of demands for changes in the terms of employment, such as wage increases or better working conditions. The employees who take part in such strikes have only a limited right to reinstatement. Of course, they normally retain their status as employees, and as such they may claim their former jobs. But there are some limitations upon these two principles.

First, the strikers retain their status as employees only until they find a substantially equivalent job. This important restriction results from sec. 2(3) of the NLRA, which provides that 'the term "employee" shall include . . . any individual whose work has ceased as a consequence of, or in connection with, any current labor dispute . . . and *who has not obtained any other regular and substantially equivalent employment.*'*

Second, the strikers may claim their former jobs only if permanent replacements have not been hired. It is here admitted that the employer, during the strike and prior to the striker's application for reinstatement, may protect his business by hiring replacements. This is the only way for him to maintain operations during the strike, and it is perfectly normal, as long as it is not a way

* Author's italics.

of retaliation against the strikers. In this case, if permanent replacements have been lawfully hired, the employer may refuse the reinstatement of the strikers without being subject to liability for unlawful discrimination. The strikers who cannot be reinstated remain entitled only to an offer of reinstatement whenever a vacancy occurs in a job that they are qualified to fill.[33]

Of course, the strikers are also deprived of their right to reinstatement if their job has been abolished during the strike because of a reduction in operations. Here again, the burden of proof lies on the employer – and the employee who is not reinstated will be placed on a preferential hiring list.

More generally, we may say that it is always up to the employer to prove that he has a legitimate justification for not reinstating the employee who has engaged in a lawful strike. In fact, the problem always arises in the course of unfair labour practice proceedings, because the unjustified refusal of reinstatement, just like the unjustified dismissal, can be regarded as an infringement on the right to strike guaranteed by sec. 7 of the NLRA and, therefore, constitutes an unfair labour practice on the part of the employer. The employee will then bring a charge before the NLRB, claiming that he has been unduly refused reinstatement; and it will be up to the employer to show that he had good reasons – in fact, a legitimate and substantial business justification – not to reinstate him.

On the whole, it appears that the worker is not completely protected in the US because he can be permanently replaced during the strike. This replacement will be a bar to his reinstatement. But in all other cases, he escapes all measures of retaliation on the part of the employer.

The limits of suspension in case of unlawful activities

We have considered until now only the case of lawful activities and we have ascertained that the principle usually admitted in such a case is the principle of the suspension of the contract of employment. Most countries, however, admit that this principle is not applicable in case of unlawful activities.

There is only one exception to this rule, and it is *Britain*. Paradoxically enough, the country which has been the latest to introduce a certain form of 'suspension' of the contracts of employment now goes further than any other by giving to this 'suspension' a very large area of application, without regard to the lawful or unlawful purpose or method of the strike. In fact, the only difference which exists in Britain between 'lawful' and 'unlawful' strikes relates to the existence or the absence of a previous notice. If the strike is not preceded by a notice, it is true that it is regarded as a breach of contract and that it constitutes a ground for immediate dismissal by the employer. But as soon as due notice has been given, the strike is lawful and sec. 147(1) and (2) apply – whatever is the object of the action and without regard to the way it is conducted. Even the fact that the strike constitutes an unfair industrial prac-

33. This solution has been affirmed in *Laidlaw Corp.*, 121 NLRB No. 175 (1968), enf'd, 141 F. 2d 99 (7th Cir. 1969), cert. denied 397 US 920 (1970).

tice does not alter the rule and does not affect the status of the individual employee. The Act, indeed, does not make, as a matter of principle, any distinction according to the purpose or the methods of the strike as to its effect on the
contract of employment. It is only the phenomenon 'strike' that is here considered and the existence or the absence of a due notice. This shows how much
the present Act is still linked with the old common law principles.

There are, however, two restrictions which must be brought to this analysis.
More precisely, there are two types of activities which are subject to particular
rules and which are not protected by the form of 'suspension' normally applicable to lawful strikes. First, it is clear that all sorts of 'irregular industrial
action short of a strike' (as defined by scc. 33(4)) havc bccn voluntarily omitted
from the text of sec. 147. Second – this is a more important exception, and has
already been mentioned – sec. 147(3) expressly provides that it will remain
possible to regard as a breach of contract '. . . any action by an employee which
is contrary to a term of his contract of employment . . . excluding or restricting his right to take part in a strike'. This is the closest we may find, in Britain, to what would be regarded in another country as an unlawful strike – and
it produces the same effect: it entitles the employer to order immediate dismissal.

It appears, nevertheless, that outside of these two cases the principle of
'suspension' receives a very large application since it concerns all types of
strikes. But it should not be forgotten that the effect of this principle is considerably limited by the already mentioned sec. 26 of the Industrial Relations
Act, which also applies to all strikes (preceded or not by a due notice) and even
to all other types of 'irregular industrial action short of a strike, and which
gives to the employer a very large power to dismiss the employee on strike,
with or without notice, as long as this dismissal does not constitute a discriminatory action directed against the union. This, in fact, leaves to the employer the possibility to take into consideration the purpose of the strike and
the individual behaviour of the striker.

It remains true, however, that the situation in Britain is very particular in
that respect, and it can easily be verified that all other countries restrict the
application of the principle of suspension to lawful activities. They set it aside
in case of unlawful activities and they return in that event to the principle of
termination of the contract. The idea is normally that the exercise of an unlawful activity is a breach of contract that allows the employer to terminate
this contract on his initiative and at his discretion.

The problem is therefore to determine what are these unlawful activities. As
a general rule, we may say that this concept includes either participation in an
unlawful strike or accomplishment of an unlawful individual act in the course
of a lawful or unlawful strike. If we want to go further into the details, we have
to turn successively to each of the countries concerned.

It is probably in the *United States* that the statutory regulation is the most
precise and complete on this point. There are many strikes which are regarded
as unlawful by the NLRA itself (such as a strike to compel someone to cease
doing business with someone else or not to bargain with the union certified as

representative); there are some which are in violation of another statute (such as a strike for racial discrimination, contrary to the Civil Rights Act of 1964); there are finally those strikes which are in breach of the peace obligation or in breach of a contract (such as a strike in violation of a 'no-strike' clause included in a collective agreement, unless this strike is caused by 'serious' and 'flagrant' unfair labour practice on the part of the employer). It is also possible that the individual worker engaged in a lawful strike commits some unlawful acts such as acts of violence, sabotage, etc.

It is certain that in all these cases, the employee on strike does not automatically lose his status as employee. He remains covered by sec. 2(3) of the N L R A. This sec. 2(3) indeed is not restricted to lawful activities: it refers to any sort of labour dispute, and sec. 2(9), which defines this expression, does not make any distinction either between what is lawful or unlawful. Consequently, it appears that even the strikers engaged in unlawful activities retain their employee status and all rights pertaining thereto.

But this principle is subject to two important restrictions. First, there may be – at least theoretically – a contract provision which expressly says the contrary. The principle that even the employee engaged in an unlawful activity retains his status as employee is not required by public policy; it can therefore be set aside by an explicit clause included in the individual contract of employment. This clause can validly provide that the contract will be terminated in the event of participation in an illegal strike or in case of misconduct on the part of the employee. The situation, however, is very rare in practice because of the very small importance of individual contracts of employment in the American system. More important is the second restriction to the above-mentioned principle. It consists of the employer's right to discharge. It is certain that such a discharge of an employee engaged in an unlawful strike does not constitute an unfair labour practice on the part of the employer, because it is not in itself an act which infringes the right to strike. The N L R B and the courts are very clear on this point. The dismissal in this case can even be summary: it need not be preceded by any sort of notice. Once the employee is discharged, then he ceases to be an employee under sec. 2(3) of the N L R A, and he loses all his rights under this Act. He naturally has no right to reinstatement. He may always be rehired, but, in this case, his status will be that of a new employee; he will have lost all rights previously acquired such as seniority rights. In fact, the situation is exactly as that which results from a break in the continuity of employment.

These rules can naturally cause severe hardship on employees, and arbitrators will often vacate or modify the discharge if there is evidence that the employer has condoned the action of the strikers or has, by his own conduct, waived his right to discipline them. The only requirement is that this condonation be clear enough. It may be deduced, for example, from the fact that the employer has permitted the strikers to return to work, has even solicited them to do so or at least has agreed to take them back. This last situation is rather frequent. There is often an agreement that is entered into by the employer and the union at the end of the strike and that expressly provides that no sanction will be taken against the strikers so that they will all be able to return to their former jobs.[34]

Of course, the employer is under no obligation to take a similar decision with regard to all workers engaged in unlawful activities, not even with regard to all those who have participated in the same unlawful strike. There is no requirement for him to act on an all-or-none basis. Therefore he will not be charged with discriminatory conduct if he chooses to make an example of some of the employees while permitting others to continue to work. The only limitation to this freedom of choice is that he should not discriminate in such a way as to engage in anti-union activity and to violate the fundamental rights of the workers (right to organize, to strike, etc.). This means two things. First, the employer can only discharge those who did take a personal part in the unlawful action. If an example has to be made, it must be properly chosen: and it is clear that the employer cannot discharge any worker who was not really a participant. At most, some courts have held that an employee's failure to repudiate an illegal strike or a violent strike, i.e., failure to 'dissociate' himself from his union's illegal action, may be ground for discharge under the rationale that, by so failing to repudiate, he became a participant, even though he did not actually engage in any of the activities. Second, it has even been held, and notably by some arbitrators, that when confronted with an illegal strike, the employer cannot single out any individual striker he chooses for discipline. He cannot single out those who have only been participants if their actual leadership is not proven. Conversely, he can single out the union officials who have a high duty not to engage in any illegal strike and to prevent others from violating a no-strike clause.

This is the general situation, but there are some special rules which apply in the case provided by sec. 8(d) of the NLRA. This sec. 8(d) forbids the union which is party to a collective agreement to resort to a strike in order to support a demand for terminating or modifying this agreement during a period of 60 days after a special notice has been given (or until the expiration date of the agreement if this date occurs later). It is a sort of peace obligation that is imposed on the parties during this period. But this peace obligation is covered by particular rules. Section 8(d) provides that 'any employee who engages in a strike within the sixty-day period . . . shall lose his status as an employee of the employer engaged in the particular labour dispute.' This loss of status is automatic and it occurs even if the employee is participating in what would otherwise be a legal economic strike (but not if he is participating in an unfair labour practice strike: for unfair labour practice strikers are not bound by this statutory notice requirement). But it only produces consequences for the purposes of sec. 8, 9, and 10 of the NLRA. This means that it deprives the employee of all the protection he normally enjoys against the unfair labour practices committed by the employer: this employee can be lawfully discharged and the discharge will produce all its normal effects. But if there is no

---

34. Such agreements sometimes also provide that the union shall take no action against employees who refused to support the strike, crossed the picket lines during the strike, etc.

discharge, the employee will recover his status of employee at the end of the strike, when he will be re-employed. Section 8(d) *in fine* provides that 'such loss of status for such employee shall terminate if and when he is reemployed by such employer.' The loss of status is therefore not definitive. In case of re-employment, everything will be as though the status had never been lost: notably the worker will regain all the seniority rights he had previously acquired. Continuity of employment will be regarded as having never been broken.

There is, on the contrary, a complete lack of statutory regulation on this matter in *Sweden*. It has therefore been up to the labour court to answer two questions:

1. When is a strike unlawful?
2. What is the effect of an unlawful strike on the individual contracts of employment?

It is not our purpose to answer here the first question. We must, however, mention the fact that a strike is not unlawful by reason only that it is not preceded by a notice. This is indeed an old problem and, as soon as the principle of the suspension of the contracts of employment was admitted in Swedish law, it was argued that such a principle should only apply to the workers who had given notice to their employer. This view was notably defended as early as in 1911 when a Bill on collective agreements was laid before the Parliament. It was then suggested that a warning should be given before the parties could resort to industrial action, but this proposal remained without practical consequences since no legislation followed upon the Bill. If the idea progressively gained more support, it was essentially at the theoretical level: the principle did not become law. The situation was not even changed in 1928, when the Act on Collective Agreements was promulgated: for there was nothing in this Act that required notice before resort to industrial action. It was only in 1935 that a rule to that effect was introduced by an amendment to the Mediation Act, 1920. Under sec. 3(a) of this Act, notice must be given to the employer and to the mediator of the district – unless it is impossible for valid reasons – not later than the seventh day before a stoppage of work is carried into effect; and this notice must state the reasons for which the strike is organized. But, in fact, this warning provision is only a rule of order, that tends to inform the employer and to make possible the procedure of mediation. This is why its non-observance is punished by a fine,[35] but it does not constitute in itself a breach of contract nor does it affect the legality of the action. It is true that, in practice, the unions ordinarily observe the rule. But if they do not, this does not change anything as to the effect of the strike on the individual contracts of employment: notably it does not produce as a consequence the termination of such contracts.

It is another problem to know whether the rules imposing a previous notice before termination of the contract of employment are applicable in the event

35. Prosecutions on this basis appear to be very rare in practice.

of a strike – in which case the strike called without notice would constitute a breach of contract and give the employer the right to terminate this contract. Of course, the statutory law does not provide any requirement of this sort. And it is quite exceptional to have such a period of notice imposed by the individual contract of employment. But it happens more commonly that the same requirement is made in a collective agreement. From the early part of the twentieth century, some collective agreements started to provide that a period of notice (usually limited to 1 or 3 weeks) should be observed in case the employment relationship should cease. It is this that has become more and more frequent today, and is the reason why there has been much discussion on whether such rules are applicable when the employees decide to go on strike. It has been claimed that these employees should (either by themselves or through their representative: the union) give notice and wait until the expiry of the period of notice, or, at any rate, as a substitute for this notice, give warning of the strike at such time in advance as corresponds to the usual period of notice. This would amount to an extension of the peace obligation normally imposed on the parties by the law – which extension is allowed by sec. 4, last para., last subdiv. of the Collective Agreements Act, 1928. However, the opposite solution has also been proposed, on the basis that the strikers actually do not want to terminate their individual contracts of employment.

The case law is clearly in favour of this second attitude. In many cases concerning collective agreements concluded by manual workers and in several different connections, the Labour Court has decided that lawful strikes do not in themselves interrupt the operation of the contract and that the strikers are still to be regarded as employees, irrespective of the fact that notice of termination has been given or not.[36] In these cases, it has never been claimed that omission to observe the period of notice provided for in the collective agreement or in the individual contract would constitute a breach of contract. The same position also prevails as to most categories of salaried employees – although it has been here more disputed. In the Bank Clerk case,[37] the Labour Court decided that there was no duty for the employees to give notice before resorting to industrial action. Of course, this solution was based on an interpretation of the collective agreement and an analysis of the intention of the parties: and there is always a possibility that the court may find that the parties really intended to read a peace obligation into the periods of notice established for the termination of their employment contracts. But it does not seem that this possibility has ever been used by the court.[38]

The principle is therefore very clear: no notice of any sort is required before

---

36. Cases cited in F. Schmidt, *The Law of Labor Relations in Sweden*, p. 203.
37. AD 1948, No. 47. This case is discussed in F. Schmidt, op. cit., pp. 204–5.
38. There is only one exception to this case law and it applies in a very special field: the merchant marine, where there are special statutory regulations. In several cases, it has been decided that merchant marine officers were guilty of breach of contract and desertion from ship service because they had gone on strike without giving the individual notice that was required of them. But this solution seems to be imposed by very particular circumstances and it cannot be extended to other categories of salaried employees. On this point, see F. Schmidt, op. cit., pp. 203–4.

the employee goes on strike; the strike can be regarded as lawful even though the contractual periods of notice provided in the collective agreements or in the individual contracts of employment have not been observed.

This does not mean, of course, that all strikes are lawful. There may be illegal strikes, notably when they violate the peace obligation. The question then is to know what is the effect of the participation in such an illegal strike on the individual contract of employment – more precisely, whether the employer can use in this case his disciplinary powers. The law indeed does not yet seem definitively settled on this point.

The matter was first brought before the Labour Court in a case where the illegal strike had been called by the union.[39] The court insisted on the idea that the individual employees can only be disciplined if they have taken a personal and active part in the illegal action. In view of the fact that the law protects the right to organize, the court expressly stated that it would be unfair to make, as a matter of principle, the individual members pay for what the union does contrary to the agreement, at least so far as these members do nothing else than what they are obliged to do, that is, follow the directions of their unions. Nevertheless, it has also stated that the employees cannot be regarded as protected against all disciplinary actions only because of the existence of this right to organize. In fact, the court laid down the principle that, in such a situation, the acts of each employee must be judged independently.

The problem has arisen more recently in the case of a strike which was not authorized by the union.[40] Some workers had been disciplined in a plant after a wildcat stoppage of work that was in violation of the peace obligation. The Labour Court held that the measures were valid as long as their purpose was not to punish the breach of the peace obligation (in which case the employer would not have been entitled to use his disciplinary power), but to punish the breach of duty committed by the employees under their employment contract.

In any case, it appears that in Sweden the participation in an unlawful strike does not bring about in itself an automatic termination of the contract; it is only a ground for disciplinary dismissal on the part of the employer.

The law concerning this problem in *France* has also been laid down by the courts, but on the basis of an important statutory provision: the famous sec. 4 of the law of 11 February 1950, stating that 'the strike does not break the contract of employment, except in case of *faute lourde* (serious misconduct) on the part of the employee'. It is necessary to define this concept of *faute lourde* and to determine its criterion before examining what is its impact on the individual contract of employment.

The definition of *faute lourde* cannot be found in the statutory law. We may infer from the case law that *faute lourde* may exist in two situations.

First, it is a *faute lourde* to participate in a strike that is not protected by law. It is essentially for that purpose that the courts have tried to determine the precise content of the 'right to strike'. Having admitted that the strike is,

39. Case 1934, No. 179.
40. Case 1970, No. 6.

in its principle, protected by law, the courts have had to decide in what exceptional cases the strike may become unlawful or abusive. In spite of a certain terminological confusion, it seems that a distinction can be made between the two notions.

Some strikes are in themselves and in all cases condemned by the courts: they are said to be unlawful (*illégitimes*). They are outside the limits of the right to strike. They may be unlawful: because of their objective (political strike or, in some cases, sympathetic strike); because of the type of pressure and methods used (for example, the slow-down strike: it is even commonly said that this type of pressure does not really constitute a strike); or because they were called in spite of a particular provision of a collective agreement.

Even when a strike is lawful in itself, it may be condemned in a particular case because of some special circumstances. In other words, it is covered by the right to strike, but it constitutes an abuse of this right. Such a strike is said to be abusive. This may be due to the methods of pressure used during the strike. Some types of strikes (short and repeated stoppages of work; strikes called by surprise; rolling strikes affecting each division of a plant, one after the other etc.) are often considered abusive in view of the particular circumstances in which they took place.

There are, however, some hesitations as to the relations between such concepts of unlawful or abusive strike and the notion of *faute lourde*. The predominant case law affirms that the mere participation in an unlawful strike – and even in an abusive strike – constitutes automatically and by itself a *faute lourde*; but this position is largely challenged today by legal commentators and it is openly rejected by some courts. The claim is that the traditional analysis does not fit with the original character of the strike, which is not a series of individual actions, but a collective phenomenon. In fact, when the law speaks of a *faute lourde*, it takes into consideration an individual behaviour: and it is true that the evaluation of the existence and of the seriousness of the misconduct can be made only at the individual level. On the contrary, when the courts have to decide about the unlawful or abusive character of a strike, they cannot do it from a strictly individualistic point of view: they have to make their estimation at the collective level. There cannot be, therefore, an exact correspondence between the two notions of unlawful or abusive strike and of *faute lourde*. It is only by way of an approximation that it can be said that the participation in a certain type of unlawful or abusive strike constitutes a *faute lourde* on the part of the individual; but this approximation is not always true and is often misleading. Besides this theoretical criticism, there is also a practical objection that can be made about the present case law: it is that it permits the employer to pick out among those who participated in the unlawful strike those whom he wants to get rid of – in fact, to engage upon anti-union and discriminatory activities. The courts indeed try to take this into account, and this is why they pay much attention to the particular circumstances of each case. Sometimes they draw a distinction between the leaders of the strike (who are charged with a *faute lourde*) and the mere participants (only charged with a *faute légère*). They notably make this distinction in case of a strike that is in violation of a clause included in the collective agreement :[41] they consider that the rank-and-file employee is not necessarily able to determine by himself whether the strike is or is not in breach of the agreement and they decide that it would be too rigorous to charge him with a *faute lourde*.

There is a second type of situation in which a striker may be charged with a *faute lourde*. Even when a strike is, as such, considered lawful and not abusive, and therefore protected by law, it may be the occasion for individual employees to commit unlawful actions. The problem does not any longer concern a collective action, but an individual behaviour – which makes easier the estimation of *faute lourde* by the court. This is, in fact, the true domain of *faute lourde*. These unlawful actions may consist in violence, fraud, sabotage, desertion from the services of security, etc. They may also pertain to the occupation of premises, the organization of unlawful picket lines (when the purpose is to prevent other workers from entering into the plant premises), etc. In some cases, they may even constitute a criminal offence (Art. 414 and 415 of the Penal Code, concerning all activities interfering with the right to work).

Once the *faute lourde* is defined, it is necessary to determine its exact effect on the contract of employment. We know that the law itself provides that, in case of a *faute lourde*, the strike causes the termination of the contract: and we have already noted that this termination is the only efficient sanction of the *faute lourde* (damages being normally quite ineffective). Some questions arise, however, as to the true nature and the procedure of this termination. Two main principles must be mentioned here.

The first one concerns the party who takes the initiative of the termination. It is no longer claimed today that the termination of the contract automatically results from the strike – and therefore that it is attributable to the employee's initiative. There is no doubt that *faute lourde* only gives to the employer a 'just cause' to terminate the contract. This involves the consequence that termination is effected on the employer's initiative: it takes the form of a dismissal. Undoubtedly this dismissal is justified by the misconduct of the employee and this is why the employer is not subject to all obligations normally imposed on him in case of unilateral termination of the contract (giving of previous notice and payment of severance pay). It remains, however, a dismissal, and it obliges the employer to comply with such requirements as the obtaining of a special permission of the Works Committee of the enterprise or, failing that, of the Inspector of Labour if the dismissed worker was a union delegate or an employees' representative. In any case, the employer cannot sue the employees for damages on the ground that they have summarily terminated the contract.

Once it is admitted that termination must be regarded as a dismissal decided by the employer, a question remains to be answered, concerning the exact nature of this dismissal. The fact is that a dismissal is a double-faced measure: it can be the mere application of the right given to each party to terminate unilaterally the employment relationship in case of a contract for an indefinite period (Art. 1780 of the Civil Code); or it can also be a sanction – the most

41. Soc. 6 May 1960 (six cases), J.C.P., 1960, II, 11692.

serious sanction indeed – taken by the employer on the basis of his disciplinary power. It is, in fact, rather difficult to make a clear distinction between these two aspects, and the courts often maintain a certain confusion. The problem, however, is of some importance – notably when a collective agreement or the written shop rules provide for a special procedure to be followed in case of a disciplinary sanction: the question arises whether this procedure is to be applied. It seems, in fact, that the answer should be affirmative, and this is the second principle that has to be mentioned here: the dismissal based on a *faute lourde* must normally be regarded as a disciplinary sanction. This opinion is supported by the fact that, if the employer does not want to go so far as dismissal, he can use his disciplinary power to pronounce other sanctions, like temporary suspension, transfer of job, reprimand, etc.

A last problem remains to be examined with regard to the situation in France: it concerns the case where there is no *faute lourde* (serious misconduct) committed by the employee, but only a *faute légère* (minor misconduct). There is no doubt that sec. 4 of the law of 11 February 1950 cannot be applied in this case. Some courts, however, take a stand that is not favourable to the employee. They decide that if the employer cannot dismiss such an employee, he can at least take other disciplinary measures less serious than the dismissal: transfer to another job, reduction to a lower rank in the hierarchy, deprivation of some particular rights or benefits, reprimands, etc. The matter indeed is not definitively settled, neither in the courts, nor in the opinion of the legal commentators.

Some courts, in fact (but they are only in a minority), even decide that, if a *faute légère* is not sufficient to allow the employer to terminate the contract on the basis of his disciplinary power (as is the case when there is a *faute lourde*), it is at least sufficient to allow him to terminate it on the basis of the power given to each of the parties to the employment relationship to terminate it unilaterally (Art. 1780 of the Civil Code). The termination would then be lawful (which means that the employer would not have to pay damages for 'abusive termination'), even though it would not appear as being justified by a *faute lourde* committed by the employee (which explains why the employer would remain subject to all obligations normally imposed on him in case of unilateral termination of the contract: payment of severance pay and giving of a previous notice or, failing that, payment of a special compensation for summary dismissal). This analysis appears subject to criticism, because it establishes between the two categories provided by the law of 1950 (existence or absence of a *faute lourde*) a new and intermediate category (existence of a *faute légère*). In fact, it is better to admit that, during the strike, the right of unilateral termination of the contract based on Art. 1780 of the Civil Code is completely suspended and that there is no derogation to this rule in case of a so-called *faute légère*.

The situation in that respect is not very different in Italy and in Germany, although there is no express statutory provision comparable to Art. 4 of the law of 1950.

In *Italy*, of course, it is also admitted (although the view was challenged at the beginning) that the principle of suspension, to the extent that it forbids discharge of the striker, is not absolute and that it does not apply in all cases: it does not apply, in fact, to unlawful strikes or unlawful individual actions. The problem has therefore been to define these two categories, and it has been up to the courts to fill the gap left by the legislator in that field. The judges have had to determine what individual actions committed during the strike are to be regarded as unlawful (such as violation of domicile, sabotage, occupation of the plant premises, violence or intimidation by way of picketing, etc.). They also have had to determine what strikes are unlawful – this being all the more important as Italian courts, following the majority of legal commentators, are traditionally hostile to the theory of abuse of rights. Therefore it was essential for them to define with precision the criterion between lawful and unlawful strikes. Sometimes, of course, there are statutory provisions (notably in criminal law) which are applicable (e.g. when strikes might be hazardous to safety or to public health). Several unsuccessful bills have been presented since 1948 in order to make some other types of strikes unlawful. In fact, it is still up to the courts to decide what strikes are unlawful in view of their objectives or of their methods. It is in the case law that we find the condemnation of such strikes as 'go-slow' strikes; intermittent stoppages of work of short duration; strikes predominantly intended to cause damage to the employer and to disorganize the enterprise; strike in reverse, etc. – although decisions have frequently been in conflict, particularly in recent years. It is also the case law that says that the strike is lawful even though it is not initiated by the union, nor preceded by a warning (except when usages make it necessary) nor by any attempt at conciliation.

What is important for us, anyway, is the fact that the immunity normally granted to the strikers as a consequence of the 'right to strike' disappears in such cases of unlawful strikes or unlawful individual activities. Of course, the individual contract of employment is not automatically terminated in such a situation, but there is a failure to execute the contract that makes it possible for the employer to resort to such a measure as a dismissal. There is no doubt that this dismissal must be justified by the seriousness of the misconduct committed by the employee and that it must be adapted to the particular situation of each individual employee. As a matter of principle, it is admitted that the mere fact of participating in an unlawful strike is not a sufficient justification for such a dismissal, unless there are some special circumstances such as the non-compliance with a precise order given by the employer. But the main problem is to know whether the dismissal in such a case must be analysed in terms of disciplinary power or in strictly contractual terms. This problem is not only theoretical, but it also has practical consequences under the new Workers' Statute of 1970. For sec. 7 of this statute provides for some rules applicable in case of disciplinary sanctions taken against the employees: notably the sanctions must be in accordance with the regulations previously announced to the workers and they must be in conformity with the provisions on the subject, if any, established by collective agreements; the worker must be previously informed of the charges against him and granted a hearing; he may appeal against the sanction to a conciliation and arbitration committee (in which case the sanction remains suspended until the committee reaches a decision) and he may finally seek recourse in a court of law. It is therefore a question to know whether the dismissal of a striker engaged in an unlawful action should fall under the scope of sec. 7, as a disciplinary action, or rather be treated as an ordinary termination of the contract and be subject to sec. 18 of the same statute. This question remains open in Italy and it is difficult to say which opinion will finally prevail.

The principle of the suspension of the employment contract is no more absolute in *Germany* than in any other country, and it is set aside in the cases already mentioned: unlawful individual action in the course of a (lawful or unlawful) strike or participation in an unlawful strike.

Individual actions are normally regarded as unlawful when they fall under the definition given by Art. 823, cl. 1, of the BGB, that is, when they violate 'the life, body, health, liberty, property or any other right of another person'.

As to unlawful strikes, we know that this category is particularly broad in Germany, since it includes all the non-union strikes (the point is now very clear since a decision of the Federal Labour Court in 1963, and it was re-affirmed in 1969)[42] and all those which are not in conformity with the criterion of 'social adequacy' as applied by the courts.

In all these cases, it appears that the employee ceases to be protected by the theory of the suspension of the contract: he may be dismissed by the employer (just as he can also be sued for damages by him). This dismissal is a sanction, justified by the breach committed by the employee; therefore, it has not to be preceded by a notice nor is it subject to the restrictions included in the 1952 law on Protection against Dismissal: for sec. 3 of this law expressly provides that it is not applicable to the dismissal which serves as a sanction in the course of an economic dispute between the employer and the workers.

There is only one problem, in fact, for the strikes which are in violation of the peace obligation. Of course, it may be claimed that such strikes are socially inadequate and consequently unlawful. But the difficulty comes from the fact that the peace obligation is not really binding on the individual employees (for it is admitted in German law that this peace obligation does not belong to the normative part of the collective agreement and, for this reason, does not become part of the employment contract). It is not sure therefore whether the criterion of social adequacy really applies in this case and whether the employees can be dismissed for having acted in violation of a 'no-strike' clause. The solution of this problem is uncertain and there is a divergent case law of the Federal Labour Court on this point (at least according to the *obiter dicta*, since the court has not yet had to answer the question directly).[43]

But it appears indeed that the same reasons for hesitation also exist in most other types of unlawful strikes. As the definition of these unlawful strikes is not very clear in German law and as it largely depends on the appreciation of

42. See Chapter 5, p. 288.
43. See Chapter 3, p. 154.

the courts, it is a heavy burden for the employee to judge by himself whether the strike is lawful or not: and experience shows that there are many cases in which the exact character of the strike cannot be sufficiently investigated by the individual worker. Therefore it seems very severe to put this employee, who only followed the orders given by his union, under the threat of a dismissal on the pretext that the strike was unlawful.

More generally and from a theoretical point of view, it can be claimed that the power given to the employer to dismiss the individual worker because of his participation in an unlawful strike is not quite in conformity with the sociological analysis of the strike and the view that it is a collective phenomenon. Such an analysis indeed normally implies that the individual action of the worker is merged into the collective action of the group to which he belongs: therefore it makes it difficult to understand why this individual worker still can be penalized through the loss of his employment.

In any event, it should not be forgotten that the employer is always entitled to use against the strikers the defensive lockout, which is presumed to produce as a consequence the termination of the contracts. Since he can use this weapon in case of a lawful strike, *a fortiori* can he do it also in case of an unlawful strike: and this is certainly the most effective way of retaliation.

A final observation can be made with regard to all of the countries here concerned. It is noticeable that all this regulation of unlawful activities connected with the strike remains, in many cases, rather theoretical and is not put into practice. At most it can be said that it serves as a threat against the strikers more than as a sanction. The reason for this is that (as we have already noted in the case of the United States) an agreement is often entered into by the two parties at the end of the strike. Sometimes (notably in Germany and in Sweden),[44] the employer states that he will not negotiate before the strikers have returned to work – so that, in fact, he waives his right to dismiss the workers or to refuse their reinstatement if they agree to go back to their jobs. In other cases, the employer agrees to negotiate while the strike is still going on: it is then the agreement itself which imposes upon the employer the obligation to reinstate all the workers engaged in the strike – even those who could be charged with misconduct and without regard to the lawful or unlawful character of the strike – and which prohibits all measures of retaliation on both sides. Such an agreement or award has a 'normative' character – which means that it gives a direct right to each individual employee. In this case, there will be no need for a new contract of employment: the worker reinstated will retain all rights that he had acquired under his former contract and this contract will be regarded as having never been terminated, but only suspended. This should be kept in mind when one is tempted to think that the legal solutions which permit the dismissal of the individual workers engaged in an unlawful strike or charged with unlawful activities are too severe. It appears,

---

44. An exception to this rule was, however, made in Sweden for the wildcat strikes of the winter 1969–70: the employers agreed to enter into informal discussion with the strikers before their return to work. See, on this point, Chapter 1 p. 35.

in fact, that it is on this point that the gap is the largest between theory and practice.

THE EFFECT OF THE LOCKOUT

The lawfulness of the lockout

The problem of the lockout is a difficult one. The law is usually much less clear on this point than it is on the strike. In some countries, there is even no statute which expressly deals with it (France, Italy, Germany); everywhere the case law is less abundant than for the strike (largely because the phenomenon is much less frequent, at least today); even the legal commentators are divided on the solutions to be given to the problem. One thing is sure: nowhere is there a general statutory provision recognizing a right to lockout or a liberty to lockout as there are concerning the right to strike or the liberty to strike.

The situation is all the more complicated as there are, in fact, many different types of lockouts. The lockout may first be defensive and be a response to a strike, a sort of 'counterstrike' (then it may concern either only the strikers or all the employees of the firm, strikers and non-strikers). It may also be offensive: as a sympathetic action in favour of another employer whose employees are on strike; as a retaliation after the end of a strike (the employer decides to lockout after the strike has ended, even though the employees are ready to resume work, in order to prove that 'he is still the boss'); as a threat, before the initiation of the strike, in order to discourage the employees from going on strike (preventive lockout); in case of a strike affecting only part of the personnel, in order to encourage the non-strikers, who will be deprived of their jobs by the lockout, to bring pressure on the strikers in favour of a termination of the strike. In some cases (offensive lockout or defensive lockout directed against the strikers), the lockout constitutes a weapon that is at the disposal of the employer to support his position in a labour dispute, just as the strike is a weapon at the disposal of the employees; in other cases (defensive lockout directed against the non-strikers), it constitutes a technical and economic decision, merely founded on the necessity to close the plant. In this respect, it appears more or less useful, according to whether the employer is given the power or not to lay off without notice and without pay the employees who have no work to perform. It is naturally much less necessary in the countries like Sweden, the United States and Britain, where the employer normally has this power – which means that he has no real duty to furnish work to his employees – than in the others, like France, Germany or Italy. Often, in fact, these two aspects of the lockout (offensive or defensive weapon; technical or economic decision) exist simultaneously (even though one or the other may be predominant): this gives to the lockout an ambiguous character.

This ambiguous character is naturally reflected in the way the lockout is regulated and it is obvious that, in the different situations that we have mentioned, the solution cannot be the same. Also and above all, we must note that there are important differences from one country to another. We find here a much greater dissimilarity in the general attitudes towards the lockout than towards the strike, according to the countries concerned. Broadly speaking, we may say that there is a main division between three groups of countries.

The first group includes Sweden and Germany, where the lockout is placed on the same level as the strike, and is regarded as equivalent to the strike and subject (*mutatis mutandis*) to the same rules. The idea is that both types of industrial action resemble each other by their objectives, the way they are conducted, the strategy and tactics used, etc., so that a parallel can be drawn between them.

In *Sweden*, the strike and the lockout have both existed for a long time. They have always been regarded as correlative weapons and considered equivalent from the legal point of view. Just as the employers have long acknowledged the right of the workers to go on strike, the workers have implicitly acknowledged the right of the employers to resort to lockout – with exactly the same restriction (notably in case of an existing collective agreement). All rules in Sweden which concern strikes also apply in the same way to the lockout – notably the necessity of a warning imposed by the Mediation Act: in fact, these rules concern all situations where there is stoppage of work.[45]

In *Germany* too, the prevailing opinion is the equivalence of the strike and the lockout. This has almost always been the case, since the last years of the nineteenth century, when lockouts started to be more frequent. It was then admitted that the employer had to give notice of the lockout just as the employees had to give notice of the strike: and the lockout was thus regarded as a collective termination of the employment contracts. Since 1945 the situation is naturally different. One could have thought that the lockout would be given a treatment different from the strike since the state Constitutions which recognize the right to strike do not refer to the lockout and there is even one state Constitution, the Constitution of Hessen, which expressly makes the lockout illegal.[46] As to the Bonn Basic Law, it only contains the already mentioned Art. 9, sec. 3, which guarantees 'the freedom of combination for maintaining and promoting labour and economic conditions'. This provision has been construed by the legal commentators and the courts as covering lockouts as well as strikes, this opinion finally receiving support from the Federal Labour Court in the famous decision laid down by its Big Senate on 28 January 1955. This decision actually concerned the strike. If it had admitted the lawfulness of the strike on the basis of a legal reasoning, the conclusion would probably have been the unlawfulness of the lockout – since the lockout appears, in fact, as a measure of retaliation which restricts the effectiveness of the strike. But we know that the Federal Labour Court actually resorted to a

45. In practice, there is a very close connection between strikes and lockouts in Sweden. It often happens that a strike is followed by a lockout covering the same group of workers and vice-versa. This is due to technical reasons: each party wants to have a word on the matter at what time work shall be resumed.
46. See Chapter 5, p. 290.

sociological analysis, and this analysis naturally led it to treat the lockout in exactly the same terms as the strike. The principles laid down by the court were those of 'equality of weapons', 'parity of combat' and neutrality of the State. These principles therefore give to the employer the possibility of resorting freely to the lockout, even to the offensive lockout, just as the unions can freely resort to the strike. They also regard the lockout (like the strike) from a strictly collective point of view and separate it from the ordinary law of individual relations: so that this lockout appears as a specific institution, quite distinct from dismissal. This is very important indeed: it means that the lockout is not subject to the rules ordinarily imposed for the individual dismissal (requirement of previous notice; special restrictions provided by statutes and notably by the 1952 Act concerning pregnant women, handicapped workers, members of the Works Council, etc.). All this explains why German law is not conceived as 'protecting' one party more than the other: it places both partners on the same level and gives them the same weapons.[47]

The important thing is that in both Sweden and Germany, where the lockout is regarded as the equivalent of the strike, the lockout is considered lawful as a matter of principle. It can only become unlawful under particular circumstances, similar to those which, according to the case law (in the absence of statute), equally make the strike unlawful.

In a second group, we find the countries like the United Kingdom or the United States, where the lockout is not really viewed as equivalent to the strike, but where it is not regarded as unlawful as a matter of principle either. It is only subject to particular rules which are somewhat stricter than those applying to the strike. But this is not very important since these two countries grant to the employer (either in all cases, as in the US, or when it is provided by contract, as in Britain) the right to lay off his workers without notice and without pay when he cannot provide them with work: the result is therefore that the lockout – at least the defensive lockout – is not so necessary.

In *British* law, the lockout is subject to the same rules as the ordinary dismissal. This means that the employer has the power to lock out his employees, but on the condition of giving previous notice to terminate their contracts. In fact, the lawful or unlawful character of the lockout is only dependent on the factor of notice, by application of the idea that, when the contract is not for a fixed term, the employer can lawfully bring it to an end, often without special ground, only by giving notice to terminate it.[48] The lockout is therefore lawful if the correct period of notice has been given, unlawful in the other case (it

47. This position is naturally criticized on the double basis: (1) that the 'social State' clause of the Bonn Basic Law should impose a different evaluation for strikes and lockouts, because a 'social State' must protect the economically weaker party, that is, the employee; and (2) that the principle of equality of weapons does not fit in with the reality: the strike indeed is necessary to protect the employee against the decisions unilaterally taken by his employer while the lockout is only a collective dismissal. Cf. T. Ramm, *Der Arbeitskampf und die Gesellschaftsordnung des Grundgesetzes: Beitrag zu einer Verfassungslehre*, 1965, G. Fischer Verlag, Stuttgart.

48. The length of this period of notice is determined in the same way as the period of notice required from the employee. But the minimum length provided by statute is here different. According to sec. 1(1) of the Contracts of Employment Act, 1963, as

is then a breach of contract).[49] There is only one situation in which the employer is excused from giving notice: it is when the employee has himself committed a breach sufficiently serious to be regarded as a repudiation of the contract. In this case, of course, he may be dismissed summarily, without notice. But this is, after all, the mere application of the law of dismissal. It appears, in fact, that in the United Kingdom the lockout is not subject to any other requirement than those required for the individual dismissal.

In the *United States*, on the contrary, the lockout is regarded as distinct from the dismissal. In fact, the situation of the lockout is not quite clear in American law. No doubt there does not exist in the present legislation a general provision that gives to the employers a right to lock-out, in the same manner as sec. 7(a) of the NLRA gives to the employees the right to strike (or at least to engage in concerted activities). Nevertheless, on the other side, it appears that the lockout cannot be regarded as a breach of contract since American law does not impose on the employer the duty to furnish work to his employees. In fact, there is some doubt as to the legal status of the lockout. This doubt is particularly great in the case of the offensive lockout resorted to in the course of the bargaining process. This lockout has long been held to be an unfair labour practice under the NLRA; some courts, however, have taken a different stand and recognized strikes and lockouts as correlative measures of economic action, which labour and management may lawfully use in the event of a bargaining impasse; as to the Supreme Court, it has held that such a lockout decided by the employer in the course of a labour dispute in support of its bargaining position is not *per se* illegal and that the real test of legality is the intention of the employer. The question, however, appears as being not yet definitively settled. Conversely, the situation is clear for two types of lockout. One is surely lawful and it is the defensive lockout, notably that which is decided by the employer in response to a strike threatening to cause unusual economic hardship: the employer is then allowed to shut down his plant in order to avoid loss. The other is certainly unlawful and it is the lockout which constitutes an unfair labour practice under the NLRA – for example, because it tends to restrain or coerce the employees in the exercise of their fundamental rights guaranteed by sec. 7 (sec. 8(a)(1) of the NLRA) or because it is discriminatorily motivated (sec. 8(a)(3) of the NLRA).

The situation is quite different in a third group of countries which includes *France* and *Italy*. In these two countries, of course, it was formerly admitted that the lockout was equivalent to the strike and subject to the same rules. But this view was completely abandoned as soon as the strike started to enjoy a special protection by law: for it appeared very clearly that such a protection should not extend to the lockout. The idea is now well-established that em-

---

amended by sec. 19 of the Industrial Relations Act, 1971, this minimum varies with the period of continuous employment: it is one week after 13 weeks of continuous employment, but it grows up to 8 weeks after 15 years or more of continuous employment.
49. In case it is unlawful, the employee can naturally obtain damages, but these damages are usually very small (as they are indeed when they are granted to the employer for breach of his contract by the employee: cf. *supra*, footnote 15).

ployers and employees are not in an equal and symmetrical position in labour relations. The emphasis is put on the differences existing between the strike and the lockout from the economic, sociological and moral standpoint, and it seems normal that these differences find expression at the juridical level. Furthermore, everybody agrees that the lawfulness of the lockout considerably impairs the right to strike: for this right does not only imply that the worker is protected against individual measures taken by the employer such as dismissal, but also against collective measures such as the lockout affecting either all the employees of the enterprise or only a group of them.

All this explains the change which has taken place in the French and Italian law of lockout, although, in the total absence of legislation, the matter has had to be decided by the courts. Of course, the lockout can no longer be regarded as a criminal offence (as it was in France until the law of 25 May 1864, which abolished the crime of coalition for employers as well as for employees – and as it still was in Italy until the repeal of Art. 502 of the Penal Code of 1930):[50] and in that respect, it can be said that there is a liberty to lockout, which is protected against the State. But there is no right to lockout as there is a right to strike. This derives very clearly from the fact that the Constitutions of both countries remain equally silent on the problem of the lockout whereas they recognize in exactly the same terms the right to strike. This clearly shows the intention of the drafters of these Constitutions to differentiate between the two types of actions.[51] It explains then why the lockout cannot be assimilated to the strike. In fact, the lockout does not appear as a specific type of action, subject to particular rules. It remains, on the contrary, subject to the general principles of the civil law. Since the employer is usually obliged to furnish work to his employees, the lockout appears as a failure on his part to perform the contract: it cannot consequently be regarded as a protected activity, it is unlawful as a matter of principle, it is a breach of contract.[52]

There are only two cases in which the lockout may become lawful, and these cases are practically the same in France and in Italy. The lockout may first be lawful when it is used against the strikers as a response to their strike, by application of the *exceptio non adimpleti contractus*.[53] This *exceptio* is admitted in all contracts where both parties assume an obligation and it makes it possible

50. It was the Court of Cassation which decided for the first time, on 18 June 1953, that this Art. 502 had been implicitly abrogated, with regard to the lockout, by the decree-law of 23 November 1944, abolishing the corporative regime. Later, the Constitutional Court, on 4 May 1960, decided to vacate Art. 502 as incompatible with the principle of union freedom guaranteed by the Constitution.

51. In France as in Italy, however, it is sometimes claimed that, in spite of the silence of the Constitution, the right to lockout is implicitly given to the employers as correlative to the right to strike. But this opinion precisely rests on the old idea of a parallel between strike and lockout: it is only a minority opinion, having less and less support.

52. The idea traditionally admitted in Italy is that of *mora creditoris* or *mora accipiendi*. Under the new Workers' Statute of 1970, it is also claimed that the lockout constitutes a violation of the right to strike and can be subject to injunction. Some courts have taken this view.

53. There are, however, some doubts, notably in Italy, as to the possibility to apply in this case the principle of the *exceptio non adimpleti contractus*.

for each party to suspend the performance of his obligation as long as the other party does not perform his. The French view is that if the employees cease to work or if they only furnish irregular work, they may be locked out. However, such a lockout loses its justification as soon as the employees are ready to resume work normally – so that these employees appear to be well protected: they finally retain the power to initiate and to terminate the stoppage of work. But the lockout may also be lawful when it is used against non-strikers because the employer is not able, as a consequence of the strike, to provide them with work. Of course, he cannot put forward a mere difficulty to supply work, but only a complete impossibility which must amount to a *force majeure*. It may be the strike of one part of the personnel of the enterprise that makes it impossible for the other party to work (and this is frequent in France and in Italy where the strikes are often partial); or it may be the strike in another enterprise – transportation, raw material or electricity supply, etc. – that forces the employer to stop production (this is also frequent because the unions often try to order a strike in those key enterprises which are vital for the whole industry, so that many other enterprises are actually paralysed). As the employer is normally obliged to pay wages even to non-strikers, he usually prefers to avoid all difficulties by locking out his employees.

These two cases of lawful lockout are indeed based on well-established principles of the civil law of contracts: it is either the *exceptio non adimpleti contractus* or the *force majeure* that justifies the non-performance of his duties by the employer. In these two cases, therefore, the lockout does not appear as a specific, original institution: and this is why it is even doubted sometimes that it constitutes a real lockout.[54]

Anyway it can easily be seen that, in France as in Italy, the only lawful lockout is the defensive lockout – whether it is used against the strikers or the non-strikers. Such a lockout may, of course, appear as useful – especially in these two countries where the right to lay off is not granted to the employer. But it is certain that under the present circumstances an offensive lockout could never be regarded as lawful.

Lockout effect on the employment relationship

In view of these various and even opposite situations, it is now easier to understand that the lockout may produce different consequences on the individual contracts of employment.

All countries make here a fundamental distinction between the lawful and unlawful lockout: but the system adopted is not the same in Britain as in the five other countries.

---

54. At the extreme, it can even be claimed indeed that, in France as in Italy, there is nothing like a lawful lockout: for the stoppage of work on the employer's initiative is only lawful when it is not a real lockout. Even the name 'lockout' tends to be abandoned in this case. In France, for example, when the closing of the plant is justified by *force majeure*, it is usually not called a 'lockout', because this word has a pejorative connotation; it is often referred to as technical unemployment (*chômage technique*).

The reason for this peculiarity is that, in *Britain*, the only difference between a lawful and an unlawful lockout is due to the existence or the absence of a previous notice. Now it is thought that this difference should not have any influence on the effect of the lockout on the individual contracts: it is admitted that in all cases, lawful or not, preceded or not by a notice, the lockout must produce the same consequences. These consequences can be summarized as follows.

Normally, the lockout produces termination of the contract: it is regarded as a dismissal – and this is why it is subject to the requirement of a previous notice to terminate the contract, like any dismissal.

But this dismissal is not conceived as being necessarily final: for, in fact, it is very rare that the employer really wants to terminate the contracts of all of his employees. Normally the employer will offer re-engagement to most of them: and this constitutes what the Industrial Relations Act calls the resumption of work (sec. 25(4) provides that the date of resumption of work is the date '. . . as from which, at or after the termination of the lockout, the other comparable employees of the original employer, or a majority of those employees, were offered re-engagement'). If, at this date, all employees are offered re-engagement, there is no problem: their dismissal will be regarded as having been only a temporary dismissal – and this is why sec. 25(1) of the Act expressly provides that it will not be subject to the rules of unfair dismissal. But if some employees are not offered re-engagement, sec. 25(2) states that they will be able to bring a complaint for unfair dismissal according to the rules provided by sec. 24. Of course, the employer is not obliged to re-engage them: but his refusal of re-engagement is equivalent to a final dismissal, and this dismissal will be subject to the ordinary rules of unfair dismissal, through the control of the Industrial Tribunals and of the National Industrial Relations Court. In fact, the only difference between this situation where the employee has been locked out and the ordinary situation where he is merely dismissed is that here the control will not be made at the time when the employee had to give up his job; it is postponed until the date of resumption of work. But it is exactly the same kind of control that is exercised: it tends to protect the employee against unfair discrimination on the part of his employer.

All this, of course, applies to the case of a lockout that was preceded by an adequate notice to terminate the contracts – that is, a lawful lockout. The question arises therefore whether the solution should be different in the case of an unlawful lockout. But the answer to this question is surely negative. It has never been suggested indeed[55] that the mere failure to give notice should change the lockout into a breach of contract and deprive it from its normal effect, which is to terminate the contract. After all, the only fault committed by the employer in this case is not to have complied with the requirement of a period of notice. This does not justify the maintenance of the employment relationship. In fact, the lockout without notice cannot be compared to the

55. Probably because lockouts are very rare in Britain.

strike without notice (this shows once more the impossibility of drawing a parallel between strikes and lockouts). The employee here has no option: he must consider himself as dismissed and he can only sue for damages – which damages will normally amount to the wages that he would have received had he been given the correct period of notice. It is, in fact, a simple case of wrongful dismissal. Through the remedy of damages, the same result is obtained indeed as if the employer himself had decided – as he could lawfully have done – to end the contract on the spot by paying the wages that should have been paid during that period in *lieu* of proper notice.

It so appears that, with this only exception concerning damages, the lawful and the unlawful lockout produce exactly the same consequences on the individual contracts of employment. In fact, the 1971 Industrial Relations Act does not provide for the lockout any equivalent of what sec. 147 is for the strike. The only notice that can make the lockout lawful is the notice to terminate the contracts. It is not therefore surprising that this notice produces the normal effect: that is, to break the employment relationship. There is no idea of suspension here. But this is compensated for by the fact that normally the employer offers re-engagement to his employees and that the refusal of making such an offer is subject to the ordinary rules of unfair dismissal.

The problem of the lockout is naturally different in the other countries where the lockout does not have to be preceded by a notice to terminate the contract. A basic distinction is there made between the lawful and the unlawful lockout.

The problem first arises as to the lawful lockout. Traditionally, indeed, except in Sweden where it has always been regarded as having a suspensive effect (because of the parallelism with the strike), this lockout was regarded as a termination of the contract and it produced all the consequences of a normal termination. But this did not correspond to the true intention of the parties, neither of the employer who did not want finally to lose his labour force but only tried to exercise a pressure on his employees, nor of these employees who did not want to lose their jobs. This is why the solution has now been largely abandoned.

The principle most commonly admitted is that of the suspension of the contracts of employment as a consequence of the lawful lockout. The employee locked out remains an employee as long as he is not personally and lawfully dismissed. Of course, the lockout may always be accompanied by some individual measures of dismissal concerning such or such employee. But each of these measures has an individual character, and its lawfulness must be appreciated in consideration of the particular situation of the employee concerned (requirement of a previous notice, control of the non-abusive character of the dismissal, etc.). It is quite independent from the lockout as such.

The principle of the suspension is no more disputed in *Sweden* than in the *United States*. In the latter country, it even appears that the express statutory provision which applies to the strikers also applies to the locked out employees: it is the famous sec. 2(3) of the NLRA according to which 'the term "employee" . . . shall include any individual whose work has ceased as a consequence of, or in connection with, any current labor dispute'. This means that the employee who has been locked out does not lose, as such, his status as employee. In fact, if the lockout is offensive (that is, decided before the employees have actually struck), it seems that the employer can only hire temporary replacements: the hiring of permanent replacements would amount to a dismissal and it would be subject to the same rules. If the lockout is defensive (that is, decided in response to a strike), the rules to be applied as to reinstatement are those that we have already discussed. Everything depends on the character of the strike. If it was a lawful economic strike, the strikers can be permanently replaced. If it was an unfair labour practice strike, the replacements cannot be permanent, for the workers are entitled to reinstatement unconditionally. All this amounts to a sort of suspension of the contracts of employment during the time of the lockout.

In spite of the great scarcity of case law on this point and the fact that there has been more discussion among the legal commentators than before the courts, it also appears that the principle of the suspension of the contract is admitted in *France* and in *Italy* in the exceptional cases where the lockout is regarded as lawful. No work is furnished, no wages are paid – but the employment relationship is not regarded as terminated. It resumes its normal course after the conflict has been settled. In fact, we have already noted that, in France as in Italy, this suspensive effect can be based on the ordinary principles of civil law (*exceptio non adimpleti contractus* or *force majeure*), without having to resort to a special concept of lockout.

But this precisely explains why the lockout is of so little interest in the two cases where it is considered lawful in France and in Italy, and why it is in fact so rarely used. The suspensive effect is, of course, understandable in the case of an offensive lockout, but it makes the defensive lockout largely meaningless – whether it is directed against the strikers or against the non-strikers. In the case of a lockout directed against employees who are already on strike, one may wonder about the usefulness of an action that will only produce suspension of the contracts since these contracts are already suspended as a consequence of the strike. It seems indeed that such a lockout cannot really constitute a response to a strike. In the case of a lockout directed against non-strikers, it may also be claimed that the lockout is useless, since the employer is already excused from paying the wages by the mere application of the theory of *force majeure*.

It appears indeed that these two arguments are not entirely convincing. First, it can be said that the lockout remains useful when it is directed against strikers who, instead of engaging in a long and continuous strike, only decide to resort to some types of strikes that suspend the contract for a very short time (so that they do not lose much of their wages) while completely and durably disorganizing the production and disturbing the functioning of the plant (repeated stoppages of work of short duration; rolling strikes; slow-down strikes, etc.): the lockout then makes it possible for the employer to suspend the contract for the entire period during which the production is disorganized, it excuses him from paying wages for a work that may be effectively furnished, but in such conditions that it is not really profitable. Second, it cannot be denied that a lockout decided against non-strikers presents at least the advantage to clarify the situation. We shall see later that the law is usually very strict in the appreciation of this *force majeure* which releases the employer from the duty to pay the wages to non-strikers. It may therefore happen that many difficulties arise when these non-strikers individually apply for the payment of their wages. The lockout permits the employer to avoid these difficulties; it makes the situation more certain and equal for all employees.

In spite of this, however, it remains true that the principle of the suspensive effect deprives the lockout of a large part of its effectiveness when it is a defensive lockout. It is this that has led the *German* courts to adopt a different position on this problem. The German law has been expressed, on this point, by the Big Senate of the Federal Labour Court, in its famous and already mentioned decision of 28 January 1955, following Nipperdey's and Siebrecht's opinion. This decision, in fact, directly related to a case implying a strike, but it dealt extensively with the problem of strike and lockout from a general point of view.

This decision has admitted, of course, the principle of the suspension of the contracts in the case of an offensive lockout or of a sympathetic lockout (in spite of the opinions expressed by some commentators). But it has been held that the defensive lockout (*Abwehraussperrung*) could, on the contrary, produce termination of the contracts. Such a termination is even to be presumed when the lockout is directed against the strikers: for the lockout in this case can hardly have any other meaning than this one. Conversely, it is only a possibility open to the employer when the lockout is directed against non-strikers – which means that this employer may, at his discretion and under the condition of clearly expressing his intention, decide that the contracts will be terminated or merely suspended.

The termination which happens in such circumstances, however, is not necessarily definitive. At the end of the strike, the employer can offer reinstatement to his employees, and in this case everything will be as though the contract had never been terminated, but only suspended: the employee will preserve all the rights (e.g., seniority rights) that he had formerly acquired, he will not have to enter into a new contract. But the employer is by no means obliged to do so, and if he reinstates some employees he is by no means obliged to reinstate them all, he can freely choose and pick among them. Since the workers have lost their status as employees, they cannot demand the application of the principle of equal treatment. The only restriction on the freedom of the employer is that he should not act in a discriminatory way: in which case he might be charged with abuse of his right and anti-union activity; but it is very easy for him, indeed, to set forth economic reasons to justify his choice (for example, a reduction in operation, the hiring of permanent replacements, etc.). In fact if not in law, he has an almost discretionary power and the employees do not appear to be sufficiently protected against the abuses he may commit.

The result is that the lockout appears, in such a case, as a collective dismissal. But it is not an ordinary dismissal. It is not subject to the rules which apply to the individual dismissal (notably the requirement of a previous notice or the special conditions made by the 1952 Act for pregnant women, handicapped workers or members of the Works Council). In fact, it is a specific institution. And this derives from its collective nature. It is certain indeed that the lockout and the dismissal cannot be compared; they are not at the same level of labour relations. The lockout belongs to the world of collective labour relations while the dismissal belongs to the world of individual labour relations. And in the view of the Federal Labour Court, there is no correspondence between these two worlds.

Here we touch, in fact, at the real foundation of the present law of strikes and lockouts in Germany. Strikes and lockouts are exclusively regarded as collective actions of a specific type; they are taken away from the ordinary law of contracts (which only applies to individual relations) and placed under particular rules. This is quite in conformity with the sociological analysis adopted by the Federal Labour Court. This analysis leads it to admit the principle of equality of weapons and parity of combat; it leads it to admit that the lockout must be as available as the strike and, since its suspensive effect would make no sense, that it may have a terminative effect.

This renders, of course, the lockout very effective; it constitutes in fact a serious weapon of retaliation that may be used by the German employers in case of strike. It is also very dangerous for the employees. It considerably reduces their right to strike. One can even say that it goes beyond what a perfect equivalence between the strike and the lockout would imply, since the employer is given the right to terminate the contracts without notice by way of a lockout whereas the employees are not given this right by way of a strike.

All this explains indeed why the present solution is strongly criticized in Germany. It must be noted, however, that it has just been confirmed, with small nuances in its application, by a recent decision of the Big Senate of the Federal Labour Court, laid down on 21 April 1971.[56] There is little hope now that it will be reversed in the near future.

But the problem of the effect of the lockout on individual contracts of employment also arises in connection with unlawful lockouts. The situation is very frequent, and it even appears as the normal one in countries like France or Italy. As a matter of theory, several possibilities may here be contemplated.

It has sometimes been suggested that such a lockout should also produce suspension of the contracts because, after all, it is the solution which is the most favourable to the employees to the extent that it prevents the disruption of the employment relationship. But it appears that this suspension would also present for the workers who are victims of an unlawful lockout severe inconveniences. Such workers would be deprived of their wages, and they would even be obliged to remain at the disposal of the employer during the time of the lockout until this employer decides the resumption of work. The employees would naturally retain the possibility to terminate their contract

56. AP Nr. 43 zu Art. 9 GG. See, on this point, Chapter 5, p. 291.

at any time during the lockout, but they could only do so under their own responsibility (which means that they would have to give previous notice to their employer and that they would lose all rights to severance pay or other compensation).

Another suggestion has been made, that the unlawful lockout should automatically and by itself involve termination of the contracts. Such a termination, of course, would produce all the usual consequences of a termination at the employer's initiative (the employer would have to pay compensation for summary dismissal and severance pay; in France, he would have to get the authorization of the Works Committee in case of dismissal of a union delegate or of an employees' representative, etc.); it would also – quite naturally – be regarded as abusive and would give rise to damages to the employee. This analysis, however, is not without danger for the workers. It deprives them of their jobs. More largely, it is in obvious contradiction with the intention of the parties, that is, to continue the employment relationship (except in case of an individual measure of dismissal).

In fact, the only possible solution, the only one that effectively protects the employee against the unlawful lockout, consists in depriving this lockout of all effect, and this can also be justified by the ordinary law of contracts. In such countries as France, Germany and Italy, it is admitted that the employer is under the contractual obligation to furnish work to his employees and to pay their wages. Now, he cannot unilaterally and without good reason refuse to perform his obligation. If he does so, he commits a breach of contract for which he is responsible. The employees then have a choice. They may regard the breach as a repudiation of the contract and terminate it without notice. But they can also (and this is the most frequent situation) ignore the breach and ask for the continuation of the contract. In both cases, they can get – either as wages or as damages – the equivalent of the sums that they have lost as a consequence of the lockout (with the possibility of complementary damages if they have suffered a special prejudice).

Whatever is the theoretical explanation, the solution anyway is very clear in all systems. In *Italy*, for example, it is on the basis of Art. 2119 of the Civil Code that the employees who have been unlawfully locked out can unilaterally and summarily terminate their contract. Normally, however, they will not do it. They will prefer to resort to the other remedy available in civil law in case of non-performance of the contract – that is, as creditors, put their employers, as debtors, into fault under the conditions provided for by Art. 1206 of the Civil Code. Their contract, in this case, will not be affected by the lockout; it will subsist as it is, without being terminated or suspended.[57]

---

57. The only problem is to know whether the sums due to the employee are due as damages or as wages. The rules applicable in both cases are not exactly the same, not only as to the payments which must be made to Social Security, but even as to their calculation (if the sums are due as damages, it will be necessary to deduct from their amount the wages possibly earned by the employee in another job during the lockout). In fact, the doubt only concerns manual workers, for a statute passed in 1924 states that the suspension due to the employer does not release this employer from his duty to pay wages to the clerical workers.

The rules are rather similar in *France*. It is also admitted that the employee has a choice either to maintain the contract (and to obtain back-pay in the form of damages) or to terminate it. In the latter case, there is some hesitation as to the true nature of this termination. A possible analysis consists in saying that such a termination, although lawful and justified by the breach committed by the employer, is, however, effected at the employee's initiative, which means that, if this employee is excused from giving previous notice to the employer, he is nevertheless deprived of his rights to compensation for summary dismissal and severance pay. But the commentators and the courts are more inclined to adopt another analysis which is more favourable to the employee and according to which it is the employer who must assume the responsibility for the termination: therefore he can be ordered to pay compensation for summary dismissal, severance pay and damages for abusive dismissal.

In the *United States*, the solution is practically the same as in the other countries, although it is not put in contractual terms. It derives indeed from the provisions included in the NLRA. It is certain that the employer who, by locking out his employees, has committed an unfair labour practice must allow these employees to come back to work and normally is subject to a back-pay order.

In all this matter, however, it should not be forgotten that the problem of the reinstatement of the workers (and even of back-pay or damages) is often dealt with in the agreement that is entered into by the employer and the union at the end of the lockout. When such an agreement exists, of course, its provisions are binding and they replace all other rules. It is often in such an agreement that the employees find, in practice, their best protection.

The effect of industrial action on employment rights and duties

The problem actually arises only with regard to employees who remain employees during the time of industrial action, that is, to workers whose employment relationship has not been terminated. There is no need, in fact, to determine the rights and duties of the parties when the relationship has been broken as a consequence of the strike or of the lockout: for the situation is exactly the same as in any other case of termination of the contract, whether it is at the initiative of the employer or of the employee. There is nothing here which is really specific to industrial action. On the contrary, it is important to see what is the exact status of those employees whose contract has not been terminated. This includes not only the employees who were directly engaged in the conflict (strikers or locked out employees), but also those whose working conditions have been indirectly affected by the industrial action – notably those who have been willing but unable to work during the strike. The situation is naturally different for these two categories of workers. But it is rather similar everywhere and it does not appear here necessary to deal separately with each of the countries concerned.

THE SITUATION OF THE STRIKERS AND LOCKED-OUT EMPLOYEES

We can immediately set aside the particular case of the unlawful lockout, for we already know that such an action does not affect in any way the situation of the parties: the wages have to be paid (normally in the form of damages) and everything continues as though there had been no lockout at all. The problem arises in all other cases where it is practically admitted (expressly or implicitly) that industrial action suspends the contract of employment. It is important to determine what are exactly the consequences of this so-called suspension on the rights and duties of each of the parties.

There are indeed some countries (Sweden, France, Germany, Italy) where the solution of this problem is relatively simple because the theory of suspension has long been applied by the courts.[58] This theory, indeed, is not even limited to the cases of industrial action: it also applies in case of illness of the employee; motherhood; requirement for a public service; temporary closing of the plant for technical or economic reasons, etc. The consequences of the suspension are then similar in all circumstances. But there are other countries where the concept of suspension is not expressly referred to in case of strike or lockout. If we can, however, use this concept, it is because the solutions given by the law are exactly those which would normally derive from it. This is notably what happens in the United States. As to Britain, the situation is more ambiguous. Although the drafters of the Industrial Relations Act have obviously avoided to mention the word 'suspension' that had been suggested to them, they have adopted as to the maintenance of the employment relationship (sec. 147) a solution that seems to imply at least a sort of suspension. It is clear, however, that this suspension is rather special, not only because (as we have already seen) it does not prevent the employer from dismissing the employee, but also because it produces limited consequences on the rights and duties of the two parties to the employment relationship. The most we can say for the present time is that these exact consequences are not yet very clear – and they will not become clear until the rather obscure terms of the new law will have been construed by the courts.

Our purpose is not here to go into the details, but only to set forth some of the general principles that are equally valid in all of the countries covered by this study.

Non-performance of work and non-payment of wages

Everybody agrees that the principal effect of the suspension is to excuse each party from the execution of the main obligation that is imposed upon him by the contract: it releases the employee from his duty to perform work and it releases the employer from his duty to pay wages.

There is no difficulty as to the non-performance of the work. Of course, it produces some consequences, notably that the striker or the locked out em-

58. It must be noted that nowhere has this theory been introduced by the legislator; it has been built-up indeed by the courts with the help of legal commentators.

ployee ceases to be under the authority and the control of his employer; therefore he cannot any longer be regarded as the agent of this employer. If he commits some tortious acts, the employer will no longer be liable for him (as he usually is – for example, in France, on the basis of Art. 1384 of the Civil Code).

The employee is commonly allowed to work for other employers during the time of the strike or the lockout. This does not normally mean that he wants to terminate his first contract (although, of course, he might have this intention: in which case he would have to observe the possibly required period of notice); the only obligation he has is not to engage himself in such a way that he would be unable to return to work on a short notice. Some courts, however – notably in France[59] – seem reluctant to admit this possibility for the suspended employee to get a temporary job with another employer: they tend to regard it as a breach of contract and they hold that the employee is compelled to give notice to terminate his first contract before entering into a new one. But such a position is normally criticized on the basis that, in fact, the suspended employee who tries to get another job should only be presumed to have the intention to enter into a temporary employment relationship – which is perfectly lawful for him; if he really wanted to enter into a new permanent relationship (which would also be perfectly lawful under the condition to give previous notice), he would have to express clearly his intention.[60]

The principle of the non-payment of wages is also accepted in all countries. Even if the employee is reinstated at the end of the strike or of the lockout, he is not entitled to any sort of back pay or compensation for the lost wages. This is not the sanction of an alleged breach of contract committed by the employee, it is only the consequence of the non-performance of work: this is why it applies to all types of strikes (without regard to their unlawful or lawful character) and to the lockout. The wages are the counterpart of the work: it is therefore normal that if no work is done, no wages are paid. It is admitted, as a matter of principle, that the reduction in wages must be exactly proportional to the duration of this stoppage (whether the workers receive an hourly payment or a monthly salary).[61] There can be some difficulties of estimation in view of the new and original types of action to which the employees resort today (such as short and repeated stoppages of work; strikes affecting successively each department of a plant, etc.): the solution of the problem then depends on the particular circumstances of the case.[62]

59. See, for example, Soc. 24 July 1952, *Droit Social*, 1952, p. 583.
60. Even in this case, it has sometimes been questioned whether that period of notice could run or not during the time the contract is suspended. But today it is usually admitted that this question must be answered affirmatively.
61. If the period of stoppage of work includes some days for which the law or the collective agreement provides that wages will be paid although no work is performed, these wages are also lost for the worker.
62. Special statutes have been passed in France in order to avoid short and repeated strikes on the part of civil servants (law of 29 July 1961) and public employees (law of 31 July 1963). These statutes provide that any stoppage of work lasting less than one day will give rise to a reduction corresponding to one day's wages.

It should be remembered that the workers actually do not only lose their basic wages, but also all accessories of these wages, such as special compensation for transportation fees, bonuses or premiums for increase in productivity, etc. It can even be provided, in the collective agreement or in the regulations unilaterally established by the employer, that the reduction in the premiums will be greater than the one that would correspond to the period really spent on strike. This is lawful, as long as it is not used as a way of retaliation and as it does not constitute an infringement of the right to strike (at least in other countries than Britain, where such a restriction does not exist).

The problem is particularly acute in *France* because of the practice which has become very common among the employers to give to their employees special premiums designed to reward them for their regular attendance at work. Such premiums are officially called 'regular attendance premiums' (*primes d' assiduité*), but they are also called 'anti-strike premiums' by the employees and the unions. The reason for this is that these premiums, in fact and by reason of their very nature, are not only reduced but completely suppressed in all cases of 'unauthorized absence' – and therefore in cases of strikes. Since the employee breaks his continuity of attendance, he loses the entire benefit of this premium. This practice is therefore very dangerous: it constitutes a tactic in order to discourage the possible strikers by threatening them with loss of an important sum. However, this practice cannot be regarded as unlawful as such. A series of 17 decisions laid down by the Court of Cassation in 1961[63] admitted its conformity with the law, on the basis that the parties have agreed on it when they have entered into an employment contract. The only condition is that such premiums do not clearly and openly appear as sanctions intended to restrict the use of the right to strike. The solution is nevertheless largely criticized by the legal commentators. It is often claimed that all benefits accessory to the wages should be reduced in the same proportion – but only in this proportion – as the wages themselves. There is no doubt that the 'regular attendance premiums', whatever the appearance under which they are disguised, constitute a limitation on the right to strike.[64]

Just as they are not entitled to wages and accessories, the employees are not entitled either to accrued vacation and retirement benefits (under private pension schemes) during the time their employment relationship is suspended. This also is quite normal. It is notably certain that the time spent on strike cannot be regarded as time of effective work for the calculation of the paid holidays. The solution can only be different if it is provided by a collective agreement or by a special agreement entered into by both parties at the end of the strike or of the lockout. It appears, in fact, that such agreements are not infrequent.

Although it is perfectly justified from a logical, legal and even moral point of view, this deprivation of wages constitutes a severe hardship for the employee:

63. Soc. 25 Oct 1961, 17 cases, D, 1961, 752, note by Lyon-Caen.
64. The problem of the validity of such premiums also arose in Italy, especially in the 1950s. It is now solved by sec. 16 of the Workers' Statute, 1970, which expressly prohibits all forms of discrimination by means of collective remuneration.

it is, in fact, the price he has to pay for engaging in an industrial action – it is the price of the strike. Of course, it also occurs in most other cases of suspension of the employment contract, such as illness of the employee or closing of the plant for technical reasons. But it is certain that in such situations, the employee nevertheless receives some sorts of benefits from the State or even from the employer (this is often provided in collective agreements), so that he can maintain himself and support his own family. The question therefore arises whether the employee engaged in an industrial action can also make similar claims and obtain some substitutes for the lost wages.

The easiest way for the employee to obtain funds would naturally be to apply to the State for unemployment benefits. But it appears that in most countries, the striker or locked out employee is not entitled to such benefits. The situation is, for example, very clear in *Italy*, where it is admitted that unemployment benefits can only be allotted to those who are inscribed on a list for obtaining a new job (this excludes the strikers and locked out employees, whose contracts are not really terminated, but only suspended, and who cannot therefore be regarded as unemployed: sec. 75 of the decree-law of 4 October 1935). It is very clear in *Germany* too, on the basis that such unemployment benefits would have an influence on labour disputes and that such an influence would be contrary to the principle of the neutrality of the State. The result is about the same in the *United Kingdom* although the law is far more complex: without going too far into the details, we may say that, as a matter of principle, sec. 22 of the National Insurance Act 1965, disqualifies from unemployment benefits the persons who have become unemployed because of a trade dispute, at least if they have been 'participating in or financing or directly interested in the trade dispute which caused the stoppage of work' – which naturally includes the strikers and the locked out employees.[65] In *France*, the law makes a theoretical distinction between the strikers, who are excluded from unemployment benefits because they are voluntarily unemployed, and the locked out employees, who may be allotted such benefits. The decree of 25 September 1967 expressly states in its sec. 3 that 'the persons whose unemployment is due to a collective labour dispute affecting the enterprise in which they are employed are not entitled to unemployment benefits'. But it adds:

65. It must be noted that, according to this section of the Act, the words 'trade dispute' only refer to 'any dispute . . . which is connected with the employment or non-employment or the terms of employment or the conditions of employment of any persons . . .'. It results from this that, paradoxically enough, the rule does not apply to political strikes. If the motive of their action is political, the strikers are thus entitled to unemployment benefits.

It is not without interest to add that, in Britain, the strikers and the locked out employees are also, as a matter of principle, disqualified from supplementary benefits by virtue of sec. 10 of the Ministry of Social Security Act 1966 – although their families (i.e. wives and children) remain qualified: but their rights have been reduced by the new Social Security Act, 1971.

Furthermore, the Redundancy Payments Act 1965, disqualifies from redundancy payment the worker laid off or put on short-time if the lay-off or short time is 'wholly or mainly' attributable to a strike or lockout whether in the trade or industry of the worker concerned or not, and whether in Great Britain or elsewhere. This disqualification is, in fact, exceptionally wide.

'However, in the case of a lockout lasting more than three days, the Minister of Social Affairs can authorize the payment of unemployment benefits to the workers, although their contract is not terminated.' The last provision is contrary to a well-established tradition: but it does not seem likely to receive many practical applications, especially in view of the fact that the lawful lockout is very rare in France. In *Sweden* also, it has been admitted for a long time that the workers on strike or locked out were disqualified from the benefit of the State unemployment insurance. This solution has been confirmed by the statute on social benefits for persons involved in an industrial dispute, 1968. In the *United States*, the matter is regulated by state laws and the solution, accordingly, varies from one state to another. The principle is that the workers unemployed as a consequence of a labour dispute are disqualified from unemployment benefits. This disqualification does not involve the question of whether the unemployment is incurred through fault on the part of the individual worker. It rests in part on an effort to maintain a neutral position of the State in regard to the dispute and, in part, on the desire to avoid potentially costly drains on the unemployment funds – especially as these funds are contributed to by the employers. But these reasons explain that the disqualification imposed is only a postponement of benefits and in no instance involves reduction or cancellation of benefit rights. The period of disqualification is usually indefinite: in 30 states, it ends whenever the stoppage of work due to the labour dispute comes to an end; in 13 states, it lasts while the labour dispute is 'in active progress', etc.; only two states (New York and Rhode Island) provide for a definite period of disqualification.[66]

Being unable to obtain unemployment benefits from the State, the suspended employees often try to obtain at least some compensation from other workers or from the public. They may receive, of course, support from the union (strike funds);[67] in some countries as in France, they may also receive funds allowed by the Works Committee and intended to be used for 'social purposes' (it is sometimes admitted that such purposes include assistance to the strikers or the locked out employees, but this raises great difficulties in practice). Finally, they may receive funds resulting from contributions collected from the public by ad hoc strike committees. All these funds can be sufficient in some countries, notably in those where the unions are well organized and well disciplined (United States, Britain, Sweden, Germany), but they are not sufficient in other countries, such as France and Italy, where the unions are not wealthy and where they are obviously unable to support long and wide strikes.

This is what has led the workers, especially in these two countries, to try to obtain from their employer himself the payment of their wages or, at least, of some substitutes.

First, it is sometimes admitted that the employer is obliged to pay a certain compensation to his employees during the course of an industrial action if this

66. If the strikers are not entitled to unemployment compensation, they remain however, in most cases and under certain conditions, eligible to welfare payments.
67. On these strike funds in the various countries, see Chapter 1.

action is due to his fault. This does not only happen in case of an unlawful lockout, as we have already seen, but also – quite exceptionally indeed – in some cases of strikes. American law accepts it for the unfair labour practice strike,[68] and the French courts admit it in very particular circumstances: for example, when the strike was originally caused by a long delay in the payment of wages already due.[69] The idea is then that the employees were compelled to go on strike in order to obtain their due; they have suffered a prejudice, which must be repaired, and the best possible reparation consists in the payment of damages equivalent to the wages lost during the strike.

Second, even when the employees have no definite right to require the payment of their wages during the strike or the lockout, they may always ask for it: and they can even try to impose it as a prerequisite to their return to work. This seems unthinkable in some countries like the United States – at least in the case of an economic strike – but it happens more and more frequently in countries like France or Italy. At least this is one of the points that comes under discussion in the final settlement of the conflict, and sometimes a clause of the agreement finally entered into by both parties provides that the wages will be paid, wholly or (more often) partly, to the employees. This is quite lawful since the principle of the non-payment of wages is not imposed by public policy. Therefore the employer can perfectly well waive it, voluntarily or under the pressure of the union.

It also happens very frequently, especially in France and Italy, that the employees ask for the possibility to work to make up for hours which were lost as a consequence of the industrial action. Of course, the employer cannot impose this 'recuperation' and the employees have no right to obtain it (this is expressly provided, in France, by the decree of 24 May 1938, sec. 1, para. 3, which is still in force and which applies equally to strikes and lockouts). Yet both parties may reach an agreement on this point, and they often do, in fact. In this case, the 'recuperated' hours will be paid at the normal rate, not at the overtime rate.

A combination of these various processes is often used, especially after long-lasting strikes. In *France*, for example, after the big strikes of 1958, there was the famous Protocol of Grenelle on which the leaders of the main unions and the representatives of the Government (headed by the Prime Minister himself) had reached an agreement. The Protocol provided some rules which have been adopted by all contracts signed in May and June 1968. The idea was to give to all workers who had participated in the strikes an advance payment of a sum corresponding to one half of the lost wages, with the possibility

68. Of course, it is not quite true that the employer, in this case, is obliged to pay wages for a work that has not been performed; it is more exact to say that he can be ordered by the NLRB to reimburse the employee in the form of back pay. The only difference is that he is then allowed to deduct from the total finally due the earnings that the employee may have made through comparable employment. The compensation is remedial, not punitive.

69. Soc. 12 March 1959, D, 1959, 241; Trib. Seine, 15 Oct. 1952, J.C.P., 1953, éd. C. I., 50402.

of paying back this advance by working overtime, but at the normal rate, before the end of the year 1968, in replacement of the lost hours.

In all cases, anyway, the right to receive the wages is returned to the employees when the conflict comes to an end – in case of a strike, when the employees offer to go back to work, at least if they have a right to reinstatement. To the extent that their right to reinstatement is an absolute one, there is no problem: the wages are due from the time the employees make an unconditional application for reinstatement; if this application is denied for one reason or another (for example, because of union activity), the wages will be due in the form of back pay for the entire period going from the offer to return to work until the date of actual reinstatement in the former job or in an equivalent job. If the employees do not have an absolute right to reinstatement, the solution is, of course, different: it depends on the willingness or ability of the employer to reinstate them. In the *United States*, for example, the economic strikers are entitled to back pay only from the date of their unconditional offer to return to work if their jobs are available at this time. If no job is available, notably because the strikers have been replaced, their right to back pay will start only at the date where they should have been recalled on the basis of seniority and availability of work. The regulation is very complex and precise on this point, because the employees must be protected against all sorts of retaliation on the part of the employers. But the principle remains that no wages are due for work not performed – so that the employers are not required to finance any strike against themselves.

There is still a problem that is connected with the problem of wages because it concerns a counterpart of the work performed. It is the allotment of dwelling accommodation to the employee by the employer when this accommodation is to be considered as appurtenant to the employment. The problem is whether the employee is entitled to keep this accommodation during the time the contract is suspended as a consequence of industrial action. Opposite arguments can here be invoked. On the one side, it is clear that, from a strictly legal point of view, the accommodation is an accessory to the wages and it should be treated in a similar way. On the other side, there are obvious human reasons that make it difficult and hardly acceptable to evict the worker and his family from the place where they live during the course of a strike or of a lockout. Such an eviction, in fact, would easily take the form of a measure of retaliation – except in the rare cases where the employer is really in need of the premises in order to allot them to other workers, for example, those who work in replacement of the strikers. In *Sweden* there is a special Act that deals with this problem: it is the Act on Protection against Eviction in Labour Disputes, that was introduced in 1936 in order to bar the employer from using eviction as a measure of industrial warfare. The principle is that such an eviction cannot take place (except in some particular circumstances) until three months have passed from the day on which the employee ceased to perform his work owing to the dispute.[70] In *France*, there is no particular statute on this

70. See, on this problem, F. Schmidt, *The Law of Labor Relations in Sweden*, pp. 168–9.

point and the problem has only been raised before the courts. Although the decisions are somewhat contradictory and although the solution seems to depend, to a large extent, on the circumstances of the case, the judges are normally reluctant to admit that the worker can be expelled since the contract is only suspended and the eviction would, therefore, only be temporary; but they often decide that the employee may be asked to pay, as a compensation, a sort of rent to the employer – especially when the allotment of the house or of the apartment has a high value and represents an important part of the remuneration.[71]

Maintenance of the subsidiary effects of the employment contract

If all the principal effects of the contract disappear as a consequence of the suspension, it is remarkable – at least in the countries where the theory of suspension is well developed: France, Italy, Germany, Sweden[72] – that most of its subsidiary effects stand during the course of the industrial action. This can be easily explained by the fact that such effects derive from the link which exists between the individual worker and the enterprise to which he belongs. It is certain that this link subsists even during the time the contract is suspended – even during the strike or the lockout.

Nobody doubts, for example, that each of the parties to the contract continues to enjoy some rights and to be subject to some duties: notably, the worker remains bound by the duty of loyalty to the employer (duty not to reveal any secrets as to fabrication, commercial transactions, etc.), while the employer remains bound by the duty to assist the employee (the medical services of the plant must normally remain open) and to abstain from anything that could cause a prejudice to him – apart from the non-payment of wages.

It is no more doubtful that, during the course of industrial action, the worker can still enjoy his rights and perform his duties as employee's representative. This is admitted in *France*, for example, for the *délégués du personnel* and the members of the Works Committees on the basis that, if the individual employment contracts are suspended, the collective labour relations continue – more than ever – within the enterprise. The same solution also prevails in *Germany*, where the workers are allowed to continue to exercise their functions as members of the Works Council during the strike or the lockout. Although these workers do not enjoy a special protection against the employer, because the special rules regarding their dismissal are also sus-

---

71. Cf. G. Vivier, *Le logement accessoire au contrat de travail*, Paris, 1953.
72. The situation is also clear in the *United States*, where the law expressly states that the worker engaged in a labour dispute retains his status as employee. There is more uncertainty in *Britain* because of the imprecision of the terms used by sec. 147 of the Industrial Relations Act (subsec. (2)(a) only states that participation in a lawful strike shall not be regarded as a breach of contract for the purposes of any proceedings in contract brought *against* the employee, not *by* him) and the fact that no article in the law provides for a real suspension. It seems indeed that everything depends in Britain on the individual contract of employment.

pended as a consequence of the industrial action, they retain their status and they continue to hold their office as long as they remain employees and as their contract is not terminated.

The most important problem, indeed, arises in connection with the requirement of a continuity of employment for such purposes as seniority, calculation of the period of notice required on both sides before termination of the contract, estimation of severance payment or redundancy payment, etc. In all these cases, the law takes into consideration the duration of the continuous employment. The general rule is that the period during which the contract was suspended is not to be included in the total length of time during which the worker has been employed – but this period of suspension does not break continuity of employment. In other words, the period of suspension because of strike or lockout is ignored for all purposes.

The solution is very clear in all countries, whether it results from statutory laws or court decisions. In *Britain*, it is expressly provided by paras. 7 and 8, Schedule I of the Contracts of Employment Act, 1963, as to the period of notice required in order to terminate the contract[73] and by sec. 37 of the Redundancy Payments Act, 1965, as to redundancy payments. As these two Acts were anterior to the campaign made in favour of the concept of suspension in Great Britain, one understands the statement made in the Donovan Report that there was no need for abandoning the principle of termination of the contract in case of a strike and that change in the law would be useless: for it is true that, in fact, these two special pieces of legislation had taken care of, and satisfactorily solved, in the framework of the existing law, the two main practical problems arising for the workers in connection with the continuity of employment; and as to the other benefits which depended upon length of continuous service and which could be provided for by the contract of employment itself – such as pension schemes, promotion structures and private redundancy schemes – the Donovan Report stated that it was always possible for the parties, if they wished to do so, to agree that strikes should not be treated as breaking such continuity. To this it can be answered that, from a theoretical point of view, such solutions were in a way illogical, since they were only exceptions to the principle of the termination of the contract (principle according to which the employee, if he was actually re-engaged by the employer at the end of the strike, had to enter into a new contract and consequently to start from scratch to acquire new rights), while they are now perfectly in accordance with the principle of suspension (even if it is a 'special' or 'limited' suspension, as resulting from sec. 147 of the Industrial Relations Act).

73. It is true that the 1963 Act had tried to make strikes in breach of employment contracts break continuity, but this attempt to penalize strikers revealed itself as futile and it was finally repealed by an amendment in 1965. This amendment restored the policy of statutory 'neutrality' towards strikes – so that now strikes count neither for nor against continuity. The Donovan Report rejected the idea (proposed by some witnesses) to reintroduce automatic rupture of continuity for strikes and other industrial action in breach of agreed procedures. And sec. 151 of the Industrial Relations Act maintains the existing rule. See, on this point, Wedderburn, *The Worker and the Law*, p. 121.

The same rule is also affirmed in the *United States*, especially in the essential field of seniority. It is admitted that the employees on strike retain their seniority rights. A denial of seniority by the employer would be unlawful because its result would be to change the relative claims of the employees to jobs in the case of later lay offs or discharges. It would therefore be contrary to the principle that when employees are on strike, the employer cannot in any way impair their job tenure or any conditions of their employment other than pay. It would be a sanction against the strikers. This is why the strikers are entitled to reinstatement with all former seniority rights. American law even goes further than that of other countries in that respect (and this is due to the particular importance of seniority in the American context), since it provides that strikers may not be deprived of seniority credit for the period of the strike if non-strikers are permitted to earn seniority credit during this time.[74] In addition, an employer may not institute a plan after a strike giving super-seniority to workers who did not join the strike and to workers who returned before the end of the strike. It is only possible to offer strike-time replacements superseniority over strikers if it is done because of the difficulty in obtaining needed replacements except by offer of permanent tenure. The basic idea of all this regulation is that, although, as a general matter, wages and other benefits growing out of wage payments (e.g. vacation pay) may be given to non-strikers and not result in a violation of the NLRA, it is forbidden to the employer to discriminate against strikers in respect of any benefit which has an effect on job tenure or any other condition of employment.

Social Security

There is a final problem that can be raised here and it concerns the situation of the individual employee with regard to Social Security laws. This is not a problem of labour relations since actually it does not affect so much the bilateral relations of private law between employer and employee as it does the triangular relations of public law between these two parties and the State. That is why we shall not deal with it extensively; we shall only briefly mention some rules that may be important from the point of view of the individual employee. The situation as regards unemployment insurance has been explained; it will be enough to summarize the regulations applicable in other fields of social security. Broadly speaking, we may say that all these regulations are based on the principle of the neutrality of the State in labour disputes; but the implications of this principle are not conceived in a similar way in the various countries.

As to sickness benefits, the solutions are very different from one country to

---

74. This is naturally a precaution against strike-breakers. In some countries, in fact, the problem of strike-breakers does not arise, because the employers prefer to close the plant completely during the course of the strike. This is notably the case in Sweden, where no employer has ever tried since 1931 to continue operation during a strike (this goes back to an incident which took place in 1931, when the police called upon for the protection of strike-breakers shot at the strikers making a demonstration and caused the deaths of several of them).

another.[75] In *Germany*, for example, the rule is that the social insurance (covering sickness, maternity, death, etc.) is interrupted by the industrial action and that the strikers lose all benefits to which they are normally entitled at the end of a period of three weeks starting with the beginning of the strike (sec. 214 of the Reich Insurance Act). But the employees are authorized to extend their insurance voluntarily after this period under the condition to pay a contribution corresponding to the addition of their own usual contribution and the employer's contribution. The situation in *France* is more favourable to the worker since it results from Art. 253 of the Code of Social Security that strikers continue to be considered employees from the point of view of social insurances (covering illness, maternity, death, etc.), in spite of the fact that their contract is suspended. Although they do not effectively work, they retain the status of insured person and they are entitled to receive normal benefits from Social Security, whatever is the duration of the strike. It must be noted, however, that the time lost as a consequence of the strike cannot be regarded as time of effective work apt to be taken into account to open to a particular worker the right to the benefit of social insurance. In *Italy*, it is admitted that the strike is without any influence on sickness benefits: it does not deprive the worker of his rights. The solution is the same in *Britain*, in application of the idea that the entitlement to such benefits is attached to the status of citizen, not of worker.

This idea, indeed, is also at the basis of the *British* system of family allowances, but it is not admitted everywhere. Yet it is true that *French* law does not contain any restriction as to the payment of such allowances during the time of a labour dispute (it considers, in fact, that family allowances are independent from the contract of employment). The same solution is also admitted in *Germany*, since the law of 7 January 1955 – although this law provides that the allowances can only be paid at the end of the strike. But the principle has been retained in *Italy* of a close connection between family allowances and the wages due to the worker: so that the non-payment of the latter as a consequence of industrial action involves the non-payment of the former. However, this rule is tempered by sec. 30 of the decree of 30 May 1955, according to which family allowances remain entirely due to the employee as long as he can prove that he has effectively worked at least 24 hours per week if he is a manual worker or 30 hours if he is a salaried employee. This rule is not without effect, in practice, on the duration and on the methods of strikers in Italy.

Another aspect of social security concerns the compensation of injury at work. Theoretically the problem does not arise in case of strike, since no work is performed (except by those who are occupied with security or emergency

75. As to the sickness benefits paid by the employer himself under private schemes, it is quite normal that they are suspended during the period of the conflict. This is the situation in Sweden, for example. In a case 1956 n. 20, the Labour Court has applied this principle to the workers of the State Telegraph Agency, who enjoyed sickness benefits under a Basic Agreement. The Court held that the Agency was allowed to cease to pay sickness allowances to all the workers, including those who were reported sick at the time when the union called the strike.

work and who naturally remain covered by the insurance). There may, however, be some exceptional cases in which the difficulty can be raised: for example if an accident happens to the employee while he is going to the plant to inquire whether the work has resumed. Although such an accident, happening on the way to the work, is normally regarded as connected with the work, the solution is different here in case of strike: and the employee will not be able to claim for the benefit of the insurance.

THE SITUATION OF THE NON-STRIKERS

Although the non-strikers are not directly engaged in the industrial action, they may be indirectly affected by this action – notably they can be placed in such a situation that it is impossible for them to perform their normal work. The situation is, in fact, very frequent for two sorts of reasons.

First it may happen that, even when all workers in a given plant are invited to go on strike, some of them refuse to take part in the action. This may be rare in such countries as Sweden, the United States or Britain, where the unions are very powerful and where their orders are actually followed by the majority of the workers, but it is very common in such countries as France and Italy, because of union pluralism (a strike can be called by one union only, and other unions do not join in the movement) and lack of union discipline – also because of the fact that many workers are not really members of any union and do not comply with the instructions given by these unions (this is particularly true in large enterprises, public or private, and for public employees). Most strikes are therefore partial strikes. But even those employees who are willing to work – the non-strikers – may be in fact prevented from working as a consequence of the strike, either because there is a close interdependence between the different jobs or because the place of work is occupied by the strikers (there may also be some picket lines at the gates of the plant which 'discourage' the entrance into the premises). In all these cases, the strike of part of the personnel can be sufficient to paralyse the functioning of the whole enterprise.

But there is also a second situation that may occur. Even the workers who have not been called out on strike by their union can be prevented from working by a strike made by other workers. This strike may be one that is limited to a particular category of employees (usually those who occupy key posts in the plant: the unions are naturally eager to call such strikes which produce the same effect as a mass strike, i.e., to paralyse the whole production, at a smaller cost – for it allows them to prolong the stoppage of work with the same strike fund); but it may also be a strike affecting another department of the same plant (for the same reasons that we have just mentioned, the unions often resort to the tactic of 'rolling strike') or another plant of the same enterprise – or even another enterprise that is necessary, for example, to supply energy or raw materials (here again, we find this practice to call strikes in the enterprises which are vital for the whole industry: this practice is rewarding when the unions want to bring pressure, not on a particular employer, but on the Government or on public opinion).

In all cases, anyway, the problem is to know what will be the situation of those non-strikers who cannot perform their work. It is certain that their employment contract is not terminated – but the problem arises to know whether it is suspended (in which case the wages will not have to be paid) or whether it normally continues (in which case the employees can ask for a normal remuneration).

In no country is this situation regulated by statute. It has therefore been up to the courts to set down some fundamental rules. There seems to be, in that respect, a fundamental (and already mentioned) distinction between two types of countries: those countries where the employer is not duty-bound to provide work, and those where the employer has such a duty.

In the first group of countries (United States, Britain and Sweden), the employer is not supposed to have such a duty. When there is a shortage of work, he can always lay off his employees without notice and without pay. In such conditions, the problem of the non-strikers does not really arise. The employer is not expected to pay anybody for a work that is not really performed.

This is notably the case in the *United States*. If the employer cannot furnish work to his non-striking employees, he does not commit a breach of contract and he is not compelled to pay them wages. The situation can be characterized, in fact, as a suspension of the employment relationship: no work is performed and no wages are due. However, the employer may agree, voluntarily or under pressure, to pay wages to the non-strikers – not only to those who actually do work (which is quite normal), but also to those who are on call but perform no actual work. The matter has, of course, been discussed, and while it has been claimed that this attitude could be regarded as discriminatory against the strikers, this view has not triumphed. It is now admitted that direct or indirect compensation may be paid to non-strikers although denied to strikers. In addition, non-strikers, even those who are merely on call, may be paid and accrue vacation and retirement benefits during the strike. In fact, we have already noted that any benefits growing out of wage payments may be given to non-strikers without resulting in a violation of the NLRA by the employer. The only restriction is that the employer should not discriminate against strikers in respect of any benefit which has an effect on job tenure or any other condition of employment – like seniority, for example.

The situation is about the same in *Britain* – although the rights and duties of the non-strikers depend more on the individual contract of employment: the main problem is therefore a problem of interpretation of this contract. As to *Sweden,* it seems that the question does not even arise in practice, because of the almost negligible number of partial strikes in that country. It is true that the unions have complete domination over all the workers belonging to a certain category (manual workers, salaried employees, supervisors) and the few workers who are not organized ordinarily follow the call of the union. There can only be a problem if, in a given industry, the strike of one category of employees makes impossible the work of another category. If the employees who cannot work are manual workers, the solution is clear: the employer is not supposed to pay them wages; actually he may lay them off at any time without notice and without pay. But the rule is different if it is a strike of the manual workers which makes it impossible for the salaried employees to perform their work. The reason for this is that salaried employees are subject to a particular regulation and that they cannot be laid off without pay. Therefore it is admitted that they can require the payment of their salary even though they have been in fact prevented from working, and even though the employer has been unable to provide them with work because of a strike of other workers. It is a settled opinion that such a strike is not an excuse for the employer not to pay the monthly salary – and that even the theory of *force majeure* is not applicable in this case.[76] The rule has already been applied by the courts, notably in a case decided by the Supreme Court in 1959.[77] It is very severe for the employer. The only possibility which remains indeed at the disposal of this employer, if he does not want to pay the salaries, is to lock out all his personnel.

At the opposite end of the scale, we find the countries which admit, as a matter of principle, that the employer has the contractual duty to furnish work to his employees. The problem then arises to know what is the situation if he does not fulfil this obligation.

There is no difficulty, of course, for the workers who are not on call (for example, because they have been prevented to come by the absence of means of transportation): there is no doubt that such workers cannot ask for the payment of their wages. But the situation is not so clear for the workers who are on call and who cannot work, for example, because of the absence of electrical power. The solutions are not exactly similar in the various countries.

German law applies here a special theory, the theory of the risk of the enterprise (*Betriebsrisiko*) as it has been set up during the Weimar Republic by the courts and the legal commentators. This risk of the enterprise is normally split between the employer and the employees. In ordinary circumstances, when the work is made impossible for a reason which is internal to the enterprise, it is the employer who has to bear the risk: he must therefore pay the wages – except if collective agreements or individual contracts provide other-

76. Of course, the rule can be modified by collective agreement. This is the case, for example, in the collective agreement entered into by the Union of Clerical and Technical Employees in Industry. It is provided, of course, that a conflict concerning another group of workers does not entitle the employer to give notice to terminate the contract to a salaried employee unless there are special reasons to believe that it will not be possible to find work for this employee after the strike. It is also provided that, if the conflict lasts more than three months, the employer will be entitled to reduce the salary: he will be allowed indeed to make a cut of 10 per cent for each additional month up to the point where the salary is reduced to 60 per cent of its original amount.
77. 1959 N.J.A., 562. In this case, the Municipal Workers' Union had decided to call out on strike the workers of the repairing shops and service stations of the municipal tramway in Gothenburg, and this strike had prevented the motormen and conductors from working: so that these employees – who were paid on a monthly basis and consequently regarded as salaried employees – were given leave without pay by the Board of the Municipal Tramway. But on the action of one of the motormen, the Municipality was ordered to pay to all of them their full salary for the period of leave. The Supreme Court stated in its decision that the Municipality would only have been released from its duty to pay if it had ordered a lockout of the motormen and the conductors (which it had chosen, indeed, not to do).

wise. But this rule does not apply if the impossibility is due to the workers themselves – namely, if it is due to a strike which has not been caused by a fault committed by the employer, whether this strike takes place within the enterprise itself or in another enterprise: the risk then has to be borne by these workers. Therefore, the employer whose enterprise is affected by a strike is allowed to reduce, by a unilateral decision, the wages of his non-striking employees and even to interrupt the payment of these wages – which is equivalent indeed to a suspension of the contract.[78] The rule has been laid down by a famous decision of the former Reichsgericht, referring not to the B G B, but to the Works Council Act of 1920, and it has been followed later by the Reich Labour Court, then by other courts. It is all the more rigorous indeed in that it applies even if the strike which creates the difficulties takes place in another enterprise; even if it has been called by a union other than the one to which the non-striking employees belong; even if it is a wildcat strike. The justification officially given for this is the solidarity which must exist among all employees: as soon as the 'risk' originates in the attitude of some workers, as it is the case for the risk of strike, it must be borne by the whole community of workers. Even if these workers are on call, but they cannot perform work, they will be deprived of their wages. The only condition is that they must be really unable to perform work – or, in other terms, that it is really impossible for the employer to furnish them work to be performed. This, of course, is the point on which difficulties can arise: it seems, notably, that the appreciation of the 'impossibility' should not be left to the discretion of the employer and that it should, on the contrary, be subject to the control of the labour courts. In spite of this, however, the principle remains well-established that the employer can refuse payment of wages to non-strikers: and even though this principle had been severely criticized and strongly opposed during the Weimar Republic, it is now almost unanimously accepted. Its relative severity can be explained by the fact that the German employer against whom a strike is organized is not allowed to lay off his employees. It may therefore be claimed that the non-payment of wages takes away from him any reason to resort to a lockout as a defensive weapon. Yet because the lockout remains possible and lawful, we may conclude that the German employer is particularly well protected.

Quite different are the principles which are applied in *France* in order to solve this problem of the obligation of the employer towards his non-striking employees. These principles are, indeed, those which derive from the ordinary law of contracts. It is clear that the employer can only be released from his duty to pay the wages to his employees if the contract is suspended – and that

78. This theory of the risk of enterprise can be regarded, in fact, as the oldest form of the theory of suspension – but it is a suspension which is to the detriment of the employee. The idea admitted in the light of the B G B is that the obligation of the employer to furnish work to his employees is suspended in case of impossibility due to an action which falls into the field of 'responsibility' of the employees. This principle indeed had been anticipated by the Court of Cassation of Rome, to the extent that this Court had admitted, on the basis of a sort of collective responsibility, the termination by the employer of all contracts of employment as soon as the majority of the workers were on strike: see, notably, the decision of 27 Dec. 1909 (cf. *supra*, n. 8), followed by two other decisions of 1912 and 1915.

the contract can only be suspended if there is a *force majeure*: that is, an absolute necessity, due to circumstances beyond the employer's control, which imposes the closing of the plant. The problem is therefore to know whether the strike constitutes or not, in itself, a *force majeure*.

The answer is, as a matter of principle, negative for the reason that the strike is neither unforeseeable nor unavoidable (conditions which are normally required in French law for the *force majeure*). The employer has not only the right, but the duty to do everything he can in order to keep the plant functioning. He must, if necessary, hire new employees (at least for a temporary period) in replacement of those who are on strike; he must try to obtain raw materials from enterprises which are not on strike; he must reorganize the internal operation of his enterprise; if there are picket lines or if the premises are occupied by sit-down strikers, he has the obligation to assure all those who are willing to work the freedom to work. He may even, for that purpose, obtain from the judge an order to evacuate the premises and, for the enforcement of this order, call the police force. If he does not use all these weapons, he is regarded as failing in his duty. This is why the strike is normally insufficient in itself to justify the non-payment of wages by the employer to the non-strikers (and this is precisely the main reason which explains the temptation of the employer to resort to the lockout – although we have already seen that the lockout is strictly limited in France and that its lawful character is also subject to the existence of a *force majeure*).

There are, however, some circumstances under which the strike may become a *force majeure*. This is notably the case when the strike presents some special features – for example, when it covers a very broad area (geographically or professionally: it may be a general strike), so that it makes absolutely impossible the hiring of new employees or the obtaining of raw materials – or when it lasts for a very long time. *Force majeure* also exists when some special events take place during the strike – for example, when the employer calls the police in order to expel the employees on strike from the place of work, but the police do not accede to this request for reasons of public order and the premises cannot be evacuated (this situation is frequent in periods of social turbulence: it happened very often in 1936 and in 1968); sometimes, it is even at the request of the public authorities themselves that the plant is closed, in order to avoid serious agitation. In all these circumstances, the employer is not responsible for the fact that the employees who are not on strike are nevertheless unable to work. Therefore, he is not supposed to pay the wages. He can invoke the doctrine of *force majeure* and claim that the contract is suspended. The decree of 24 May 1938 only provides in such a situation for the possibility of 'recuperating' the hours wasted because of the strike. This recuperation must be made within the twelve following months. But it is only at the employer's discretion: it depends on the needs of the enterprise, of the economic situation, etc. If the employer proposes this recuperation, the employees are compelled to accept it; their refusal would be regarded as a refusal to work.

These are the normal rules. But they are modified when one of the parties has committed a fault. If it appears that the strike was caused by a fault committed by the employer, or that it was prolonged because of such a fault, this employer will be under the obligation to pay the wages to the non-strikers without any possibility of invoking a *force majeure* in order to escape this obligation. If, on the contrary, a fault has been committed by the non-strikers, special rules are also applicable. There may be, for example, a sort of collusion between strikers and non-strikers, resulting in successive strikes affecting in turn the various departments of a plant (rolling strike). Each stoppage of work affects only one department at a time and only the employees in this department are considered strikers; but it is notorious that all employees in other departments are, in fact, prevented from working. If it can be proved that all employees were in agreement about such tactics, they will all be regarded and treated in the same way. Even those who are not officially on strike will be treated as though they were on strike. The solution is sometimes criticized by commentators, and it is true that it raises difficult problems of evidence: but it seems perfectly justified in practice.[79]

It seems that, as a whole, the results obtained by French law are not very distant from those obtained by German law in that respect. It is admitted in both countries that the real impossibility of the employer to furnish work to his employees releases this employer from his duty to pay the wages, and the difficulty turns, in fact, on the determination of this impossibility in each particular case. The only difference is that in Germany the impossibility is presumed, whereas in France it has to be proved by the employer (and the burden of this proof can be a heavy one).

There is not much difference between the French law, as we have now just described it, and the *Italian* law on this point. A distinction is also made in Italy between two situations. If the employer can bring evidence of an absolute impossibility to furnish work to his employees, the rules applicable are those relating to *force majeure*: the employee is then excused from performing work (Art. 1256, para. 2, of the Civil Code); and the employer is released from his duty to pay wages (Art. 1463 of the Civil Code); the contract is then suspended. It is, of course, necessary that the strike which creates the impossibility is not due to the fault of the employer, but it does not matter whether it is justified or not and whether it is lawful or not. On the contrary, if the employer is not in a position of absolute impossibility, but only in great difficulty to furnish work to his employees, he is not excused from paying wages. All he can do is to terminate the contracts of the non-strikers, under the ordinary conditions (previous notice, severance pay, etc.). But if he does not do so, the strikers will be entitled to back-pay or damages.[80]

---

79. This explains why 'rolling strikes' have been made unlawful for all public employees by the law of 31 July 1963. Cf. *infra*, Chapter 6, p. 374.

80. It must be noted indeed that the Italian courts deal with this problem from a rather individualistic point of view: they look at the particular situation of each employee to see whether he really was unable to work. This may involve difficulties, notably in the case of a rolling strike: for it is a question as to whether the non-strikers were really in a position of finding it impossible to work or whether they were in fact in collusion with the strikers.

The system adopted in France and in Italy is all the more severe indeed because the lockout is strictly regulated – and even made unlawful as a matter of principle. The solution which consists of compelling the employer to pay wages to the non-strikers may thus be regarded as putting on this employer a heavy burden.

Yet the matter should not be considered only from the employer's point of view. It is clear that it is also important to protect the non-strikers, especially as they are not always allowed to obtain unemployment benefits. In *France*, for example, the legal formula according to which such benefits are refused to all 'persons whose unemployment is caused by a collective labour dispute' is broad enough to include at the same time strikers and non-strikers. The situation, however, is better in *Germany* (where certain benefits can be granted to non-strikers, although only to a small extent and under very strict conditions). In *Italy* workers made idle temporarily enjoy the benefits of a Social Security fund providing up to 80 per cent of normal wages in case of involuntary suspension.

As to the other countries, they make a distinction between the workers according to whether they are or are not employed in the place where the dispute takes place. In *Britain*, it results from sec. 22 of the National Insurance Act 1965, that the disqualification from unemployment benefits does not apply to workers at an establishment different from that at which the trade dispute exists.[81] In the *United States*, the laws of the various states usually provide that the disqualification concerns only the workers who were last employed in the establishment where the labour dispute takes place; workers employed in other establishments are not disqualified. This raises problems as to the interpretation of the word 'establishment' and as to the relative integration of the various establishments owned by the same employing unit. The solutions depend on the exact wording of the various state laws and on the particular circumstances of each case. But the principle is that if the non-strikers have clearly no common interest with the strikers, they remain entitled to unemployment benefits. The solution is not very different in *Sweden*. It was formerly admitted that all workers unemployed as a consequence of a strike or of a lockout were disqualified from the benefit of the state unemployment insurance – and this applied to all workers, even those who were not directly interested in the dispute: in case they were laid off, these employees were not entitled to any benefit. But a new law enacted in 1968 provides that the disqualification con-

---

81. Sec. 22 also states that the disqualification does not apply, even in the case of a person who works at the establishment where the trade dispute takes place, if this person can prove '(*a*) that he is not participating in or financing or directly interested in the trade dispute which caused the stoppage of work; and (*b*) that he does not belong to a grade or class of workers of which, immediately before the commencement of the stoppage, there were members employed at his place of employment any of whom are participating in or financing or directly interested in the dispute . . .'.

It must also be mentioned that, according to sec. 7(3) of the Redundancy Payments Act, 1965, the worker laid off or put on short time is 'wholly or mainly' attributable to a strike or a lockout whether in the trade or industry of the worker concerned or not, and whether in Great Britain or elsewhere. This naturally applies to the non-strikers who lose their employment as a consequence of the strike.

cerns only the workers who are on strike or locked out or those whose conditions of employment are directly affected by the dispute:[82] so that the workers
who are only indirectly affected by the dispute retain all their rights in case of
a lay-off due to the strike or the lockout. This may naturally constitute in
certain situations an incentive for the employer to lock them out (notably if he
wants to extend by sympathetic action the primary dispute).

This problem of the non-strikers is all the more delicate as it is often difficult to make a clear distinction between strikers and non-strikers. We have
already seen that the unions try to make this distinction still more difficult
today by resorting to various tactics which result in letting the bulk of the
workers call for work – and consequently ask for the payment of their wages –
but under such conditions that they are unable to perform any actual work because production is stopped by the strike of a small number of employees occupying key posts: thereby ensuring that the employer, by paying the non-
strikers, is often led, in fact, to finance a strike against himself. This explains
the movement of opinion which is developing in some countries (for example
in France) in favour of a stricter regulation of the right to strike. It is only such
a regulation indeed that could make useless – and would allow the declaration
in all cases as unlawful – the resort to lockout.

It would, of course, be quite illusory to think that such a regulation could
definitively solve the problem. All regulation in this field is bound to have
only limited effects. This is a general statement that can be extended to all the
problems concerning the status of the individual employee in case of industrial
action. The rules enacted by the legislature or laid down by the courts in each
country are certainly very important for the individual worker; they are even
necessary to make effective the official proclamations about the right to organize and the right to strike. But their importance should not be exaggerated
in practice, and one should never forget the fundamental impotence of the law
in such matters. It is beyond all doubt that the best protection of the employee
still lies in the strength of his union and the ratio of forces which exists between this union and the employer: for, in fact, it is this relation of power that
will determine the content of the agreement which will be finally entered into
by both parties at the end of the conflict, and it is this agreement that will
determine in a sure and definite way the status of the individual worker.

82. Such workers are also deprived of several other state benefits; they remain entitled to ordinary social aid, but only in case of urgent need.

The legality of industrial actions and the methods of settlement procedure
by Thilo Ramm

Introduction

This chapter deals with the following questions: Which legal instruments against industrial actions are offered by the law? Shall they be used against all or only against special industrial actions? Are they reserved to the State or may they be employed by one party in the bargaining against the other? Is their use intended to suppress labour disputes or merely to help avoid them?

Before these questions can be answered it is necessary to investigate the legal status of industrial actions either in general or as restricted to specific actions. However, legal machinery may be used not only against unlawful actions but also to prevent lawful actions or to avoid their continuation. The procedures for the settlement of collective labour disputes will be separately described. Lastly, legal machinery itself will be discussed: sanctions and remedies for prevention.

It is impossible, first of all, to maintain a strict line of demarcation between remedial sanctions and preventive actions. Certainly reference to well-known legal institutions are at hand: to punishment; to the obligation to pay damages; to legal invalidation of contracts, and to injunctions or police actions. While theoretically sanctions refer to the past, preventive actions refer to the future. They cannot, nevertheless, be separated, either theoretically or practically. Penal sanctions effect prevention by threat of their use and by their permanent imposition. On the other hand there is no effective action of prevention without a sanction. The best evidence for their close connection is the history of industrial actions, in which the most effective method of prevention was the prohibition of employees' associations.

This chapter avoids special problems investigated by other chapters, although they will be touched upon since otherwise this contribution would give an incomplete picture. The characteristic of the investigation of comparative law is not the comparison of special norms and institutions. Very often the same problem is solved differently by the different national laws – sometimes in our case by the construction of the peace obligation of collective agreements and sometimes if we remain in the field of Civil Law, by the law of torts. Another difficulty is perhaps even more important: studies in comparative law cannot give a snapshot view of the present legal situation. The present law of one country possibly corresponds to the earlier law of another now replaced by a new law. It must be asked whether there is a legal development and in which direction it is going. Will individualistic law be forced out by collective? Will penal sanctions be replaced by civil ones? Will injunctions of the courts replace police actions? These are only some of the many questions which arise – and how else can they be answered than by comparative labour law investigations?

Certainly, this contribution gives only a partial picture, as no communist countries have been described. All countries investigated have a capitalistic economy, or, in Sweden, a mixed capitalist-socialist. However, in two countries, Germany and Italy, this economic situation was restored after the Second World War. For nearly 20 years (1926–44) Italy prohibited all strikes and lockouts and made labour organizations into State institutions. In Germany 12 years of Nazi government repressed, with its legal institutions, collective labour law. Later a special period, the period of reconstructing a nearly completely destroyed economy, followed. These events have influenced later developments, in these two countries especially as in both of them collective labour law was given up without a fight.

Liberalism and industrial disputes

It becomes necessary to pose the question – as Benjamin Aaron has already done in Chapter 2 – how did liberalism face industrial disputes? how did it suppress them? how did it manage to integrate them? Or to ask the opposite question: How did the existence of labour disputes influence liberal politics and liberal theories? It seems to me that this last question gives the basis for this investigation. Economic liberalism means free competition among individuals, the determination of the price of products by supply and demand. The liberal principle of *laissez-faire, laissez-aller* was opposed to the guild system of the Middle Ages and to the mercantilism of the absolute monarchy or the enlightened Prussian 'welfare' State, both of which had regulated economy and labour relations. The historic development of liberalism therefore consists of three periods – all taken as abstract patterns. First the concept of the new system had to be realized. It was necessary to break with the corporative system of the Middle Ages. The absolute prohibition of labour disputes and labour organizations therefore was the beginning. In 1796 Mr. Justice Grose in Britain expressed this idea in these classical words:

> Each [journeyman] may insist on raising his wages if he can, but if several meet for the same purpose it is illegal and the parties may be indicted for conspiracy.

The prohibition, however, had different meanings: For the workers it was the continuation of the law, as it was, with a new reason, because their organizations had also been prohibited in the feudal system. For the employers who had controlled wages by the guilds or by the magistrates, it was new. After the general recognition of liberalism as the new concept of order, the old legitimacy to protect the economic order became superfluous. The time approached for overcoming the contradiction between the prohibition of combinations and the liberal theory. Was not the freedom of combinations a natural part of the individual freedom ? And was it possible to prohibit actions – which were as legal as individual actions – only because they were committed collectively, by a group of persons ? Again, the British Trade Disputes Act of 1906, sec. 1, contains the classical description:

> An act done in pursuance of an agreement or combination by two or more persons shall, if done in contemplation or furtherance of a trade dispute, not be actionable unless the act, if done without any such agreement or combination, could be actionable.

The other question was: how was it politically possible to refuse the freedom of combination to that part of the population whose distress was the result of the free determination of the wage by supply and demand ? The liberal economists insisted that competition should bring the price of the good 'labour' to the lowest level. The pressure of competition among the employers as entrepreneurs additionally aggravated this situation. Those who were able to reduce the costs of production – and among these, wages – had better chances of success. In this period the combination of the workers, who as individuals were weaker than the employer, that is, their 'social self-help', might appear at least as a means of mitigating the social question if not solve it. The repeal of the laws prohibiting labour disputes and labour organizations seemed to be the lesser evil because it was more closely connected with liberalism than was State intervention in economic and labour relations. With the end of that era began the second period: the open struggle between social opponents, between the employers and the employees. Liberalism thus lost much of its individualistic character. But the competition between different organizations emerged, especially on the employees' side, and, more important, the State remained neutral.

The third period is characterized by State intervention in labour disputes. There may have been different reasons. The State, which also underwent substantial change by the introduction of universal suffrage, might have wanted to support the workers because they still seemed to be the weaker party. Or the State may have wanted to restrict labour disputes because they were considered to violate common interests – generally or in certain cases only.

Freedom to organize and freedom of trade

This division into three periods at first sight does not seem to make the description of the legal developments of the different countries easier because there were no sharp breaks between them. France, however, is the famous exception.

The French revolution brought recognition of the freedom of combination. After the fundamental declaration of the 'assemblée constituante' in the night of 4 August 1789 to dissolve all corporations, the decree of 21 August 1793 recognized the right of all citizens, 'to assemble peacefully and to form free associations provided that they obey the statutes applying to all citizens'. The hope that freedom of trade and competition would be practised without difficulties, however, was shattered by the great strikes of 1790 and 1791 in Paris. Therefore, the Constitution of 1791 only guaranteed 'the freedom of the citizens to assemble peacefully and without arms in accordance with statutes on police power'. The Le Chapelier Act of the same year prohibited the factual reconstitution of corporations as well as deliberations and decisions of citizens of the same profession or trade because of their 'pretended common interests'. In all other legal systems in which no revolutionary break occurred with the feudal system, the description of the typical development as described above helps to specify the particularities of the national legal developments. Some factors can be clearly observed: the importance of the recognition of freedom of trade with respect to the position of the labour organizations is shown by a comparison between Germany and the United States.

In Germany this was a long process, although it began early (in Prussia in 1810). However, the guilds remained unchallenged, and an attempt was even made to meet the social conflicts of the first half of the nineteenth century with their help. In Prussia, after 1849, the guilds had control of the industrial qualification of most of the handicrafts, but in the repeal of the Prussian statute in 1869 by the *Reichsgewerbeordnung*, they were kept as voluntary organizations. During Nazism they again became corporations with compulsory membership – and membership was the condition to work in one's trade. Today the guilds are again voluntary associations, but they are responsible for the 'master examination', without which nobody is allowed to establish a handicraft workshop (Handicraft Order of 1953/65). These guilds are also recognized by the Federal Constitutional Court to be employers' associations.[1]

The continuation of the guilds exercised a strong indirect influence on German collective labour law. It certainly favoured the establishment of the industrial employers' associations after 1890 and it may also explain the fact that before the First World War there was no German anti-trust legislation or case law.[2] That is, if the guilds were recognized as economic associations, how could trusts be condemned?

No investigation of the factual relations between employers' and entrepreneurs' associations or of agreements on competition within the employers' association has been undertaken so far – although the importance of this question is evident because of the double position of employer and entre-

1. Decision of 19 October 1960, BVerfGE, vol. 20, p. 312.
2. The *Reichsgericht* (Supreme Court) declared in its famous decision of 4 February 1897, RGZ, vol. 38, p. 155, that the formation of trusts is included in contractual liberty.

preneur. How relevant this problem is may, however, be demonstrated by an attempt (which was made before 1933): The guarantee of Art. 165 of the Weimar Constitution (which is nearly literally the same as Art. 9, sec. 3 of the Bonn Basic Law) of the 'freedom of combination in order to maintain and to promote the labour and economic conditions for everybody and for all professions' was argued to be a constitutional guarantee for the trusts.

In the United States free competition became a matter of national faith although it never has been recognized as a fundamental right under the Constitution. It corresponds to the reality, to the ever-present chance to begin a new trade and to remain independent. This delayed the development of the American trade unions as well as the formation of employers' associations. The United States again demonstrates the close connection between antitrust legislation and collective labour law. The Sherman Act of 1890, which was directed against combinations in restraint of trade, was also applied to the American trade unions.

Industrialization began in the various countries at different times, and proceeded with different speeds. In the nineteenth century Great Britain was the leading industrial nation, followed by France and Germany. This explains why Great Britain also influenced the development of the law of industrial disputes in other countries. After the British repeal of the prohibitive legislation against the existence of labour associations (1824/25), France (1864) and Germany (1869) followed. The model nature of labour legislation of the leading industrial nations is important for a comparison of labour law in the nineteenth century, since after that time it has been replaced to a certain degree by international agreements within the International Labour Organization and, now, within the European Economic Community.

Political structure of the State and industrial disputes

The political structure of the various States is also very important, ranging in many fields from the role of monarchy to the influence of fundamental rights for labour law and to the question whether the legislator or the judge makes the law.

Great Britain, very early, and Sweden took the step to establish a parliamentary monarchy, but Germany and Italy created a constitutional monarchy where the prevailing power was still in the hands of the king; in both countries his influence was increased by the national unification achieved by the monarchy. While the Italian king was allied to the *bourgeoisie*, the German emperor did not favour one social party exclusively. He protected the nobility as land owners, and even after the abolition of servitude and serfdom the rural labour force was kept in very strong legal dependence. Until 1848, the big land owner, who was usually a nobleman, had jurisdiction over such workers, and even until 1927 he was the police authority on his estate. The right to 'reasonable bodily correction' of servants remained until 1896 – while for industrial workers it had been abolished in 1869. In the Germany of the nineteenth century the labour law of the towns and of the land were clearly separated. Contrary to Sweden and Great Britain, Germany had special Master and Servant Acts for agricultural and domestic workers, the *Gesindeordnungen*. They provided penal sanctions for breach of contract – which had been repealed for the trade in 1869. All these Acts remained in force until the revolution of 1918.

The monarchy used the labour movement as a weapon against the *bourgeoisie*. It tried to win the workers by labour security and especially the social security legislation of the 1880s – the latter relieving the trade unions of their task of mutual aid and consequently increasing their power in labour disputes. The reaction was the formation of employers' associations. The indirect influence of the monarchy may have been, perhaps, even more significant. The monarch was the decisive figure on the political scene, and his example was transferred to labour relations where it re-emphasized the patriarchal structure of the individual labour relationship – the 'master-in-the-house' viewpoint – or, indeed, even strengthened that view. And even after the proclamation of the Republic, this effect continued because the Reich President was a kind of 'substitute emperor'. Nazism, of course, reinforced this tradition.

Sweden may be compared with Germany as a country having a similar social situation, but without a powerful monarch as the head of an 'Obrigkeit'-State. In the last decades of the nineteenth and the first of the twentieth century, a political vacuum existed and Parliament could not agree upon actions against industrial disputes. This was the basis for the establishment and full development of Swedish collective labour law, while such law in Germany has always been considered to be contrary to the power of the State.

In this context it is, however, also necessary to mention the political aims of workers' associations. As long as the labour movement constituted the extreme left wing of the *bourgeoisie* in the fight against the monarchy, the fight against all political associations included workers' associations as well. We may observe that the same attitude was expressed by the courts in prosecution of workers' organizations, for example the Chartists, for a short period in the British legislation following the great French Revolution after the repeal of the prohibitive acts (1824/25).

In France, after the June rebellion of the Paris workers (1849), the Government was authorized to prohibit all assemblies and to dissolve all associations which could possibly endanger public peace. This authorization, which was limited to one year, was twice renewed. Similar special legislation was enacted after the rebellion of the Paris Commune and remained in force from 1872–84. Germany followed with the Anti-Socialists Act (1878–90).

In Italy a three-year prosecution of socialists and trade unions commenced in 1898 after riots induced by an increase of bread prices. This reveals the deeper reasons of all prosecutions: as long as the trade unions did not consider themselves to be integrated, they – as mass organizations – could be considered a permanent threat.

The picture of the law of industrial actions therefore remains incomplete if these political prosecutions are not considered as well. To some extent they made suppression of industrial disputes for economic reasons superfluous, and sometimes they were used as additional weapons.

The recognition of liberal rights, especially by the constitutions, had different – both unfavourable and favourable – results for the legal evaluation of industrial actions. It has already been mentioned that in the United States and Great Britain the suppression of industrial actions and of labour associations was justified by the theory of freedom of trade. On the other hand, the open contradiction between the recognition of the 'freedom of general action' and the prohibition of association has certainly promoted the repeal of the prohibiting legislation. In the United States the constitutional guarantee of freedom of speech was used in order to ameliorate the laws against picketing.

Another development took place where liberal rights were protected against the social side: the right to organize was recognized by the German constitution of 1919; National Industrial Recovery Act of the USA (1933); Swedish Act respecting the right to organize and the right of collective bargaining of 1936; preamble of the French Constitution of 1946 which is still referred to by the Constitution of 1958; Italian Constitution of 1948, Art. 39; British Industrial Relations Act of 1971, sec. 24(4).[3] France and Italy combined this recognition of the right to strike while some German State Constitutions after 1945 restricted the recognition of the right to strike to official strikes.

The law-making power

The most important question is who in the different States has the law-making power; the legislator or the judge. This problem has various aspects, and it does not help very much to say that the legislator makes only one decision while a plurality of judicial decisions exists because this distinction becomes very doubtful in practice. More important is the fact that judicial decisions are based on single cases which demand an answer, while the legislator often avoids clear answers and tends toward compromise.

In Great Britain and in the United States the law of industrial actions has been the subject of a struggle between the legislature and the judiciary. The legislature – as a consequence of universal suffrage – took the side of the employees, while the partisanship of the judges against industrial disputes may be explained – though not entirely – by their background affiliating them to the *bourgeoisie*. In Great Britain, the Trade Disputes Act of 1906 ended this development but was challenged by judicial decisions in the 1960s and then reversed by the Industrial Relations Act of 1971. In the United States the struggle lasted longer and displayed more variety. The courts did not accept the Clayton Act of 1914, which tried to avoid the application of the Anti-Trust Act of 1890 (Sherman Act) to the trade unions. And at the beginning of the New Deal era, the National Industrial Recovery Act (NIRA) of 1933 was

3. The statute, however, restricts protection against those discriminatory dismissals to members of registered trade unions only. Members of unregistered trade unions may be in a weaker position because of the new regulation against strikes – strikes which might otherwise have protected them.

declared unconstitutional by the Supreme Court. The same fate threatened the National Labor Relations [Wagner] Act (NLRA) of 1935. In 1937 the serious conflict between the Supreme Court, and the executive and the legislature came to an end with the Court's ruling on the NLRA as constitutional.

France, Germany and Italy started with the primacy of the statutory law. But these countries left the judges a wide range of discretion by vague legal notions and general clauses, and by the recognition of the immediate obligation of Constitutional provisions as being parts of the substantive law; this was, in Germany, the reaction against the disappointments of the Weimar Constitution, the promises that had not been fulfilled by the legislator. The judicial power was enforced by the establishment of constitutional courts (in Germany and Italy). In Germany the law-making power of the supreme courts was recognized by the institution of the Big Divisions (1935), and the judges were ordered not to apply the liberal regulation of the German Civil Code but to develop a new Nazi law. After 1945 their task changed; they now had to denazify the Acts that had been promulgated between 1933 and 1945. The German Federal Labour Court has certainly profited from these developments in its decisions on industrial disputes.

The law-making power may best be discovered by the expression of public policy. In Great Britain in 1796 this was done by a judge, and in 1906 by the legislator; in the USA by the legislature with the Norris-La Guardia Act of 1932 (NLGA); in France the constitutional provisions were applied by the judiciary and later on sanctioned by the legislator. In Germany the Big Division of the Federal Labour Court decided the public policy on industrial conflicts (in its decision of 28 January 1955). In Sweden the fundamental principles on industrial disputes are contained in the Act of 1936, but also – and this is unique to Sweden – in the basic agreement between the Swedish Employers' Confederation and the Confederation of Swedish Trade Unions of 1938.

Unlawfulness of industrial actions according to penal law

The era in which a general negative attitude toward industrial disputes and labour associations prevailed belongs to the past. Such negative legal evaluations could be found in penal codes and, at first, in special penal acts which clearly showed that industrial disputes were considered a foreign intrusion within a liberal legal system. As concerns France, the Chapelier Act of 1791 may be cited here.

In Great Britain the Combination Acts of 1799 and 1800 – which were repealed as early as 1824/25 – are the corresponding events.

For Germany the Prussian Trade Order of 1845, which, however, was applied only to industrial workers, may be quoted. This Act was repealed by the Reich Trade Order of 1869.

It is impossible to consider the various statutes in isolation. In France the separate statute became part of the penal code (Arts. 414 and 415 until 1864), and France became the model for the penal codes of the Italian states, among them the Penal Code of Sardinia (1840–89), which became the first Italian penal code. Besides that code, the Penal Code of Tuscany, which had repealed the prohibition of industrial disputes, remained in force. Italy's next penal code (1889) incorporated this repeal.

In Great Britain the criminal conspiracy doctrine (which originated in the feudal and monarchical legislation and developed in the Common Law) had preceded the special legislation and had survived it. The doctrine was then abolished in trade disputes by the Conspiracy and Protection of Property Act of 1875.[4] This British doctrine was received by the judiciary of the United States, but ceased to be applied after 1842.

Similar to the British the German courts continued the fight against strikes after the repeal of the special legislation. This was facilitated by the provision on blackmailing of the German Penal Code (sec. 253):

> Whoever, in order to procure an unlawful economic advantage to himself or to a third person, coerces another person by force or intimidation to undertake an action, a forbearance or a non-performance will be penalized for blackmailing with imprisonment of not less than one month.

In its decision of 6 October 1890,[5] the German Supreme Court considered intimidation together with work stoppage in order to get better wage and work conditions as blackmail if the workers' demand exercised 'a pressure on the will'. Also the court saw such a pressure in the unilateral demand of the workers and in the 'disdainful and impudent way in which they brought it forward'. The language is remarkably similar to that used by the judges in *R. v. Bunn*, 1872 in Britain.[6]

The Supreme Court's interpretation of the law, which was bitterly attacked by the unions, remained within the letter of sec. 253 of the German Penal Code: 'unlawful' was interpreted to mean that no legally recognized claim existed; that is, the general intention of the interpreters was to furnish wide protection against all forms of coercion and to secure the freedom of will. Thus, the lower courts, encouraged by the Supreme Court, could also use secs. 253 and 240 (concerning coercion) of the Penal Code against the strike.[7] Several times the attempt was made – without success – to change the criminal law prior to the First World War.[8] In the commentaries of the draft for a new

4. The same Act repealed the Master and Servant statutes which had been a common source of prosecution of workers.
5. RGSt, vol. 21, p. 114 (117).
6. cf. K. W. Wedderburn, *The Worker and the Law*, 2nd ed., Penguin Books, 1971, p. 311.
7. The best description of the decisions is given by *Nestriepke, Das Koalitionsrecht in Deutschland. Gesetze und Praxis*. Without date (1914). It is the official report of the General Commission of the Trade Unions of Germany.
8. Surveys are given in the dissertation of Hans Carl Nipperdey, *Grenzlinien der Erpressung und Drohung unter Berücksichtigung der modernen Arbeitskämpfe* (1917) and by the publication *Koalitionsrecht und Strafrecht* (1917), part 1 of the comprehensive work *Das Recht der Organisationen im neuen Deutschland*. This work contained the reform proposals for post-war Germany which were made by the very influential progressive 'Society for Social Reform'. They were issued by the subcommittee for labour law. Among the members were the former Prussian Minister of the Interior Freiherr von Berlepsch, the Professors Zimmermann and Herkner and the famous German labour lawyer Hugo Sinzheimer.

Penal Code of 1909, it was even declared that this interpretation was contrary to the trend of sec. 152 of the Reich Trade Order on the freedom of labour organization, and that it would violate the interest of employers and workers, making industrial disputes more bitter: 'For both parties will herewith be discouraged from using conciliation and resort to dismissals and strikes because they must fear that expressions which are natural at preliminary negotiations will be prosecuted as blackmailing'.[9] It was curious enough that the strike itself – according to this doctrine which was continuously applied by the courts until after the First World War – was not considered to fall under the Penal Code because it was not 'coercion' (*Noetigung*): sec. 240 required for unlawful coercion that intimidation accompanies crime or an offence.[10] The turning point was not the change of the text of sec. 253 of the Penal Code, which came relatively late during the Nazi period (1943). A change of the general legal evaluation was introduced by the November Revolution (1918) and was expressed by the provisions of the Weimar Republic on labour organizations though they were very cautiously drafted and did not involve a constitutional guarantee of the right to strike. This precaution was useless, however, because the link between labour associations and industrial disputes had been clearly shown by the previous social struggles.

The general condemnation of industrial actions under Criminal Law was followed by the general condemnation under Civil Law.

Unlawfulness of industrial actions under civil law

This development is especially clear in the Anglo-Saxon countries, where the criminal conspiracy doctrine was superseded by the civil conspiracy doctrine – which means that only the sanctions were replaced. The sociological basis of this development was the gradual formation of permanent workers' associations, which were able to finance longer strikes by strike funds, and which substituted planned strikes for spontaneous strikes. In Great Britain the development caused a dispute between the legislature and the courts. The Conspiracy and Property Act of 1875 was – according to its letter – only concerned with conspiracy as a penal action. But, did this exclude civil actions in court? As long as the criminal conspiracy doctrine was recognized, it was possible to derive a new liability in tort. Yet, could this be done after the statutory abolition of the criminal conspiracy doctrine?

This question was also discussed in Germany after the repeal of the separate penal statutes against labour associations and industrial actions: Did this mean the recognition of the freedom to strike, or was the strike merely declared to be relieved from penal sanctions – as was suggested by the Secretary of the Interior in a speech before the Reich Parliament of 10 December 1912. Was only a penal privilege created, as stated by the Supreme Court in one of its decisions?[11] In several decisions the British courts interpreted their statute

9. Quoted from *Koalitionsrecht und Strafrecht*, p. 1.
10. Both expressions refer to the German classification of criminal actions according to the nature and extent of penal sanctions provided by the sections of the Penal Code.
11. 3.12.1889, RGSt 20, 63 (69 f.), p. 268.

restrictively as well – until *Quinn* v. *Leathem* and especially the *Taff-Vale* decision of 1901 shocked public opinion and led to the Trade Disputes Act of 1906 which practically abolished all civil sanctions against industrial actions. Nearly 60 years later in 1964, however, the conflict between the judiciary and the legislature broke out again. The decision of the House of Lords in *Rookes* v. *Barnard* considered – quite similar to the decisions of the German Supreme Court on blackmailing before the First World War – a strike threat to be a tort. One year later the legislature intervened and blocked this interpretation. But in later decisions between 1965 and 1970 British courts intervened by use of the liabilities for interference with commercial contracts, not protected by the Trade Disputes Acts.

In the United States at a very early stage and without intervention of the legislator, the criminal conspiracy doctrine was replaced by the civil conspiracy doctrine. The new doctrine went parallel to the application of the Sherman Act of 1890 and was, in a way, confirmed by it. The Clayton Act of 1914 was directed against this interpretation in declaring that human labour is not a 'commodity or article of commerce'. But the courts did not adhere to this when, after the First World War, the economic situation was normalized. Only the NLGA of 1932 changed this attitude.

There is no similar development in France, though the comprehensive provisions on damage caused by tort (Art. 1382 and 1383) of the Civil Code could have served as a basis: according to them even negligently or carelessly committed actions which cause damage oblige the wrongdoer to pay damages. The reason why French law developed differently was probably that the French trade unions did not succeed in establishing strike funds, the strike being financed by the employees themselves therefore remained the ordinary strike form.

In pre-Fascist Italy the situation was the same – legally and factually – and Italy, too, did not use the law of torts (Art. 2043 Codice Civile) against the trade unions.

The trade unions in Germany had become very powerful before the First World War and could concentrate on industrial actions because social insurance legislation relieved them of the task of supporting their members. The legal situation, however, was very similar to the French: two provisions of the German Civil Code, sec. 823(1) and sec. 826, may be applied to industrial disputes. The first provision imposes liability to pay damages on any person who intentionally or negligently and unlawfully violates the life, body, health, liberty, property 'or some other right' of another person. The second provision concerns an 'intentional violation of *bonos mores*' which causes damage. The important distinction in practice between these two sections consists in the legal evaluation of negligent error in industrial action and in the general legal evaluation of those actions. Section 826 of the German Civil Code means that actions – and this includes individual actions, too – are generally lawful and become unlawful only in exceptional cases in which there is general moral condemnation. The situation is reversed in sec. 823(1) of the code: actions which fall under this provision are unlawful except in cases in which there is a special reason of justification. Until 1933 industrial disputes were considered according to sec. 826. Sometimes, for example, in the Act on unlawful competition, the 'right of enterprise', or more precisely, the 'immediate intervention into the right of an established and practised enterprise' (a concept more close to the right of property[12] than to the right of trade) fell within the category 'some other right'. But this recognition was not applied to social struggles in industrial relations, because strikes were considered to constitute breaches of the individual employment contracts (mostly strikes were performed without previously given notice). Even the unions' call to boycott, which was combined with requesting their members to strike, was not considered as a violation of sec. 826, German Civil Code, *per se*, but only in special cases. After 1945, however, the legal and the factual situation of official strikes changed. With the recognition of the right to strike, if the union called the strike, the work stoppage and the proclamation of the strike were considered parts of one united action. The increasing professional specialization, the growing division of labour among enterprises, and full employment made boycotting of employers unnecessary. The calling of a strike does not any longer necessarily include a boycott. It is now only an appeal by the union to its members – an internal action. On the other hand, by this time the discipline of the union members had also changed the form of strikes: the periods of giving notice were observed, or at least the possibility existed to do so. Industrial action had been adapted to the established legal system and now new instruments against them had to be developed. The instrument created by Hans Carl Nipperdey, a labour law professor at Cologne who had acquired his high reputation during the Weimar Republic and who became first president of the newly established Federal Labour Court (1954), was the recognition of the right of enterprise as 'some other right' in the sense of sec. 823(1), German Civil Code, now constitutionally justified by references to general liberty and liberty of exercising a man's profession (Arts. 2 and 12, Bonn Basic Law) in the law on industrial actions. But this would have resulted in making strikes *per se* illegal and in demanding special reasons of justification for them – and this would have been an open contradiction to the constitutional recognition of the right to strike by some State constitutions after 1945. Therefore, it was necessary to avoid the consequence of unlawfulness of industrial actions which was the normal consequence of the recognition of the right of enterprise as 'some other right'. A new legal notion was created,[13] namely that of 'social adequacy' (*soziale adaequanz*). It was a new general clause, a blank cheque which left the decision to the judges' discretion. Since that time it has not been clear whether the strikes are *per se* illegal and only the socially adequate strikes are legal, or, conversely, whether the strike *per se* is legal and only the socially

12. Property is defined by sec. 903, German Civil Code, to be tangible property. The so-called 'mental property' – in which patents, authors' rights and comparable rights were included – are considered to be 'some other rights' as well.
13. More exactly it has been the transfer of a well-known notion of penal law to civil law. The functions of this notion in penal law has been the restriction of penal unlawfulness in certain cases of common life. For instance, the operation on a patient is a 'socially adequate' action, not an unlawful bodily injury.

inadequate strike is illegal. However, this question cannot receive a definite answer, because the Federal Labour Court has sidestepped the constitutional recognition of the right to strike and based its decision on a sociologically-founded doctrine of collective industrial action. Moreover, the formula of social inadequacy comes close to that of violation of *bonos mores*, but it mitigates the negative legal evaluation – and it breaks with the case law of the Reich Labour Court which was abolished in 1945. The Federal Labour Court could begin anew without the burden of precedents.

This new German doctrine on industrial actions is also very close to the old civil conspiracy doctrine of the Common Law countries; but it is flexible, and it is more difficult to attack because it avoids an open general condemnation of industrial actions. Certainly, in Germany the clear distinction between lawful and unlawful industrial actions will be abandoned only for a period of transition. The Federal Labour Court creates new law, and from its decisions a new general legal evaluation of industrial disputes will be obtained by abstraction, with the help of academic writers. The trend, however, is already visible in the leading decision of the Big Division of the Federal Labour Court of 28 January 1955:

> Industrial actions (strikes and lockout) are generally undesirable, because they are accompanied by damage to the economy and disturb social peace which is required by the common interest. But they are permitted within certain limits, they are accepted in the liberal, social basic order of the German Federal Republic.[14]

Sweden does not know the problem of a general civil condemnation of industrial disputes because the general principle is recognized concerning peaceful actions *per se* lawful. If an action is permitted as individual, it is also permitted as collective.

Another general condemnation combining civil and penal law was provided during the nineteenth century by the penal sanctions against breaches of the employment contract. But they only applied where strikes broke out without previous notice having been given.

A last attempt was made by the German Supreme Court – that the call to strike could be considered as a demand to disobey the statutes (which would violate sec. 110 of the German Penal Code)[15] – but this doctrine did not find any followers.

Withdrawal of the State or State intervention?

If industrial actions are not considered to be unlawful *per se* it is possible either to abstain from legal evaluations or to distinguish between legal and separate illegal industrial actions. Both ways have been used.

14. BAG, vol. 1, p. 291 (p. 300), the leading decision.
15. supra n. 11.

Great Britain took the first with the Conspiracy and Protection of Property Act of 1875 and with the Trade Disputes Act of 1906. The State withdrew, first in respect of criminal conspiracy and then in tort, from the evaluation of industrial actions. It subjected them to the penal law without discriminating between them. Trade-union actions were kept out of the law and received an immunity from tort liabilities. The State saw its task mainly in regulating strikes in certain public utilities.[16]

The second way, used by the other countries, is of more interest because it leads to essential problems of industrial strikes and displays that in many points the legal solutions of those countries were the same. But before the problems and the solutions are described, it is necessary to say one word about the sources. The main source is, of course, the legislature, but there it depends whether the statutes are rather specific – as they are in Great Britain and in the United States – or whether they permit wide discretion by general clauses – as in France, Germany and Italy. The other question is who applies the statutes: judges, amongst whom it is necessary to distinguish between professional judges (who always set the rules in the supreme courts of France, Germany and Italy) or Labour Court judges? The United States operates with a mixed system of administrative decisions under the control of the courts.

The National Labor Relations Board, an independent administrative agency, was originally established by the NLRA. LMRA amendments increased the size of the Board from three to five members, appointed for five-year terms by the US President, by and with the advice and consent of the Senate. A panel of three members is sufficient to adjudicate a dispute before the Board, although in important cases the Board usually sits *en banc*. The amended NLRA also established the office of General Counsel, an independent official appointed by the President, by and with the advice and consent of the Senate, for a four-year term. The General Counsel is the final authority as to whether, and on what basis, unfair labour practices shall be prosecuted; he also supervises all attorneys and employees in the regional offices of the Board; applies to the courts for injunctions in certain types of cases; seeks compliance with the orders issued by the Board; and applies to the appropriate courts for enforcement of the Board's orders. Complaints in unfair labour practice cases are filed by regional directors of the Board and heard by Trial Examiners, autonomous officials appointed for life and placed directly under the authority of the Civil Service Commission. The specific functions of the Trial Examiners are to conduct hearings upon complaints and to render an official decision upon the facts. In the absence of exceptions by any party, a Trial Examiner's recommendation becomes the order of the Board. In the majority of cases, however, exceptions are taken either to the findings or the recommendations of the Trial Examiner, or both; in that event, the Board decides after a review of the entire record. If upon the preponderance of the evidence the Board concludes that any person named in the complaint has engaged in or is engaging in any unfair labour practice, it sets forth its findings of facts

16. See Chapter 6.

and issues an order requiring such person to 'cease and desist' from such unfair labour practice, and to take such affirmative action, including reinstatement of employees with or without back-pay, as will effectuate the policies of the Act. In the absence of voluntary full compliance by the respondent with the Board's order, the Board may petition the appropriate federal court of appeals for enforcement. Conversely, the respondent may petition that court to review and set aside the Board's order. The reviewing court has the power to grant such temporary relief or restraining order as it deems 'just and proper' and to make and enter a decree enforcing, modifying, or setting aside in whole or in part the order of the Board. The findings of the Board in respect of questions of fact are conclusive if supported 'by substantial evidence on the record considered as a whole'. The decision of the court of appeals is reviewable by the Supreme Court of the United States upon writ of certiorari; that is to say, the reviewing power of the Supreme Court is discretionary. Generally, the Court will grant certiorari only if the case is one of unusual importance or if there is a conflict in the decisions of the several circuit courts of appeals.

In Sweden the statutes on collective agreements (1928) and on the right to organize and on the right of collective bargaining (1936) are supplemented by the Basic Agreement between the Swedish Employers' Confederation and the Swedish Trade Unions' Confederation (1938). Its Chapter IV 'Limitation of strikes, lockouts and other direct action' regulates many problems which are statutorily decided in other countries. The openly declared policy of the Swedish labour organizations is to avoid State intervention as much as possible. They include even disputes threatening essential public services. As Chapter V of the Basic Agreement prescribes, they shall be 'jointly taken up for prompt consideration'.

No doubt a distinction between these different methods of handling industrial disputes is neither complete nor entirely accurate. It is incomplete because in all cases in which the police intervene, statutes are applied which give much discretion to the police and the judges are practically restricted to controlling abuse of this discretionary power. The distinction cannot be entirely accurate, because in all systems which recognize collective agreements the possibility is granted by the peace obligation to follow the Swedish model. But the realization of this possibility depends upon many factors, the power and the structure of the labour organizations, especially the strength of the top organizations, and the activity of the courts. In Germany, for instance, the attempt of the Federal Labour Court in the Schleswig–Holstein Metal Workers' case to extend – by interpreting a very unclear conciliation agreement – the term *Kampfmassnahme* (industrial action) as to include strike balloting[17] has certainly deterred the trade unions.

It is not the function of the constitutions of the labour associations to express the lawfulness or unlawfulness of industrial actions. Statements, however, made by trade unions, that strikes shall be used only after the exhaustion

17. See p. 133.

of all possibilities to bargain, can be used by the courts as the basis for a new rule – as the German Federal Labour Court has established the so-called *ultima ratio* doctrine: the interior rule thereby becomes an exterior obligation. The following part of this chapter tries to approach systematically the different problems of industrial actions. It begins with the strike, which in liberal economies is mainly the target of attack. Here two questions must be answered: (i) the protection of the employees who want to continue work and (ii) protection of those employees hired as replacements. Then is discussed the extension of the strike (as a work stoppage) to the economic field: by the boycott of the strikers in their capacity as customers and the request to the public to join, and by secondary strikes and boycotts. Finally it will be shown how industrial disputes gradually became institutionalized. This development includes the recognition of the labour associations and the intervention of the social State which calls in question the classical action of the employers: the lockout.

Strike and boycott of the enterprise

The employers, of course, are interested in protecting employees who want to continue work during the strike or who have been hired as replacements for the strikers, because they want to continue production; consequently the strike will be ineffective and break down. But the employees themselves are also interested in legal protection: some want to continue work and receive the wages, especially if no strike funds exist or they are excluded as non-members from union strike support. Others, previously unemployed, want a job. The strike, therefore, is the test of the solidarity of employees. The greater the amount of unemployment and therefore the easier the exchange of workers, then the more this solidarity is threatened because it is opposed by the elementary interest to keep alive by work.

This partly explains the inefficiency of many strikes especially in the nineteenth century, although the violence and animosity of the early industrial actions were certainly enlarged by political and religious influences. Considering the lasting impact of those fights even after the termination of the industrial action, it seems wise that after a bloody confrontation between military force and parading strikers (1932) the Swedish employers gave up their policy of hiring replacements. It can be generally expected that the possibility to change the labour force of an enterprise will be reduced in the future by the progressive specialization of work performance and by full employment.

The strike therefore is changing its nature. The intervention of the employer by hiring replacements ends, and the strike becomes the decision of a minority or majority of employees. So far the strike is closely connected with the disciplinary power of a trade union and its position within the enterprise, the percentage of its members among the employees being important as to its legal position as a bargaining unit.

This is the factual background of the legal development which contains two elements: the protection of contractual freedom of the employer and of the newly-hired employees, and the confrontation between competition and solidarity on the employees' side. The legal evaluation concerned picketing and the strike call of the union, which included demands to boycott.

According to the French Le Chapelier Act of 1791 (Art. 7) a person was penalized who restrained the freedom of labour and trade by threat or force. This provision essentially agrees with the Italian Penal Code of 1889 (until the Fascist Penal Code of 1931) concerning industrial disputes 'caused or continued by force or intimidation' (Arts. 165 and 166) and with Arts. 414 and 415 of the French Penal Code of 1810 in their texts after 1864; but it was completed by a third qualification of restraint, fraudulent manipulation, which includes the publication of falsehoods or defamatory assertions in the press.

The British Combinations Acts (1799/1800) were more concrete: giving money, persuasion, solicitation or intimidation or other means were the disapproved forms. And in addition to preventing another person from hiring himself or from hiring a third person, a third possibility concerned refusal to work together with another employee. The British provisions changed very often and thus displayed the great practical importance of these regulations.

The amendment of the repealing Act (1825) contained a new description: 'Violence to the person or property, threats or intimidation, molesting or in any way obstructing in order to force or to endeavour to force.' These broad provisions rendered it possible to prosecute all strikes. Therefore, the Molestation of Workmen Act (1859) made an exception for 'endeavouring peaceably' and persuasion 'in a reasonable manner, and without threat or intimidation, direct or indirect', and without inducing break of contract.

This position, however, was corrected by the Criminal Law Amendment Act of 1871, which redefined molestation, obstruction and intimidation. The Conspiracy and Protection of Property Act 1875, passed after complaints by the trade unions, granted only the right to meet at a place for the purpose of communicating or receiving information. Finally the Trade Disputes Act, 1906, introduced the right of peaceful persuasion (now Industrial Relations Act, 1971, sec. 134 – subject to sec. 96 in the case of unregistered unions).

In Germany the Reich Trade Order of 1869 addressed itself against the 'use of bodily force, intimidation, violation of honour, or declaration of boycott'.

The substantial question behind all these provisions was answered most clearly by the courts of the United States in the early nineteenth century. Picketing *per se* was considered unlawful. The exhibition of collective force, the confrontation of the individual strike-breaker with the collectivity of pickets was incompatible with individualistic legal thinking. The Swedish Åkarp amendment of 1899 (amended again in 1914) showed this attitude best. It extended the term 'illegal constraint' of its Penal Code (Chapter 15, sec. 22) by a legal definition. It included even the attempts to coerce another person to participate in a work stoppage or to abstain from returning to work or to accept work at another workplace – this was the only case in which the attempt to commit an illegal constraint was made a crime in Sweden.

It is interesting to observe that this amendment was introduced at the very time when the German Emperor, William II, demanded hard labour for all persons who threatened an employee wanting to work. In Germany picketers were prosecuted as guilty of 'gross misdemeanour' or by the police, who were authorized by a general clause (of the Prussian General Code of 1794 – but this provision has served as model for all other state police statutes): 'It is the office of the police to take the actions necessary in order to maintain public peace, security and order and to prevent danger imminent to the community or to any member of it.' Certainly, the Government emphasized the neutrality of the State, but actually the discretionary power was very wide and at that time not even subject to judiciary control in most German states. It was possible, for instance, to prohibit picketing under the pretext of traffic regulation on public streets.

Generally this former legal situation may be characterized by saying that the individual statutory provisions were not used to distinguish between different industrial disputes but to suppress strikes.

Today the legal situation varies from country to country. Special Acts do not exist any longer in Germany where the provisions of the German Reich Trade Order were abolished in 1918. The Swedish Åkarp amendment was repealed in 1938. In Great Britain the Conspiracy and Property Act of 1875 is applicable but, after 1971, in the new definition of industrial disputes (Industrial Relations Act, sec. 167(1)). In France we find special provisions within the Penal Code. In Italy sometimes the police tried to take action according to Art. 650 of the Penal Code, which punishes the 'non-compliance with an order of such a public authority' (in such cases the order was to breach the picket line insofar as it hampered circulation). The courts, however, released the strikers.[18] Resort to violence and threat is prosecuted under general provisions of the Penal Code.

Regardless of these different legal situations, the factual problems remain the same. Everywhere the right of pickets to peaceful persuasion is recognized. The first country to grant recognition was Great Britain (Trade Disputes Act of 1906, now substantially repeated by sec. 134 of the Industrial Relations Act). The NLGA of the United States (1932) admitted this right in its sec. 4(e), which concerned 'giving publicity to the existence of, or the facts involved in, any labour dispute, whether by advertising, speaking, patrolling, or by any other method not involving fraud or violence'. The Supreme Court considered this provision to be in accordance with the protection of the freedom of speech by the first amendment to the constitution.

In Italy Art. 507 of the (Fascist) Penal Code prohibited the inducement of persons not to conclude labour contracts 'by propaganda or by utilizing the preponderance and the power of parties, associations or combinations'. But this provision was, as far as propaganda is concerned, considered by the Constitutional Court[19] to be contradictory to the recognition of the freedom of speech (Art. 21 Italian Constitution).

18. See Chapter 2 for further development.
19. 17 April 1969, Nr. 84.

It is also possible in Germany to justify peaceful picketing by the principle of freedom of speech – and, in case of a union strike, by the right to organize (Art. 9, sec. 3 Bonn Basic Law and before 1933, Art. 159, Weimar Constitution). Nevertheless this has not influenced the result of the legal evaluation: Since the enactment of the Civil Code (1900) and even before, according to Roman law as applied to Germany, the inducement to break an individual contract – including the employment contract – has not been considered a tort. The same is true for Sweden as well.

On the other hand, it is agreed that the employees who want to work must have free and secure access to their working places. This means physically – as the case law shows – that pickets are not allowed to use force and that mass picketing may not block the route to the factory. Decisions of German lower courts often determine the breadth of this. Other problems arise out of the question whether buses shall pass or only the individual workers. But free and secure access to the premises of the employer also includes a psychological dimension, and here it is very difficult to draw the line between permitted influence on the decision to work or to strike and threats or insults. Especially on the point of insults, many factors should be regarded: the colloquial speech within an enterprise, which generally is rougher than on the outside, the feeling of violated solidarity, provocations, and last but certainly not least, considerable difficulties of getting evidence – all these aggravate the evaluation by the judges. Swedish court decisions go very far in prohibiting 'defamation' by insulting people to be strike-breaker or boycott-breaker, probably because they expect those persons to be blacklisted.[20]

In France, the court of Lyon has tried to give an objective description of intimidation (which does not correspond to the conditions required by Art. 305, French Penal Code): 'a person who is of normal energy must be led to act against his own will and to do what he does not want to do because he would have serious reasons to expect an attack against his person, his family or his property'.[21]

The British Conspiracy and Protection Act of 1875 added other important aspects when it made a criminal offence the use of violence and intimidation, even against the wife or the children; the injury of property; watching or besetting; the persistent following about from place to place; and the following with two or more persons in a disorderly manner; the hiding of tools, clothes, or property, or the depriving or hindering in the use thereof. Also mass picketing is not protected by the Act of 1906 (now sec. 134 of the 1971 Act which also prohibits picketing of a domicile).

In the United States mass picketing is still considered to be coercion or restraint and therefore is an unfair labour practice.[22]

Boycotting of replacements did not occur before the gates of the factory only. The most efficient kind was the occupation of the factory in the form of a

20. Cf. Folke Schmidt, *The Law of Labor Relations in Sweden*, Harvard UP, 1962, p. 470.
21. 8 May 1931, D 1932.2.63.
22. See Chapter 2.

sit-down. These strikes, widespread in the nineteenth century especially in the Romanic countries but now rare, are generally considered unlawful – as trespassing (*Hausfriedensbruch*) according to the German Penal Code (Arts. 123 and 124); as a tort in Great Britain;[23] or in Italy, 'invasion into an agricultural or industrial enterprise or its besetting for the only purpose of hindering or of disturbing the natural development of labour' (Art. 508 Italian Penal Code, which was declared by the Cassation Court not to be contradictory to the Constitution). The courts, however, did not apply this provision with its heavy sanctions[24] and resorted rather to Arts. 610 (violation of domicile), 633 (invasion). Also in these cases courts try to avoid condemnation on the ground of lack of malice (*dolus*) etc.

In France trespassing presumes that the entering has been done by threat or violence; therefore this provision is not applicable if the workers simply remain in the factory. The question need not be raised whether the recognition of the right to the workplace similar to the right of property would possibly change this view. This right can be derived from the protection of the employee against unjustified dismissal – if this protection is more than a limitation of the abuse of the employer's freedom to dismiss the employees.[25] Then again the factory can be regarded as the domicile of the worker, as the Italian Pretura di Roma has already done;[26] Pretura di Fiorenzuola,[27] on similar ground denied possessory actions against employees. The boycott of replacements eliminates competition between workers for the purpose of improving wages or working conditions by a strike, and this explains why especially the United States opposed the legal recognition of this type of industrial action: it was due to their strong protection of the freedom of competition – which is meant by the words, 'freedom of trade'.

In Germany, however, because it never completely broke with the collectivism of the Middle Ages, the boycott *per se* was not considered to violate the principle of *bonos mores*. Exceptions were made 'if either the measure which was used to achieve a permitted aim violates the *bonos mores*, as inciting misrepresentations, or if the harm created for the adversary involved a considerable risk of ruining him economically, or if there is no tolerable relationship of the harm and the advantage demanded and even, if in the situation concerned the result which is to be achieved by the pressure does not appear any longer as a justified aim'. This very old interpretation of the 'blank cheque' provision of sec. 826, German Civil Code, by the Supreme Court[28] is still used – it is merged into the new formula of social adequacy and is also now applied to industrial actions.

23. See K. W. Wedderburn, *The Worker and the Law*, p. 324.
24. See ultimately Tribunale Prato 19.12.69 and others.
25. In Germany, some academic writers, among them Nipperdey, recognize the right of the workplace to be 'some other right' in the sense of sec. 823(1) Civil Code – but they do not draw the consequences indicated as possible by the text.
26. 6 March 1970.
27. 23 April 71.
28. Supreme Court, 17 Sept. 1908, JW, 1908, p. 679.

Industrial actions and third parties

All industrial actions are economic disputes, not only because they exercise economic pressure but also because the employer has a double position as employer (considering the relation to his employees) and as entrepreneur or as a party to commercial contracts with third persons. Both parties to bargaining, of course, try to profit from this fact for the purpose of strengthening their own position in the industrial dispute and in order to weaken the position of the adversary.

Work stoppages will mostly delay the delivery of the products of the enterprise or even make it impossible altogether. If in these cases the employer can be made liable to pay the damages of his contractors, the economic pressure on him is increased. This liability is much disputed in all countries by civil lawyers and sometimes by the courts, but in fact these decisions are rather unimportant because the employers generally include in their contracts an exclusion of liability for damage caused by industrial actions.

Another problem, the combination of strike and suppliers' boycott, may also be omitted here. It had general importance in a time of an underdeveloped division of labour in industry. Nowadays it is restricted to enterprises which render personal services, such as restaurants, hotels, shops, etc. It seems, however, that it has kept some importance only in the United States, because there picketing in the form of handbilling has always been used for the purpose of influencing public opinion and this appeal to the public can always have the effect of a suppliers' boycott.

Commercial contracts may be used differently in order to improve the chances of success in an industrial action: the employer may conclude new contracts with other entrepreneurs for the purpose of receiving the goods from them which he cannot produce himself because of the strike. Are the workers of this second entrepreneur entitled to refuse work because they do not want to act indirectly as strike-breakers? They may prefer to stay neutral and may not even wish to support the workers of the primary dispute.[29]

On the other hand, the employees of the primary employer may take action equivalent to his entering into commercial contracts by demanding – with or without a strike – that another employer break his contract with the first employer or they may induce him not to conclude a contract at all.

The last extension would be a strike of employees of other enterprises for the purpose of supporting the demands of the striking workers of the primary enterprise; or in reverse corresponding lockouts.

The solutions of the different legal systems are based upon separate ideological and sociological approaches. It is, of course, important to know whether industrial actions are essentially considered to be class struggles in which at least all workers act or should act in solidarity, or to be part of collective bargaining and therefore principally restricted to the parties to bargaining. Solidarity or sympathetic strikes[30] must be regarded within the con-

29. Otherwise, if they had the intention of support, this would be a sympathetic strike (cf. *infra* text).
30. The terminology is different in the different countries. See also Chapter 2, p. 90.

text of the structure of the trade unions and of the employers' associations.[31] Also we must keep in mind that in the United States one of many competing trade unions may be elected by the workers of an enterprise (NLRA, sec. 9) and certified by the NLRB as their exclusive bargaining representative. But the system of company collective agreements, of course enlarges the area of sympathetic actions. In Germany the field of sympathetic actions is much more restricted mostly because trade unions are organized as industrial unions and the existence of employers' associations permits resort to combined industrial action on their side as well as on the unions' side.

The legal approach is less important. Sometimes it is even misleading. The recognition of the right to strike by the French and Italian Constitutions opens a wide and fruitless field of discussion as to whether this recognition should be restrictively interpreted to primary *strikes*, but not to *boycotts* at all and not to secondary strikes; or whether an extensive interpretation should not include all these types of industrial actions. Needless to say, all theories can be developed and they are often little more than a cover for political decisions. Even more worthless is the German solution of creating the new tort of 'socially inadequate violation' of the right of enterprise – because it substantially does not mean anything but leaves the decision to the courts, or more specifically, to the Federal Labour Court which openly established by this doctrine the claim to be the final authority of the legitimacy of industrial actions. One point, however, is sure: the new law will be more restrictive than it was before 1933, when sec. 826 was used.

The restrictive tendency seems to be an international development which can be clearly observed in Sweden, and even more so in the United States and in Great Britain. Sweden began by including in the peace obligation all industrial actions 'in order to assist others in cases in which those may not themselves commit offensive actions' (Act on Collective Agreements, sec. 4(4)). This meant a very wide recognition of all types of industrial action because there was no limit on them when the peace obligation had been terminated and also during the existence of such a peace obligation for sympathetic actions. Under the threat of legislative intervention the Basic Agreement of 1938 regulated the problems in a very detailed way – based upon the statutory drafts. It still, however, kept the recognition of sympathetic strikes for the purpose of assisting a party bargaining for a new collective agreement (Chapter IV, secs. 8 and 10), but then generally protected the neutral third party in industrial disputes. It made the exceptions by defining the non-neutral third party in its sec. 9.

In the United States the restriction was made by 'no-strike' clauses in collective agreements[32] and by supplementing the NLRA by the LMRA and the Labor-Management Reporting and Disclosure (Landrum-Griffin) Act (LMRDA) of 1959. The NLRA now forbids the unions to induce or encourage the employees of the second employer to engage in a strike or another

31. See also Chapter 1, p. 8.
32. See also Chapter 3, p. 145.

industrial action for the purpose of forcing or requiring him to boycott the first employer who is party of the industrial dispute.[33] Certainly, according to its letter, this provision does not include all types of secondary boycotts, but it is rather doubtful which of them are actually covered by the broad words 'induce or encourage'. Possibly even sympathetic strikes can be included when the only effective method of 'influencing' the first employer by the second is the boycott.

Very close to these provisions is the British Industrial Relations Act which severely restricted the freedom of action previously enjoyed by the trade unions under the Trade Disputes Acts 1906 and 1965 – although this freedom had already been considerably diminished by case law decisions on interference with commercial contracts in the 1960s.

The principle is that inducing a breach of any contract is illegal, unless the union doing this is registered (sec. 96); and, for any union, the calling, organizing, procuring or financing of industrial action 'in contemplation or furtherance' of an industrial dispute or even the threat to do so is prohibited when the purpose is knowingly to induce any other person to break a commercial contract with the party of the industrial dispute or to prevent him from performing it (sec. 98). Exceptions are made for an extraneous party – and here the British Act meets the same questions like the Swedish Basic Agreement (Chapter IV, sec. 9), but answers them in a very different way. Contrary to Sweden, in Great Britain membership of the same employers' organization to which the party of the industrial dispute belongs is still compatible with neutrality. Even the payment to a fund available to the party of the industrial dispute for compensation of the economic losses suffered by it is only considered to be an 'action in material support' to this party if the payment is made with specific reference to that dispute. Also another point of disagreement seems to be important: Sweden regards as a non-neutral third party anyone who has assisted the party to the industrial dispute 'by converting or otherwise altering his own pursuits or activities'. Great Britain does not consider it to be 'any action in material support' when the supply of goods or the provision of services is in pursuance of a contract entered into before the industrial conflict began – even if this means a requirement under an optional contract.

While Great Britain also regards an associated employer in relation to the employer who is party to the industrial dispute to be an extraneous party, Sweden pushes through the legal forms of company law. It considers as a non-neutral party

> anyone who has a controlling interest in a company being a party to the dispute, or who is a partner without limited liability . . . and a company in which a party to the dispute owns shares or a partnership in which the party is a partner provided that the operations of the company or partnership must . . . be considered to be maintained on behalf of the party concerned.

33. See also Chapter 2, on this subject and the problem of 'hot cargo' (p. 106).

Reflecting upon those different efforts to limit industrial actions to the 'primary' parties and therefore to increase the 'extraneous' or neutral parties, this seems to be more than a comprehensible reaction to the ideology of class struggle – which it certainly is. It must also be seen against the background of the advancing division of labour in industry which more and more connects the separate enterprises – economically as well as legally. Therefore the restrictive tendency of modern law must be regarded as an attempt to decrease the efficiency of industrial actions, or more specifically, of strikes.

Another development took the opposite direction, the recognition of the right to organize.

The recognition of the right to organize and to take industrial actions

The history of the right to organize and of the right to strike is the same. When prohibitive laws were repealed the employers attempted to prevent strikes by fighting against the unions. The forms were different, and the workers succeeded in prohibiting them gradually. State intervention so far also became favourable to them, but this required a change in State structure. In Germany at the end of the First World War the monarchy, and with it the former authority of the State, broke down. In a critical situation, under the threat of a Communist revolution, the employers' associations, in the agreement of 15 November 1918, recognized the socialist trade unions to be the representatives of the workers. This agreement was the basis of collective labour law of the Weimar Republic (and, therefore, still is of the present collective labour law of the Federal Republic of Germany) after the collapse of the monarchy and the authority of the State. In the United States the liberal society broke down in the Great Depression and the 'New Deal' legislation became the turning point, although its intervention in favour of the employees has been balanced by the legislature after the Second World War.

Systematically we have to distinguish between: (*a*) the interference in the organization of the opposing social group; and (*b*) the prevention of such an independent organization. The employers created or promoted labour associations depending on and especially financed by them. These were the 'works associations' or 'company unions' with members of a single enterprise only; the 'free labourers' or the 'economically peaceful' associations, or the 'yellow unions', as they have been otherwise called. Their great time was in Europe before the First World War and in the United States after that war; then they disappeared. But a newly established powerful French trade union is suspected to be financially supported by the employers, especially by the Simca Motor Corporation. It seems that two main reasons explain their frequency, especially in France and in Germany: the strong tendencies of the unions to promote social revolution and the patriarchal attitude of the employer. In Germany the employers gave up the support of the works' associations in the agreement of 1918, mentioned above. The question must be left unanswered here concerning whether these works' associations have not been replaced to some extent by the works councils, which were established during the First World War and were finally regulated by the Works' Council Act of 1919 on which the present Works' Constitution Act of 1952 is based. These councils represent the employees of one enterprise which depend upon the employer and they are not allowed to call strikes. It may be disputed whether these qualifications which the former works' associations also had, are satisfactorily balanced by the statutory regulation of the election of the works' councils and by their special protection against dismissals. This question is important because the works' councils conclude works' agreements which can cover the same substance as collective agreements concluded by the trade unions. Certainly, the legislature has given a legal (but not sanctioned) priority to the collective agreements of the trade unions; factually, however, these often compete with works agreements.

In the United States the NLRA makes it an unfair labour practice for employers 'to dominate or interfere with the formation or administration of any labour organization or contribute financial or other support to it' (sec. 8(a)(2)).

Italy gives in its Workers' Statute of 1970 the same legal solution, only using other words: 'Employers and employers' associations are forbidden to establish or support by financial means or otherwise, labour unions' (sec. 17). The definition of an 'independent' trade union (which alone can be registered) in the British Act of 1971 (sec. 167(1)) is rather more narrow and only concerned with the 'domination' of the employers. The French Labour Code (Book III, Art. 1a 3) is not so precise. It prohibits the employer to resort to any form of pressure 'for or against any union', but this provision is considered to include all forms of interference in union activities. Germany had to resort to the constitutional recognition of the right to organize (Art. 9, sec. 3, Bonn Basic Law), but this includes, according to the letter of the law, also an equal protection of the employers' associations. The employers' prevention of the formation of independent employees' organizations offered an alternative to the foundation or promotion of dependent employees' associations. The instruments used by employers were: blacklisting of unionists; the agreement on clauses in the employment contracts to abstain from entering a union; the agreement to 'no-strike' clauses and the dismissal of union leaders or members or the leaders of strikes.

Blacklisting has been a strong weapon, especially when the employers had their own employment agencies and unemployment existed. It had not been considered illegal by the German Supreme Court which only demanded that such a powerful intervention must have proportionately compelling reasons.[34] One exception, however, was made in the time before the First World War, namely, the secret notations of work books (which were issued between 1897 and 1937 for industrial workers under 21 years of age) or of dismissal certificates was considered illegal (former sec. 111 and 113(3), Reich Trade Order). Now, however, blacklisting is considered a violation of the right to organize or

---

34. 17 March 1904, RGZ 57, 418 (427 *et seq.*).

of the right of free choice of the working place (Art. 9, sec. 3, and Art. 12, Bonn Basic Law). Evidently legal development leads to inclusion of the special case of blacklisting in the general provision protecting the right to organize. We observe this, too, in the United States, when the National Labor Relations Board (NLRB) considers blacklisting an unfair labour practice because it violates the employees' right to self-organizations, especially the right to engage in concerted activities (NLRA, sec. 7). This is also true for Sweden, France and Italy (Workers' Statute, sec. 8).

The former legal treatment of 'no-strike' clauses in the individual labour contracts can be observed by the fate of the Social-Democrats' demand that they should be expressly treated as void in the German Civil Code. This demand was rejected on the ground that those clauses would be void as a violation of *bonos mores*. The courts, however, did not follow this view, and anyhow this legal discussion made no sense at all because the employer possessed the right of free dismissal. The Weimar Constitution (Art. 159) and Bonn Basic Law (Art. 9) broke with this legal view by recognition of the freedom to organize and its protection against the social adversary. Parallel to this provision the Constitution also recognized the labour associations themselves, but this last provision is not contained in the Bonn Basic Law. Therefore, the Federal Constitutional Court derives the protection of the labour associations from the individual freedom of labour association.

Sweden arrived at the same point with its law on the right to organize (1936). It is interesting that this recognition also followed the guarantee of inviolability by the Collective Agreement of 1906 – as in Germany where the constitutional recognition had followed the basic agreement between the employers and employees' associations of 1918. Section 3 of the Swedish Act on the right to organize very clearly and comprehensively defines the right to organize as an individual right consisting: of the right to belong to the association; to exercise the right as a member; to work for the association; to form an association. This right is protected against infringements, which are specifically enumerated: all measures taken in order to cause someone 'to refrain from becoming a member or to resign from an association, to refrain from working for an association or for the formation of an association and all disadvantages for these reasons.' Dismissals or similar legal acts are considered to be null and void. Violation of individual rights, however, also concerns the association itself, provided that it has members or prospective members whose individual rights were violated. 'An association shall not be bound to tolerate any infringement of the right of organizations which constitutes interference with its activities.'

The German and Swedish provisions generally recognize the right to organize and to treat equally employees and employers alike. In Great Britain the recognition of the rights of workers and employers to organize in different sections of the 1971 Act (e.g. sec. 5 – workers) seems to be accidental. The preamble to the French Constitution of 1946, to which the Constitution of 1958 refers, also states: 'Everybody may defend his rights and interests by the associative action (*action syndicale*) and join an association of his choice.' Book

III, Art. 1(a) of the Labour Code, however, protects the right to organize against the employer. The same distinction can also be observed in Italy: Art. 39 of the Constitution of 1946 recognizes the free formation of labour associations. The Workers' Statute of 1970, however, protects the employees against discriminatory actions of the employers only (Art. 15).

The distinction is even clearer in the United States: The NLRA of 1935 speaks only of the employees' right of self-organization 'to form, join or assist labour organizations' (sec. 7) and considers it an unfair labour practice for an employer to 'interfere with, restrain or coerce employees in the exercise of this right' (sec. 8(1)). Twelve years later the employers were protected by the LMRA – against restraining or coercion in the selection of their representatives for the purpose of collective bargaining or the adjustment of grievances (sec. 8(b)(1)(B)) and against forcing or requiring anyone to join any labour or employer organization (sec. 8(b)(4)(A)).

This distinction between the right to organize of the employees and of the employer (also seen in the International Labour Organization (ILO) Agreement 98 of 1951 (Art. 1), serving as a model for the Italian Workers Statute) leads to the origin of collective labour law: the necessity to protect the workers against the economic superiority of the employer. The same problem will come up again when the different types of industrial actions, strikes and lockouts, are discussed.

Another question, however, remains: how efficient the legal protection of the employees' right to organize actually is. If the reason for dismissal is openly declared to be for union activities, this protection seems to be easy. But it must be questioned whether actually the reinstatement of the dismissed workers can be compelled. The British Industrial Relations Act provides for a recommendation by an industrial tribunal, but if the recommendation is not complied with, the industrial tribunal is restricted to an award of compensation (sec. 106(4) and (5)). The French Labour Code (Book III, Art. 1(a)) provides for damages too, but not for reinstatements. In the United States reinstatements seem to work, possibly because the employers' authority in personnel problems is less respected – numerous binding decisions of arbitrators may have contributed to this result. Certainly it may be often very difficult to prove that union activities are the reason of a dismissal. The US Supreme Court has declared that specific evidence of the employer's intent to encourage or discourage union activity is not an indispensable element of proof of violation of sec. 8(a)(3) of the NLRA, and that 'an employer's protestation that he did not intend to encourage or discourage' must be unavailing where a natural consequence of his action was such encouragement or discouragement.[35] The current tendency of court opinions and of scholarly articles is to stress the balancing of the employer's interest against the extent of likely interference with union membership.[36]

35. *Radio Officers' Union* v. *NLRB*, 347 US 1745 (1954).
36. See T. Christiansen and Swanoe, 'Motive and Intent in the Commission of Unfair Labor Practices: The Supreme Court and Fictive Formality', 77, *Yale Law Journal*, 1269 (1968).

The Swedish Labour Court has established a general division of the burden of proof:

> It is for the workers to show plausible reasons that the right to organize has been infringed, and if such reasons have been produced, the employer must prove that the dismissal has taken place upon reasonable grounds independent of the question of the right to organize.[37]

It is a division which is very close to the German when the general context of the right of dismissals is also regarded. If the employee cannot prove that the reason to dismiss him was a violation of his right to organize, the general rule of the Act on Protection against Dismissals of 1951 will be applied and the employer has to prove that the dismissal is not 'socially unjustified', namely not required by reasons which lay in the person or conduct of the workers or in 'urgent necessities of the enterprise' (sec. 1(2)). The British Industrial Relations Act shows even better the close connection between general and special law by providing that whereas the employer must prove a sufficient reason to avoid a charge of unfair dismissal (sec. 24), the burden of proof is shifted to an employee who alleges that the unfairness took the form of discrimination in a strike (sec. 26). Needless to say that the effect of these different efforts to distribute the burden of proof is always limited. It gives no protection against well-camouflaged dismissals, the reason for which are actually union activities.

Much weaker is the protection of union members against discrimination at hiring – unless, as Italy provides, the free choice of hiring is generally restricted. It does not help much that the British Industrial Relation Act considers the refusal to engage as an unfair industrial practice (sec. 5(2)(c)) – the remedy granted by the industrial tribunals is an order determining the right of the employee and an award of compensation. French labour courts considered discrimination as 'abuse of rights', and the Labour Code (Book III, Art. 1(a)) provides for damages. The German Works' Constitution Act of 1952 provides protection only against union discrimination of persons occupied in the enterprise (sec. 51) and gives the works' council the right to oppose the hiring of a person being hired in order to disadvantage other qualified employees for union activities (sec. 61(3)(c)). In Sweden the refusal to hire a union member is not recognized as a violation of the right to organize.[38]

Having treated the right of the *individual* employee to organize and the right of the organization to take action if it was considered to be the prerogative of the organization – a prerogative which exists only in Sweden – we must now discuss the rights of the organization to have activities within the enterprise and its right to bargain.

The Italian Workers' Statute (Art. 25) and a French statute of 1945 oblige the employer to permit the union the use of the notice board of the enterprise. The recruiting of members, the distribution of publications, and the collection of fees as well as the use of the rooms within the enterprise formerly required his permission, but is now permitted by the French Statute of 27

37. 1937:57.
38. cf. AD 1952 Nr. 18, 1955 Nr. 16 II.

December 1968 and by the Italian Workers' Statute (Arts. 20, 22, 26, 27). The German Federal Labour Court has authorized the employees to distribute recruiting and other information-material to their colleagues during the breaks and outside of working time.[39] It is an open question, however, whether even members of the works' council may do it – because the Works Constitution Act obliges them to abstain from anything which could endanger labour and the peace of the enterprise (sec. 49(2)).[40] In the United States the NLRB and the courts have generally ruled that an employer may normally enforce non-discriminatory rules prohibiting his employees from soliciting union membership during working time, but not during non-working time on the employer's property. Distribution of union literature in working areas during either working or non-working time may be banned on a non-discriminatory basis, but distribution in non-working areas (such as parking lots) during non-working time may not be prohibited.[41] The foregoing applies only to employees; non-employees may normally be prohibited from soliciting or distributing on the employer's property on a non-discriminatory basis at all times.[42] In special cases, such as retail sales operations, an employer may lawfully ban union solicitation by employees in selling areas at all times.[43]

The refusal to bargain with the employees' associations can be discovered everywhere as a weapon of the employers. In 1890 the manager of the Central Organizations of German Employers emphatically declared: 'The German employers will not resist the organization of workers, but they will never accept negotiation with representatives of these organizations or other persons outside on an equal status.' Twenty-eight years later in their agreement with the trade unions they revoked this opinion by recognizing the unions as the 'competent representatives of the workers'. Since that time, especially since the establishment of the unity union system after 1945, the actual pressure of the unions is so strong that the employers bargain. However, one problem exists: if different unions are competing – which may happen in the case of white-collar workers or in the public service – the employers negotiate with one union of their choice, regularly with the most representative, and then conclude with the other unions a so-called 'adhesion collective agreement', which consists of one sentence, namely, that the collective agreement concluded with the first union is extended to this collective agreement. When a small union which had not been admitted as partner to the negotiations went to court, the Federal Labour Court declared that the right of association did not include the right to bargain and that no obligation to make collective agreements is provided for by statute.[44]

39. 19 February 1967, AP Nr. 20 zu Art. 9 GG.
40. An indication of this tendency is made for the members of the personnel representation of the public services (the equivalent to works' council) by the Federal Constitutional Court, 26 May 1970, p. 772 and by the Federal Administration Court, 23 October 1970, 1971, p. 288 (even outside of the labour time!).
41. *Republic Aviation Corp.* v. *NLRB*, 324 US 793 (1945); Stoddard–Quirk Mfg. Co., 138 NLRB 615 (1962).
42. *NLRB* v. *Babcock & Wilcox Co.*, 351 US 105 (1956).
43. *Marshall Field & Co.*, 98 NLRB 88 (1952).
44. 2 August 1963, AP Nr. 5 zu Art. 9 GG.

Sweden recognized the right to bargain as an additional right to organize and even expressed it in the name of the statute: Act on the Right to Organize and on the Right to Bargain Collectively. In the United States employers have the duty to bargain in good faith over rates of pay, wages, hours of employment, or other conditions of employment. The scope of mandatory bargaining now comprehends a wide variety of subjects, including overtime pay; shift differentials; paid vacations; pensions; severance pay; Christmas bonuses; stock-purchase plans; merit wage increases; seniority; contracting out; management rights clauses; grievance and arbitration provisions; and a host of others.[45] But this right to bargain is restricted to the union which has been elected for collective bargaining by the majority of the employees (NLRA, sec. 9). Both countries, Sweden and the United States, give a very detailed description of the obligation to bargain. In the United States unilateral wage increases by the employer are considered to violate the obligation to bargain, except when the collective agreement has come to an end, although the employer had negotiated in good faith. In Germany such wage increases are not unlawful. In Britain the Act of 1971 allows an employer or a registered union to apply for a 'bargaining unit' in which, after a ballot of the employees, the union acquires an exclusive right to bargain; but the definition of the employer's duty to bargain is vague and the remedy for breach of that duty is limited to an application by the union for arbitration on the terms of employment. The employer cannot be ordered by the Industrial Court to bargain (secs. 45; 55(1); 105(5)).

The 'negative right to organize' and union-security clauses

In the discussion of the right to organize the right of the individual employee to abstain from membership is often included, sometimes also called the 'negative right to organize'. Contrary to the questions which have been answered up to now, the present problem concerns the protection of the individual against his own social group. The purpose of industrial action here is to strengthen organization, and this may be achieved by preventing disadvantages to union members at hiring as well as by the guarantee that only those union members will be employed (union security clauses). At least unions try to fight against the 'free riders', who profit from their activities, and especially from the union strikes, because the employers treat all employees equally and grant the same wages to organized as well as to non-organized employees who do not pay membership fees. Therefore the unions demand either 100 per cent membership or 'solidarity contributions' from the non-organized employees, or financial advantages from the employers which are reserved to the union members.

The question does not exist in countries such as France where the trade unions have practically no strike funds and therefore do not support their members during the strike. It is very important in Germany where the trade

45. See *The Developing Labor Law*, C. J. Morris (ed.), Washington, 1971, pp. 389–434.

unions succeeded in getting better wage and labour conditions without a strike and in the United States with its system of competing unions. It naturally becomes more complicated if, as in France and Italy, the competition between the unions is based upon political or ideological reasons. In this case objections against any form of coercion to acquire membership become stronger.

The solutions are different. In the United States, employees select the union to represent them in collective bargaining in secret ballot elections conducted by the NLRB. The union so selected becomes the 'exclusive bargaining representative', which means that it represents the employees within the 'appropriate bargaining unit', whether or not they are members of the union. The employer has the affirmative duty to deal exclusively with that union on all matters within the scope of collective bargaining, and the negative duty to refrain from dealing in respect of such matters with any other union or any single employee or group of employees. The 'closed shop' (an arrangement under which no employee may be hired unless he is a union member) is illegal in the United States. A so-called 'union shop' arrangement is permitted, under which employees may be required either to join the union or to pay the equivalent of the regular initiation fee and union dues. Where the union shop exists, an employee may be lawfully discharged for failure to accede to this requirement. On the other hand, a union member expelled for other reasons may not be discharged if he continues to make the necessary payments. If the employer discharges an employee under these circumstances, he is guilty of an unfair labour practice. Similarly, the union is guilty of an unfair labour practice if it causes or attempts to cause the employer to discharge the employee for this reason. It is also an unfair labour practice for a union to require of employees covered by a union shop agreement to pay an initiation fee 'in an amount which the Board finds excessive or discriminatory under all the circumstances'.

Dealing with the same subject matter, an exception is made in the case of agreements requiring membership in a labour organization as a condition of employment. Section 14(b) of the NLRA permits states or territories to forbid the execution or application of such agreements within their boundaries. State laws to this effect are popularly known as 'right-to-work' laws – a misleading description, inasmuch as they have nothing to do with the right to work.

The British Industrial Relations Act generally considers pre-entry closed-shop agreements to be void (sec. 7). The effect of this law on the existing closed-shop practices – lawful until 1971 – remains to be seen. But closed-shop agreements may be approved by the Industrial Court if the agreement enables the workers to be organized and to get reasonable conditions of employment or stable arrangements for collective bargaining (sec. 17; Schedule 1, para. 5). The approval demands an initial, joint application of one or more employers and registered unions, but also a qualified majority of the workers concerned in a ballot. And the same control by balloting is provided for the continuance of the closed-shop agreement. This agreement does not force the workers to become members of a union; if they object on ground of conscience they may make in lieu appropriate contributions to charity.

The 'agency shop agreement' which the Act allows between an employer and a registered union may be made either after application to the Industrial Court and a ballot or voluntarily. But under it, an employee has the right either to apply to contribute to an appropriate charity or merely to pay his contribution to the union (secs. 11–16) without becoming a member. If he does one of these things he may retain his membership in another registered union by virtue of sec. 5(1)(*b*) of the Act.

France has not experienced coercion to join even a determined union, although it has competing unions and the legislature has introduced a system of most representative unions (Labour Code, Book I, Art. 31(f)). Since 1950 the collective agreements must include provisions on the 'free exercise of the right to organize' in order to be subject to the procedure of declaring those agreements to be generally applicable by ministerial regulation (Art. 31(g)), e.g. of extending them even to employees who are not members of the union. And the Labour Code (Book III, Art. 1(a)) prohibits the employer to take union membership as a criterion of his decision.

In Sweden the Act on the right to organize does not deal with the question as to whether an employee should be protected against actions from his fellow workers to persuade him to join a union. The Social-Democratic Government which introduced the Bill, rejecting the view of the conservatives that there existed a right to remain outside the union, decided that the ordinary crime of defamation or physical threat should apply.

The German Works Constitution Act prohibits unequal treatment of persons because of union activities or sympathies (sec. 51), but it has not considered protection against union-security clauses. The Big Division of the Federal Labour Court[46] refers to Art. 9, sec. III of the Bonn Basic Law: the right to organize should also include the right of not joining an organization and even indirect influence by agreements providing special benefits to the union member (for instance additional vacation pay) is considered illegal. In two state constitutions after 1945 – of Hessen and Bremen, both governed by the Social-Democratic Party – the right of not joining an association was expressly guaranteed. Evidently the guarantee was a reaction to the forced membership of the Nazi period.

The Italian legal situation is very similar to the German. A practice of benefits reserved to union members had just started when the unions shifted to the ideology of acting as representatives of the whole working class and not of their members only. Many collective agreements, however, provide for payment of solidarity contributions from non-organized employees. According to the prevailing opinion among legal writers the right not to organize is included in the right to organize. The French Labour Code, Book 3, Art. 1(a) which was introduced in 1956, treated equally the right to organize and the right not to organize. One may ask whether this is a concession to the French ideal of

46. 29 November 1967, AP Nr. 13 zu Art. 9 GG, p. 18.

personal liberty, one more consequence of the lack of disciplined union organization in France and Italy. Historically, however, the right not to organize and the right to organize, which has to be protected against the social opponent, must be clearly separated. The social state (which is recognized as a fundamental principle of the German Federal Republic) certainly legitimates the effort of the unions to strengthen their power in the social conflicts with employers.

Unofficial and official strikes

The most important State intervention is the protection of the employee who participates in a strike against sanctions of the employer – usually dismissal. In the German Weimar Republic this had been attempted twice: by the recognition of the right of 'coalition' in the first state constitutions, and by efforts of legal writers to state the superiority of obligations arising out of union membership to the contractual obligation to work. Both, however, failed. The term right of 'coalition' was received from the French prohibitive legislation, i.e. from the Le Chapelier Act of 1791, and included combinations as well as strikes and lockouts, but it was not used in the Weimar Constitution. That Constitution used as a substitute the words 'Vereinigung zur Wahrung und Förderung von Arbeits- und Wirtschaftsbedingungen' (combination in order to maintain and promote labour and economic conditions) in order to avoid any justification for public officials and for the employees of vital industries to participate in a strike.[47] This terminological distinction of the Constitution which has been taken over by the Bonn Basic Law, meant the separation of the trade unions from strikes and caused confusion which still exists because the lawyers had the choice between obedience to the Constitution and recognition of the historical and sociological fact that trade unions and strikes are very closely connected. Potthoff[48] tried to solve this conflict by giving the obligation to strike as a union member priority to the contractual duty to work as an employee, but he failed. The German state constitutions which, after 1945, recognized the right to participate in a strike if it had been proclaimed by the unions, stated it in separate provisions. This recognition, also drafted for the Bonn Basic Law, but finally not accepted, was achieved by the Federal Labour Court. But this court used another – sociological – reasoning, referring to the collective nature of industrial disputes. This, however, did not mean that participation in a union strike and in an unofficial strike are treated equally – although both are collective actions and only sociologically distinguished in their organization. The Federal Labour Court considers unofficial strikes *per*

47. For details of the history see T. Ramm, *Das Koalitions- und Streikrecht der Beamten*, 1970, p. 67 *et seq.* See also Chapter 6.
48. Hans Potthoff (1875–1945), economist, and one of the leading legal politicians in labour law of the Weimar Republic. Author of *Die Einwirkung der Reichsverfassung auf das Arbeitsrecht*, 1925; *Arbeitsrecht, Das Ringen um werdendes Recht*, 1928, 2nd ed., 1931.

se to be torts[49] – which, as shown later on, leads to extremely hard sanctions for all participants. It is very doubtful, however, whether this decision is compatible with the Bonn Basic Law: Art. 9, sec. 3 speaks of the right to organize, and strikers form by the strike itself a combination during the time of the strike. The possibility that permanent new unions may arise from those temporary combinations which corresponds to the historical development of unions is sufficient to prevent the present unions from constituting a monopoly. A social order based upon the philosophy of liberalism must guarantee a permanent chance to establish new labour organizations.

It may, however, be a sign of the general development of law that the close connection between individual and collective law established by the British Trade Disputes Act of 1906 is repealed now by the Industrial Relations Act (Schedule 9). The statute considers inducing or threatening to induce the breach of an individual labour contract an unfair labour practice unless it is done by a trade union which must be entered in the provisional or final register (sec. 96). Registration is more than a pure formality which would not have touched the substance of the liberty to organize. It involves considerable control by the registrar over the content and observance of a registered union's rules. Advantages are offered to the registered union, as in sec. 96 or sec. 97(3), which permits it to make 'unofficial' strikes 'official'. But these advantages may be seen as the price for an increase in regulation by the State over the right to form workers' organizations with an effective legal capacity to engage in bargaining and industrial action.

The United States and Sweden do not go so far. Their solutions are very similar. In the United States a wildcat strike without union sanction in violation of a 'no-strike' clause is illegal. In Sweden it is considered to be a breach of the peace obligation in the collective agreement which, in accordance with the agency doctrine, is incumbent upon the individual employees as members of the unions (Collective Agreements Act, sec. 2). In a situation in which no collective agreement exists, the unofficial strike will be considered lawful. In the Basic Agreement, however (Chapter II, Art. 8, sec. 2), there is laid down a provision that no individual action should take place unless authorized by the national unions.

In the United States a defensive strike of unorganized employees in order to protest against working conditions is a protected activity under NLRA, sec. 7. For all these countries industrial actions have become an institution of collective labour law. German legal discussions among scholars show this very clearly. The statute of 1918 provided collective agreements with immediate binding force for employment contracts. From this time onwards, German lawyers tried to make the connection between industrial actions and collective agreements. The legal function of industrial actions was seen in the achievement of collective agreements; and, therefore, the conclusion was drawn by lawyers that action with aims which could not be realized by the making of a collective agreement must be illegal. The statutory restriction that

49. For details see T. Ramm, *Der nichtgewerkschaftliche Streik*, Arbur, 1971, p. 65 *et seq.* and 97 *et seq.*

only unions could conclude collective agreements was deprived of its original meaning so as to exclude labour associations which were dependent upon the employer. It has not been overlooked that unofficial strikes can be often terminated by improving individual employment contracts or (in Germany) by concluding works' agreements.

Exceptions are made by the Romanic countries in which – due to the lack of support by their members in industrial actions – the sociological distinction between official and unofficial strikes is much less important. The French (Preamble of 1946) and the Italian (Art. 40) Constitutions recognize that the right to strike may be exercised within the ambit defined by statutory law. In both countries strikes are, according to this wide recognition, not privileges for union members or, to use the German approach, the unions are not considered as organizations responsible for social peace. These countries see as the reason to protect strike participation the socially inferior position of the individual workers. However, even in France a change can be observed for the public service sector which covers, as may be recalled, a very large labour force much larger than the public service sector of other countries. An Act of 31 July 1963, demands previous notice of five days before a strike by the most representative trade unions can be called.[50]

Lockouts

Protection of strikers is closely connected with the legal treatment of lockouts. The old individualistic doctrine of industrial actions required that the employers, as well as the employees, had to give previous notice of terminating the employment contract – and the German employers complied before 1933 when unemployment guaranteed that after the end of the industrial actions the employees generally wanted to be rehired. Lockout therefore was – according to law and practice – the collective giving of notice to employees. As lockouts were prevailingly used as defence against strikes, one may ask now, after the recognition of the right to strike, whether the prohibition of individual sanctions also includes the prohibition of collective sanctions such as lockouts since it is generally acknowledged that illegal individual action will not become legal because it is an element in concerted action.

Neither French nor Italian nor German State Constitutions nor the European Social Charter (Part II, Art. 6, sec. 4), which all recognize the right to strike, speak of the right to lockout. One German state constitution (of Hessen) considers the lockout illegal. But German labour and constitutional lawyers nearly unanimously claimed this provision violated the principle of equality and declared it to be void. The Big Division of the Federal Labour Court developed in its decision of 28.1.1955 the doctrine of 'equality of weapons' or 'parity of combat'[51] and considered – as the Collective Agreements Act did in

50. See Chapter 6.
51. BAG, vol. 1, p. 291 (p. 300) the leading decision.

respect of the capacity to conclude collective agreements – that both collective parties should have an equal position in industrial actions. This doctrine could only be based, however, upon the sociological doctrine of the collective nature of industrial actions and of the 'social adequacy' of those actions which also refer to the 'framework of the socially ethical orders of community life as they have been historically developed'. But this definition did not hinder the court from considering unofficial strikes illegal, regardless of their solution before 1933. However, the employers succeeded in enlarging the right to dismiss the employees collectively (all together or in single groups), and now dismissals do not even require previous notice. Lockouts may be limited to the same suspension effect which is applied by German, Swedish and United States laws; to union strikes and to unofficial strikes by French and Italian laws. A recent decision, 21 April 1971,[52] of the Big Division of the Federal Labour Court changed the old decision somewhat. That left reinstatement after the end of an industrial dispute to the discretion of the employer and gave the employee a right to be reinstated only in the case of an 'evident abuse of the discretionary power'; now the employee is entitled to demand re-instatement according to 'equitable discretion'. This prevents discrimination against old or sick employees or against strike leaders. However, the employer may still fill working places with other employees during the industrial dispute or may abolish such working places by rationalizing the enterprise in the meanwhile without being subject to the provisions of the Works' Constitution Act as usually required. The employer still retains the power to change his labour force during industrial action. Very similar to that German legal situation is the one found in Sweden. The lockouts are as legal as strikes. The United States which held offensive bargaining lockouts illegal now seems to approach this same view.[53]

Great Britain distinguishes between the lockout by an employers' association which is considered legal (Industrial Relations Act, sec. 96), and of the single employer, which may be an unfair industrial practice if employment contracts are broken. This solution may be compared with the draft of the German Act on Collective Agreements, in which was repealed the legal capacity of the single employer to conclude collective agreements. This provision which, however, did not become a part of the statute[54] would certainly have promoted treatment of the lockout by an individual employer as similar to the unofficial strike.

In France labour lawyers consider only a defensive lockout legal: if the employer cannot any longer provide the employees with work – for instance if the strike is carried on in a key department of the enterprise on which activities in the other department depend. Otherwise the employer would finance the striking union by continuing payment of wages to union members and other strikers. But he may also lock out when a strike disorganizes his enterprise, as the rotating strike especially does.

52. AP Nr. 43 zu Art. 9 GG.
53. See Chapter 2, p. 118.
54. T. Ramm, *Die Parteien des Tarifvertrags*, p. 61.

The Italian Penal Code (Art. 502) repressing lockouts as well as strikes was abrogated by Art. 40 of the Constitution. The Constitutional Court also considered the prohibition of lockouts as incompatible with the abolition of the corporative order of Fascism. The Court did not speak of a right to lockout, but only of a freedom to lock out – which is part of the general freedom of action. Nevertheless, as actions in courts for payment of work hours lost by a lockout show, lockouts are considered to be a civil wrong.

One may ask whether the language of the European Social Charter (Part II, Art. 6, sec. 4) which only uses the term 'collective actions' for the employers' side does not show the way to a reasonable solution. It seems that a concerted action of the employers, which is not allowed for offensive purposes (to decrease wages and to depress employment conditions) or to terminate the individual employment contracts, does not deserve the name lockout.

Another point which is especially important for Germany should be mentioned in this discussion. In this country the employer may choose between the possibility of locking out and the 'doctrine of the risk of enterprise', which was first developed by the Supreme Court and the Reich Labour Court before 1933, but has been taken over by the Federal Labour Court. According to these decisions, which had been strongly opposed by many labour lawyers before 1933, 'impossibility to work' exempts the employer from payment when its reason does not fall within his responsibility but within the responsibility of the employees – and the latter is recognized not only for strikes within the same enterprise but also in enterprises supplying energy on which the first enterprise depends. In these cases which are justified by the principle of 'solidarity' of workers and thus touch the ideology of sympathetic strikes, duties under the employment contract are 'suspended'. The employer must not resort to industrial actions for the purpose only of avoiding damage, and it is a question to be decided by the courts, how strictly 'impossibility to work' is interpreted, and especially to what degree the court will accept the employer's assurance that work has become 'impossible'.

Industrial actions and 'social self-help'

In the history of modern collective labour law strikes have been introduced by the philosophy of 'social self-help'. Certainly the old distinction between self-help and 'State-help' has become critical because the State also intervened in industrial action in favour of the employees when it prohibited dismissals of strikers and even placed limits upon lockouts. But the term of self-help has another meaning, a legal meaning, too – for penal law and the law of torts. There it justifies acts which otherwise would be illegal and is restricted to the exceptional cases in which the State cannot assist or in which its aid would come too late. German labour lawyers consider both terms, the political and the legal one to be equal; and this is more than a naivety, it is a philosophy.

Behind this idea stands the idea of a State governing the economy. It has served as a basis for the German *ultima ratio* doctrine which considerably diminishes the ambit of the liberty to strike. According to this doctrine, which is not used in France or Italy, employees and employers who resort to industrial action must have regard to the availability of any legal procedure for settlement of the dispute. In Germany this refers to the availability of the labour courts. The essence of this doctrine cannot be disputed. It is also to be found in the peace obligation laid down in the Swedish Act on Collective Agreements (sec. 4(1)). Moreover, in the Swedish Basic Agreement (Chapter IV, sec. 3) industrial action is prohibited if it aims at preventing a person from pleading before a court or other public authority or from giving testimony. These last actions would also violate the German rule of *bonos mores* (Civil Code, sec. 826).

Here there is the question whether the *ultima ratio* doctrine does not go too far in including all cases which can be legally decided. German legislation has limited the field of collective labour law; incidentally, enactments with that effect have often been initiated within the Federal Parliament by union representatives and especially by the members of the German Federation of Trade Unions (DGB) which is too weak against its affiliates[55] and, therefore, prefers to use political methods instead of promoting basic collective agreements for all industries. But such statutes often – especially if dealing with managerial prerogatives – give only 'blank cheque' provisions authorizing the judges to use their discretion. In a way German labour courts – as boards with representatives of employers and employees with a neutral president – can be considered as a kind of compulsory conciliation. Furthermore the works' council must be heard prior to personnel decisions and it has therefore the chance to influence them; its consent, however, is not required.

The *ultima ratio* doctrine also tries to make sure that before resort to industrial action all possibilities of negotiations are exhausted. Otherwise the action is considered illegal. Commentators justify this result by referring to the declaration of the German Federation of Trade Unions, that a strike is only the final weapon. Legal evaluation is used for the purpose of enforcement or as a substitute for conciliation procedures. The same result is attained by German courts and academic writers; it is also achieved by the Swedish Basic Agreement (Chapter II, sec. 8) by the parties themselves. Industrial action is not permitted for a party to a grievance who has either forfeited his right to negotiate or has not fulfilled his due obligation to negotiate. In practice those 'blank cheque' provisions of Sweden and Germany make doubtful the distinction between the disputes over interests – in which strikes are permitted (see European Social Charter, Part II, sec. 6(4)) – and the disputes over rights. They really substitute for the arbitrary decisions of the parties those of the judges. They only mean that industrial actions must be avoided, even without requiring special conciliation procedures. The law of industrial actions also approaches conciliation in another way: no sudden attack shall take place – at

55. See Chapter 1.

least not in cases of public interest, as in the French Act of 1963 which requires a previous notice of five days. Otherwise the chance of peacefully settling the dispute would become smaller. The idea of the individual giving notice as required by the individualistic theory for industrial actions has been transferred to the collective level.

The term 'industrial actions'

Up to now industrial actions have been considered as strikes, lockouts or similar collective actions. They were understood in the sense that they were collective acts, or, to speak more exactly, a collective abstaining from work, or refusal of payment for collective non-working. The German Federal Labour Court tried to enlarge the field of industrial actions when it interpreted a very unclear provision of a conciliation agreement as to include even a strike ballot and indicated this to be a general rule.[56] Very close to this idea is the decision of the British House of Lords in *Rookes* v. *Barnard* which reminds one of the old German penal law cases considering the threat of an industrial action to be a crime – but not the action itself. The British Act of 1971 gives the Industrial Court a wide power to prevent by order a 'threat' to commit an unfair industrial action or any 'threat of a like nature' (sec. 105(3)). Certainly, we should ask whether now, under the present economic conditions, those threats have the same effect as had actions in former times. But one must also ask whether this reason alone will justify an equal treatment – because the general development of social law favours the workers. Furthermore, the distinction between an action and the formation of the will of an association remains, and the 'liberty of creating will' must be recognized – not only for the individual and the State, but also for the association and especially for the union because of its social function.[57] Sweden makes this distinction and this avoids an intervention in the internal affairs of the associations.

This is another very dangerous approach which must be seen in the context of the German efforts to make the unions, the employers, and the employers' associations part of the economic administration. The frequently used words 'social self-government' which now – contrary to the time of the Weimar Republic – include collective bargaining too, imply the original responsibility of the State for economy and permit its control – they give up the original basis of liberalism.

The meaning of industrial actions, however, suffers other changes, too. Germany again may be used as an example, because here the change of meaning has the same function as the 'distinctions' between precedents in Great Britain and in the United States. At first the legal term 'industrial action' and the sociological term corresponded – this correspondence existed at the time of those actions being repressed, regardless of whether repression was

56. 31 October 1958, BAG 6, 321 (Schleswig–Holstein metal workers' strike). See T. Ramm, *Kampfmassnahme und Friedenspflicht im deutschen Recht*, 1962 and Chapter 3, p. 133.
57. See T. Ramm, 'Die Freiheit der Willensbildung ein Grundprinzip der Rechtsordnung', *Neue Juristische Wochenschrift*, 1962, p. 465.

made by the State or by the employers. Legal writers tried to cover all forms of collectively committed disturbances of social peace by which pressure upon the will of the addressee could be exercised. Now, after the intervention of the social State in favour of the workers, expressed by the constitutional recognition of the 'right to strike' or other forms of protecting strikers against sanctions by the employers or even against lockouts, legal writers change the meaning of the word 'strike'. It is no longer used as a *description* of the facts, but as a *justification* for a concerted action – if there is no justification, there is no strike; and this justification is now only found in the demand to conclude a collective agreement. The term 'strike' is reserved to the area of collective bargaining. Certainly, Germany exaggerates the British and American distinction between economic strikes and unfair industrial or labour practices and, therefore, meets new difficulties. Unofficial strikes are illegal even if they comply with the provisions of the employment contract by previous notice being given in the time agreed upon. They are not 'strikes'. But it cannot be ignored that there are unofficial strikes which must be recognized by the law, for instance, in case of defence against collective actions of the employer. Therefore, it is necessary to have a new expression – the *kollektive Zurück-behaltungsrecht* (the right of collectively refraining from work). Objectively it is a strike, but a subjective distinction from the strike may be seen in the aim of maintaining the present situation without even obtaining its formal recognition by a collective agreement. The same happened with lockouts. Certainly, the employer's giving collective notice to his employees in order to decrease or to abolish wage drift between the wage paid and the wage agreed upon in collective agreement is a lockout. But its recognition as a lockout would have raised the question why, then, the similar action of the workers to increase wage drift would be unofficial and, therefore, illegal strike, as the German Federal Labour Court had decided.[58] Therefore, a new name instead of lockouts has been found: the *kollektive Aenderungskuendigung* (giving collective notices for modifying the employment contracts). A 1969 amendment to the Act of Protection Against Dismissals has taken up this decision, but submitted those notices to the Act – the labour courts having to decide whether they are 'socially justified' or not. Again, as in the 'risk of enterprise' doctrine, the question arises whether the judge as the economically inexperienced person should not trust the assurance of the employer that otherwise the enterprise will be ruined.

Regardless of the special German problems which show how critical judge-made law is – at least if it claims to set the general policy – the general development can be clearly observed. It is the restriction of the area of lawful industrial disputes, and the increase of State intervention – not by administration. The same development can also be found in the United States, not by developing concepts of unlawfulness but in respect of the remedy of injunction. The NLGA, 1932, had prohibited injunctions in Federal courts against strikes in order to enforce the peace obligation. After the LMRA (sec. 301)

58. 28 April 1966, AP Nr. 37 zu Art. 9 GG, Arbeitskampf.

had confirmed Federal jurisdiction over collective agreements as contracts, the Supreme Court in 1957 was willing to order specific performance of an arbitration clause in such an agreement. In the *Boys Market* decision, 1970, reversing a previous decision of 1962, the Court granted an injunction against a strike undertaken by a union in breach of its peace obligation under such an arbitration clause. In this way the Court has reconciled the different legislative purposes of the LMRA and the NLGA. This general development of judge-made law, however, must be seen together with settlement procedures, because both have the same aim – the avoidance of industrial actions.

Settlement procedures

Settlement procedures are, theoretically, sharply distinguished from court or arbitration procedures, because the former concern disputes over interest and the latter disputes over rights, that is, disputes in which only existing legal provisions have to be applied. This distinction, however, is largely not true in countries such as Great Britain and France.[59] Even in the other countries legal 'blank cheque' provisions make this distinction – at least – less clear than it seems. The efforts of the judges to acquire more independence from written law, too, makes the distinction even more problematical. In collective labour law, another special point should not be overlooked, namely that the provisions are very often a compromise which has been deliberated for days. Sometimes the parties are not able to evaluate the meaning of the last formula on which they agreed, and sometimes the formula has been created to camouflage the dissent of the parties, both of whom do not want to give up their contradictory standpoints. This means that a labour court or any other board must decide the matter themselves. They do not apply law but arbitrate a legally unsettled case – a dispute over interests – and thus create, if a collective agreement is concerned, new law. Nevertheless the author will follow the traditional distinction as a possible demarcation of the main problems and try to limit himself to settlement of disputes over interest.

One idea is common for all countries investigated in this study. At the present time the State has withdrawn compulsory settlement of industrial disputes – public service and emergency cases excepted.[60] Compulsory settlement had existed in France (between 1936 and 1939) and in Germany during the Weimar Republic. In both countries it did not revive after 1945, but the past is differently evaluated – positive in France, negative in Germany. In France, as a first step, conciliation took place: the conflict was brought before a board composed of assessors of both parties with the prefect as president, and the board had to decide within a week. If its proposal was not accepted, arbitration proceedings followed immediately before an arbitration board

59. See K. W. Wedderburn and Davies, *Employment Grievances and Dispute Procedures in Britain*, California UP, 1969; X. Blanc-Jouvan, *Settlement in Labor Courts and Grievance Settlement in Western Europe*, California UP, Aaron (ed.), 1971.
60. Chapter 6.

which had to be preliminarily appointed by a collective agreement. If the arbitrators disagreed the final decision was made by another board of at least five persons who were also appointed by a collective agreement. The competence of the arbitrators concerned disputes over interest as well as over rights – in the first case they decided on equity, in the second according to the law. Appeals against the arbitration award were made to the Supreme Arbitration Court which controlled the legality of the awards and quashed illegal ones.

In Germany during the Weimar Republic the draft of a Settlements Act had been rejected by the employers and workers, and State settlement was introduced by an emergency decree of 1923 'until final legal regulation' (which never came). The Settlement Boards established by the Reich Labour Minister had assessors of both social parties and neutral presidents who were appointed by the state labour ministers or by the Reich Labour Minister. They intervened on the application of one party or *ex officio*. The president himself at first had to mediate. If no new collective agreement was concluded, the case was to be negotiated before the Settlement Board. If there the parties still disagreed, the Board was authorized to arbitrate. The award, if not accepted by the parties, could be declared to be binding by the State conciliator, 'if the provision made by it was equitable under just consideration of the interests of both parties and if its performance is required for economic and social reasons' (sec. 6 of the Decree of 1923).

German compulsory settlement has been criticized as having promoted a feeling of lack of responsibility, and certainly it prepared the end of collective labour law – together with the wage regulation policy of the 'emergency ordinances' of the Reich President between 1930 and 1933. After 1945 trade union and employers' associations therefore agreed on decided opposition against all attempts to reintroduce compulsory settlement.

The reaction against all State intervention was so strong that when the Allied Control Council promulgated the Law Nr. 35 on Conciliation and Arbitration Machinery in Labour Conflicts (1946) most German states did not even enact executive ordinances.[61] Indeed, it was not necessary, because there were only a few industrial actions and trade unions and employees' associations concluded settlement agreements.[62]

The present basic agreement of 7 September 1954 (*Margarethenhof* agreement) has been concluded by the German Federation of Trade Unions (DGB) and the Confederation of German Employers' Associations (BDA).[63] This model has been adopted by agreements of their affiliated organizations, though mostly in a modified form – after the first basic agreement of 1950 (*Hattenheim* agreement)[64] had not been adopted by them and the Federal Labour Ministry had threatened to proclaim a Settlement Act. Among the agreements of the

61. Exceptions are the states Nordrhein–Westfalen, Berlin, and the former states Württemberg–Baden and Württemberg–Hohenzollern (which are since 1951 part of the state Baden–Württemberg). Rheinland–Pfalz and the former state Baden (which now also belongs to Baden–Württemberg) promulgated their own Settlement Acts.
62. See Chapter 1, p. 37.
63. Published RdA 1954, p. 383.
64. RdA 1964, p. 216.

affiliated organizations the agreement of the metal industry of 12 May 1964 is especially remarkable. It was concluded as a part of the compromise between the metal trade union and the employers' association of the metal industry which settled the Schleswig–Holstein metal workers' strike case. In this agreement the metal trade union gave up its former opposition against the automatic commencement of settlement procedures; that opposition had been based on the view that it was a confession of weakness for the union to be under an obligation to commence those procedures once negotiations failed and not to be able to take industrial action.

German settlement agreements[65] are based upon three common principles:

(a) The commencement of settlement procedures requires that preliminary negotiation between the collective parties have failed. Settlement procedures then follow automatically.

(b) Settlement Boards equally composed of members of both sides. They do not negotiate publicly. They submit a proposal to the parties – if it is accepted it has the effect of a collective agreement. The parties also may (but are not obliged to) agree to accept the decision of the Board in advance.

(c) During the settlement procedure a peace obligation is imposed – the parties may not resort to industrial actions for the matters which they want to be settled by a collective agreement.

Settlement agreements mainly differ in regard to the form of the automatic introduction of the proceedings and the personality of the president of the Board (alternately by a party representing one side or the other to the agreement according to the terms of the model agreement, or by a neutral president according to the terms of the agreement in the metal industry). The election of a neutral president – if the parties disagree – is also differently regulated: by drawing lots (as in the agreement of the metal industry) or by a third party, for instance the president of a state Labour Court or a Civil Court. Although the state is kept out of the settlement procedure, it plays an important role, however, in informal settling of industrial disputes, especially in important branches which usually follow the failure of a formal settlement. Very often the state Labour Minister intervenes, but in the last conflict in the chemical industry the office of the Federal Chancellor, headed by a minister, asked the president of the Federal Social Court to mediate, and the president was successful.

In Italy the aversion against compulsory or even statutorily regulated settlement of industrial disputes is very strong – possibly, as in Germany, strengthened by opposition against the political past. Nevertheless the demand for informal mediation by the Minister and the Secretary of State is increasing. Often a trade union asks him for settlement, but he may take up the case himself. Proceedings, and especially the way of obtaining information on the

65. They are investigated by Koenigbauer, *Freiwillige Schlichtung und tarifliche Schiedsgerichtsbarkeit. Eine rechtstatsaechliche Untersuchung*, Stuttgart, Gustav-Fischer-Verlag, 1971.

economic situation independently from the parties, entirely depend upon his personality or on the official who is charged by him with settling the dispute. He has to decide whether to negotiate separately with the parties or jointly, and whether he wants to submit a proposal to the parties or not. But his proposal will take into consideration the possible negative consequences of a disapproval by one party. The employer especially may fear that he will not obtain a subvention or orders from the Government. A very old policy of influencing labour law which is a reminder of the fair wage clauses in public contracts, here appears in a new form.

Only in a few collective agreements of Italy are settlement procedures regulated[66] and the situation seems similar to France where only few collective agreements provide for settlement procedure and most settlement procedures serve as an introduction to State settlement.[67] The United States did not develop a system of settling industrial disputes by the parties to collective bargaining – and here the reason is that the State offers mediation and conciliation by a special branch: the Federal Mediation and Conciliation Service (FMCS) which originated in the Department of Labour established during the First World War and was reorganized by the Taft-Hartley Act on the basis of the proposals of the National Labour Management Conference of 1945. The head of the Service assigns qualified mediators and advises the parties about other possibilities of settling the dispute: to choose arbitration or to submit the last offer of the employer to the ballot of his employees (LMRA, sec. 203). This last possibility, however, seems to be very uncommon. The State does not intervene directly, but just offers its good services to the parties which remain independent in their decisions. So far the United States is much closer to the German solution than it seems to be at first sight.

Sweden has no settlement procedures in collective agreement. Incidentally the Basic Agreement deals with grievances exclusively. But this country has a long tradition of State conciliation originating from the Act of 1906 which has been substituted by the Act of 1920.

The situation in Great Britain is more complicated. State settlement procedures are provided by two statutes: the Conciliation Act of 1896 and the Industrial Courts Act of 1919. Both authorize the Minister of Labour (since 1970 called the Secretary of State for Employment) to intervene in industrial disputes but they are distinguished by the degree of intervention. The Act of 1896 enables the Secretary of State (formerly Minister of Labour) to inquire into the causes and circumstances of the case and to attempt to bring the parties together with a view to amicable settlement (sec. 2(a) and (b)). The ini-

---

66. See Chapter 3, p. 142.
67. The act of 11 February 1950, however also provides settlement by a binding arbitration award if it is accepted by a collective agreement. The statute of 1950 is restricted to main principles of the proceeding and to the award which is characterized to be a 'decision in equity' (Art. 215). The violations of these principles are subject to the control of a supreme arbitration court which works as a kind of appeal court on legal questions. Its nine members – appointed for three years – are, in equal proportion, members of the State Council or judges of higher courts, the president is the vice-president of the State Council or the president of a department of the State Council.

tiation of conciliation or arbitration, however, needs the application by both parties (sec. 2). The Act of 1919 is less reluctant and offers more formalized procedures – but these also demand the consent of both parties.[68]

Since 1968 it has been possible for the Government to refer any question concerning industrial relations to the Commission on Industrial Relations (now sec. 121 of the 1971 Act); and use has been made of this method to obtain recommendations from the Commission for settlement of difficult disputes between employers and unions. Such recommendations, however, cannot be enforced by any legal sanction.

Further, under the 1971 Act both the industrial tribunals and the Industrial Court are instructed to ensure that efforts are made to settle cases by conciliation between the parties before proceeding to judicial hearing and adjudication (Schedule 3, para. 18(3) and Schedule 6, para. 4(c)). It must also not be forgotten that the same Act allows an employer or the Secretary of State to apply to the Court for an order imposing procedures upon the bargaining parties where their existing procedures are construed to be 'inadequate', and that an order is to operate 'as if' it were a contract made between them (secs. 37–41).[69] Such imposed procedures might include provisions for arbitration as a last resort for settling disputes.

France distinguishes two forms of settlement as well, conciliation and arbitration – both only optional, however.[70] France also relies upon the position of the mediator, though in a much more advanced way, as it will be shown later.

It seems best to begin the description of the main principles of State settlement procedures with the two questions which are general for all settlement: how to obtain qualified conciliators and what are the underlying assumptions of the proceeding? A relevant third question is only concerned with State settlement: How can the parties to an industrial dispute be influenced by public opinion? This question reveals the principle of State settlement and connects it with the problems of illegality of industrial disputes: industrial disputes are not considered to be 'private affairs' of the parties for the public is interested in their settlement.

Two forms of electing conciliation are given: the *ad hoc* nomination in case of need and the permanent provision of conciliation. The distinction between them is not due to the reason that industrial disputes are abnormal or normal events in social life, but it is due to the different efforts to avoid these conflicts in order to ensure social peace. It does not surprise one therefore to find that all countries agree on the necessity of permanently providing for conciliation. The continuation of the form of *ad hoc* conciliation as an additional form of intervention therefore receives a new meaning; some conflicts need, because of their importance or the special situation, an especially qualified conciliator outside of the established bureaucracy of conciliation.

State conciliation can be provided either by a special branch or by the use

68. Cf. Wedderburn and Davies, *Employment Grievances and Dispute Procedures in Britain*, 1969.
69. See Chapter 3, p. 129.
70. The system is entirely described by X. Blanc-Jouvan in *Settlement in Labor Courts and Grievance Settlement in Western Europe*, Aaron (ed.), 1971.

of the general administration. The first solution prevails. It exists in the United States, where the head of the F M C S is a director appointed by the President by and with the advice and consent of the Senate.

In Great Britain the Industrial Court Act of 1919 permits the Minister of Employment normally with the consent of the parties to submit the case to the competent Industrial Court, or as it is now called since the Industrial Relations Act (sec. 124) to the Industrial Arbitration Board. This board has a permanent full-time president, assessors of employers, employees and independent ones all appointed by the Minister of Employment.

France incorporates conciliation in the general administration. Three levels are distinguished on national, regional and department basis. The boards are always equally composed of six representatives of the parties to the dispute, and also of a maximum of three representatives of the public authorities. The national board has among these three additional members the Minister of Social Affairs as president and the Minister of Economy or one of his officials; at regional level the labour inspector and at department level the head of the labour office preside and they are assisted respectively by a judge of the administration court and by an official.

In Sweden a State agency for conciliation exists. The agency coordinates the service of eight district conciliators. The appointment of special conciliators is provided for and left to the King in council, actually to the Minister of Interior if an industrial dispute involves special danger of a breach of industrial peace or if, for other reason, it seems expedient (Conciliation Act, sec. 12).

In Great Britain the appointment is generally left to the discretion of the Secretary of State, provided that the parties consent to conciliation.

In France the *ad hoc* appointment is not necessary, because there another, although similar, way has been used by the 'mediation' procedure which, however, is considered to be a part of the general settlement procedure and will therefore be described later on.

The principles of proceedings can be neglected. There are no problems of special interest. The idea of an objective and fair negotiation is common. Settlement procedures agree on the obligation of the parties to negotiate which is statutorily expressed in Sweden (Conciliation Act, sec. 4), the United States (Labour Management Relations Act, sec. 204), France (Conciliation Act, sec. 9) and Great Britain (Industrial Court Act, sec. 2). They do, however, give different answers to the questions: how to start the procedure and how to conduct conciliation.

In Great Britain the Secretary of State needs the consent of the parties in order to introduce any settlement. He may, however, submit the case to the competent Industrial Arbitration Board for advice.

In all other countries the initiation is either *ex officio* or the parties are forced to apply for initiation.

In Sweden the conciliator is obliged 'to follow with close attention the conditions of work within his sphere' (Conciliation Act, sec. 2). If a dispute arises, which leads or threatens to lead to an industrial dispute, he has to contact the parties and to procure information. He has to summon the parties for negotiations (sec. 3). If a party refuses to appear, the conciliator must report his refusal to the Labour Court, which may order the party, under threat of a penalty, to meet the conciliator (Art. 6).

In the United States, the party that wishes to terminate or modify an existing collective agreement has to inform the other party 60 days before the modification or the termination of the collective agreement shall take place and has to offer negotiations. Thirty days after giving notice the FMCS or a state conciliation office must be informed.

France stands between these two solutions. All collective labour disputes have to be reported to the prefect who in conjunction with the labour inspector has to attempt amicable settlement. Conciliation will be initiated by him, the Minister of Labour or the Department inspector of labour or by one of the parties (Conciliation Act, sec. 8). But law does not provide that reports of the parties to the industrial dispute must be made before the beginning even of an industrial action, so that this obligation is without effect.

Special regard is paid in Sweden and in the United States to avoiding industrial actions.

Sweden demands that one party give notice to the other party and the conciliator seven days before the work stoppage begins 'if urgent obstacles do not prevent that' (Conciliation Act, sec. 3(a)). This provision is designed for the time when no collective agreement and therefore no peace obligation exists. In the United States the peace obligation is not an implied condition of a collective agreement. A 'no-strike' clause must be expressly agreed upon, but the provision that during the 60 days after the notice a 'cooling off' period begins – during which time no strikes or lockouts are permitted (NLRA, sec. 8(d)(4)) – does not pay regard to whether 'no-strike' clauses are concluded. The law in Sweden seems to approximate to the idea of a 'cooling-off period'. The first step has been made in the public service sector by extending the ordinary peace obligation. A strike of university teachers, teachers of higher schools and of State employees of the railways was suspended, but was in fact, terminated by a special Act of 11 March 1971. This Act put the expired collective agreement between the parties in force again for a limited period and thus restored the peace obligation.[71] It is exactly the same method of State intervention in contractual liberty of the social parties which was used by the Weimar Republic in its last three years in order to decrease wages by 'emergency ordinances'.

The task of conciliators can differ. The first and historically oldest form is conciliation between the parties. This means that the conciliator has to establish a basis for communication, and to prevent the display of hostile attitudes. Next is the extension of his duties to make a proposal of his own. All this belongs to his normal functions. Sweden then takes the decisive step of making the conciliator independent from the parties, as it has made the procuring of information a duty of the conciliator. The parties, on his request, have to give him extracts of the accounts and other documents, together with statistical data and to grant him access to the workplace (Conciliation Act, sec. 7).

71. See Chapter 6, p. 302.

France even goes one step further, developing a special 'mediation' procedure by the Act of 7 July 1957. This procedure is separated from conciliation. It begins after the failure of conciliation and can be initiated either by the president of the conciliation board or the Minister of Labour, even if neither party applies for it (sec. 12). If the parties do not agree upon a mediator, who can be selected from a special list, the Minister or prefect will appoint him. This mediator 'has the widest authority to be informed about the economic situation of the enterprises and employees'. He may proceed with any inquiry and demand all documents and information necessary to accomplish his task (Art. 13). If conciliation fails again the mediator has to submit a recommendation, with reasons, to the parties (Art. 15).

All national regulations on state settlement have to answer the question as to the way industrial actions can be avoided without resorting to compulsory adjustment.

Sweden provides for the 'suggestion' of the conciliator that the parties shall agree upon arbitration (Conciliation Act, sec. 8), which incidentally is rarely applied in present days. This is one of the solutions which can also be proposed in the United States by the F M C S. But the chance that the parties will agree upon this proposal is not very great after conciliation has failed. Another common method of making conciliation effective is the use of publicity for the purpose that public opinion should exercise pressure upon the parties. Information of the public can be part of the normal proceeding or of special procedures.

In France the mediator's proposal, if it has not been accepted, has to be sent, together with a report, to the Minister of Labour who will publish both within three months (Art. 16).

In Sweden no immediate report by the conciliator is made, but he has to keep a record of events and has to submit a yearly report, which will be published, to the Agency for State Conciliation (Conciliation Act, sec. 13).

A special procedure is provided in Great Britain; the Secretary of State can establish an investigation committee and decide whether its sessions shall be public or not. The report of this committee including dissenting opinions will be submitted to Parliament and become public by parliamentary discussion.

Obviously the State avoids exercising pressure as much as possible. The explanation may be that public opinion or informal use of discretionary power by the Government, as may be seen in Italy, are considered to be sufficient. More probably, however, it seems that a strong antipathy against State intervention still exists. On the other hand when settlement procedures are provided by collective agreements their violation as a violation of the peace obligation is subject to the ordinary sanctions. In this way sanctions also concern settlement procedures.

Sanctions

The term 'sanction' will be used in the following pages as covering disadvantages[72] imposed upon a party by law on the ground of certain behaviour

72. It is sometimes difficult to distinguish disadvantages from advantages which cannot be obtained on grounds of a certain behaviour. This is especially important for

in the past which is considered to be unlawful. The decision upon whether sanctions will actually be called for, may depend upon their initiation either by the State or by the injured party.

The main forms of sanctions are penal sanctions and damages. They cannot be sharply distinguished from one another, as the civil fine provided by penal courts and exceeding compensation in order to give satisfaction to the injured person (the German *Busse*) shows. When legal development leads to a clear distinction between penal sanction and civil sanction, this mixture of both types loses importance. Its old function – to give satisfaction is then often, however, taken over by the compensation of non-material damage.

Besides penalty and damages a third legal institution exists which was historically connected with penalty but has survived it: civil avoidance of agreements and engagements on industrial conflicts and combinations. This will be described as well, although one may ask whether it should be included in the term sanction.

As has been demonstrated in the first part of this chapter, industrial action no longer entails criminal sanctions. In the view of the legislature industrial action is on equal footing with ordinary actions. Whether this is true for the practice of the courts or whether or not old aversions against industrial actions will influence their decisions, is a question which could only be answered by special investigations for the separate countries, but must be left open here.

When we go back to the history of the law on industrial disputes and investigate the former special penal provisions, we discover that the two social parties had been unequally treated. In the French Act of 1803 and the original Art. 414 and 415 French Penal Code (until 1849) sanctions against the employees were harder, by providing not fines but stricter imprisonment or more comprehensive provisions.[73]

This inequality which can be observed in prosecutions as well, can certainly be explained by the frequency of strikes – in liberal economic systems the employees are forced to attack and therefore sanctions will primarily be used against them. Moreover the guild system, in which the employers stated the wages, will have exercised a lasting effect – legal tradition always influences new law. Finally, fines against the employees who had no assets and whose wages were only sufficient to keep them from starving must remain without effect. On the other side was not the fine imposed upon the employer a serious

the law of social security. Nevertheless the distinction remains theoretically legitimate. The investigation will also set aside the demands (which were important for the history of trade unions) to observe the law on insurance companies (because the union supported their members). Legally these demands have been justified by the aspect of equal treatment with other associations. In reality they often served however as instruments of repression used against the trade unions. Incidentally, in this context the influence of changing legal evaluation of other collective action must be observed too. Certainly mitigation of anti-demonstration law will also mitigate the legislature on other collective criminal action.

73. British Combination Acts, however, did not provide for unequal treatment. Prussian Trade Order of 1845 provided for the same penalties for strikes and lockouts (Arts. 181 and 182) but prohibited only the journeymen's associations – the masters' organizations were accepted as part of the guild system.

disadvantage from his point of view, when we consider that this period of history adored property? Or, to ask the reverse question, was not the same punishment for employer and employee an inequality because the employer also suffered the loss of the chance to win new assets and was he not the person who was punished more strictly?

Nevertheless this legal inequality could not be maintained – politically it was said to express 'class justice' and it was also incompatible with the liberal principle of equal rights.

History has proved that penal sanctions against industrial actions and labour organizations are ineffective. They were unfit instruments – at least for the time in which the 'workers' question' was a social question, and the misery of the workers created a permanent threat of revolutionary change of society while, on the other hand, the contradiction within the liberal conception was obvious. It was impossible to advocate liberty and to suppress the right to organize for the workers at the same time. This is the basis on which to observe the enforcement of penal sanctions – in other words, to answer the question about the efficiency of police intervention. In authoritarian States police intervention offered, and still offers, no problem – as long as industrial conflicts are generally rejected, and the policeman considers himself to be the faithful servant of authority, and therefore remains at a distance from the workers. This picture changes, however, when industrial conflicts are no longer *per se* crimes, and the police feel themselves to be workers who claim the improvement of their social conditions by strikes. They are, of course, less disposed to attack striking employees. But if they are prohibited to strike, and therefore think they are disadvantaged as compared with other workers, a feeling of resentment may increase their activities against strikers.

Another problem is posed by the democratic structure of government and administration. Strike intervention can be unpopular and therefore cause the loss of voters in the next election. In Germany, in Hessen – a state with traditional social democratic government – the employers therefore discussed the question on how they should act if the police refused to intervene, for instance, in order to protect strike-breakers. The police president refusing to give the orders could be charged for 'abettment in office' (sec. 346, Penal Code). Also, a civil suit could be filed against the State for 'violation of the official duties of a civil servant' (sec. 839, Civil Code and Art. 34, Bonn Basic Law). The same regulation exists in France, where additionally, according to the Act of 1894, the municipality has to pay damages caused by rioting, and this is applied in the case of strikes. Great Britain seems to approach this view (as in the Roberts Arundel strike, 1970), while Germany never applied the corresponding statute[74] upon strikes – probably because strikes were either performed in a well disciplined manner or suppressed by the police.

Together with the provision of penal sanctions, agreements and covenants on industrial actions, and even on combinations, were declared to be void by

---

74. cf. the Act on Damages caused by interior riots of 1920 which was applied upon actions committed in connection with the Nazi revolution and State's renewal.

the British Combinations Acts of 1799 and 1800 and the French Le Chapelier Act. But when a statute failed to provide for this limitation of contractual liberty – as, for example, the Prussian Trade Order of 1845 – it meant nothing. Obviously, agreements or combinations or activities prohibited by penal law had no civil efficacy without any express statutory provision. After the repeal of penal prohibitive laws, civil avoidance was maintained. This was stated by sec. 153 German Reich Trade Order of 1869 (*Reichsgewerbeordnung*), which remained in force until the Supreme Court considered it to violate the constitutional recognition of the freedom to organize and of the collective agreements.[75] The efficacy of this provision, however, was small. It may be quoted as an example of over-estimating civil law prohibitions. It could prevent neither the formation of powerful German trade unions which even preferred to refuse the usual registration requirements for associations (which incidentally were connected with police control before the Weimar Republic) nor strikes.

Civil avoidance has practical importance only in cases in which a party may use it as a weapon against another. Avoidance used against union security clauses or against dismissals which violate the right to organize – as is provided by the German Bonn Basic Law, Art. 9, sec. 3, the Italian Constitution Art. 39 (implicit) and the Swedish Act on the Right to Organize (1936), sec. 4(4) for both cases, and also by the British Industrial Relations Act, sec. 7, for the first case – is therefore living law. But one may ask whether this will be also true in cases in which trade unions and the employer agree – will the average unorganized worker, for instance, always dare to fight for his right, for instance not to organize, against both? Here we come to the factual limits of law.

Today compensation must be regarded to be the civil sanction against industrial actions, as far as they are legally considered to be collective actions.[76] The provisions stating the obligation to pay damages arising from violation of individual and collective contracts and arising out of tort liabilities have already been described. This different source will be reconsidered only as far as necessary for considering the kind of damage, the extent and the range of persons covered.[77] Another important question cannot be clearly answered – i.e., how practically important suits for damages really are. It generally seems that they are not very important. The real economic losses caused by an industrial action are never paid and mostly they are not even demanded. Obviously the parties to collective bargaining use suits for damages more for obtaining legal decisions on the legality of certain industrial actions than to get compensation – provided that there is no special procedure, as in Great Britain and in the United States, on unfair industrial or labour practices. In Germany the form of model lawsuit is therefore used in which only a share of the real damage is demanded – it must exceed 6,000 DM in order to

75. 2 July 1925, R G Z, vol. III, p. 199.
76. This chapter does not deal with sanctions which relate to an individualistic understanding of industrial actions as violations of the individual employment contract. See also Chapter 4, p. 179.
77. Generally known distinctions which have no special importance for individual actions will be set aside here – for instance, the duration of prescription which is generally longer for contractual liabilities than for torts.

guarantee that the Federal Labour Court will finally decide it. This form of proceeding saves a considerable amount of court and attorney fees.[78] Possibly this attitude is changing, however. When the Leather Union took over an unofficial strike and was therefore sentenced to pay damages, the employer actually demanded them and the union finally agreed as a compromise to pay 240,000 D M. After the Schleswig–Holstein metal workers' strike decision the employers demanded 34 million D M using this demand as a pressure to get a more favourable conciliation agreement. In the final compromise the employers' associations which were the plaintiffs gave up the claim, but some entrepreneurs, especially of smaller enterprises, had opposed this. It may be that in future, when industrial action increases in Germany, the employers may proceed against the financially potent unions. Also an increase of illegal strikes could lead to demands for real compensation.

The different countries have different basic positions in the question of the extent of damage: whether only material or non-material damage is to be paid for industrial actions. The first solution is accepted by Germany, Great Britain, Italy and the United States, the second by Sweden and France. But the discretionary power of the judge is still more important and here Sweden takes the lead.

The Swedish regulation is contained in the Collective Agreements Act of 1928 and in the Act on the Right to Organize of 1936. The first statute creates a special notion for compensation of loss in industrial action as far as it connects this problem with the interest of maintaining industrial peace – which could be threatened by a very severe liability. Therefore 'in determining whether and to what extent loss has been incurred, regard shall also be paid to the interest of the persons concerned in the maintenance of the agreement' (sec. 8(2)). The question of non-material damage is also touched by this provision: 'Circumstances other than those of a purely financial nature' shall be considered as well and the Act on the Right to Organize includes 'compensation for personal suffering and for encroachment upon the interest of the injured party in carrying on his occupation without disturbance' (sec. 23). Both Acts enable the judge to reduce the amount of the damages

> if this appears reasonable in view of the actual degree of culpability of the person who has caused the loss, the attitude of the person who has suffered loss in respect of the occurrence of the dispute, the extent of the loss in proportion to the means of the person who has caused it or other circumstances.

The reduction may even amount to a complete exemption to pay damages.

Very close to the Swedish regulation is the British which demands a just and equitable consideration of

> all the circumstances having regard to the loss sustained by the aggrieved party in consequence of the matters to which the complaint relates, in so

78. See T. Ramm, *Labor Courts and Grievance Settlement Procedures in Western Europe*, Aaron (ed.), 1971, p. 124.

far as that loss was attributable to action taken by or on behalf of the party
in default (Industrial Relations Act, sec. 116(1)).

In assessing damages which are limited to economic loss the Court must consider whether the defendant has acted reasonably in order to mitigate his loss
and also must consider the extent to which acts by the complainant (whether
lawful or unlawful) have contributed to the matters in issue (sec. 116(2) and
(3)). Both factors can provide a reason for reducing the damages. The latter in
particular gives the court a very broad discretion in fixing the amount of the
damages.

This broad power of decision is not given to the German labour courts. The
judge has absolute discretionary power in evaluating the damage (sec. 287,
Civil Procedure Order), but he has to state the real damage, and the question
of what is included in the term 'damage' has never been answered by a court
for the reasons explained before. When damages were demanded from the
metal union on the ground of the Schleswig–Holstein metal workers' strike
only the contributions paid by the employers' association to their members
were demanded; but these contributions had been assigned by the members
as a kind of strike insurance and remained in the firms' assets until they were
called upon at the outbreak of the strike. The employers considered these
amounts to be the damage, or at least a part of it, of the employers' association,
while the metal union was interested in looking into the economic condition
of the enterprises by forcing them to give precise and detailed information on
their damage – and they would have certainly used this information for the
next round of bargaining on wage increases. These problems remained un-
solved as the lawsuit was not carried on but concluded by a compromise and
they have never been investigated by the lawyers.

All the difficulties of determining the damage suffered by an industrial
action are raised by the question of whether the loss of production is generally
equivalent to damage. Until now the term damage has been related to individualistic legal theory, and that background, of course, is competition. If
one competitor is excluded from competition and his place is taken by another,
then he suffers a loss and may claim for its compensation. It may be difficult to
determine the amount of damage if competition is changing rapidly. This,
however, remains only a task of evaluating the evidence. Another completely
different problem comes up when competition is temporarily interrupted by
an industrial action in a branch of industry on a national or a regional basis
(provided that no other branch or no other international or inter-regional
competitor profits of this situation). If the demand for the product remains
constant, then, in fact, it may be asked, whether the strike has caused a loss at
all or whether the demand has not been postponed only and can be balanced
by an increase of production after the end of the industrial conflict.

The actual loss also depends upon the liability of the employer as entrepreneur, if he cannot deliver his product in time because of an industrial action. The question put to all legal systems is whether or not industrial conflicts are considered to be *force majeure* in the commercial contracts of the

entrepreneur, which means that no such liability would follow. This question is answered by the Civil Law in different ways. Article 1147 of the French Civil Code used, for instance, the term 'external reason' which had been adopted by Italy, but the Civil Code of 1942 then turned to the German doctrine of 'conditions for which the debtor does not have to answer' (German Civil Code, Art. 275, Italian Civil Code, Art. 1218). These distinctions are only of theoretical interest, because everywhere, in the United States, Great Britain, Germany and Italy liability for damages caused by a strike is generally, or at least, rather frequently excluded by contract. At first the legality of those clauses was denied in France – they were interpreted to refer to the Civil Code, because it was contradictory to original liberal thinking to entrust the decision of *force majeure* to the discretion of the parties. Now the legal validity of the clauses is no longer disputed, although French, Italian and German constitutional provisions permit the question of whether the social function of the strike to improve labour and wage conditions of the employees must be accepted by Civil Law. Even if this question were positively answered and contractual liberty limited that far, solidarity among the entrepreneurs could be strong enough for no claim for damages to be made.

One may argue, however, that Civil Law is sufficient when its principles are applied to industrial actions, too. Thus the German Civil Code (sec. 254(2)) and the British Industrial Relations Act oblige the injured person to mitigate his loss. The German civil lawyers understand the provision to include use of the legal remedies. For industrial action this would mean that in case of a strike the employer should require an injunction. But this idea has been rejected, although it resorts to the *ultima ratio* doctrine. The German Federal Labour Court even denied the obligation of an employer to apply for conciliation to the conciliation board, because this would be an 'unreasonable demand'.[79] The reason may be that the appeal to a conciliation board is considered as confession of weakness and that the employers' right to lockout, as implied by the doctrine of 'parity of weapons', should not be endangered. Behind this doctrine certainly stands the understanding of industrial actions as a combat in which the same regulation must be applied as is individual self-defence in penal law. Here it becomes important that industrial actions are subject to the law of torts in Germany.

If we compare the Schleswig–Holstein metal workers' strike case and generally the case law of the German Federal Labour Court with the decisions of the Swedish Labour Court another very important distinction will be discovered. In Sweden reasons for reducing damages or complete exemption from payment were found in unclear formulation of collective agreements or in the different previous practice of the parties or in a defendant's belief that he had acted lawfully. In Germany the risk of understanding the law correctly is entirely imposed upon the attacking party – and this risk is tremendous because of the wide discretion of the labour courts given by the recognition of the right of enterprise and the new general clause of social adequacy and,

79. 31 October 1958, BAG 6, p. 321 – AP Nr. 2 zu 1 TVG, p. 23, reverse side.

last but not least, by the definition of negligence (which is sufficient for the violation of the right of enterprise) as 'the care required by the public'. When, for example, the Federal Labour Court first stated the illegality of unofficial strikes (they had been considered legal by the jurisdiction of the Reich Labour Court and academic writers) the Federal Labour Court made the strikers liable for damages. It was negligence not to have foreseen the court's future decision.

The economic situation of the party which inflicts losses is very important if we consider that in liberal economies the employees always attack. The Swedish Labour Court therefore reduces the obligation of the trade union to compensate the full loss when the payment of full compensation would have resulted in a levy being made on the members.[80]

The British Industrial Relations Act gives a normative solution by a limitation of the compensation awarded against a trade union which corresponds to the number of members. These appropriate limits are:

Membership	£
Less than 5,000	5,000
Between 5,000 to 25,000	25,000
Between 25,000 to 100,000	50,000
100,000 or more	100,000

This privilege in respect of liability (sec. 117) is, however, reserved only to registered trade unions and the limit applies only to each claim by each complainant which means that every capable plaintiff's lawyer may evade the privilege.

In the German Weimar Republic the draft of the Act on collective agreements had provided a limitation for violation of the peace obligation (sec. 17) similar to the present Swedish law. But the draft did not become a statute and this provision was never revived or even discussed again.

Very close to the question of limiting liability is the problem how far the collective parties are able to decide upon the amount of damages. This is important for Sweden and Germany, because in both countries a wide field of contractual liberty is given by collective agreements and settlement agreements. An example is the agreement upon a contractual fine in the settlement agreement of the German metal industry in 1965, but the claim for damages is then excluded except in a case where a party culpably does not execute a decision of the arbitration board concerning the violation of the agreement (see sec. 16(4) and (5) of the settlement agreement). Generally parties to collective agreements enjoy full contractual liberty if the legislator does not restrict it. The aims as well as the reasons for those restrictions could be different, depending upon the decision whether industrial actions should be avoided in the public interest – this would favour a system of contracting high contractual fines – or whether they should be encouraged or at least tolerated as necessary instruments of improving social conditions – this would imply a control of contractual liberty as far as high contractual fines are agreed.

80. AD 1946:8.

One may also ask (in Germany and Sweden, but not in the other countries) about pretended equality of the social parties and especially the function of the employers' association in industrial actions. German and Swedish labour lawyers have neglected this problem because employers' associations have not acted as offensive parties for decades. But does the association only coordinate the actions of the individual employers ? Or do real corporate decisions exist – i.e., majority decisions which are performed against the will of individual employers ? The answer depends upon the efficacy of competition. If it still functions, then the basis of agreement among the employers is small, and as far as lockouts are connected with the termination of individual employment contracts the answer is clear: the individual employer is the one who locks out – not his association. If, however, the suspensive effect of lockouts is recognized, then at least this former difference from strikes will be abolished and the legal treatment of strikes and lockouts would be nearly the same. But they will even then not be exactly the same, because the suspended worker must further obtain the right of terminating his contract without giving previous notice, as he must always have the chance to earn wages for himself and his family's support.

The previous position which concerned labour organizations only must now be supplemented by describing the obligation to pay damages which exists for the parties to the individual employment contract. This is especially important for Sweden because its agency doctrine – as part of the combined effect of the collective agreement, for the contracting parties as well as for their members – establishes liability of each member for violations of the peace obligation committed by the association. In Sweden this liability, however, is limited to 200 Kroner (Collective Agreements Act, sec. 8, III (3)). In Germany after 1891 (sec. 124(b), Reich Trade Order) an obligation of the industrial employee to pay damages for breaches of contract was established. But this obligation has been limited to the daily wage as it is usually paid at the location of the enterprise – for each day of his abstention from work up to a maximum of eight days. It is not necessary to prove that damage of this amount was really caused by the worker. This liability excluded claims for higher damages. The same right against the employers breaking the contract was given to the industrial employees.

This regulation was bitterly attacked by the workers, and remained a dead letter. It is now overruled by the collective doctrine of industrial actions as well as by the application of the law of torts on them, because tort liability would not have to pay regard to the restriction imposed for contractual liabilities. This will possibly become important for the compensation of losses which are caused by unofficial strikes. Formerly those strikes were considered only as torts *per se*. Similar problems arise for the apportionment of damages among several liable persons.

The Swedish Acts on Collective Agreements (sec. 9) and on the Right to Organize (Art. 24) both agree that liability shall be divided among the parties in proportion to the greater or less degree of culpability. When this concerns only the individual employees, it has to be asked whether some of them, for instance, because of their position in the enterprise, could more easily recognize the illegality of the action, otherwise damage is equally distributed. On the other hand minority or reduced means of partial disablement have been considered to diminish liability. If the trade union and their members are jointly liable the Labour Court imposes the larger portion on the union and the rest on the members. Joint liability means that the strike has been initiated by the members. If they merely acted in accordance with the union's decision, damages cannot be claimed by the employers against individuals.[81]

In Germany liability for industrial actions is not separately regulated. Therefore the provision of the Civil Code must be applied – and this means, according to the decisions of the Federal Labour Court, the law of torts. According to sec. 830 of the Civil Code the person who, together with others, has caused damage by committing a tort, is responsible for the damage. This means according to sec. 840 that all these responsible persons are liable as collective debtors. The creditor is permitted to claim total or partial payment from each and is also free in his choice among them (sec. 421). This very strict liability is applicable both for the trade union and among the members and among the participants in an unofficial strike. Until now German employees have been very reluctant to take action in court. In the period of full employment the employer wants to avoid the stigma of being anti-social in which case he would take the risk of losing his employees. But this regulation could become an important weapon of the employer against strike leaders if social conflicts were increased by unofficial strikes – provided that those strikes were not joined by a great number or even the majority of the employees.

Summarizing, it seems that civil sanctions as dealt with in this chapter do not play an important role for industrial actions. They certainly have not acquired a greater importance because a new weapon had been developed: the injunction.

Prevention

Repression and prevention of actions appear to be only two sides of the same thing. Similarly it seems to be obvious that legal prevention stands beside legal sanction. Consequently the only relevant question would be to ask who decides upon prevention: administration (or more concretely the police) or courts. This alternative is, however, not convincing. Certainly history displays that at first the police tried to prevent industrial actions and this form of fighting lasted longest where the pre-liberal State was maintained – the 'Obrigkeits' state, in Germany until 1918. Today, however, the police try to prevent other penal actions. But just as in the fight against preventive censorship it shows that liberalism does not easily accept a legal institution which prohibits a future action. The first reason may be a doubt as to whether it is possible to predict human action with certainty; second is the fear of limiting

81. AD 1970:7.

free individual decision. Therefore liberal Civil Law is very reluctant about preventive measures. The French Civil Code does not mention them and protects individual freedom also in another way, which has some impact on the question of injunction. The suit for enforcement of performance of personal duties imposed by a contract is unknown in France, Great Britain and the United States – a violation of these duties will only cause liability to pay damages – and in the United States only in the instance of an individual contract of employment, which is rarely found. Sweden accepted French law and therefore did not develop the law of injunctions. The same is true for Italy.

This situation proves how important is the impact of general political convictions on law – because France, Italy and Germany had the same provisions in their Procedure Orders providing temporary court orders for the purpose of regulating the relations between parties to litigation. But only Germany developed the right of injunctions for industrial conflicts. However, three other reasons may explain this development: The first is the recognition of an injunction by the German Civil Code in order to protect tangible property and similar rights – as a part of the proprietor's sovereignty. The second is the more pragmatic and unpolitical approach to contractual law as part of the social system. The rule *pacta sunt servanda* was considered prior to the protection of personal freedom. Performance of a duty seemed to be the natural consequence of a contract voluntarily agreed upon. The third source was the Act of 1896 (now of 1909) against unfair competition which established the idea of preventive damage as one of the consequences of industrial revolution. Greater technological development increases the dimension of damage. The law has to recognize more extensively an interest in prevention of damage because often it can never compensate the defendant and, moreover, because the determination of damages in all competition cases is difficult.

In Germany the provisions of the Civil Procedure Order on the *einstweilige Verfuegung* have been applied to industrial conflicts – rarely in the time before the First World War or during the Weimar Republic, but increasingly after the end of the Second World War. Due to the small number of industrial disputes in Germany the number of injunctions is also small.

The very close connection between the law on competition and the law on industrial disputes is probably shown best in the United States. Injunctions directed against trusts by the Sherman Act of 1890 were increasingly used by the courts against industrial actions. The epoch of 'Government by injunctions' was practically terminated by the NLGA of 1932. And NLRA carefully avoided the word injunction when it introduced restraining orders against unfair labour practices – but at that time they concerned the employers only. The Taft-Hartley Act supplemented these provisions by extending unfair labour practices on the union side. But the turning point seems to be the *Boys Market* case, because according to this decision the violation of an arbitration agreement in a 'no-strike' clause can be subject to an injunction. This means that an exemption has been made from the rule of Civil Law that an order of enforcement is unusual for breach of contract.

In Great Britain development was very similar, although the Trade

Disputes Act 1906 (sec. 4) had prohibited all remedies for torts against a trade union. But the courts, even though this remedy was barred as against unions, used injunctions against trade union officials to prohibit actions involving tortious liabilities that were not protected in trade disputes by that statute or, later, by the Act of 1965 – torts which were from time to time 'discovered' or 'developed' by the courts. Although protection is now provided in cases of tort in the ordinary court, similar types of liability can arise in the Industrial Court in respect of unfair industrial practices under the Act of 1971; and orders of that court will operate in a manner parallel to injunctions.

British law, however, still does not have any experience of injunctions against violations of the peace obligation.

The idea of enforcing the peace obligation by injunctions does not seem unusual to German lawyers. Moreover the German Federal Labour Court had indicated the tendency in some *obiter dicta* to consider violations of a peace obligation as socially inadequate violations of the right of enterprise[82] – a finding which would abolish the traditionally sharp distinction between contractual and tort liability in yet one more case.

In the United States and Great Britain the injunction is enforced by 'contempt of court' procedure. In Germany the sanctions for disobedience are similar – fines and imprisonment (maximum of six months).

All six countries accept that orders that compel an employee to do any work are not allowed. The British Industrial Relations Act (sec. 128) states it plainly. In the United States it would be considered as 'involuntary servitude' (13th amendment of the Constitution). Germany, Bonn Basic Law, Art. 12, also guarantees the liberty of choosing the working place. But the Civil Procedure Order interdicts the execution of an award to perform the duties of an employment contract (sec. 888(2)) and this excludes the ordinary sanctions of injunctions, fines and imprisonment. One may have to ask for the actual importance of this provision after the German collective labour law gave up individualistic doctrine. The collective doctrine of strike combines three actions which had been previously clearly separated: the call of the trade union to strike – which formerly was a boycott too; the work stoppage; and the financial support of the strikers in case of an official strike. After boycott of replacements had disappeared the consideration of the democratic structure of trade unions requires us to consider work stoppage as the main point upon which the decision about legality has to be based.

Here we meet the question as to the nature of the trade-union strike: Is this strike a direct action of the workers or is it an action ordered by union officials and executed by the members? The German Federal Labour Court has adopted the second view, and this entails the full application of the law of injunctions upon trade-union strikes. Following the first view, we were able to

82. Decisions are, however, not unanimous. While the decisions of: 4 May 1955, BAG 2, 75; of 5 September 1955, AP Nr. 3 zu Art. 9 Arbeitskampf; and of 17 December 1958, AP Nr. 3 zu 1 TVG Friedenspflicht, consider the violation to be socially inadequate, decisions of: 27 July 1956, BAG 3, 99 (p. 103); of 31 October 1958, BAG 6, 321 (p. 379); and of October 1960, still distinguish between contractual and tortious liabilities.

see another reason for the lack of injunctions in industrial actions in France and Italy – that view cannot be reconciled with the strike as a direct and spontaneous action, even if a union strike is involved.

Injunctions against industrial actions offer some more problems. The first is closely connected with the question of spontaneity. An order prohibiting a strike – even if the order is only for a certain time – could mean, that after the repeal of this order it could become impossible to continue a strike, because the workers could change their mind. A parallel problem exists when the period of a short boom is over or if the surprise effect of a strike is destroyed. In all these cases the temporary order adopts a definitive character. This view, however, seems to be overlooked, although the German Federal Labour Court has used the argument of the surprise effect as one of its justifications for recognizing the collective character of a union strike and therefore for granting the 'suspensive effect' to those strikes. It must be seen, however, that the provisions of the United States NLGA (sec. 7), which now gains new importance for violations of 'no-strike' clauses, restrict the application of injunctions to 'substantial and irreparable injury to the complainant's property', requiring that the damage caused by the denial of relief would be greater than by granting it and that there is a lack of adequate legal remedy or other sufficient public protection. In Germany none of these restrictions exist, because, as already mentioned, injunctions against industrial actions have been developed from the Civil Procedure Order which did not pay regard to these questions. The tremendous practical impact of an injunction must be compared with substantial law on industrial actions – the problem of legal errors of the applicants of law must be considered. The United States legislature gives specific provisions, certainly not as specific as the Swedish Basic Agreement of 1938. But after the NLRA, a double check is provided for injunctions against unfair labour practices. The NLRB decides upon unfairness, but then its General Counsel is required (sec. 10(e) NLRA) or has the discretion (sec. 10(j) and (l) NLRA) to seek an injunction and a court has to issue the injunction and may refuse if it is not convinced of the legality of the board's decision. In Germany no control exists although legal decisions on the unlawfulness of strikes are much more difficult than in the United States, because Germany has practically no statutory law and a poor case-law, but a judge-made general clause. Nevertheless, the professional judge of the lowest instance, the labour court, may issue the injunction – without his laymen of the employers' and employees' side. And in 'urgent cases' – and all industrial actions are such urgent cases – even the judge of the ordinary court, the *Amtsgericht*, is authorized to issue an injunction. Furthermore, Germany has kept one type of injunction (abolished by the United States Norris-La Guardia Act (sec. 7) and the British Industrial Relations Act (Schedule 3, para. 22(3)): namely, the interim injunction issued only on the basis of a sworn or para-sworn statement of the applicant without giving the defendants an opportunity to be heard. This injunction cannot even be suspended for bail, 'special cases' excepted. The injunction, however, is limited, regularly to a period of five to ten days until a preliminary trial is being fixed.

In the trial the opponent is heard. The judge then decides whether the order shall be maintained until the termination of the legal dispute. This stage is the same in the United States and Great Britain, where the decision of the judge is called a 'temporary injunction', 'interlocutory injunction' or 'injunction *pendente lite*'.

After this decision the procedure becomes different in the United States and Great Britain on the one side and for Germany on the other side. In Germany the procedure is terminated – an appeal excepted. However, the issue of an injunction always carries with it the imposition upon the favoured party of the obligation to bring the case to trial in a fixed time; otherwise the injunction will expire. In the United States and Great Britain the procedures are not separated. After the second step which terminates preliminary procedure a 'permanent injunction' may be issued in the dispute, which can thereafter be appealed.

In Germany and Great Britain the application for the injunction remains throughout the task of the party to the industrial dispute, usually the employee. This can be the case in the United States in a few situations; but in that country where the NLRB decides that an unfair labour practice has been committed, its General Counsel becomes the person to apply for the injunction. In this way a private industrial dispute takes on a public character.

The basis seems to be the liberal approach of the United States legislature, the attempt to restrict injunctions, because the attacked social party is certainly inclined to apply more for injunctions than a public authority. But despite this important distinction between both types of injunctions, it may be that after the *Boys Market* decision of the Supreme Court the scenery of collective disputes will be changed and injunctions against unfair labour practices will lose importance and be more and more replaced by injunctions against violations of 'no-strike' clauses.

The development of the law of injunctions may continue – Italian Workers' Statute of 1970 (Art. 28, sec. 1) has introduced injunctions against the employers ordering them 'to cease and to desist from illegitimate actions (against trade unions and the right to strike) and to eliminate their effects'. This could be regarded as the crossing of a Rubicon. Sweden, however, shows that injunctions against employers need not be followed by those against employees. Section 700 of the Italian Civil Procedures Act, which alone could be taken as the basis for this development, does not provide for sanctions if the court's order is not performed. Thus a thorough change of the policy on injunctions does not seem very probable, although the extensive application made of the injunction under the new law has somehow awakened Art. 700 from its long-lasting sleep. In a few cases attempts are made to use the latter against alleged unlawful strikes.

In Germany the status of the law on injunctions is much behind Great Britain and especially the United States, and it may surprise us to find that the considerable number of union members and union officials in the German Federal Parliament have not even attempted to change the law. They did not even react against the substantial changes of the law on industrial actions made by the Federal Labour Court. Several reasons may explain this attitude: the small number of strikes in post-war Germany, or the readiness of employers to yield to trade-unions' demands on the ground of possible price increases and full employment. But the main point is that Germany has not developed one system of collective labour law based on industrial disputes – as have all the other countries. Besides this system, another one has been built up, as expressed by the Act on Codetermination in the Steel and Coal Mining Industry. It is the concept of codetermination of workers within the enterprises – the concept of industrial democracy. The entrepreneur, as the absolute monarch of the enterprise, is to be replaced by a system of constitutional monarchs. These two concepts, however, are strictly opposed to each other and trade unions which ask for more codetermination which implies cooperation, lack credibility when they also demand a law of industrial actions more favourable to them. Moreover, another question may be asked in this context – whether trade unions which own (not all but the most important unions) large funds, because the funds of the old German trade unions dissolved by the Nazis in 1933 were restored and non-performance of strikes has saved strike benefits for which membership fees are calculated, have not changed their social role and functions. The unions have become businessmen themselves, and are 'capitalistic' trade unions really interested in developing the law on industrial disputes? In approaching this question one should also realize that strikes are generally unpopular in Germany.

But this question about future developments leads to the general question which was posed at the beginning of this investigation: Is there any development in the law on industrial disputes, and if so what is its pattern?

Conclusions

The first part of this chapter has shown that there has been a general development of the law on industrial actions. The age of condemning them generally has been terminated. The time of State intervention by penal sanctions is over, and countries evidently even avoid creating the impression that there is any exceptional law against criminal acts committed during a strike. Italy with its partial retention of the Fascist Penal Code providing for those sanctions is one, France with its law of 1864 is the other exception; and both may be explained by the law of immobility which governs collective labour law as a whole. But law used as the only approach to these problems will give an incomplete and therefore untrue picture. It must be supplemented by a more sociological and political approach, and if they are all taken together the picture will be different. The epoch of general condemnation of industrial actions has been followed by another one in which the employers felt themselves able to suppress strikes and union – and here they used the instrument offered by Civil Law. Civil Law became the law of industrial actions. And this epoch is still with us, especially in France and in Italy. State intervention in favour of the workers tried to help – by limiting the area of industrial actions. This was done with the recognition of the right to organize and of the right to strike. Both rights mean the protection of the workers against the economically more powerful employer; but sometimes, especially in Germany, this concept has been spoilt by a legalistic approach providing 'equality' of rights for the collective parties. This development leads to a new consideration of industrial actions. When law recognizes unions and strikes, then necessarily one may ask after the function of both in the legal system.

This question remains open, or may not even be put at all, especially if strikes are not organized by unions and preserve their spontaneous character – as is still the case in France and Italy and has also been in Great Britain before the Act of 1971. A strong feeling of personal liberty also demands that attention be paid to the personal decision of each individual striker to participate. This helps us to understand the situation of the United States and Sweden – and prevents us considering union strikes as a separate problem as Germany does. That country in this regard still keeps the medieval tradition of corporations as a unit between individual and state. But if unofficial and official strikes are separated then one decisive step is made to integrate the unions into the State. France and Italy do not take this step. The United States tries to avoid the problem by the system of having the union as elected bargaining agent for all workers in an enterprise. Britain, which was unique in the abstention of its law from industrial disputes, now moves towards a legal distinction between unofficial strikes and strikes authorized by registered unions. Germany illustrates this development in the strongest manner. The terminology of 'social self-government' or of the parties to collective bargaining as 'social partners' reveals it; the impact of traditional State ideology strengthens it.

The development of integration can be observed in Sweden as well, even though the traditions of that country are rooted not in State ideology, but in liberalism. Sweden may retain for many years a form of 'collective liberalism', which has taken the place of 'individualistic liberalism'; but this may be only another road to 'social partnership' and integration.

6

Industrial action,
the State and
the public interest
by K. W. Wedderburn

Introduction

The law in each of the six countries sets frontiers across which the right to take industrial action must not pass by reason of some over-riding 'public interest' or the necessity to protect 'the State'. In one sense most of the limits already discussed in this book on the right to strike or lockout could be defended on this ground. In Britain, for example, the new limitations introduced by the Industrial Relations Act 1971, especially those inhibiting strikes by unregistered unions, were defended by the Government as necessary in the national interest. Although it is impossible in this chapter to compare all aspects of the six different systems for which such a reason might be given, there is one distinction at the centre of most systems which serves as an interesting focus for a comparison between the different laws and between law and reality. It is frequently stated, or taken for granted, that industrial action should be permitted only for 'economic', 'industrial' or 'socio-economic' ends and not for 'political' purposes. Comparisons in this area reveal increasingly intransigent problems of definition as to what is 'political' and what is not, and lead to a re-evaluation of the very distinction.

Secondly, many of the legal systems place special limitations in situations declared to be 'emergencies'. Laws of this character establish prohibitions upon, or procedures governing, industrial action which are imposed in the 'national interest'. The search for the confines of an 'emergency' or a 'socially dangerous' situation or the 'essential' industry, has not, as we shall see, been very successful. Moreover, in five of the countries under review the 'emergency' laws cannot be discussed sensibly except in the perspective of other laws governing 'public employees'. In many of the six systems, that discussion opens up a vast hinterland of public law of which no more than a sketch can be provided below. Nevertheless, it is an area of law which cannot be overlooked; the denial to public employees of the right to strike is in some societies a most important reflection of interests of the 'State' or 'public interest' in the positive law governing labour relations. Sometimes, as in the

United States, the discussion of the 'political' strike becomes identified with the debate about strikes by public employees.

These three areas illustrate attempts of the law to confine industrial action within socially acceptable areas, or (to put the point in another way), by forbidding certain types of industrial action or prohibiting offensive action by certain groups of employees, to integrate the parties within a particular social consensus. With that in mind, one would expect to find today in the 'mixed' capitalist economies under discussion, increasingly direct legal intervention by Government to regulate industrial conflict by reference to national policies on 'prices and incomes' or economic policies as a whole. So far there have been few direct interventions of this character though recent events suggest that we may soon see more. In societies in which the trade unions represent a challenge in whole or in part to the character not just of wage-levels but of society as a whole, such laws are likely to meet with resistance – a resistance which inevitably raises the question of 'political' confrontation with the Government.

This chapter, therefore, comprises four parts:

Political strikes and other industrial action;
Emergency laws governing industrial action;
Public employees; and
National economic policies and labour law.

Political strikes and other industrial action

In all six systems of law a distinction is taken between what may broadly be called action for 'economic' and 'political' ends by way of industrial pressure. The latter may on a simplistic view be said to be repugnant to the interests of the community in a democracy because 'political' ends must be pursued by the duly constituted political machinery. But on further examination this simplistic view is shown to be crude to the point of falsity. The main reasons for this are two. First, the direct or indirect intervention of Government in the workings of the economy renders difficult the attempt 'to draw a line between the sphere of the "State" and the sphere of "Society"' – indeed, it has been said: 'Today any attempt to do so is doomed to failure'.[1] The second reason relates to the fact that most of the trade union or workers' unofficial movements have long had, or are fast developing, social interests which often compel them to challenge in fact the theoretical boundaries that lawyers place around prohibited 'political action' on the industrial level.

If these are truly the reasons that make for difficulty, one would expect to find least discussion of the problem in the United States; for there the bulk of the labour movement has never developed into a working-class movement with the broad social aims which challenge the consensus of the society at

1. O. Kahn-Freund, *The System of Industrial Relations in Great Britain*, Flanders and Clegg (eds.), 1st ed., 1954, p. 127.

large but has remained a form of 'business unionism' accepting the socio-economic framework. Nor has Government played so direct a role as in most European countries (at least in theory) in attempts to plan the economy. This expectation is indeed realized. Two senses of the term 'political' strike are often found – namely a strike against the Government as such (the definition by way of the *parties*) or a strike for policies or objectives of a 'political' and general social ends as opposed to 'economic' ends of direct interest to the parties. In both senses this type of strike has been almost unknown in the United States. The National Labor Relations Act (NLRA) does not deal with them because they pose no problem. True, student strikes in recent years have sometimes attempted to forge links with workers but (as in other countries) have met with little success.

In America strikes for political purposes, for example against a policy of Government, would be protected neither by labour legislation nor by any provision of the Constitution. They would therefore be subject to injunction and punishment by fine against the union, or even in some cases imprisonment of the strike leaders. The reason appears to be not that the political strike is *per se* illegal, either at Federal or state level but because, without the protection from the labour legislation, the old Common Law governs the position. Thus the striker could be dismissed and lose his status as an 'employee engaged in a labour dispute'. Presumably also, as we shall see in Britain, liabilities might arise in tort or even in crime, for example by way of unlawful conspiracy. This has never been tested probably because such political or 'general' strikes as have occurred have involved acts or threats of violence or the like – e.g. by dock workers – which immediately attract such liabilities.[2]

The situation is in certain respects parallel in Britain where no 'right' to strike exists but where the 'liberty' to take industrial action emerges from those actions which are protected in contemplation of furtherance of (in the past) trade disputes within sec. 5(3) Trade Disputes Act 1906 or (after 1971) 'industrial disputes' under the Industrial Relations Act. The definition of the latter is similar to the former, with the exception that it no longer includes disputes between 'workmen and workmen' or their unions acting as their agents. Industrial dispute is now defined to include:

(a) as to parties, a dispute between one or more employer or organization of employers and one or more worker or organization of workers; and
(b) as to content, a dispute which 'relates wholly or mainly' to one of a list of issues which cover almost all employment questions.[3]

2. cf. W. F. Dunne, *The Great San Francisco General Strike*, Workers Library, New York, 1934.
3. Terms, conditions or physical condition of employment; engagement, non-engagement, termination, suspension of employment; allocation of work; procedures agreements; consultation machinery for negotiation or arbitration on terms of employment or relating to 'other questions arising' between employers and workers; negotiating rights; facilities for union officials including shop stewards; procedures relating to dismissal, discipline or a worker's employment grievances: secs. 167(1) and 166(5), Industrial Relations Act 1971.

This definition is wide as regards content; but it remains to be seen how far the courts will demand that the dispute must relate mainly and *directly* to such employment questions.

'Political' strikes in either of the main senses here discussed (that is (*a*) against the Government or (*b*) for general social or political objectives) might well not fall within the sphere of 'furtherance of an industrial dispute'. The only previous discussion of the problem in Britain has concentrated upon the General Strike of 1926, ten days in which two million workers struck without success in support of miners whose wages were reduced after Government subsidies to coal owners were removed. On one side, it was argued that this 'so called general strike called by the Trades Union Congress is illegal'[4] because there could be no trade dispute between (as parties) workers or the TUC and the Government and because its content was 'unconstitutional' and unlawful under the general law of conspiracy. On the other side, it was argued that the TUC was as it put the point itself, 'engaged in an industrial dispute' in support of the miners and therefore protected against Common Law liabilities (e.g. for inducing breach of employment contracts) by the old Trade Disputes Act 1906. A political element did not displace this fundamental economic nature of the dispute being 'furthered' by the General Strike. Moreover, commentators have argued that even if the strike went beyond 'furtherance of a trade dispute' it was not *per se* illegal. It was not treason or sedition or some other offence against the State in the absence of violence or a threat to overturn the constituted authorities. Indeed it was said that all that distinguished a General Strike was 'that it is more likely to succeed'[5] and was not illegal *per se* even as a residual criminal conspiracy. But to this we must return below. Certainly, however, in recent years judges have interpreted the concept of 'furthering' a trade dispute in a very narrow fashion so as to deprive the protections of the Trade Disputes Act 1906 (and what would now be to some extent its successor in the jurisdiction of the High Court, secs. 132 and 134, Industrial Relations Act 1971). Deprived of those protections organizers of a strike will certainly risk injunctions or damages for tort (e.g. conspiracy or inducing breach of contract). Thus in 1969 the Court of Appeal followed earlier decisions in restricting the concept of 'furtherance', holding that workers in dispute with one hotel who picketed another hotel whose manager they thought had intervened to support his colleagues had 'furthered' not the original dispute but 'their own fury' in order to punish the second hotel.[6] In recent years there have been a number of strikes which many commentators have called furtherance of political not 'trade' purposes, e.g., a strike in 1969 in protest against the removal of a politician from the 'Shadow Cabinet' of the opposition Conservative Party (i.e. its leadership group) and a

---

4. Astbury J., *National Sailors' and Firemen's Union* v. *Reed* [1926] Ch. 536, 539; and Sir John Simon, *The General Strike: Three Speeches*, London, 1926.
5. A. L. Goodhart, 36 *Yale Law Journal*, 464, 1927; reprinted *Essays in Jurisprudence and Common Law*, 1937, at p. 241.
6. *Torquay Hotel Ltd.* v. *Cousins* [1969] 2 Ch. 106; see K. W. Wedderburn, *The Worker and the Law*, 2nd ed., 1971, p. 335; and also pp. 327–31.

strike in 1970 to demand full nationalization of the docks and workers' representation on the docks' boards at a time when a Bill for partial nationalization was before Parliament. Though in the latter case it was arguable that this 'furthered' a dispute connected with the workers' employment, the attitude to be expected from English judges is exemplified by a judgment concerning printing workers who organized a strike in December 1970 in protest against the Industrial Relations Bill proposed by the Conservative Government. The judge commented that to include a strike objecting to proposed legislation (albeit on labour conditions) within the area of a 'trade dispute' would be an 'impossible construction' of the statutory definition;[7] and the same principle would undoubtedly apply to furtherance of an 'industrial dispute' under the Act of 1971.

This reasoning would have three main effects under the new Industrial Relations Act 1971. First it removes the protection of the sections similar to the Act of 1906 in the jurisdiction of the High Court. Secondly, however, it paradoxically removes (with one possible exception)[8] the liabilities for 'unfair industrial practices' administered by the new Industrial Court. Those unfair industrial practices are invariably defined in terms which include only acts that contemplate or further an industrial dispute. For example, strike, lockout and 'irregular industrial action' are so defined; and specific unfair practices, such as inducing breach of contract, preventing performance of an employer's commercial contracts, putting pressure on an employer to discriminate against non-unionists, or the like, always include the same phrase.[9] Thus, if strike action were held to be taken for furtherance of predominantly *political* objectives the new Industrial Court would effectively lack jurisdiction. Nor would the provisions apply relating to the Government's power to seek a 'cooling off' order against industrial action in an 'emergency' (discussed below), because those too apply only in case of action in contemplation or furtherance of an industrial dispute. So, in a society where the assumption that one can easily separate predominant economic from political motives or action was said in 1954 by Professor Kahn-Freund to be 'plainly untenable', the new Act has created an Industrial Court to administer a code of labour law that does not apply to 'political' disputes. The British law therefore still rests upon an insistence that economic and political motivations are separable and distinct legal categories.

All this makes very remarkable the third consequence which flows from the new Industrial Relations Act. In a special sub-section added to the Act at a late stage[10] it is made illegal for any organization of workers to take disciplinary action of any kind against a member on the ground that he failed to take part in a strike or irregular industrial action organized by the union 'otherwise than

7. *Associated Newspapers Group Ltd.* v. *Flynn* (1971) 10 K.L.R. 17, 21.
8. Breach of a legally binding collective agreement under sec. 36 where the Industrial Court retains jurisdiction under sec. 129. This matter involves the 'peace obligation': see Chapter 3.
9. See respectively secs. 167(1), 33(4), 96, 98 and 33(3) of the 1971 Act.
10. Section 65(7)(b) and (c).

in contemplation or furtherance of an industrial dispute'. By this section the new Act prohibits all workers' unions from using their rule book to enforce solidarity in anything which could be called a political strike. The unusual nature of this provision of the Act is illustrated by the fact that the section has to redefine 'strike' and 'irregular industrial action'. It has to omit from the definition, for the purpose of this section alone, the restriction of those words to action taken in an industrial dispute.[11] This special provision will be seen by British trade unions as a sharp attack upon their right to maintain solidarity in all types of action; and it can be seen to introduce the fragile distinction between industrial and political action for the first time into the British law governing trade-union rules.

British law places 'political' disputes, therefore, outside both the protections and the new liabilities that attend industrial conflict, and appears to ascribe to the notion of 'political dispute' a wide meaning. It certainly includes industrial action taken primarily to influence Government policy or legislation. Many commentators also include such action even if it directly affects the working conditions of those concerned, such as the threat by a union to strike in 1970 if an airline was taken over by a private firm rather than a nationalized corporation. In 1966, the Prime Minister himself even alleged that a general strike of seamen organized by their trade union was controlled by a 'tightly knit group of politically motivated men' and was a 'strike against the State'. In 1970 in proceedings that were abandoned, a court granted an interim injunction against shop stewards who threatened a strike against the award of a servicing contract at London Airport to a private firm because it threatened employment prospects and was evidence of 'creeping denationalization' in the airways industry on the ground that the dispute did not affect the workers' employment conditions in a direct manner.

It was in this context that Britain faced the likelihood in 1971 of industrial action by workers with wide social implications. At the TUC conference 1971, the powerful engineering union unsuccessfully moved a resolution calling for strikes to support demands for higher pensions – a type of industrial action which, as will be seen below, has been common in Italy. Stoppages of work, moreover, were called for in Scotland against the rising rate of unemployment. Workers at certain Clyde shipyards 'occupied' the workplace (for the first time in recent British history) to stop dismissals and the closing down of most of the yards. How far these could be seen legally as 'political' has not so far been tested. But in so far as they are 'political', liability might arise for the organizers under the principles of the old Common Law. Those principles are not entirely clear but they may be summarized as follows.[12] In respect of civil liability in tort, a combination which does damage for an illegitimate purpose is an unlawful conspiracy; and among illegitimate purposes at Common Law is probably to be found the purpose of injuring a person because of his political beliefs. Similar liability in tort arises from deliberate interference with contracts or from any intentional damage done by use of 'unlawful means'

11. Section 65(11).
12. See Clerk and Lindsell, *Torts*, 13th ed., 1969, Chapter 11.

– included therein by use of a breach of contract.[13] Such liabilities would not be easy to avoid for the organizers of strikes found to be 'political'.

More difficult is the problem of criminal responsibility. There is old authority for the view that a strike, even to bring pressure to bear upon the Government by peaceful means, is not *per se* unlawful in the judgments given in prosecutions of some of the Chartist leaders who demanded the 'People's Charter' in the nineteenth century.[14] But other judicial statements of the same era suggest that there may be such liability in the event of a union 'compelling' members not to work for example 'until the Charter becomes the law of the land'.[15] Certainly such acts would not be protected against the general doctrine that a conspiracy for illegitimate objects is criminal; for that protection was given in 1875 only for acts furthering trade disputes and exists after 1971 for acts furthering 'industrial disputes'.[16] In modern times influential voices have suggested that a strike not protected by labour legislation in this way can amount to criminal conspiracy. Lord Shawcross, when Attorney-General in 1951, suggested to a court (which did not decide the issue) that it was a crime to strike in a way calculated to 'interfere with or affect the policy of the State'; and in 1970 he wrote that the 'starkly political' strikes against the proposed Industrial Relations Bill could render the organizers liable to both civil sanctions and to fines or imprisonment 'for conspiracy is also a criminal offence'.[17] Such a view could not be said to command universal agreement; indeed, most commentators reject the view that strikes against Government policies are *ipso facto* criminal at Common Law. But after the enactment of the Industrial Relations Act 1971, it is possible that many persons, possibly many judges, will take the same view as Lord Shawcross on the ground, as he put it, that in such strikes 'it is not only the rule of law but Parliamentary Government itself which is at risk'.

The position in the Federal Republic of Germany, for all the differences in terminology and concept, is not dissimilar to that which the less liberal commentators would wish to describe as British law. As a preliminary point we may note that jurisdiction over 'political strikes' is, once again, generally not vested in the Labour Courts but in the ordinary court.[18] Secondly, as in most countries, the matter has given rise to very little litigation in the courts; and a

13. This could probably include using a breach of a legally binding collective agreement, e.g. to inflict damage for political ends, despite secs. 96, 129 and 132, Industrial Relations Act 1971. The High Court is not prohibited from taking note of a contractual status of such an agreement.
14. *R.* v. *Cooper* (1843) 4 St.TR. (N.S.) 1249, per Erskine, J., p. 1316, discussed in Citrine, *Trade Union Law*, 3rd ed., Stevens, 1967, p. 618.
15. ibid. p. 1328, per Patterson, J.; but Citrine suggests that the compulsion involved violence: p. 619, n. 57.
16. Section 3, Conspiracy and Protection of Property Act 1875; now amended by Industrial Relations Act 1971, Schedule 9. The protection was introduced because courts had held it was a criminal conspiracy to organize workers to 'molest' an employer: *R.* v. *Bunn* (1872) 12 Cox 316.
17. Quoted in K. W. Wedderburn, *The Worker and the Law*, p. 393, where a different view is advanced.
18. See T. Ramm in *Labor Courts and Grievance Settlement in Western Europe*, B. Aaron (ed.), California U.P., 1971, pp. 94 and 105.

variety of social situations involving strikes more or less 'political' have not been tested in law. An interesting example arose in June 1971 when a trade union chairman, Mr Kluncker, urged dockers to abstain from unloading cargoes of salad from California in order to show solidarity with rural workers in California employed on allegedly starvation wages. Such a strike would probably be unlawful according to the majority German opinion as a sympathetic action which lacked a 'socially adequate' cause, even if it was regarded as an industrial rather than a political event. In Britain, too, under the Industrial Relations Act 1971 such an act of solidarity would be unlawful as preventing the performance of commercial contracts with 'extraneous parties' even if in furtherance of an industrial dispute.[19] Clearly in Germany, action would be unlawful if taken in solidarity with workers who were striking against social policies, including perhaps the failure of their national government to control the activities of a multi-national enterprise – a problem which is likely to become the dominant issue of the next decade. Alone of neighbouring European unions, the appropriate German union claimed to be unable to offer sympathetic action to the British dock workers in their national strike of 1970, even though that was a straightforward industrial dispute.

The primary test in German law of the 'political' character of industrial action is the party at which it is aimed. Is it aimed at the employer or is it mainly directed at the State in order to influence the legislature or its policies or to alter the political structure or situation? Apart from a few political strikes after 1945 aimed at policies pursued by the occupying (military) government, none of which gave rise to ordinary litigation, modern German law appears to have had only one instance of such a political strike. This occurred in 1952 when the printers' trade unions organized a work stoppage on the newspapers (though their members continued to work on other printing work) for some three days in order to promote changes in the Bill then before the legislature concerning works' councils and 'co-determination', that is to say the right of workers to be represented upon the supervisory councils of German enterprises. The matter did not go before the Federal Labour Court which had not by then been established. Even after it was established, however, in order to prevent an action being taken before that court the printing union voluntarily settled the question by paying damages following a majority of lower court decisions and (more important) of various expert professors' opinions pronouncing such a strike unlawful as a tort in civil law. Three decisions of the lower courts[20] all in effect followed the fundamental opinion of the leading German authority, Professor Nipperdey, who wrote an opinion for the employers and who was later President of the Federal Labour Court. Although not all commentators agreed[21] Nipperdey's opinion in effect gave to German labour law on industrial conflict a wholly new direction. Until 1953, it had been

19. Under both sections 96 and 98, Industrial Relations Act 1971.
20. Frankfurt, 20 February 1953 and 29 April 1953 (*Recht der Arbeit* 1953, p. 195, p. 354); Freiburg, 13 April 1953 (*Neue Juristische Wochenschrift*, 1953, p. 1278); Bavaria, 17 April 1953 (*Arbeitsrechtliche Praxis*, 1954, Nr. 59; and *Amtsblatt des Ministeriums für arbeit und Soziale Fürsorge*, 1953, p. c/77).
21. Professor W. Abendroth (Marburg) and Schnorr von Carolsfeld (Erlangen)

argued that industrial action was only illicit if it contravened the provision in the Civil Code, para. 826, prohibiting intentional acts that are *contra bonos mores*. But the new view, later adopted by the Federal Labour Court, rested upon para. 823 by which liability to pay damages applies to anyone who intentionally, or even negligently, and unlawfully violates the life, person, health, liberty, property 'or any other right' of another.

It was upon this 'other right' that Nipperdey seized. The new theory, basing itself on the 'right of enterprise' (the employer's personal right to conduct his undertaking)[22] demanded that before a strike could be regarded as lawful it must rest upon some 'socially adequate' basis. One concrete element in this 'social adequacy' test is the requirement that the industrial action must not be 'of such a nature as to make it impossible to terminate it by the conclusion of a collective agreement'.[23] On this ground alone, strikes aimed at the Government and its policies could be said to be unlawful. But what if the Government policies concern the very rights and duties of the workers themselves – such as their right to participate in works' councils or on supervisory boards? Nipperdey's opinion[24] found no social adequacy in that circumstance. Indeed, the new theory adds to the collective-agreement test the demand that the strike must be 'adequate' also in the sense that it is an *ultima ratio* and that no other lawful method of achieving the required objective could reasonably be pursued. The new theory of social adequacy was firmly adopted by the Federal Labour Court in 1955. By 1961 an orthodox jurist could write quite simply that in Germany 'the political strike is absolutely forbidden'.[25] An alternative formula is to say that a political strike is not an industrial dispute at all, because it does not put pressure primarily on the employer, and is on that ground illegal.[26]

An alternative explanation, albeit a minority one, which leads to the same conclusion that the 1952 newspaper strike was unlawful is that of Professor H. Meissinger.[27] He accepts that another Article (9, sec. 3) of the Bonn Basic Law establishes freedom of association and, according to the view prevailing in the Constitutional Court, that this could have justified the association of the printers if they kept their strike (as appears to be the case) within the bounds of 'maintaining and promoting labour and economic conditions'. But Meissinger adds that this freedom of association in industrial affairs is granted to the 'social partners' in collective labour relations by way of a right of delegated legislation. If that be so, then it must always be open to the supreme

contra: but Professors Forsthoff (Heidelberg) and Hueck (Munich) advanced the same view as Nipperdey.
22. See Chapter 5, p. 267.
23. T. Ramm in *Labour Relations and the Law*, O. Kahn-Freund (ed.), 1964, p. 207.
24. 'Die Ersatzansprueche für die Schaeden, die durch den von den Gewerkschaften gegen das geplante Betriebsverfassungsgesetz geführten Zeitungsstreik vom 27 bis 29 Mai 1952 entstanden sind' (1953).
25. Boldt et al., *La Greve et Lock-out*, p. 115, 'Droit du Travail dans la Communauté' (Collection du Droit du Travail), Luxembourg, CECA.
26. Hueck-Nipperdey, *Lehrbuch des Arbeitsrecht*, Vol. II, Ch. 1, p. 884, n. 10a.
27. 'Grundlagen und Grenzen der gewerkschaftlichen Machmittel' in *Recht der Arbeit*, 1956, p. 401 (Meissinger was a former President of the Bavarian Land Labour Court).

legislator to regain at will his competence as legislator on labour matters; and on this ground a strike against *labour* legislation could not be valid. The odd consequence of this view seems to be that other political strikes might be lawful. Some jurists offer an extreme view of a different kind, namely that even stoppages aimed at the employer to improve employment conditions can become unlawful as 'political' strikes if they result in endangering the State by reason of their general character and the gravity of their consequences.[28]

A preferable minority view seems to be that advanced in 1953 by the Berlin lower Labour Court and a parallel argument of Professor Ramm. The Berlin Court[29] considered that it was precisely legislation on social policy and labour law that trade unions should have the right to influence by means which included a short 'demonstration' stoppage which did not break any peace obligation in a collective agreement. To draw a line to exclude so-called strikes because they were addressed to the legislature on a matter which might be regulated by a collective agreement would 'establish an arbitrary border between economic and political strikes'. So long as its legislature had not laid down a precise prescription of political strikes it was not proper for the courts to outlaw a stoppage of which the subject matter concerned labour conditions even if aimed at indirectly influencing the legislature. Professor Ramm adds to this argument an insistence upon the distinction between an ordinary strike and the 'demonstration stoppage of work'. The latter he associates with the right of freedom of speech, itself protected by Art. 5 of the Bonn Basic Law. Such demonstration stoppages should normally be limited in duration; but, contrary to the prevailing opinion of Nipperdey and his school of thought, Ramm insists that these collective actions by workers ought not to be placed within the same category as 'strikes' strictly so-called, for in the latter the objective is to put pressure upon an opponent (the employer) until he capitulates to or negotiates a settlement upon a particular set of demands. The distinction between a normal strike and demonstration, however, is not conterminous with that between a strike for employment objectives and a political stoppage. Thus, in 1969 a group of women workers held a short meeting but returned to their workplace without working by reason of their dissatisfaction with the dismissal of the Work's Council chairman. There was no evidence that they intended to strike until he was reinstated; but the court[30] held that this stoppage was a 'strike'. But because it was 'unofficial' – without trade union authority – therefore, under the German concepts of unlawful and 'socially inadequate' strikes, it was *ipso facto* unlawful. Even so, Ramm argues that by reason of the absolute protection given constitutionally to freedom of speech, a limited 'demonstration stoppage' must be lawful, more especially for political purposes.[31] But unless the Constitutional Court delivers a judgment upholding

28. J. Kaiser, *Der politische Streik*, 2nd ed., 1959, p. 32; and Brox-Ruethers, *Arbeitskampfrecht*, 1965, p. 33.
29. Berlin, 17 August 1953; *Recht der Arbeit*, 1954, p. 76.
30. Federal Labour Court, 21 October 1969. Unofficial strikes were declared *per se* unlawful by the Federal Labour Court in 1955, a complete breach with German law before 1933: see Chapter 5, p. 288–9.
31. See T. Ramm, 'Der nichtgewerkschaftliche Streik', *Arbeit und Recht*, 1971, 67.

this view in the industrial field it seems clear that such an argument is a minority view facing a solid wall of opposing arguments accepted by the Labour Court under which political strikes are unlawful. By the same token the majority view would regard a 'political lockout' (if such can be imagined) as improper; and perhaps more important, then a general strike would inevitably take on a 'political' character and become unlawful.

A further dimension to the German problem is added by the constitutional right accorded by the Bonn Basic Law, Art. 20, sec. 4 (which will be mentioned again below) of a 'right of resistance against anybody who attempts to eliminate the constitutionally established order if no other means is available'. This Article looks back to the 'putsch' of Kapp in 1920 when a general strike of workers was called, and it was clearly inserted into the German Constitution to provide some ultimate weapon against a recurrence of the events of 1933. A 'political strike' called within the terms of this law should surely be lawful.

So far we have considered mainly the civil consequences of political strikes. What of the criminal law? Apart from questions germane to 'emergencies', there is one German decision of 1955 which suggests that a wide interpretation might be put upon certain provisions relating to criminal law so as to inhibit political action at industrial level, though the case itself did not concern merely the problem of industrial conflict. It involved two secretaries of the communist 'Free German Youth' who had planned 'demonstrations and strikes, including a mass or general strike' with the aim, so the court held, to 'eliminate the Federal Government and Federal Parliament' by making their activities impossible. The question arose whether they could be sentenced for high treason under (now sec. 83, Penal Code) for attempting 'with force or intimidation by threat of force . . . to change the constitutional order . . .'. The Federal Penal Court[32] refused to limit 'force' to a 'display of physical energy' and held that having regard to other sections of the Penal Code

> demonstrations and strikes cannot be looked upon as 'typical measures of non-violence'. Every strike is, and is meant to be an active display of energy . . . Whether an effect that is comparable to a display of physical energy is intended and achieved will depend on the quality and the size of the strike and on the question at whom it is directed. This has nothing to do with the question whether a strike is itself lawful.

The court added that a local strike would generally not imply such 'force' against the constitutionally constituted organs even if aimed at their policies; but a mass strike or general strike was different. In a heavily industrialized country like the Federal Republic of Germany, certain types of cooperation were needed to supply vital goods and services. If essential parts of that mechanism were paralysed, as in a general strike, an orderly working of the State would become impossible and chaos would result. Moreover, 'Government and Parliament will feel they are no longer able to control the situation and may be forced to surrender to hostile forces to prevent further suffering to the population.' The authors of this progamme were therefore guilty of an un-

32. Sixth Penal Senate, 4.6.1955; *B.G.H.St.*, Vol. 9, p. 102.

lawful plan to use coercive force against the regime, and it was irrelevant that they had planned no acts of violence of the like. This decision provides the possibility both of Government intervention by prosecution and also of applications by employers for injunctions in the Labour Courts against those who are about to engage in mass strike action. Short of emergency provisions, German law here provides an extreme illustration of a general and flexible weapon which could be used almost without limit against a labour movement which decided to use its strength on a mass basis for general social purposes.

When one turns to the situation in the other three European countries one finds a remarkable contrast, at least in practice, and, it is suggested, a more realistic and liberal attitude. Perhaps the country in respect of which the most liberal theory can be advanced is Sweden. In Swedish law mere combination cannot bring about liability in tort; the issue will arise in relation to contractual principles. The question can be ventilated only before the Labour Court since that court has exclusive jurisdiction over questions arising under collective agreements. Because the court assumes that the 'Common Law principles' of employment are silently incorporated into a collective agreement in so far as they are not expressly limited, including for example the prerogative of the employer to allocate work among workers or to dismiss workers,[33] these 'invisible clauses' in the collective agreement will cover the area within which the legality of political industrial action must be judged. The issue will therefore appear, if at all, as one between employers and unions or workers; the Government has no opportunity to bring an action.

Two propositions concerning Swedish law must first be clearly enunciated. Collective agreements[34] fall under the Collective Agreements Act 1928 and that statute is based upon the assumption that collective industrial action is permissible – that is to say, one starts from the unusual base that there is a Common Law 'right' to strike, to lockout, to boycott, etc. Four particular limits are imposed by sec. 4 of the Act: banning stoppages in disputes about interpretation of the agreement; to effect an alteration; to enforce provisions which are to apply only after termination; or to assist others acting unlawfully. Secondly, Common Law students of labour law must remind themselves that, although the collective agreement may be binding, there is in Swedish law no equivalent in tort to their Common Law 'remedies against a third party who induces a contracting party to commit a breach of contract or assists him in committing such infringement'.[35]

The debate in Sweden about political strikes is particularly useful because it has for some years taken in the international dimension that will be so important in a world dominated by multi-national enterprises. Folke Schmidt[36]

33. F. Schmidt, *The Law of Labor Relations in Sweden*, Harvard U.P., 1962, p. 184 *et seq.*; and Suviranta, 'Invisible Clauses in Collective Agreements', Vol. 9, *Scandinavian Studies in Law*, 1965, 177.
34. For their general effect see F. Schmidt, op. cit., and the summary by him in *Labor Courts and Grievance Settlement in Western Europe*, pp. 161–74.
35. F. Schmidt, *Law of Labor Relations in Sweden*, p. 193–4.
36. *Politiska Strejker och Fackliga Sympatiåtgarder* (Political Strikes and Trade Union Sympathetic Actions), Stockholm, 1969.

has offered as a definition of a 'political strike': 'a stoppage of work directed against the Swedish Government or a Swedish public authority or against the Government of a foreign country or a foreign public authority'. As usual this definition is couched in terms of the party against whom the action is launched; and it allows for a wide variety of content. It assumes that the mere existence of a general social purpose does not by itself disqualify industrial action aimed at an employer as the addressee. Examples in Sweden have been rare and litigation, as elsewhere, almost non-existent. In 1902 a mass strike to demand universal franchise lasted three days. A joint demonstration by the Social Democratic Party and the central trade union body (LO) in 1928 against the Collective Agreements Bill led to a one-day general strike in the entire country; but, contrary to the British experience, no court proceedings resulted. In 1967, the Transport Workers' union threatened to boycott Greek ships for a day in support of Greek workers but the boycott did not eventuate. In August 1968, at the request of the International Transport Workers Federation, the leaders of various transportation workers' unions decided to boycott lorries, ships and aircraft from Russia and certain other countries to support the Czeckoslovak transport workers and people. Although, once again, the boycott did not take place in fact, the decision did give rise to considerable discussion which is considered below. Similarly in 1963 there was discussion in Parliament of a possible refusal by Swedish dock workers to load or unload ships with cargo from South Africa.

The prevailing view in Sweden (though, as will be seen, not a view that goes unchallenged) is that the political strike is not unlawful so long, at least, as it has a temporary rather than a permanent character. This additional requirement arises from the one judicial decision of the Labour Court relevant to the central problem, the so-called *Dagsposten* case (1945/62). By way of preface, it should be stated that the Basic Agreement of 1938 between LO and the Swedish Employers Confederation (SAF) accepts the legality of sympathetic action[37] and that the Labour Court held that sympathetic industrial action was permissible in favour of a foreign party on the same terms as support for a party in dispute in Sweden (Case 1961/30). Again, the mere fact that pressure is collective will not in the Swedish Court give rise to an action in tort for damages even if it arises from a general boycott and causes damages which could well be foreseen (Supreme Court, 1935 N.J.A. 300; Schmidt, op. cit., p. 173). In the *Dagsposten* case the printers' union had organized a boycott of the printing office where the *Dagsposten*, a pro-Nazi newspaper, was produced in order to prevent its publication, their reason being the unpatriotic attitude of the paper. To support the printers, the Union of Commercial Workers ordered its members employed by the Press Bureau not to distribute or bundle *Dagsposten*. This sympathetic action was held by the court to be unlawful as violating sec. 4 of the 1928 Act because it was intended to bring about a change in the collective agreement between the Press Bureau (which distributed newspapers) and the union. Great stress was laid upon the *per-*

37. Agreement, Chapter IV, Article 10.

manence of the intended sympathetic boycott and, indeed, it is only by stressing that part of the decision that the judgment can be reconciled with the other cases which permit sympathetic action.[38] The issue of the 'political' character of the strike was raised but was touched upon only by one of the 'official' members of the Court who did hold that sympathetic action was unlawful if it was taken in support of industrial action undertaken, as here, for 'political reasons'. But this opinion has played little part in the subsequent Swedish debates and would not be followed by prevailing opinion, perhaps because it was concerned not with a 'political' strike as defined above (an attack on the Government, etc.) but with the 'political' *motives* of the printers who were taking action otherwise lawful against a private adversary in industrial conflict. On the other hand, the *Dagsposten* decision was clearly influential in that it underpins an assumption of the modern Swedish discussion on 'political' strikes aimed at Governments of their policies, namely that the strike will be of limited duration and not 'permanent'. In the latter case it seems to be assumed that, despite the existence of other 'political' machinery, such strikes could well be lawful. This is a particularly interesting view in a country where the democratic sensitivity of ordinary 'political' machinery is highly developed.

After the decision of 1968 by transport unions to boycott Soviet and other transportation, the legal adviser of LO prepared a memorandum in which he expressed the view that politically motivated action of this kind was unlawful as a violation of the peace obligation laid down in the collective agreement. The LO therefore circulated its affiliated unions with the statement that it could not support sympathetic industrial action of this character. Folke Schmidt's study[36] was prepared as a contrary opinion for the Transport Workers' union. In this study he advanced four dominant reasons for concluding that the political strike, as so defined, was not unlawful, namely:

1. The assumption on which the 1928 Act is based that collective industrial action is permitted unless enumerated as wrongful. This is the exact opposite of a system of law (such as the traditional British approach) which protects industrial action against common law liability only in 'trade disputes' or 'industrial disputes'.
2. The fact that the *Dagsposten* case rests upon the point about permanence whereas a political strike is a demonstration of opinion intended to be of short duration. (This argument echoes the minority German school of thought.)
3. No Swedish statute regulates political strikes; and on the introduction of the 1962 Penal Code it was made clear that peaceful political strikes were not an offence against the State. (We may contrast here the wide possibilities of the German penal law, and the 'Shawcross school' in England in respect of conspiracy.)

---

38. For detailed criticism of the decision, see F. Schmidt, *The Law of Labor Relations in Sweden*, p. 187-8.

4. Academic opinion has hitherto been unanimous in supporting the legality of the political strike.

Schmidt accepted that provisions in collective agreements could of course limit this right (as in the case of an agreement banning every type of industrial action by seamen); and he added that public officials fell into a separate category (see *infra*) and could not engage in political strikes. On the other hand, where a political strike *supported* the Government e.g. in fulfilling its international obligations (say) in applying sanctions against Rhodesia, there was a fifth and over-riding reason supporting its legality.

Schmidt's opinion was challenged in 1969 by Professor Tore Sigeman.[39] He argued that there was nothing in the Act of 1928 or its background to prove the legality or illegality of such strikes. While accepting that the political strike is not unlawful merely by reason of its purpose, he continues that a strike can acquire an unlawful character if it infringes established commercial norms, e.g., the prerogative of the employer to choose his customers, Russian, South African or other.

> Which rule shall prevail – the rule that the workers have a right to resort to offensive actions or the rule that the employer is entitled to his managerial prerogatives?

The fact that the Swedish Court had accepted sympathetic strikes – 'for a long time part of the rules of the labour market' – put it under no obligation to make the same choice so as to tolerate political strikes. Finally, Sigeman cites the opinion of the Minister of Foreign Affairs in Parliament in 1963 to the effect that to accept as lawful the refusal of dockers to work on South African cargoes would 'take the risk of introducing a new element which might disturb industrial peace'.

Folke Schmidt replied to this[40] by suggesting that the Minister had in mind a *permanent* refusal to handle such cargo. As for policy, the labour court should refrain from inventing new prohibitions in labour relations. Moreover, in the events of 1968, one trade-union leader had informed the SAF of the intention to boycott and after consultation the head of SAF had telephoned that SAF would 'not object to a boycott of short duration'. While this might not imply acceptance of legality, it certainly meant that the SAF did not want to take legal action on the matter.

Finally, Folke Schmidt's view is partly supported by Professor Sten Edlund.[41] The legislative history in his view supports legality. But looking to the present day realities, Edlund in a remarkable passage suggests that political strikes on *domestic* issues should not be lawful in days when so many other channels exist for expression of opinion and pressure.

> [On domestic issues] a political strike does not seem – to use a German term – 'sozialadekvat'. With regard to international issues the situation is

39. In *Dagens Nyheter*, 15.11.1969.
40. *Dagens Nyheter*, 25.11.1969.
41. In *TCO-Tidningen*, 1969.

somewhat different. A greater international solidarity should be developed and this could be an argument why political actions should be permissible when ordinary channels are not available.

This interesting use of the German notion of 'social adequacy' – standing it almost on its head so that its father Professor Nipperdey would hardly recognize it – clearly refers to the need to develop trade-union action in a world of multi-national enterprises. The 'national interest' is no longer an adequate test of industrial action. The power relationships at international level should play their part in moulding our view of the law. Most important, the value of the Swedish debate lies in its disclosing so much more clearly than British legalism or the conceptualism of the German approach, that our view of the legality of a 'political strike' is based on often unspoken assumptions about the policy which we favour as to the nature of a national – and now international – society.

In both France and Italy the description of the political strike must commence with the expected statement of abstract principles. But what distinguishes both countries at the present day is the acceptance of a wide variety of 'political' industrial action in practice, in a manner so pragmatic that the uninformed student could be excused if he had expected to find it, not in those countries, but in a country such as Britain which avowedly places pragmatism above concepts in such matters. Both Italy and France are of course distinguished by two features in common – first, a 'right to strike' stated in the Constitution (Italy) or its Preamble (France); and secondly, a trade-union movement divided along ideological lines in which the more militant members have kept alive the concept that trade unions are more than business-men with dirty hands and have wide social objectives as well as the fight for higher wages and shorter hours. No doubt both the British and Swedish trade unions to some extent share the latter trait; but their actions have not compelled their legal systems to accept *sub silentio* the fact of 'political' industrial action whatever legal theory may say. That is just what seems to have happened in both France and Italy.

In France, case law has limited the constitutional guarantee of the right to strike. That right is guaranteed by sec. 7 of the Preamble to the Constitution of 1946 (reaffirmed in 1958) and is supplemented by the Law of 11 February 1950 which guarantees continuity of the employment contracts for a striker unless he commits a 'serious breach' of his contract (*faute lourde*). But the courts have limited lawful strikes to those promoting 'les intérêts professionels' of the strikers (of which the best translation is perhaps 'the industrial or economic interests' of the collective group of workers concerned).[42] From this it was a short step for the Cour de Cassation in 1953 to argue that the right to strike did not include the right to play the role assigned constitutionally to political institutions and that political strikes were therefore unlawful.[43] Many

42. Cour de Cassation, Sec. Soc., 23.6.1951. *Droit Social*, 1951, p. 532.
43. Cour de Cassation, Sec. Soc., 23.3.1953; D 1954, p. 89 (Levasseur); see generally H. Sinay, *La Grève*, Dalloz, 1966, Part 3, Chapter II; and ibid., p. 187 on this development.

judicial decisions followed in the same direction, both in the ordinary courts and in administrative law.[44] But it is to be noticed that the French definition of a legitimate strike does not include the requirement that it must be directed at the employer of the strikers.[45] Thus a strike against a decision of a public authority can remain lawful so long as it remains a defence of the 'intérêts professionels' of the strikers; and it was said by the leading authority in 1961 that in periods of planning – including Government planning affecting wages – strikes directed not against an employer but against Government decisions led to a test of whether the stoppage led 'as a *direct* result to modifications in working conditions'[46] in which case it was not a political strike.

Moreover, for a period in the 1950s the French courts took a view that was perhaps even more relaxed. Of all the countries under review France understands best the fact that 'most strikes are at one and the same time political and industrial and it is very difficult to disentangle the one characteristic from the other'.[47] In this period therefore case law condemned as illicit strikes of a 'mixed' character only if the 'intérêts professionels' appeared to be so secondary as to be a mere pretext for the pursuit of the political objective. Going further, in 1959 the Cour de Cassation held that 'intérêts professionels', even if secondary, could prevent a strike being unlawful even if it had clear political aims.[48] The Conseil d'Etat took a similar view in the *Bernot* case of 1955,[49] and that seems still to prevail in administrative law.

But in 1961 the Cour de Cassation returned to a more strict view. As usual in France the issue involved the legal problem in respect of which the political strike problem arises, namely whether the strike is unlawful so as to break continuity of employment despite the Law of 11 February 1950 and to allow the employer at once to dismiss the striker. In *S.N.C.F. c. Cluzel*[50] the court refused to accept as lawful the stoppage of work by a widow, Mme Cluzel, even though the stoppage was connected with a refusal to increase wages and redundancy among railway employees. The strike was also called in connection with the arrest of trade union leaders and protests against the general political policy of the Government. The Court held that participation in this strike constituted *faute lourde* since it did not have as its 'principal object' an altera-

44. G. H. Camerlynck and G. Lyon-Caen, *Droit du Travail*, 4th ed., Dalloz, 1970, pp. 531–2. The Superior Court of Arbitration took the same view. See on that court: X. Blanc Jouvan in *Labor Courts and Grievance Settlement in Western Europe*, p. 65 et seq.
45. The same is true of the definition of 'strike' in Britain: Industrial Relations Act, sec. 167(1) (concerted stoppage by workers whether 'parties to the dispute' or not); but in such a system this provides no extra protection – since protected acts are largely defined by reference to other judicial concepts, e.g. inducing breach of contracts – but extra liabilities, e.g. strikes for unfair industrial practices.
46. P. Durand in Boldt et al., *La Grève et Lock-out*, op. cit., p. 42.
47. H. Sinay, *La Grève*, p. 188.
48. Sec. Soc. 4.6.1959; *Bull. IV*, No. 660, p. 530.
49. *Affaire Bernot*, C. E., 18.2.1955, 'Receuil Arrêts C.E.', p. 97. (Worker employed by Defence Ministry stopped work on the same date as a series of political demonstrations against the incoming American Admiral commanding NATO forces in France held to be on lawful strike, there having been industrial demands formulated concerning working conditions.)
50. Civ. Sec. 10.3.1961, *Bull. IV*, No. 333, p. 269.

tion in employment conditions; without such object the strike was an 'abus de droit'. This test of the need of a 'principal object' of an industrial character was accepted by certain commentators.[51]

But in the last ten years no strict adherence to that rule can be said to have dominated French practice. While cases have retained the doctrine that purely political strikes are illegal, commentators have attempted to refine further the definition of 'political'. Thus Professor H. Sinay poses three main requisites:

1. That the strike is not aimed at the employer and the demands cannot be met by him but only by Government or other public authority;
2. That the protest has an 'essentially negative' character, without precise positive alternative policies ('all political strikes have the character of strikes to *oppose* something'); and
3. That the strikers act not in their role as workers but in their capacity as citizens.[52]

The second test would seem to give rise to difficulties, and it has to be added that decisions have made lawful strikes in *support* of Government policies, such as the one hour stoppage invited by the President in 1961 against the insurrection in Algeria, although in that case the court was careful not to speak of the stoppage as a strike. Many judicial decisions have regarded mere participation in a political strike, as in other unlawful strikes, to be *faute lourde* on the part of each participant. A minority of cases insist upon an individual assessment of the nature of each particular worker's participation. Some commentators criticize the majority case law as a departure from the normal French rule that *faute lourde* should always be judged by reference to each individual (for in France, the right to strike, although a right to join in a collective act, is nevertheless an *individual* right and the question of *faute lourde* is normally judged not by the collective nature of the strike but by the individual conduct of the participant).[53]

Whatever the judicial decisions say, however, the fact that the only major legal consequence of illegality is the subjection of a striker to dismissal by reason of his *faute lourde* explains why the letter of the case law may not represent the reality of the law in action. Whereas in local or unsuccessful strikes a few strikers may be dismissed and actions brought in court, in national or successful strikes the employers will prefer to reach a solution that does not raise these issues at all.

In fact, the most important strikes, those that really made the history of labour relations in France, were political strikes: strikes against rightist movements in 1934, strikes at the Liberation in 1944, strikes in 1958, 1961,

51. See A. Brun, *Jurisprudence en Droit du Travail*, 1967, pp. 638–9.
52. H. Sinay, *La Grève*, pp. 181–4 and pp. 190–1. For a bibliography of the French discussion see Sinay, p. 179, n. 1.
53. See G. H. Camerlynck and G. Lyon-Caen, *Droit du Travail*, p. 543: in political strikes the courts make use of a kind of *faute lourde collective*. See also Chapter 4, p. 216, on *faute lourde*.

1968 etc. .... Most of these strikes were never declared unlawful and they never produced any of the effects of an unlawful strike.[54]

Indeed, the attitude of French courts had become more ambiguous even before the great stoppages of 1968; and matters can hardly be the same after the events of that year. The 'Accords de Grenelle', a new species of 'Protocol' short of a collective agreement proper made by unions and employers under the chairmanship of the Prime Minister in the presence of other ministers, resulted from the general strikes of 1968 without any suggestion that they were unlawful, though they illustrated above all others a mixture of 'political' and 'industrial' objectives.[55] The Accords de Grenelle concerned both employment conditions and projected reforms in labour law and resulted in other industrial agreements – 'gentleman's agreement du type anglo-saxon' – rather than collective contracts of the traditional French kind.[56]

After these developments it is not surprising that new strength has been added to the reasoning of commentators who have attacked the very notion that 'political strikes' should be excluded from the constitutional right to strike. Why should a strike dominated by 'disinterested motives' be less legitimate than a stoppage of work which seeks merely an increase in wages for the workers concerned.[57] Commentators such as Sinay have been critical of the continuing practice of the Cour de Cassation (though not the Conseil d'Etat) of condemning as illegal some strikes with 'mixed' objects – especially because the court refused in this one case only to follow the traditional French law of examining the objects of each individual striker.[58] By 1968, Savatier put in this way the increasing doubts of French commentators on whether the old law could survive the new social facts:

One wonders first whether the distinction established in the case law between industrial strikes and political strikes will be able to be maintained. This distinction, for many years a difficult one, seems to have been made outmoded by the type of strike we have seen where a struggle against the established political authority and its reactions to the student or workers' movement has been intimately bound up with the industrial demands. What led to new elections was not a vote of censure in Parliament but the pressure of strikes. Can the courts, after that precedent, still consider illegitimate any strike that makes demands of a political character? Must we not recognize that, in our society, trade unions constitute the great engine of opposition that can serve as a countervailing force against a governmental authority which is now very little controlled effectively by Parliament?[59]

54. Communication from X. Blanc-Jouvan, citing Sinay *La Grève*, p. 180–1.
55. See Chapter 1, p. 48. On the strikes see D. Singer, *Prelude to Revolution*, Cape, 1970, pp. 152–275
56. J. Savatier, *Droit Social*, 1968, p. 442.
57. Ripert, *Les Forces créatrices du droit*, No. 101, p. 261. See also Boitel, 'Pour la licéité de la grève politique', *Droit Ouvrier*, 1952, p. 293; and 'Grèves politiques benies et grèves politiques maudites', *Droit Ouvrier*, 1962, p. 71.
58. H. Sinay, *La Grève*, pp. 198–9.
59. J. Savatier, 'La "Revolution" de Mai et le Droit de Travail', *Droit Social*, 1968, July–August, p. 438 at p. 440; see too G. Lyon-Caen, ibid, 'Les journées de Mai et les

In Italy the story is similar. One begins with the Constitution of 1948: 'The right to strike shall be exercised within the limits of the laws regulating it' (Art. 40). No such laws have since been passed; but the courts have placed limits by case law, since 1951 accepting the right but claiming also the right to control it by interpretation of what is a 'lawful' strike. Their fundamental definition of a lawful strike related to 'the power, collectively and by agreement, to abstain from work in order to further *economic* interest'.[60] From this definition it followed that a political strike was unlawful either because it was not a 'strike' or because, even if a strike, it is not for the correct, constitutionally protected objectives. For some time the required 'economic' interest was tested in a manner similar to the test applied by German law, namely that the subject matter of the strike must be something which could form the subject matter of an agreement with the employer.[61] In similar fashion it was said that to be lawful a strike must be aimed at the employer and not at some third party, for example the State.[62] The consequences of engaging in a political strike are found in civil law, e.g. the power of the employer to discipline or dismiss strikers, and the right of third parties to sue in tort. Articles of the Penal Code (503 to 505) suggest that criminal liability could result; but as with so many other parts of this bequest from the Fascist régime the validity of these Articles is not clear, the better view in this case being that criminal liability no longer arises.[63] But a political strike which aimed at a general coup d'Etat would remain criminally punishable under Art. 207 of the same Code.

A decision of the Constitutional Court in 1962, however,[64] not only accepted any interest as 'economic' which fell within Chapter III of the Constitution (a very wide list) but also upheld the validity of strike action for those purposes even if directed against the Government and its policies, e.g. in support of a minimum wage law or for social security legislation. That decision involved, as we shall see, public employment; but in general terms it, and a later decision of 1969, gave support to those writers who had argued that not all 'political' strikes were illegal. First, it made clear that the test by way of party was no longer tenable. The other party aimed at by a lawful strike could well be the Government. But what, secondly, of the content of the strike? On this matter Italian writers appear still to be divided. Taking the most extreme position, Professor Natoli argues that Art. 40 of the Constitution must be read with

Accords de Grenélle', p. 446, with the text of the Accord at p. 448. For an early expression of such a view see Lyon-Caen, 'Il diritto di sciopero e il contratto individuale di lavoro', *Rivista Giuridica di Lavoro*, 1952, Vol. I, p. 53.
60. G. Giugni, in 'Labour Relations and the Law', O. Kahn-Freund (ed.), p. 212.
61. G. Giugni, *Diritto Sindacale*, Bari, 1969, p. 197–8.
62. L. Mengoni in Boldt et al., *La Grève et Lock-out*, op. cit., p. 276, but see the following paragraph in text.
63. See G. Pera, 'Lo Sciopero e la Serrata', in *Nuovo Trattato di Diritto del Lavoro*, L. Riva Sanseverino and G. Mazzoni (eds.), Padua, 1971, Vol. 1, p. 561. A Bill of 1971 aims to repeal these criminal sanctions in the old Penal Code. But the new Bill includes a provision similar to the old Art. 504 whereby it would be unlawful to take mass action to influence public authorities. This liability, if reinvigorated by such a new law, could be even wider than the German law discussed above, p. 330.
64. Case 123; 28.12.1962. The 1969 decision (see below, p. 372) extends 'economic' to 'socio-economic'.

Arts. 2 and 3 (which guarantee 'the inviolable rights of man' social and individual, including the development of human personality, and the right to equal
social dignity and equality before the law). From this he argues that the right
to strike must encompass every case in which workers need to be safeguarded
from economic domination. That is why there is no equivalent right to lockout
found in the Constitution, for there is no equivalent need on the other side of
the employment relationship. In effect, he rejects the very distinction between
'economic' and 'political' action for today there is no area of economic activity unaffected by politics and vice versa.[65] Although Natoli would not uphold
a purely political strike (e.g. the demonstration against a visit by Vice President Humphrey) as a 'strike', he considers this legitimate within the provisions relating to free expression of opinion;[66] but other commentators would
support it even as a *licit* strike, arguing that it is a participation in political
activities protected by Art. 3, sec. 2, of the Constitution.[67]

A more limited view which also derives support from the 1962 decision and
which is probably nearer the doctrines of the majority is that advanced by
Professor Mengoni.[68] While a political strike in the sense of a strike against the
Government or its political orientation remains for him illegal, he accepts as
lawful a strike which has as its aim the acquisition of benefits of a social welfare character from Government. The events of 1969 to 1971 certainly required some such theory. In these years very large strikes were called to press
for legislative reforms on pensions, housing and a national health service; and
strikes were launched on a number of other social issues, such as the demand
to enlarge tax relief on low incomes – all done with few suggestions that workers
concerned were acting illegally. Such a doctrine would, however, justify neither
a strike against the Government on a political question in which the workers
could be said to have a direct social or economic stake; nor even against an
employer by reason only, for example, of his supporting a particular political
group.[69] In a decision of 1970 a court upheld the lawfulness of the action of an
employer in tearing down placards put up in the workplace by workers despite
the Law on Workers' Rights giving to employees the right to put up posters;
but that Law (in Arts. 20 and 26) expressly limits workers' rights to meet or
put up placards to matters promoting trade union or labour interests in
general, while the placards in that case protested in general terms against the
war in Vietnam.[70] On the other hand, when dockers refused to handle Spanish

65. See U. Natoli, in 'L'Esercizio del diritto di sciopero' (Proceedings of Seminar at
Istituto di Diritto del Lavoro, Universitá di Firenze; Milan, 1968), pp. 141–6.
66. U. Natoli, ibid., pp. 171–2 criticizing a lower court decision which held that strikes
against the electoral laws of 1953 were unlawful.
67. See Onida, 'Lo Sciopero politico è un diritto', *Relazioni Sociali*, 1970, No. 4–5.
68. L. Mengoni, *Il diritto di sciopero*, Milan, 1964; *La Grève et Lock-out*, op. cit.,
p. 278; G. Branca, 'Reflessioni sullo sciopero economico', *Rivista di diritto civile*,
1968, I, p. 151.
69. Compare the English doctrine that it may be at Common Law a wrongful conspiracy to combine to injure a man only because of his political beliefs: see above,
p. 325.
70. F. de Ambri Corridone, F. Fabbri and G. Veneto, 'Rassegna critica delle decisioni concernenti la legge, 20 Maggio 1970', *Rivista Giuridica del Lavoro*, 1970, II,
p. 817.

ships during the notorious Burgos trial in 1971, it was not suggested that this was an unlawful strike.

The Spanish ships example introduces three further doctrines of Italian law which are to be found in areas contiguous to the political strike. The first is the law on sympathetic action, or 'solidarity strikes'. The Constitutional Court decision 123 of 1962 recognized the legitimacy of this form of action once there is a community of interest between two groups of workers. Sufficient community of interest can be found where, without the two groups joining forces in their struggle, the needs of the workers concerned will not be met.[71] Professor Giugni points out that not only does this extend the right to strike beyond action taken against the primary employer; it also means that the existence of a common interest will be evidenced effectively by the decisions of the workers themselves, and that to have it judged by some other body, e.g. the court, would infringe the rights of 'collective autonomy' of the workers under Italian law. As in the case of Sweden, Italian writers do not seem to limit the community of interests to national frontiers. A sympathetic strike, for example, to assist workers in another country or a boycott (e.g. of South African goods) in support of them seems to be lawful within this doctrine.

Secondly, however, there is the doctrine of 'unreasonable damage', a doctrine not dissimilar to that which we shall meet elsewhere in German law (p. 358). The essence of this uncertain and criticized doctrine is that the damage which can be permitted by strike action must not be out of proportion to that which would be caused by a straightforward stoppage of work for the permitted objectives.[72]

Thirdly, there is, in the view of some Italian commentators a form of strike which is neither fully 'political' nor merely 'economic', namely the 'protest strike'. It may be, however, this term is no more than a label to be attached to 'political' strikes which fall within the limits of legality. Mengoni appears so to use the term.[73] Professor Riva Sanseverino defines the term more narrowly to include abstentions from work that express dissent from decisions by management which do not affect the workers directly. Such strikes are lawful in her view, and some 'political' strikes could arguably fall into the same category, when, for example, the expression of dissent includes demands for the enactment or repeal of laws relating to labour or social legislation.[74] In this way her view approximates to that of Mengoni.

In the Italian experience, therefore, as much as in the French, we find a legal system and its expositors struggling with old-fashioned concepts against the social fact that a strong trade-union movement is determined on occasion to use its industrial strength to push for social reforms as well as for higher wages. As early as 1953 one commentator stated that again and again it was to

71. Court's decision quoted in Suppiej, *Fonti per lo studio del Diritto Sindacale*, Padua, 1970. See also Pera Lo sciopero e la serrata, op. cit., p. 561.
72. See Chapter 2, p. 94.
73. See 'Grève et Lock-out, op. cit., p. 278.
74. See L. Riva Sanseverino, in *L'Esercizio del diritto di sciopero*, Milan, 1968, pp. 129–33 and pp. 137–8.

be found that 'there are no neat categories of political strikes and economic strikes; there exists a whole range of mixed and intermediate forms and it would be impossible finally to give to some strikes a definitive economic label as against political demonstrations'.[75] Another added that given the close links between economic and political affairs in a modern society, it was extremely difficult to distinguish the two, for there was scarcely a strike that does not affect the general social situation.[76]

The Italian commentators end where we began – with the nearly 'untenable' character of the basic distinction between lawful (economic) action and unlawful (political) action by which, in one form or another, each of the systems under review tries to confine its trade unions. Even when we know that the two concepts are almost meaningless, we apparently have to keep them as legal props or legalistic myths. It appears almost as if judges and legislators in these Western societies, with the possible exception of the deeper thinking of our Swedish colleagues, would feel psychologically insecure to the point of collapse if they could not fall back into the arms of the unlawful 'political' strike as a safety net for the protection of the society which they know against an unduly powerful demand from trade unions for social change. For it can be seen in all these systems that the illegality of the 'political' strike – not being matched by any equivalent prohibition against the use of capital to change society in a fundamental manner – is a protection of the 'national interest' in the sense only of the *status quo*. If that can be justified by reason of the possibility of changing society radically through the ballot box (and since that has never happened yet, Professor Savatier's question remains to be answered), there still remains the need to allow international 'political' and solidarity strike action, as Professor Edlund argues, as the necessary corollary of the multi-national organization of capital in Western countries.

Emergency laws governing industrial action

Each of the legal systems has some provision relating to industrial conflict that gives rise to an 'emergency', but they are extremely difficult to compare. All, for example (except perhaps for Great Britain), must have their 'emergency' provisions reviewed in the context of the laws prohibiting strikes by public employees (p. 364) with which the emergency laws often overlap. In each, the emergency provisions rest squarely upon the particular social and industrial relations system in question and here above all it is indeed 'fruitless to try to decide which nation has the "best" laws'.[77] Nevertheless there are compar-

75. M. Ruini, *L'organizzazione sindacale e il diritto di sciopero nella Costituzione*, Milan, 1953, p. 109. The author was a former President of the Senate and member of the Committee which drafted the Constitution.
76. G. Pera, *Problemi Costituzionali del diritto sindacale Italiano*, Milan, 1960, pp. 197–8 et seq., for a useful discussion of Art. 40.
77. D. Bok, 'Reflections on the Distinctive Character of American Labor Laws', 84 *Harvard L. R.*, 1971, 394, p. 1459; who nods therefore when he describes the British tradition of resistance to legal regulation of labour relations as a 'fetish', p. 1461.

able problems that emerge – not least the question whether labour laws seeking to defend the national interest can effectively define an 'emergency' situation in advance in which the ordinary economic sanctions available to the parties must be displaced. It may be that the introduction of the very term 'emergency dispute', as opposed to other concepts such as a 'major' work stoppage, gives rise to almost insoluble definitional questions as it appears to have done in the United States.[78] Despite the long American experience since 1947, of which a summary appears below,

> There is still no consensus as to when a dispute truly imperils the national health and safety. If primarily economic criteria are applied, few cases would meet the test; but the line between emergency and inconvenience is frequently hard to draw and public resentment against strikes in the key industries, regardless of their effect on the national health and safety is a political force which cannot be ignored.[79]

Until the new British law of 1971, it could be said that this search for a separate class of dispute and procedures laid down for 'emergencies' was primarily an American phenomenon.[80] But other countries have passed through attempts to define such categories. In the 1930s prolonged debate in Sweden failed to define disputes 'dangerous to society' and illustrated only that sometimes a conflict involving a whole industry 'is easier for the majority of citizens to tolerate than a dispute which concerns a small number of persons in such key positions that in addition to its other effects a strike would result in unemployment for a great number of persons'[81]. That is not to say that each of the systems does not provide methods for prevention or prohibition of various types of 'emergency' disputes as such. Indeed the European Social Charter, despite its recognition of a 'right to strike' (Art. 6(4)) accepts the propriety of laws limiting such rights in time of 'war or other public emergency threatening the life of the nation' (Art. 30) and laws 'necessary in a democratic society . . . for the protection of public interest, national security, public health or morals' (Art. 31). It is convenient therefore to look at the experience of the four continental european systems before turning to that of the United States and, finally, to the strangely changing situation in Britain.

In Sweden, as in other Scandinavian countries,[82] from an early date the Goverment's response to a 'general' strike or lockout has often been the threat of introduction of special legislation. This threat to intervene by *ad hoc* legislation is the only method for direct Government legal intervention. In 1955, for example, a Bill was introduced in Parliament providing for compulsory arbitration in a dispute between shipowners and officers of the merchant navy and was withdrawn when the parties speedily reached agreement in their

78. H. Wellington, *Labor and the Legal Process*, Yale, 1968, p. 272.
79. B. Aaron, 'Public Interest Disputes and Their Settlement', 14 *Labor Law Journal*, 1963, 746, p. 748.
80. J. Dunlop, 'Procedures for the Settlement of Emergency Disputes' (Paper at Rome Conference on 'Automation, Full Employment and a Balanced Economy', 29.6.1967), p. 9 (referred to below as 'Rome Paper').
81. F. Schmidt, *The Law of Labor Relations in Sweden*, 1962, p. 206.
82. See W. Galenson, *The Danish System of Labor Relations*, Harvard, 1952, pp. 130–7.

dispute. But until recently such intervention has not been a central feature of the Swedish industrial relations scene. Of much greater importance have been the limitations upon the ambit of industrial conflict by the trade unions and employers. In the general strike of 1909 in which the emergent L O, faced with a lockout of some 70,000 workers, called a strike of over 300,000 members, in which it was supported by the unaffiliated typographers' union who stopped the daily press, Government action went no further than mediation.[83] The trade unions were defeated; but the L O laid down as a general rule that work should not stop where it concerned the care of sick persons, maintenance of livestock, or continuance of lighting or water supplies or of garbage collection. By 1935, when Sweden had moved into a phase of rapid industrialization, proposals for laws to regulate disputes 'dangerous to society' led to appointment of a Royal Committee which suggested that a distinction be made between strikes in profit and non-profit making enterprises. But no such laws eventuated. Instead, in the Basic Agreement, 1938, between L O and S A F the parties agreed that the Labour Market Board (composed of three persons from each party) shall promptly consider any dispute referred to it for 'protection of the public interest' by either party *or* by 'a public authority or other similar body representing the public interest' in order 'so far as possible to prevent labour disputes from disturbing essential public services'. Each side agreed to implement immediately any decision reached by a majority on such public interest disputes.[84] In 1953 a unanimous decision by the Board for the settlement of a strike in privately owned electricity plants along the lines of proposals made by a State mediator at once saw the end of the strike.

As we shall see later (pp. 370–1) public employees obtained new rights of negotiation under the State Officials and Municipal Officials Acts of 1965. Within the limited area of industrial action allowed to them, special provisions are made for disputes potentially dangerous to society. But these provisions are made not in the statutes but in collective agreements made by the authorities and the unions representing various State and municipal employees (the S F, T C O-S, S R, and S A C O) which came into effect at the same time as the statutes. Of the four unions, S F is affiliated to the main union organization (Confederation of Trade Unions) and represents mainly lower-paid manual workers; T C O-S represents mainly salaried white-collar workers; S R comprises certain other salaried employees such as railway-controllers and Army officers; and S A C O comprises higher-paid professional workers. The making of these agreements was in effect a condition imposed by the Government for agreeing to the new law. A Municipal and a (State) Public Service Council (with equal membership of unions and employing authorities, four on each side) were set up under the agreements, and provisions made for such disputes similar to that in the Basic Agreement 1938. But there are significant differences.[85] First, only one of the parties (not another 'public authority')

83. Bernt Schiller, *Storstrejken 1909: Förhistoria och orsaker*, 1967; Ragner Casparsson, *L O under fem årtionden*, 1947, Vol. 1, p. 313 et seq.
84. Text in F. Schmidt, *The Law of Labor Relations in Sweden*, p. 277.
85. 'Basic Agreement between the State and Main Organizations of State Officials on

may raise an issue as to a dispute 'calculated unduly to disturb important social functions'. Secondly, the primary obligation after such a request is to negotiate in order to 'avoid, limit or end the dispute'. (A limitation may result in the union agreeing that a certain proportion of its members will not strike so as to relieve a dispute of its socially dangerous character.) Thirdly, if negotiations bring no solution the question of its 'social dangerousness' shall be referred to the Public Service Council and no 'offensive action' (strike, lockout, etc.) of which notice has been given shall be taken for a period of up to three weeks. But a majority vote once again can decide the issue and where that decision pronounces a dispute socially dangerous the party concerned is put under strong pressure to limit or end the dispute.

In the severe industrial conflicts of 1971 various cases were taken to the Public and Municipal Service Councils, some with curious results. A tied vote left undetermined the question whether a strike of TCO-S workers in the Postal Giro (banking) Service would disturb a vital social function. The Public Service Council ruled that a strike of SACO veterinary inspectors in slaughter-houses did have that character whereupon SACO withdrew its strike notice. But by a seven to one majority the Council ruled that a lockout of teachers was not socially dangerous, a decision which led the chief SACO negotiator to comment that pigs were apparently of greater social value than children! The Municipal Council had to rule upon a dispute concerning social workers at the instance of the Municipalities' Association *after* the municipal authorities had locked out the employees. The Council by a majority ruled that conflicts within the administration of social assistance were socially dangerous unless limitations were placed on the ambit of the dispute.

These disputes arose in the course of several months of industrial conflict that have tested to its foundations the Swedish system of labour law. Government and LO policy in 1971 aimed at much greater equality of incomes. But great resistance was encountered, especially from SACO and SR. By March these organizations had called strikes of certain administrative and legal State officials, railway organizers (thereby closing passenger transport) and marine pilots, together with municipal social workers. The National Collective Bargaining Office and the municipal authorities responded by locking out thousands of other SACO and SR members including teachers in schools and universities, and giving notice even to selected groups of Army officers. On 11 March, after a one-day debate, Parliament enacted a Law giving the King in Council power to order that in a case of a dispute threatening essential interests of the community, lapsed collective agreements should come into force again for up to six weeks but in no case beyond 27 April. The collective agreements affecting SR and SACO members were renewed by proclamations on the following day. The Government had not, as in 1909, been able to stand aside as an observer; nor, as in the 1950s, to rely upon the mere threat of *ad hoc* legislation. This time the statute was passed – though, as can be seen, with a

Negotiations etc.' ('Slottsbacksavtalet'), Stockholm, 1966, Art. 16, 17 and 18. See the text in S. Jägerskiöld, *Collective Bargaining Rights of State Officials in Sweden*, Michigan, 1970.

strict time limit to its validity. Three mediation Committees had been appointed, one each for the State, municipal and private sectors of industry; and (as a matter of no small importance) the chairman presiding over each was ordered to consult with the other chairmen – a clear indication that the Government intended to enforce its incomes policy of 'equalization' as far as it could. In the State sector an agreement was reached with SF and TCO-S giving higher increases of salary to lower paid workers. But SR and SACO refused to sign. Moreover, they challenged as unlawful a clause in the agreements, which had been put into force, whereby the increase between 1 January and 13 March should not be paid to members of SR and SACO because they had resorted to strike action.[86] As for the private sector LO presented its claims but waited for the State to operate as the wage leader. When the employers refused the claims, LO first banned overtime and then gave a strike notice for some 10 per cent of its membership. But on 22 June a new three-year agreement was signed between the LO and SAF, by way of a compromise. So far, therefore, the 'voluntary' institutions of the Swedish system backed by brief *ad hoc* legislative intervention have survived the perils of social emergency disputes.

The German system has not yet been so tested. A brief summary of German law must distinguish the interesting but theoretical discussion of the emergency laws and one very practical institution which may be of much greater importance. First, as to the emergency laws, under the Bonn Basic Law, as amended in 1968, various situations are defined in which the Government might intervene directly. These situations may be summarized under three headings:

1. *Defence* or *crisis* where the Federal territory is attacked or stands in imminent danger of attack by foreign forces.[87] But such a situation must be proclaimed by a two-thirds majority of the Federal Parliament (and also in the case of actual attack, by the Federal Council or by an international organ acting within the framework of a treaty to which the Federal Government has adhered). In this case, the legislature appears able to go as far as the conscription of workers if this is necessary.
2. *Natural catastrophe*: where natural forces have produced an emergency situation and assistance is requested by one of the states;[88] and
3. *Internal dangers*: where there is an 'imminent danger to the continued existence of the liberal democratic basic order' of either the Federal régime or of one of the constituent states.[89]

In the two latter cases no prior proclamation by Parliament is required and the Government may legally use military or police forces for civil purposes: but this activity must cease on the request of the Federal Council and, in case 3, also on the request of Parliament.[90] Clearly the most important question

86. The Labour Court dismissed the action: case 1971/34.
87. Arts. 115(a), 12(a), sec. 3, 4 and 6; as applied by Art. 80(a).
88. Art. 35, sec. 2 and 3.
89. Art. 87(a), sec. 4; and Art. 91, sec. 1.
90. Art. 87(a), sec. 4, 91; sec. 2, 35; sec. 3.

arising is the meaning of 'imminent danger to the continued existence of the liberal democratic basic order'. No definition appears in the Constitution, but discussions which preceded the new Articles suggest that there is to be included any threat by an organization that falls within another Article declaring unconstitutional parties which, 'either by their aims or by the activities of their adherents' aim at endangering or eliminating that order.[91] This has been interpreted by the Federal Constitutional Court by contrasting a 'liberal democratic' regime with policies aimed at establishing an authoritarian State which rejects the dignity of man, freedom and the equality of citizens. Essential principles of this *rechtsstaatliche Herrschaftsordnung* include, the Court said:

> respect of those human rights set out in the Basic Law, especially rights of personality, of life and of free development, the sovereignty of the people, the separation of powers, the acceptance of the rule of law, the independence of the courts, the principle of a plurality of political parties each of which must have an equal right to exercise constitutional opposition.

The question arises, however, what is it that puts these five principles into 'imminent danger'? Prevailing opinion seems to include situations of 'intimidation by force' or 'coercion upon a constitutional organ', phrases which we have seen can assume a wide meaning in German Law (see above, p. 331). Because of the fears of trade unions that such provisions would allow for executive or legislative action against major strike action two provisions were inserted into the amended Basic Law, providing

(a) 'All Germans have a right to resist anyone who attempts to eliminate this (constitutional) order, if no other means is available.'[92]

(b) 'Measures must not be directed against labour disputes which are carried on by associations, in the sense of sentence 1, in order to maintain or improve labour and economic conditions' (Art. 9, sec. 3, sentence 3).

Here everything turns upon the meaning of 'association' (*Vereinigung*) a question much debated by German lawyers. The same word is used in sec. 2. The preceding sec. 1, however, refers to *Vereine und Gesellschaften*. If both of these are forms of 'association' in sec. 1, it can be argued that the association can be an informal one, temporary as well as permanent. In that case the protection applies not merely to official trade-union action but also to industrial action by unofficial groups. But the opposite view appears to be that *Vereinigung* includes only a permanent official trade union, especially when the Federal Labour Court has already declared 'unofficial' strikes to be *per se* unlawful.[93] According to ordinary labour law principles unofficial groups can-

---

91. Decision 23.10.1952 (on the Socialist Reich Party).
92. Art. 20, sec. 4. See above, p. 330.
93. But see T. Ramm, 'Die nichtgewerkschaftliche Streik', *Arbeit und Recht*, 1971, who argues that historically *Vereinigung* has the wider meaning, and that this was accepted as good law before 1933 (p. 97).

not be brought within the protection.[94] Furthermore, orthodox opinion (such as Professor Nipperdey) demands that the 'labour dispute' must be lawful as a dispute that could lead to a collective agreement. By the nature of the situation, one of 'imminent danger' to society, this is unlikely to be a test that such a strike could easily meet because it is almost bound to take on the appearance of a 'political' character. Opponents of this school of thought stress, however, that freedom of association is secured by Art. 9, sec. 3 and this must include freedom to represent collective interests even against State power. Even in such emergency cases, therefore, political strikes should be protected within this Article. The Federal Labour Court has not finally pronounced upon the ambit of Art. 9, sec. 3.

A further principle of German law can, however, here be relevant, similar to the questionable principle introduced in another context by the judges in Italy (see above, p. 341). The Federal Constitutional Court demands that a principle of 'reasonable proportion' shall govern all State interventions connected with public welfare. Thus it must not excessively burden citizens beyond what is required to reach the necessary objective. Decisions of the Constitutional Court have so far not concerned strikes in this connection, though the Court has accepted that the constitutional right 'to choose freely a profession', which is made subject in the Constitution to 'control by law', can be limited by the legislature to the extent that is reasonably required for other social purposes, for example to the extent that it is necessary to regulate the supply of certain goods such as pharmaceutical products.[95] It is not clear how far such principles might control the Federal Labour Court's interpretation of 'association' in connection with the emergency laws. Such questions of interpretation are, however, of little practical importance in the light of the extensive control over the right to strike of public employees (*Beamte*) and of the simple fact that, short of a major innovation by the Constitutional Court, the Government's action under such emergency laws, once effected, would be difficult to challenge subsequently.

Of greater practical importance is the *voluntary* control in emergency situations exercised by the German trade-union movement, a control which is not, as in Sweden, effected through bilateral agreements with employers but by means of *unilateral* provision in the rule books of the unions themselves. The origin lies in the history of the German trade-union movement in the Weimar Republic. As early as 1918 the Berlin Workers and Soldiers' Council had prohibited strikes in enterprises which were 'vital for life' including traffic, transport and food stores. In 1920 the umbrella organization of social democratic unions, the General German Trade Union Federation declared that the

94. Federal German Labour Court, 28.1.1955, BAG, Vol. 1, p. 291; 20.12.1963; BAG, Vol. 15, p. 174; and Hueck-Nipperdey, *Lehrbuch des Arbeitsrechts*, Vol. 2, p. 641: the right to be a party in a labour dispute can apply to an employer or organization of employers or workers but not 'an indeterminate and riotous mob in a temporary association'.
95. Decision 11.6.1958, B.Verf.G.E., Vol. 7, p. 405, S., on Art. 12, sec. 1 (the 'pharmacy' decision); and Decision 14.12.1965, B.Verf.G.E., Vol. 19, p. 337.

'vital interests of the public must be protected' and declared that the trade unions would 'themselves take over the necessary protection of the public interest against grave excesses of strike action and will require their members to furnish assistance which is made necessary by unofficial strikes'. Directives of 1922 designated water supplies, public health, funerals, railways, coal mining and even public administration and social insurance among the vital public services protected. No strikes were to occur within that area without conciliation and the authority of the Federation; and members of affiliated unions who refused to do emergency work were to be regarded as in serious breach of their union duties.[96] The origin of this self-regulation lay in the attempt by German unions to avoid the use of para-military groups for 'Technical Emergency Service' which were greatly feared by the unions as a mechanism for strike-breaking.

A tradition which had clearly sprung from days when (for example in 1918) workers were looking to the problems of taking power, was revived in a different setting after 1945. Partly in order to resist the attempts of the occupying Military Governments (especially in the French zone) to impose laws for compulsory arbitration and partly to avoid the resurrection of the Weimar experience of para-military anti-strike organizations, the trade unions revived these rules about maintenance of emergency services. Their efforts largely succeeded, the Law on 'Technical Aid Work' in 1953 being limited to cases where the 'social partners' (employers and unions) or public authorities were unable to maintain vital supplies, in which case the State could intervene to do the necessary work. The price, however, was the insertion of sec. 19 of the rules of the Federation of Trade Unions in 1949 providing for a set of guiding principles to bind member unions in industrial disputes. Section 6 of these principles states:

> The main union boards are obliged to report to the Federal Board before industrial action is taken in plants vital to sustain life, such as food or production, gas or water supplies, sewage, public health, funeral, traffic or coal mining enterprises, etc. They must inform the Federal Board of the reasons, the nature and planned extent of the proposed industrial action and the execution of emergency work in case of a strike. If in the opinion of the Federal Board the public interest involved in such industrial action appears to require it, the Board may take any measures necessary to conciliate in order to settle the dispute. The industrial action must be suspended until all suitable methods of settling the dispute are exhausted. In case of a difference of opinion which cannot be resolved in such a case between the Federal Board and the unions involved, the matter shall be taken to the Federal Advisory Council.

All German trade unions, therefore, have rules requiring their members to execute emergency work of the kind prescribed by the main Federal Board. A refusal by a member to execute such work is a 'grave violation of his duty' as

96. S. F. Nestriepke, *Die Gewerkschaftsbewegung*, 2nd ed., 1923, Vol. 2, p. 238 et seq.

a union member for which he can be expelled.[97] No court decisions have tested the result of a refusal by a union to maintain such emergency services. But the prevailing opinion seems to be that this breach would amount to a tort actionable by any injured third party by way of an action for damages or even an injunction. (Even if a trade union were to repeal its rule on this matter, the tradition is now so strong that it seems likely that the Federal Labour Court would hold that strikes which did not provide for the maintenance of essential public services were wrongful as lacking in 'social adequacy'.) Paradoxically, therefore, at the centre of a system of labour law which relies heavily upon legal regulation, the practical question of 'emergencies' in the sense of strikes which endanger vital social services, seems to be settled by a unilateral self-denying ordinance imposed upon itself voluntarily by the German trade-union movement. Although we find examples in other countries of unions voluntarily placing a limit upon their industrial actions (for example, the railway unions in Italy[98]), this seems to be one of the highest points of 'integration' of a Western trade-union movement into the society which surrounds it and a feature which, not being dependent in the Swedish fashion upon agreement with the employers, constricts its ability to confront that society with its full power.

The situation is very different in Italy and France, where such a rule in the fragmented trade-union movements would be unthinkable. Most of the discussion of the law of Italy is reserved for the later section on 'Public employees' – or what in the Italian context is more strictly described as 'service of a public character' (see p. 371), since it is impossible to make the division between such 'public servants' and workers who maintain essential services in Italian law. For the present it suffices to insist that the social *function* of the law relating to maintenance of services of a public character, although defined by the juristic category of 'public' employment, is precisely similar to that fulfilled by the rules of law which in other systems refer to the 'emergency' or 'socially dangerous' character of the industrial dispute or its consequences. We shall note that, in respect of workers in such 'public services', strikes are not necessarily justified by the presence of an 'economic' objective.

Italian law, does, however, include certain provisions that relate to emergencies by reference to the social situation rather than the public status of the workers. For example, the Government has a general power to use military forces for public purposes. This power it has used, without conscription of strikers or requisition of property, to continue work brought to a halt by strikes – for example, the running of buses and other transport. In the post-war years police were on occasion sent to milk cows in urgent need of attention. So too, if strike action has an effect upon periods of time or limitation required by law (such as the time limit on tax returns) the Government may extend such periods by Decree where it is urgent and necessary for action to be taken. But here the constitution demands that within five days the Emergency Decree

97. Grote, *Der Streik, Strategie und Taktik*, 1952, p. 98.
98. Compare Chapter 3, p. 142: maintenance of safety work.

must be presented to Parliament which has power to reject, accept or amend the text promulgated. Of more general and practical importance, local authorities (the Mayor or Prefect of a district for example) have important powers an matters connected with public health, housing and local police affairs.[99] Also, if a service is declared by administrative order to be essential for public purposes under Article 360 of the Criminal Code, then Article 330 becomes applicable, within the limits set by the courts (below, p. 371). Frequently action has under these powers been taken to guarantee a minimum service in hospitals, occasionally by means of a direct order to work, breach of which amounts to a misdemeanour; and in some of these cases the unions have not raised objection to such local interventions of the executive authorities.

In France we find a large area of 'emergency' law which, in practice, has fallen into disuse. In earlier decades from 1919 to 1938 the French Government possessed the power to conscript and mobilize strikers; but this gave way to a power of 'requisition' under the Law of 11 July 1938, now made permanent in the form of the Ordinance of 7 January 1959 and the Law of 21 July 1962. The law is usually discussed under the heading of 'Employees in Public Services'[100] but, while most orders of requisition have indeed been made in the public sector, the legal power to make them is not limited to that area of employment. The history of the development of this power to requisition 'not the man but the human machine'[101] from a power introduced for wartime purposes into a general control of emergencies in peace need not here concern us.[102] What is important is that disobedience to an order of requisition amounts not merely to *faute lourde* but also to a crime on the part of the worker who refuses to obey. What then are the limits of this power? The Government may make such an order only in regard to 'persons employed in a service or an enterprise regarded as indispensable to provide for the needs of the nation' – *les besoins du pays*. This power is not regarded by the courts as an infringement of the right to strike; but the administrative courts, ultimately the Conseil d'État, will confine the use of the power within the limits of the 'needs of the nation'.

The actual procedure involves three stages. First, a Decree made by the Council of Ministers opens the way to use of the power to requisition. Secondly, the Minister concerned decides upon a requisition by way of an Order (*arrêté*); and thirdly, on the basis of this order, the Prefect at local level serves the orders of requisition upon the workers either individually or collectively (e.g. at the factory or over the radio). In the latter case it is required that all available means be used to inform workers; and it is a method suitable only if all the workers of a plant or enterprise are under requisition.

Originally intended as an exceptional measure, the order of requisition was gradually used more and more frequently between 1948 and 1963. In 1953

99. Based upon Royal Decrees No. 148, 4.2.1915, Art. 153; No. 383, 3.3.1934, Art. 20; and No. 773, 18.6.1931, Art. 2.
100. H. Sinay, *La Grève*, 1966, Part IX, Chapter III, p. 411 et seq., 'Les Réquisitions'.
101. R. Escarpit, *Le Monde*, 5.3.1963.
102. See G. Lyon-Caen, 'La Réquisition des salariés en grève', *Droit Social*, 1963, April, p. 215, for a useful summary.

alone some 21,000 workers were involved; but the pace accelerated after 1958.[103] In some cases the orders were either ignored by strikers and in others their cancellation was a natural part of an agreement settling a dispute; but without doubt some strikes were broken by use of this blunt instrument of the criminal law. Nor were the courts quick to use their power of control by restricting the meaning of 'needs of the nation'. Indeed, the first time that the Conseil d'État (and, slightly earlier, indirectly the Cour de Cassation) set aside a Decree for requisition was in the *Isnardon* case which arose from the strike of tramway workers in Marseilles.[104] The strike, a *grève tournante* where groups struck in different places on various days, did not sufficiently affect the continuity of the service or otherwise strike at the needs of the people to justify a Decree, the court held. This was for a time thought to be a new liberal turn in the case law, but the expectation was short-lived. In 1962 in the *Moult* case, the Conseil d'État again gave, as in most of its decisions, a wide interpretation to the power to requisition. Moult was one of the pilots employed by Air France to navigate Boeing aircraft.[105] The strike was launched not by the whole staff of Air France but by all personnel who flew Boeing planes. The court held that having regard to the importance of the interruption in air travel and to the serious risk that its continuance could affect the whole of air transport, the 'needs of the country' were sufficiently affected; and that it made no difference that the Government may have had in mind the financial interests of Air France, including its own stake in the company. Professor Lyon-Caen asked: 'Where was the threat to public order?[106] Was not this just a question of avoiding financial loss to a public company or a loss of prestige to French airways'.[107]

In 1963 the Government appears to have over-reached itself. Orders of requisition were made on 2 March 1963 against thousands of coal miners who were on strike; but the response of the miners was to ignore the orders and the strike, now a celebrated precedent, lasted six weeks. Communications are slow in comparative labour law; for it seems impossible that the French authorities could not have heard of the precedent that leaps to the English mind – the strike of 4,000 Kent coalminers in 1941, illegal under a war-time order which led to the prosecution of 1,000 men, all of whom pleaded guilty, most of whom were fined and whose three leaders were sentenced to a month's imprisonment or more, events which led to a settlement of the strike (on the terms demanded by the strikers) by an agreement made between the leaders and the management in a Kent prison after a short visit to the gaol by the Minister and the Union's national secretary; to the release of the leaders after eleven days.[108] But the lessons in France were much the same. If diminu-

103. See H. Sinay, *La Grève*, p. 412.
104. *Rec. C.E.* (26.2.1961), p. 150; *Droit Social*, 1961, p. 356 (Savatier).
105. C.E. 26.10.1962, *Droit Social*, 1963, p. 224 (noted by Savatier).
106. This had been the test used by the Court of Cassation.
107. *Droit Social*, 1963, p. 218. The converse problem was raised in February 1971 in connection with a lockout of pilots.
108. See the delightful description in Appendix 6, Report of the Donovan Royal Commission, Cmnd. 3623, 1968, pp. 340–1.

tion in the supply of coal was enough to justify a requisition, what, demanded Professor Lyon-Caen, was left of the right of coal miners to strike when their strike could only be made effective by causing just that result? Moreover, he said:

> The efficacy of requisition lies in the threat of criminal sanctions; but public opinion will not for ever tolerate that those who exercise their rights should be dragged before criminal courts. Thus we can see that the chosen weapon (requisition) was inadequate for the desired objective – the control of the strike. In the law, procedural method must always conform in fact to the purposes pursued.[109]

Indeed, since the prolonged struggle of the miners in 1963 little or nothing has been heard in France of orders of requisition.[110] It had no place in the events of 1968. As to the future, discussion seems to have arisen mainly around the question whether requisition could ever be used against an employer who has conducted a lockout. Opinions on this differ; but since orders have been made against independent businessmen (e.g., bakers in 1950 and butchers in 1953) there would seem to be no essential objection to this being done, though it is scarcely conceivable in the case of a public enterprise.

One point may be added. In addition to the power to use police to enforce public order (including, at least theoretically, their use to permit non-strikers to pass through picket lines) the Government has a clear power to use troops to do the work left undone by strikers. Military trucks, for example, have often been used in Paris for public transportation during strikes; but, as in other countries, this replacement of ordinary workers by troops is hardly an effective or efficient method of solving the problem of emergency strikes.

As already indicated, in the United States the quest for a definition of the 'emergency dispute' and for an adequate procedure for dealing with it has given rise to a jurisprudence of vast proportions. The result seems to be largely negative; or at least, as one authority concludes: 'it is obvious that there is no single "correct" answer, no "final" solution to the problem'.[111]

The two major legislative provisions[112] are found in the Railway Labor Act 1926, covering interstate railways and also, from 1936, the airlines, and the 'Taft-Hartley' Labor-Management Relations Act 1947, Title II, secs. 206–10. The Railway Labor Act applies to controversies over changes in collective agreements, known as 'major' disputes. Collective agreements in the railroad industry have the rather 'British' feature, abnormal in the United States, of being of no fixed duration. A National Mediation Board has authority to intervene either on its own initiative or at the request of any party and, during

---

109. *Droit Social*, 1963, p. 219.
110. An order was made against air-controllers in October 1963; but a special Law of 2 July 1964 later made strikes illegal on their part.
111. B. Aaron, 'National Emergency Disputes: Is there a "Final Solution"?', 1 *Wisconsin Law Review*, 137, 1970, p. 147, agreeing with D. Cullen, *National Emergency Strikes*, New York, 1968, p. 125, n. 7.
112. For full material on 'The Protection of Public Interests' in US labour law see C. W. Summers and H. H. Wellington, *Labor Law*, 1968, Chapter 7, pp. 818–904.

its attempt to mediate in a dispute, the parties must maintain the *status quo*. As a next step, the Board urges voluntary arbitration; but if the parties refuse that, they must observe a 30-day waiting period when an Emergency Board sits, again with maintenance of the *status quo*, and reports to the President of the United States. The President may appoint such Emergency Board only after the Mediation Board reports that the dispute threatens to interrupt interstate commerce 'to a degree such as to deprive any section of the country of essential transportation service'. That Board examines the facts; may obtain an extension of time; and may, and usually does, include recommendations for a solution in its report which the President usually makes public to influence public opinion. But at the end of this procedure, if unions and employers reject the recommendations they are free to engage once more in industrial action. Between 1934 and 1967, 186 Emergency Boards sat in railroad disputes, the majority on issues that were local or concerned with one railroad company only: and from 1936 to 1967, 37 were appointed in airline disputes.[113] Few recommendations produced settlements in railway disputes of a national character (e.g., when unions made national wage claims); and the rejection rate by airline unions of recommendations in the 1960s reached 60 per cent, strikes occurring in all the principal disputes. There has emerged a general consensus that the Railway Labor Act has not achieved 'adequately the functions for which it was designed'.[114] Above all, the employers and unions have been criticized for 'ritualistic' refusals to consider the offer of voluntary arbitration and for failing to bargain at all until after the Emergency Board has reported; and the machinery is said to freeze normal bargaining and obstruct mediation, so much so that critics have 'compared not unfavourably the emergency board performance to a kabuki theatre'.[115] The Nixon Administration has, as we shall see, proposed changes for transportation 'emergencies'.

On some occasions, rather than allow the parties to relapse into ordinary industrial conflict at the exhaustion of the rituals under the Act, Congress has enacted special legislation; and on many more occasions it has threatened to do so. Thus in 1963, compulsory arbitration was directed by a Joint Resolution of Congress between national rail carriers and unions; in 1967 Congress, after directing postponement of a strike by six shopcraft unions, imposed a procedure for settlement by a 'Special Board'; and in 1970 laws were passed in one dispute to force a recalcitrant craft union into line first by postponement of a strike deadline and then by imposing upon it a settlement agreed by other unions, and, in December, compelling the postponement of another strike and imposing a settlement in a holiday season.[116] But union resistance has not in all these cases been quickly broken. In December 1970, for example, the railway clerks stayed out despite the law banning strikes, signed by a President reluctant to grant in effect a $13\frac{1}{2}$ per cent wage increase. Under the threat,

113. D. Cullen, *National Emergency Strikes*, p. 70-1.
114. American Bar Association's Special Committee Report, on 'National Strikes in Transportation', 13 June 1969.
115. J. Dunlop, 'Rome Paper', 1967, pp. 3-4.
116. Respectively Public Laws 88-108 (1963); 90-54 (1967); 91-203, 91-226, and 91-541 (1970).

however, of $200,000-a-day fines which could be imposed by the courts the union capitulated. As we shall see, these are not the only cases where *ad hoc* legislation has been discussed in the United States. In May 1971 the President responded to a nationwide signalman's strike paralysing the railways by asking for emergency legislation which would allow the executive power to take control of any means of transportation. But in July 1971 the threat of a national rail strike occurred again and the President's response this time was to state his belief that 'this industry can, should and is able to solve its own problems through the collective bargaining process'.

The Taft-Hartley Act 1947 applies to all other industries affecting interstate commerce. Here the emergency dispute procedures may be invoked by the President whenever in his opinion a threatened or actual strike or lockout 'affecting an entire industry or a substantial part thereof' will 'imperil the national health or safety'. If he so decides, he may appoint a Board of Inquiry which reports on the facts and issues in dispute but which is expressly forbidden to make recommendations. After such a report, the President may (in effect, does) direct the Attorney-General to seek from the relevant Federal Court an injunction against the strike, and this the court grants if it agrees with the President's opinion (as it invariably does). An argument that the sections must be limited to cases where the nation was in real jeopardy, and where the court was satisfied that no other means for solution of the dispute, was rejected by the Supreme Court in 1959, even though in the case in question only 1 per cent of the industry's product (steel) was used for defence purposes with which the peril to the nation was connected.[117] In practice, the only requirement needed to set the procedures in motion is the opinion of the President[118] and the decision to declare an emergency 'is essentially political and is as much a reflection of the incumbent President's temperament and style as of the actual or potential economic impact of the dispute'.[119]

This dominance in American experience of the subjective and policy element in the declaration of a dispute as an 'emergency' illustrates most clearly the impossibility of any clear anterior definition and – in the broad sense – the political character which Government intervention is bound to acquire under such laws.

After a Taft-Hartley injunction has been granted the Board of Inquiry is reconvened and it is the duty of the parties to attempt to settle their differences with the assistance of the Federal Mediation and Conciliation Service (FMCS), an independent public agency created by the same Act. The mediators appointed by the Service can make recommendations to the parties. The testimony of an author who was for many years director of that Service suggests that mediation may be easier if no injunction is sought. Sixty days after the injunction – the so-called 'cooling off' period – the Board is to make

117. *United Steel Workers* v. *United States*, 361 US 39, 1959; Douglas, J., wrote a powerful dissenting judgment.
118. See generally J. E. Jones, 'The National Emergency Disputes Provisions of Taft-Hartley Act', 1 *Western Reserve Law Review*, 1965, pp. 133–256.
119. B. Aaron, op. cit., 1 *Wisconsin Law Review*, 1970, p. 141.

a report on the parties' current position and what is the employer's 'last offer'; and within 20 days after that, a poll of the workers is to be held by the National Labor Relations Board (NLRB) on their willingness to accept that offer. The same author states that in the typical case 'cooling-off occurs for a period of time not exceeding the first half of the 80-day period. Thereafter "heating up" is a more appropriate term'.[120]

Various other parts of the procedure have been criticized by prevailing opinion. Professor Dunlop regards the whole procedure as 'uncommonly inept'; the Board of Inquiry, prohibited from recommendations, has sterile functions; while the required vote on an employer's last offer is 'simply silly' since it fails to understand the nature of collective bargaining.[121] Moreover, as Dunlop points out, a little-noted feature of the Taft-Hartley Law requires the President at the end of the 80-day period to submit a report to Congress with recommendations for action, so that an industrial dispute is inevitably 'transmitted into a political and public policy issue'. Despite these curiosities, however, the record of the Taft-Hartley procedures has not been as disastrous as might be expected. This may be largely due to the reluctance of some Presidents to invoke them, and, more, to the patient work behind the scenes of mediators such as the FMCS. Between 1947 and 1970, the provisions were invoked 29 times in disputes, in 22 of which strikes actually occurred. In four cases disputes were settled before the injunction; in thirteen other disputes settlement was reached within the 80-day period and in twelve *after* that period. Of the twelve, seven involved strikes all in the docks and maritime industries. But in two other cases (in bituminous coal) the injunction failed to end strikes.[122] And the dock strikes occurred at various intervals of time and included a 'three-month shutdown of Pacific Coast shipping . . . and several total or partial shut-downs of East Coast ports', from ten days to two months.[123] But no proceedings were taken in many other strikes which might well have been thought to 'imperil national health and safety' such as a 63-day strike at a General Electric jet engine plant. (It is no obstacle to use of Taft-Hartley that only one plant is involved as was proved when an injunction was upheld in 1952 against a strike at one American Locomotive plant supplying components to the Atomic Energy Commission.[124]) The machinery has in practice been used against strikes in coal, steel, water transportation, communications, and some plants important for military purposes.[125]

In 1970, President Nixon proposed to Congress a new law – the 'Emergency Public Interest Protection Bill' – to deal with the transportation in-

120. W. Simkin, *Mediation and the Dynamics of Collective Bargaining*, Washington, 1971, p. 205; and see Chapter X generally.
121. J. Dunlop, 'Rome Paper', p. 4. Simkin, op. cit., p. 210, also regards the 'last offer' vote as 'less than worthless'. In no case has the vote gone in favour of the employer's last offer!
122. L. H. Silberman, 'National Emergency Disputes', 4 *Georgia Law Review*, 673, 1970, p. 674.
123. D. Cullen, *National Emergency Strikes*, p. 61.
124. *US* v. *American Locomotive Company*, 109 F. Supp. 78 (DCNY 1952).
125. See R. Levin, 'National Emergency Disputes under Taft-Hartley', *Labor Law Journal*, 29, 1971, p. 40.

dustry. This would effectively bring transport, including the railroad and airline industries, under a system similar to the Taft-Hartley Law, except that after an 80-day 'cooling off' period the President would have three clear options: (*a*) to extend the period for up to 30 days; (*b*) to order partial operation of the industry concerned; and (*c*) to order the parties to submit their final offers to the Secretary of Labor, and, if no agreement could be reached, to have a panel of three arbitrators (appointed by the parties or, if need be, the President) choose between them. (The proposed law would also try to strengthen voluntary methods of reaching agreement in the railroad industry.) This proposal moves in the direction that appears to be approved by most American commentators, namely to give the President an 'arsenal of weapons' so that he has a much wider discretion in treatment of disputes which he dubs 'emergencies'. So serious is the crisis of emergency disputes thought to be that the Secretary of Labor in 1971 spoke of the choice of a new law – 'compulsory arbitration or . . . something like our Presidential option system including Final Offer Selection' – as involving a 'historic watershed' and the question: 'Can collective bargaining survive?'[126] In one sense it is curious that such anxiety should have been caused by strikes in a country where by 1968 collective bargaining covered no more than about 30 per cent of the non-agricultural labour-force,[127] a figure smaller than that of the 1950s and very much lower than that for the European countries under discussion. On the other hand, it may speak to the great strength of union organization in the crucial areas of industry in the United States.

Since the discussion in America has recently turned to the search for a new 'arsenal of options' in emergency cases, various other methods have come back into prominence. One proposal (by Senator Smathers) would give a new Court of Labor–Management Relations power to impose not merely an injunction but also a solution, fixing rates of pay and other conditions of employment that are 'fair and equitable . . . (and) within the employer's ability to pay'. A less extreme solution would be compulsory arbitration. Certain states passed statutes in the late 1940s prohibiting strikes in public utilities and providing for compulsory arbitration; but the Supreme Court held these to be unconstitutional if they covered fields to which the Federal National Labor Relations Act applied.[128] Proposals have been made for compulsory arbitration to be an 'option' available to the President via a proposal to Congress for *ad hoc* legislation.[129] In the past, apart from the use or threat of such legislation, two other types of Presidential intervention have been used. The first is *ad hoc* intervention to put pressure upon the parties, if necessary with the

126. Address by J. D. Hodgson to American Bar Association, London, 14.7.1971. On other proposals for amendment to the emergency laws see B. Aaron, *Labor Law Journal*, 1971, 461.
127. See Chapter 1, p. 17; and D. Bok and J. Dunlop, *Labor and the American Community*, Harvard U.P., 1970, p. 42.
128. *Amalgamated Association of Street etc. Employees* v. *Wisconsin Employment Relations Bd.*, 340 US 383 (1951). Some seventeen states have such laws; but they are valid only to the extent that they do not overlap with the NLRA, e.g., in regulating emergencies affecting interstate commerce.
129. B. Aaron, op. cit., 1 *Wisconsin Law Review*, 1970, p. 145.

appointment of a special Presidential *ad hoc* board of inquiry (something resembling the British 'Court of Inquiry'[130]). Such *ad hoc* interventions were frequently used by President Kennedy, in some cases even before a dispute proper had arisen between the parties.[131]

The second and different form of Presidential intervention is *seizure* of a plant which is then operated by the Government.[132] Various seizures were made under wartime powers in both World Wars or other special statutory authority; in fact the leading study discloses that between 1867 and 1967 some 94 cases of 'required production' can be found, 71 of them by means of seizure of the plants.[133] But when in 1952, President Truman attempted to use the power of seizure to take over steel plants without express statutory authority from Congress, his action was declared unconstitutional by the Supreme Court.[134] Similarly, since the power to authorize seizure vests in Congress, a State statute providing for seizure of plants in which the employees are covered by the National Labor Relations Act is also unconstitutional.[135] While the Taft-Hartley Law is widely criticized for certain features (the 'last offer' vote, for example, and the restrictions on inquiry boards) there are some, but fewer, critics who would prefer to introduce a new power of Presidential seizure in the place of its injunction remedy.[136]

Two final points may be briefly mentioned. There is clear statutory power for the President to use troops, including the 'Ready Reserve', to do the work of strikers.[137] The National Guard was, for example, used to do the work of postal workers during the national mail strike in 1970; and a threat to use troops was one of the weapons used by the President to break a rail strike in 1946. At state level, the same phenomenon has occurred, as in the Boston police strike of 1919. Lastly, there remains the possibility of conscription of strikers themselves. The President asked Congress to legislate that power for him in 1946, the request being for power to use mobilization as a punitive measure. Although the provision was never legislated, speakers in the debate supported the constitutional propriety of such laws; and while punitive conscription remains doubtful, judicial authority[138] seems to support the right of Federal or even state governments to legislate for the conscription of strikers to secure the performance of essential work.

130. See K. W. Wedderburn and P. L. Davies, *Employment Grievances and Disputes Procedures in Britain*, California U.P., 1969, Chapter 11.
131. C. W. Summers and H. H. Wellington, *Labor Law*, Foundation Press, New York, 1968, pp. 845–60 contains a useful summary: 'The great advantage of *ad hoc* intervention over existing statutory law . . . is its flexibility': p. 860.
132. See A. Cox, 'Seizure in Emergency Disputes', Chapter XII, in *Emergency Disputes and National Policy*, Bernstein (ed.).
133. J. Blackman, *President Seizure in Labor Disputes*, Harvard, 1967.
134. *Youngstown Sheet & Tube Co.* v. *Sawyer*, 343 US 579 (1952): (a minority of the Justices thought the President might have power of seizure in serious emergencies, but that here the Taft-Hartley Act had impliedly excluded that power.)
135. *Division 1287, Street etc. Employees* v. *Missouri*, 374 US 74 (1963.)
136. See Rehmus, 'Operation of the National Emergency Provisions', 62 *Yale Law Journal*, 1047, 1963. For the Nixon proposals, however, see p. 357, above.
137. Title 10 US Code, secs. 673; 3500; 8500; constitutionality upheld in *Morse* v. *Boswell*, 393 US 1052 (1968).
138. *In re Debs*, 158 US 564 (1895).

Of the American provisions on emergencies, the Taft-Hartley Law is without doubt the most important; and there is 'a fairly broad consensus that Taft-Hartley emergency provisions have not worked too badly'.[139] On the other hand, the number of situations in which they have been used has not (given the size of the workforce and the high incidence of strikes in the United States) been very large. In the middle of July 1971, for example, there was a national telephone strike, a strike of copper workers, of telegram employees, of West Coast dockers, and other impending strikes (once more the possibility of a national rail strike). But no emergency powers were being employed. One leading commentator, after discussing the alternatives concludes:

> Paradoxically then nearly *any* of the strike controls described . . . might have endured over the post-war period as tenaciously as the 80-day injunction of Taft-Hartley and the emergency board procedures of the Railway Labor Act . . . if Congress in 1947 had adopted some other strike control which had then compiled a mixed record over the next twenty years, imagine how difficult it would be today to argue for a change to such a one-sided and inconclusive technique as an 80-day injunction![140]

Despite this inconclusive history, Britain in 1971 adopted for the first time a new law on emergencies plainly modelled on the Taft-Hartley precedent. Until that year 'emergency' situations were met by three main provisions in British law.[141] First, the Emergency Powers Act 1920 allows the Government special powers after a Royal Proclamation of an 'emergency' in the sense that action has been taken or is threatened so as to be likely, by interfering with food, water, or lighting supplies or the means of locomotion, 'to deprive the community or any substantial portion of the community of the essentials of life.' The special powers include power to make any Regulations necessary to avoid this result and for 'purposes essential to the public safety and the life of the community'; but the Regulations must at once be laid before Parliament for approval and cannot continue for longer than seven days without a resolution in both Houses. If so approved the Regulations can create criminal offences but not so as to allow for punishment without proper trial. Moreover, two provisions expressly limit the range of the Regulations:

(*a*) No such Regulation may impose any form of 'compulsory military service or industrial conscription'; and

(*b*) No Regulation may make it an offence to take part in a strike or peacefully persuade others to take part in a strike.

Emergencies have been proclaimed under the Act of 1920 on six occasions between 1945 and 1971, three times in dock strikes, and on other occasions in the electricity, railways and shipping industries.[142]

139. B. Aaron, 1 *Wisconsin Law Review*, 1970, p. 146.
140. D. Cullen, *National Emergency Strikes*, p. 123.
141. Summarized in K. W. Wedderburn, *The Worker and the Law*, 2nd ed., 1971, pp. 388–95.
142. See for example The Emergency Regulations 1970; SI 1864/70, on the electricity industry under which Orders were in force for two days.

In 1964, a statute widened the Act of 1920 to include emergencies created by natural catastrophe. But more important the same statute made permanent the Defence (Armed Forces) Regulations, 1939, which had hitherto been regarded as temporary powers.[143] These regulations enable the Government to use the armed services without any consultation with Parliament on any 'urgent work of national importance', and this can clearly include the injection of troops to do work left undone by strikers. Troops have been used in certain cases, such as the dock strike of 1949 and gas strike of 1950, where the legal basis of their employment can only have been this unusual power, which was originally intended to be no more than a 'stop-gap' power[144] but which has now been made permanent.

Although it is not possible in this chapter to examine all special laws dealing with special groups of workers in each country, one other British Statute demands attention. The Conspiracy and Protection of Property Act 1875 (which, in sec. 3, protected simple 'criminal conspiracy' liability in trade disputes) provided that it was a crime for a worker employed in gas or water undertakings wilfully to break his

> contract of service. . . . knowing or having reasonable cause to believe that the probable consequence of his so doing, either alone or in combination with others, will be to deprive the inhabitants of that . . . [area] . . . wholly or to a great extent of their supply of gas or water. (Sec. 4.)

A statute of 1919 added workers in electricity enterprises to the list. The offence was committed only if employment contracts were broken; and this frequently led to strike notices being given by unions in these three industries in the form of notice to *terminate* employment contracts. Nevertheless, many gas and electricity strikers must have broken this law: but in 1968 the Donovan Commission had evidence of only one case in which criminal proceedings had ever been taken[145] – in 1950 against gas strikers – and in that case after a conviction the proceedings were withdrawn, the furore consequent upon the trial having made a settlement more difficult.

The Industrial Relations Act 1971, has repealed this criminal liability (sec. 133) but has retained in modified form the following section (5) of the 1875 Act. This makes it a criminal offence for any person wilfully to break a contract of service *or hiring* (a wider area) having cause to believe that the probable consequence of his so doing alone or in combination will be 'to endanger human life or cause serious bodily injury or to expose valuable property . . . to destruction or serious injury'. There must have been thousands of strikes in which this liability was risked by workers; yet there is no single recorded prosecution under the section. But the new British Government of 1970 considered that the abolition of sec. 4 of the 1875 Act was justified because 'the necessary safeguard against action leading to serious harm is pro-

143. Section 2, Emergency Powers Act 1964.
144. C. Grunfeld, *Modern Trade Union Law*, 1966, p. 478.
145. Royal Commission Report, H M S O, Cmnd. 3623, pp. 222–3.

vided by sec. 5'.[146] Accordingly the Industrial Relations Act 1971 retains the section, modifying it merely to the extent that a 'due notice' of strike action (i.e. notice equivalent in length to the notice contractually required from a worker to terminate his contract of employment) shall, for the purposes of sec. 5, cure any breach of a contract of employment (though not, it seems, other contracts of 'hiring') provided that the breach does not also include the breach of a 'no-strike' provision or any other obligation in that employment contract restricting the worker's right to strike.[147] Since many British strikes involve breaches of procedure that are now more likely to be part of a worker's employment contract,[148] it seems that the Government foresees that prosecutions under sec. 5 of the 1875 Act may well be brought in the future. On their face, the words of that statute are very wide and severe criminal liabilities could be created by hostile courts[149] if prosecutions were ever brought.

Until 1971, all that was to be added to the above was the power of the Government to use its conciliation services or to influence the parties and public opinion by the setting up of a 'Court of Inquiry', the recommendations of which had no binding force.[150] After 1969, there might also be a reference to the new Commission on Industrial Relations of any question concerning industrial relations; but once again, the findings of such an inquiry did not, and still do not, have any legal force.[151] Nor did the Donovan Report consider that there was need for further laws on emergency disputes. It recorded that proposals had been made to it (the Royal Commission) for laws similar to 'the power which the President of the USA has had since 1947 under the Taft-Hartley Act' but concluded that, in the light of the Government's wide range of conciliation and inquiry powers, the Commission did 'not think it has been shown that its powers need to be increased'.

> The record under the Taft-Hartley Act in the United States has been worse than the record in our country. We have been singularly free from strikes in recent years which would have come within the scope of a 'Taft-Hartley' kind of procedure.[152]

As for compulsory strike ballots, the Royal Commission decisively rejected proposals to introduce a law making them compulsory either generally or in selected cases.

The Industrial Relations Act 1971, however, has enacted in Part VIII both types of provision, which it is open to the Secretary of State to use either separately or cumulatively. First, he may apply for an order prohibiting in-

---

146. 'Consultative Document' on the Industrial Relations Bill (5.10.1970), para. 73; reprinted in K. W. Wedderburn, *The Worker and the Law*, Appendix, p. 485.
147. The effect of sec. 147(1), (2)(c) and (3).
148. By reason of sec. 20(2)(b) and (c) of the 1971 Act.
149. Prosecution would be in the ordinary criminal courts not before the new Industrial Court.
150. See K. W. Wedderburn and P. L. Davies, *Employment Grievances and Disputes Procedures in Britain*, Part III.
151. See now secs. 120–2, Industrial Relations Act 1971.
152. Donovan Report, paras. 420, 423 and 425.

dustrial action for a period of up to 60 days. Before he does so he must take the view:

(*a*) that a strike, or 'irregular' industrial action by workers, or a lockout, has begun or is likely to begin, in contemplation or furtherance of an industrial dispute;[153]
(*b*) that it would be conducive to a settlement if such industrial action were deferred; and
(*c*) that the industrial action has caused or would cause an interruption in the supply of goods or services as to be likely

    (i)   to be gravely injurious to the national economy; or
    (ii) to imperil national security or create serious risk of public disorder; or
    (iii) to endanger the lives of a substantial number of persons or expose them to risk of disease or personal injury.

These provisions are set out in sec. 138(1) and (2).

It can at once be appreciated that the new British law is markedly wider than the 'health and safety' formula of the Taft-Hartley Act, especially in that part that speaks of the 'national economy'. On the other hand, the Minister, in order to obtain his order, must prove to the new Industrial Court that there are 'sufficient grounds' for his belief that one of the conditions listed under (*c*) above does exist. If he does so the Court must make the order, specifying the area of employment and persons bound by it. The latter may include registered or unregistered unions and officials of the latter; but they may *not* include either workers that have no 'responsibility' for organizing the strike or irregular action or officials of a *registered* trade union who have acted within the scope of their authority.[154] The order will direct the persons specified that, during the period, they shall not organize, procure, finance or threaten the strike, irregular action or lockout in question; and it may require them to take any necessary steps to have the action deferred, such as withdrawal of instructions given to members of a trade union. Failure to observe such an order will not be merely an 'unfair industrial practice' under the new Act. It will rank as contempt of court and since the new Industrial Court has the same status as the High Court,[155] the penalties of this would be the normal ones of a fine or imprisonment or, in the case of a union, sequestration of its assets, of its officers' assets and their imprisonment. Power is given to the Court to extend the order, on the application of the Minister, to persons other than those specified in the original application.

The explanatory Government 'Consultative Document' which preceded the Act of 1971 explained that these provisions were aimed at disputes where 'whatever the merits or demerits of the case, the Government's prime duty and responsibility is to protect the public interest'. It is, perhaps, ironic that at

153. This at once excludes 'political' strikes: see above, p. 324.
154. Section 139(3) of the Act.
155. Industrial Relations Act 1971, Schedule 3, paras. 13, 27 and 28.

precisely the time when the American debate has turned to the search for a flexible 'arsenal of weapons' in the hands of the Executive to deal with emergencies, the new British law allows for only one type of remedy, namely an order against the organizers of industrial action that can last for only 60 days. While such traps as 'last offer' ballots have been avoided, no specific provision is made for the methods to be used in the stated period of settling what, by definition, is already a grave dispute. Whether such a period would lead to 'cooling-off' or 'heating-up' remains to be seen, though the latter seems more probable in view of the strong opposition of the British trade union movement to the whole Act. Few observers expect extended use of these powers by the Secretary of State. It is, perhaps, not insignificant that neither the first draft of the *Code of Industrial Practice*[156] nor the first booklet of guidance issued to employers by the Confederation of British Industries[157] makes any reference whatever to the steps that are desirable during the period of an Emergency Order.

The Act of 1971[158] also allows the Secretary of State to apply for a compulsory ballot of workers who are or are about to be engaged in a strike or irregular industrial action if he considers that there is doubt about the wishes of those workers. Once again he must apply to the Industrial Court for an order; but in this case he must show grounds for believing either that one of the conditions set out in (*c*) above exists or that the effects of the industrial action are or are likely to be 'seriously injurious to the livelihood of a substantial number of workers' in a particular industry. Before making such application he must consult any employer or employers' association or 'trade union' appearing to him to be a party to the dispute (but that does not include unions which refuse to register. The Court makes an order for a ballot among specified workers and for 'the question on which the ballot is to be taken', matters on which it may invite the assistance of the Commission on Industrial Relations. During the period of the ballot, the order will direct that no registered or unregistered union, employer, or other person (excluding a registered trade union's officials acting within their authority) shall call, organize, procure, finance or threaten a strike, irregular industrial action or lockout in respect of the workers concerned; and it may, again, require the withdrawal of instruction already given in that respect. Provision is made for the taking of the ballot fairly and secretly; but nothing in the Act limits the parties' persuading of workers to vote one way or another. In particular, nothing prevents an employer from stating that he will dismiss the workers if they strike. On the contrary, his right to do so (except in cases where he discriminates against trade-union members by way of 'unfair dismissal') is expressly preserved by the Act.[159] The result of the ballot is then reported by the

156. *Code of Industrial Practice* (Consultative Document, June, 1971, Department of Employment). The Code will be taken into account in interpreting the Act and in assessing the degree of responsibility of parties in breach of it.
157. *Guidance to Employers on the Industrial Relations Bill*, CBI, June 1971.
158. Sections 141–4.
159. Section 147(4).

Commission to the Court and the Court then publishes the result. No further legal consequences ensue.

These sections on strike-ballots are also enshrined in Part VIII of the Act headed 'Emergency Procedures'. It seems more than likely that such a compulsory ballot would merely increase the tension of such a crisis. As the Donovan Report suggested, such evidence as there is suggests that workers will vote for rather than against a strike in such a ballot; and once that happens a settlement may be impeded. The Report, echoing American experience, added a question to which the Industrial Court will have to find an answer:

> Moreover how is the question on which the vote is to be taken to be framed? If the vote is, for instance about whether to accept the employer's latest offer, its result can be stultified if the employer subsequently makes a slightly improved offer.[160]

Public employees

In order to examine the notion of the 'national interest' in the context of industrial conflict one must clearly examine the law and practice concerning persons employed by public authorities, national or local, and workers regarded as having a special 'public' status. For one thing, the State can control their activities and often their wages and conditions of work being at one and the same time the source of law and either their employer or the power in practice behind their employer (as in the case of nationalized companies). But in all the countries under discussion except Britain, this topic involves a wide area of law which would demand a separate study of its own.[161] Here we can only touch upon a bare outline. Often as in Germany, France, or the United States, the 'public servant' is judically in a quite distinct category. True, the facts today are causing some jurists to question this deep-seated division in their traditional concepts. In 1968, Professor Lyon-Caen declared:

> The Accords de Grenelle for the first time rightly joined together in the same document relating to civil servants (*fonctionnaires*), employees in the public sector and employees in the private sector. Should we not draw from this fact certain conclusions as to the unity of Labour Law? . . . Why not decide that the whole of Labour Law is applicable to the public sector?[162]

To British ears this may not sound so strange; to many Continental and American lawyers it may still be little less than shocking.

Perhaps Germany illustrates the Continental tradition most strongly. The German *Beamte* (public official) is distinguished by a special status. He may be employed by the Federal or a state authority or by any of the national or local public bodies or public corporations. He includes for example a railway

160. Donovan Report, para. 429.
160. See F. Schmidt, 'Public Officials as a Separate Category of Employees', Report to Sixth International Congress of Labour Law and Legislation (Stockholm, 1966).
162. *Droit Social*, 1968, p. 447.

employee in a position of responsibility alongside the civil servant proper. He carries with him the features even today of a servant of an absolute monarch, having no employment contract but a status governed by public law. The traditional view is that by reason of his status he has no right to strike, a prohibition made explicit in the constitutions of two of the states (Rheinland-Pfalz and Bavaria). But the normal justification of the prohibition is found in the very principles governing public officials (*Bernufsbeamte*) or in their 'obligation of fidelity' which allows for no collective offensive economic action. This principle is mentioned in the Constitution.[163] Nevertheless, as in the 1920s in Germany and in other countries with similar concepts of State Officials, industrial action by public officials does occur. Various cases of 'working to rule' and refusal to work overtime (e.g. by teachers) have occurred in recent times, and traditional sanctions are not now always applied even to those who strike. The traditional sanctions include reprimand, fines, a temporary reduction in salary, transfer to a post with lower salary, reduction or loss of pension or dismissal.[164] With the exception of the first two, these sanctions can be applied to Federal officials only by a decision of the Federal Disciplinary Court from which an appeal lies to the Federal Administrative Court. But the equivalent sanctions at state level were not applied in 1970 to university assistants who, despite being public officials, went on strike[165] to influence the legislature of their state (Hesse) in respect of prospective legislation on the universities. The reason, however, lay not in any weakening of the law, but in the reluctance of the Minister of Education to initiate disciplinary proceedings against a group with whose objectives he sympathized. There has arisen in fact a much greater general reluctance to discipline public officials. This appears to be the reason for paucity of judicial decisions in recent years.

The status of the German public official is such that, in the absence of a breach of discipline, he cannot be dismissed. Traditionally this status, under which the State secured for him life-long employment, was given as the distinguishing mark that divided him from the ordinary employee. But today the gap has narrowed for the German worker is legally protected generally against unjust dismissal and in particular against dismissal by reason of a lawful exercise of the right to strike. This change in the social climate has led a minority of German jurists to argue that there should be no general prohibition upon strikes by public officials[166] and that any prohibition must be justified by virtue of the social function fulfilled in a particular job not merely by reason of the existence of the status of public official applicable often for merely historical reasons, to a particular worker. They call in aid the

163. Bonn Basic Law, Art. 33.
164. The Federal Discipline Order (*Bundesdisziplinarordnung*), 1967, para. 5.
165. For other examples see W. H. McPherson, *Public Employee Relations in West Germany*, Michigan, 1971, pp. 177–87 (air controllers, teachers, municipal workers and medical 'assistants' though most of these were not strictly Beamte).
166. W. Benz, *Beamtenverhältnis und Arbeitsverhältnis*, 1970; W. Daeubler, *Streik im öffentlichen Dienst*, 2nd ed., 1971; T. Ramm, *Das Koalitions und Streikrecht der Beamten*, 1970.

European Social Charter (ratified by Germany) which in Art. 6(4) appears not to exclude public officials from the right to strike. The First Report of the Committee of Experts of the Council of Europe declared that the German Report to them which stated that public officials had no right to strike was a 'state of affairs ... incompatible with the Charter' since 'the complete suppression of the right to strike for public servants was not permissible' and rejected the argument that this was justified in the interests of 'public order and State security'.[167] In a manner curious to British eyes, traditional German law distinguishes entirely between the right to strike and the right to organize. German public officials enjoy with other workers full freedom of association by way of the right to organize. Indeed, that right extends even to members of the armed forces many of whom are trade-union members. But collective bargaining is limited to groups of manual and white collar workers in the public service; and it is not thought illogical by orthodox lawyers even then to deny such workers the right to strike. So strong is the division between the categories of public and private law.

From different origins the law in the United States has encountered similar problems. On the one hand, jurists encountered difficulty with the very concept of collective bargaining to which the Government (Federal or State) was a party, for this was felt to impinge upon the 'sovereignty' of the legislature. On the other hand:

> At Common Law no employee, whether public or private, had a constitutional right to strike in concert with his fellow workers. Indeed, such collective action on the part of employees was often held to be a conspiracy. When the right of private employees to strike finally received full protection it was by statute, sec. 7 of the National Labor Relations Act. ... It seems clear that public employees stand on no stronger footing in this regard than private employees and that in the absence of a statute they too do not possess the right to strike.[168]

The Court mentioned that, while public employees had the full right to free association, among the reasons why Government might properly deny a right to strike to public employees were the 'prerogatives of the sovereign'; the 'higher obligation associated with public service'; the need to assure 'continuing function of the Government', and to protect 'public health and safety'. No American judges ever seem to have put the German position better. As in other systems, the United States has gradually extended to public employees the right to organize and the right to bargain; but it stops short of granting the right to strike. Any doubt upon the matter at Federal level was put to rest by the Taft-Hartley Act 1947 which made it unlawful for any individual employed

167. Supplement to Conclusions I (Strasbourg, February 1970), p. 27. For the general interpretation of Arts. 6(4) and 31 see First Report (8 December 1969), pp. 43–5. The right of States to limit strikes by persons employed in 'essential public services' or by certain public servants such as 'police, armed forces, judges and senior civil servants' was, in the Committee's view, consistent with the Charter: ibid., p. 44.
168. *United Federation of Postal Clerks* v. *Blount (Postmaster General)*, 325 F. Supp. 879 (D.D.C.).

by the Government or any Government agency including a wholly-owned corporation to 'participate in any strike', and added that such a participant 'shall' be discharged, forfeit his civil service status and be ineligible for Government employment for three years (sec. 305). In addition, a strike by Federal employees is a felony:[169] and such an employee must swear an oath that he is not participating and will not participate in a strike against the United States Government, breach of which can be sanctioned by a prosecution for perjury. Since the Norris-La Guardia Act 1932 does not apply, the Federal Government can obtain an injunction against unions of public employees which strike. At state level provisions of a not dissimilar character are found. Twelve states totally prohibit employee strikes,[170] and in general, state courts are able to enjoin such strikers even without the aid of statutes. Some states, such as New York, have punitive penalties which forfeit twice the daily pay of a public employee on strike for each day on strike. Two States (Hawaii and Pennsylvania) have made limited forms of state-employee strikes lawful, and one other (Vermont) recognizes such strikes by municipal employees only so long as public health safety or welfare are not endangered. It is a notable feature of the American scene that the concepts of political sovereignty and public welfare came to be applied down the line, from Federal to state to municipal level in such a way that, on the right to prohibit strikes, each 'sovereign' township operates as if it were a national state. The Committee of the Federal Bar Council on Labor Law suggested in 1971 that: 'the traditional inhibitor of strikes against the Government – that is respect for the sovereignty of Government – still retains greater applicability to the Federal Government than to local governments.'[171]

But of course there has been a massive increase, in fact, in strikes by public employees. Between 1958 and 1968 they increased from 15 to 254 stoppages involving respectively 7,510 and 2,545,200 'man-days idle'. By 1970 the hitherto predominantly State-employee strikes had spread to the Federal service; and that year saw massive stoppages by the national postal workers and by the air controllers (including a mass 'sick-out' on their part – a novel form of industrial struggle by concerted reporting of illness by the employees). The sanctions just have not worked; and the same Committee commented that the severe penalties of Federal law were not imposed on the mail strikers 'because postal services could not be restored by adjudging 160,000 postmen felons and firing them'. The same fate overtook the United States' laws on public-employee strikes in 1970 as that which hit the French 'requisition' in 1963. Accordingly, American jurisprudence is beset by the quest for a new basis for public-employee bargaining (which has, as we note below, developed lawfully and powerfully). But most of it is still concerned to find a reason why public employees should *not* be allowed more than the most limited rights to take industrial action. The conceptual apparatus of 'sovereignty' is clearly

169. Chapter 390, 69 Stat. 624, 18 US Code, sec. 1918.
170. J. Seidman, *State Legislation on Collective Bargaining by Employees*, Labor Law *Journal*, 13, 1971, p. 18.
171. *Labor Law Journal*, 173, 1971, p. 181.

inadequate in the face of modern social facts. As Secretary of Labor Wirtz said in 1966: 'This doctrine is wrong in theory; what's more, it won't work'. It has now largely given way to attempts to find a profound economic or social distinction between the character of private and public-sector employment – in the former (it is said) the employer being 'motivated by the necessity to maximize profits', whereas the public sector model is taken as either the municipality whose Mayor bargains against a background of political not market pressures or the central governments, where strikes by public employees necessarily threaten sovereignty in the sense of the 'normal American political process.'[172] Not all lawyers are ready to accept these limitations[173] Public employment is not conterminous with 'essential services' (for example santitation-workers in Philadelphia are employed by private contractors and seem to have a right to strike denied to colleagues in most other municipalities). Nor can the division between a 'public' and 'private' sector be regarded as a chasm in days when the great private corporations are maintained by public 'defence contracts'; and one hardly needs to be a disciple of Professor Galbraith at least to question the model of the private entrepreneur who always aims to maximize his profits. As for the injection of an 'alien element' into the normal legislative process, such statements merely apply *a priori* solutions upon a social situation in which political and industrial power-problems are inextricably intertwined. Even so, few American jurists can swallow the idea of a right to strike for public employees, for they conceptualize the basic question in question-begging terms, such as 'whether the strike, which in the United States has been viewed primarily as an economic weapon is equally appropriate when used as a political weapon'.[174] It is thus in the context of the illegality of public employment strikes that the illegality of the 'political' strike tends to be discussed in the United States – as an attack upon the public authority by its own employees.

Both at municipal, State and Federal level the answer has been sought in laws which allow for collective bargaining while not opening the way to lawful strikes. In New York, for example, the 'Taylor Law' of 1967 developed that method. Similarly the Postal Reorganization Act 1970, setting up the Postal Service, allows for collective bargaining agreements of up to two years duration with recognized trade unions and provides that industrial disputes are ultimately to be referred to the FMCS which has power to appoint a 'fact-finding panel' of three persons to report with recommendations on the dispute. If no agreement is reached on the basis of that report, the dispute is referred to an Arbitration Board of three other persons of which the decision 'shall be conclusive and binding upon the parties' (sec. 1207(c)(2)).

172. H. H. Wellington and R. K. Winter, 'The Limits of Collective Bargaining in Public Employment', 78 *Yale Law Journal*, 1107, 1969, especially pp. 1119–26; and the same authors in 79 *Yale Law Journal*, 805, 1970.
173. See the criticism of H. H. Wellington and R. K. Winter, 79 *Yale Law Journal*, 418, 1970, by J. Burton and C. Krider. (Since the completion of our study Wellington and Winter have developed their views in: H. H. Wellington and R. K. Winter, *The Unions and the Cities*, Brookings Institution, 1971.)
174. J. Steiber in *Challenges to Collective Bargaining*, L. Ulman (ed.), 1967, p. 83, nevertheless a most valuable survey.

A similar solution is sought in the Federal Executive Order 11491, which has since October 1969 governed labour-management relations in Federal employment. All strikes, 'slowdowns', picketing and the like are prohibited, together with disciplinary action by a union against members who fail to engage in any type of industrial action (sec. 19(b)). Moreover, no union is to be recognized which asserts the right to strike against the Federal Government or any of its agencies (sec. 2(e)(2)). With that limitation, employees – other than supervisory and higher grades – are given the right to join a labour organization. The Order establishes a Federal Labor Relations Council and a Federal Services Impasses Panel. The former determines which organizations have sufficient membership to entitle it to the stated rights of consultation in any area of employment, and after a ballot a union may, in the characteristic American fashion, become the exclusive agent of a unit of employees. Federal agencies are obliged to confer upon certain matters relating to employment conditions with recognized unions; but a list of topics is excluded from consideration. This list narrows bargaining severely since it includes the 'mission' and budget of the agency, its organization, the number of employees, numbers and grades of workers assigned to a unit, the 'work project or tour of duty', the technology of the agency's work or its internal security practices, though agreements providing against the adverse effect on workers of technological change are expressly allowed (sec. 11(b)). A long list of management prerogatives is set out, including the right to hire, discipline and dismiss, and to 'maintain the efficiency of the Government operations entrusted' to the agency. Grievance procedures may be agreed; but where there is an industrial dispute, the first step is an attempt at settlement by the FMCS. In the absence of voluntary agreement, either side may request the Federal Impasses Panel to consider the matter and that Panel may 'in its discretion' settle the impasse 'by appropriate action'. Report to arbitration of third-party fact-finding is allowed only when authorized by the Panel (sec. 17). Thus there is no right even to arbitration; and it is a strange form of collective bargaining which, having deprived the unions of the right to use their economic power, leaves the settlement to the discretion of a Panel appointed by the President. It seems unlikely, when government employment is the fastest growing sector of the workforce and with public-employee unionism having risen from 915,000 in 1956 to 2,155,000 in 1968 (from 5.0 to 10.7 per cent of total union membership), that this scheme will be the final solution of the problem.

> To achieve a viable system of [public] labor relations . . . will require more than orderly procedures for recognition, for the establishment of negotiating relationships and for impasse resolution; it will also demand the development within public agencies of skilled management concerned with constructive relationships with employee organizations and with aggressive ideas to reduce labor costs rather than with rights of sovereignty.[175]

The English observer is tempted to add that it may also demand a right to strike.

175. D. Bok and J. Dunlop, *Labor and the American Community*, p. 339; see pp. 312–41 for a valuable survey of the problem.

As we have already seen, the rights of public employees in Sweden are now dealt with in the State Officials' Act and Municipal Officials' Act of 1965. As in Germany, the Swedish 'public official' (*ämbetsman*) was from the seventeenth century regarded as quite distinct from the employee. Governed by public law, he could not be removed except for serious misconduct; and the concept that he held his office in almost a proprietary fashion predominated. Naturally the counterpart was provision of a severe kind in the Penal Code against certain misconduct, including industrial action. But by 1937, public officials had organized in trade unions; and an Order of that year allowed for minimal rights for State employees by way of consultation before employment conditions were determined. In 1940, similar rights to information and prior consultation were granted to municipal officials; but there was no bargaining in either sector, still less a right to strike. Nevertheless, social fact again ran ahead of the letter of the law and bargaining did begin. By the 1950s certain national federations were recognized by the Minister of Civil Affairs and the *de facto* agreements made between them on State officials were accorded legal recognition on a yearly basis, provided the approval of the King in Council and of Parliament was given. Such agreements included a 'no-strike' clause. By 1962 a working party was set up to consider reforms on the basis that State and municipal officials should be granted bargaining rights on salaries and related benefits but otherwise employment conditions should still be unilaterally regulated.

The Acts of 1965 were the result. The State Officials Act[176] on which we concentrate here was, as we saw (see above, p. 344) promoted by the Minister on condition that the unions entered into the Basic Agreement of 1966 establishing the special procedures for 'socially dangerous' disputes. The Act provides that questions of remuneration and related employment conditions shall be determined by collective bargaining, but other questions (such as distribution of work, number of employees, or even working hours) shall remain the prerogative of the State for unilateral determination (Art. 3(1)(2)). In industrial disputes which concern matters which may be the subject of bargaining, it is expressly made lawful for the parties to engage in strikes or lockouts except in breach of their collective agreements; but otherwise no industrial action may be taken. The limitations in the 1965 Act are additional to the normal 'peace obligations' arising in Swedish law from the Collective Agreements Act 1928. Moreover, a State official is permitted to strike only 'officially', i.e. after a decision to strike by a trade union (Art. 15). It is to be noted that only strikes and lockouts are permitted. Sympathetic action is lawful in support only of other unions in State employment where their strike is lawful. Action in solidarity with private employees is unlawful.

The operation of the Basic Agreement, 1966, which accompanied this legislation, and the strikes of 1971 which have been the first major test of the new system, have already been discussed (see above, p. 345). Although the

176. Published with the Basic Agreement of 1966, as 'Collective Bargaining Rights of State Officials in Sweden', Stockholm, 1966. See also S. Jägerskiöld, *Collective Bargaining of State Officials in Sweden*, Michigan, 1970.

right to strike effectively granted to public officials is in practice severely attenuated, the events of 1971 show that is likely to be used increasingly. What is remarkable about the Swedish solution is that, commencing with all the theoretical disadvantages of German theory, it has sought a pragmatic solution which has dared, as American law has not, to accord to the public employee at least the basic right to engage collectively in industrial conflict.

A not dissimilar contrast may be drawn between Italy and France. In Italy commentators dispute the extent to which the right to strike may be extended. Some argue that it should be extended only for workers in a weak position in bargaining (such as salesmen and dockworkers in cooperatives), others that it must be seen as a legitimate form of self-help and therefore include attorneys and doctors and similar groups. The latter groups in practice certainly do organize strike action. But groups of public employees such as civil servants of the State, the police and armed services are considered not as employees but as public officials enjoying a special status. Police and military personnel were traditionally denied the right to organize in trade unions and, naturally, the right to strike; and a special statute of 1946 confirmed this position for the police. On some occasions courts have avoided the imposition of sanctions demanded by the laws relating to such persons, as in the case of a strike by municipal policemen in 1965 who were 'excused' by reason of their honest mistake of law in believing that they had a right to organize and strike. In 1966, however, a much criticized decision of the superior court of public law reaffirmed that even civil servants in police organizations had no right to organize in trade unions, the reasoning of the court being based on the odd ground that such trade unions would be 'political' organizations.[177] Although the conditions of their employment are theoretically regulated by law, bargaining does in fact occur between unions and the State, and collective agreements are often the real basis of those conditions. From this, commentators now argue that such 'public officials' should have a legal right to organize. On the other hand, traditional doctrine is so harshly opposed to strikes by public officials that other writers apply to them the law relating to rebellion or mutiny.

But Italian law makes use of a further classification. Under the Penal Code of 1931, Art. 330, it is a crime punishable by imprisonment for two years for three or more persons to leave their work collectively or to act in any other way so as to disturb the continuity of work if they are either public officials proper or persons charged with a public service, including private employees exercising public services or employed in enterprises of public service or essential to public needs. Among the latter, Art. 359 includes specifically attorneys and medical personnel. The organizers of such strikes are liable to imprisonment for up to five years, or even more if the strike has a 'political' rather than an industrial objective.[178]

This Article, also dating from the Fascist era and even earlier, covers much of the ground dealt with by the 'emergency' provisions of other countries'

177. *Cons. di Stato*, 4.2.1966.
178. Article 333 also renders individual cessation of work a crime in similar circumstances.

labour laws. It has, however, been subjected to interpretation of some complexity by the Constitutional Court. In 1962 the Court refused to hold that the Article was completely unconstitutional, but held that its application was limited by 'general interests recognized by the general principles of the Constitution'. The Court held on the same day (in a decision prohibiting seamen's strikes during voyages) that the Article applied wherever serious damage would be caused to the interests or security of the community of a kind recognized in the Constitution.[179] From this it concluded that certain categories of employees had no right to strike since their stoppage would endanger community interests. Professor Giugni has criticized this conclusion on the ground that there may well be workers within those categories who can strike without causing such danger,[180] for example groups of office workers employed in public service enterprises. In a later decision of 1969, the Constitutional Court further limited Art. 330[181] declaring that the Article is unconstitutional in so far as it aims to punish the exercise of the right to strike. This decision, which amounts to a partial repeal of the Article, found legitimate those strikes by employees in the public service sector which aimed at achieving legitimate 'socio-economic objectives'; and it is a prevailing view among commentators that the latter may include wider 'economic' interests than those expressly mentioned in the Constitution. Even in 'economic' strikes, however, the normal principle that a public servant is entitled to his salary by virtue of his status and not in return for work is displaced, the Court having held in 1967 that payment need not be made during a strike.[182] The extent to which Art. 330 of the Penal Code and associated Articles currently limit the right to strike of employers in the public service industries is, therefore, not wholly clear. Its effect is likely to be small in the area of ordinary economic strikes even if certain public services are interrupted. Professor Miele has supported a wider application of Art. 330 arguing that it applies wherever a strike infringes any of the rights expressly or impliedly protected by the Constitution, including safety; freedom; dignity; equality, and the right to work.[183] Naturally, in certain cases specific crimes might be committed contrary to Articles other than 330 and in that event the strikes would not be justified.

Recent laws mark a growing recognition of collective labour law generally in the public sector. In 1968 a Law (No. 249) protected against discrimination the organization of trade unions by public officials in State administration and certain trade union activities by them. No mention was made of the right to strike and this question was left, as Miele points out, in a position of obscurity. But although the 1968 law protects such officials it does not seem to have been a consequence that they are also protected against administrative sanctions such as suspension and dismissal.

Lastly, a Law of October 1970 (No. 775) provides that the wages, salaries

179. Decisions No. 123 and No. 124, 28.12.1962.
180. G. Giugni, *Diritto Sindacale*, p. 191.
181. Decision No. 31, 1969. See also, Onida, 'La Sciopero politico è un diritto', op. cit.
182. Decision No. 470, 22.3.1967; also see Chapter 4.
183. See *L'Esercizio del diritto di sciopero*, Milan, 1968, p. 183.

and pensions of both white collar and manual workers in the public sector may be regulated by collective agreement. The juridical method adopted makes a genuflection to traditional concepts by declaring that such conditions of employment are to be determined by Government regulations which incorporate the terms of collective agreements negotiated between the Government and trade unions (Art. 24). But public officials proper in the narrower category, who occupy a position similar to the German *Beamte*, are not covered by this provision.

In France, too, we find two different categories in the public sector. Of the 2·4 million public employees in France about half fall into the category of *fonctionnaires* (civil servants) employed by the State, departmental or municipal authorities. These civil servants are governed not by the normal labour law but by public law. As in Germany and Italy, and in Sweden before 1966, they are seen to be not in a contractual employment relationship but the holders of offices of which, fundamentally, the relevant authority is in control. The remaining half are *salariés des services publics* (public service employees), employed by such bodies as nationalized enterprises or enterprises in which the State has partial ownership, or even by private enterprises if they operate a public service (such as certain agencies concerned with social security). In this category, normal labour law applies but with modifications from enterprise to enterprise. The category is of special importance by reason of the primary role played by bargaining in the public sector in France, which acts as a wage-leader for the rest of industry. A decree of 1 June 1950 listed among these enterprises the Bank of France, Air France, the coal mines, electricity and gas enterprises and other major enterprises; and the Government has power to add to the list.[184] Such enterprises are known as *entreprises à statut* (controlled enterprises) because the conditions of employment in them can be controlled by a 'statut', either by way of a Law or an Order of the relevant administrative authority. Thus, their employees are *sui generis*, being controlled by a law which is partly private (labour) law and partly public law.[185]

It might be expected that French law would start out from the basis that one or other of these groups has no right to strike. Exactly the opposite is the case. Such is the force of the constitutional right to strike that even the civil servant enjoys it. The Conseil d' État recognized in the *Dehaene* case, 1950[186] that this right extended to all citizens including civil servants. Indeed, it has been remarked that public service employees have made more frequent use of the strike weapon than workers in private industry, possibly because they do not ordinarily enjoy the ordinary laws relating to collective bargaining and agreements. Given the nature of the status of civil servants and the character of the work done by public service employees, however, it is hardly surprising that the courts have accepted as valid statutory or regulatory limitations upon the right to strike of particular groups. For example, statutes or ordinances have deprived of the right to strike, members of the police forces, judges of

184. G. Belorgey, *Le Droit de la Grève et Les Services Publics*, 1964, p. 89.
185. H. Sinay, *La Grève*, p. 369; see Part IX generally on ' Salariés des services publics'.
186. C.E., 7.7.1950; *Droit Social*, 1950, p. 317. See generally F. Meyers, *The State and Government Employee Unions in France*, Michigan, 1971, Chapter III.

all types, prison warders and air-controllers.[187] Each Minister may by way of regulation (*arrêté* or *circulaire*) place limitations upon the right to strike in public service enterprises which come under his authority. Such limitations have been applied to the railways, public transport in Paris, and to the Post Office (in which the workers are civil servants). The *Dehaene* case accepted the constitutionality of laws and ordinances limiting the right to strike (in that case of the police); but in the case of Ministerial regulations the Conseil d'État demands proof that the regulation in question, which may place either temporary or permanent limits on strikes, is justified by the requirements of the public interest. This limitation has rarely been used. Regulations have required notice of strike action or prohibited certain types of strike such as *grèves tournantes* (rotating or 'rolling' strikes, taking place in different plants on different days). Certain commentators have argued that both the legislative and regulatory method should be regarded as limited further by the law of 1963 (which is mentioned below);[188] But the Conseil d'État refused to accept the 1963 law as a complete definition of the right to regulate the right to strike and in 1966 upheld the earlier case law accepting both the legislative and regulatory method of limitation.[189]

In 1963 Parliament intervened to place a restriction upon public employees working for the State or for departments and communes with more than 10,000 inhabitants, and workers in public service industries, in particular those controlled enterprises listed in the Decree of 1 June 1950.[190] Two major prohibitions are laid down in this Law of 31 July 1963. First, strikes without notice are made unlawful, a minimum of five days' notice being required. Moreover, notice can be given only by the 'most representative' trade unions in the relevant enterprise or service – a concept which has given rise to a wide variety of interpretation. (One difficulty is caused by the text speaking of the most representative union 'at national level, in the industrial category concerned or in the enterprise service', etc. Majority opinion favours the construction 'either at national level in the industrial category concerned, or in the particular enterprise, service', etc.) Whatever is the correct interpretation, the 'most representative' union acquires in the public sector a monopoly of the right to call strikes.

Secondly, the 1963 Law declares unlawful all *grèves tournantes* (or 'rolling' strikes), but in words which leave the precise limits uncertain. The text is capable of comprising even strikes by different shifts in turn in the same plant. In respect of both these prohibitions, sanctions are provided for civil servants and public service employees. (It remains an open question whether the normal disciplinary sanctions can additionally be applied to civil servants.[191])

187. Respectively Laws of 27.12.1947 and 28.9.1948; Ordinance 27.12.1958 and 6.8.1958; and Law 2.7.1964. Members of the armed services are also effectively deprived of the right.
188. H. Sinay, *La Grève*, pp. 402–6.
189. *Arrêt Syndicat Unifié de Techniciens de la Radiodiffusion Télévision Française*, 4.2.1966.
190. H. Sinay, *La Grève*, p. 378 *et seq.*; G. Belorgey, *Le Droit de la Grève et les Services Publics*, p. 88 *et seq.* But for this purpose there can be no additions to the 1950 list.
191. H. Sinay, op. cit., pp. 393–9.

Participation in such strikes is clearly *faute lourde*. In addition, the 1963 Law states that employees who stop work for less than one day must lose the equivalent of one day's pay, extending thereby to all public employees a law first introduced for civil servants in 1961. This provision is aimed at stopping repeated short strikes.

Not unnaturally the Law of 1963 has been harshly criticized by trade-union leaders. More important, it has been observed or enforced very little in connection with strikes in the public sector in 1968 and the following years. The agreements settling the 1968 strikes expressly included clauses whereby public authorities renounced its enforcement. In practice it remains to be seen whether it will be important in future. In August 1971, one leader of a French police union declared: 'We are firmly determined to recover our right to strike which was taken from us by the Law of 1948.' In the spring of 1971 the postal unions even launched a series of official *grèves tournantes* without legal consequences ensuing. But in theory the French law marks an unusual development in the 1960s towards severe restriction of the right of public employees of all kinds to engage in strike action. It cannot have been mere coincidence that the novelties were introduced in precisely the same year which saw, as already described, the final exhaustion of the viability of the use (mainly in the public sector) by the Government of the remedy of 'requisition'.

Only in Britain has the civil servant or public official not been singled out for special treatment in strike law. Nor are the employees of public corporations regarded as different from other employees. The fact of civil service employment being employment by the 'Crown' (theoretically terminable at pleasure) and the failure of any separate code of public 'administrative' law to develop in Britain concerning such employees has contributed to this position. Moreover, since the establishment of the Councils recommended by the Whitley Committees of 1917, joint consultation and bargaining have been widespread and dominant in all areas of the public service.[192] The 'density' of white-collar trade unionism in the public sector is over 80 per cent[193] and among manual workers even higher. The Government encourages membership of trade unions taking the view that 'fully representative associations . . . [are] essential to effective negotiations on conditions of service'.[194] The 'spirit of Whitleyism' spread joint councils throughout the national civil service[195] in such a manner as to give a lead towards voluntary collective bargaining and a final arbitration body was accepted – also on a voluntary basis – by unions and the Government, which became in 1936 the tripartite Civil Service Arbitration Tribunal.[196] Trade-union confidence in that Tribunal was somewhat

192. See for the best general account, B. Hepple and P. O'Higgins, *Public Employee Trade Unionism in the United Kingdom: The Legal Framework*, Michigan, 1971. See too R. Loveridge, *Collective Bargaining by National Employees in the U.K.*, Michigan, 1971, pp. 92–5.
193. G. Bain, 'The Growth of White Collar Unionism', Oxford, 1970, p. 39; in private industry it is just over 10 per cent.
194. *Staff Relations in the Civil Service*, HM Treasury, 1968, p. 5.
195. See S. J. Hayward, *Whitley Councils in the UK Civil Service*, London, 1963.
196. See H. D. Hughes, 'Settlement of Disputes in the Public Service', *Public Administration*, 45, 1968, p. 51 for a comparative view of the Tribunal.

weakened when in 1971 the Government failed to re-appoint the independent chairman, Professor Clegg, after some awards which offended Government policies on wage increases; but the Tribunal is still regularly used by the unions.

Strikes in the public sector, including employees of local and national government, have, however, become increasingly common in the last few years. Thus, in 1969 major strikes took place among teachers, ambulance personnel, hospital workers, firemen, naval dockyard workers, university technicians and post-office workers; and the two years that followed saw major stoppages on a national scale by municipal dustmen and sewage workers and by all postal workers (just after the Post Office ceased to be a Government department and became a public corporation). None of these strikes gave rise to legal sanctions or consequences.

In practice, therefore, the 'right to strike' of public employees was accepted. In one sense, this was peculiarly pragmatic because it could be argued that many of these groups did not enjoy the protection of the Trade Disputes Acts 1906 and 1965, since these applied only to 'persons employed in trade or industry' (1906 Act, sec. 5(3)) and it was arguable that most civil servants and local government employees did not fall within that definition. Moreover, in most of the strikes the employees concerned will have acted in breach of their employment contracts; but the legal consequences of this remained theoretical. It has never been finally decided whether civil servants of the Crown have a true 'contract' of employment;[197] but although successive Governments have adhered to the view that they have power to take any disciplinary action required against striking civil servants, such action has rarely, if ever, been used. The new Industrial Relations Act has dealt expressly with 'crown employment' without bothering finally to resolve the issue of the 'contract'. Crown employees and Crown employment are declared to be subject to the benefits and liabilities of the statute in the same manner as other employees (sec. 162 and 167(2) including Health Service employees). In general, therefore, British law now recognizes the unity of labour law, just as British practice has long recognized it, in the public and private sectors of employment.

There are, naturally, certain exceptions. The Industrial Relations Act 1971, for example, limits the remedies available against the Government for an 'unfair industrial practice' to declaratory orders or reference of certain matters to arbitration, thereby excluding the power of the Industrial Court to award compensation or make mandatory orders (sec. 162(4)). So, too, a Minister may, on grounds of national security, by certificate exclude groups of employees from the provisions of the Act (sec. 162(7)), justify a dismissal which would otherwise be actionable as 'unfair' or refuse an otherwise enforceable request for information required for collective bargaining (sec. 159). Moreover the new statute retains some limitations previously applicable to certain groups (though as we have previously seen, p. 360, it repealed the special criminal laws applicable to gas, water and electricity workers, all of them nationalized industries). Of these the most important are:

197. K. W. Wedderburn, *The Worker and The Law*, 1971, p. 70.

(a) *The Armed Forces*: while mere membership of a trade union is not expressly prohibited, trade-union activity and anything resembling industrial action would infringe the statutes and regulations applicable to the armed forces. The 1971 Act expressly excludes them from the Crown employees to whom it applies (sec. 162(2) and (4)).

(b) *The Police*: By virtue of a statute of 1964, renewing the original Act of 1919, industrial action or even membership of an ordinary trade union is a criminal offence (though a new recruit may with permission *retain* an existing trade-union membership). Police forces are organized on a local not a national basis. The 1964 Act sets up a special Police Federation to represent members of police forces; and at the 1970 conference of the Federation a resolution demanding a right to strike was overwhelmingly defeated. Severe penalties can be encountered by anyone inciting 'disaffection', which would clearly include a strike.

(c) *Postal Workers*: The Post Office Act 1953, passed when the Post Office was still a Government department, makes certain acts criminal on the part of postal workers, for example for wilfully endangering or retarding the delivery of the mail. Even though no exception is made in that statute for industrial disputes, the Post Office authorities were at pains to deny, during the national postal strike of 1971, that any strikers had acted unlawfully. It seems unlikely that somewhere an infraction of the 1953 Act had not taken place. What was in truth being said by the authorities was that the technicalities of this statute, aimed at individual misconduct, were not going to be used to impede a strike which, on the industrial level, the same authorities fought with ruthless vigour until the Union of Post Office Workers was forced, by lack of funds, into what can only be called a defeat.

These exceptional laws do little to qualify the assertion that British labour law acknowledges the right (though since 1971 within new limits) of public employees to take collective industrial action in equal measure to those employed in the private sector.

National economic policies and labour law

In the light of the preceding paragraphs it is ironic to note that until 1971, of the six countries, only in Britain had the Government attempted to introduce by law a statutory 'incomes policy' which had direct legal impact upon the right to take industrial action.[198] As with most Western countries, including all those at present under discussion, the British Government had long before 1966 been 'in the business' of influencing wage and price levels. Indirect or (as in Italy) direct influence upon the parties or mediators and arbitrators in collective negotiation; fiscal measures to influence wage demands; the incorporation of trade unions where they will agree to sit on national

198. See K. W. Wedderburn, *The Worker and The Law*, 1971, pp. 211–18.

boards or committees to 'advise' Government on economic policies;[199] resistance by the Government-as-employer to high wage demands in the public
sector – these have in varying degrees been the common experience of the six
national economies. By these and other means, the various Governments have
put such pressures as they saw fit to check inflation and stop wage increases.
In Sweden price control was even imposed in October 1970 by law, but without
any concurrent control of wages. Statutory control of wages must involve legal
limitation in the 'national interest' upon the right to strike for those wages.

It was that Rubicon which the British Prices and Incomes Act crossed in
1966. The Act was repealed at the end of 1970. It gave the Government for
one emergency year the power to prohibit all wage increases (though bad
drafting led to successful court actions by workers who had been promised
increases); and later it gave a power to the Minister to order that particular
agreed increases should be postponed – so-called 'standstill' orders. At first
the maximum period of a standstill was to be three months; but as the Act was
renewed and amended at yearly intervals, the standstill period grew by 1969
to a possible twelve months after a reference to the advisory National Board
for Prices and Incomes (now also defunct) and an adverse report from that
Board. Standstill orders could, after 1967, be made even in respect of wage
increases already implemented by employers; but, more important, it was
never unlawful for the employer to pay (and in advance agree to pay) the increases *retroactively* once the standstill order was over. Thus the order often
acted as a mere dam behind which the flood of wage entitlement built up until
some months later. Even so, what the Government called its 'reserve powers'
to put standstill orders on wage increase agreements that offended its stated
maximum 'norms', had some effect, though how great is still disputed. The
sanctions used were primarily the threat of criminal prosecution though none
was ever brought. In civil law, apart from destroying the workers' contractual
right to any increase, a standstill order was carefully excluded from giving
rise to further tort liabilities. Moreover, disputes about standstill orders or the
Act were expressly made 'trade disputes' – a marked shift towards inclusion of
political disputes within the protected area.

Any attempt by strike action or otherwise 'with a view to compel, induce
or influence' an employer to pay an increase contrary to a standstill order
during the relevant period was a crime remediable by fines of up to £100. But
workers had to have that 'view'; so that when a group of lorry drivers stopped
working extra hours, they claimed that that had no such object, but were
merely withdrawing from their end of a bargain of which the wage increase
had been 'frozen' by an order. Although no one was prosecuted, the Act caused great tension between the Labour Government and the trade unions who
had opposed it. Indeed, this struggle, together with the severe battle between
the same Government and the Trades Union Congress over rather minor reforms in labour law in 1969, shows that the fact that the trade-union movement
has a direct affiliation with a political 'labour' party (as in Sweden, Germany

199. See e.g. Reynaud, *Les Syndicats en France*, 1963, p. 246 *et seq.*

and Britain) does not prevent or even inhibit the harshest confrontation between the two when the party pursues, as a Government, economic policies in what it considers the national interest that are unacceptable to the unions.

The actual administration of the Act of 1966 was in fact rather strange. Orders often appeared to be directed or threatened against groups that were strongly organized but hardly at the centre of economy, for example busmen and building unions in 1967, while other groups escaped. By 1970 the statute was being 'phased out' by the Labour Government, and the Conservative Government is committed to not reintroducing an 'incomes policy' by direct legal controls. The policy failed not merely because it would have been difficult to fine or imprison thousands of workers had they defied the Act.

> The reason is that a law enforcing an incomes policy has to create some novel offences which upset cherished principles of democratic thought.... What offence are workers committing if, having given notice and observed the [agreed] procedure, they come out in support of a claim for an increase in their own pay? If we subject them to legal penalties, what liberties are safe? Then there is still the employer ... what kind of crime is it for a man to agree to pay his employees higher wages?[200]

It is surely for this fundamental reason that those who have, with pre-eminent logic, proposed that reforms of labour laws must now be overtly dovetailed into national Government's overall economic policy, have met with little positive response. In the United States, for example, Professor Wellington has suggested in 1968 that the national policy of 'guide posts' for wage increases should be 'integrated with collective bargaining' by adding to the American duty to bargain 'in good faith' a *legal* duty to bargain with reference to those 'guide posts', thereby preserving the collective bargaining system but changing it so as to effect 'viable accommodation between the parties' responsibilities' as employers and unions and their duty to the national interest.[201] Furthermore, the difficulty about using the 'emergency provisions' of the American and of the even wider British law, as instruments of economic policy clearly lies in the same fundamental area; and the political character which is inevitably acquired by the very definition of 'emergency' is not unrelated to that fact.

Notwithstanding the British experience, in August 1971 the President of the United States embarked upon a new policy which had an appearance not dissimilar to the British statutes in the period 1966 to 1970. Acting under authority based upon the Constitution and the Economic Stabilization Act 1970, he issued Order 11615 whereby

200. H. Clegg (for long himself a member of the National Prices and Incomes Board), *How to run an Incomes Policy – and why we made such a mess of the last one*, London, 1971, p. 57–8.
201. H. H. Wellington, *Labor and The Legal Process*, Yale, 1968, pp. 322–7. Compare on G. Schultz and R. Aiber, *Guidelines, Informal Controls and the Market Place*, Chicago, 1966, especially J. Dunlop, pp. 81–97; A. Ross, pp. 97–141; and P. Kurland, pp. 209–41.

Prices, rents, wages and salaries shall be stabilized for a period of 90 days from the date hereof at levels not greater than the highest of those pertaining to a substantial volume of actual transactions by each individual, business, firm or other entity or any kind during the 30-day period ending 14 August 1971 for like or similar commodities or services (sec. 1).

Although Secretary of the Treasury Connally declared this was a 'different animal entirely from wage-price controls', the '90-day freeze' clearly brought positive law to bear directly upon bargaining and, probably, upon industrial action. Administration of the Order was vested in a specially created 'Cost-of-Living Council' which was given power to 'prescribe definitions', make exceptions, 'issue regulations and orders', and take any other action that it deemed necessary to carry out the Order. Enforcement involved both fines for wilful violation of the Order or any such regulation and an application for an injunction by the Department of Justice on the request of the Council to prevent persons acting in violation. The latter remedy thus introduced a dimension of even greater width than the criminal remedies of the British Acts.

In its first Circular[202] the Council made it clear that it took the injunction remedy very seriously, declaring that the United States Government might apply for temporary or permanent injunctions, even in mandatory terms, against anyone about to act in violation. The words both of the Order and of the Circular seemed apt to include industrial action of any kind which aimed to bring about such a violation. Thus, sec. 1 of the Order prohibited persons 'to use any means to obtain payment of wages and salaries in any form, higher than those permitted hereunder, whether by retroactive increase or otherwise'; and the Circular prohibited 'any practice which constitutes a means to obtain a higher price, wage, salary or rent than is permitted . . .'.[203]

Not surprisingly, the Council was immediately thrown into a vast sea of interpretative declarations. In Memoranda issued in the 10 days that followed the initial Order, the Council interpreted 'wages' to include all forms of 'fringe benefit' from stock-options to cost-of-living allowances; forbade changes in working conditions that would lead to higher pay per hour worked; and froze wages even in industries where collective agreements accorded to workers the right to automatic increases as the cost of living rose, in effect nullifying agreement for the 90-day period. Whilst bargaining might continue during that period, the Council was insistent that the Order meant what it said and did not allow for negotiated pay increases which would be retroactive after the freeze was over.[204] This factor was, we saw above, one of the legal reasons why the Prices and Incomes Acts in Britain led to a dam behind which retroactive rises built up. The American Order met the problem head on, and it will be an essay of no small interest in the effect of legal regulation to see

202. Economic Stabilization Circular No. 1, 23.8.1971, para. 900(b).
203. ibid., para. 900(a).
204. Memorandum 19.8.1971: 'Cost-of-Living Council: Q. & A., List 2'. The President's statement of 7 October 1971 proposed to extend provisions controlling prices and wages after the 90-day freeze which would clearly entail some limitations upon industrial action. (See below, note 204a.)

whether the parties in industry do not find, in the long term, a way of providing for such increases where the employer either wishes to pay or is faced with strong union pressure.

The immediate response of most United States unions was of protest against the Order (not least because there was no legal control of profits). But, although a conference of their lawyers announced that they were examining the constitutionality of the Order and the Council, and even of the 1970 Act on which both purported to be based, they made no immediate challenge in the courts. Nor was battle immediately joined on the industrial front. Whether legal action could be taken to prosecute or enjoin strikes, in some or all cases, and if so how far it would be effective, remained to be tested. But the 90-day freeze Order, whatever was to follow its limited life, opened up a new arena of conflict between unions and Government about economic policy in which the latter began by using the law and the former might well end by using industrial action. If that occurs, we may expect the American silence in the debate about 'political' strikes in the private sector to be broken.[204a]

204a. [The subsequent experience of President Nixon's 'Phase Two' policy, in-augurated by Executive Order 11627 after the 90-day freeze (and therefore after the completion of our study), can only be summarized here up to the end of March 1972. Two main new bodies were created, responsible to the Cost of Living Council: The Price Commission with seven members, and The Pay Board with five 'public' members, five members from industry and five from the labour movement. (A special Commission dealt with problems of the construction industry.) After initial disagree-ments, in November 1971 the Pay Board decided by a majority (the five labour mem-bers dissenting) on a 'guide line' norm of 5.5 per cent as the ceiling for annual wage increases. The Board also set its face against most retroactive settlements without special permission. Violation of the Board's decisions could give rise to legal offences, though President Nixon stressed that this 'Phase Two' policy should be enforced by 'voluntary' means and 'not by an army of bureaucrats'. The decisions of the Pay Board, in which from the outset the different factions were locked in combat, were erratic. In November 1971, it approved by 10 votes to 3 pay increases for miners of over 16 per cent immediately (39 per cent over three years); but in January 1972, it rejected a 12 per cent settlement for aerospace workers.

The Board's history became inextricably woven into the texture of the longest dock strike in United States' history. Strike action in East Coast ports began in October 1971; the President, after attempting to solve the dispute by sending a special mediator, obtained an 80-day injunction under the Taft-Hartley statute (described above in this chapter) on 25 November 1971; but a settlement above the norm of 5.5 per cent was negotiated only in January 1972. The West Coast ports were paralysed for much longer. The strike there began on 1 July 1971. An application for a Taft-Hartley injunction was not made until 6 October; but the 80-day injunction, far from settling the strike, saw its fierce resumption on the expiry of the Court Order; and after two abortive postponements for negotiation, the strike was fully resumed in January 1972. By 4 February 1972, President Nixon felt constrained to propose to a reluctant Congress special *ad hoc* legislation to compel the West Coast dockers to return to work and to compel arbitration of the issues in the strike. By the third week of February, however, a settlement of the strike has been negotiated; but, since it was a settlement involving pay increases of about 26 per cent, the Pay Board early in March 1972, refused to endorse it. Two weeks later, three of the five labour members of the Pay Board resigned.

For the purposes of our study, two points stand out in this unfinished story: first, the ineffectiveness once again of the Taft-Hartley 'cooling-off' injunction in the case of strikes by dock-workers (a recurring theme in United States' industrial experience); and, secondly, most relevant here, the reluctance of Government to use direct legal sanctions against those who, by industrial action, might well be in violation of the

Apart from direct intervention, most Governments have of course been not unwilling to utilize indirect legal weapons to support their economic policies. The control over action by public service employees in many countries, especially in France; and the very restructuring of labour legislation as a whole – as in the case of the British Industrial Relations Act 1971 presented by the Government as part of its policy to stop inflation (its major role being to reduce the power of workers' groups at plant level) – are both examples which may be called direct or indirect, according to taste. The United States even before the 90-day freeze in 1971 provided a rather different illustration. In 1971 President Nixon suspended by proclamation the 'Davis-Bacon Act 1931' for one month, a law which guaranteed to workers throughout the construction industry the 'prevailing wage' negotiated in areas covered by collective bargaining. During the month of suspension he imposed an Executive Order establishing a 'Cooperative Mechanism for the stabilization of Wages and Prices', forcing employers and unions to establish joint boards to consider wage agreements with reference to stated 'criteria' of economic policy.[205] Lastly, in France, since 1968 there have evolved new types of collective agreements (*contrats de progrès*) which make reference to yearly percentage increases in income determined at national level. This system had begun in 1964 with the 'Toutée Report' on nationalized industry, spread in 1965 to the private sector, and gave rise to the contrats de progrès in the public sector after the 'Martin Report' of 1968. In 1969 and 1970 these agreements incorporated a clause whereby unions agreed to give two months' notice of strike action; but in 1971, this clause (probably legally enforceable) was dropped in order to win the accession to the system of the most powerful union federation, the CGT. So far, however, this new style of collective bargaining with direct reference to national economic policies is confined to the public sector; and while the CGT is a party it is unlikely to include any control of the right to strike.

The signs that pressures of national policy on labour law and collective bargaining will increase are, however, clear. That is the reason why the discussion of 'emergency' laws does indeed pose the question 'can collective bargaining survive?' Each Government will use the rhetoric of its own system – laws on 'political' strikes and on 'public officials', or the creation of 'unfair' industrial actions – to justify the shaping of its legal system in the 'national interest'. Two points must however be kept firmly in mind if reality is not to be mystified by rhetoric. First, that 'national interest' is today intimately con-

---

'Phase Two' legal order on incomes policy. 'While it is against the law to strike to obtain or to enforce destabilizing wage settlements, and while the sanctions against strikes are virtually unlimited, there has been no test of the Board's ability to withstand a strike challenge. Unlike the war-time experience, the co-operation of organized labour has not included a commitment not to strike against Board recommendations, and the experience in peacetime with legal restrictions on strike activity has not been encouraging.' P. B. Doeringer, *Pay Policy in the United States – 1971: A Speculative View*, p. 21, a paper written in January 1972 which will be included in a forthcoming volume to be published by the National Institute for Economic and Social Research, London.
205. See *Labor Law Journal*, 1971, pp. 240–5.

nected with international commerce, not least through the activity of the multi-national corporation for which none of the labour laws of the six countries seem so far to have made provision. Secondly, the problems of an 'incomes policy' are policy and political questions which cannot be settled merely by appeals to reason or even reasonableness. In such policies

> Labour is really being asked to give its consent to a particular type of social order. There is no reason why it should willingly do so – or for that matter why the owners of capital should positively assent to any alternative proposed. . . . But what a fully fledged 'incomes policy' really implies is the equivalent of a new Social Contract.[206]

In so far as such political demands are made upon labour, it is clearly illogical to prohibit the use of their power by collective labour organizations for 'political' purposes or purposes which upset 'normal' political processes, if the great mass of working people do not subscribe to that new Social Contract; and no appeal to the democratic national interest can in the modern world be expected to convince free working-class movements to the contrary.

206. A. Shonfield, *Modern Capitalism*, London, 1965, p. 218.

Index